Why Do You Need this New Edition?

If you're wondering why you should buy this new edition of *The Art of Being Human,* here are 8 good reasons

1. **A new chapter on critical thinking** will help you to develop the skills you need to understand, evaluate, and appreciate the arts—and encourage you to discover new ways to apply these skills to your daily life.

2. **Updated examples throughout** expose you to today's **emerging artists and contemporary works,** including films like *The Departed* and *Ratatouille*, multiple-Tony-award-winning plays like *The History Boys* and *Spring Awakening,* and music by artists like Aimee Mann and U2.

3. **More examples by non-Western, minority, and female artists** are designed to help you understand and appreciate the universal appeal of the humanities.

4. **More color images—**and a different layout that brings the images closer to the text discussing them—bring renewed visual interest.

5. **A new chapter, Conflicts about Art,** explores strategies for approaching controversial subjects with an open mind and critical eye.

6. **New Topics for Writing and Discussion** help you practice your critical thinking skills, and **updated marginal quotations** serve as thought-provoking reminders of how the humanities relate to your daily life.

7. **Expanded coverage of architecture** (Ch. 5) looks at landmark buildings around the globe, including Dubai's Burj-al-Arab, one of the world's most extravagant (and controversial) hotels.

8. **A refreshed art program** offers over 40 color photos and over 160 black and white photos, including 75 images new to this edition.

PEARSON
Longman

NINTH EDITION

THE ART OF BEING HUMAN

The Humanities as a Technique for Living

Richard Janaro
New World School of the Arts

Thelma Altshuler
Professor Emerita, Miami-Dade Community College

New York San Francisco Boston
London Toronto Sydney Tokyo Singapore Madrid
Mexico City Munich Paris Cape Town Hong Kong Montreal

Senior Sponsoring Editor: Virginia L. Blanford
Executive Marketing Manager: Joyce Nilsen
Associate Development Editor: Erin Reilly
Production Manager: Stacey Kulig
Project Coordination, Text Design, and Electronic Page Makeup: Electronic Publishing Services Inc, NYC
Cover Design Manager: Wendy Ann Fredericks
Cover Designer: Nancy Sacks
Cover Image: Portrait of a Jester with a Lute, Frans Hals/Louvre, Paris, France, Peter Willi/ The Bridgeman Art Library
Photo Researcher: Linda Sykes
Senior Manufacturing Buyer: Roy Pickering
Printer and Binder: Von Hoffmann Graphics
Cover Printer: Coral Graphics

Janaro, Richard Paul.
The art of being : the humanities as a technique for living/
Richard Janaro, Thelma Altshuler.—9th ed.
p. cm.
Includes bibliographical references and index.
ISBN 978-0-205-60542-2
1. Conduct of life—Textbooks. 2. Humanities—Textbooks. I. Altshuler, Thelma C.
II. Title.
BJ1581.2.J36 2008
001.3—dc22
2008019806

Please visit us at www.ablongman.com.

ISBN 13: 978-0-205-60542-2
ISBN 10: 0-205-60542-7

2 3 4 5 6 7 8 9 10—VH—11 10 09

This book is dedicated to

Laura and Rocky

David and Patti

Julia and Jim

Brief Contents

Detailed Contents

Preface

The ninth edition of *The Art of Being Human*, like its predecessors, introduces students to the joys of the humanities. As always, our aim is to communicate our enthusiasm for the humanities as experience for the mind and emotions. By becoming acquainted with the creative arts and learning to think critically about them, students will also better understand themselves and the world they live in.

The Art of Being Human tells the story of outstanding achievements in the humanities throughout history and across the world's many cultures. We acknowledge the contributions of the past because people very much like us lived there, and what they said and did can shed light on the present. We continue to find new reasons to rejoice, new stimuli for the senses in work from the past and the present, from different cultures and peoples around the world, and from women and men.

New Features of *The Art of Being Human*

This text has remained popular through nine editions because the humanities are alive and will be alive forever—and as a part of our daily lives, they must grow and change. Thus, the present text includes a number of important revisions necessary to keep our special approach to the humanities vital.

New Chapter on "Critical Thinking"

In response to numerous reviewer requests, a new chapter, *Chapter 2: Profile of the Critical Thinker*, has been added in Part One. This chapter will help students develop the skills they need to understand, evaluate, and appreciate the arts, as well as encourage students to apply these skills to their daily lives.

New Layout for Color Inserts

The text now contains three eight-page color inserts. This new layout brings each piece closer to where it is discussed in the text and allows for more color images than in previous editions.

More Examples from Non-Western, Minority, and Women Artists and Philosophers

Diverse text and visual examples help students better appreciate the worldwide reach and universal appeal of the humanities. Popularly requested by reviewers and adopters alike, the new examples serve as an integral part of the discussions throughout the book and are not isolated to a particular section or chapter. Among the new additions are in-depth discussions of Khaled Hosseini's *The Kite Runner* (2003), Alaa Al Aswany's *The Yacoubian Building* (2002), and Nadine Gordimer's "The Beneficiary" (2007).

More Contemporary Examples

It has always been one of our aims to expose students not only to the great artists of the past but also to great artists just emerging. Creative examples from our own time help students understand the connection between the arts of today and the great works of the past. The text now includes films such as *The Departed* (2006) and *Ratatouille* (2007); plays such as the Tony award winners *The History Boys* (2004) and *Spring Awakening* (2007); music by artists such as Aimee Mann and U2; and countless other influential modern works from all genres.

Updated Pedagogy

Our Archetypes in This Chapter, Topics for Writing and Discussion, and marginal quotations have all been updated for this edition. An expanded art program presents over 40 color photos and over 160 black-and-white photos—including 75 images that are new to this edition.

Revised Subtitle

"The Humanities as a Technique for Living," highlights, reflects, and emphasizes the humanities as a way of living one's life.

Other Updates and Revisions

We have endeavored to keep the book as fresh as possible with updates and revisions throughout the text. In response to reviewer requests, we completely reworked Chapter 3, "Struggles in the Humanities," to become a new Chapter 15, "Conflicts about Art," in Part Three. We have almost doubled our coverage of architecture in Chapter 5 to include discussion and photos of more landmark buildings than in previous editions. Lastly, many of the explanations and analyses, identified by numerous reviewers, have been simplified to be more accessible overall and engage students in a meaningful way.

Enduring Strengths

The ninth edition of *The Art of Being Human* retains the many strengths that have made it a highly respected and easy-to-use text.

- *Full coverage of the humanities*: *The Art of Being Human* discusses all the important disciplines and examines connections to issues that remain of vital importance. Students are encouraged to explore how the arts and social themes relate to their own life.
- *Individual treatment of disciplines and themes*: The book's topical organization allows students to explore one artistic mode or theme at a time, rather than having to cover multiple disciplines and themes in each chapter, often the case in chronologically organized texts.
- *Flexible organization*: Each chapter stands on its own, so the book can be taught in any sequence and can be easily customized to meet the goals of any number of introductory courses on the humanities in two- and four-year colleges.
- *Diverse range of traditional and contemporary examples of all the arts*: *The Art of Being Human* strives to familiarize students with the reach of the humanities by including many examples of literature and art from cultures around the globe. We include the work of women and minorities as well, and we address issues that remain of vital importance for an increasingly global society.
- *Accessible writing style*: The authors explore the world of the humanities in a contemporary idiom that students can easily understand.
- *An impressive visual program*: The more than 160 black-and-white photos and 45 color plates (presented on three eight-page inserts) provide students with a rich visual appreciation of the arts. All of the images and their captions are tied directly to discussions within the text. Each color plate includes a page reference identifying where the work is discussed within the text.

Supplements

A rich array of supplements is available for *The Art of Being Human* for both instructors and students.

For Instructors

An Instructor's Manual and Test Bank (020561647X) includes over a thousand test items and questions, timelines, checklists of major concepts, and suggested teaching strategies.

For Students

- An **audio CD** (0205616755) features arias and instrumental selections, both old and new, as well as poetry readings and dramatic scenes. All of the content on the CD is discussed in the text; discussions are marked with a marginal CD icon. This CD can be packaged at no additional cost with *The Art of Being Human.*
- *Evaluating a Performance*, by Michael Greenwald (0321095413), guides students through watching and reviewing theatrical performances with a

critical eye. Available at no additional cost when packaged with *The Art of Being Human*.

- Add a classic or contemporary novel to your course by selecting from a variety of Penguin titles in our **Penguin Discount Novel Program**. To review the available choices, visit www.pearsonhighered.com/penguin and consult your local Pearson Arts and Sciences representative to set up a value pack.

Acknowledgments

Our fervent hope is that, after reading this book, students will have gained the assurance of discovering much about themselves and learned about features of the humanities that will prove rewarding in their ongoing development. If, as Katherine Mansfield once said, a great poet must first be a great poem, what shall we say of the fully realized human being? Won't such an individual be not only a poem but also a song, dance, painting, play, movie, or new idea? These are distant stars at which to aim, but a journey too easily accomplished may not be worth the effort.

The "we" of this preface includes not only the authors but others who have worked long and hard helping to improve the book. Matt Wright, our acquisitions editor, stayed diligently on top of the project from its inception and helped guide us through the complexities we faced. Erin Reilly, our development editor, provided us with useful text suggestions. Cheryl Besenjak adroitly handled our text permissions, as Linda Sykes did our photo permissions. Rebecca Coleman was our meticulous production editor, overseeing copyediting and design. All became part of a team, and through their efforts we discovered the true meaning of *synergy*.

Still others contributed to the emergence of the final product: the many dedicated employees at Longman who took care of thousands of details. Both Haley Pero, Matt Wright's assistant, and Joyce Nilsen, executive marketing editor, played key roles.

We would also like to acknowledge the letters from students and teachers who support what we are doing and made valuable comments about how we could do it even better, and the detailed, thorough, caring reviews by those who saw the manuscript in various stages of preparation: Janice Stockard Dargan, North Carolina Central University; Connie La Marca-Frankel, Pasco-Hernando Community College; Ileen L. Linden, Lakeland Community College; JoAnna Falco-Leshin, Miami Dade College; Debra Bergeson-Graham, Rocky Mountain College; David Carney, Salt Lake Community College; Flora Carter, Modesto Junior College; Adrien Cuellar-McGuire, Brookhaven College School of the Arts; Margaret Dahl, Austin Community College; Charles L. Darr, University of Pittsburgh at Johnstown; Robert L. Doxtator, Chadron State College; Rita Gagelman, Park University; Sarah Garman, Miami-Dade College; Kristine Haddox, Richland College; Jerry Hamby, Lee College; Victor Hebert, Fayetteville State University; Carolyn A. Johnson, Montcalm Community College; Sharron Kollmeyer, California State University, Northridge; Thomas A. Marshall, Robert Morris University; Bernadette McInnis, Neumann College; Charles J. Olson,

Midwestern State University; Betsey Pender, Florida Community College at Jacksonville; Barbara Rhoades, Elon University; Dr. Julie Rodakowski, Rochester Community and Technical College; Stephanie Satie, California State University, Northridge; Gregory Seltzer, Villa Julie College; Kathryn Sheffield, Mesa Community College; Carlo V. Spataro, Muskegon Community College; Karen Taylor, Genesee Community College; Kathryn L. Valdivia, Cuyamca College; Carolyn B. Wilkinson, Northern Virginia Community College.

To write a humanities text is perhaps the best way to discover the humane characteristics of others and the secret of all meaningful endeavor, which is that *no one can work alone.*

Richard Janaro
Thelma Altshuler

PART

I

Exploring the Humanities

1 The Humanities: Still Vital

Overview of This Book

Some believe that in the twenty-first century, humans must adapt to the rapid, almost daily, advances in technology—to what Alvin Toffler more than thirty years ago called "future shock"—and that those who don't will be lost in a bewildering world of iPods, BlackBerries, and even computers being developed not only to think as efficiently as the human brain (or more so) but to experience emotion as well. New television screens as thin as sheets of paper; remote controls so powerful that you can start your dinner cooking while you are driving home; robots performing a brain operation in Fort Wayne, Indiana, controlled by a surgeon in Rangoon—and the list goes on and on.

Toffler predicted that the rate at which advances are made would accelerate to dizzying proportions, but perhaps only an Einstein could have imagined the speed. Some are wondering whether this technological takeover will eventually leave humanity behind in the dust, as if to say "All right, you invented us, but you've done your job, and now we don't need you."

Not only humanity but the *humanities*, the subject of this book, could be left in the dust unless we realize that those who love the humanities are often people who know how to use technology not for its own sake but for the betterment of human life. Poets of today may use a computer to give us memorable words and images. Visual artists may use not only computers but video, even fax machines, to express themselves and add new shapes to the world around us. In short, there is still a place for humanity. Machines can assist composers, but they can't come up with the music. Well, maybe they can, but they will be using notes and scales programmed by human beings. And if a composer doesn't like what a machine is turning out, there is always the delete button.

While we are marveling at the infinite potential of Google and the rest of the Internet, let us not forget that human beings created them. If we relax our minds and let them rust from lack of use, we are forgetting that the people who have given us the machines to work for us have not relaxed *their* minds. Let us use the creators and the innovators as our role models, not just use the amazing products of their intellectual labors. Yet one could wish they had thought to paste labels advising us, for example, "In addition to downloading Bon Jovi, you might also download Beethoven's Eroica Symphony."

The goal of this book is to show you there is a wonderful, magical world of human devising that has existed as long as humanity has existed.

Source: © Fotosearch.

The goal of this book is to show you there is a wonderful, magical world of human devising that has existed for as long as humanity has existed, and that it is still here, waiting each day to be discovered anew. It is the world of the humanities. The humanities are just outside your door, waiting. They are also inside *you* if you know where to look. All you have to do is open that door or get in touch with your creative self and extend a welcoming hand. If you do, your life will be changed very much for the better. And you will want to run out into the street and share the wonder with everyone you meet!

Defining the Humanities

The humanities can no longer be defined in a simple statement. At one time they were said to be the best products of the best minds. The word **humanities** grew out of the term **humanism**, which did indeed once mean the study of what great artists, writers, and philosophers had accomplished. During the Renaissance, that huge artistic and political revolution that swept over Western Europe beginning in the fifteenth century, there was a revival of interest in the culture of ancient Greece and Rome—a culture that had been left largely unexamined during the thousand-year span following the fall of Rome. (Actually, *renaissance* means "rebirth.") The intelligentsia of the Renaissance believed that only through a study of classical art, literature, and philosophy could a person become *fully* human. Thus these **disciplines** became known as the humanities. In time, the term had to be extended beyond the study of Greek and Roman culture to include that of major Western European countries: first Italy, then France and Spain, then Britain, and finally Germany. As cultures multiplied, so did the disciplines people needed to study in pursuit of humanness. Music, theater, and dance began to flourish during the Renaissance, and scholars realized that these disciplines were also part of the ancient world's legacy.

The term *humanities* must now be broadened still further. Yes, we still need to pay attention to extraordinary artistic and intellectual achievements that have been singled out for special praise and that now represent what is sometimes called the "humanistic tradition." All of us belong to the human race and should want to know as much as possible about the distinguished contributions of those who have gone before. Yet we also need to recognize that the "humanistic tradition" usually was limited to the contributions made by *men* of the classical and then the Western European worlds. Plato and Michelangelo and Shakespeare continue to deserve our admiration and reward our study, but think of those persons, both male and female, past and present, who may be little known or not known at all but nevertheless left behind or now offer a myriad of wonderful songs, poems, and provocative thoughts waiting to be appreciated.

The humanities are also the creative and intellectual expressions of each of us in moments of inspiration, whether they happen in the shower or just walking down the street on a balmy day when our spirits are lifted by the sheer joy of being alive. In these times of global fears and a future of uncertainty, in these times of dizzying technological advances that can be both marvelous and bewildering, when it can be hard to pinpoint our identity in time and space, the humanities offer a safe haven, a quiet harbor where we can moor our vessels and, at least for a time, confirm who we are.

Each of us is more than a gender, an age, an address, an occupation. Each of us is thoughts, expressed or not, the capacity to be moved, the need to laugh or cry, longings for things just beyond our reach. The humanities give us stories to stimulate our imagination, ideas to stimulate our intellect, musical sounds to excite our passions. Exposure to the humanities helps us foster our ability to respond to the creativity and thought of others and to look inwardly to see what *we* think and what creative impulses lie dormant and cry out to be released. All of this helps us confront our true identity. A major aim of this book is to show how a study of the humanities can be the starting point for the journey into self-knowledge.

The humanities are inspiring achievements in themselves, but we also find value in the *study* of those achievements, in the *critical process* by which scholars and critics interpret the humanities and communicate their findings to others so that these achievements will never be forgotten. This is also the critical process by which we ourselves look squarely at and come to appreciate what is there for us to read, see, or hear. This process, often called *critical thinking*, is essential to being effectively human, the more so as the world's tempo increases. In fact, so crucial is critical thought and so important are the humanities in developing it that Chapter 2 is devoted solely to the subject.

The humanities can also be called a technique for living, accessible to every human being who wants to do more with life. They offer a way of life filled with moments of critical thought and aesthetic pleasure, and they are urgently needed in our world.

We are healthy only to the extent that our ideas are humane.

—Kurt Vonnegut

The humanities are addictive. Once you let song and story, music and dance, words and ideas into your life, you can never live without them. And you should never *have* to. The humanities are best appreciated in our quiet moments, and quiet is also addictive in a noisy world. *If only everyone on Earth would insist on these quiet moments, wouldn't the world be a happier (and a safer) place?*

In a world that has become a global village, in a world with all its hovering threats of terror attacks and dirty bombs, with so many who are more than willing to sacrifice their own lives to kill others, in a world of environmental woes, a world in which cynics wonder about the value of living—in such a world there are always the humanities to lift our spirits. Art and music and literature, stories and songs, all the marvels of the human mind, the architectural and engineering achievements—or just noticing the first robin of the year—they keep reminding us that, as American novelist William Faulkner said when he accepted the Nobel Prize for Literature in 1949, humanity will not only survive, "it will prevail."

But humanity will not prevail just because we are living longer. Genetic scientists expect to replace the gene responsible for aging and promise life expectancies that were once found only in literary fables. (Perhaps some of us may live to celebrate our "eleventy-first birthday," like Bilbo Baggins of *The Hobbit.*) Existing on and on without coming to terms with who we are and without knowing how to reach a safe haven inside when the world gets maddeningly chaotic about us—maybe that wouldn't be the best technique for living. The humanities help make longer life spans abundantly richer.

The key to the richer life is to be as open-minded as possible. One of the dangers of living longer is becoming too firmly enclosed by the values many of us have held since our earliest days. The humanities cannot fail to inspire open-mindedness. The literature of other cultures, not to mention their music, art, and patterns of thought—becoming aware of the problems they face and *their* way of prevailing—are indispensable to our own development. Why? The answer is simple: the world has grown too small for us not to care what is happening all around us. And the world is just that—all around us. So we need to balance a sharper awareness of who we are with a broader understanding of who *they* are, for they are part of us, and we of them.

The ancient Greeks . . . were convinced that an explanation of, and definition for, Beauty was as concrete and discoverable as the answer to why the days got shorter in winter . . .

—**Bruce Maddox**

The cultural history of Western civilization as traditionally presented will no longer suffice. During the time of the ancient Greeks, for example, were there not many women who thought great thoughts and wrote great poems, even if unknown today? While the much heralded early civilizations, like those of Egypt, China, Japan, Rome, and Greece, have received abundant attention and been the subject of countless critical and historical studies, they do not tell the whole story of human genius. Rich cultures flourished in Africa, South and Central America, the North America that was inhabited long before Columbus "discovered" it, and in the lands that produced Islamic art, science, and philosophy—lands once thought too mysterious for the Western mind to understand. We find vestiges of rich cultures as well in Stonehenge in England and in the thirty-foot statues that stand in eternal attention on Easter Island. In our more recent history, while some were sipping juleps on plantation verandas in the American South, slaves in their humble shanties were weaving elaborate tales and singing complex songs to keep their heritage alive.

The traditional humanistic disciplines have been art, music, literature, and drama, and these are discussed in Part Two, along with the musical stage (opera, musical theater, and dance) and the cinema, because each has by now contributed works that are considered of lasting excellence or, at the very least, represent steps in the direction of art—works that are also valuable in our quest for self-knowledge. Part Three deals with issues and themes that cross disciplinary and cultural boundaries: religion, morality, love, happiness, death, and subjects and art forms that have caused much controversy.

The book concludes with a chapter on freedom—how it can be defined and how it can be achieved and held. The life enriched by the humanities presupposes freedom of choice. We cannot know who we really are if someone else determines who that shall be.

Gifts of the Humanities

Economics tells us that the wants of people are insatiable, but resources are limited. Because almost everything is scarcer than we would like, treasured possessions, as well as basics like food and shelter, come with a price tag. Do we have enough money to buy everything we want? The answer is usually NO!

With the humanities the problem is reversed. *The resources of the humanities are unlimited*, but all too often our wants are meager. In the economic world you can't always be rich by choice, but in the world of the humanities you can be poor by choice.

Several years ago, when the U.S. economy was in a severe recession, banks attracted savings deposits by offering gifts to those who would forgo spending and open CD accounts instead. People were walking out with new toasters, blenders, steam irons, and luggage, and of course bank reserves swelled. Such incentives are cyclical in nature, but the humanities always have gifts that are there for us regardless of what the economy is doing. Here are some of them.

Beauty

The shiny new car stands in the driveway, attracting envious glances from the neighbors. The owner glows with pride. Is it that the newly acquired possession is a sign of the buyer's apparent prosperity? Is it simply that people are genetically prone to owning things and the more the better? Although the answer may be yes, isn't something else involved? Is it something we call **beauty**?

Ever since philosophy began, ever since thoughtful people started inquiring into the meaning and purpose of life, the question of the beautiful has arisen. Its close connection with pleasure has always seemed apparent. It is pleasant and desirable to see beautiful things and beautiful people. People prefer to live amid beauty than amid ugliness.

Though people may debate whether a particular person or piece of music is beautiful, there is widespread agreement that something deserves to be called beautiful if the arrangement of the parts is pleasing, if it seems *right*. The rightness of the arrangement determines the pleasure that it gives us. When there is something in an arrangement that seems *not* right, we are less attracted, possibly even repelled.

Is judging an arrangement—of a painting, a person's face, a story, a dramatic moment—as right or not right entirely subjective? Yes and no. There is widespread agreement about the rightness of *certain* arrangements. Leonardo da Vinci's *La Gioconda*, more popularly known as the *Mona Lisa* (Color Plate 1), has earned the reputation as the world's most famous painting. Each week thousands flock to the Louvre Museum in Paris to see the portrait of the lady with the enigmatic smile. Yet in the centuries since it was created (1503–1505), innumerable art historians and critics have given their opinions of what makes this a great work. They often differ in the specific elements they praise—such as the haunting face or the ambiguity of the gaze—but they tend to agree that the way the artist has assembled the various elements has turned a flat canvas into the illusion of a living, breathing, three-dimensional human being. They tend to agree that *Mona Lisa* is a beautiful work of art.

The pleasure that beauty inspires in us is called **aesthetic**. Yet what kind of pleasure is it? One answer is that the beautiful inspires within us *a feeling of well-being that is its own justification*. True, the attraction of a shiny new car may have less to do with its pure beauty than with the pride we feel in owning it or, if it belongs to someone else, by the envy we feel. When a beautiful face passes by, we might long for closer contact with it, but we would not have such a desire if we did not first make an aesthetic judgment. Even if we are denied closer contact, we probably won't change our opinion of its beauty. The critics who have written volumes about the "secret" of the *Mona Lisa* have already made an aesthetic judgment and are now trying to find the words to describe why the arrangement of the parts is right. A universal definition of beauty that fits every example may be impossible to find, but few of us would deny that the beautiful does indeed exist.

The humanities are, *in part*, a catalogue of works that have tallied a host of positive votes from people who have spent their lives in pursuit of the beautiful and who hold up road signs for us in our own quest. Be advised, however, that the pursuit is endless, the catalogue needs almost daily updating, and the road signs often vary from one culture to another. If we are to expand our capacity for aesthetic pleasure, we need to experience many versions of the beautiful and try to see them from other points of view.

Sharply differing portraits of women considered beautiful in widely separated times and places.

Source: Left: Halle Berry. Credit: Reuters/Corbis. Right: Kitigawa Utamaro, *The Beauty*. Credit: Burstein Collection/Corbis.

Though we travel the world over to find the beautiful, we must carry it with us or we find it not.

—Ralph Waldo Emerson

Study the two portraits of women on this page. The photo on the left is that of Halle Berry, a popular Hollywood star, famous not only as an award-winning actress but as an acknowledged beauty. The image on the right is from a woodblock engraving by Japanese artist Kitagawa Utamaro (1753–1806), representing a late eighteenth-century Japanese popular trend in which artists celebrated the beauty of women. Utamaro is known for his 1794 collection called *Physiognomies of Ten Women*. Definitions of what constitutes true female beauty are clearly different here, but each woman, for her time and culture, can be said to illustrate what many have agreed to call beautiful.

In the Asian Wing of New York's Metropolitan Museum of Art, tucked away in a corner that the visitor can easily miss, is a sculpture called *Water Stone* (see photo) by the Japanese artist Isamu Noguchi (1904–1988). It is a gray stone fountain of uneven shape with a perpetual flow of water that, at first glance, appears to be a sheet of clear glass sitting motionless on top but, in reality, trickles slowly down the side so that the escaping water is always equal to the new supply being pumped up from below. The trickle creates a soft sound that soothes and mesmerizes the visitor who takes the time to sit on the bench provided. One woman reported that she sat there, entranced, for nearly an hour.

The arrangement of parts in *Water Stone* includes the shape and texture of the stone, the varying shades created by the falling water, and most important, the

A beautiful arrangement of parts: the shape of the sculpture, the serenity of the water, and its soothing sound as it slowly trickles down the sides.

Source: Isamu Noguchi, *Water Stone,* 1986. Credit: The Metropolitan Museum of Art, Purchase, Anonymous Gift, 1987. (1987.222).

sound itself. But you don't have to be in a museum to experience the beauty of similar arrangements. A woodland stream, flowing over rocks of different shapes, will create varied shadings, and if you shut your eyes and really listen to the water, you will discover that it has a variety of sounds, depending on wind and the different rocks over which it flows.

All you need to do to experience in full how the humanities can take you to that quiet oasis we mentioned is find a stream in the woods, or study closely the different colors in rainwater gushing alongside a curb. When you search for the beautiful, you will be astonished to realize how close it is.

Let's say you go to a popular movie on a Friday night. Sitting there with your popcorn and soda, you might be hoping for nothing more than a few hours of escapist entertainment—just something to whisk you away from worrying about a job or school or a troublesome relationship. Perhaps you are watching (or half-watching) the usual slam-bang car chase while enduring the ear-splitting sound of a spray of bullets magnified by gigantic speakers. Then a car suddenly blasts its way through a huge glass window and divebombs straight into the river below. Just as suddenly, the music stops, and the car falls in slow motion, gracefully contradicting the expected explosiveness that often leaves you indifferent. The moment is justified for its own sake. It is a sudden moment of aesthetic beauty, sometimes employed by an artistic director to soften the horror of the death that will happen within the car. Both movie and television history are filled with unanticipated beautiful moments, most of them soon forgotten. Perhaps you can think of some you have experienced recently. Really noticing is a first step in appreciating the humanities.

Of course, the arts can do more for us than providing an aesthetic moment. Sometimes they may convey a message the artist believes is imperative that we understand. In fact, some take the position that meaning is what we primarily look for in any work. Yet it does a disservice both to the artist and to us the viewers if we always insist on looking for a message. (After all, what is the message in a car diving in slow motion?) Many graphic artists, poets, and novelists object to critics evaluating a work solely in terms of the important—or unimportant—meanings they find.

The painting *Mississippi Monday* (Color Plate 2) by the American artist Romare Bearden (1912–1988) illustrates how an artist's intent can be misunderstood. By his own admission, Bearden was interested primarily in creating aesthetic pleasure. Here he recreates a familiar scene: women hanging up laundry. What appears to be central to the painting is the color and design of the clothes themselves: that is the *arrangement* of the parts. Doubtless the artist would say, "If you want to talk about what the standing woman is tossing from the bag or what the seated woman is doing with her hands, or to ask whether the painting is a commentary on the subservient role of women, go right ahead, but that's not what I'm up to."

The humanities can be enjoyed for both their aesthetic and communicative function. Learning to distinguish one from the other is an important part of *critical thinking*, the subject of Chapter 2.

Beautiful Movement

The best art always seems effortless. . .
—**Stephen Sondheim**

The perfection of movement cannot fail to inspire a sense of awe and admiration. Movement is as much a part of being human as breathing. Few of us move in perfect synchrony, but almost all of us experience joy when we see it done right. Even though our own movements may lack the coordination of, say, the skilled dancer, we find aesthetic pleasure in not just watching others but in getting up and swaying, gliding, or shaking to a rhythm. We have patterned our lives to meeting deadlines and reaching destinations. Perhaps that's why people like, for a change, to be on the dance floor and simply move in rhythm. Are they trying to get somewhere in particular? No. The pleasure of the movement is its own reason for existing.

The French artist Edgar Degas (1834–1917) loved to paint dancers. He seems to have had no message to convey beyond the beauty of the women and the elegance of their movements. Ballerinas gave him aesthetic pleasure. His paintings give that same pleasure to us.

So do the graceful leaps of a figure skater such as the young Japanese star Fumie Suguri. Like all great skaters and dancers, Suguri makes her body do what bodies seem never meant to do. In her leaps she defies gravity. In her spins she defies analysis. To the non-skater (most of us) it becomes nearly impossible to see how two rigid blades attached to her shoes can seem to disappear as she twirls. In this respect, figure skaters are akin to great magicians like David Copperfield. The arrangement of the parts in a given trick seem right if we don't see their function. If the rest of the world were not more often clumsy than otherwise, if our feet didn't get in each other's way from time to time, if we didn't drop things conspicuously, then the art of the figure skater or the magician would perhaps seem less than beautiful.

Language

Words in varied combinations are the means by which we communicate to ourselves and with each other. Through language we make ourselves understood to others, and we are able to understand what we read and what others are saying. The need for language becomes apparent at an early age, and we develop a love of language if we are fortunate enough to be around adults who talk to us (but not in baby-talk), who enjoy reading, and who read to us.

Children develop through recognizable and documented stages. Most children between the ages of two and three become word-conscious. The need to attach

Ballet performances provided the artist with aesthetic pleasure, and the painting can offer us the same experience.

Source: Edgar Degas, *Rehearsal on Stage,* 1876. Credit: Giraudon/Art Resource, NY.

a name to everything in sight appears to be an inborn instinct. Parents as well as older siblings can be annoyed at hearing the persistent "What's that?" throughout the day, even as they are happy that the insatiable demand for words is proceeding as it should. At this stage, children like to repeat sentences and phrases they hear in their surroundings, even if they have no idea what the words mean. Children like the sound and the "taste" of words. Nature supplies the need to acquire words, for the ability to think and to communicate are strategies for our survival.

How or when some of us lose the need for more words is a complex mystery. Unraveling it is perhaps less important than the awareness that *it does not have to happen*. That's where the humanities come in. Through reading, and through listening to great language on the stage or screen, we acquire models of how to say things in ways that make others sit up and take notice. People experienced in using the humanities as a technique for living sometimes make a point by directly quoting well-known lines, assured that their friends will catch the reference.

True wit is Nature to advantage dressed:
What oft was thought, but ne'er so well expressed.

—Alexander Pope

One of the most famous lines in all of drama is the beginning of Hamlet's third soliloquy: *To be or not to be: that is the question*. When people on similar wavelengths are discussing whether, for example, to stay home and watch television or go downtown for a costly evening of eating out and seeing a movie, the comment "Ah, that is the question" communicates instantly that the speaker is not leaning one way or the other but is wide open to suggestions. Directly quoting or providing variations on famous lines that you know others will recognize is not only fun, but it cuts down on the need for details and circular discussions.

Great dancers and skaters like Fumie Suguri seem to transcend the role that nature has given to the human body.

Source: Ng Han Guan/AP Photo.

Reading is to the mind what exercise is to the body.
—Joseph Addison

The most popular work of the medieval English poet Geoffrey Chaucer (1340–1400), *The Canterbury Tales*, contains not only a collection of unforgettable stories but also famous descriptions of the people who tell them. Chaucer was a master at capturing the essence of his characters with swift strokes of his pen, many of which are part of the reservoir of language in the minds of people who read. One of the characters is a lawyer who is always in a hurry and apparently so busy that he could easily have been the envy of lazy people. After describing the man and his behavior in detail, Chaucer adds: "Yet he seemed busier than he was." Who knows how many thousands of readers over the last 600 years have used this line as a reference to people who display feverish but essentially meaningless activity? A high school student is asked why he is not doing his homework. His reply: "I'm very busy with other things." One parent then tells the other, "He seems busier than he is."

The sixth century B.C.E. Greek philosopher Heraclitus is famous for having said: "You cannot step twice into the same river." By this he meant that life is constant change, that the only thing stable in the entire universe is the fact of change itself. A contemporary environmental expert, addressing a college graduating class and wishing to underscore the growing dangers of water pollution, echoed Heraclitus and remarked: "You cannot step *once* into the same river." Clearly, the versatile language derived from the humanities even increases the chance that an urgent cause may win more supporters.

The humanities help us to appreciate a variety of ingenious phrasing and offer us models of how language can be expertly manipulated. One of the greatest comedies ever written, Oscar Wilde's 1895 *The Importance of Being Earnest* (discussed in Chapter 7), is a storehouse of witty lines illustrating that one way of saying something is not necessarily as good as another. In one scene the hero, Jack Worthing, is being interviewed by his fiancé's mother, a social lioness with biting wit, who investigates his credentials as a suitor. At one point she asks the nervous young man whether he smokes. Sheepishly he admits that well yes, he does smoke. Her unexpected reply: "I'm glad to hear it. A man should always have an occupation of some sort." Not only is the lady staying one step ahead of him with her wit, but she is making an indirect statement about the indolence and lack of purpose of the upper classes.

Playing with language has evolved into a high art. Like the beautiful, good language needs no further justification. A person characterized by others as someone with "a way with words" or "a flair for language" generally earns respect (unless, of course, it turns out that the person never has anything else to offer *except* words).

Yet just as a novel or play or movie can be spoiled when authors use words and idioms that have become so commonplace they are no longer effective, so too is the everyday language of most people littered with terminology employed over and over. "I'm so tired I could die" belongs in the category of the no-longer-usable. Yet such hackneyed language keeps slipping from our tongues without our even noticing. "Like" has become the most frequently spoken word in our language, whether used appropriately or not. "I felt like a worn-out dishrag" no longer makes any kind of impression but is at least grammatically sound. What, however, are we to make of "After she said she decided not to go to the dance with me, I was, like, this can't be happening"?

In addition to "like," ordinary speech is now littered with "y'know" and "go" in place of "said"—as in "I go . . . and then he goes . . ." Hollywood and television perpetuate the idea that lines of dialogue are good if they reproduce the way people actually speak. But do we listen closely to that speech, whether it's in real life or on a screen? Does it startle us with its cleverness or a memorable turn of phrase? Does it help us grow? Listen carefully to the speech patterns of people with whom you are conversing. If their language tends to be fresh and interesting, chances are they spend a lot of time reading. Perhaps your own language reflects the same habit. We hope so.

Ideas

Language is not only the vehicle through which we can display our savvy in everyday dealings with others; it is also the means by which we formulate ideas. Still, all of us have flashes of ideas that we can't quite catch hold of because the words aren't there. A philosopher once said, "If you can't say it, you don't know it." When someone explains a complicated idea such as the theory of relativity and we nod to signify understanding, we are more or less guaranteeing that we would be able to deliver the identical explanation in our own words. Very often we cannot do this.

The most beautiful thing we can experience is the mysterious. It is the source of science.

—**Albert Einstein**

Words are the means by which we think. If we have no words, we cannot have ideas. We can have *intuitions* without words, but they are not the same as ideas. Intuitions are, of course, vital human resources. We don't need words to find a piece of music exciting. Intuitions are necessary for a full appreciation of much that the humanities have to offer. But through our philosophers, novelists, and poets, we derive a love for exciting ideas. After reading a stimulating book that makes an explosive point, one may say: "Oh! I wish I'd thought of that!" And don't we glow with pride when we advance an idea that meets with approval, even admiration?

Difficult things of the world can only be tackled when they are easy. Big things of the world can only be achieved by attending to their small beginnings.

—**Lao-tzu**

When people talk about "the mind," they are really talking about a supposed place inside the brain where ideas are formulated and stored. It is probably better to refer to the formulation and storing of ideas as "thinking." This capacity, once thought to be unique to human beings but now a matter open to question, remains nonetheless the cornerstone of humanity.

Thinking helps us keep our sanity—even in our world of rapidly accelerating change and technological marvels that are said to think *for* us. Fortunately, the brain can still be what makes us want to do more than just survive. Thinking keeps us in touch with ourselves and the world around us. Thinking comes in a variety of forms. Rigorous studies like mathematics, physics, and economics provide powerful exercise for the brain, but not all of us are adept at these disciplines. Yet happily, we have the humanities, which widen both our emotional range and our understanding of many things: the past, the present, human behavior, the workings of the creative mind, and the many unanswered questions that philosophers, scientists, and theologians have asked for centuries. A recently founded movement, the Society for Philosophical Inquiry, is the brainchild of Christopher Phillips, author of *Socrates' Cafe* (2003). In various venues, all with the name Socrates' Cafe, members gather to discuss and share ideas. The format for the meetings is inspired by the teaching methods of Socrates (469–399 B.C.E.), mentor of Plato (427–347 B.C.E.).

Socrates and his young students would gather in an Athenian grove called Academe and discuss specific questions, such as "What is justice?" As recorded by Plato—since the master himself, as far as we know, wrote nothing down—the discussions took this form:

> *The question is posed by Socrates. One student says "Justice is whatever is in the best interest of the ruling party."*
>
> *Socrates answers: "Can the ruling party ever pass a law that is for some reason* not *in its best interest?"*
>
> *Student: "I suppose it could happen."*
>
> *Socrates: "If it* did *happen, would the people be justified in breaking that law?"*
>
> *Student: "I don't think so. A law is a law."*
>
> *Socrates: "In other words, it would be wrong to break a law just because somebody thought it was not in the best interest of the ruling party."*
>
> *Student: "Well . . . maybe it* could *be broken."*
>
> *Socrates: "If* you *thought the law could be broken and I said it couldn't, which of us is right?"*
>
> *Student: "I guess in that case we're both right."*
>
> *Socrates: "Is this your idea of a just society—one in which anyone can decide whether to obey a law or not? Would you want to live in such a society?"*
>
> *Student: "I . . . suppose I wouldn't."*
>
> *Socrates: "Then justice really has to be defined as something that is absolute and not only in the best interest of the ruling party or the individual who decides not to obey a certain law."*

The point of a discussion at a Socrates' Cafe is not to solve all the problems of the world. It is to adapt the technique of the ancient philosopher as well as those of other thinkers to puzzling questions of the past and present. Clearly "justice" is one. It has never been defined to everyone's satisfaction. Whether one agrees or not that justice is absolute and unchanging or that there is no applicable principle other than "might makes right," the discussion and defense of ideas are ways of strengthening our mental faculties. Like dancing, thinking needs no further justification.

If birds of a feather flock together, they don't learn enough.

—Robert Hall

Deeper Sense of the Past

The humanities allow us to see more than our personal past. Through the humanities we may immerse ourselves in the firsthand experiences of those who actually lived and often struggled in the past, lived and struggled with many of the problems that face us today. These experiences help each of us to better understand what living is all about. *The realized human being is an accumulation of what has gone before and how that affects the present.*

Becoming familiar with treasures of the past inspires in us the pride of belonging to the community of our species.

Source: Venus de Milo, second century B.C.E. Credit: Erich Lessing/Art Resource, NY.

Through the humanities we can live more than once: here and now, and yesterday as well. Those who refuse to browse among the cumulative treasures of human expression have only themselves to blame if they find themselves trapped in one solitary existence.

Like all of us, the past has its right to be heard. It did not, we know, allow for the *full* representation of its genius, for the contributions of both men and women from a variety of cultures. Still, the past has its own glory, even as it stands. The *Venus de Milo* statue has been around for many hundreds of years. It no longer has arms, but gazing at it, we cannot help seeing the idealism, the adoration of the female form that must have motivated the unknown classical artist. Becoming familiar with treasures of the past not only brings us closer to those who came before us but also inspires in us the pride of belonging to the continuity of our species. The love of beauty is timeless and universal, and the past, as reflected in the humanities, has more than its share of beauty, not to mention ideas and great language.

Some treasures from the past embody issues that still face us. *The Oresteia*, an epic tragedy by the Greek dramatist Aeschylus (525–456 B.C.E.), is based on a very ancient myth about the murder of a mother and her lover by a son seeking revenge for his father's death at their hands. In the final segment of the work, the playwright creates the world's first courtroom drama, in which the hero is acquitted on the grounds that his mother's crime had been greater than his. She had killed a man who was a great warrior and leader of his people. He had killed an adulterous woman and her lover. The decision to acquit the hero was made nearly 2,500 years ago and delivered from the stage at the Theater of Dionysus; it is still discussed today. Teachers of theater history often point out that the acquittal does not sit well with everyone. Feminist scholars, for example, argue that it discriminates against the gender of the victim and ignores the fact that the murdered husband had a mistress. Nevertheless, the work is a milestone in the early history of democracy. There was, after all, a trial. Reading or watching a performance of *The Oresteia* can generate a discussion of whether the law, even in a democracy, judges all persons equally.

Developing a profound respect for the work of Socrates, Plato, Aeschylus, the sculptor of the *Venus de Milo*, and others from the past does not mean that we choose to ignore the achievements of everyone else, including many contemporaries. At the same time, having profound respect for today and a wider vision of tomorrow does not mean that we ought to ignore what can be justly celebrated from yesterday.

Becoming an Infinite Person

By sharpening our awareness of the present—the issues, the important themes and varied ways of presenting them—and by linking us to the past, the humanities widen our view of life. As this book unfolds, you will be learning much more about the humanities and what the various disciplines are and how they can deeply affect your life. Your view of the humanities and the world will continue to expand.

Developing this perspective is of crucial importance in the twenty-first century, a time of amazing technology that changes almost daily. Every day the world grows smaller and the lives of the diverse populations become more interconnected. In such a world we must resist the temptation to concern ourselves exclusively with our own interests and the limited time we have to pursue them. To study the humanities requires time, time that could be spent doing other things. For some, pausing to reflect on art, music, literature, and drama might at first seem like *wasting* time. Who wants to stay inside and read a book when there is so much pulsating life out there? A cellphone call away? A mouse click away?

History has accorded Leonardo da Vinci that rarest of titles, *uomo universale*.
Source: Biblioteca Reale, Turin, Italy. Credit: Alinari/Art Resource, NY.

To answer those questions, let us consider the very model of humanism, the very essence of the infinite person, Leonardo da Vinci (1452–1519). So broad was the range of his curiosity and creative genius that history has accorded him that rarest of titles: *uomo universale*, universal man. He is also called a **Renaissance man**, meaning a man of the broadest possible learning and a widely diverse range of interests and achievements. Since Leonardo's time, that label has been given to many people, both famous and not-so-famous, who refused to be limited to just one field of endeavor, though it is doubtful that many will ever match what Leonardo accomplished: plans for early versions of the airplane and submarine; speculating about the human circulatory system long before William Harvey "officially" discovered the circulation of the blood; building the first hydrometer to measure the displacement of water; inventing the science of meteorology long before there were the proper instruments to make accurate predictions. And on top of all the scientific and technological contributions there are the works of art, including the world's most famous painting, the *Mona Lisa*.

The example of Leonardo da Vinci suggests that, while few may hope to approach his genius, all of us can do more with our lives than we are doing at this very moment. There are so many books to be read, so much music to hear, so many plays to see, so many great films that line the shelves of the video stores, orphans silently begging to be taken home. We may not become Renaissance persons, but infinite choices await us. The more we absorb from the humanities, the more we expand our knowledge, our capacity for understanding both ourselves and others. In a sense, we become infinite, intertwining with innumerable lives in myriad combinations.

Some of us rush through life, and some of us saunter through life. Mrs. Vesey sat through life.

—**Wilkie Collins**

There are many advantages to becoming an infinite person. Here are just three:

- The infinite person commits no crimes against humanity. He or she is no longer narrowly preoccupied with the self and its immediate needs, its sense of having been unfairly used, its desire to avenge wrongs against itself.
- The infinite person is free of rigid prejudices and never works consciously to restrict others from exercising their right to assemble, speak their minds openly, practice their own religion, and follow their own preferences, as long as, in being free, they do not themselves limit the freedom of others.
- The infinite person does not jump to quick conclusions but looks at all sides of an issue before making a judgment, recognizes that no judgment is final, and is always willing to reconsider in the light of new data. This person is therefore not constrained by family and social traditions and willingly seeks out the source of imposed or inherited beliefs so as to reevaluate them. "That's how we've always done it around here" is not the mark of the infinite person.

The book you are about to read is thus not only a visit to the treasure house of the humanities, the stupendous creative and intellectual achievements of human beings. It has the underlying purpose of convincing you that you cannot fail to want to expand your life, to fill every moment with art and thought, once you realize that all it takes is the willingness to do it.

Key Terms

aesthetic an experience in the arts or in life, such as watching a sunset, that we value for no reason beyond itself.

beauty a pleasing arrangement of parts that affects us aesthetically.

discipline in the humanities, a given art form—literature, visual art, music, drama, dance, cinema—as well as a field of academic study, such as "literary theory" or "history of dance."

humanism a movement begun in the early Renaissance that extolled and studied the creative and intellectual legacies of Greece and Rome, leading to the conviction that only through such study could one become fully human; the term *humanism* is now expanded to include the study of contributions from all cultures.

humanities once limited to "the best products of the best minds," narrowly defined as Greek or Roman, but later expanded to include Western European achievements and, more recently, the creative expressions of men and women around the world.

Renaissance man a label often applied to Leonardo da Vinci, indicating his display of genius in many areas from art to science; now used as high praise for anyone who has earned a reputation for high achievement in several fields.

Topics for Writing and Discussion

1. The text states: "Each of us is more than a gender, an age, an address, an occupation." Explain what this means and how it relates to the study of the humanities.
2. How do you define *beauty*? Give two examples, citing how you would use the term to describe a person and an object.
3. Reread carefully the section called "Ideas." Then restate Socrates' definition of justice in your own words.
4. What does it mean to be an "infinite" person? Describe either someone you know personally or a famous person in the news who seems to fit the label.
5. Briefly give a profile of someone for whom the humanities function as a technique for living. Or do a profile of someone who has no interest in the humanities.

VII-'53

2 Profile of the Critical Thinker

Overview

In the introductory chapter we said that the study of the humanities includes understanding the critical process by which professional critics and scholars interpret and evaluate cultural achievements and communicate their thoughts to others. In this chapter we will elaborate on the elements of professional criticism, presenting examples of what the critic notices when he or she is reviewing a given humanities event. But we will also be dealing with ways in which most of us who are not professional critics can enrich our lives by using some of the same techniques: becoming objective in how we evaluate what we see, read, or hear; separating rational and emotional responses; delaying a final judgment until we have all the data. The critical skill has a strong carryover into everyday life as well. We should find ourselves not making snap judgments about other people or blindly accepting opinions expressed in the media just because we like the commentator. And, of vital importance to the conduct of our own lives, we should find that we are listening carefully to what others tell us before we make up our minds. All too often we are guilty of deciding something is true or that other thing is poppycock, or he is not to be trusted but she always knows what she is talking about. Worse, we often place people in the wax museum of our mind, attaching labels that never change: liar, cheat, double-crosser, tightwad.

Critical thinking sharpens the mind. If we start early enough in life and continue to exercise our critical faculties throughout our lives, chances are good that our mind will not desert us late in life. Toward the end of William Wharton's novel *Dad* (1981), the main character, en route to his father's funeral, has a sudden glimpse of his own aging. "I'll become a bore to others, a drag in conversation, repeat myself, be slow at comprehension, quick at misunderstanding, have lapses in conceptual sequences. All this will probably be invisible to me. I won't even be aware of my own decline."[1]

The older one gets, the more precious does the mind become. Many, early on, seek what they term "altered states," achieved through substance or alcohol abuse. A reason often given is that life is too complex; one has too

Relativity.

Source: © The M. C. Escher Company–Holland. All rights reserved. www.mcescher.com

many responsibilities—school, parental problems, relationship problems—so escape is not only pleasant but absolutely necessary. Even if the use of such escape mechanisms is relatively moderate and there are no lasting effects, the mind, that most fragile and wonderful instrument, is not being used. The danger here is that when one finally is old enough to make important decisions, the critical faculties, so necessary for those decisions, won't be there. Those who miss the chance to develop critical thought can be called *non-critical thinkers.* They do think, of course, but most of the time they are narrowly concerned with the specific details of their everyday life. Decisions are based on what seems most personally important at the moment: for example, *What shall I wear to the party*? The critical thinker might wonder about the purpose of going to a party: in other words, might move from the particular moment to finding a general principle at work. *My acquaintances seem to like parties because . . . Am I just blindly following because . . . ? Why are there so many parties in our society*?

This chapter is dedicated both to those who believe there will be plenty of time in the future to think about weightier matters and those who believe in thinking now.

Apollonian and Dionysian Responses to the Humanities

You miss all the fun if you obey all the rules.

—**Katharine Hepburn**

The German philosopher Friedrich Nietzsche (1844–1900) wrote a book in 1872 titled *The Birth of Tragedy from the Spirit of Music*, in which he revisits the great age of drama in fifth century (B.C.E.) Athens. He points out that the art form began as choral music and dance, without spoken dialogue. As it evolved, certain soloists became distinct from the Chorus, and through their dialogue they told stories based on ancient myths. *The Oresteia* by Aeschylus, discussed in the previous chapter, is one such story. Most popular were the tragic myths, stories of powerful and rich men (often rulers) who, because of a fatal flaw of character, would fall from the heights, would in fact reach the depths of despair and ruination. Not all of the tragedies, including *The Oresteia*, fit this description exactly, but they are all filled with horror, suffering, and the extremes of human pain. They have scenes that are among the most shattering ever devised.

Music does not depict scenes or describe objects or tell stories, but it mysteriously embodies the continuous motion and emotion that we experience at the sight of objects and scenes and events.

—**Jacques Barzun**

What bothered Nietzsche was that, in lecturing or writing about tragedy, teachers and critics sometimes forgot that the roots of the art form were in dance and music. He believed the proper response to viewing a tragedy was to allow oneself to respond emotionally, the way we respond to music. He found that viewers and critics alike were focusing on the central characters' moral failings, on the breaking of moral law as the cause of their tragic fall. As a result, Greek tragedies were evaluated and taught in terms of their moral messages, not their strong emotional impact. Nietzsche believed it was wrong to encourage people to view tragedy through reason rather than emotion—wrong to insist on the moral philosophy behind a play at the expense of appreciating the force and the fury that drive it.

He then made a famous distinction between two ways of responding not only to drama but to events in real life. He identified as **Apollonian** that side of the human personality dominated by disciplined, analytical, rational, and coherent thought: in short, the side that responds to Greek tragedy by seeking

Apollo, god of the sun, and Dionysus, god of the vibrant energy of the earth.

Source: Left: Villa Valmarana, Vicenza, Italy. Credit: Scala/Art Resource, NY. Right: Uffizi/Florence, Italy. Credit: The Bridgeman Art Library.

its meaning. He dubbed as **Dionysian** that side of the human personality dominated by emotion, intuition, and freedom from limits: the side that responds emotionally to music as well as the force and fury of tragedy.

Real knowledge is knowing the extent of one's ignorance.
—**Confucius**

These opposing terms are derived from Greek mythology. Apollo was the god of the sun (hence of light and truth) and Dionysus was the god of the vibrant energy of the earth (hence of emotion, spontaneity, and intuition). Nietzsche believed the goal of life was to achieve a balance between reason and emotion: to be able to think clearly, to be steady, reliable, and responsible for one's actions, AND be able to feel, to enjoy the fruits of the vine (so to speak), to express both love and hate (when necessary), unguided by a concern for rules.

Throughout this book we will refer many times to Apollonian and Dionysian elements in the humanities. If critical thinking is a major goal of studying the humanities, the distinction between the two sides of our personality is always the starting point. It is *impossible* to study the humanities without seeing how one or the other or sometimes both together inform a given work.

The Apollonian response means looking at a work objectively before evaluating it. Critical thinking begins on the Apollonian side; writing a critical analysis is always Apollonian, even though a strong emotional response may have inspired the analysis. One can be enraptured by a musical performance *without* wanting to analyze it further. If this is the case, however, the comment "It was great; I was carried away by it" must not be confused with a full critical statement. It has to be recognized for what it is: a statement of a personal experience. "I liked it" is personal and Dionysian. "I liked it because it had . . ." may be introducing an Apollonian evaluation. Both are valid, but they must not be mistaken for each other.

A wise skepticism is the first attribute of a good critic.

—**James Russell Lowell**

The Popcorn Syndrome

A word of caution. It is all too easy to give the critical mind a vacation, to surrender to the Dionysian excitement of the moment and decide that further considerations are not important. But doing so will not stretch our mental capacities. However, sometimes a given work clearly does not warrant time and mental energy. More seductive is the popcorn experience, usually at the movies. "This is strictly a popcorn movie" means that one should be able to sit back, munch on popcorn, and be entertained without having to think. A huge number of films and television shows belong to this category, as indeed do many novels called "good reads."

Dan Brown's *The Da Vinci Code* (2002), one of the most widely read novels ever written, topped the best-seller list for almost two years and sold well into the millions of copies. The story of a secret organization, oppressed by religious authorities because it can supposedly prove that Jesus was married and sired a family, is told in such fast-moving, cinematic prose that the reader cannot wait to turn the page. Exciting? Yes. Suspenseful? Indeed. A great novel? Here one must pause and reflect. Is the story totally believable? Is there any depth to the main characters? Does the novel leave the reader with what we may call "residual thoughts"? Or is it, like many others, just popcorn fun? Perhaps. Yet one may also decide that any novel *so* entertaining to read is certainly worthwhile. Popular music, films, novels, cartoons in newspapers and magazines, the "funnies"—all that entertains and amuses us for even a short time can be called, at the very least, the "temporary humanities." Like all emotional responses, fun is a legitimate way to spend some time. Nobody gets hurt, nobody dies.

Dionysian enjoyment may also lead to a morning-after headache, what we can call the "popcorn hangover." The night before at the movies, the big bucket of popcorn, the pleasant company, the fast-moving, car-chase plot, the nerve-jangling soundtrack that brings one into a la-la land of no stress. "What a great evening. What a terrific movie!" Then tomorrow dawns. Subliminal replay of the movie on the semiconscious screen of the half-awake mind. The sudden sitting up. The flash of truth. "*How could I possibly have liked that awful film?*" This often happens, and it is a perfectly valid response. The difference between popcorn fun and critical thinking, however, is that, engaging in the latter, determining why the film does not remain in the museum of one's fondest aesthetic experiences, provides a far different sort of pleasure (now that the big bucket of popcorn is empty).

The critical thinker eventually finds a deeper, more satisfying definition of "entertainment." Having enjoyed *The Da Vinci Code* as a good read, you might have looked forward to the 2006 film version, expecting to find not a work of high screen art but at the very least an engrossing, fast-moving thriller. Instead, let us say, you emerge from the theater *without* a popcorn hangover, without any sense of having been involved. You can let it go at that or, preferably, spend a little time pondering why the transference of the novel to the screen did not work for you, especially since the author's prose had been more than once praised as "cinematic." The story line was the same. But wasn't the action slower than you expected it to be? Didn't it lack the pulsating rhythm of popcorn movies you usually enjoy?

The critical mind, perceiving that a response has been largely Dionysian, looks further. After hearing a thrilling interpretation of Beethoven's Ninth Symphony in a concert hall, the critical mind seeks, in the later tranquility of musing on the exciting experience, to consider those elements which caused the response: the beauty of the singers' voices? the unexpected shifts in tempo?

the alternation between the majesty of the musical crescendos and the sudden silences that follow? No two analyses will be exactly the same. Nor need they be. Critical thinking is valid as an ongoing process, not as the road to absolute determination of good or bad. The important thing is that the unexamined Dionysian response may be limited to "Gee, that was terrific!"—okay as far as it goes, but not likely to contribute much toward balancing the two forces in our lives. At best, the unexamined response ought to be restricted to experiences that defy words.

Empathy and Alienation

Empathy, the process by which we identify with a character or a performer so that for a short time we believe we are that person, is a Dionysian trick of our nature. On the one hand, it lures us away from our problems and therefore offers a valuable escape from stress. Empathy is crucial to the entertainment process. If you, for example, should arrive late for a circus performance, sitting down just as the tightrope-walker's act has begun, what you would see is not only the death-defying stunter higher up than you might ever care to be but hundreds of seated patrons swaying back and forth. They would be projecting themselves into the precarious journey, gasping each time the performer (as part of the act) appears about to fall. In similar fashion, you and your fellow audience members in a movie theater may be in a car careening wildly out of control and dodging oncoming traffic in the streets of New York. Filmmakers know about Dionysian empathy and readily design opportunities for indulging in it. If the main character, trapped in a mountain ravine with floodwaters inching upward, attempts to scale the rock wall, she has to be successful at first and then *must* slip when she is halfway up and appear to be doomed. You give free reign to your empathetic imagination because deep down you know all will be well in the end—but you will feel cheated if all is well from the start.

It is the rediscovery of the world of which I have the joy of being a part. It fills me with awareness of the wonder of life, with a feeling of the incredible marvel of being a human being. The music is never the same for me, never! Each day it is something new, fantastic and unbelievable. That is Bach, like nature, a miracle!

—**Pablo Casals**

Just why empathizing with near-death experiences should qualify as entertainment has been debated for centuries. It may be traceable to the eighteenth-century shift away from the onstage blood and gore of popular tragedies, including many of Shakespeare's, which featured hands being chopped off, tongues and eyes being ripped out, horrors that could rival the bloodiest slasher movie of today. The eighteenth century on both sides of the Atlantic introduced a more genteel way of life for the upper classes and those who imitated them. The works of Shakespeare and his contemporaries went into a period of decline, or else were revised with all the horrors eliminated. But little by little, as society became more and more "respectable," stage entertainment began reintroducing melodramatic elements for audiences that enjoyed escape from their morally upright lives. In the late-eighteenth century the circus was born, with its empathy-inducing trapeze and highwire acts and its wild animal

The bloodier the scene, the more many in the audience may feel they are being royally entertained.

Source: Celador/Crawlspace Productions/The Kobal Collection.

encounters. All of this led inevitably to the current Dionysian orgies on film and television, and to circuses with ever more dangerous acts.

The flip side of the Dionysian coin, when it comes to such entertainment, can be called Apollonian alienation. The term **alienation** was coined by Bertolt Brecht, a major German playwright of the early twentieth century, about whom much more will be said in Chapter 7. Brecht wanted to make sure audiences did not become so emotionally involved in plot and character that they failed to heed his messages. He often injected vaudeville slapstick, songs, and dances into very serious material. In this way he hoped to prevent empathetic responses.

What is written without effort is in general read without pleasure.
—**Samuel Johnson**

As critical thinkers, we are not so restricted. Attending a play or film with strong emotional undercurrents or reading a powerful novel filled with moving, tragic moments, we may appreciate the feelings evoked but can also sit back and look objectively at the work. Questions raised might be: *Why is the hero's downfall so terrifying when he is not a very good person? How does the author make us care about what is happening to him?* When the author's technique becomes transparent, the viewing or reading experience becomes that much richer. And we have seized the opportunity to expand our mind. Critical thinkers tend to retain stronger memories of their experiences and find enjoyment in discussing works with other critical thinkers who may have the same or sharply differing views. Mutual agreement doesn't matter. The process of building "brain muscle" does.

When a Purely Emotional Response Is Appropriate

We are not insisting that it is always better to analyze, Apollonian fashion. To enter the Sistine Chapel at the Vatican and see Michelangelo's ornate fresco ceiling is, quite literally, to be bereft of words. None are necessary. Something inside tells us that these artistic arrangements are right, magnificently right. It is to experience what Plato would have called "pure beauty." Time stops for the viewer. Practical concerns disappear. The experience doesn't have to be explained or analyzed. It is the quiet joy of being conscious at the highest level. When you get to a summit like this, you *know* it!

Seeing these famous works may well defy words and make analysis irrelevant.

Source: Michelangelo, *The Creation of Adam*, Sistene Chapel, Vatican Palace. Credit: Erich Lessing, Art Resource, NY.

Great works like the *Venus de Milo* (p. 15), the *David* (p. 132), the symphonies of Beethoven, or the tragedies of Shakespeare have powerful emotional effects on us long before we begin to exercise sober critical judgment. Even professional critics, whom we shall be discussing presently, no doubt allow themselves to be so affected before they stand back and begin a rational analysis of a work. Often there is no point to the rational analysis if the emotions have not first been stirred. What is unfortunate is that, in writing about or teaching the humanities, many fail to mention emotional appeal.

Here is a poem by the American e.e. cummings (1894–1962), famous for dismantling standard English grammar and finding alternate ways to express feelings and ideas. In this poem, "may my heart always," he delivers a clear Dionysian message but in off-the-wall language that can be intuitively understood without requiring further analysis.[2]

may my heart always be open to little
birds who are the secrets of living
whatever they sing is better than to know
and if men should not hear them men are old

may my mind stroll about hungry
and fearless and thirsty and supple
and even if it's sunday may i be wrong
for whenever men are right they are not young

and may myself do nothing usefully
and love yourself so more than truly
there's never been quite such a fool who could fail
pulling all the sky over him with one smile

Analysis here is not only irrelevant but unfair to the poet. What cummings is expressing all of us can feel. Does he not awaken the Dionysian impulse to "do nothing useful" and believe truly and deeply that being in love is all that really matters? Don't we know, without having to be directly told, that it's better to do what your instinct tells you even if you're wrong than to be self-righteously "right" all of the time? Is cummings irresponsible? Perhaps, but if we find ourselves joyously agreeing with him, then he's allowing us to express—along *with* him—feelings that we usually have to hide. And isn't it better to be a little irresponsible in *art* and save our responsibility for society, where it's needed?

The Importance of Responding Critically

Critical thinking carefully defines, describes, and analyzes something: an election, an important decision, a question that has puzzled or intrigued philosophers for centuries, a new electronic invention, a movie, a novel, the Number One song on the Top 40, or a determination to move into your own apartment. Critical responses, as we have said, build our mental strength. They usually involve the following steps:

Take each man's censure but reserve thy judgment.
—**William Shakespeare**

1. Defining what it is we want to determine. Example: *Why did this film work for me?*
2. Putting aside instinctive, emotional responses.
3. Collecting and analyzing all pertinent factors.
4. Evaluating the work or the topic in its proper context.
5. Forgetting how it relates only to you. Example: *I know it's good because the main character is young like me.*
6. Having an informed opinion.

Developing the skill of analysis and objective evaluation helps us to deepen our appreciation of the humanities and also to have a better sense of who we are and what seems to be truly worth our time.

Exercising the Mind

Most of us get up and go when we feel the need to exercise our bodies, especially when something has prevented our moving about (such as being cramped for three hours in an airplane seat). Those who have suffered illnesses charged to a lack of exercise may be encouraged to alter the way they live, urged to run, walk, do basketball layups, a host of activities to avoid that sluggish feeling well known to non-exercisers, who usually experience guilt even if they cannot bring themselves to engage in even the briefest of workouts. Yet far too many of us experience no guilt while allowing our minds to be sluggish. The critical responses discussed in the previous section come much easier to minds that are trim and fit. And getting there doesn't even involve a diet!

Critical thinking is enhanced as we engage in three important activities: solving problems, challenging assumptions, and recognizing contexts.

Solving Problems

Problems are only opportunities in work clothes.

—**Henry J. Kaiser**

Critical thinkers are always solving problems, even hypothetical ones. One day the late American philosopher Richard Rorty was relaxing in a backyard hammock, hazily listening to the radio. A DJ announced he was going to play "that golden oldie 'Everybody Loves My Baby,' " which begins with these lines:

Everybody loves my baby
But my baby don't love nobody but me

Suddenly the philosopher's active brain, which had been allowed to float in a reverie, snapped to attention. It knew that something was wrong with the lines, something that did not make sense. He quickly solved the problem. The next day he repeated the lines to a class of philosophy majors and asked them to determine why the lines made no sense. We suggest you cover the following paragraph and try first to find the answer yourself.

Here's Rorty's answer. Since the first line states that *everybody* loves the singer's baby, that baby is logically included in the totality of everybody. It is then permissible to change the line to read *My baby loves my baby*. But if, regardless of the double negative, it is also true that the "me" is the only one loved by the baby, then the second line can be changed to read *My baby loves only me*, and thus baby = me. Professor Rorty, whose active brain was very sharp indeed, realized in a flash that the song was saying "I am my baby," which he assumed was unintentional.

Exercises like Rorty's are the stuff of critical thinking. To solve such problems helps strengthen the brain for times when real problems confront us. Having developed the habit of critical analysis, we are prepared to confront a real problem in our own life. The family member who needs help is a problem thousands face each day. Suppose you have a brother who constantly overspends, is heavily in debt, and cannot curb this extravagance. One reason is that he always counts on being rescued by responsible relatives—for example, *you*.

The first step in solving such a problem is to determine whether a problem actually exists. Whether or not to pay off your brother's debts may not be a problem if you decide not to assume ownership of it. Whose problem is it? It's yours if you wish to avoid the pain of guilt you think you'll experience if you turn your back. But the problem belongs to your brother or to other family members if you decide to withdraw with a clear conscience. If the rest of the family also declines, with a clear conscience, then only your brother has something to solve.

Family bonds are likely to be pretty strong, but you have to weigh all the factors. Does your brother overspend very often? Is your brother capable of earning enough money to pay the debts? If not, will he listen to a rational argument in favor of spending within his limits? Merely to pay off the debts to "avoid the hassle" may send the wrong signal.

No ultimate answer will be found here, but we have just engaged in the act of reasoning. Sometimes easy solutions evade us and we must finally settle on one, hoping for the best. Yet we are less likely to find a successful answer if we have not fully analyzed the problem—if we have not been critical thinkers.

Challenging Assumptions

Assumptions are a fact of everyday communication. They are the beliefs on which opinions are based and conclusions drawn. Often these are *buried*: that is, they lie underneath what people are saying without being acknowledged as assumptions, and often they are the real message that is being communicated. The critical thinker listens carefully, always seeking what is actually being said.

Suppose a newspaper reader turns to you and says that a convicted murderer has been released after being confined to a mental hospital for ten years. In the opinion of the medical staff, that person is no longer a menace to society. The reader then observes, "There ought to be a law against letting people escape the death penalty with a plea of insanity and then releasing them so they can kill again."

The above statement makes no pretense to be factual. It is understood that the speaker is expressing an opinion. The buried assumptions behind the opinion, however, may not be recognized. Here are some possibilities:

1. The question of insanity should have no bearing on a court case.
2. The defendant was not really insane anyway.
3. The state or federal legislature should control how defendants plead.
4. Once a murderer, always a murderer.
5. Those in charge of mental hospitals are not qualified to make accurate judgments about the future behavior of a released patient.

Non-critical listeners are likely to nod in agreement with the reader's observation, because careful debate in this instance involves careful analysis of the buried assumptions. Many do not wish to invest the time needed for making this analysis.

Now suppose that the newspaper reader and the listener in the above example are both seasoned critical thinkers, people who are knowledgeable about the humanities and who exercise their mental faculties as often as possible, knowing how to balance their inner Apollo and Dionysus. A critically thinking reader would no doubt communicate a different version of the newspaper story, such as "Abel Parsons has been released from the mental hospital where he has spent the last ten years. If you remember, his lawyer pleaded not guilty by reason of insanity."

The critically thinking listener might then respond: "Does the article cite any reasons for his release?"

"One. The psychiatrist who has observed him for the whole time called in three consultants, and they all agreed that Parsons appears to be totally rehabilitated."

"Have they provided any sort of monitoring system to keep tabs on what he does at least for a while?"

"It doesn't say."

"They'd *have* to set something up, don't you think?"

The two critical thinkers have not solved a thorny legal problem. What they *have* done in this hypothetical conversation is exercise critical thinking to get at the objective facts of the newspaper story rather than make assumptions about it.

Recognizing Contexts

Each of us lives within contexts: family, circle of friends, religious affiliation, political allegiances. . .

Everyone and everything exist in a **context**, a framework of circumstances and relationships. A sentence is a context, a relationship among words, their individual meanings, and how they come together to express a thought. A forest fire threatening nearby homes is a context for those living in the homes and for those fighting the fire. The Great Depression of the 1930s was a huge context enveloping the entire population of the United States, as well as the countries that depended on the health of the American economy. A college course is a context, and the circumstances of it involve the professor, the syllabus, grading policies, and the grade point average of you and your classmates. Each of us lives within many contexts: family, circle of friends, religious affiliation, political allegiances, and so on and so on.

Knowing that nothing exists independent of one or more contexts, critical thinkers try to avoid making large-scale generalizations and absolute evaluations. Even so, like many others, they are at times not above simplifying, distilling contexts down to something manageable. This is likeliest to be true when past events are recalled and related. *Selective memory* is a universal trait. People, including critical thinkers, can obscure the truth, not only of the past but of what happened just yesterday when the full context of an event is unpleasant or embarrassing to relate. Using the well-practiced skill of **rationalization**, they tell others (as well as themselves) a convenient and palatable version of an event—say, a bitter argument with a sibling. In this version, the absent family member is usually the culprit and the speaker is the victim. By the time the speaker is finished, the context within which the argument took place has become fixed in the speaker's mind exactly as it has been described, and chances are that it doesn't come close to what *really* happened. While dedicated critical thinkers are not immune to reinventing contexts or selecting those that can be comfortably dealt with, they are less likely, upon reflection, to feel good about substituting imagination for reality.

One of the gifts of the humanities we described earlier is a sense of the past, which provides us with *historical context.* A casual browser in a secondhand store filled with attic discards might grow impatient because none of the items belongs to today. Those with a sense of the past, however, would be interested in examining a phonograph, a doll, or a pair of shoes that reveal much about bygone periods. Examining pictorial records from publications of the past increases our interest in and knowledge of earlier times.

Turn to Color Plate 3 and study the 1945 cover for the *Saturday Evening Post,* once among the most popular magazines in the United States. Norman Rockwell (1894–1978), the artist, achieved fame as an interpreter of middle-class life. To see his work is to gain invaluable knowledge of how a large segment of the population lived in twentieth-century America. Notice the way the people are dressed. Look closely at the various objects in what appears to be a repair shop of some kind. Which are hard to recognize now? Why are the flags important? Which have been replaced by updated versions? If nothing else, spending some time with old pictures like this adds to our critical thinking skills.

The more we learn to recognize historical contexts, the less likely are we to evaluate everything in terms of today. In reading books or watching movies from the past, the critical thinker knows better than to judge them in terms of the present. *Gone with the Wind* (1939) is still recognized by professional critics as a milestone in movie making, even though a contemporary viewer may find some of it sentimental and dated. Without overlooking these failings, the critical thinker tries to view the film in the context of 1939 and enjoys what is still to be enjoyed, such as the marvelously advanced (for its time) use of color, the sweeping symphonic score, and the still believable performance of Vivien Leigh as Scarlett O'Hara. Whether a given work belongs to the past *or* the present, we can appreciate its positive achievements without endorsing all of its ideas or techniques.

The ability to appreciate historical context makes one more tolerant of art forms in unfamiliar styles: for example, most operas. Viewers who are visiting an opera house for the first time might easily lose patience with a three-hour performance in which every word is sung in a foreign language and performers are chosen for the power of their voice, not their physical appearance or acting ability. Opera companies throughout the world try to update some classic works, such as Mozart's *The Abduction from the Seraglio*, in order to accommodate modern tastes, but even though a recent production changed the setting from a Turkish harem to a trans-European railroad, the cast still sang in German. In times past, English-speaking audiences did not base their opera-going pleasure on whether or not they could understand the language, and informed audiences of today are still expected to watch most operas in their original language.

The ability to appreciate historical context makes one more tolerant of art forms in unfamiliar styles: for example, most operas.

The plots of even the most celebrated operas are likely to seem ridiculous. Critical viewers concentrate on the glorious music, the quality of the voices delivering it, the ingenuity of the staging, the imaginative use of scenery, the visual effect of the costumes, and the appropriateness of whatever updating the director has chosen.

Occasionally a work from the past is staged or even totally rewritten in a modern context. One of the most enduringly popular operas is *La Bohème* by Giacomo Puccini (1858–1924). Since its 1896 premiere, it has been performed hundreds of times throughout the world. Audiences seem never to tire of its lush romantic score and its touching, tragic tale of the love between Rodolfo, a poet, and Mimi, a seamstress, living in the shabby bohemian section of Paris along with a number of friends, most of them artists, all of them poor but always hopeful of selling a poem or a painting. The story captures for all time the myth of starving artists living in a garret; and its main characters are, like Romeo and Juliet, doomed to be separated. The final scene in which the fragile Mimi dies from consumption in Rodolfo's bitterly cold attic room has probably brought even the most alienated Apollonian viewer close to tears.

The free lifestyle of the bohemian artist is not, however, limited to the context of 1830 Paris. There continue to be rebellious young people dedicated to innovations in music, art, and theater. New York, in particular, is home to thousands of young hopefuls, often living in cramped, shabby apartments, often without much food, but always trying, like the characters in *La Bohème*, to sell their work or to get work in the theater.

In 1996 what appeared to be a modest, low-budget, rock-musical retelling of *La Bohème* called *Rent* opened in a tiny off-Broadway theater. It was the brainchild of Jonathan Larson, who wrote the book and lyrics and composed the music. Larson died suddenly of an aortic aneurysm after the final dress rehearsal, thus never living to enjoy his show's phenomenal success. To accommodate the crowds, it moved to a large theater on Broadway and later became a successful film.

Similar story but vastly different music in startlingly contrasted historical periods.
Source: Left: Perrin/Sygma-Corbis. Right: Sony Pictures/The Kobal Collection.

With an infectious and unrelenting rock beat and its twenty-first-century cast of characters, *Rent* would have bewildered Puccini's original audiences. In the modern version, Rodolfo is transformed into Roger, an HIV-positive rocker determined to write a great song before he dies. Mimi keeps her name, but now she is a drug addict, also HIV-positive. Their friends include a gay couple, a lesbian couple, and a transvestite. Like the bohemians of Puccini's Paris, Larson's characters live together in blissful poverty, singing wildly joyous songs pulsating with hope for the future, though the shadow of death is slowly encroaching.

If one could view both *La Bohème* and *Rent* on successive nights, one would need no further lesson to understand two startlingly contrasted historical periods. Arguments have been raised about which version is more enjoyable. This in itself is one of the pleasures offered by the humanities: the ability to contrast two versions of the same story and defend a preference for one or the other. Yet those who slip easily into different historical contexts will probably find the strong points of both.

Critical Viewing

Before moving on to explore the humanities in greater depth, we will examine the skill of critical viewing. Though professional critics are people who devote much time to the analysis and evaluation of the work of others, we do not have to be professional critics to engage in their art.

How the Professional Critic Responds

The best critics have widely respected opinions. Their work can be found in the pages of leading newspapers like the *New York Times* or *San Francisco Chronicle*, magazines like the *New Yorker*, *Film Comment*, or *Opera News*, as well as Internet sites such as *Prodigy* and *Slate*. What professional critics have to say about something can help us decide among the many choices open to us. In the world of the humanities, with so much that is Dionysian to stir the emotions and, sometimes, to cloud our judgment, the professional critic is an Apollonian voice that can serve as a model for our own growing critical skills.

In 2007 the director Michael Winterbottom made a widely anticipated film version of the book *A Mighty Heart* by Mariane Pearl, widow of Daniel Pearl, the correspondent who in 2002 was kidnapped and gruesomely executed in Pakistan. There had been widespread speculation about which actress would be chosen and have the credentials to play the woman who was in the news on an almost daily basis and whose face and mannerisms were already familiar to millions. When it was learned that most-hounded and photographed celebrity couple in the world, skeptics shook their heads at what they immediately decided was gross miscasting before the first scene was ever shot.

So it is not surprising that Anthony Lane, a highly respected film critic for *The New Yorker*, should begin his **review** of the film with an indictment of contemporary media-directed mass culture, in which preconceived opinions of celebrities such as Jolie make open-minded critical viewing difficult indeed. Lane, in other words, stacks the cards against Jolie at the outset, and we fully expect his review to be a quotable pan.

> *We brace ourselves for a star turn, a hundred minutes of vanity project, but here's the thing: it never happens. Jolie slips into the part, ducks in and out of the action, and generally plays second string to the onrush of events.*[3]

Lane marvels that a superstar allows herself to play second string to what is most important, the violent events in Pakistan. In this way, Lane skillfully paves the way for what will surely be a favorable notice, one that will no doubt impress readers who, like him, had previously made their minds up about the casting. He sees a bright future for someone who had never been taken seriously as an actress.

In the popular press, as well as on the quickie reviews of morning show critics, whose job it is to deliver a fast-talking, two-minute "analysis," such superstars may be praised or panned, but never given minute scrutiny of the kind offered by Anthony Lane. This is the reason the critical viewer seeks the guidance of intelligent opinion and knows how to recognize it.

A professional, widely read film critic decides that a superstar can also be an actress.

Source: Plan B/Revolution Films/The Kobal Collection.

Howard Cohen, pop music critic for the *Miami Herald*, regularly reviews the latest rock, rap, country, jazz, and rhythm and blues CDs. Since so much music is released each week and since we could not possibly sample every CD in order to decide which ones to buy, Cohen's informed opinions are a service the paper offers. His mini-reviews appear on a weekly basis, and they are loaded with catchy evaluations his readers have learned to trust. He has paid his dues and is saying in so many words: "I am a professional critic. I can be forthright about my likes and dislikes. That's what I'm paid for, and will be so long as I retain your trust."

In reviewing a CD called *Zeitgeist* (a term employed by philosophers as a reference to the soul or guiding spirit of an age), Cohen brings his dissenting fist down immediately: "With a gift for pretension that always overshadowed his musical ability, leader Billy Corgan hasn't mellowed with age."[4] Cohen handles prose expertly and, as we can see, with a vocabulary that is neither pretentious nor condescending. It tells us his readership includes genuine lovers of rock music who are accustomed to thinking about what they listen to and what critics say about it. But he also backs up his general indictments with some specific details—always the mark of the professional. He is sorry to announce that several former musicians "who helped temper Corgan's excesses . . . are gone." And "there's no finesse in his playing the way . . . Jack White brings textured noise to The White Stripes. Corgan's nasal whine remains one of rock's most annoying sounds."

The type of music reviewed by Cohen and other such critics is presumably well known to many readers. Reviews of an unfamiliar work can also be rewarding because it expands our knowledge of the vast range of musical offerings. Alex Ross, for example, music critic for the *New Yorker*, reviewed the premier performance by the Boston Symphony Orchestra of a work called *La Pasión según San Marcos* (*The Passion of Jesus Christ According to Saint Mark*) by an Argentine composer named Osvaldo Golijov. Ross begins by describing the wild ovation, something rarely seen at a concert featuring a new and avant-garde work. "This level of euphoria is sometimes encountered at the Met, when a favorite singer has an exceptional night. It is not found at concerts of new music."[5] Very probably, not many readers knew much about Golijov at the time of the performance. Mention of the ovation sends a signal: *Pay attention; here is somebody who's going to be very important.* Then Ross adds that the ovation lasted for twenty minutes at the first performance of the work in Stuttgart, Germany, the year before. He also shares his delight in rediscovering Latino concert music:

> *this Latino passion carries two messages: one is that Golijov is a huge talent . . . and the second is that Latino America has a fabulously rich tradition, one that will become a dominant force in coming decades. "Pasión" drops like a bomb on the belief that classical music is an exclusively European art. It has a revolutionary air, as if musical history were starting over, with new, sensuous materials and in a new, affirmative tone.*

The professional critic is likely to bestow extravagant praise on something he or she considers to be a masterpiece, and such praise raises our level of interest.

The professional critic is likely to bestow extravagant praise on something he or she considers to be a masterpiece, and such praise raises our level of interest. In this case one asks: *How tolerant am I of new music? How much do I really know about new music, especially from South America?* Reading this review can excite our curiosity about what young composers, especially from other cultures, are doing, and it should enhance our awareness of the "rich tradition" from which their work springs.

Ross does his homework. He follows his enthusiastic opening comments with a detailed biography of the young composer. We learn that Golijov composed a choral work called *Oceana*, a musical setting of poems by the Chilean poet Pablo Neruda, the 1971 Nobel laureate, and that *La Pasión* was commissioned by the orchestra of Stuttgart—high recognition for an artist not in the European mainstream.

Last, and perhaps most important, Ross dissects the work in detail, explaining what makes it so special. He comments that Bach might have written like this had he been born in Latin America at the end of the twentieth century. The descriptions are enough to entice us into downloading the album. "Brazilian shakers and musical bows, conjuring an ancient world; eerie moans from the accordion, representing the voice of God; then the entry of the chorus, braying in Africanized Spanish over *bata* drums. The listener is thrown into the middle of a Lenten street festival, with three processions of singers, converging into an antiphonal clamor."

Ross describes a "Bachian-Brazilian aria," sung near the end of the work, "and the piece moves for a long spell into the interior world of Jesus's suffering. At the very end, Kaddish is sung for the man on the cross, and the music undergoes an even more mysterious metamorphosis: the language is now Aramaic, the cantillation is Jewish, and the centuries have slipped away like sand."

When confronted with the unfamiliar, those who are new to critical viewing and listening are tempted to think that modern composers go out of their way to sound bizarre. Thus it is reassuring to note that Ross finds a timeless quality in great art. Though some artists, composers, and writers do indeed deliberately seek out novelty, this review reminds us that great works always arise from the passionate need to express something of huge importance, something geniuses have in common, even if their language seems bizarre and unfamiliar in the beginning.

Notice that Ross exhibits considerable knowledge about the elements of music. He hears more than those of us without substantial musical backgrounds. The best critics display their credentials in everything they write and thus they earn our trust.

One could say that professional criticism is an art form in itself. As authors and composers as well as actors and visual artists put themselves on the line whenever they come forth with new work, so too is the critic exposed to the applause or condemnation of the public. The seeming arrogance we often detect in critics' writing may well mask their own vulnerability. If we understand that they are human beings like all of us, we can read them with better understanding and can profit by what they have to teach us.

The Personal Critical Response

One does not have to be a professional critic to engage in the process of evaluation after a careful and fair viewing, listening, or reading. Here is "The world is too much with us," a poem by William Wordsworth (1770–1850), who lived in England's lake country at a time when the Industrial Revolution was beginning to have an impact and many people were moving from the country to the cities seeking a more lucrative lifestyle.[6] Though Wordsworth preferred to live amid the wonders of nature, he was aware of the dangers posed by the promise of economic gain.

The world is too much with us; late and soon,
Getting and spending, we lay waste our powers:
Little we see in Nature that is ours;
We have given our hearts away, a sordid boon!

This Sea that bares her bosom to the moon;
The winds that will be howling at all hours,
And are up-gathered now like sleeping flowers;
For this, for everything, we are out of tune,
It moves us not.—Great God! I'd rather be
A Pagan suckled in a creed outworn;
So might I, standing on this pleasant lea,
Have glimpses that would make me less forlorn;
Have sight of Proteus rising from the sea;
Or hear old Triton blow his wreathed horn.

The first step in becoming an informed critic is not to jump to hasty conclusions.

The first step in becoming an informed critic is *not to jump to a hasty conclusion*. "I don't like it" or "I love this poem" is an irrelevant remark at this early stage in the process of critical thinking.

The next step is to determine what it is you have just read. Describe the poem as clearly and objectively as possible. A possibility: The poem contains (or appears to contain, which might be a more cautious approach, at least in the beginning) a regretful realization that, in a concern for material welfare, we no longer live on close terms with nature. It reminds us that the natural world is a place of wondrous beauty and should be a source of inspiration.

Beauty, of course, is its own justification. To spend all day working for economic gain is to deny oneself one of the major aesthetic joys in life: intimacy with nature. Noticing how the seasons affect the landscape, how plants and flowers will grow and bloom wherever they are given space, costs nothing and yields treasures that money cannot buy.

Wordsworth could not have known about *environmentalism*, but he is already aware that the commerce of everyday life, the "getting and spending," is creating a danger that the natural world will be ignored, uncared for. And so he thinks of an ancient time when mythology turned nature into a wondrous force that we are to be dazzled by and always respect.

A modern artist is seeing a world that would probably have appalled Wordsworth.

Source: Fernand Léger, *The City*, Philadelphia Museum of Art/Art Resource, NY.

If you are adventurous and enjoy probing a little deeper, you can obtain information about the poet's life from the library or Internet. You would learn that, as Wordsworth grew older, he feared he was losing the inspiration he used to feel when he was out in nature. You would also learn that this poem was written in 1804, perhaps during a transitional phase in the poet's development—that is, at a time when, in reaching full maturity, he might have begun to fear that, though he was profiting from writing, he was doing so at the cost of his inspiration. If you wanted to advance this idea, you would do well to tread softly, however. Though many literary scholars take the plunge and read autobiography into every work by an author, the poet in this case might have been making a general statement applicable to all people.

In any case, speculation about ideas in a work sharpens our critical faculties, even if it doesn't say the last word about what we are reading. The important thing is to separate probability from possibility. It is virtually certain that Wordsworth is upset about the pursuit of material gain, and it is possible that, at the age of thirty-four, he fears he might be losing the passion that fired his youth.

I do not feel obliged to believe that the same God who has endowed us with sense, reason, and intellect has intended us to forego their use.
—Galileo

The next stage in the critical process is to look at the poet's *craft*—that is, the handling of language and **imagery** (the pictures in your mind that the poem communicates). What makes poetry different from prose is that poets are able to compress a great deal into fewer words than prose requires. They do this by taking shortcuts—sneaking past our commonsense barriers and heading directly into the Dionysian region of intuition, where we understand something without having to be directly told, or without going through an extended process of reasoning. When we grasp something intuitively, we "catch on" right away. One of poetry's gifts to us is thus to sharpen our intuitive faculties.

In this poem Wordsworth does considerable direct talking, as in "Getting and spending, we lay waste our powers." But he also communicates through intuition, as in the famous final lines, beginning with the explosive "Great God!"(which forces us to sit up and pay closer attention). Instead of talking directly about ancient times when people, through their myths, endowed nature with electric super-forces, the poet says he wishes he could have lived back then and shared the imagination of these people as well as the awe and respect they felt in the presence of nature. Instead of mentioning mythology directly, he invokes the names of two mythological sea gods, Proteus and Triton. The old religion made nature come alive and filled believers with inspiration, something sadly lacking in an age of restless commerce and profit-seeking, when nature has been abandoned.

Wordsworth's poem is a **sonnet**, a demanding literary form in which the poet is restricted to fourteen lines. In Wordsworth's time, poets also challenged themselves by using rhyming lines and writing in a definite rhythm. One way of identifying a good poem is to determine whether the rhythm and the rhyme are forced, whether they are deliberately imposed by the poet to meet the requirements, or whether they seem to be the only possible way of expressing the thought.

If you read the poem aloud to find the rhythmic pattern, you discover that unaccented syllables are followed by accented ones, that there never are two accented or unaccented syllables side by side. At the same time, when you read it without stressing the rhythm, the words flow naturally and manage to keep the rhythm unnoticed. The rhyming pattern is also quite regular (the first and fourth lines rhyme, as do the second and third, the fifth and eighth, the sixth and seventh, and finally, the ninth, eleventh, and thirteenth, and the tenth, twelfth, and fourteenth). Yet in reading the poem aloud, following the natural progression of it, you don't find the rhymes jumping out of their context. (There will be much more about the craft of poetry in Chapter 4.)

Being aware that the poet has carefully concealed the artistry behind the poem happens to be one of the pleasures of responding critically. When a pianist performs a complicated jazz solo or a sonata by Mozart, we should not have to think about the years of practicing eight hours a day. When the ice skater glides across the arena in perfect sync with Debussy's "Clair de Lune," we should believe that we can strap on a pair of skates and do the same thing. *Art is the illusion that there is no art.* Only when the skater attempts a triple axel and falls do we then watch future leaps with apprehension, painfully aware of the difficulty involved.

Track 1

In the critical thinking process, you can now make your personal assessment of the poem as a worthwhile or non-worthwhile experience for the reader. In the case of Wordsworth's sonnet, you are dealing with a poem that is 200 years old. You might want to comment on whether the thought it expresses is relevant to our times. You can ask yourself, "Do the sentiments expressed by the poet have anything to do with me, with the twenty-first century?" Perhaps it is fair to say that humanity's estrangement from the natural world has only increased as time moved on.

Yet, granted that the poem does indeed have contemporary relevance, does it hold any personal value for you? In this last stage of the critical process you are free to make your own assessment. Perhaps you are most taken by the language or the imagery. Perhaps you have become more inclined to look for concealed artistry. Perhaps what is most important is that it made you think about such pressing concerns as global warming and the industrial pollution of air and water. Perhaps you have read other things that you thought spoke with greater force to the modern reader. Or perhaps you have always wanted to try your hand at writing, and Wordsworth's poem made you wish you could spend more time exercising your imagination. *Your personal assessment is your own business.* But remember: it should not get mixed in with the way you describe what you have read. That is not being fair to the work. In a sense, you the reader are part of a jury, expected to be open-minded about the work you are evaluating.

Literalists and Figuratists

How, then, does involvement in the humanities lead to critical thinking? The answer is that it may not if one's responses are limited to the emotions, if one *never* wants to be analytical. Yet it is difficult to believe that there would not come a time when a clash of opinion occurs and when the generally intuitive viewer is asked to defend a positive or negative view. After a time "I didn't like it; I know what I like, and I didn't like this" becomes inadequate. Continued experience in the humanities inevitably broadens our perspective, and we become increasingly skillful in defending our likes or dislikes as well as listening carefully and critically to others.

If you start chatting with a stranger in a theater lobby, and your casual chit-chat leads to comments about the movie you've just seen, you can usually tell whether you're conversing with a critical or a non-critical thinker *by that person's use of language.* The non-critical often relate all experience, whether at the movies or in real life, to themselves. "The movie was too gory for me. I prefer a nice love story." Or it could go the other way: "I hate gooey love stories; give me good old-fashioned horror any time." The critical, however, speak in or imply general principles. This comes from seeing, listening, or reading a great deal and thinking about what has been absorbed.

The non-critical may also be called **literalists**, a term derived from their habitual way of *not* seeing general principles. They are tuned into what is happening at the moment, and their opinions are often shaped by popular views expressed by friends who are just like them or by what a favorite commentator has been saying about global warming, homeland security, the state of the economy, and so on. They prefer supermarket-type, plastic-wrapped ideas that can be taken in whole and never analyzed. For their part, the critical may be termed **figuratists**, a term derived from the fact that their language is colorful and suggests wide experiences in many fields, including the humanities. If they are talking about the present moment, the likelihood is that they will see it in broader terms. There is a vast difference between "The cream in my coffee looks sour" and "Looks as if the world was too much with this cow."

Responding to the literalist's "I know what I like," the figuratist in the lobby may begin with "This movie's dialogue was riddled with clichés," and then give a list of them. The general principle, which is implied and easily defensible, is: *Cliché-riddled dialogue is not the sign of talent; it is visiting familiar territory, which is not worth the viewer's time.* An answer like "Well, I don't have anything else to do, so I don't mind what you call clichés" quickly identifies the speaker as a non-critical literalist.

Literalist Speech

Literalists are limited to what we may call the "everyday concrete." They are also likely to listen haphazardly to what a figuratist is *generally* saying, latching on to the very last thing that was mentioned.

> *One must be able to transcend the narrow confines of a self-centered existence and believe that one will make a significant contribution to life . . .*
>
> —**Bruno Bettelheim**

F: *So many of the so-called professionals I run into don't seem to be what I would call experts. I'd love to meet one who could give me sound answers to important questions: where to live, whether to change jobs, what suntan lotion is most effective, where my children could get the best education.*

L: *I didn't know you had children.*

F: *I don't.*

(Blank stare)

The figuratist may not be personally involved in *any* of the examples mentioned in the list given. They are meant to introduce the general subject of incompetence in areas where you would expect to find the opposite. The figuratist is also implying that there is no certainty—that in a philosophical sense we are all alone to stumble our way through the world. The figuratist uses specific experiences to arrive at general principles. Friends of "F" may have children, but not necessarily. Being broadly interested in what's happening in the world, "F" knows a good deal about educational systems, has read widely on the subject, has viewed panel discussions, and so on. In the same way, a novelist may begin by writing about her own childhood memories, but if she is a good novelist, she will impart some wisdom that will help all readers make sense out of life, wisdom that comes not necessarily from her own life but from being immersed in reality. Literalists generally don't write books.

F: *I think my students don't know the difference between the classroom and their bedroom.*

L: *My neighbor says her son likes to sleep in class.*

F: *The least their parents could do is send them to school with pillows.*

L: *I don't think that would be wise.*

Figuratist Speech

Figuratists, especially those who devote considerable time to reading great literature, use fanciful, often metaphoric language—that is, language that means something other than what is being directly said. Effective ways of communicating occur more naturally to them than to people who have spent less time in libraries. For example, at a recent opening of a bad play, a figuratist, talking to friends afterward in the lobby, was overheard commenting: "Watching this, I thought I was giving CPR to a statue." Somehow, "The play was boring" just doesn't have the same *zing*.

Figuratists are adept at twisting words that in their original context were just mildly clever, making them shine with brilliance. Many years ago the celebrated

In this world there are only two tragedies. One is not getting what you want, and the other is getting it.
—**Oscar Wilde**

(and somewhat arrogant) British dramatist Noel Coward wrote a personal note to then prime minister Winston Churchill, who was famous for cleverness and quick wit, inviting him to the opening night of his play. He ended the note this way: "Oh, and feel free to bring a friend if you have one." Not one to take an insult lying down, Churchill replied: "I won't be able to make the opening, but I will come the second night if there is one."

An added bonus for the avid reader of great writers is that clever remarks like Churchill's are in the public domain. They can be absorbed into one's own repertoire of shining comments. It is also fun for the figuratist to converse with other widely read friends and either quote from instantly recognizable sources or, even better, come up with a personal variation. Shakespeare has probably penned more frequently quoted lines than any other writer in the English-speaking world, so many in fact that the figuratist feels obliged to allude to but not to repeat them verbatim one more time. The queen in *Hamlet*, tossing flower petals into the heroine's grave, cries "Sweets to the sweet: farewell!" A figuratist, much addicted to chocolates, was heard to say, just before giving in to the temptation of one more delectable piece: "Sweets to the sweet: farewell, teeth!"

Put all your eggs in one basket and--WATCH THAT BASKET.
—**Mark Twain**

The most often repeated of the great lines are those which contain wisdom behind the wit, so that the critical thinker is quick to claim ownership of them, knowing there is no way to improve upon them. The legendary Yogi Berra is credited with many now famous, if not always grammatically respectable, remarks. Much of his wisdom sprang from the observations of a folk philosopher, thinking about his beloved game of baseball. "It ain't over till it's over" is now, despite the grammatical lapse, *the* best way to imply that there is always hope. There is, after all, always a ninth inning, with three outs.

"It ain't over till it's over" just seems more effective than "There's always hope."

Source: Bettmann/Corbis.

Nor is every saying attributed to Yogi Berra the mark of an untutored philosopher with bad grammar. One suspects that, as he grew older and realized his comments were becoming famous, he gave them more depth and an entirely original style. "In theory there is no difference between theory and practice. In practice there is." This sly bit of wisdom sneaks up on us. It could be rephrased like this: "People who spend their lives talking theories really need to see what's out there." But it wouldn't have the *zing* of the seasoned figuratist that Yogi Berra really was. And the critical thinker is always looking for clever uses of language, whether from the libraries or from the baseball stadium.

Critical thinking is indispensable to the art of being human, though the critical thinker is always going to run into an uncritical acquaintance who insists, "I'd rather not think about what I read or see; I'd rather just enjoy myself." Is there no way to convince the acquaintance that it's possible to both think and enjoy—that, in fact, thinking just *might* be the ultimate way to enjoy living? Those who think well speak well, and those who do both will remain avid lovers of the humanities, a perennial reservoir of inspiration that sharpens our critical faculties.

Key Terms

alienation the term used by Bertolt Brecht to describe the ideal, non-emotional state in which the viewer is best able to derive the author's message.

Apollonian a term derived from the Greek god of light and truth; used to describe something or someone that is orderly and rational.

context as used in this chapter, the environment, background, or special circumstances in terms of which a given work is best understood; historical context is the influence that the ideas, values, and styles of a particular time have on a society, work of art, or philosophy.

critical thinking the faculty of rational and logical analysis; looking at subjects objectively, gathering all information, and then drawing conclusions about the subject based on evidence; the opposite of jumping to hasty conclusions based on a purely emotional response.

Dionysian a term derived from the Greek god of wine and vegetation; used to describe spontaneity as well as a lack of order and structure, signifying the passionate and creative (often impulsive) aspects of art, society, or an individual.

empathy the quality of identifying with another (an actual person or a character in a book, film, or play), becoming, in a sense, that person and being involved in his or her problems.

figuratist a critical thinker whose use of language is characteristically colorful, often playful, filled with metaphors that suggest a greater interest in the general than in just the particular.

imagery found especially in poetry, the pictures that the words create in your mind and communicate what ordinary prose cannot, or at least not as economically.

literalist the non-critical person whose language reflects a concern for the immediate moment, especially as what is happening or being viewed relates to the self.

sonnet a fourteen-line poem that originally imposed on poets tight rules of length, rhythm, and rhyming pattern.

rationalizing often mistaken for critical thinking, it is justifying something we have done that our conscience may disapprove of, or explaining away something others do or say that would otherwise damage our ego.

review a careful evaluation of a work of literature, drama, visual art, music, or cinema by a professional or non-professional critic, the former earning a salary for his or her opinions because of demonstrated knowledge of a particular field.

Topics for Writing and Discussion

1. The evaluation of both the novel and film version of *The Da Vinci Code* in this chapter is that of a hypothetical critical viewer. You may have a different, equally valid opinion. Defend it.
2. May we say that the critical person is Apollonian and the non-critical person is Dionysian? Why or why not? Explain.
3. It has been said: "Wisdom is rooted in the figurative." Explain what this might mean.
4. Take stock of your personality as it is right now, in terms of Apollo and Dionysus. Do you think you have achieved a balance between the two? Does one side predominate? Does one side need work?
5. What made Richard Rorty realize that "My baby don't love nobody but me" didn't make sense?
6. Give an example of a "popcorn hangover" you have experienced.
7. Explain, in Brechtian terms, how you may be alienated while watching a movie.
8. How do you recognize when someone is giving an informed opinion?
9. Briefly indicate and describe the steps in the personal critical process.
10. Write an imaginary conversation between a literalist and a figuratist.

3 Myth and the Origin of the Humanities

Overview

Long before there was print, before the formal arts existed, there were the humanities in the form of **mythology**. Music and dance probably began as rhythmic accompaniments to stylized movements in which people honored and appeased the gods and observed certain stages of life, such as the transition from youth to adulthood. Early forms of the drama occurred when people pretended to be hunting wild animals needed for their survival or heroic warriors battling evil spirits. In Neolithic cave drawings, such as those found in Lascaux, France, our ancestors depicted both the animals on which their survival depended and themselves in the act of hunting those animals. In reimagining the hunt, they endowed their deeds unwittingly with mythic significance.

Early people, in societies that were of necessity closely knit, preserved their history by weaving stories of their past—stories about where they may have originated and their relationship to the gods; stories about great hunters, warriors, and leaders; and eventually, stories designed to illustrate the difference between right and wrong.

Mythology underlies much of the work created in *all* disciplines of the humanities. Literature, visual art, music, drama, cinema—all may have roots in **myths** that are sometimes unique to a given culture but in many instances are universal, found in one version or another in most cultures. For this reason, mythology is an appropriate starting place for our study of the humanities.

What, then, *is* mythology? Webster gives us two ways of defining it. One is "the science or study of myths." The other is "a collection of all the myths of a specific people or about a specific being." Myth can also be defined as "a traditional story of unknown authorship, ostensibly with a historical basis, but serving usually to explain some phenomenon of nature, the origin of humanity, or the customs, religious rites, etc., of a people." Thus we can speak about the mythology of a Native American nation or the mythology of a specific figure such as King Arthur.

The 1959 Brazilian film *Black Orpheus*, a modern retelling of the Greek myth, shows the enduring relevance of ancient tales.
Source: The Everett Collection, Inc.

In this chapter we discuss the role mythology played in shaping the humanities. We'll conclude by sampling mythic elements in some famous literary works. We also discuss the fact that all of us have our own personal mythology, beginning in early childhood when we objectify our fears and our secret longings, when we divide the world into good and evil and have our heroes and, for the most part, identify with them. Our myths stay with us for life and grow up with us, fulfilling psychological needs at every stage of our development.

We need, at the outset, to demolish some common misconceptions about myth. It has become a deceptively simple four-letter word used in a variety of ways not necessarily related to the humanities, though closely tied to our personal needs. In popular usage, myth is *something erroneous yet widely believed*—something to be refuted by rational adults, such as "The Myth of Mental Illness," or "Myth of calories exposed; eat all you want and get thin!" Another misuse of the word is patronizing, in the sense of "old stories once believed by naive people in a prescientific age that didn't know better."

Myths are clues to the spiritual potentiality of the human life.
—**Joseph Campbell**

If myths could be thus dismissed as just false and outmoded beliefs, they would not be the subject of this chapter. But mythology belongs to and affects large numbers of people. Knowledge of myth is basic to cultural literacy. Writers assume that readers will understand mythic references. For example, *romance*, love that goes far deeper than just sexual attraction, is an archetype we can date back to the Middle Ages. In describing *Eternal Sunshine of the Spotless Mind* (2004) as "romantic," *New Yorker* film critic Anthony Lane says that the film suggests "every one of us harbors an inextinguishable need, and that we helplessly swing back toward our soulmates."[1] Intrinsic to the romantic love archetype is the belief that each of us is destined to meet the right person eventually.

That humankind is the mythmaking species is not saying too much. Myths are as necessary for survival as breathing and eating. In addition to influencing both the humanities and, as we shall see, psychology, myth affects the behavior of people all over the world. This chapter examines basic myths about creation, birth, death, the afterlife, love, power, magic numbers, the importance of circles, the arduous journey, and the unspoiled garden. Some of these myths date back to very early people, but all of them recur in many forms. They are symbols in our culture and in our unconscious minds that help to shape the way we view ourselves and our world. They are vital to the study of the humanities.

Archetypes in Mythology

Even if myths were only a collection of stories about recognizable families, feuds, passion and revenge, they would be enjoyable as literature. Reading them, we are struck by similarities in stories and characters. We might ask ourselves why certain of these are found again and again and often influence the way we ourselves think and react to what others do. Scholars expect even more. They seek in myth a common thread, a chance to learn if the stories tell us something important about the human condition. For this they turn to a theory of psychologist-philosopher Carl Jung (1875–1961), who maintained that all persons are born with an instinctive knowledge of certain **archetypes**, the models by which people comprehend experience and cope with the enormous and often baffling task of being human. Jung believed these models are shared by societies all over the world, though they may take different forms. Archetypes are mythic characters, events, symbols, and buried assumptions transmitted from one generation to another through what Jung labeled the **collective unconscious**.

Plate 1 Leonardo da Vinci, Mona Lisa. Louvre, Paris, France. Credit: Réunion des Musées Nationaux/Art Resource, NY.

The complexity of her expression has made this the most famous work of art in the world. (See page 17 for more on da Vinci.)

Plate 2 Romare Bearden, *Mississippi Monday* (1941). Credit: Copyright © Romare Bearden Foundation/Licensed by VAGA, New York, NY.

Bearden claimed he was more concerned with aesthetics than with social commentary. What do you think engaged him aesthetically about this scene? (See page 100 for more on Bearden.)

Plate 3 Norman Rockwell, Marine Homecoming (1945). Credit: Printed by permission of the Norman Rockwell Family Agency Copyright ©1945 The Norman Rockwell Family Entities. Photo: The Curtis Publishing Company.

To see Rockwell's work is to gain invaluable knowledge of how a large segment of the population lived in the early twentieth century and to recognize the importance of historical context. (See page 30 for more on Rockwell.)

Plate 4 Dante Gabriel Rossetti, *Pandora Holding Her Box* (1869). Credit: AFP/Getty Images.

Two depictions of how the world's troubles began. Above, Dante Gabriel Rossetti's *Pandora* shows the moment just as the mythical woman opens the box releasing evil into the world. Below, Gabriel Alix's *Food for the Spirit* portrays the biblical first man and woman in the Garden of Eden prior to the Fall. (See page 61 for more on Rossetti and Alix.)

Plate 5 Gabriel Alix, *Food for the Spirit* (1992). Credit: Courtesy of Macondo.

Plate 6 Leonardo da Vinci, *The Last Supper* (1495–1498).
Credit: © Superstock, Inc.

Two renditions of the same subject. Da Vinci's (above) has won universal acceptance for its reverential treatment of Jesus and the disciples. Van der Woestyne's modern rendering of the scene seems primarily concerned with its bold technique. (See page 132 for more on da Vinci and page 134 for more on Van der Woestyne.)

Plate 7 Gustave van der Woestyne, *The Last Supper* (1927).
Credit: Photographic Service City of Bruges, Jan Termont - Dirk Van der Borght. Groeninge Museum, Bruges, Belgium.

Plate 8 Wassily Kandinsky, *Composition VII* (1913). Tretyakov Gallery, Moscow. Copyright © 2003 Artists Rights Society [ARS], New York/ADAGP, Paris. Credit: Bridgeman Art Library.

An abstractionist, Kandinsky believed that what mattered is form, not meaning—a pleasing arrangement of lines and color existing for no purpose other than aesthetic experience. (See page 148 for more on Kandinsky.)

Plate 9 Raphael, *The School of Athens* (1510). Stanza della Segnatura, Stanze di Raffaello, Vatican Palace. Credit: Scala/Art Resource, NY.

The two figures in the center, top level, are Plato (left) and Aristotle, his pupil. (See pages 366, 397, and 467 for more on Plato.)

Plate 10 Artemisia Gentileschi, *Judith Beheading Holofernes* (1620). Uffizi, Florence, Italy. Credit: Scala/Art Resource, NY.

Example of late Renaissance realism by a feminine artist scandalous in her own time. (See page 138 for more on Gentileschi.)

Plate 11 Francisco Goya, *Family of Charles IV* (1800). Museo del Prado, Madrid, Spain. Credit: Erich Lessing/Art Resource, NY.

This painting is far from the idealization of royalty found in traditional portraits, but the royal family didn't seem to notice. (See page 140 for more on Goya.)

Plate 12 Francisco Goya, *Saturn Devouring His Children* (1819–1823). Museo del Prado, Madrid. Credit: Scala/Art Resource, NY.

Paintings such as this one raise questions about the meaning of art that is intended to provoke revulsion and horror. Does art have to be beautiful to command our respect? (See page 140 for more on Goya.)

Plate 13 Claude Monet, *Impression: Sunrise* (1872; Musée Marmottan, Paris). Credit: Museé Marmottan, Paris. Photo: A.K.G., Berlin/Superstock.

The painting that gave Impressionism its name. Monet avoids photographic realism in favor of depicting his personal experience of light and color. (See page 143 for more on Monet.)

Plate 14 Berthe Morisot, *The Psyche* (1876). Fundacion Coleccion Thyssen-Bornemisza, Madrid. Credit: Copyright © Nimatallah/Art Resource, NY.

Only partially influenced by Impressionism, Morisot combines light and color with domestic realism. (See page 144 for more on Morisot.)

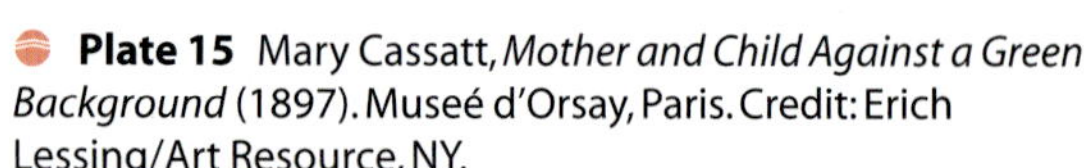

Plate 15 Mary Cassatt, *Mother and Child Against a Green Background* (1897). Museé d'Orsay, Paris. Credit: Erich Lessing/Art Resource, NY.

American Impressionist Cassatt uses her subjects as designs and events of light and color. The background is more important for its color than its detail. (See page 144 for more on Cassatt.)

> *From the unconscious emanate determining influences which, independently of tradition, guarantee in every single individual a similarity and even a sameness of experience, and also of the way it is represented imaginatively. One of the main proofs of this is the almost universal parallelism between mythological motifs.*[2]

Jung's theory is not accepted by all psychologists or scholars of myth, but without it or another comprehensive theory to replace it, we have a difficult time accounting for the continued appearance of certain myths and myth elements: tales of a terrible flood and the salvation of one good man; the stories about dangerous journeys into the land of death and darkness; and above all, tales about the major stages in the life of a singular human being—sometimes partly divine—known as the *hero*. There are, however, some alternative explanations.

> *These heavenly archetypes were felt to be true in the same way as the events and forms that inhabit our imaginations often seem more real and significant to us than our mundane existence.*
>
> **—Karen Armstrong**

One is the *external* theory, the most scientific of the possibilities. According to this theory, stories were spread along migratory routes. Myths originated in specific places and then were transported as people warred, traded, and intermarried with each other. In general, we do find myth similarities among certain cultures whose migrations can be traced.

An example of the migratory spread of old stories is the way the myths of the African Yoruba tribe were transported to Cuba, where they were modified and adopted by a whole new body of listeners. These stories gradually became systematized into both a religion and a philosophy known as *Santeria*, which offers an explanation of universal origins that combines Catholic monotheism with an African belief in multiple deities. Santeria continues to be practiced in Cuba, and its pantheon of heavenly protectors includes both African gods and Christian saints.

Yet another explanation for the universality of myth is the predictable one that human beings share common needs, regardless of geography and level of cultural sophistication, and thus certain elements found in all myths must play their part in helping people cope with the conditions in which they find themselves. Similar needs do not necessarily imply contacts between cultures or a mandatory belief in a collective unconscious. If human needs are very much the same everywhere, why shouldn't myths be?

The Hero as World Myth

In examining the mythic roots of many works in the formal disciplines of the humanities, we can see that Shakespeare's portrait of King Henry V is one of a nearly perfect hero, the champion and defender of a people, the one who seems indestructible. But so is Frodo, the tiny hobbit of *The Lord of the Rings*, who sacrifices home and security and ultimately his very life to save Middle Earth from the terrible Sauron. And the term *hero* applies to women as well as men. Think Sigourney Weaver in the *Alien* trilogy. The Chinese film *Crouching Tiger, Hidden Dragon* (2000) featured a woman who was almost supernaturally adept at the martial arts and could even fly.

The hero is an archetype found in almost every culture–hence the label world myth.

The hero is an archetype found in almost every culture—hence the label *world myth*. The Irish novelist James Joyce, of whom we shall have much to say in Chapter 15, used the term **monomyth** to convey his belief that the concept of the hero is the same everywhere. (There *are* similarities, of course, from one culture to another, but there are also significant differences.) Regardless of how each culture views existence and its particular survival needs, stories of heroes seem to be essential. As early as 1909, Otto Rank, a disciple of Freud, indicated the characteristics of the hero in Western mythology.

> *The hero is the son of parents of the highest station. His conception takes place under difficulty. There is a portent in a dream or oracle connected with the child's birth. The child is then sent away, or exposed to extreme danger. He is rescued by people of humble station, or by humble animals, and reared by them. When grown, he discovers his noble parentage after many adventures, and, over-coming all obstacles in his path, becomes at last recognized as the hero and attains fame and greatness.*[3]

The human passions transform man from a mere thing into a hero, into a being that in spite of tremendous handicaps tries to make sense of life.

—**Erich Fromm**

Freud, a pioneer in the psychological interpretation of mythology, maintained that the two families in the monomyth—the noble and the common—represent the parents as they appear at different stages of the child's development. But Jung went beyond this interpretation, arguing that the components, or motifs, of this pervasive myth were primordial images, "or—as I have named them—archetypes." For Jung, they were not narrowly connected to individual children but were a profound part of universal expectations of life. In short, *everyone* is prone to believe in and await the coming of a hero.

Birth of the Hero. The hero's birth occurs under wondrous circumstances: bowing trees; a shower of gold penetrating the ceiling of a room in which a young girl has been confined; the visit of a god in the guise of some other creature, animal or human; mysterious prophecies. Usually the hero has been sired by a supernatural being.

The ultimate meaning of these stories is psychological rather than concrete, and the stories themselves serve only as metaphors for the myth, expressing something that is deeply felt but not easily said.

—**David Leeming**

From the beginning of human awareness, the phenomenon of birth has preoccupied and baffled people. Eventually they came to know the causal sequence that led to reproduction. But they must have marveled over the sequence, that such a miracle could be possible! Even for "ordinary" mortals, the birth of a child is a glorious event; announcements are mailed, friends offer congratulations, and a birthday remains a special day throughout life. In a real-life version of the prophecy that attends the birth of a hero, the parents are offered best wishes, a way of urging providence to take note of the infant, to destine the child for love and success. Those whose glorious future does not materialize may even believe themselves to have been cursed by fate.

Early Recognition of the Hero. The hero destined for greatness must be recognized early in life, often after accomplishing a spectacular physical deed—such as the young Arthur's removal of the sword Excalibur from the stone that had held it until the rightful owner should come along, or the superhuman ability of Theseus to lift a heavy stone that covered a golden sword and sandals, evidence that he was a king's lost son. (One version of the myth, however, credits him not so much with strength as with ingenuity in lifting the stone by devising a lever.) Sometimes recognition comes through fulfillment of a prophecy, as when Jason arrives in the kingdom wearing only one sandal.

The theory behind the monomyth is that the theme of early recognition identifies a universal need for acceptance. In the painful stages of early adolescence, the child asks, "Who am I?" and fears that the answer will be, "You're nobody." Children are so small compared to the adults around them that it's no wonder they lack a sense of worth.

Many of us later admit that in childhood we harbored fantasies of secretly being children of a prominent, even royal, family, stolen from the cradle by gypsies or given away by our true parents. This unknown identity allows the extraordinary child to live with such average people and to perform dreary domestic tasks unsuited for noble beings. One day, the child-turned-adolescent feels, the recognition of special status will surely arrive. One only has to look at the popularity of the Harry Potter books for proof of the widespread appeal of such fantasies.

The Hero's Great Deed. It always occurs in young adulthood, at a time when the hero has left home and is separated from the parents. It is a mythical version of the universal rite of passage: the attainment of adult status at puberty. All mythologies recognize the importance of the transition to adulthood.

Almost every early culture required the accomplishment of an arduous task to signify the end of childhood: enduring bitter cold, surviving in the wilderness, recovering a magic item from a ferocious guardian, conquering a predatory beast. Theseus destroyed the Minotaur of Crete, a creature with the head of a bull and the body of a man, which had demanded the regular sacrifice of the finest Athenian young men and maidens. In order to kill the Minotaur—an extraordinary feat in itself—Theseus had first to find him by making his way through the labyrinth, a series of deceptive passages, which Freud-oriented myth commentators have viewed as the journey through the maze of childhood sexual stages. According to Freudian interpretation, the ultimate discovery and killing of the Minotaur thus becomes the young adult's arrival into sexual maturity.

The first condition that any mythology must fulfill is that of cleaning the doors of perception to the wonder of ourselves and the universe of which we are the ears and eyes and the mind.

—Joseph Campbell

Many of the great deeds in mythology are physical, but others are purely mental. Oedipus, the protagonist of the great Sophoclean tragedy (discussed in Chapter 7), achieved greatness by solving the riddle of the Sphinx—half monstrous bird, half woman—who devoured anyone unable to give the correct answer to this question: *What creature goes on four feet in the morning, two feet at midday, and three feet at twilight, and goes slowest when on the most feet?* When Oedipus arrived, Thebes was in a chaotic state of panic, for no one could solve the riddle. But Oedipus did. The answer is *man, who crawls on all fours as a child and therefore goes slowest, walks upright as an adult, and uses a cane near the end of life.* The furious Sphinx kills herself, and Oedipus is made king, only to suffer disastrous consequences.

The celebration of a hero's successful and wondrous feat is a need that stays with us through life. We love to watch and empathize with milestone achievements: the inauguration of the new president; the Academy Award ceremonies; the placing of a ribboned gold medal around the neck of an Olympic champion. We mark the milestones in our personal lives: birthdays; graduation; the first date; the first kiss; a letter of acceptance; getting the desired job; marrying.

The Hero's Loss of Power. Myths of the West seldom end when the heroes are happy and successful. Fairy tales do. (After Cinderella marries, we never hear a word about her relationship with her family, in-laws, or children.) In adult mythology, however, the hero, like Oedipus, usually falls from greatness. King Arthur must live on to see Camelot destroyed, his noble kingdom shattered. In the West, the story of the hero tends to be tragic.

When the best leader's work is done, the people say, "We did it ourselves."

—Lao-tzu

If heroes lose their power, a possible compensation is that their death is usually glorious and their former greatness acknowledged. When Oedipus, who blinds himself so that he might never again look upon his misbegotten children, says, "I am the unclean one who has defiled this land" and makes his way to exile in the desert, the Chorus asks the fearful question: Why does this happen?

Why is Oedipus guilty of patricide and incest when he was doomed by a prophecy to perform these deeds? Why not blame the gods for his unkind fate? Yet, in accepting full responsibility for his deeds, he retains his noble status. In Sophocles' play, the doomed hero walks *unbowed* from the city. The grieving citizens make a respectful path for him. A vast presence is departing, and he will be mourned for many years to come.

After the fall of Camelot, the body of King Arthur is placed on a ship that will sail to the mystic land of Avalon. Great heroes fail, but their failures only testify to the bigness of their lives. It's almost as though mythology is saying "You can't have it both ways. You are either uncelebrated but perhaps content, or you take the risk of greatness, knowing that it doesn't last."

Recognition of the hero's nobility is seldom there during his or her lifetime. In fact, there is sometimes outright hostility toward the hero. Before he undergoes a violent death, Theseus is blamed by his once loyal subjects for the Spartan invasion of Athens at a time when he was gone from the kingdom. They even drive him out of the city, forcing him to seek the hospitality of the rival king who eventually kills him. But later the citizens realize the mistake they have made and erect an enormous tomb to honor his memory.

The history of Western civilization has recorded many instances of actual heroes, rejected or highly controversial during their lifetime but revered after death: Joan of Arc, Galileo, John F. Kennedy, to name a few.

The Hero in Non-Western Mythology. Asian and Middle Eastern cultures have hero stories, but they seldom concern the exploits of a singular mortal who is to be revered and celebrated to the exclusion of ordinary human beings. The Buddha (by birth, a prince named Siddhartha) achieved great humility, never sought power, and discouraged his followers from looking upon him as a deity of some sort.

Joseph Campbell has pointed out that whereas

> *the typical Occidental hero is a personality, and . . . necessarily tragic . . . the Oriental hero is the monad [a simple indivisible unit]: in essence without character . . . untouched by . . . the delusory involvements of the mortal sphere. And just as in the West the orientation to personality is reflected in the concept and experience even of God as a personality, so in the Orient, in perfect contrast, the overpowering sense of an . . . impersonal law . . . harmonizing all things reduces to a mere blot the accident of an individual life.*[4]

Judaic and Islamic traditions contain many stories of Moses and Mohammed, respectively, and their feats of leadership, but both prophets are regarded as spiritual forces, not as mighty conquerors. Before his death, Moses asked that his burial site be concealed so that no elaborate memorial could be built in his memory. The Islamic laws taught by Mohammed assume "the brotherhood of man . . . [the] equality of all believers . . . and absolute submission to the will of God [Allah]."[5]

In Chinese mythology, great dynastic rulers are cited for their virtue and their social achievements, such as in the case of Huang Ti, the "Yellow Emperor," who made agriculture possible and encouraged the development of a musical scale. He is celebrated for having driven out the barbarians, but his success came not from his unique superhuman valor but from the help of the gods, who looked with favor on his virtuous character. Confucius occupied himself not with metaphysical beliefs about the spirit behind the universe but with practical advice for those who would rule: walk the straight and narrow and live for the good of society. In Western mythology, King Arthur comes close to the Confucian ideal, but he was also a brave warrior of consummate fighting skill and would have been less revered if he had not been. He certainly meets the Western "requirement" that the hero be a singular individual capable of astonishing physical feats.

Dreams are private myths. Myths are public dreams.
—**Joseph Campbell**

The Hero Today

The archetype of the hero is still very much with us. Celebrities, today's demigods, may not be the literal progeny of deities and mortals, but they are as vivid in the public mind as their bygone counterparts. Their exploits are followed in magazines, gossip columns, and television interviews, and they set the trend in clothes, hair styles, and language.

We keep looking for that special someone who solves all problems.

There are still those who perform Herculean tasks and win admiration: the new home-run king; the world's fastest runner; the first astronauts in space; the first woman to walk the length of Tibet on foot; the first blind climber to reach the top of Everest; actors who receive Oscars for their first screen roles; and Nobel prize winners, often unknown before their achievements catapulted them to celebrity status.

We keep looking for that special someone who solves all problems. The archetype of the mysterious stranger has been important in American mythology because of the early dangers encountered in settling so vast a land and the democratic structure of frontier societies in which leaders were not born into their roles but had to prove themselves. That they often failed to do so made the myth that much more intense.

A classic example of the "special someone" hero myth can be found in George Stevens's 1952 film version of Max Brand's popular Western novel *Shane*.

Alan Ladd as the mysterious stranger in *Shane* who rides out of the hills and rescues a peaceful community of homesteaders from a ruthless killer hired to drive them from their land.

Source: The Everett Collection, Inc.

The film features a retired gunfighter who rides out of the Wyoming hills on a white horse, rescues a group of peaceful farmers from the lawless cattlemen intent on driving them off their land, shoots the leader of the bad guys, and then rides back into the misty land of his origin.

One interpretation of word significance is male jealousy over female reproductive powers. In myth, the power of the uttered word could be supreme. Men could talk. Perhaps that is why men have traditionally insisted on having the last word.

Today we still long for that wonderful presidential candidate with precisely the right qualifications, honest to the marrow, who will suddenly materialize at the Iowa caucuses, untainted by past political compromises, and be instantly recognized as the new political messiah. On the other hand, we can quickly desert charismatic orators who announce their candidacy, then are forced to withdraw when they are found to be error prone like the rest of us.

Magic

Almost always present in myths, especially but not exclusively those of the West, is the archetype of magic. Myths the world over are filled with objects like magical rings and weapons of supernatural power when wielded by a hero. Wizards, witches, and sorcerers appear and disappear at will, cast spells, and become close allies of mortals with righteous causes, endowing them with the strength and courage to accomplish their marvelous feats. The hero often has a magic sword with which to conquer opponents. King Arthur has Excalibur and Shu Lien in *Crouching Tiger, Hidden Dragon* has her Green Destiny.

One interpretation of magic-as-archetype may be the need to believe that the resources for coping with life are, like the magic sword, virtually at hand. Another is that only singular individuals can do the big tasks, and since they have magic on their side, the rest of us should not feel ashamed if we cannot live up to their example. In our mythology, magicians like King Arthur's Merlin or Gandalf in *Lord of the Rings* reassure us that, though many tasks appear to be impossible, someone is always there who has the resources to accomplish them.

Magic still captivates audiences, as in the 2004 film *King Arthur.*

Source: © Orion/The Everett Collection, Inc.

The Power of Words

Language of a special kind is another recurrent archetype. "In the beginning was the Word," so begins the Gospel of John. "It is written . . . " is found in speech the world over to represent absolute authority. Cultural anthropologists theorize that our male ancestors, in jealous awe of women's reproductive powers, believed that language was literally man-made and that words uttered by men were more miraculous than birth itself. In early cultures, when birth was considered a magical event, men may well have sought ways to match or even surpass this phenomenon in which they seemed to play so small a part. In many myths, the male hero is able to move heaven and earth because he knows secret words. Perhaps this myth helps explain the male tendency to insist on having the last say in all matters.

The words *Open Sesame!* yielded wonders for Ali Baba, even as *Sesame Street* serves as a modern archetype—the thoroughfare that takes children from ignorance to knowledge through the magic of letters and the fantasy creatures that attend them. Rumpelstiltskin was an elf whose magic name had to be guessed to save the queen's firstborn child. Special words also have their uses in real-world settings. For example, unless you are told "Simon says," you may not imitate the leader in the child's verson of that game. A sneeze often receives the blessing "Gesundheit!" from well-wishers. When two people happen to say the same thing at the same time, each might immediately exclaim "Jinx!" Presumably, bad luck will attend those who fail to carry out the verbal ritual.

For thousands of years, the world of human affairs has counted on the reliability of someone's word, as when a pact is made over a handshake and the inevitable "I give you my word" is uttered. There are still places in which insisting upon a written contract instead of accepting a spoken promise is greeted with suspicion and hostility. Most of us have yet to dismiss as insignificant the giving of our word, or to minimize the disappointment when others break theirs. In fact, *break* is an interesting verb to use in conjunction with *word*. In myth, a broken magic wand can be disastrous.

Sesame Street is the long-running television show that shows children the magic of words.

Source: Yoshikazu Tsuno/AFP/Getty Images.

The Power of Numbers

The belief in the magic of words is closely associated with the magic of numbers. Humanity long ago discovered that numerical units were basic to the design of both the earthly and the heavenly universe. In *The Divine Comedy*, Dante makes abundant use of the number 3, representing the Trinity. The poem is divided into three parts—*Inferno, Purgatory*, and *Paradise*. The last two parts contain 33 cantos, or chapters, corresponding to the age at which Jesus died; the first part has one extra canto to bring the total to what was considered the perfect number, 100.

In Hebrew tradition, there are mystic numbers. The letters of the Hebrew alphabet have number equivalents, and certain combinations of numbers are believed by some to hold the secrets of the universe. A school of Hebrew mysticism called Kabbalah studies the numerical complexities of Hebrew scripture. For example, some scholars have determined that there are 620, not just 10, commandments: 613 that were present in the five books attributed to Moses and 7 that were added later by rabbis. Not by coincidence, these scholars observe, is the fact that the 10 commandments contain 620 letters.

When the 999th person jumped off the Golden Gate Bridge, the authorities quickly announced that a mythical 1000th had followed suit right away.

People still have mystic feelings about numbers and sequences, expecting, for example, that the news of two deaths will lead inevitably to news of a third. The Golden Gate Bridge in San Francisco was a popular place for suicides, and when authorities discovered that the 999th person had leaped to a watery grave, they quickly announced the 1000th suicide as having already occurred, gave the person a fictitious name and occupation, and said services would be private. They knew all too well that a real 1000th would have shown up in no time—so powerful can numbers be.

The ancient symbol of the mandala may have suggested completeness and order in the universe. For Jung, it suggested the organization of the mind.

Source: The Newark Museum/Art Resource, NY.

Tomorrow, and tomorrow, and tomorrow,
Creeps in this petty pace from day to day,
To the last syllable of recorded time;
And all our yesterdays have lighted fools
The way to dusty death.
—**William Shakespeare**

The Circle

The circle is an archetype that affects our lives profoundly. Because the circle is an unbroken line without beginning or end that encloses a uniform space, people have used it to symbolize oneness, completeness, and eternity. In myth, it appears as a shield, a ring, a pendant, the sun, and the moon, as well as in markings on cave walls or on stones. Countless circular structures, some dating back many millennia, are found throughout the world: temples, stone circles, and that most intriguing of all round monuments to ancient humanity: Stonehenge, a large circle of heavy stones on Salisbury Plain in southwest England, once thought to have been a place of human sacrifice but now known to have almost certainly been the means of identifying the seasons of the year by the changing positions of the sun.

One universal form of the circle archetype is the *mandala*, found in the art of almost every period and every culture. It is an enclosed circle, often with an intricate design representing the organization of the universe and the various deities that control it. The exact nature of the design is perhaps less significant than the implications of the circular shape. It told people that the universe is an entity—one thing—as indeed the word itself—*uni*verse—suggested. It told them that, if it could be viewed from an alternate universe, it would be an enormous round object, something like a gigantic crystal ball, self-contained and distinguishable from anything else hovering in space.

Eastern and Western minds apparently came to similar conclusions about the universe. Both decided on the circular, geometrically perfect shape, which made the universe seem somehow *manageable*—that is, within the scope of human comprehension, if not control. Contemporary science continues to debate the nature and extent of the universe, and indeed whether the word does or does not really apply. Is it a random collection of planets and suns formed in the aftermath of an original explosion? Does it extend infinitely? At the same time, physicists continue to seek uniformity in physical laws. Einstein's general theory of relativity maintains that space is both infinite and *curved* and that gravity so warps space that no object can travel in a straight line forever.

Carl Jung saw in the mandala a universal symbol of not only cosmic but psychic organization. He believed that, just as humanity appears unwilling to exist within a shapeless, infinite universe, we also resist disorder in human existence. We reject the idea of discontinuous sensations, a hodgepodge of sensory reports, emotions, and thoughts. The circular shapes in myths, according to Jung, are projections of an inner need to identify a coherent self, a shaped self, one that can be thought about and discussed. In a sense, even our concern with memory is related to the mandala symbol. When we forget a name, for example, we sometimes ransack our minds as if the elusive words were hiding there, as if the mind were a self-contained circle preserving every memory. On this point, East and West have different opinions.

For the East, the circle has traditionally been a symbol of the order behind *nature*. The *yin* and *yang* of Taoist philosophy, which represent the attraction of opposite forces that keep the universe in balance, are artistically depicted as a black and white mandala. (See Chapter 10 for more on Taoism.) But in this philosophy, the human mind is not a self-contained circle. The boundaries between the mind and the outside world are not distinct, as they are in much Western thought. Consciousness is like a flowing river. Thoughts and feelings come and go. Human intelligence is something inherent in the order of nature. It is there when a problem needs to be solved or when a sustained thought process focusing on a particular thing is required. The Western idea of the personal ego as a walled city is a strange concept to the traditional Eastern mind.

In the East, the circle is often a symbol of the oneness of nature and the living beings who inhabit it. In the West, the vocabulary of circles is often narrowly related to self. We have "holistic" medicine that treats the "whole person." When we feel unsure of where we want to go with our lives, we speak of trying to "get it together," and if we feel that we are losing control, friends might offer to help us "pick up the pieces."

Except for different images of the mind, East and West seem to have always liked the idea that everything makes sense; the circle does not suggest chaos. Universal humanity does not want to think of itself as adrift and abandoned in an existence that cannot be comprehended.

The circle also represents immortality. The Hindu and Buddhist concepts of reincarnation and the cycles of existence, shared by many Westerners, are obvious examples. And what is the belief in an afterlife, found the world over, but the concept that existence has no end—like a circle?

The Journey

One of the major archetypes in Western mythology offers a non-circular view of the meaning of existence. The difficult journey is another way of depicting the course of human life. Life-as-a-journey implies both purpose and a final destination, as opposed to a random series of disconnected happenings. We think of life as moving from one stage or "phase" to another; again, this implies that we can make sense of it. The French educator Jean Piaget is famous for having set forth the stages of child development, and his ideas form the basis for much educational theory.

Life as a journey implies both purpose and a final destination, as opposed to a random series of disconnected happenings.

The mythic hero usually sets out on a journey fraught with danger and has a challenging task that must be performed at the conclusion. Fearful obstacles usually threaten the hero along the way: dense, maze-like forests; dangerous beasts; magical potions that induce slumber and prevent motion. But sooner or later, the journey continues.

Our expectations thus formed by the myth, we look for progress in our own lives and in those of others. We expect the obstacles. We say, "No pain, no gain." We are sure the journey will prove worth the effort. Accomplishing the big task will mean recognition and approval. When others seem not to succeed in their journey, we say, "He is stuck in adolescence" or "She's still at the same old job!"

The mythical journey is also a quest. The hero searches for his or her homeland, a buried treasure, the Holy Grail. Attainment of the goal gives shape and purpose to life. And here we note a conflict in the two key symbols. Whereas the circle guarantees life without end, the journey is supposed to yield important results. We don't mind applying the circle to universal order or to the shape of the mind as a self-contained whole, but we resist thinking of life as just one thing after another without purpose, without direction. We hate to think of ourselves as "going around in circles." We like to think that, regardless of life's continual changes, its ups and downs (there are always mythical mountains to cross), life *does* come to something after all.

The journey in Eastern mythology, on the other hand, is a series of happenings, not necessarily in a sequence and without a necessary final task. In the myth of Bodhidharma, the monk who supposedly brought Buddhism from India to China, the hero stops to meditate on a mountain top for nine years, during which his legs fall off. But the story merely points out that this is what occurred. It does not call it a tragedy. For the East, life is indeed one thing after another, and each day has to be accepted for what it is. For the West, a journey without a successful destination is worthless. "She died before her time" is a Western mythic observation. So is "Here he is, thirty-five years old, and what has he done with his life?"

The Garden

We must tend our own gardens.
—Voltaire

In the West, as we have said, journeys are supposed to have successful destinations, but related myths question these destinations. Some myths say we are heading down the "wrong path." Some myths look back to the past and say: "Would that we had never embarked on this journey; we have lost too much."

Myths of a Golden Age, when things were better, extend far back in the Western tradition. In fact, the usual downfall of the hero implies that what was once good is now gone. With the death of King Arthur went all hope of another Camelot. Many myth scholars believe that the archetype of the Golden Age had its origins in the Hebrew Bible's account of the Garden, the earthly paradise Adam and Eve called home until they were cast out for eating the forbidden fruit from the Tree of Knowledge.

The Hebrew Bible also contains a countermyth with a countersymbol to the Garden. Adam and Eve are expelled from *their* Garden, but Abraham and his descendants are offered the hope for a Promised Land, Canaan, the fertile land of milk and honey. Moses leads the Children of Israel out of captivity in Egypt, but he does not live to reach his destination. His followers, however, find that Canaan is anything but a joyful paradise where they can live happily ever after. It is constantly attacked, conquered, and occupied. Yet the promise made by God to Abraham projects the Garden into the future. The Golden Age has yet to come, but come it will.

In the eighteenth century, writers in Europe and America revived the Garden myth as they mourned the shift from rural to urban living. They lamented the wretched lives of the urban poor, densely packed into crime-ridden, filthy slums. The teeming cities represented for these writers the antithesis of the Garden, and they celebrated the unspoiled countryside and the happy, unschooled innocents who lived there, uncorrupted by the greed and arrogance of cosmopolitan life. Literature and drama began to cast their eyes far afield, imagining the paradise of remote lands, where the sun shines warmly all year long, food is abundant, and inhabitants live in perpetual harmony.

This literary movement was inspired by the philosophy of *primitivism*, which held that those who lived far from cities in what was called the "state of nature" were happier, less apt to commit crime, and more willing to share the fruits of the land than their educated and wealthier counterparts. The key spokesperson for primitivism was the French philosopher Jean-Jacques Rousseau (1712–1768), whose contributions to the idea of freedom are discussed in the final chapter of this book. For now, we need to know that Rousseau restated the myth of the Garden, blaming government and social controls, both products of so-called civilization, for the corruption of humanity. In doing so, he created the archetype of the *noble savage*—untutored but astute in the ways of nature, infinitely resourceful, and able to provide food and shelter for the family.

Primitivism led to the popularity on the stage and in fiction of this new mythic figure. Robinson Crusoe's "man Friday" was far more adept at living without the comforts of civilization than the shipwrecked British gentleman who depends on him for survival. Mark Twain (1835–1910) created Huck Finn and his wonderful raft, and sent them floating down the Mississippi River—a way of life representing a perpetual escape from civilization, its moral codes, its social demands, and its unhappy inhabitants. James M. Barrie gave the world Peter Pan, who eludes the aging process and lives a boy's carefree existence in Never-Never-Land. More recently, Steven Spielberg gave us E.T., the extraterrestrial, an adorable, unspoiled being from outer space who manages to escape the clutches of humanity, which is—except for one tender and understanding little boy—unworthy of his purity. He waits somewhere "up there" for a true believer who will find a way out of the mess we humans have made of the once beautiful Earth.

I am pessimistic about the human race because it is too ingenious for its own good. Our approach to nature is to beat it into submission. We would stand a better chance of survival if we accommodated ourselves to the planet. . .

—E. B. White

The "discovery" of America in 1492 gave rise to a new version of the Garden archetype—*the New World*—which continues to influence us today. First came the explorers, proudly planting their nations' flags on the "virgin" soil (while Native Americans watched). Then came boatloads of pilgrims seeking a new start in life. Then by the thousands came immigrants seeking prosperity in streets supposedly paved with gold. As the eastern half of the United States became densely populated and the dream of prosperity gave way to the reality of long hours of work and crowded tenements, the archetype of the Garden was moved out to the frontier, the wide-open American West. Pioneers left their homes by the thousands, seeking a new Canaan. Some prospered, many did not. The promise of the New World still holds out hope for millions throughout the globe.

When they come to a promised land, modern immigrants, like their predecessors, bring with them a strong archetype—the family—as well as the customs, traditional beliefs, and rituals that hold families together. Sometimes the newcomers are received with enthusiasm, and sometimes they are rejected. Often, members of the younger generation drift away, become part of the new culture. The elders sometimes intensify the traditional rituals, hold even more tightly to their customs, close themselves in for fear of losing their identity, self-respect, dignity. Disenchanted by the New World, they remember the old country, where things were better, where people were nicer and the streets safer. Like Dorothy in the Land of Oz, they discover that maybe their original home wasn't so bad after all. The Garden always seems to be somewhere else. But if this archetype can cause disillusionment, it can also be the source of hope.

Gods as Human Beings

As an archetype, the Greek god is written about and depicted in statuary as a larger-than-life mortal. Unlike most other early cultures, the Greeks had ambivalent feelings about their deities. They feared them because of their enormous power and because they could be unpredictable, striking down anyone they chose, at any time, and for any reason. They also resented them. The Greeks believed that nothing in the universe was as important as human beings. If there were to be

In humanizing their gods, the Greeks in effect deified themselves.

gods, why, they must be made in the image of humanity (not the other way around as in Judaism, Christianity, and Islam).

The archetypal term *Greek god*, used to describe a very handsome man, usually refers to Apollo, who was always portrayed as the epitome of physical perfection and whose name itself has become an archetype of male beauty. *Greek goddess*, or just *goddess*, used to describe a woman of surpassing beauty, usually means Aphrodite or the Roman Venus. Although we don't run into an Apollo or a Venus every day, the enduring myth is that such physical perfection, though godlike, *is* attainable by certain mortals.

The Greek deities were thought of as residing on Mount Olympus, which is a very real place, in much the same way that our own deities of the entertainment world live high up in the Hollywood Hills or on the slopes of Aspen or along the Grande Corniche, the topmost road on the French Riviera and home to the wealthy (*and* "beautiful") people of this world. Zeus and Hera, the king and queen of the other Greek deities, were married celebrities who fought bitterly and held grudges against each other. Many human woes were ascribed to the "fact" that Zeus and Hera were often on opposite sides in a war, with each plotting against the other. *In humanizing their gods, the Greeks in effect deified themselves!*

Myth as Explanation

Mythology consists of much more than the archetypes that shape the way we interpret our world and what happens to us in it. For our ancestors, two major aspects of being alive must have been very baffling. One was the mystery of natural phenomena. The other was how to account for all the trouble that seemed to be part of life. Mythology was their way of understanding the mystery of the universe and the pain and hardships of living in it.

If science had been at the disposal of our early ancestors, they might have turned away from mythmaking in favor of observation and experimentation. Lacking science, they created stories to account for what they could not otherwise explain. We should be grateful that they did, for these ancient stories, along with the music and dances that must surely have accompanied group ceremonies, became the foundation on which the humanities now rest securely. The myths they wove made the natural world and its amazing phenomena seem less remote and frightening and helped remove the fear that life was innately evil, that bad things happened without cause.

The need for acceptable explanations for life's tragedies remains with the humanities. Often these explanations are at odds with scientific evidence. For example, in 1927 the American author Thornton Wilder, most well known for his innovative play *Our Town* (discussed in Chapter 7), published the novel *The Bridge of San Luis Rey*. Significantly, the book appeared just ten years after the outbreak of World War I, while people were still searching for reasons for that conflict.

The bridge in the novel is a footbridge built across a steep gorge in the Andes Mountains of Peru. Thousands traveled across it for years, but on one particular day the bridge collapses, and five travelers are hurled to their deaths. The novel then presents the story of each victim and poses the question "Why this person?" Although scientific explanations are abundant, the author prefers to leave the door open for the possibility that divine intervention was responsible. Is it more comforting to believe everything happens for a reason instead of believing that life is a series of random, senseless occurrences? Our ancestors must have thought so and may have left explanatory myths as their legacy to us.

Creation

Even the greatest scientists and philosophers have wrestled with complex questions about life and our beginnings. Why is there something when there might have been nothing? Is there an essential principle that requires existence to exist? Or did it spring accidentally from nothing? And if so, how and why? Why are *we* here? Why haven't we discovered intelligent life anywhere else in the universe—at least so far? Mythology supplies a number of different answers, and the quest continues.

Accounts of creation are present in almost every early culture. One myth, as recounted in the *Upanishads*, sacred books of India, begins: "At first he was lonely and afraid but, above all, he lacked delight (therefore, we lack delight when alone) and desired a second . . . . This Self then divided itself into two parts; and with that, there were a master and a mistress."[6] But this first woman was afraid to be touched and so hid from her male Self. She turned into various animals, but he pursued her and mated with each of her manifestations—until the natural world, as we know it, was formed. The story does not explain where the Self came from, but once that is accepted, everything else follows in a cause-and-effect sequence.

Most Asian mythologies have no clear-cut story of creation. The Buddhist *dharma* constitutes the orderly principle that guides the universe, and it had no beginning. Therefore, the natural world, which is the outer garment of this order, must have always existed. Confucianism, a major Chinese philosophy, stresses the social world and one's duties within it and avoids the question of how it began, which does not matter as much as how life is lived. However, in another major Chinese philosophy, Taoism (or Dowism), we find a creation story that resembles those of non-Asian cultures, giving further credence to Jung's theory that early cultures developed similar myths without traceable communication with each other. In this story, the universe, as in the Hebrew Bible, was at first a dark, formless void. Within this void, a single egg came into being, inside of which was the fetus of what would eventually become the giant Pan-Gu. After attaining colossal size, Pan-Gu stretched his arms, the egg broke, and the lighter half floated upward to become the sky, while the heavier part sank downward to become the earth. Ever since, the operation of the universe has depended on the attraction of opposites—astonishingly prophetic of the modern electromagnetic theory of nature!

In Greek mythology, precreation is depicted in a similar fashion. It is called the "formless confusion of Chaos," existing only in darkness. Chaos in some mysterious way gave birth to children: one was Gaea, or Mother Earth. Others were Night and Erebus, or Death. Night placed an egg in the depths of Erebus, and from it was born Love (though we are not sure how this love was defined). Love's first act was to create Light and Day.

Greek myths tell us that the gods came after the creation, but this order is not surprising when we consider that, in the Greek myths, the power of Fate appears to be greater than that of the gods. For the Greeks, the power of Fate always existed, was responsible for the coming of Night and Death, and must therefore be reckoned as *the* divine force.[7]

According to an Aztec myth, before the universe was formed, there were gods. A fight developed over who would create which part of the world. Eventually a snake divided in half—one half to create the upper part, the other half to create the lower part. The half that created the earth felt she was less important and began to quarrel with the half that made the heavens. As compensation for her inferior position, the gods added to her importance by allowing different parts of her body to be the source of important elements—the rivers and streams coming from her eyes, for instance.

Many other cultures attribute the origin of the natural world to a divinity that preceded its existence. Judaism, Christianity, and Islam share a common belief that the world was brought into existence by an all-powerful and singular creator. Working within this tradition, the English poet John Milton (1608–1674), in his epic poem *Paradise Lost*, assumes the preexistence of both God and a chaotic universe, which was then transformed into the orderly cosmos the poet knew. According to Milton's interpretation, in the beginning there was

> *the vast immeasurable Abyss,*
> *Outrageous as a Sea, dark, wasteful, wild,*
> *Up from the bottom turn'd by furious winds*
> *And surging waves, as Mountains to assault*
> *Heav'n's highth, and with the centre mix the Pole.*
> *Silence, ye troubl'd waves, and thou Deep, peace,*
> *Said then th' Omnific Word, your discord end.*[8]

In the modern world, a debate continues between those who believe the universe had no known beginning and those who believe it cannot have always existed. Modern science is deeply committed to the law of cause and effect, yet when it comes to the question of whether there was a *first* cause, a deep division of opinion remains. The theory that the origins of the universe can be traced to a big bang, a huge explosion of perhaps a single particle, is widely held. Once this explanation is accepted, the theory manages to explain all that followed. But where, some ask, did the single particle come from? One answer has been that it came from nothing, and that we need not assume "nothing" is empty.

It is interesting to note that one of the crucial unsolved questions about our existence is remarkably similar to those asked by our earliest ancestors.

The Natural World

> *Every part of the earth is sacred to my people. Every single pine needle, every sandy shore, every mist in the dark woods, every meadow, every humming insect. All are holy in the memory and experience of my people.*
>
> —**Chief Seattle**

Once believed to be an ancient site of human sacrifice, Stonehenge—that remarkable stone circle on the Salisbury Plain in southwestern England—is now believed to have been erected as a means of predicting the seasons according to the position of the sun with respect to the stones at various times of the year. When the sun shone directly through the archway formed by the prominent pair of stones in the center, this regular occurrence was taken as the beginning of summer. Yet Stonehenge could not explain why there *were* seasons. Why was it not always summer? Why the bitter cold, when people could freeze to death and food was scarce?

Nature was surely something to inspire wonder, apprehension, and worship. Many early myths sought to explain nature, and early rituals—ceremonial dances as well as animal and human sacrifice—were efforts to control it.

Stonehenge has stood on the Salisbury Plain in southwestern England for thousand of years; believed to have been an early means of predicting the seasons, it could not explain why there had to be seasons.

Source: Bob Krist/Corbis.

In Scandinavian communities, for example, the fertility deity was Freyr, who was thought to bring rich harvests to the earth. He did so by wooing a maiden symbolizing the union of earth and sky. Rituals that honored Freyr and the abundance he gave were, Scandinavians thought, essential to survival. In almost all early cultures, help from the gods was needed if crops should fail or were insufficient. If the weather did not cooperate, food could be found in the sea if the storm god could be appeased.

In Greek mythology, Apollo, the sun god, drove his chariot across the sky each day, thus accounting for the rising and setting of the sun. Apollo's sister Artemis presided over the moon at night. The king of gods, Zeus, was responsible for hurling thunderbolts, and Poseidon controlled the sea. But these phenomena could be altered at the whim of the gods. Thus the sea might be made so calm that no ships could move when Poseidon wished to punish a fleet that failed to honor him. Or a sea monster might appear, sent by Poseidon in response to the prayer of a mortal to whom he owed a favor, as when Theseus prayed for the destruction of his son, who he believed had committed adultery with his stepmother.

Early peoples performed what was called "sympathetic magic," the acting out of ceremonies designed to affect the behavior of the gods. Thus during the winter solstice, the longest night of the year, people in countries throughout the world

What more natural than if a beautiful boy had thus been killed, than to think when later the ground blossomed with Narcissus or hyacinths that the flowers were his very self?

—Edith Hamilton

attempted to evoke the return of the sun through lighting candles, as if the sun—or the powers in charge of light—would imitate the lesser light below. Similarly, the Native American rain dance is a ritual designed to bring an end to drought.

A Greek explanation for the seasons was the love of Demeter, goddess of the earth, for her daughter Persephone. So joyful was Demeter at the very thought of her daughter that she provided a superabundance of all the good things the earth could yield. One day, however, the girl was glimpsed by Hades, lord of the underworld, who captured her and took her to be his bride. Demeter so mourned her loss that the earth came to be covered with the ice and snow of perpetual winter. If Zeus had not intervened, all human life would have ended, but he was so touched by Demeter's grief that he arranged for Persephone to live with her mother for all but four months of the year, those she owed to her husband. When Persephone is in the underworld, the earth freezes over, and when she returns, her happy mother allows the earth once again to bloom.

Another explanation occurs in the myth of Dionysus, the deity who governed the abundance of the earth. Winter came about because he died and, in the underworld, was torn to pieces and eaten. Still, when he was somehow resurrected and became whole again, spring returned—but only temporarily, for each year Dionysus met his terrible fate again.

The descent into the underworld of both Persephone and Dionysus can be regarded as sacrifices that ensured rebirth. This idea, that without sorrow or death there can be no springtime joy, was an early belief that has captured the minds of writers and philosophers ever since.

For the Greeks, vegetation could be connected to the involvement of gods with beautiful mortals. The blooms of the hyacinth and the narcissus celebrated the transformation of their namesakes from death to eternal life in nature. Hyacinthus was a beautiful young mortal dearly loved by Apollo, who accidentally killed him while they were playing a game of discus throwing. (Note that once again the Greeks attributed human failings to their gods.) Apollo then transformed the dead body into the hyacinth. The narcissus commemorated the death of another beautiful young man, who saw his own reflection in a pool, fell madly in love with it, and pined away from sorrow because he could never possess it.

Mythologist Edith Hamilton interprets such transformation stories in a somewhat ominous way. They are, she speculates, vestiges of ancient human sacrifice rather than of accidental death. Ancient people did offer a select number of handsome young people in sacrificial rituals designed to appease the gods. According to Hamilton, when the Greeks told their myths in later years, they revised the stories to rid themselves of this violent era in their past:

> *It might happen, if the fields around a village were not fruitful, if the corn did not spring up as it should, that one of the villagers would be killed and his—or her—blood sprinkled over the barren land. . . . What more natural then, if a beautiful boy had thus been killed, than to think when later the ground blossomed with narcissus or hyacinths that the flowers were his very self, changed and yet living again? So they would tell each other it had happened, a lovely miracle which made the cruel death seem less cruel.*[9]

The sacrifice of animals was probably performed each year at the spring festivals honoring Dionysus to ensure the god's return and the renewal of the growing season. At the drama festivals, when the tragic protagonist fell from his high position, he became a kind of symbolic sacrifice so order could return to the state.

From what is now Ghana, in West Africa, comes a story of how the country flourished and was prosperous because each year a beautiful young woman was given to a devouring serpent. One year, however, when the woman was led to the pit where the serpent waited, rescue came in the form of a brave young man engaged to marry her. He stood by while the serpent appeared and twice spat venom on the woman, because he knew that only on the third try could the reptile be destroyed. At the appropriate moment, the young man beheaded the serpent, only to find that it kept growing new heads—seven in all. The young woman was saved, but the serpent had its revenge. As the last head was cut off, it flew away, saying, "For seven years, seven months, and seven days, Ghana will receive neither water nor rains of gold." A drought ensued, destroying the populace and a once great empire. In this myth we do not find the cycle motif of Persephone and Dionysus but rather an unhappy explanation for a catastrophe that must have actually taken place.

In Native American mythology, human sacrifice was needed in order to make the heavens work properly. After four worlds failed, a fifth world was revealed. It was discovered that the sun and moon could be set in their courses only by the death of a Navajo each day and another each night. Later, when human beings claimed credit for the prosperity of the world, they were punished by plagues and monsters.

Human Suffering

Evil enters like a needle and spreads like an oak tree.

—**Ethiopian proverb**

Sometimes known as the *problem of evil,* suffering caused by natural catastrophes (such as the devastating tsunamis of 2004 that took more than 200,000 lives in southeast Asia) and by the inhumanity of regimes (such as that of the Nazis in the early twentieth century) continues to be analyzed by philosophers, theologians, and creative writers. Our ancestors asked the same questions we hear now. Why are some people consumed with hatred, envy, and greed? Why are there famines, plagues, and wars? Like many contemporaries, they wanted to believe there were reasons for the suffering people had to endure. The idea that terrible things happened without cause was unacceptable because it suggested a universe ruled by chaos, a universe in which humankind was powerless. In creating stories that explained suffering, our ancestors were able to reassure themselves that order did indeed prevail in the universe and that, if they acted in an appropriate manner, they might escape misfortune.

A common explanation for suffering was an early act of transgression against divine law—offending a god or disobeying a command. The Greek myth of Pandora explains how human misfortune came about because of curiosity. Beloved by Zeus, Pandora was given a magical box in which all of the gods had placed something, but she did not know what the contents were, and she was not supposed to open the box. Frustrated by the gnawing desire to discover what treasures were concealed inside, she disobeyed Zeus and opened the box, out of which flew death, sorrow, plagues, war, and every other calamity visited upon mortals ever since. Alarmed, Pandora slammed the box shut, not knowing that trapped inside was the gift of hope.

Color Plates 4 and 5 show two visual interpretations of trouble's origin. In the portrait of Pandora by the nineteenth-century English artist Dante Gabriel

Rossetti (1828–1882), the mythical Greek woman appears strong-willed and determined to have her own way, whatever the cost. In *Food for the Spirit*, Haitian artist Gabriel Alix (b. 1930) shows Adam and Eve as equal partners in sin. Given the colorful lusciousness of the fruit hanging over their heads, the viewer may find it hard to blame the first man and woman for failing to obey God's command.

In the Judeo-Christian tradition, God commands Adam and Eve not to eat the forbidden fruit growing on the Tree of Knowledge. (The fruit, often depicted as an apple, is not identified in Genesis, and apples are not native to the Middle East.) Tempted by the serpent, Eve eats the fruit, and Adam does the same. Genesis does not say that Eve prevailed upon Adam to follow her into sin, though later versions turned the story into a myth of woman's weakness. In Milton's *Paradise Lost*, God judges Adam more harshly than he does Eve because, even though Eve has sinned first, Adam, being a man, should have known better.

In an African myth of the Burundi tribe, a woman is again blamed for bringing about human suffering. In the long-ago time in which the myth is set, human beings are not touched by Death because divine dogs protect them. One day Death approaches a woman and promises to give her and her family special protection. When the woman opens her mouth to speak, Death jumps in. Questioned by the chief of the gods concerning the whereabouts of Death, the woman lies and says she has not seen him. The chief of the gods, being all mighty and all knowing, recognizes that the woman is lying and allows Death to dwell inside the woman and all of her descendants.

According to another tale found in the oral tradition of many African cultures, Kintu, the first man, and his wife Nambi are hurrying to leave the land of the sky in order to flee Death. They have been warned not to delay their escape, but Nambi decides to go back for grain. Death follows her as she attempts to rejoin her husband. As a result, death becomes the punishment for all future generations, a motif notably similar to that found in Genesis.

The traditions of the East do not speak of human suffering as caused by disobedience to a divine command; rather, they blame selfish acts by individuals for the world's ills. In Hindu belief, what happens to a person is the result of **karma** (see Chapter 10 for a fuller discussion), a summation at death of how one's life has been conducted. If it has been less than morally satisfactory, the spirit is reborn into a new body and a less fortunate social position in which hunger and poverty dominate. If it has been mainly satisfactory but not perfect, the spirit is reborn with a chance to live a better life. Thus Hindus speak of "good karma," which means a life blessed by good deeds in a past existence, while "bad karma" is just the opposite.

A legend found in Mexico and in Central and South America is that of *La Llorona* ("The Weeping Woman"). So popular is this figure in oral storytelling that numerous versions of her persist. In one version, she is a phantom, never seen, but heard weeping at night, mourning her children, for whose deaths she is responsible. In another version, she is a spirit doomed to wander forever in search of the children she neglected during her lifetime. Still another version shows her to be blatantly evil, a woman who lures men to follow her only to suffer violent death. In this telling, the woman resembles the Sirens of Greek mythology, the sea maidens whose seductive singing lures sailors to their doom, and the Lorelei in Germanic myth, a lovely maiden who sits on a rock, combing her hair and singing so beautifully that sailors wreck their ships trying to reach her. The tales of

La Llorona are often told as a warning to unmarried pregnant women who, finding themselves abandoned, have no recourse but to give up their babies. Presumably, repeating the story of a mother mourning her lost children reminds young women of what can happen when they indulge in practices forbidden by religion and family.[10]

The tragic results of curiosity and disobedience are also found in two other famous myths, one from the Greeks and the other from the Hebrew Bible. Both illustrate a universal belief that some things are better left unknown. In the Greek myth, an extraordinary musician named Orpheus, later the subject of the operas we discuss in Chapter 8, is in love with the beautiful Eurydice, who dies and is taken to the underworld. Orpheus follows her down and uses the gorgeous strains of his lute to convince the king of the underworld that Eurydice should be returned to the land of the living. His request is granted, with one condition: Orpheus must walk straight up the path without turning around to make sure that Eurydice is following. He almost keeps the pact, but at the last minute, unable to bear the suspense, he turns around, only to see his beloved being reclaimed by the powers of darkness, lost to him forever.

The prizewinning 1959 Brazilian film *Black Orpheus* (see the opening image in this chapter) tells essentially the same tale, set during the night of Carnivale in Rio de Janeiro. A figure wearing the mask of Death pursues the modern Eurydice through a crowded street, finally seizing her and carrying her into an empty building and down an endless spiral staircase. The modern Orpheus follows them, but instead of being given the chance to return to life with her, he dies also. The morning finds the two lovers, together, impaled on the sharp spikes of an aloe plant. In this modern retelling, death is not the result of curiosity or disobedience, but—more tragically—something that occurs without any purpose at all.

The Orpheus and Eurydice story continues to fascinate writers and public alike. In 2000 there was Mary Zimmerman's fanciful stage adaptation of the Roman poet Ovid's *Metamorphoses*, itself an updating of Greek myths. Eurydice is now a modern, liberated woman who decides she is *not* going to follow meekly behind her lord and master, Orpheus. She pays the price, but the assumption is that her independence is worth it.

In a biblical tale, Lot and his family are allowed to escape the destruction of Sodom and Gomorrah, with one condition—that they flee the city without turning around to see what is happening. Lot's wife, however, cannot resist the temptation, and when she turns around, she is transformed into a pillar of salt.

Cursed by Fate

The Greeks personified Fate as three sisters, one of whom wove the thread of life, another stretched it, and the third cut it–presumably on a whim.

The Greeks introduced another way of accounting for human woes, and that was Fate. It was visually represented as three sisters: one wove the thread of life, another stretched it out, and the third cut it. In addition to having a person's lifespan determined by the whim of Fate, Greek mythology also developed the concept that many people were followed throughout their lives by the unkindness of Fate because of a transgression they had committed in the past, or one that was committed by an ancestor for which they were paying the price. Two of the greatest Greek tragedies are trilogies about noble families cursed by Fate because of past sins.

The Oresteia by Aeschylus (525–456 B.C.E.) consists of three plays about the doomed family of Atreus, who killed his brother's children and then served them to him as food. He committed this atrocity as an act of vengeance against the brother for having forced his wife into adultery. The two sons of Atreus, who must bear the consequences of their father's sin, are Menelaus, king of Sparta, and Agamemnon, a Greek warrior. Menelaus marries the beautiful Helen, who runs off with the Trojan prince Paris, thus precipitating the Trojan War. Agamemnon fights the ten-year war on his brother's side, returning home only to be lured to his death by his wife, whose lover stabs him. The two adulterers are in turn murdered by Agamemnon's son Orestes with the assistance of his sister Electra. The Furies, ferocious mythic women whose duty it is to haunt and terrify evil-doers, pursue Orestes, taunting him demonically day and night until he is exonerated by the goddess Athena in the world's first known trial scene.

The doomed family of Cadmus includes his descendant Oedipus and the four children borne to Oedipus and his wife Jocasta, who was also his natural mother. Cadmus had been a wealthy citizen who offended the gods by bragging that, because of his business success, he was just as powerful as those deities. The disasters visited upon his descendants were punishments for his arrogance.

Greek myths and tragedies are of enduring relevance because the question of whether any of us really has free will is still very much alive.

The tragedy of the doomed Oedipus is told in three plays by Sophocles (discussed in Chapter 7): *Oedipus the King* (or *Oedipus Rex*), *Antigone*, and *Oedipus at Colonus*. By the fifth century B.C.E., Athenians had developed a highly sophisticated urban civilization, and though the old myths still formed the basis for many plays of the period, they were subject to question. In particular, the Oedipus plays dealt with the issue of whether the protagonist, suffering because he had long ago killed his father and then married his mother without knowing the truth of his parentage, should accept responsibility for his actions when he was doomed by Fate to commit them. Sophocles resolves the issue by having his protagonist willingly accept responsibility as a means of maintaining his dignity. "The gods willed that I should slay the man I didn't know was my father," he says, "but the hand that struck the blow was mine."

Greek myths and the tragedies they inspired remain of enduring relevance because the question of whether any of us really has free will is still very much alive. Free will is at the core of many a court case involving dilemmas of responsibility. Inherited traits, family abuse, poverty, and a bad environment frequently enter into arguments for the defense. In Chapter 16, Freedom, the reader will find much more about this problem, which crops up continually in literature and film.

Myths of Childhood

Our earliest encounters with literature, the stories told or read to us, probably influenced our expectations of later life. Childhood tales—despite their frequent violence and terror—usually satisfy the child's (or even the parent's) need for security by bringing the action to a happy conclusion. How often did we hear "And they all lived happily ever after"?

Adults like to escape from the demands of everyday life by giving in to their childhood love of magical kingdoms, witches, wizards, and perils that are inevitably overcome. The Harry Potter books seem to be as widely read by the adult population as they are by the young. Fables from distant childhood have been kept alive, particularly by the Disney company. Both the young and the not so young have made huge box-office successes of *Snow White, The Little Mermaid,*

Beauty and the Beast, Aladdin, and *The Lion King*. This section deals with some childhood tales that are too important not to be considered as valid introductions to the humanities.

The Need for Reassurance

Children who hear about the Three Little Pigs learn that hard work and diligence, not fun and frivolity, pay off in the long run. And Red Riding Hood's journey to Granny's house would certainly have been a lot safer if she had heeded the advice about not speaking to strangers. Similarly, the mother goat in "The Wolf and the Seven Kids" goes off, leaving her children home alone with the admonition not to open the door to anyone. Most of the seven goats pay for disobeying this instruction by being eaten. Of course, as often happens in fairy-tale land, they are rescued, none the worse for their ordeal. Sleeping Beauty, threatened with awful consequences if she pricks her finger on a spindle, cannot resist the temptation to explore a hidden spinning wheel and so suffers the inevitable wound. But like so many childhood myths, that of Sleeping Beauty contains not only dire warnings about disobedience but also the reassurance that nothing *really* bad is ever going to happen.

The Harry Potter stories offer a combination of myths. Harry, the orphan kept under lock and key by relatives who do not understand him, is a modern version of Cinderella. Though neglected and consigned to a bleak future, he has magical powers that will eventually make a difference. In this respect, he also resembles the young King Arthur, the only person able to pull the sword Excalibur from the stone. Both myths appeal to our secret desire for hidden powers that make us superior to others.

The fairy tale takes a child's anxieties and dilemmas very seriously and addresses itself directly to them: the need to be loved and the fear that one is thought worthless; the love of life and the fear of death.

—Bruno Bettelheim

Modern children's mythology tends to be less blatantly optimistic than popular myths of the past. Perhaps the stress of modern life filters down into bedtime stories. Or perhaps modern readers (or listeners) have developed a higher tolerance for conflict. Characters can face very real dangers and frightening villains. Sauron, who guards Mount Doom in J.R.R. Tolkien's *Lord of the Rings*, is evil incarnate and ultimately conquered, but only after a furious battle sequence. Maurice Sendak, also known for his imaginative stage and opera sets, has written a number of children's stories, such as *Where the Wild Things Are*, in which a little boy, sent to his room without supper, flies out of his bedroom (without adult permission, of course) and encounters weird, fantastic, sometimes frightening creatures, all vividly illustrated by the author. But, despite the odds, the boy manages to return safely—and to find his supper waiting for him. The myth appeals to the need for escape from humdrum—sometimes burdensome—reality, as well as the need for reassuring safety and love.

The Importance of Being Attractive and Rich

The old fairy tales reinforce stereotypical gender roles, class distinctions, and the notion that good and evil are based on physical appearance. People named Charming, Beauty, and Snow White are beautiful to look at and morally pure. The names Wicked Witch and Stepmother are given to unattractive characters who are up to no good. Cinderella is both breathtakingly beautiful and hard working. By contrast, her stepsisters are selfish, ugly, and possessed of unfortunately large feet. Old people seldom fare well in fairy tales, and critics point to this fact to explain why children often shy away from close contact with the elderly and the wrinkled, who resemble fairy-tale witches.

Red Riding Hood's journey would have been safer if she had heeded the advice about not speaking to strangers.

Source: Gustave Doré, *Little Red Riding Hood.* Credit: Archivo Iconograpico, S. A.Corbis.

Fairy tales take place in magic kingdoms dominated by a class system, for, after all, they originated in a time when it was believed that nobility was inborn. People may not have believed literally in the blue blood of one small segment of the populace, but they were reminded time and again that "class will tell." The heroine of "The Princess and the Pea" is so innately sensitive—so clearly a member of the upper class—that she spends a sleepless night because one pea is under the pile of mattresses on which she has been lying. The pea has been deliberately placed there as a test of her true aristocracy.

The Importance of Names

In one folk tale, a lower-class heroine, a miller's daughter, marries a prince on the strength of a false promise—that she can transform flax into gold. She is locked in a room and told to fill it with the precious metal, but of course she doesn't know how. Help comes from a little man who tells her he can perform the magic, provided she promise to give him her first-born child. Since the poor girl is not yet married and is in danger of losing her life if she doesn't perform the task before morning, she agrees. The gold appears, the marriage takes place, and in due time a child is born. When reminded of her agreement, she begs for another chance, which she gets! The condition is that she must tell the little man his name. Her first guesses are not even close, but she eventually is victorious when she overhears him boasting, "Rumpelstiltskin is my name."

The myth probably appeals to children of an age when language is becoming important. During dramatic presentations of the story, young audiences continually scream the name to the actress playing the heroine. Perhaps it helps children affirm their own identities, for they too have names, and names, as they are learning, are all-important, especially unusual names that make one unique.

The Dark Side

Though modern childhood mythology does not shy away from confronting real dangers, even the time-honored fairy tales must have evoked multiple responses. As well as magic kingdoms and beautiful characters, there are dangerous forests where lurk goblins, bats, and skulls. Through these and other dark elements, children learn that life is not always sunny.

The beautiful Snow White appears to die from biting into a poisonous apple given to her by her jealous stepmother. She is placed in a glass coffin, though in real life, children are often shielded from close contact with death. Of course, the kiss of a prince restores Snow White to life and leads to the usual proposal of a royal marriage.

In fairy tales, much emphasis is placed on the threat of being eaten. In *Hansel and Gretel*, still popular as children's theater and as opera, the wicked woman in the tempting gingerbread house warms her oven in dreadful preparation for roasting the two children. In the nick of time they are rescued and the wicked woman is consigned to a painful death.

In his 1983 musical play *Into the Woods*, Stephen Sondheim brings together all of the major characters from the fairy tales and puts them into small houses on the edge of the woods, a symbol of the true dangers in the world. Mythical illusion is continually shattered in the play. After their marriage, Cinderella discovers that Prince Charming is having many affairs. When confronted, he explains: "I was raised to be charming, not faithful." Jack's excursion up the magical beanstalk nets no fortune, and the hand of the dead giant falls on and kills the baker's wife. Traditional myths help the makers of the humanities to communicate dark messages.

There must be more to life than having everything.
—**Maurice Sendak**

Roald Dahl's *Charlie and the Chocolate Factory* has been filmed twice in recent times: as the 1971 *Willy Wonka and the Chocolate Factory* and director Tim Burton's 2005 *Charlie and the Chocolate Factory*. Neither version is precisely the wholesome entertainment the title appears to promise. The fable about a wondrous world of unbelievable candy was turned it into a dark story of how greed destroys. The children who can't resist the many temptations drown in a chocolate river or are crushed in mixing machines. The purity and common sense of the young hero, however, are recognized by the factory's proprietor, and he is allowed to ride a magic elevator into a land free of greed and corruption.

Some parents seek to avoid frightening their children (especially at bedtime) by eliminating all threatening motifs, by making sure that hungry wolves are not allowed to eat either little pigs or old ladies. One mother was distressed, however, when her child burst into tears at the end of a bland retelling of "Red Riding Hood" by demanding to know whether the wolf was still hungry!

Is it important for each generation of children to be taught the old fables? Writer Leonard Courier apparently believes so. His 1961 short story "A Christmas Morning" concerns a science-minded father who decides to eliminate all fairy-tale illusions in order to make sure his son will be able to face a harsh world. "The story of Santa Claus is nonsense," he says, and forces the child to stay awake all night so that he will observe the true source of his presents. The child, rubbing his eyes, watches as his parents assemble the gifts under the tree. At dawn he pleads to be allowed to sleep, but his father insists that he have breakfast and then play with his toys.

Before he may eat, however, the boy is required to show that he has learned his lesson. "Finish this sentence," says his father, "There is no—." When the boy keeps silent, the father becomes angry and threatens to beat the child if the correct answer does not come forth. "Well, what is it?" he repeats. "There is no what?"

Wearily, the little boy looks up and says, "There is no father."

Popular Mythology

Much of what we say and how we react to certain situations have roots in mythology, both past and present. Whether we know it or not, we keep creating and perpetuating myths. The fables of the Greek writer Aesop (sixth century B.C.E.) contain many stories and morals that stay with humanity from age to age. There is the story of the tortoise who wins a race against the swifter hare, proving that slow and steady can win a race. And there is a fox who decides that the grapes he is unable to reach are probably sour anyway—hence the continued use of "sour grapes" applied to anyone claiming "I didn't want it anyway." Aesop gave practical advice, but it was often contradictory. "Look before you leap" is the opposite of "He who hesitates is lost." Still, either can contain wisdom, depending on the situation.

Many popular beliefs are quoted without regard to their origins. Discovering the roots of popular mythology is not a plea for being more realistic. Its purpose is to encourage the *habit* of identifying certain thought and emotional patterns so they can be more readily evaluated as either still vital or no longer useful. In a sense, it is also an introduction to the critical appreciation of the humanities.

Common Sayings

Truth is one, the sages speak it by many names.

—**The Vedas**

All of us hear them; nearly everyone uses them. Life would be different without them. They are expressions of beliefs that may have originated in ancient stories, religious teachings, or frequently repeated slogans. They may be considered misconceptions by some, but indeed most of them are not challenged at all. Even those who scoff, however, may not be analyzing why the belief has found such wide acceptance. The following is a selective listing of some common beliefs that constitute our everyday mythology.

"*What goes around comes around.*" In Hindu and Buddhist belief, as we have pointed out, *karma* is connected to a past life. People who have not led exemplary lives must continue to live in a new incarnation, as repayment for past deeds. As commonly used, the expression explains and approves of justice, as when the criminal who seemed beyond the law is discovered and punished, thus "getting what was coming." The saying also helps many of us account for bad things that happen. Apparently it is easier to believe that bad things are not random like a lightning strike but are the logical result of a misdeed. Thus, if we avoid such misdeeds in the future, all will be well.

The other side of the coin is how this belief helps us cope when good deeds are not recognized. Everyone likes to be given credit when it is due, and the popular myth assures people that eventually a reward will come.

"*Leave it to Mother Nature.*" If nothing else, this saying supports the notion that nature is warm, caring, and nurturing. Mother Nature, or Mother Earth, is important in many cultures. Mongolian mythology, for example, has a Mother Earth who is gentle, in contrast to Father Sky, a stern disciplinarian who uses lightning to show his displeasure. In Greek mythology the goddess Gaea, who became Mother Earth, was the daughter of Chaos and mother and wife of both Uranus (the sky) and Pontus (the sea). In early myths, she is a monster, but over the centuries she evolved into a benevolent force. She lives on as the mother of all things, and as Gaia she is often featured by environmentalists on Earth Day to emphasize the need to love and protect the planet.

We like to think that Nature, like a good mother, will somehow forgive her children for pollution, overcrowding, and global warning. Indeed the myth of Mother Nature is the myth of motherhood in general, influencing how many women view their role in life and the expectations of their children. Mother is supposed to look after people's needs, and if she does not do so to their satisfaction, she will be accused of behaving unnaturally.

"They'll think of something." The ending of some Greek plays resolved terrible problems by having an actor dressed as a god come down to the stage. The device, as discussed in Chapter 7, was known as a *deus ex machina*, and it has become a standard critical term for plot contrivance. In popular mythology, the *deus* is sometimes medical research. Like the cavalry riding to the rescue, like the mysterious stranger who appears just in time, science will solve every problem, find a cure for every disease in the nick of time. Because "they" have helped so often before, they can be expected to help every time. If rescue is inevitable, every rule of good health can be violated for our bodies or our cities while we wait for our rescuers.

"What do THEY know?" This popular expression is the opposite of expecting miracles from science. Disrespect for, even ridicule of, professional authority is the source of continual tension in the world. It is the Dionysian component in many people that makes them shout down speakers, hurl cream pies, and defy those who are said to know better. Literature and films have often endorsed the hero who is shown to be right by defying rules, while the person in authority has been depicted as unrealistically rigid and deserving of overthrow. This popular myth suggests that a healthy dose of skepticism is important. The sentiment can indeed fuel beneficial social change but, when applied indiscriminately, can lead to anarchy.

"All you need is love." Whether love is defined as the sweetest thing, whether it makes the world go round, or whether it's all you need, a popular belief is that love is as important as breathable air. Even the high divorce rate has not interfered with the widespread belief that living alone is unnatural or that there is no happiness outside commitment to one other person. A first mistake requires the search for the right choice next time, and a newly single person's claim of being happy is met with disbelief and offers of matchmaking. The myth is not only that there is someone for everyone, but that love and talk of love can substitute for any other human concern.

Just as the universe is filled with positive and negative particles, myths frequently have their own negative counterparts. In this case, the popular belief in love at all costs is often rejected by those who believe that love is a delusion or that the search for love will always fail and leave one bereft and miserable. If successive attempts have produced unhappy results, there may be comfort in thinking that love itself is to blame for what happened, that it is wiser never to expect a relationship to succeed.

"It must be fate." Also called destiny, fate plays an important role in Greek mythology and is one of its major legacies. It is still present in the way people react to events. The idea of destiny can offer comfort, relief, and freedom from responsibility because, if something is "meant to be," it will certainly happen, and no one is to blame. There is a positive side as well. If destiny can bring disasters, it can also bring good fortune, love, and happiness. It can be the source of perpetual hope.

In the popular film *Somewhere in Time* (1980), two lovers, separated by a century, finally meet because it is their destiny. The man, who is of the modern world, is at first restless and brooding, as if he knows that his life is incomplete. As soon as he finds himself in another part of time and sees the beautiful woman who seems to be waiting for him, he knows that all is as it should be.

To believe that one is meant for better things, that the answer to prayers is just around the corner, can be uplifting to the spirits, but of course if nothing turns that corner, the result can be a quick flip of the coin, back to "facing the fact" that life is *never* under one's control; life means just waiting for "what will be." The myth can also trap people in defeatist attitudes.

"Just deserts." Deserts in this saying is related to *deserve* rather than an after-dinner sweet. Early on, we learn that Santa Claus rewards only good children, while naughty ones receive a piece of coal, getting what they deserve. Life without the myth of deserving is unimaginable. It underlies our whole system of justice, for example. It probably acts as a deterrent to untold numbers of people who might otherwise commit crimes, or even provides secret comfort to people who are serving long sentences in prison: "After all, I *deserve* this."

On the other hand, this belief can be the source of much personal unhappiness. "What did I do to deserve this?" is a question frequently asked in the midst of a crisis. The answer might be that "it was destined" or that somehow the system has broken down and an innocent victim unjustly treated. This is a myth of entitlement, and it's particularly strong among those who expect payment for good deeds. The myth of the red-suited jolly man with the white beard is as pervasive as a myth can be. A wise course might be to ask ourselves *why* we are doing something. Is it for the implicit rightness of the deed or an expected full stocking on the mantelpiece?

"Us versus them." The desire to be part of a group and therefore at odds with people in another group is well established. It may encourage school spirit and often promotes family unity, but it can also lead to wars, mob violence, and a lifelong distrust and hatred of "the other." Coaches and army sergeants urge their charges to fight more ferociously by reinforcing the "us/them" distinction, and in time of war it can help to bring about both national unity and inflexible mistrust of the enemy.

The us/them distinction can also be seen in zoning disputes, laws about immigration, and matters of territorial boundaries. It can be found in stories, plays, and novels about children in prominent families who disappoint their parents by failing to realize how lucky they are to be privileged. It underlies the racism implicit in films of the early twentieth century in which ethnic minorities are treated as stupid, bungling, or endearingly childlike. The belief presupposes the superiority of one group over the inferiority or even non-humanness of another.

"There's always room at the top." Belief that unlimited success should be possible for everyone is a spur to ambition as well as a cause for major disappointment in those who never achieve wealth or fame. The very word *top* is loaded with preconceptions and expectations. At the top are star entertainers, athletes, corporation executives, and political leaders. The pervasiveness of the belief is indicated by sales of how-to books and enrollment in seminars promising a quick and guaranteed road up. Of course if the *top* is to have any meaning, there must be a lot of people *below*.

Literature abounds with tales of those who buy into the mythology of upward mobility. The Horatio Alger novels of the early twentieth century all have heroes who start off poor and become wealthy either by hard work or accident. They are success novels, and their counterparts are films about aspiring performers who inevitably became stars after their early disappointments. The myth is so deeply ingrained in Western culture that many believe it is their *duty* to move up.

"Isn't that just like a man/woman?" **Gender roles**—models of appropriate behavior and functions for men and women—were for a long time codified and

unchanging. In many cultures these have been religiously defined, and failure to observe the rules can have serious consequences. Even among those who consider themselves enlightened, old myths that men are this and women are that often lurk in the background.

Gender reversals are not uncommon in mythology and literature, usually as a source of amusement. In one story, the Greek hero Achilles, dressed as a woman to avoid being drafted into military service, reveals his masculine identity when he brings his knees together to catch something thrown to him instead of catching it in his lap by spreading his skirt as a woman would have done. In Shakespeare's *Twelfth Night* (more fully discussed in Chapter 7), a shipwrecked woman disguises herself as her twin brother so she can safely travel alone. The duke who hires "him" as a servant becomes inexplicably attracted to "him." A modern update of *Twelfth Night* was the 1968 off-Broadway musical *Your Own Thing*, which advocated that it doesn't matter whether a man loves a woman or another man, as long as both are happy.

Still, many popular myths continue about gender. Men are expected to like adventure films, while films about love and betrayal are called chick flicks. Men are thought to never ask directions when lost. Women are not supposed to pass a clothing store without examining the window display. In 2004 business mogul Martha Stewart, called the queen of the domestic divas, was arrested, tried, and convicted in an insider-trading scandal. Her supporters argued that she had been the victim of the masculine cultural mythology that resents a woman's success. In this mythology, the woman who gets ahead is called "pushy" and "unfeminine," while a successful man is called "assertive."

"*Nice guys finish last.* The equation that goodness equals weakness accounts for the perhaps cynical acceptance of cheating, or at least "cutting corners," as an understandably human practice at all ages and places: on the playground, in class, in a courtroom or personnel office. Using test answers dishonestly acquired is only one example, and "everybody does it" furnishes the rationale. It is, after all, the way of the world. To the victor belong the spoils, presumably, regardless of how the spoils are obtained. A bumper sticker reads: "Do unto others before they do unto you."

Does anybody think mythology has no relevance to ordinary living?

How Myths Influence the Humanities

Throughout the rest of this book, especially in Part Two, which introduces you to the formal disciplines, you will see that myths and archetypes underlie a given work. In this final section of Chapter 3, we want to offer some prominent uses of myth found in literature, the theater, and film. You will see how a knowledge of mythology greatly enhances the appreciation of what is read or seen.

> *I've always preferred mythology to history. History is truth that becomes an illusion. Mythology is an illusion that becomes reality.*
>
> —**Jean Cocteau**

A reading of the poem "Leda and the Swan," for example, by the Irish poet William Butler Yeats (1865–1939) is more meaningful if we know the myth of how a woman named Leda was raped by the all-powerful god Zeus, disguised as a swan. Leda bore him two daughters, one of whom was Helen, whose adulterous love for the Trojan prince Paris led, mythically at least, to the Trojan War.

Literature comes alive through our understanding of how Venus, goddess of love, became obsessed with a handsome mortal, Adonis, and begged him not to go hunting, or how the young man disregarded her plea and was mortally wounded, leaving Venus to mourn. Shakespeare was inspired by their story and made it the subject of one of the world's great love poems.

We can read *Endymion* by the English poet John Keats (1795–1821) more easily if we know the fable about the handsome shepherd who, while sleeping on a hill, so arouses the moon goddess with love for him that she casts a spell causing him to sleep forever. He will never wake up, but he will never grow old. The myth of eternal youth is universal—and for obvious reasons.

A reading of the poem *Prometheus Unbound* by the English poet Percy Bysshe Shelley (1792–1822) is enhanced by knowing the story of the mythical Titan who stole fire from the gods and gave it to mortals. Prometheus was punished for his transgression by being shackled to a gigantic rock; every day thereafter a huge vulture ate his liver, which would grow back the following day while the vulture waited to devour it once again, the cycle of torture repeated without end.

Even when death comes in mythology, there is always the question of what comes afterward. Two major kinds of afterlife are described: one sometimes known as paradise, the other a dark, often dismal—and in many stories, eternally painful—place.

In Greek mythology the souls of brave warriors were believed to reside in an eternal paradise called the Elysian Fields after having been spared the pain of death. When it came time for them to die in battle, a benevolent god lifted them up and escorted them to a place of peace. In the medieval legends, after King Arthur is slain in battle, his body is placed on a magical ship that bears him to the far-off land of Avalon, where he will presumably live on forever. In the modern mythic trilogy *Lord of the Rings*, Frodo, the hobbit hero, embarks on a long and treacherous journey to destroy the magic ring that has caused so much pain and death. After bringing peace to Middle Earth, his world, he must leave. In an ending that resembles Arthur's fate, the author J.R.R. Tolkien describes Frodo's final seaward journey in unforgettable terms:

> *Then Frodo . . . went aboard; and the sails were drawn up, and the wind blew, and slowly the ship slipped away down the long dark firth; and . . . went out into the High Sea and passed on into the West, until at last on a night of rain Frodo smelled a sweet fragrance and heard the sound of singing that came over the water. And then . . . the grey rain-curtain turned all to silver glass and was rolled back, and he beheld white shores and beyond them a far green country under a swift sunrise.*[11]

In view of today's environmental concerns, the myth of a green afterlife has much appeal.

The Greeks also had Hades, or the Underworld, where the souls of non-warriors had to live after crossing the River Styx, which led from the land of the living to the land of the dead. Although the Underworld was dark and cheerless, it was not a place of torment.

The Divine Comedy by the Italian poet Dante Alighieri (1265–1321) has given us the popular image of the inferno, or hell, where souls must suffer for their sins. The narrator is led through descending levels by his guide, the Roman poet Virgil. After describing in vivid detail the punishments for various sinners, the poet comes to the place reserved for the greatest sinner of all: Satan. Instead of fire, the archenemy of humankind is fixed for all time in a frozen lake, which symbolizes pure hate. Purgatory, the place where lesser offenders are allowed to do penance for their sins, is described as a a mountain that eventually leads to paradise in the upper regions of the sky. It should be noted, by the way, that Dante's view of the next world came from his extensive grounding in Islamic mystic writings.

John Milton's *Paradise Lost* (1670–1672) begins in heaven, from which the devil, here called Lucifer, again the archetype of pure evil, is evicted after rebelling against God. After declaring that he would rather reign in hell than serve in heaven, he inhabits the palace of Pandemonium, where he, his followers, and all who will die without redemption are granted asylum. Then Lucifer enviously observes the Garden of Eden, which has been created as a paradise of unending beauty and tranquility, the abode of the newly formed Adam and Eve. Disguised as a serpent, he manages to entice them into disobeying God's commandment that they not eat from the Tree of Knowledge and thus bring about their downfall.

Christian writers have probably done the most to make hell an enduringly vivid concept, yet even those who dispute the theological view are apt to use *hell* in their everyday vocabulary, if only as a convenient way to describe a bad day at school or the office, or the frustration of plane delays, reservations lost in a computer malfunction, or luggage sent to an airport a thousand miles away.

Yet what would literature be without the principal resident of hell in all of his villainous manifestations? The medieval legend of the person who sells his soul to the devil in exchange for unlimited knowledge or special skills or non-stop sexual pleasures (depending on the version of the story) appears over and over. The classic use of the legend is *Dr. Faustus* by the tragically short-lived Christopher Marlowe (1564–1593), but it became the toast of Broadway in the 1955 musical comedy *Damn Yankees*, in which a loyal fan of the worst team in baseball history (the now defunct Washington Senators) sells his soul to Mr. Applegate, secretly known as Satan, in exchange for vigorous, athletic youth, allowing him to become a star player and help the Senators win the World Series, beating, of course, the perennial winners, the New York Yankees of the title. In everyday parlance, people speak about selling their souls in the workplace, often meaning they play up to their superiors in hopes of higher pay or a more prestigious title.

Conversely, stories about the triumph of good over evil keep that mythology alive in innumerable forms: movies, television, plays and musicals, children's stories, romance novels, and detective fiction. Usually the victory is predictable and not quite believable, but readers and viewers enjoy the feel-good experience anyway.

All cultures do not have the equivalent of Satan, though most of them *do* have stories illustrating goodness, as in this deceptively simple Buddhist fable:

> *Once there was a monk named Ryokan living a simple life of poverty and meditation. One night a thief enters the monk's little hut and steals his food as well as the clothes off his back. Instead of being angry, Ryokan says: "I only wish I could give you the moonlight on my floor."*[12]

As we have seen, myths, originating in the depths of the unconscious, in the primordial prehistory of our species, and in common beliefs, can become part of

"Goodbye," said the fox. "And now here is my secret. It is only with the heart that one can see rightly; what is essential is invisible to the eye."
—**Antoine de Saint-Exupéry**

our everyday awareness. We can find mythology in films, television shows, literature—even comic strips. Myths, ancient and modern, are tales about characters and events that help to define who we are and where we want to go. Unearthing underlying myths is a vital aspect of critical appreciation, for even if a given work fails for some reason to satisfy us aesthetically, it may still contribute to our expanding knowledge of ourselves and the kind of world we inhabit.

Psychologists studying the phenomenon of the Harry Potter books and the film adaptations point out that children become engrossed in the tales, which represent for them victory over the authority and control of the adult world through magical powers. They agree that children need to identify with heroic figures. Nor do adults ever outgrow their ties with mythology. Fortunately, the humanities are always there to rekindle the magic fires.

Surely we know, in our lucid moments, that no myth contains the full truth. Some mythology interferes with our judgment, and some is downright superstition. Even so, there are those dazzling mazes and those magic rings and the wonderful stranger we keep expecting to arrive.

Key Terms

archetype a model (e.g., the hero, the circle, the journey) that, through mythology, becomes part of our subconscious and an addition to the way we organize our thinking about ourselves, human beings in general, and the nature of the universe.

collective unconscious Jung's phrase for the universality of many myths and archetypes among cultures, some of which could not possibly have had any contact with each other.

gender roles the way acceptable male and female behavior and functions are defined in a given culture.

karma in Hindu and some Buddhist belief, a tabulation of people's deeds throughout their lifetime such that, if they have been mostly good, they are reincarnated into a better existence, and if mostly bad, into a worse existence.

monomyth James Joyce's term for a fundamental myth of all cultures (e.g., that of the hero). Also known as a *world myth*.

mythology (1) the collective myths of a specific culture or group of cultures; (2) the organized study of myths, either those of world cultures or of a specific culture.

myths tales and beliefs transmitted from generation to generation, or springing up as part of the popular mind in a current generation, many containing psychological truth or fulfilling some deep-rooted need.

Topics for Writing and Discussion

1. The purpose of this chapter has been to encourage you to seek out myths that may underlie works in the humanities. It could be argued that the enjoyment of a given work should not depend on knowing its mythic roots. What argument can you give in *favor* of it?

2. Write a short paper about three myths from your early childhood that helped shape your expectations of life. Do you still have them? If so, what role do they play in your life? If not, what happened to make you discard them?

3. Write a short fable about an animal hero who must undertake a dangerous journey to accomplish a task. Share it with the class and see whether they can grasp your meaning or perhaps recognize some contemporary issue in it.

4. Some myths have environmental subjects. In the stories of Demeter, grieving for her daughter Persephone, and Dionysus, descending annually into the underworld, we have an explanation of winter and the return of spring. Make up a fable to explain what happened to the ozone layer, the rain forests, the polar ice caps, or the planet's non-renewable resources.

5. Discuss a recent public figure whose life fits the pattern of the rise and fall of the hero, as described in the chapter.

6. Like the ancient Greeks, we know that the lives of prominent personalities often are filled with tragedies or, at any rate, many troubles. In many of the old myths, troubles beset those who offend the gods. What do you think accounts for the problems of celebrities now?

7. The chapter discusses the myths of the wizard and the mysterious stranger. Are these outmoded now? Still relevant? Found but in different forms?

8. Briefly write your autobiography in mythic terms. Describe your birth, your mission in life, the villains you must outwit, and your magic powers.

9. Take an old fairy tale and rewrite it (seriously or comically) in terms of how it might fill a psychological need of today.

10. The section on "Common Sayings" is not exhaustive. Think of at least two others not mentioned, and explain their purpose as myth.

PART

II

Disciplines of the Humanities

4 Literature

Overview

We are storytelling animals–who we are, what we are, and why. When we die we become part of other stories. This residue is our immortality.

—**Salman Rushdie**

The child, resisting bedtime and not wishing just yet to be left alone in a darkened room, makes a frequent request: *Tell me a story*. The parent obligingly sits down and says, "All right, but just one. Close your eyes and listen. Once upon a time . . ." The child has a need. It may be inconvenient for the parent at the moment, but the parent knows the need must be met.

The child also will tell stories. Perhaps they will be tales of ghosts and witches, told to other children happily scared and huddled together on Halloween. Perhaps they will be tales told to the parent: "I was trick-or-treating, and this giant with only one eye came to the door, and he tried to steal my candy, but I was too fast for him." Both parents and child know this is fiction. We are all creators of literature at one time or another. Who has not greatly elaborated on an incident that occurred, "jazzing" it up by giving it more drama than it had?

How did it all start? What was the first kind of literature? Our guess is that the literary impulse was being felt long before there were written languages to preserve the earliest expressions of it. In the visual arts, there are cave drawings that date back thousands of years prior to the beginning of written history. Using our imaginations, we can suppose that early (*very* early) people were dancing, chanting, and pounding away with stones and sticks. And there they were: music and dance! It is hard to imagine, however, that some form of literature did not happen along with these other arts.

Let's assume that people are natural-born poets and storytellers (and by natural progression, readers) and therefore there is no good reason to look upon literature as something locked away in libraries. We'll look at a few examples of the major types, or **genres**, of literature: the poem, the novel, and the short story. We'll see how they might have evolved, and the needs they may have served. We'll discuss drama, a major genre of literature, in Chapter 7.

Some of the works we shall study are **classics**, in the sense that they have outlived their time and continue to be relevant. Some have earned the right to be called **masterpieces**. A masterpiece is a work that in style, execution, and resonance far exceeds what other writers were doing at the same time. For example, though many sonnets were successful in Shakespeare's time, many

Imagination taking flight.

Source: © Fotosearch RF.

of *his* sonnets tower above those of his contemporaries in profundity, sophistication of technique (handling of meter and rhyme), and the intricate use of words. Many classics are also masterpieces, but they don't always have to be. Time and circumstances give continuing relevance to a classic. A masterpiece can always stand on its own, and it will find admirers in any age.

This chapter addresses itself to literature of the past and present that springs from the soul of human beings and through which we come to understand ourselves and others with whom we share the amazing condition of being alive. We are going to discuss a few representative works that have achieved literary distinction, some well known, others less familiar but with much to offer.

Literature as History

At some point many thousands of years ago, groups must have felt the need to identify, to *define* themselves. They knew they had common bonds that came from their strivings. Imagine how you would feel if you suddenly developed amnesia and had no clue about your past. Wouldn't you become obsessed with the desire to locate yourself in time and space?

The Basic Literary Impulse: Identity

Literature transmits incontrovertible condensed experience. . . from generation to generation. In this way literature becomes the living memory of a nation.

—**Alexander Solzhenitsyn**

Early in *The Grapes of Wrath* (1939), by American novelist John Steinbeck (1902–1968), a simple incident illustrates how important it is that people leave behind a record of themselves.[1] Steinbeck saw the westward migration of dispossessed Oklahoma farmers of the 1930s as an example of how human society developed. Trying to get to California, the longed-for promised land of abundant work and prosperity, they were despised nobodies robbed of their roots and their identity and given the collective designation *Okies*. When a family pulled into a large orchard looking for work, the question was always "How many hands for picking?"—never "What is your name?"

During the arduous journey, Grampa Joad, patriarch of the novel's central family, dies and has to be buried by the side of the road in some desolate and nameless place. Tom Joad, a grandson, writes a brief note and puts it on the body. It says with all the simplicity of a folk poem:

> *This here is William James Joad, dyed of a stroke, old, old man. His fokes bured him becaws they got no money to pay for funerls. Nobody kilt him. Just a stroke an he dyed.*

Leaving the body unidentified was unthinkable. If Tom had had a literary bent, he might have wanted to say more.

The pharaohs of ancient Egypt spent most of their adult lives designing their own monumental tombs, which survive to this day. The great pyramids identify not only the rulers, but the culture that bore them. Egypt established its past and present identity through art and architecture. Other cultures did it through literature, usually in oral form, and in some cases their efforts can be traced back thousands of years. The literary impulse was originally the same thing as the need to establish identity and a history.

The First Epic: *Gilgamesh*

The **epic** is a genre that can be found in the literary heritage of most early societies. An epic is a long narrative poem recounting the actions and adventures of a hero who exemplifies strength, courage, and cunning, but not necessarily moral virtue. When survival was the predominant concern of a people, their myth heroes had to seem unconquerable.

One of the oldest of literary works is the epic *Gilgamesh*, the story of a tyrannical king who lived around 4,000 years ago in a land that is now Iraq. Inscribed on twelve tablets, dating from the seventh century B.C.E it was discovered in the ruins of an Assyrian library. Classical scholars believe the story has its origins in a cycle of songs and poems created to celebrate the deeds of a real person, Gilgamesh, a king in the city of Uruk in 2750 B.C.E. Over the course of a thousand years, the songs and poems became popular throughout Mesopotamia, and eventually Babylonian poets transformed them into a singular epic poem. It is believed the definitive version of the epic was compiled by a Babylonian priest named Shin-eqi-unninni.

Gilgamesh is *one of the oldest of literary works, discovered in the 7th century B.C.E. but probably much older than that.*

Central to the poem are the swashbuckling exploits of a superman. So formidable did Gilgamesh become, so devastating to all who stood in his way, that even the gods were intimidated. So they created a gentler, more compassionate counterpart named Enkidu. Some scholars have interpreted Enkidu as Gilgamesh's other self, the side with humane principles. The climax of the epic is a tremendous wrestling match between the two superheroes, ending in a tie, suggesting that both aggressiveness and kindness are necessary for human existence.

Enkidu finally dies in the story, but Gilgamesh lives on, undefeated, and still a mortal problem for the immortal gods. Was the author saying that, even though kindness is a necessary element in the human personality, it is less likely to outlast aggressiveness?

The Iliad, which we consider next, marks a considerable change in the nature and purpose of the genre. It does indeed, like *Gilgamesh*, have a climactic showdown between two supermen, but in this case the one who dies is the central character. His opponent, with far less likeable traits, lives on. It is a work intended, as usual, to provide its audience with a history and an identity. It did just that, but it also extolled the glory and the virtue of an enemy.

An Early Masterpiece: Homer's *Iliad*

The Iliad is not only a prime example of early literature but one of the treasures of human culture. It has been traditionally attributed to Homer, who may have lived any time between 1200 and 850 B.C.E. For a long time classical scholarship tended to believe that the poem was composed over several centuries and therefore cannot be attributed to one poet. More recent scholarship suggests the poem is too unified *not* to have been the work of a single genius. Nothing is definitively known about the poet, except that, according to legend, he may have been blind.

Homer is new and fresh this morning, and nothing perhaps is as old and tired as today's newspaper.
—**Charles Peguy**

Track 2

The Iliad was an ambitious effort to give the nation of Greece a cultural history, a sense of continuity. It was probably not composed before the unification of related but often warring tribes that finally settled in the Greek peninsula, the nearby islands, and along the coast of what is now Turkey. You can see why a country made up of so many different strands of people would want to think of itself as having a definite, single history; otherwise, how would anybody have been able to talk about a heritage? *The Iliad* describes the events leading up to and then the waging of the ten-year Greek war against Troy, a city known to Homer as Ilion. Hence the poem's title, which means "The Song of Ilion."

Why song? The answer may be that those who performed the poem could remember the lines better if they were sung. Most of us learned the alphabet because it was set to a simple tune and had the added advantage of rhyme. The absence of written languages is therefore a most important point to remember about much early literature. A minstrel—or rhapsodist—was a professional performer hired by powerful rulers and their court to present their "history." Naturally that history was about the exploits of ancestral rulers who were also brave warriors. Common people don't enter the literary scene in any major way for more than 2,000 years. Homer not only relates his audience to a proud tradition of rulers but relates those rulers to the gods themselves. The war against Troy was fought as part of the expansion and unification of Greece, but Homer tells it as if it were the consequence of a conflict among gods on Mount Olympus.

When power narrows the area of man's concern, poetry reminds him of the richness and diversity of his experience.

—John F. Kennedy

Three goddesses get into an argument over who is the most beautiful: Athena, goddess of wisdom; Aphrodite, goddess of love; and Hera, queen of the gods and wife of Zeus, the power of the universe. They ask Paris, a Trojan prince, to make the determination and present a golden apple to the winner. Each goddess appears to him privately and offers him a bribe: Athena promises him glory in battle; Hera, money and power. But Paris cannot resist Aphrodite's offer to make the most beautiful woman in the world his wife. Presenting Aphrodite with the apple, he infuriates the other two goddesses.

Unfortunately, the most beautiful woman turns out to be married to King Menelaus, a Greek. Aphrodite causes the wife, Helen, to fall in love with Paris and run away with him to Troy. Both Menelaus and his brother Agamemnon lead the Greek army in pursuit of the adulterous pair, and thus the Trojan War begins. This and other Greek myths were in circulation long before Homer, and as in most cultures, little distinction was made between mythology and history.

Myth/history indicates that the Greeks had a difficult time defeating Troy, waging a decade-long siege. According to legend, to end this stalemate, the Greeks offered the Trojans a huge wooden horse as a peacemaking gift. Hidden inside were Greek soldiers, who crept out in the middle of the night, slaughtering everyone they could find. Historians believe that the story of the horse is totally fictional, but that the war itself actually took place during the twelfth century B.C.E.

Interestingly, the story of the Trojan horse is not included in *The Iliad*, and it is only alluded to in the other epic attributed to Homer, *The Odyssey*. Only much later was the story part of a great literary work, the Roman epic *The Aeneid* by Virgil (70–19 B.C.E.), which attributes the founding of Rome to Aeneas, a Trojan prince who manages to escape the slaughter. A Roman writer would have been only too delighted to depict the Greeks as devious, dishonorable warriors. If the seeds of the Roman empire were in Troy and Troy had been conquered, it is in the spirit of literature-as-history to show that the conquest was an inglorious one.

Why leave out the story of the Trojan horse? Perhaps Homer believed the Greek victory was anything but heroic or flattering to the Greek side. After all, his purpose was to create a nationalistic epic, *right*? Throughout *The Iliad*, Homer establishes Achilles as a Greek hero of titanic proportions, giving his prowess in battle ample treatment. The disarray into which the Greek army fell, perhaps necessitating the trickery of the horse, is explained in terms of Achilles' resentment toward what he considered unfair treatment by Agamemnon. That Achilles is characterized as a brave but strong-willed individual would not in itself have made him less heroic to the listeners. Epic characters, as we have seen, are braver than they are virtuous. Gilgamesh was hardly a model human being. Had the victory over Troy been accomplished by Greek superiority on the field of battle, *The Iliad* might have been a prime example of literature meant to glorify a nation's past. And Homer may have intended it as such. However, it can also be read as a tragedy of the losing side.

Engraving on a Greek jug, c. 510 B.C.E., showing a relaxed Achilles receiving payment for Hector's body.

Source: Erich Lessing/Art Resource, NY.

Hector, a prince and Troy's most important defender, is treated so sympathetically that the true climax of the epic is Hector's death at the hands of Achilles, who ties the body of the slain warrior to his chariot and drags it ignominiously around the walls of Troy, afterward selling it back to the Trojans. *The Iliad*, while rooted in Greek history, is essentially a tragic poem about a fallen hero—a hero who was not Greek! In contrast, *The Aeneid* portrays its hero, Aeneas, as the perfect hero—strong, brave, and intelligent. Troy is shown to have fallen because the destiny of Aeneas was to found a city much greater than Troy. Virgil's *Aeneid* is a nationalistic poem. *The Iliad* is not. And although *The Aeneid* is as thrilling and as wondrous as an epic should be, it is the human drama of *The Iliad* that grips the reader.

There exists, of course, the possibility that *The Iliad* went through several centuries of change as a memorized poem, sung generation after generation by unknown minstrels. It may have been gradually altered to become a tragic epic. The Greeks, after all, developed the art of tragic theater, indicating that as a nation they loved to be moved by stories of noble people who suffer a downfall. In the plays, as we shall see in Chapter 7, the fall of the hero comes about because of a fatal flaw in an otherwise good person. *The Iliad*, as we have it today, anticipates the age of Greek tragedy.

Does Hector have a tragic flaw? In a sense, he does. He is characterized as a brave warrior who goes beyond what is expected of him because, like all warriors, he wants to be remembered for great deeds of valor. The ambition to be known for bravery is characteristic of a hero, to be sure, but it can also be a fatal weakness. Pride would become the major theme of the Greek—and indeed many later—tragedies. *The Iliad* may be said to be the first major work in the literature of the Western world, not only for its soaring poetry, but for the humanization of its major characters, Hector in particular.

Humanization in this sense explains what makes certain literary characters stand apart from others. It is very close to a term that actors often use to define what they are looking for in a character they're going to play: *polarity*, or the binary extremes that exist in our natures. In playing a role, the actor first determines major characteristics defined by the playwright—for example, *he is a jealous husband*; *she is a faithful wife*. Then the actor tries to locate the opposite of these characteristics—*he loves his wife very much and doesn't want to lose her; though faithful, she resents his jealousy and secretly wishes she could have a fling.* Great writers have always known that human beings are never just one thing. If characters are given certain unwavering traits instead of the contradictory natures we all share, the result is melodrama rather than tragedy.

The Iliad *deserves its place of honor as the first literary masterpiece of the Western world because*
the poet goes beyond strict nationalism, whatever may have been his original intent

the poet establishes a fundamental principle of great literature: life is not a simple struggle between good and evil.

Like all tragic heroes, Hector has a blind side. Several times before his mortal combat with his archenemy Achilles, he has been warned that he almost certainly will die. His wife, Andromache, pleads with him not to leave her and their son, but Hector is resolute. He firmly believes that he and he alone has the strength and courage to defeat Achilles.

> *Go home, attend to your own handiwork*
> *at loom and spindle, and command the maids*
> *to busy themselves, too. As for the war,*
> *that is for men, all who were born at Ilion,*
> *to put their minds on—most of all for me.*[2]

"*Most of all for me.*" This is not only courage but pride as well. Here is the polarity in Hector's character; here is Homer's humanization of him. Hector *assumes* he is the only one who can save Troy, just as so many human beings close their minds to the possibility that someone else might be able to perform a difficult task better than they can. His supreme self-confidence causes Hector to fight with reckless abandon against overwhelming odds—and to fail, weakening his city's defenses as well.

To create a great tragic figure like Hector is to create an ironic contradiction. The very thing that destroys Hector (and Troy) is his bravery, but bravery is also the source of human greatness. The suggestion—to be echoed over and over in many enduring literary works—is that *to be great is to be tragic.* If this is a truth of existence, then the question is whether it is better to have failed at something tremendous than to have stayed within limitations and won trivial successes. Great literature inspires big, unanswerable questions like this.

The Iliad deserves its place of honor as the first literary masterpiece of the Western world for a number of reasons. First, the poet goes beyond strict nationalism, whatever may have been his original intent. If that intent had been to inspire the listener with a love of country, the poet became far more concerned with what drives human behavior, how humans interact, and the consequences of those actions. Homer is a born tragic dramatist, though the theater as we know it did not exist in his time.

Second, the poet establishes a fundamental principle of much great literature: *real life is not a simple struggle between good and evil.* If Hector is the hero of *The Iliad*, Achilles is not the villain. The subtitle of the poem is "The Wrath of Achilles," and the warrior's outrage against Agamemnon over a certain prisoner Achilles did not wish to return is indeed the force that drives the plot. Homer as historian presents, without judgment, the story of Achilles' anger. If the author is less compassionate toward the Greek warrior than toward Hector, he duly recognizes the man's strength and courage as well as his place in Greek history.

What makes *The Iliad* not only a great epic but also a great tragedy, however, is the struggle inside Hector between his desire for glory and his understanding of his wife's anguish, his sensitivity to her ardent pleas, born out of his deep love for her. As a reader, you will find that the impact of many masterpieces arises from conflict *within* the characters, not *between* them.

The Russian playwright Anton Chekhov (1860–1904) observed: "Evil flows *through* people, not *from* them." Hector's pride leads him into a violent battle in which not only he but many others are slain. Achilles' refusal to fight costs the Greeks many lives and a more honorable victory. Both men believed their cause was righteous. Neither man could be described as evil, yet their actions had disastrous consequences. That is the way of tragedy and, as the great writers such as Homer knew, the tragic way of humanity.

If Homer had lived in the modern world, how might he have responded to the Holocaust, the My Lai massacre during the Vietnam War, the September 11 terrorist attacks, or the bitter fighting in Iraq? Big questions, difficult answers. Great literature, whether from the past or the present, makes us feel, makes us think, and inevitably we are changed.

Evil flows through men, not from them.

—Anton Chekhov

Poetry

Though classified in this chapter as a form of history, the epic is also narrative poetry, telling a story in rhythmic language. Narrative, as found in *Gilgamesh* and *The Iliad*, was probably the earliest genre of poetry. But as early societies grew in sophistication and produced artists who could be identified by their style, technique, and typical themes, poetry evolved into numerous forms. By the time of the Greek poet Sappho in the sixth century B.C.E., poets were highly trained and respected members of society. They worked in a written language expected to be elevated above everyday talk—that is to say, above *prose.*

Lyrical Poetry

The Romans inherited from the Greeks the desire to cultivate the arts of civilization. Especially popular among the Romans was **lyrical poetry**, so named because it was usually sung to the accompaniment of a *lyre*, a stringed instrument similar to a small harp.

Lyrical Greek poetry is found in the work of Sappho, who may have been the first poet on record to write about deeply personal feelings, even referring to herself by name in prayers to the gods. Sappho is known to have accompanied herself on a lyre and may have composed most of the music as well. She would have used the kind of musical notation that we know existed at the time, but so far none of the music has survived.

The stars about the lovely moon hiding their shining forms when it lights up the earth at its fullest.

—Sappho

Among Sappho's favorite subjects are the joys and the sorrows of being in love. Apparently a woman of strong physical needs, she introduced into literature one of its most enduring themes: unrequited passion—a theme that, as we shall see, became wildly popular during the Renaissance and can still be found in contemporary popular songs.

In one of her most famous poems, *Ode to Aphrodite*, Sappho implores the goddess of love to have pity on her as she languishes in the agony of romantic frustration:

Then didst thou, Divine one,
Laugh a bright laugh from lips and eyes immortal,
Ask me, What ailed me—wherefore out of heaven
Thus had I called thee?
What it was made me madden in my heart so?
Question me, smiling—say to me, "My Sappho,
"Who is it wrongs thee? Tell me who refuses

"Thee, vainly sighing.
"Be it who it may be, he that flies shall follow;
"He that rejects gifts, he shall bring thee many;
"He that hates now shall love thee dearly, madly—
"Aye, though thou wouldst not."[3]

Other writers, especially William Shakespeare, would carry this theme to greater heights, but Sappho will always be remembered as a distinguished pioneer in poetic art (as well as the founder of the first known school for women).

Lyrical poetry flourished in Rome, and again the primary subject was love, a popular Roman pastime. Much of the poetry is highly artificial: high-flown words that professional poets knew would please their public. Since, in Roman society, upper-class women acquired power and independence, the theme of unrequited passion was often expressed from the male point of view, as in this poem by Catullus (87–54 B.C.E.), one of many written to and about a lady named Lesbia.

TRUE OR FALSE

None could ever say that she,
Lesbia! was so loved by me.
Never all the world around
Faith so true as mine was found.
If no longer it endures
(Would it did!) the fault is yours.
I can never think again
Well of you: I try in vain.
But . . . be false . . . do what you will.—
Lesbia! I must love you still.[4]

To the theme of unrequited passion, Catullus and other Romans added that of betrayal and infidelity, of a sworn lover's being false. Instead of swearing vengeance and wishing harm to befall his lady, however, Catullus merely suffers.

The lyric poetry of Greece and Rome was forgotten during the early and late Middle Ages. Poetry became for Christians a way of expressing the mystic experiences of the devout as they tried to escape from worldly temptations and find God. But the classical themes of love were revived during the Renaissance (beginning in the fourteenth century) when women of the aristocracy again attained stature and claimed the right to reject men's pleas for their favors. The pain of scorned love reemerged as a popular subject.

The Sonnet

The **sonnet** is a fourteen-line poetic form invented by the Italians in the early Renaissance, during the revival of interest in classical art and literature. Although the form was new, the usual subject—the pain caused by unsatisfied love—was of classical origin. The poet Francesco Petrarca (1304–1374), known to the English-speaking world as Petrarch, played a large part in the classical revival. He recognized the genius of *The Iliad* and had it translated into Latin. He is best known, however, for having developed the sonnet. The demands of the form, the discipline of having to put all his thoughts and feelings into fourteen rhymed and rhythmic lines, challenged him, as it has challenged poets ever since.

Over the centuries a number of variations on the sonnet have emerged, but the basic form is the Petrarchan. The rhythm, called **iambic pentameter**, also became the fundamental rhythm of English poetry, closely identified with the sonnets and plays of William Shakespeare, who was heavily influenced by Petrarch.

In *iambic pentameter*, each line has five repetitions of an unstressed followed by a stressed syllable. Each pair of syllables is called a *foot*, similar to a bar of music. The word *decide* is an iambic foot. The line "Decide on when to go or not, my dear" has five repetitions of the pattern and is therefore an example of iambic pentameter. Read aloud, the line heavily accents every other syllable. The poet has the difficult task of writing fourteen lines in this pattern without letting the rhythm or rhyme seem heavily forced or obvious. (A listener would soon grow very tired of rigid repetition!) In good sonnets, the lines have a sense of inevitability about them and give no suggestion that the poet was straining to keep the rhythm going or to seek rhymes. When read aloud, the poem should not sound overly rhythmic. Instead, the meter should strike the listener as a happy discovery. In the following lines from an obscure poem, the rhythm (not to mention the rhyme) hits you squarely in the face.

He writes to us most every day, and how his letters thrill us!
I can't describe the joys with which his quaint expressions fill us.

The English language falls easily into iambic patterns. (Ordinary speech tends to be iambic.) Great poets in the language, like Shakespeare, know that rhythm has an emotional effect (as it does in music), but they don't want it to overwhelm the words. Compare the above lines of poetry with the opening lines from one of Shakespeare's most famous sonnets (XVIII). Note that to discover the iambic meter, you have to distort the natural flow of the words.

Scorn not the sonnet: critic, you have frowned,
Mindful of its honors; with this key
Shakespeare unlocked his heart.
—William Wordsworth

Shall I compare thee to a summer's day?
Thou art more lovely and more temperate

The challenge to the writer of a Petrarchan sonnet grows more rigorous still. Not only must each line fit the rhythmic pattern, but the poet must find five or seven line-endings that rhyme. Though rhyme may have originated as an aid to memory, it remains an essential ingredient of poetry, still employed by many poets who like the musical resonance that rhyme can create, as well as the challenge of having the rhymes not seem forced. In Petrarchan and Shakespearean sonnets, rhymes are placed in certain sequences and cannot be varied. The great poets are somehow able to stay within the bounds of the rhyme scheme and still find freedom of thought.

Two of Petrarch's schemes can be outlined as follows, using letters of the alphabet to represent the rhyming line-endings: the first is *abba abba cddcee*; the second is *abab cdcd efef gg*. In other words, a poet writing in the first scheme must rhyme the final sound of the first line with that of the fourth, fifth, and eighth lines (*a*), the final sound of the second line with that of the third, sixth, and seventh lines (*b*), while there are two new rhymes for the remaining six lines, represented as *cddcee.*

Shakespeare's own favorite was the second scheme, perhaps because it allows more rhyming options. In Spanish or Italian, for example, many words have the same endings, making rhyme that much easier. In English, however, fewer words have multiple rhymes. Perhaps for this very reason, much English and American poetry—most of the speeches in the plays of Shakespeare, for example—abandon rhyme altogether. **Blank verse** is poetic language that has rhythm but not rhyme. You probably wouldn't want to listen to a play in which the dialogue rhymed like an Italian sonnet. But one of the marvels of the Shakespearean play is that the rhythm is there underneath the dialogue—like a faint drum—but it too is seldom obvious.

Here is one of the famous sonnets written by Petrarch to the love of his life, a young married woman he called Laura. "Love's Inconsistency," translated by Thomas Wyatt, captures the mixture of pain and joy well known to everyone who has fallen deeply into a love that is not returned.

I find no peace, and all my war is done;
I fear and hope, I burn and freeze likewise;
I fly above the wind, yet cannot rise;
And nought I have, yet all the world I seize on;
That looseth, nor locketh, holdeth me in prison,
And holds me not, yet can I 'scape no wise;
Nor lets me live, nor die, at my devise,
And yet of death it giveth none occasion.
Without eyes I see, and without tongue I plain;
I wish to perish, yet I ask for health;
I love another, and yet I hate myself;
I feed in sorrow, and laugh in all my pain;
Lo, thus displeaseth me both death and life,
And my delight is causer of my grief.

Many of the rhymes are not exact, but we may assume the translator had a difficult time being faithful to Petrarch's original words in Italian. "Done" and "seize on" are stretching verse conventions quite a bit, as are "prison" and "occasion" and "life" and "grief" in the concluding couplet.

To read literature in translation is often to lose the essence of the work. The content is there, but some subtleties can fall by the wayside. This is not to say that the experience is useless. Without translations, many of us could not read *The Iliad* or *Don Quixote*, to name just two great works in the humanities. The problems of translation, however, are particularly acute for poetry, which is so dependent on the music of the words.

Even if you can't understand Spanish, for example, you can first read a Spanish poem in an English translation to get some idea of what the words mean, and then you can read the original aloud to get some sense of the music. Such an experience is richer than ignoring the original language altogether. Here, first in translation and then in the original Spanish, is a sonnet by Federico Garcia Lorca (1898–1936), one of the greatest Spanish poets. The subject is similar to that of the Petrarchan sonnet, and even in English the directness of Lorca's passion is intense and startling.

WOUNDS OF LOVE

This light, this fire that devours,
this gray landscape that surrounds me,
this pain that comes from one idea,
this anguish of the sky, the earth, the hour,

and this lament of blood that decorates
a pulseless lyre, a lascivious torch,
this burden of the sea that beats upon me,
this scorpion that beats within my breast

are all a wreath of love, bed of one wounded,
where, sleepless, I dream of your presence
amid the ruins of my fallen breast.

And though I seek the summit of discretion,
your heart gives me a valley spread below
with hemlock and passion of bitter wisdom.

LLAGAS DE AMOR

Esta luz, esta fuego que devora,
este paisaje gris que me rodea,
este dolor por una sola idea,
este angusta de cielo, mundo y hora,

este llanto de sangre que decora
lira sin pulso ya, lúbrica tea,
este peso del mar que me golpea,
este alacran que por mi pecho mora

son guirnalda de amor, cama de herido,
donde sin sueño, sueño tu presencia
entre las ruinas de mi pecho hundido.

Y aunque busco la cumbre de prudencia
me da tu corazón valle tendido
con cicuta y pasión de amarga ciencia.[5]

Lorca's sonnet has a rhyme scheme: *abba abba cdcdcd.* There is none in the translation, because the translator's goal is to convey the poet's meaning without imposing English rhymes that might distort it.

Among the glories of literature in our language are the 154 sonnets penned by William Shakespeare (1564–1616), universally acknowledged as the master of English verse, not only for the complexity of his thought but for the unsurpassed manner in which he handles both rhythm and rhyme.

Shakespeare's plays are written for the most part in blank verse: unrhymed iambic pentameter. When Shakespeare ends a scene with a **couplet**, two lines that rhyme, he is using a poetic scheme that might seem obvious and undramatic in lesser hands, but he manages to make the rhymes seem perfectly natural. Here is Hamlet's famous couplet spoken after he learns that his uncle murdered his father, whose ghost has demanded vengeance, a violent crime that the young man is afraid he may not have the will to commit:

The time is out of joint: O cursed spite,
That ever I was born to set it right!

Though Shakespeare takes rhyming liberties in his sonnets from time to time, one aspect of his genius certainly has to be an extraordinary vocabulary (said to have included over 30,000 words) from which he was able to draw forth words that perfectly fit rhythm, rhyme, and meaning. The sonnets are generally expressions of love, sometimes obsessive adoration, which is not always returned.

Shakespeare, with his open candid nature, laid bare his soul.
—**A. L. Rowse**

The identity of the person (or persons) to whom these poems are addressed has aroused considerable debate among Shakespearean scholars. However, poetry was popular during the Elizabethan age (sixteenth century), and the subject matter was generally love in both its positive and negative guises. In this respect Elizabethan poetry is similar to today's rhythm and blues ballads, with lyrics that either extol the beauty of the beloved or the heartbreak of a broken romance. Like present-day songwriters, Elizabethan poets did not always write from personal experience. Writing good poetry was a profitable business, and the youthful Shakespeare, who came to the big city of London from the small town of Stratford-upon-Avon without a great deal of money, realized he might be able to support himself with his skills as a writer of plays and poems.

Here, in Sonnet XXIX, he speaks of the joy that love can bring.

Track 3

When, in disgrace with fortune and men's eyes,
I all alone beweep my outcast state
And trouble deaf heaven with my bootless cries
And look upon myself and curse my fate,
Wishing me like to one more rich in hope,
Featured like him, like him with friends possess'd,
Desiring this man's art and that man's scope,
With what I most enjoy contented least;
Yet in these thoughts myself almost despising,
Haply I think on thee, and then my state,
Like to the lark at break of day arising
From sullen earth, sings hymns at heaven's gate;
For thy sweet love remember'd such wealth brings
That then I scorn to change my state with kings.

His vocabulary was large–almost 30,000 words–but he usually chose small, common words–although in shocking juxtaposition, to describe Juliet, Harriet, or anything else important.
—**Jaronde Lanier**

The meter of the poem eases only here and there. "And trouble," for example, is an iambic foot with an extra, unstressed syllable, but the rest of the line follows the rhythmic pattern. Often the rhythm of a poem is apparent only through **scanning**: marking a line's syllables as stressed or unstressed, and counting them to determine the pattern. Sometimes you can determine the pattern only by exaggerating the meter as you read a line. Shakespeare does not want his lines to sound *overly* rhythmic. The secret of Shakespearean verse is to read it as if it were prose. Meter and rhyme are often only quietly there. They function like subtle background music in a well-directed film. The genius of the poet is his ability to merge form and content into a unified whole.

Shakespeare uses only two semicolons in Sonnet XXIX. Other lines (except for the final line, of course) use either commas or no punctuation at all. In either case, the thought extends beyond the rhyming word, as in lines 9–12. The rhyming of "despising" and "arising" is glossed over, because there is no pause after "arising." Shakespeare writes prose while adhering to the rules of poetry. He does, as we have said, take liberties here and there, as in "myself almost despising," because clearly a rhyme for "myself" would have posed more of a challenge than a rhyme for "despising." For the most part, however, his fertile mind was able to make rhythmic and rhymed lines fit together logically and inevitably. Larks *do* arise!

In Chapter 7 we look at examples of how Shakespeare's mastery of poetry is overwhelmingly evident in his plays.

Metaphors and Conceits

A **metaphor** is a form of expression in which something is explained in terms of something else. An abstraction such as justice, for example, or a feeling that can only be vaguely expressed, such as love, might be described in terms of something else that is concrete and visual. To say "There is no justice" fails to communicate very much. Saying "Justice for some defendants is the blind lady dropping her scales" is much more effective.

Shakespeare, as we have said, possessed an enormous vocabulary. The linguistic resources stored in his brain gave him the power to express and investigate complex ideas, and often the reader is surrounded by abstractions. So Shakespeare also experimented with metaphor, to create a more visual and concretized way of saying something for which there were no satisfying abstractions. His *Romeo and Juliet*, arguably the world's most enduring romance, cried out for a rich linguistic expression of love in all its complex facets: as lust, as a spiritual bond between two people, as a sweet sensation that does not last, and much more—too much, in fact, for lesser writers to handle as effectively.

Discover magazine columnist Jaron Lanier made use of recent scientific research concerning metaphor to examine one particular metaphor in *Romeo and Juliet*. His example centers on the famous balcony scene, in which the two young people declare their devotion in unforgettable metaphors. When Juliet emerges from her bedchamber, Romeo wonders "what light through yonder window breaks?" Then he answers his own question: "It is the east, and Juliet is the sun." In his column, Lanier considers the appropriateness of comparing a young woman to the sun, and how such a metaphor relates to our ability to make connections across our various senses.[6]

Lauren Ambrose and Oscar Isaac speaking great metaphors in the Public Theatre's 2007 outdoor production of *Romeo and Juliet*.

Source: Sara Krulwich/*The New York Times*, June 25, 2007/Redux Pictures.

Later on in the scene, Juliet indicates that she is not altogether happy about the feelings she and Romeo are expressing. She is afraid that their infatuation with each other is "too swift, too like the lightning / Which doth cease to be ere one can say it lightens." But there is no going back. They are committed to each other. They must part for the moment, yet "parting is such sweet sorrow / That I shall say good-night till it be morrow." "Sweet" has become a time-honored metaphoric alternate to "nice," but it was Shakespeare who used it in an unexpected context and gave the metaphor a complexity that casual usage rarely captures.

A generation younger than Shakespeare, John Donne (1572–1631), is famous for a special kind of metaphor called the **conceit**, an extremely elaborate and extended association between two dissimilar things. The varied life Donne led helps to explain his unique manner of communicating complex feelings and ideas with references to widely separate human experiences. In his youth, he served as a soldier in English expeditions against the Spanish. In later life, he became an Anglican priest and eventually the dean of St. Paul's Cathedral in London. The development of his poetic works reflects his contrasting modes of living. The poems of his youth express sensuality, cynicism, and a humorous approach to life, while those of his later years exhibit a fervent spirituality. The deeply religious older man, however, retained a strong undercurrent of the younger man's sexual urges, and in the following sonnet, one of his most celebrated, the two sides of his nature merge. The struggle to achieve mystic exaltation and free the self from sin is described in sexually explicit terms.

Donne's poems furnish a curious record of his emotional, intellectual, and spiritual progress through life. He brings all the resources of a mind rich in learning to a focus in his poetry.
—**Alexander M. Witherspoon**

Batter my heart, three person'd God; for you
As yet but knock, breathe, shine, and seek to mend;
That I may rise, and stand, o'erthrow me, and bend
Your force, to break, blow, burn, and make me new.
I, like an usurpt town, to another due,
Labor to admit you, but Oh, to no end,
Reason your viceroy in me, me should defend,
But is captiv'd, and proves weak or untrue.
Yet dearly I love you, and would be loved fain
But am betroth'd unto your enemy:
Divorce me, untie, or break that knot again,
Take me to you, imprison me, for I
Except you' enthrall me, never shall be free,
Nor ever chaste, except you ravish me.

Donne expands his conceit to include not only a violent sexual encounter ("except you ravish me") but a startling plea to God to divorce him from Satan or else to "untie" him, suggesting a kind of mystical adultery. Donne seems to have been deeply in love with his wife, perhaps explaining why it may have been natural for him to associate the sexual and spiritual bonds between two people. But only a great poet would have had the creative audacity to make God one of those people.

John Donne has fascinated critics and scholars for centuries as a writer of great complexity with a hidden self that may never be completely understood apart from what he wrote. Poetry is the key that unlocks the door to the hidden self, which has no language until a poet finds a way to liberate it.

A Modern Love Sonnet

After her graduation, Miss Millay became a resident of Greenwich Village and symbol of "flaming youth."
—**Norman Foerster**

Shakespeare's sonnets may or may not be personal. Donne's certainly are, and as the sonnet form has continued to develop over the years, the content has become almost always an expression of a poet's deepest feelings. At least such expression is characteristic of sonnets by Edna St. Vincent Millay (1892–1950), an American poet who lived a free-spirited life in Greenwich Village. Many of her sonnets are about lost love. Here is one of them:

Time does not bring relief; you all have lied
Who told me time would ease me of my pain!
I miss him in the weeping of the rain;
I want him at the shrinking of the tide;
The old snows melt from every mountain-side,

And last year's leaves are smoke in every lane;
And last year's bitter loving must remain
Heaped on my heart, and my old thoughts abide,
There are a hundred places where I fear
To go,—so with his memory they brim.
And entering with relief some quiet place
Where never fell his foot or shone his face
I say, "There is no memory of him here!"
And so stand stricken, so remembering him.[7]

Note that the poet adheres closely to iambic pentameter and has a definite rhyme scheme: *abbaabbacdeecd*. Note also that, here again, meaning comes first. The first sentence of the second stanza is five lines long, not stopping to punctuate the rhymes. And as is true of the Shakespearean sonnet, the strict rhythm does not intrude on the thought.

Haiku

The Japanese **haiku** is founded on oneness with the natural world. It is a short poem of seventeen syllables, distributed over three lines—five, seven, five—in which the writer captures an incisive thought or an image derived from direct observation of nature, but in words that ordinary language cannot match. The thought or the image becomes fixed forever in the reader's memory. Its nearest counterpart is Zen painting, in which the artist captures the essence of an object in a few brushstrokes.

Much of this poetry springs from the Buddhist tradition which discourages lengthy rational sequences in favor of sudden intuitive insights. Many poets use haiku as a vehicle for exploring their inner self, and for bringing them into closer contact with nature. Haiku also delights children, many of whom learn to love poetry from the apparent simplicity of the form.

Almost a contemporary of John Donne was Matsuo Basho (1644–1694), who pioneered in the development of haiku.

Detestable crow!
Today alone you please me—
black against the snow.[8]

Here is a haiku by a later poet, Kobayashi Issa (1763–1827):

Oh, don't strike the fly!
See? With knees bent and hands clasped
he prays for his life.[9]

The first poem illustrates the Japanese art of capturing both an image and a thought at the same time, and the second imparts a moral admonition to understand, not harm the natural world.

Much Japanese art is, like haiku, apparently simple but conveying a depth of meaning.

Source: Miyamoto Niten, detail from *Shrike*. Credit: Burstein Collection/Corbis.

Parallels to haiku are abundant in the world of visual art, especially among artists who like to create a scene or express a thought using as few details as possible. In the painting shown here, *Shrike*, by the Japanese artist Miyamoto Masashi (pseudonym, Niten), a Samurai and Zen

Buddhist (1585–1645), the focus is on just two central objects, a bird and a caterpillar crawling up the tree branch, apparently unaware that the shrike perched atop the branch will soon end its life. Like many haiku, the painting says more about life than a great abundance of words could match.

To see a world in a grain of sand
And heaven in a wild flower,
Hold infinity in the palm of your hand
And eternity in an hour.
—**William Blake**

Simple Forms, Profound Meaning: William Blake

In the centuries that followed the tremendous literary and dramatic achievements of Shakespeare's age, many different poetic forms became popular. William Blake (1757–1827) was fascinated by what a serious writer might do with nursery rhymes. Blake, who was both an artist and a poet, shows in some of his verse how a simple, popular form becomes, in the hands of a master, an unforgettable way of expressing a truth that is both personal and universal.

Unlike today, when modern poets can set down their thoughts and feelings in whatever form they deem suitable, in Blake's time it was customary for a poet to choose among available verse models and adhere closely to their requirements. In two of his most famous achievements, collections known as *Songs of Innocence* (1789) and *Songs of Experience* (1794), Blake met the challenge of simple, childlike verse, heavily rhythmic and forcefully rhymed (unlike the Shakespearean sonnet). But underneath their sing-songy music lies Blake's sorrow over the inevitable loss of childhood innocence and the adult's unavoidable confrontation of what life holds.

The most famous poem in *Songs of Innocence* is "The Lamb," and it is paralleled in *Songs of Experience* by another, equally famous poem, "The Tiger." Taken together, they make a powerful statement. Both poems speak to religious themes, but their contrasts could not be greater.

THE LAMB

Little Lamb, who made thee?
Does thou know who made thee?
Gave thee life and bid thee feed,
By the stream and o'er the mead;
Gave thee clothing of delight,
Softest clothing, wooly, bright;
Gave thee such a tender voice,
Making all the vales rejoice.
Little Lamb, who made thee?
Dost thou know who made thee?

Little Lamb, I'll tell thee,
Little Lamb, I'll tell thee.
He is called by thy name,
For he calls himself a Lamb.
He is meek, and he is mild;
He became a little child.
I a child, and thou a lamb,
We are called by his name.
Little Lamb, God bless thee!
Little Lamb, God bless thee!

Even though the poem suggests a nursery rhyme and is written in a childlike style, lurking behind the surface innocence of the poem is the knowledge that lambs were sacrificial animals and also that Christ, who "calls himself a Lamb," was himself a sacrifice. The poem suggests the darker world of experience that is to come.

In the *Songs of Experience* Blake uses the same childlike style but expresses emotions that come to us as we grow and begin to experience the world's evil. Here is the companion piece to "The Lamb."

THE TIGER

Tiger! Tiger! burning bright
In the forests of the night:
What immortal hand or eye,
Could frame thy fearful symmetry?

In what distant deeps or skies
Burnt the fire of thine eyes?
On what wings dare he aspire?
What the hand dare seize the fire?

And what shoulder, and what art,
Could twist the sinews of thy heart?
And when thy heart began to beat,
What dread hand? and what dread feet?

What the hammer? what the chain?
In what furnace was thy brain?
What the anvil? what dread grasp
Dare its deadly terrors clasp?

Did he who made the Lamb make thee?

Source: Henri Rousseau, *Tiger in a Tropical Storm (Surprise!)*. Credit: © National Gallery Collection; By kind permission of the Trustees of the National Gallery, London/Corbis.

When the stars threw down their spears,
And water'd heaven with their tears,
Did he smile his work to see?
Did he who made the Lamb make thee?

Tiger! Tiger! burning bright
In the forests of the night:
What immortal hand or eye,
Dare frame thy fearful symmetry?

The poem combines simple language, childlike patter, and *huge questions.* Blake was thirty-seven when he wrote this poem. The child's narrative viewpoint of "The Lamb" is now that of a grown-up, sobered by the world. "Did he who made the Lamb make thee?" is as electrifying a line as exists in the entire range of the humanities and will always speak deeply to anyone who has ever asked the awful question: "If God is good, why is there evil in the world?" Philosophers have pondered this question, and millions of words in complex prose have been written in answer to it. But it took poetic genius to ask it in eight short words that echo through time, defying an answer.

As with all great literature, explanations only scratch the surface. Just as the innocence of "The Lamb" is tempered by the dark reminder of sacrifice, so too is the fearfulness of "The Tiger" tempered by the recognition of the animal's magnificence: "burning bright." Is this a compensation? Does evil fascinate even as it terrifies? Or do the two poems, taken collectively, hint at a divine order behind the universe that is beyond our ability to understand? Great literature unsettles, disturbs, makes us wonder, even as it thrills us with its power.

Religious Poetry

Religious rituals with their rhythmic chantings provided the foundation for much poetry.

The urge to communicate with and sing the praises of a deity is as old as humanity itself and, like dance and music, an early component of the humanities. The key word here is "sing," for much prayer was and continues to be sung or at least *intoned* (expressed as a prolonged monotone or chant). The precise kind of intonation varies from religion to religion as well as among the different sects within a particular faith. Buddhist monks, Roman Catholic clerics during Mass, the cantor in a synagogue, priests in a tribal ceremony, worshippers in a mosque—all chant in their own styles.

What is chanting but intoning words in rhythm and often in rhyme: in short, poetry? Protestant believers singing a hymn are putting poetry to music. Great composers like Mozart and Beethoven adapted prayers and chants into enormous symphonic works requiring full orchestras and large choirs. Words in rhythm, the building blocks of poetry, are integral to human religious experience.

The psalms in the Hebrew Bible, attributed to King David, contain many personal expressions of joy in God's creation and faith in the transcendent power of God's love. Here is one of the most enduring of the psalms in the 1611 King James version of the Bible:

Psalm 23

The Lord is my shepherd; I shall not want.
He maketh me to lie down in green pastures;
He leadeth me beside the still waters.
He restoreth my soul:
He leadeth me in the paths of righteousness for his name's sake.

Yea, though I walk through the valley of the shadow of death,
I will fear no evil: for thou art with me;
Thy rod and thy staff they comfort me.
Thou preparest a table before me in the presence of mine enemies:
Thou anointest my head with oil; my cup runneth over.
Surely goodness and mercy shall follow me all the days of my life:
And I will dwell in the house of the Lord for ever.

This psalm has achieved immortal status. It has been translated into just about every language in the world, as well as rewritten from the perspective of particular cultures. Here is a Native American version.[10]

The Native American version of the familiar psalm shows the universality of the theme as well as its simple power.

The Great Father above is a Shepherd Chief.
I am His and with Him I want not.
He throws out to me a rope
and the name of the rope is Love
and he draws me to where the grass is green
and the water not dangerous
and I eat and am satisfied.

Sometimes my heart is very weak
and falls down
but He lifts me up again
and draws me into a good road
His name is Wonderful.

Sometime, and it may be very soon,
it may be very long, long in time
He will draw me into a valley.
It is dark there, but I'll be afraid not,
for it is in between those mountains
that the Shepherd Creator will meet me
and the hunger that I have in my heart
all through this life will be satisfied.

He gives me a staff to lean upon.
He spreads a table before me
with all kinds of food.
He puts His hand upon my head
and all the "tired" is gone.
My cup He fills till it runs over.
What I tell is true.
I lie not.

These roads that are way ahead
will stay with me through life and after,
and afterwards I will go to live
in the Big Tepee and sit down
with the Shepherd Chief forever.

Though this version is easily recognizable as the 23rd Psalm, notice that the poet has not followed the more well-known King James translation exactly. The poem is localized. God, who is a Shepherd Chief, throws out a rope. The water is not dangerous—neither to drink nor flood the land, perhaps. The valley of death lies between two mountains, but in this case the poet doesn't have to fear an ambush or a sudden rockslide. In the King James translation, God is carrying the staff; but in the Native American version God gives the staff to the narrator, who is presumably old and "tired." The House of the Lord is now the big Tepee. The heartfelt simplicity of this version is touching, illustrating the human need to attain through poetry a higher spiritual consciousness.

Beginnings of Modernism: Emily Dickinson

If I feel physically as if the top of my head were taken off, I know that is poetry.

—**Emily Dickinson**

Poetry is often called *modern* if it has been written within the last hundred years or so. *Modern* can also imply "less accessible than poetry used to be." The fear for many is that modern poetry, like modern art and music, will prove too difficult for the average person to understand. Though some modern poems may be obscure on first reading, most of them *are* approachable if the reader is patient—and, above all, if the work is read aloud. Many modern poets, abandoning traditional forms such as the sonnet, do not use strict rhythm and rhyme. Some, like e.e. cummings (discussed in Chapter 1), distort standard grammar. We need, however, to grant poets the right to create their own forms and their own way of using language.

The American poet Emily Dickinson (1830–1886), an introverted, reclusive woman, found in poetry an outlet for the thoughts and feelings she kept locked away inside her. She wrote for herself. Few of her poems were published during her lifetime, but many of them were found, after her death, in little packets hidden away in a drawer. She is now considered one of the greatest poets of the nineteenth century.

Dickinson had the uncanny ability to take simple, universal experiences and translate them into poetic form:

After great pain a formal feeling comes—
The nerves sit ceremonious like tombs;
The stiff Heart questions—was it He that bore?
And yesterday—or centuries before?
The feet mechanical
Go round a wooden way
Of ground or air or Ought, regardless grown,
A quartz contentment like a stone.
This is the hour of lead
Remembered if outlived,
As freezing persons recollect the snow—
First chill, then stupor, then the letting go.[11]

Dickinson is on the very threshold of modern poetry, except that she, unlike some of our contemporaries, anchors her feelings in traditional iambic meter, and with half of the lines rhyming in couplets. Her *premodernism* is suggested by the fact that the other lines do not rhyme and there is no consistent pattern. The poem begins with two consecutive rhyming couplets, followed by a non-rhyming couplet, followed by a rhyming, followed by a non-rhyming, concluding with a rhyming couplet. To have a pattern, Dickinson could have alternated rhyming with non-rhyming, but there is something magical about the coupling of "snow" and "go." "Letting go" so obviously follows after chill and stupor that it seems almost by accident that "go" should be a rhyme. Try thinking of a non-rhyme that would work as the final line. As we have said before, art is the illusion that there is no art. The words of a great poem just seem to have fallen into place by their own accord. Behind a bad poem we can often detect a poet's hard work.

We might call Dickinson a transition poet. She has one foot in the world of the lyrical poem and the other in the coming world of modern poetry, in which rhythm and rhyme schemes, if they exist at all, are not allowed to get in the way of what the poet wishes to express. Many modern poets turn increasingly to an almost proselike sentence structure, but they can suddenly do a grammatical about-face, as Dickinson does in "The feet mechanical / Go round a wooden way / Of ground or air or Ought, regardless grown." Here the old Apollonian-Dionysian split is evident. The sentence has a standard grammatical structure of subject and verb, but note that the poet uses the adjective "mechanical" instead of the expected adverb form "mechanically." And then we have the three nouns, "ground," "air," and "Ought"—the latter usually a verb but here used as a noun and then strangely capitalized, perhaps to make us focus on its underlying meaning: no matter how much great pain has numbed us, there are duties we have to perform whether we want to or not. The poem is both simple and complex, proselike and poetic in the highest sense of the word. The pairings are Dickinson's signature style, making much of her work instantly recognizable as hers.

To move beyond the strangeness of some of the words is to realize that the poet is crystallizing the universal experience of grief. Anyone who has felt the pain of losing a loved one or the agony of rejection or defeat knows about the numbness that follows the shock. Dickinson makes the numbness seem normal, reassuring those who share her thoughts that they are part of the human fellowship. Here we join forces with a poet who is sharing her very soul.

Poetry of the Harlem Renaissance

From time to time there emerge conscious literary movements, brainchildren of people drawn together by the common aim of bringing their culture, their statements, to the attention of a wider audience. One such movement was the Irish Renaissance of the early twentieth century. Another was the Harlem Renaissance, which, from the mid-1920s to the mid-1930s, launched the careers of dozens of African American artists, including a number of poets. African American poets, for the most part, had been writing in traditional forms, using rhythm and rhyme. The poets who ushered in the Harlem Renaissance often wrote in traditional forms, but the content of their poems was anything but traditional.

On the night of March 21, 1924, Charles S. Johnson, editor of the literary magazine *Opportunity*, invited a number of distinguished white literary figures, including playwright Eugene O'Neill, to attend a celebration of African American literature. Also present to read some of their work were about a dozen relatively unknown poets. Word spread rapidly, and soon Manhattan was buzzing about the astonishing array of talent that had been assembled. Through newspaper articles and radio interviews, many hitherto obscure personalities began to make their presence felt.

Georgia Douglas Johnson (1886–1966) was one such presence. Now considered the first major female African American poet of the twentieth century, she adapted the traditional style of the lyric poem, while communicating anything but lyrical images of the painful hardships endured by a neglected but crucial sector of America. "Black Woman" illustrates how a modern poet makes the reader see life with a different set of eyes.

After you read the poem, look at the painting by Romare Bearden reproduced here. (Bearden also gave us "Mississippi Monday," Color Plate 2.) The two artists complement each other: the painting intensifies our understanding of the poem mother's sorrow.

"Black Woman" shows us that a good modern poem is never over until we reach the final, enlightening line.

BLACK WOMAN

Don't knock at my door, little child,
I cannot let you in,
You know not what a world this is
Of cruelty and sin.
Wait in the still eternity
Until I come to you,
The world is cruel, cruel, child,
I cannot let you in!
Don't knock at my heart, little one,
I cannot bear the pain
Of turning deaf-ear to your call
Time and time again!
You do not know the monster men
Inhabiting the earth,
Be still, be still, my precious child,
I must not give you birth![12]

A modern version of the madonna and child theme. Here the face of the mother suggests the hardship of their life, and that of the child shows a sad wisdom beyond his years.

Source: Romare Bearden, *Black Mother and Child.* Credit: Art © Romare Bearden Foundation. Licensed by VAGA, New York, NY. Founders Society Dr. Lula Belle Robinson African Art Fund. Photograph © 1986 The Detroit Institute of Arts.

Although Johnson gives her theme away early in the piece, the poem is not really complete until the shock of the final line, in which she suddenly abandons the metaphor of someone knocking and confronts us with the reality of the woman's plight. Johnson's structure almost defines modern poetry, which is intended to move, startle, and give sudden insight. And it does so with ever increasing complexity. Having to compete with other linear media and, more particularly, with visual media requiring little thought, a good many modern poets go their own way, knowing they will reach a small, understanding audience, one that is accustomed to seeing with new eyes and will work, if need be, to grasp what can be the mystery of that last line.

Johnson's poem is a direct appeal for greater understanding of the pain many women endure. Much modern poetry is far less direct (sometimes maddeningly so!), and poets might be asked why, if the audience for poetry is small anyway, their work is so inaccessible. The answer, we suspect, is that, except for some isolated cases of deliberate obscurity, most modern poets do not consider their poems inaccessible. They are looking for new ways to speak, otherwise why should they write at all? It is our job as readers to broaden our expectations of what a poem should be.

Poetry in Our Time

Great poetry is still being written. In its storehouse is the wisdom accumulated in the process of living. Much of this wisdom is familiar, at least once we get past the barriers, because most readers will find they have had the same experiences as the poet. But unlike the poet, they do not store it away in a memorable form. A great poem is a reminder and, because of a fine poet's genius for language, often an unforgettable one. Carefully reading a poem, we are likely to discover a shared humanity.

Though some poets, such as John Ciardi (1916–1986), have argued for a return to the days when people read poems aloud, the fact is that poetry has become a largely silent art. For this very reason modern poetry need not be grasped immediately; it can be read and reread, studied, thought about, and returned to days later. It occupies its own space, its own corner of the world, into which the reader is invited, a space where a private dialogue takes place between the poet's thoughts and the reader's mind. Such dialogue creates a special kind of bond that exists nowhere else but in the humanities.

While with an eye made quiet by the power
Of harmony, and the deep power of joy,
We see into the life of things.
—**William Wordsworth**

Because they consider their work accessible to the patient reader, modern poets usually prefer that their work not be analyzed and translated into a prose equivalent that cannot do justice to the whole. The American poet Archibald MacLeish (1892–1982) wrote his own manifesto for poetry.

ARS POETICA

A poem should be palpable and mute
As a globed fruit
Dumb
As old medallions to the thumb
Silent as the sleeve-worn stone
Of casement ledges where the moss has grown—
A poem should be wordless
As the flight of birds

A poem should be motionless in time
As the moon climbs
Leaving, as the moon releases
Twig by twig the night-entangled trees,
Leaving, as the moon behind the winter leaves,
Memory by memory the mind
A poem should be motionless in time
As the moon climbs
A poem should be equal to:
Not true
For all the history of grief
An empty doorway and a maple leaf
For love
The leaning grasses and two lights above the sea—
A poem should not mean
But be[13]

Reading this poem out loud, slowly, tasting the words, leads to an immediate understanding of why a poem is a "globed fruit." Here's a prose translation: *Poetry is an experience; it is not reducible to its prose meaning.* How's that? Does that do justice to the poem? We hope the answer is NO!

What is amazing about this poem is that it becomes the very thing it talks about: a poem that is equal to itself and nothing else. Analyzing it further is like asking what

Collins is often very funny–but more startling than the wit is the way his mind makes unexpected leaps and splices.
—**The Boston Globe**

a bird means, or a sunset, or a Louis Armstrong jazz improvisation. The American philosopher Ralph Waldo Emerson anticipated modern poetry in the early nineteenth century when he said that the function of the poet is to adorn nature with a "new thing." You can ask, "What is it?"—not "What does it mean?" There is a difference.

In a sense "Ars Poetica" is simplicity itself, the kind of simplicity that is found only in great art. Here, "simple" means "indivisible." Physicists speculate that all matter may have erupted from a simple cell, but what have you said when you've said *that*? A cell that contained everything that could ever be is hardly simple in the ordinary meaning of the term, yet its enormous potential would not have been evident, even if there *had* been someone around to see it! A good many poems are something like that simple cell—maybe the best ones.

Another poet whose work illustrates the complex simplicity that sometimes makes modern poetry seem "difficult" is Billy Collins (b. 1941), who served in 2001 as Poet Laureate of the United States. He is fond of using colloquial American idiom—the language of everyday speech—as a way of inviting the reader in. Once there, however, we realize we are not reading straightforward prose after all, and we have to adjust our consciousness, precisely what the modern poet wants.

My Number

Is Death miles away from this house,
reaching for a widow in Cincinnati
or breathing down the neck of a lost hiker
in British Columbia?

Is he too busy making arrangements,
tampering with air brakes,
scattering cancer cells like seeds,
loosening the wooden beams of roller coasters

to bother with my hidden cottage
that visitors find so hard to find?

Or is he stepping from a black car
parked at the dark end of the lane,
shaking open the familiar cloak,
its hood raised like the head of a crow,
and removing the scythe from the trunk?

Did you have any trouble with the directions?
I will ask, as I start talking my way out of this.[14]

In addition to its colloquial style, the poem is filled with details drawn from a world we are all familiar with: a hiker, car brakes, garden seeds, a roller coaster, and the death figure so common in Halloween decorations. The final two lines also suggest a familiar situation: trying to persuade the nice police officer not to write a ticket. Billy Collins is one of us, isn't he? Not some lofty genius perched inaccessibly above our heads. Oh, and the title. Straight out of the colloquial way of talking about death, with its suggestion of a lottery. In a lottery only a few people win, most lose, except that *perhaps* in this case it's turned around. Most of the time we win, and only a few don't. There is hope after all. But on the other hand, the random nature of death cautions us against overconfidence. The tendency is to think always that it happens to that widow in Cincinnati or that hiker in Canada, who had no business hiking alone anyway. Still, there's always the chance, slim though it may be, that the car at the end of the lane is *not* there by mistake.

What, then, is the final answer? Shall we go through life, worrying that any moment might be our last? Or do we keep a sense of humor, as in trying to talk our way out of a ticket? Chances are, when your number is up, there's not much you can do about it. But look! Maybe the driver of that black car *will* realize he's got the wrong house. On the other hand . . . we don't need to say it. Billy Collins already has.

We close this section with a poem by Michael Blumenthal (b. 1949), former director of the Creative Writing Center at Harvard and now a resident of Budapest. Though his name is unfamiliar to a large segment of the population, he has attracted a small circle of followers. Like almost every poet, Blumenthal relies on metaphor to communicate thoughts and feelings both to himself and to his readers. As we would expect from a contemporary writer, he seeks to avoid poetic clichés and tired metaphors that have been used so often they have become abstractions themselves.

The poet is the priest of the invisible.

—**Wallace Stevens**

Like many modern poets, Blumenthal withholds the full statement of his theme until the very last lines, and we discover, to no surprise, that defining and understanding the complexity of love is still an important concern. A goodly number of the poems we have chosen to illustrate the art of poetry do in fact ask variants of the same question he asks in his final four lines: *Is there such a thing as love?*

THE TIP OF THE ICEBERG

Say language really does
what it says it does:
That the bird in your hand
is really a bird, that it takes two
to tango, that whoever digs
his own grave will have to sleep in it.
Say you have a fool for a friend,
feckless and dissipated and greedy
beneath the stars, and that it takes one
to know one. Say that might
makes right, that the best offense
is a good defense, that fools rush in
where trepid angels stammer
in front of the doormats. Say
that life's unfair, that that's
the way it is, that someone tells you
"have a nice day" and really means it.
What would it be like: the word,
reticent and calm, urged out
once again toward its true meaning—
"the worst" really the worst,
"the best" the best, the sum of all
your "everythings" really, now,
everything, *even the blurbs*

on the back of your own books
as true as their good intentions?
What would it mean if "until death
do us part" really meant until all breath
leaves me, love, *if "forever" meant*
until the tides cease? *What would signify*
if "love" could only mean love *once again,*
not just the tip of the iceberg, sinking
and in all sincerity.[15]

I have this image.
It's not a generator
It's not a power plant.
But it's like they have
these different points in between.
So it's a place,
it's a poem, like a globular,
like a circle with center points all over.
All poems are like that.
They have circuits.

—**Joy Harjo**

The poem's title gives us a clue, but it isn't until the final three lines that we understand the relationship between an iceberg and love. Both the word and the emotion are the tip of the iceberg, and underneath, undetected at first, are the dark if not sinister aspects, so that once we have a picture of the iceberg's enormous size, we realize, to our sorrow, that the word and the emotion are relics of an old and tired romanticism. But oh! the poet would so like to go back to a time when one could believe in them and not be disillusioned.

As you explore modern poetry, you will find that analysis and interpretation are less and less necessary. Your Dionysus—your intuitive grasp—will take over, and you will "know" what you are reading. Investigate some more. Go to the library or bookstores, browse, and select a collection of contemporary poems that intrigue you. Some of them will be poems that, when you turn the page to continue reading, have already ended without your knowledge. Okay, so you missed something. Go back and read the poem again and again, out loud. Give it a fair shot. The communication is there, waiting for you. Above all, never ask why the poets don't come right out and say what they have on their mind. After all, if there were another, simpler way of saying what they feel, they wouldn't have had to write the poem in the first place.

The Novel

The emergence of the *novel* as a literary form was inevitable. The novel is essentially a long narrative, and the great epics discussed above are long narratives of adventures, battles, conquests, and complicated human relationships—all the stuff of fiction. In this respect, *The Iliad* and *The Aeneid* could be considered forerunners of the novel, and they certainly are not the only examples. Throughout the world, every culture has produced stories, either written or communicated orally. Much of the Hebrew Bible contains long narratives: for example, the story of Moses leading the people of Israel out of bondage, and the story of the patient Job whose faith is put to a severe test.

Between 400 B.C.E. and 400 C.E., India produced its great Sanskrit epic *The Mahabharata*, a vast tale of family struggles over inherited lands and fortunes, with more episodes than any novel that can be precisely dated. The 800 years of its development tell us that an enormous number of writers were involved. Similarly, both China and Japan have literary traditions that preceded Homer, indicating that the storytelling instinct developed along with human communication skills.

Many literary historians believe that the world's first novel was *The Tale of Genji*, written by a Japanese aristocrat, Lady Murasaki Shikibu, over a thousand years ago. Like the great epics of Homer and Virgil, it is filled with brave deeds and heroes, but it is written in prose.

France in the late Middle Ages produced a number of prose tales called **romances**. These were stories of knighthood, chivalry, and love affairs between brave knights and fair ladies (often married to other men). From England came the tales of King Arthur and the knights of the Round Table. Not only were they artful narratives but they created a whole mythology that continues to influence the human dream. In addition to Camelot, these tales gave prominence to the search for the Holy Grail, which has become a lasting symbol of the elusive prize for which human beings keep searching.

In Western literary history, the word *novel* comes from the Latin *novellus*, meaning new and unfamiliar. Early in the Italian Renaissance, the author Giovanni Boccaccio (1313–1375) used the Italian word **novella** to describe the short prose narratives he wrote. It is very possible that the sense of "novelty" contained in the term was intended to distinguish fictional stories from those that, like the epics, supposedly had a basis in truth.

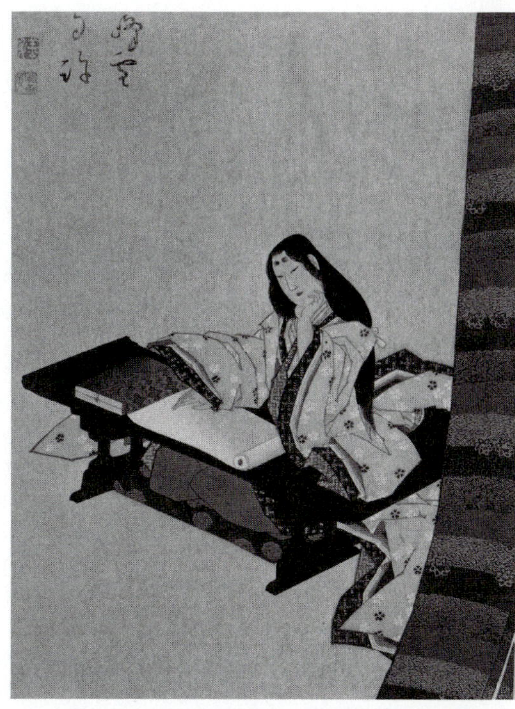

Many credit Lady Murasaki with writing the world's first true novel, *The Tale of Genji*, some 1,000 years ago in Japan.

Source: Ogata Körin, *Portrait of Murasaki Shikibu*. Credit: Private Collection, Paris/Dagli Orti/The Art Archive.

Early Western Novels

During the sixteenth century, literature flourished in Spain, especially the *picaresque* tale, often quite long, which narrated the adventures of a carefree soldier of fortune, living the free life on the open road and getting involved in all sorts of intrigues and love affairs. The Spanish also had tales similar to the King Arthur legends, dealing with the adventures on the road of brave and dashing knights, who were superheroes, tremendous in battle and noble and chivalrous toward their true loves.

The storyteller takes over to recount the event, and this is the one who survives, who outlives all the others. It is the storyteller in fact that makes us what we are.

—Chinua Achebe

The first known major novelist of the Western world was Miguel de Cervantes Saavedra (1547–1616), whose lifespan closely parallels Shakespeare's. His *Don Quixote* (written between 1612 and 1615) remains one of the most popular and beloved of all novels. The central character is an old man who has read so many stories of brave knights that he has gone mad and believes himself to be one of them. Riding a broken-down old horse named Rocinante and attended by his faithful squire Sancho Panza, he goes off in search of glorious adventure. Intended originally as a satire on the ridiculous excesses of the wandering knight story, *Don Quixote* became, in the opinion of many, a tragic tale of an idealist who sees the world not as it is, but as it ought to be: a world in which people are driven by the noblest of motives, chivalry prevails, and love means forever. *Don Quixote* influenced the work of many novelists who followed, setting the pattern for long, loosely structured adventure yarns, which would find a home in the magazine serials of the eighteenth and nineteenth centuries. The serial was a publishing gimmick, each episode ending with the main character in a perilous strait, and thus keeping the reader coming back to purchase more issues.

The English novel had its true beginnings in the eighteenth century. The coming of the magazine fostered a passion for fiction that had potential novelists busily scribbling. But the period was also one of a passion for science and its search for truth. Those who dictated the taste of the reading public insisted that a lengthy published work, to be worth the time spent in reading it, must be a true story. Consequently, much fiction was passed off as biography or autobiography, and this meant that the author's real name was often omitted. For example, *Gulliver's Travels* by Jonathan Swift (1667–1745) and *Robinson Crusoe* by Daniel Defoe (1659–1731), two enduringly popular works of fiction, pretended to be nonfictional accounts of actual adventures.

The Novel in America

American writers were slow to gain recognition and respect abroad. In the early nineteenth century, a British critic asked, "Who reads an American book or goes to see an American play?" The question incurred the wrath of native authors, who promptly responded. There was Washington Irving (1783–1859) and his satiric novel masquerading as nonfiction, *A History of New York, by Dietrich Knickerbocker* (1809), which took an irreverent swing at Thomas Jefferson's democratic ideology. Irving may be considered the first American writer to win the long-awaited praise abroad. His achievement was followed closely by that of James Fenimore Cooper (1789–1851), who romanticized the American wilderness in such novels as *The Last of the Mohicans* (1826) and *The Deerslayer* (1841). Then came Nathaniel Hawthorne (1804–1864), who, with *The Scarlet Letter* (1850) and *The House of the Seven Gables* (1851), won almost unanimous praise in England. Herman Melville's *Moby Dick* appeared in 1851, though Melville was not hailed as a great novelist until many years after his death in 1891.

By the end of the nineteenth century, American novelists William Dean Howells and Henry James were making their presence felt on both sides of the Atlantic. Mark Twain had already written *Huckleberry Finn*. American writers no longer had to play catch-up with their European counterparts. Important novels could return a publisher's investment. That's why an eager young writer named F. Scott Fitzgerald (1896–1940) could sit down with great deliberation and resolve to write "the great American novel." We are all familiar with that phrase, which has become for many the great American myth, something to be aspired to but never quite realized. In fact, the pursuit of the great American novel became itself a theme for many American writers, whose heroes usually shed their youthful idealism, confront a harsh world, and realize that the perfect novel can never be written. Yet there was also the influence of the icon created by James Fenimore Cooper: the rugged individualist, not intellectual but schooled in the realities of life, someone who stood head and shoulders above the genteel heroes of European fiction.

> The Great Gatsby *does not proclaim the nobility of the human spirit; it is not politically correct; it does not reveal how to solve the problems of life; it delivers no fashionable or comfortable messages. It is just a masterpiece.*
>
> —**Matthew J. Broccoli**

Two novelists of the early twentieth century, F. Scott Fitzgerald and Ernest Hemingway, exemplify two kinds of writers, different in their style and themes, but both representatively American nonetheless. Fitzgerald wrote in rich, complex prose, evoking a still classic portrait of the 1920s: the Jazz Age of short-skirted flappers, bathtub gin, sleek roadsters, and endless rounds of wild parties—a carefree period that would come to a crashing end in 1929, when the stock market dropped through the floor and countless investors jumped out of windows.

Fitzgerald was an observer and critic of this careening culture, and in *The Great Gatsby* (1925) he wrote a tragic story of a man who dedicates his life to the pursuit of wealth (though the source of his money is probably outside the law), seems to have achieved the American dream, gives lavish parties which are the talk of affluent Long Island society, makes love to a woman he knows is married, and meets his own predictably violent death.

The final passage of the novel illustrates Fitzgerald's frequently imitated, never duplicated style, and it provides a glimpse into Jay Gatsby, one of the few truly tragic figures in American literature:

> *He had come a long way to this blue lawn and his dream must have seemed so close that he could hardly fail to grasp it. He did not know that it was already behind him, somewhere back in that vast obscurity beyond the city, where the dark fields of the republic rolled on under the night.*[16]

Vastly different from Fitzgerald but of equal stature is Ernest Hemingway (1899–1961), who recreates the rugged individualist hero of earlier times but places him in a number of different locales where he is tested for courage. In *A Farewell to Arms* (1929) he appears as Frederic Henry, an ambulance driver in World War I, who falls in love with a nurse only to see her die. Bitter and angry at the civilization that has ruined his life, not to mention the world, he deserts the army and thus becomes the first in a long line of alienated American heroes who drop out of society.

As Hemingway grew older, however, his sensibilities and values changed. Some Hemingway scholars believe that he became obsessed with maintaining his physical conditioning as well as his magnetic appeal to women. His heroes were transformed into a strong, silent, intensely masculine figure, stoically able to experience and conquer extreme dangers, always falling in love with, then losing, strong women. Biographers see the Hemingway hero as a portrait of the man he longed to be. A *New Yorker* cartoon showed a hairy, muscular arm with its hand holding a rose. The caption read: "*The soul of Ernest Hemingway*."

Perhaps the alienation of Frederick Henry in *A Farewell to Arms* weighed heavily on Hemingway's conscience. The death of Catherine as well as the futility of war motivate his running away, but to the later Hemingway, it would have been an act of cowardice. The theme of the mature Hemingway novels and stories is the attainment of a courageous stand against not only war but all of life's brutalities.

Hemingway's 1940 novel about the Spanish Civil War, *For Whom the Bell Tolls*, offers the author's most memorable portrait of the stoical, courageous hero, one who is willing to die for a cause that is not his own. The American Robert Jordan joins a band of Spanish guerrillas battling a repressive government. When the superior forces seem to have them trapped in the mountain, Jordan orders them to escape while he mans a machine gun to hold off the advancing army long enough to ensure the guerrillas' safe exit. The scene includes a moving farewell to Maria, a woman with whom he would have gladly lived for the rest of his life. Like all of Hemingway fiction, this novel cannot have a traditional happy ending, yet it does have his characteristic take on what constitutes happiness. For Ernest Hemingway, happiness is having conquered the coward who lives inside each of us. One literary historian has observed that Robert Jordan is Frederick Henry redeemed. Henry saves himself when he deserts the army; Jordan, who might have saved himself, chooses not to.

Archetypes in This Chapter

Icons and Symbols in Literature

American Dream The belief that anyone, even the poor and new immigrants, can become wealthy and successful in the United States if they apply themselves with sufficient drive and ambition. F. Scott Fitzgerald's character Jay Gatsby represents a tragic interpretation of the American dream.

Sacrificial lamb The lamb was an animal frequently sacrificed in religious rites throughout the ancient world. In time, the lamb became a symbol of all sacrificial victims. As a symbol, the lamb is also associated with Christ, with his crucifixion and death often interpreted as a form of sacrifice. Explicit references to this archetype can be found in William Blake's poem "The Lamb."

Superhero An extreme version of a hero who transcends regular human limitations and may be endowed with a supernatural special power. Gilgamesh, Achilles, and Hector are all ancient versions of the superhero.

Trojan horse A mythical ruse by which the Greeks finally conquered Troy. Greek soldiers hid inside a massive wooden horse, which was taken inside Troy as a gift; the soldiers emerged at night when the city slept. Today, a tactic by which a person, thing, or even a computer virus gains entry to a site through voluntary admission by those protecting it.

The next novel we consider also has a central character seeking to redeem himself, but his choices are more subtle and complicated by the once unknown horror of modern warfare.

An Afghan-Born Novelist

Early in the nineteenth century, when American fiction was young and American writers were trying to shake off their inferiority complexes, their focus was almost exclusively on their own culture. The rest of the world seemed not to exist. Today, however, with television and the Internet, what happens in far-off lands is reported immediately. You can be in your living room and on a street in Baghdad at the same time. Of course, as soon as you shut down the computer or turn off the television, you may, if you choose, return to your own little corner of the world, involved only in your own daily tasks and problems.

One writer, born in Kabul, Afghanistan, has brought the Mideast to startling life in a work of fiction that renders it impossible for a reader to be only sporadically concerned with devastating upheaval in far-off places. Once you become engrossed in this novel by Khaled Hosseini (b. 1966), your understanding of his native country and the turmoil that has engulfed it for three decades deepens and expands, and you will finally close the book a much wiser person. We have chosen to end this section of the chapter by discussing *The Kite Runner* (2003), the book that first brought Hosseini to the attention of the American public.

It was by far the hottest day of the year. The mountains trapped the bonescorching heat, stifled the city like smoke. Power had been out for days. All over Kabul, electric fans sat idle, almost mockingly so.
—**Khaled Hosseini**

Hosseini lived in Kabul for the first eight years of his life. In 1974 his father moved the family to Paris, because of better employment opportunities. When communist insurgents overthrew the Afghan monarchy, his family decided against returning to Kabul. Granted political asylum in the United States, the family arrived here with only the clothes on their backs, and they were so poor they relied on welfare and food stamps to survive. Eventually Hosseini was able to put himself through college and medical school. Then, this brilliant refugee from an embattled nation abandoned the profession that was guaranteeing him a comfortable income for life to pursue his writing. Why?

The answer lies in the fact that, in addition to developing a careful scientific eye, Hosseini sprang from a culture of born storytellers. When he was growing up, fiction was his escape from poverty. He knew there was a book locked inside him that had to be written. Life was good in his adopted country, but there were the memories of his boyhood in Kabul, where he must have seen kite runners, and he remembered what life was like before the communist coup. The writer's imagination could readily piece together the fragments of memory and link them into a narrative thread.

Hosseini's central character is Amir, a sensitive, bookish, motherless youth and the despair of his father, who wants a stronger, more athletic son, able to protect himself against bullies. The two, Sunni Muslims, live in relative luxury compared to the Shi'ites. The Sunnis and the Shi'ites form the two main branches of Muslim faith. Each traces itself to a different patriarch and claims to represent the one true religion. They have been enemies for centuries. (For further discussion, see Chapter 10, Religion.) In Amir's Afghanistan, those who owe their allegiance to the Sunnis are the privileged class, while Shi'ites are regarded as second-class citizens. Amir's only friend is Hassan, the housekeeper's son. Their close ties earn the disapproval of the class-conscious society. Hassan and his father are Hazaras, Shi'ite Muslims who work mainly as farmhands and, in cities, as domestics; they are social outcasts, deprived of even the most basic skills such as reading and writing.

Both boys want to become adept in the kite-flying competitions that, next to soccer, are the principal sport in Afghanistan. As hundreds of kites flood the sky, the object is to get your kite to force as many of the others out of competition as you can. This goes on until there is one kite left and its owner is crowned champion. But there is another competition, kite *running*, the object of which is to chase down the fallen kites and collect as many as possible. This of course involves pushing and tripping your opponents. Hassan, much to the disapproval of the Sunni boys, becomes a star kite runner. It would seem at this point in the story that the two boys, despite the difference in their class, are leading an idyllic existence. Then the novel turns tragic.

As in many celebrated novels, what drives *The Kite Runner* is a mistake that will cast a shadow over everything that happens afterward. The mistake stems from tragic weaknesses in Amir, both cowardice and the tendency to put himself down at every opportunity, like Hamlet, perpetually analyzing what he is doing wrong, self-criticism that paralyzes his will. When Hassan is raped by a local bully, Amir hides helplessly and watches.

To ease his inner torment, Amir decides to do away with the visual embodiment of his guilt by forcing Hassan to leave. He hides an expensive wristwatch and money under Hassan's mattress so that his friend will be blamed for theft and disgraced.

These lapses haunt Amir throughout his life. And paralleling the torment inside him is what happens to Afghanistan. The monarchy is overthrown in a communist coup, and the class-protected Sunnis no longer dominate. The Taliban take over through violent struggle and impose a repressive society. When Amir, who has been living in America, eventually returns to Afghanistan to try to make things right between himself and Hassan, he arrives to a devastated homeland. Hassan, he discovers, has been massacred, along with his wife, while his son, Sohrab, lives amid squalor in a run-down orphanage. With great difficulty, Amir finds Sohrab, who is deeply scarred by his troubled upbringing in Kabul, and cannot adjust to the comfortable life Amir provides for him in America.

The Kite Runner *ends on a note that is remotely upbeat. It is comforting to know that out of upheaval and devastation there can emerge a work of such beauty, showing us the humanities survive even while some cynics are predicting the end of civilization.*

The novel ends on a note that is remotely upbeat. Hosseini does not tie the complex strands together into a neat package. There is no author-manipulated happy outcome, no gift to the reader that says, "I know you want me to show you how their new life in America makes up for the past." Amir, approaching middle-age by now, is still able to beat some children in a kite-flying competition, noting that his adopted son, Sohrab, is showing a little interest. And the boy smiles!

Kabul, Afghanistan, before and after the devastation of war, parallels the psychological path of Amir's life in *The Kite Runner*.

Source: Left: Time and Life Pictures/Getty Images. Right: Cheng W. Lee/*The New York Times*/Redux Pictures.

> *It was only a smile, nothing more. It didn't make everything all right. It didn't make* anything *all right. Only a smile. A tiny thing. A leaf in the woods, shaking in the wake of a startled bird's flight. But I'll take it. With open arms. Because when spring comes, it melts the snow one flake at a time, and maybe I just witnessed the first flake melting.*[17]

As you noticed, the author is also a poet, who uses his scientifically trained observations of the smallest detail to express himself, not only in traditional narrative, but in metaphors as well. It's hard to imagine a more effective way to say that there is always some hope, even if it's "one flake at a time."

It is comforting to know that out of upheaval and devastation there can emerge a work of such beauty, showing us that the humanities survive even while some cynics are predicting the end of civilization.

The Short Story

A case could be made—in fact, *has* been made—that the short story is essentially an American invention, along with jazz, which we discuss in Chapter 6. We have to be cautious, however, because much depends on what we mean by the short story. If we simply mean a brief tale featuring one central action, then we'd have to concede that the Bible got there long before there *was* an America. The stories of Cain and Abel, Joseph and his brothers, Ruth, Abraham's near sacrifice of Isaac, not to mention the Garden of Eden, must be considered literary masterpieces as well as religious writings, models of tales that waste few words. That is precisely what great short stories do.

Magazine Fiction

A woman is sitting in her old, shuttered house. She knows that she is alone in the whole world; every other thing is dead. The doorbell rings.

Source: A short tale of horror attributed to Thomas Bailey Aldrich

The short story form gained recognition and respectability early in the nineteenth century with the growing popularity of the magazine. Along with weekly or monthly installments of long novels, magazines printed pieces of short fiction that could be read in one sitting, presumably because writers could not produce lengthy fiction fast enough to meet the demand. Besides, large sums of money awaited those who could devise a fantastic story, especially one involving murder and ghosts in eerie castles and building to a shattering climax. Financial returns on a novel came much more slowly.

When we think of such stories, the name Edgar Allan Poe (1809–1849) immediately comes to mind. With his dark and brooding atmosphere, his old castles with their locked doors and cobwebs, his ghostly voices echoing down dark hallways, Poe made enough money to support his two tragic habits, substance abuse and gambling. Though he appears never to have been very happy in his brief lifetime—something that may explain the fantastic world of the imagination into which he continually escaped—he left behind a treasury of short fiction that clearly established American preeminence in this field.

Later, in France, the short story became swept up with a literary trend known as *realism*—a strong reaction against the earlier novels and stories of sheer fantasy. Character became as important as plot, if not more important, and the short story was expected to climax in a revelation, offering an insight into some aspect of human nature or life itself. The revelation was often an ironic one.

Epiphany

The sudden insight into life or human nature which short stories often give us is called an **epiphany**, a term borrowed by Irish novelist James Joyce from its biblical meaning: the sudden appearance of Jesus to his disciples after his resurrection. Joyce and subsequent literary critics used the term to mean an action or a line of dialogue that reveals a truth.

A literary epiphany is an action or line of dialogue that reveals a truth.

One story that has achieved international renown, largely because of its shattering epiphany, is "The Lottery" by Shirley Jackson (1919–1965), who often combines the chilling aspects of Poe with climactic meaningfulness. "The Lottery" exists on a number of levels. While it rewards the discerning reader with an epiphany that deepens with each reading, it also offers a suspenseful and realistic surface tale of an annual prize-drawing ceremony in a typical, peaceful small town, with the nature of the "prize" carefully withheld until the horrifying climax. As townspeople gather for the drawing, each one takes from a black box a small scrap of paper. All of the scraps are blank except one, which has a black mark on it. The one who draws this is declared the winner, and the person is then stoned to death by all the others.

Early in the story, the symbolic nature of the events is hinted at. There are rumors being discussed that some towns are thinking of abandoning the lottery. Then an elderly denizen comments that this is a bad idea: "Lottery in June, corn be heavy soon." After the horrifying revelation and the first stone is hurled at the victim, we realize that the author is showing us the survival of an ancient sacrificial ritual in which one person is slain so that the gods will provide an abundant harvest. Yet why write such a story? *That* ritual is no longer practiced in the civilized world. We think about it, discuss it, then realize that the story is not about an agricultural ritual. It is about the survival of many primitive instincts we believe are long buried. Why, for example, does traffic slow to a crawl so drivers can gawk at police cars and an ambulance on the side of the road, the signal of a dreadful accident? Why are disaster films so popular?

Many stories published in recent years have dispensed with the once required epiphany. The modern short story can be just that—a *story*—a brief narrative that doesn't have to lead anywhere. It can be about people and their relationships, not requiring the reader to wonder what it *means*. Modern short story writers are often fond of ending their pieces in a puzzling manner. They write the kind of thing that, according to one professor of literature, "when you turn the page, you find out it's over." They claim the same right granted to modern poets—the right not to be analyzed. But there are still readers who think analysis is an art form in itself and enjoy the added pleasure of thinking about and discussing what they have read. And there are still writers who want to share their insights with readers and want their stories to offer some understanding of life.

A Master of Style and Meaning

Not only is epiphany not "out," but some of the most celebrated contemporary short story writers combine meaning with elegance of language and complexity of character, demonstrating the literary heights which this art form can reach. One such writer is Nobel laureate Nadine Gordimer (b. 1923), one of the most recognized names in the literature of South Africa, with numerous novels and short

. . . and I joked, 'Lucky she doesn't look like me'....my wife picked her up, away from me, and told me, 'She's not your child.'

—**Nadine Gordimer**

story collections to her credit. One of Gordimer's recent stories, published in the *New Yorker*, enables us to say with considerable pleasure that the form is still thriving in the hands of masters.

"A Beneficiary" shares with *The Kite Runner* a theme that runs through much literature of both past and present: *the search for one's roots, for a true family*. The theme ties in with that of the alienation and loneliness which are inevitable effects of a rapidly changing world. Charlotte, the main character in Gordimer's story, does not live in a war-torn country like Afghanistan or confront the inhumanity that ancient hostilities continue to breed. In her late twenties, she lives in a comfortable urban environment. Her mother, Laila de Morne, was a self-centered stage actress who never quite achieved the recognition she thought she deserved. Charlotte was raised untraditionally, her irresponsible mother having divorced her neurologist husband and been far too busy to attend to the duties of motherhood. After Laila's death, the neurologist comes back into Charlotte's life, and the two develop the family relationship Charlotte has never known.

Then Gordimer makes use of a classic literary device: the discovery of an old letter that contains a startling revelation. Written by the neurologist to his attorney after Charlotte's birth, it indicates that Laila had told him the child was not his, that the true father was the leading actor of her theater company. But the neurologist, believing the exact paternity could not be proved, wanted to sue for custody. The suit had obviously been unsuccessful.

Charlotte is in a quandary: how does she find her true father? The story couldn't have gone anywhere at this point had Gordimer not availed herself of an author's license to impose a happy coincidence. The actor in question is to appear in a season of plays at a local theater. Charlotte attends each performance, swept away by the man's genius for embodying himself in a host of very different characters. In a certain sense, she falls in love with him, and we naturally expect the inevitable meeting, the finding of the real parent, the traditional happy ending. After all, the family is a sacred unit, is it not? But Gordimer is far too serious an artist to bow to convention. Charlotte is at a loss as to how to proceed. Or should she proceed at all? Must she really have a biological parent?

In fact, the neurologist, meeting the actor, sets up the climax. The neurologist tells the actor that he remembers his powerful performance in the play *Marat/Sade* (discussed in Chapter 7) and that "Laila de Morne was Charlotte Corday." The time has come to please the reader with Charlotte's long-awaited "Laila de Morne was my mother." But the actor's only response is to remind Charlotte that, while Corday was the knife-wielding assassin of Marat, "you're not a Charlotte to carry a knife, spoil your beautiful aura with that, frighten off the men around you." A compliment, nothing more, and not a trace of a guilty conscience, or even a slight memory of the night spent with her mother.

And what has Charlotte learned? What have *we* learned? In an exquisitely wrought final scene, Charlotte drives the neurologist home and, at his doorstep, she "went to him and he saw, without understanding, that he should take her in his arms. She held him. He kissed her cheek, and she pressed it against his. Nothing to do with DNA."[18]

This is the stuff great fiction is made of. In this scene Gordimer captures the subtleties and ambiguities of human consciousness and behavior. What exactly is Charlotte feeling at this moment? Is it an inner joy that she has at last found a father? Is there a sexual current here as well? There is surely something we could call "love," but it's a long way from the standard, abstract way we define the word. And what matters in the long run? To say that one is no longer an orphan? Or perhaps that finding a nest, a place where one belongs is the only thing that matters, regardless of who is tending that nest?

Maybe the story is really not about finding a parent, at least not primarily. Maybe it's about the difficulty of understanding our true selves, our wants and needs, and the complexity of our longing. Is it enough to have located one's biological parentage? What does one expect from a parent anyway? Is a deep feeling for another better than to tell the world that one is not an orphan? Like her colleagues at the highest literary levels, Gordimer is not satisfied with easy answers. She knows that life doesn't provide them.

Aside from its many layers of possible meanings, "A Beneficiary" offers rich examples of a major writer's literary style and insights that come at us so fast we have a hard time absorbing them in a first reading. In the hands of a lesser writer, Charlotte's response to reading the letter to the attorney could have been factual and bland. "She was overcome by feelings of anger toward her mother. She deserved to know who her real father was." But Gordimer frankly can't find the words that belong in this situation, so she asks the question: "How do you recognize something that is not in the known vocabulary of your emotions?" Instead of glossing over the moment, she makes us wonder and perhaps feel a little guilty over our own tendencies to gloss.

Much of the time, however, Gordimer's sentences are long and complicated, forcing the reader to go very slowly, deliberately, so as not to miss the point. Here is Charlotte's reaction to her first meeting with the man who may or may not have been her natural father: "He was wittily critical at other people's expense, and so with him she was free to think—say—what she found ponderous in those she worked with: the predictability among her set of friends, which she usually tolerated without stirring them up."

The casual reader is likely to be one who wearies of prose that doesn't flow rapidly and superficially toward answering the only important question: well, what happens? The Gordimer reader is as interested in the flow as in the destination. Her highly literate style, like that of other major writers, gives evidence of wisdom behind the words. She knows what she is doing. We know we are in good hands.

A tip-off comes to us from the title itself: Charlotte is *a*, not *the*, beneficiary. The latter is someone named in a will, the one with all the legal rights, but not necessarily the one most loved. To be *a* beneficiary without legal, but only voluntarily granted, rights may in the long run be better than to inherit an estate, especially if *the* beneficiary lucked into the role purely by accident of birth.

This chapter has offered an introduction to a very complex subject by focusing on particular examples from major genres of literature. It makes no claim to being an exhaustive study. We have sampled a few important works by way of encouraging you to make the reading of fiction an ongoing part of your life. We hope you will take it from there. Once you open the pages of literature, short or long, prose or poetry, you will discover infinite worlds and dimensions of reality that can carry you to a place only the humanities know about: your own private island of imagination.

The consequences of slavery only artists can deal with. There are certain things only artists can deal with, and it's our job.

—Toni Morrison

Key Terms

blank verse poetry that has an iambic pentameter rhythm but does not rhyme.

classic a literary work that continues to be read even centuries after its initial appearance because it is still relevant.

conceit an elaborate, extended description of something in terms of something else; e.g., in Donne's sonnet "Batter my heart," mystical exaltation is expressed in sexually charged language.

couplet two consecutive lines of poetry that rhyme; often used by Shakespeare to conclude a sonnet.

epic a genre of literature; a long narrative poem recounting the actions of a hero who exemplifies strength, courage, and cunning, but not necessarily moral virtue.

epiphany a sudden insight into life or human nature that often serves as the climax in a work of fiction, particularly a short story. The author James Joyce adapted this term from its original religious context.

genre any distinct category within a discipline such as, in literature, the epic, poetry, the novel, the short story; a genre generally imposes certain requirements on the writer: e.g., a sonnet must have fourteen lines; a haiku must have seventeen syllables.

haiku Japanese poetic form that presents one image, usually derived from an observation of nature, with an underlying thought; usually limited to three lines totalling 17 syllables in the pattern 5, 7, 5.

iambic pentameter classical rhythmic scheme, widely used in English verse, consisting of five repetitions in a poetic line of an unstressed syllable followed by a stressed syllable, as in the line "Shall I compare thee to a summer's day?"

lyrical poetry rhythmic, often rhymed verse, musical in nature, usually dealing with the poet's feelings, especially of love. *Lyric* means "of a lyre," an ancient musical instrument, indicating words sung to music.

masterpiece here, a literary work acknowledged to tower above others of its time in its style, execution, memorable characters, or profound meaning; not necessarily recognized in its time

metaphor widely used literary device in which something abstract is described in terms of something that is more concrete.

novella a work of fiction that is shorter than a novel but longer than a short story.

romance a literary genre popular in the Middle Ages, revolving around the exploits of a brave knight and his love for a beautiful lady, often married to someone else.

scanning marking a line's syllables as stressed or unstressed, and counting them to determine the pattern, sometimes exaggerating the rhythm to do so.

sonnet a fourteen-line verse form controlled by a strict rhythm and rhyme scheme; invented by Renaissance Italian poets and adapted by Shakespeare and later poets.

Topics for Writing and Discussion

1. Achilles and Hector are the heroes of the *Iliad*, but they couldn't be more different. Describe the characteristics of each one, then indicate why each is a hero in the context of the age that produced the epic.

2. Write a sonnet using iambic pentameter and the rhyme scheme of Shakespeare's "When in disgrace with fortune and men's eyes." Try to make your sentences flow from line to line rather than stop at the end of each line. In other words, try to make your rhyme scheme as low-key as possible.

3. Write a poem, not necessarily observing strict rules of rhythm or rhyme, using one of the following themes:
   a. a romantic involvement you want to break off
   b. a romantic involvement you would like to have
   c. advice to someone who is depressed over a lost love
   d. a verse letter to someone who has stolen your love
   e. a verse letter to the loved one who has been stolen

   It would be interesting to have the poems read aloud to the class by people other than the poets, then ask the class whether the writer was male or female.

4. Reread Blake's "The Lamb" and "The Tiger." With or without rhythm and rhyme, write a short poem about another animal, using it as a symbol for something else you should not name directly. Share the poem with the class and see whether your audience catches your meaning.

5. Traditional haiku presented an image derived from an observation of nature, but modern poets often have fun with the genre. Write some haiku of your own on one or more of these subjects: pollution; a rock concert; an after-school job; a shopping mall. Or choose your own subject. Your poem must be written in three lines and observe the 5/7/5 syllable format.

   As an example, here is a contemporary haiku by poet Fred Witkoff.

   The bird sings because
   it has a song, not because
   it has a message.

6. What do we mean when we say that in good poetry the rhymes seem to be there by chance? Illustrate, using Shakespeare's "When in disgrace with fortune and men's eyes." Be sure you make it clear what you mean by "chance."

7. Reread the material on the *conceit*. Write a short poem in which you describe something (falling in love, breaking up with someone, wishing you had not made a promise that you do not want to keep but feel you must), using an extended metaphor. Hint: The entire poem should focus on one situation or action that is clearly something else.

8. Explain the original religious context of *epiphany*, then indicate why James Joyce thought it an appropriate way to define the most important element in a short story.

9. From what you read about *The Kite Runner* in this chapter, would you say that Amir has found redemption for the tragic mistakes he made early in life? Explain your answer.

10. From what you learned about "A Beneficiary" in this chapter, why do you think many readers might be dissatisfied with the ending?

5 Art

Overview

What makes a true artist? Who decides?

At an exhibition of works by the modern Russian abstract painter Wassily Kandinsky (Color Plate 8), two friends were staring in confusion at one of the pieces. One of them asked the other, "What is that supposed to be?" His friend replied, "I think it's two electric light bulbs." The first man stared some more, then finally nodded in agreement. "You're right. It's two light bulbs, and it's very good, don't you think?" If the artist had been standing by, he might well have thought: *Whatever they see is just fine as far as I'm concerned.* On the other hand, he might have hoped that, with increasing exposure to visual art, these visitors would come to view a work on its own terms.

Most of us share a definite bias toward realism, defined as *that which copies or at least approximates the appearance of objects and persons.* Comic strips, while exaggerations of reality, are nonetheless recognizable facsimiles of the real thing. Animated cartoons may take us to fantasy lands, but there, however distorted, animals are still animals, people are people, and trees are trees.

Yet even the most meticulous efforts to imitate the appearance of the real world are just that: **imitations**. A photograph is not the real thing. Greek and Roman statues *resemble* real people, but their bodies are often perfectly proportioned, as most people's bodies are *not*. Photographic realism—art that so closely imitates real scenes that we feel we could walk right into the canvas—was perfected during the seventeenth and eighteenth centuries. For artists of today, photographic realism may be a starting point from which they depart as they find new ways to express themselves. Nevertheless, many people still judge art in terms of how real it looks.

At its first showing, viewers were disgruntled because *Nude Descending a Staircase* did not seem to show what its title promised.

Source: Marcel Duchamp, *Nude Descending a Staircase #2* (1912). Philadelphia Museum of Art, Pennsylvania. Credit: © 2005 Artists Rights Society (ARS), New York/ADAGP, Paris/Succession Marcel Duchamp/Superstock.

What makes a true artist? Who decides? Sometimes the judgment of history decides, as in the case of Vincent van Gogh, who died obscure and penniless but whose work has since been acknowledged all over the world. Sometimes acclaim comes during the artist's lifetime: witness Michelangelo, Leonardo, and Picasso. Sometimes judgments vary both during and after an artist's lifetime. The jury is still out when it comes to Andy Warhol, a pop artist who stirred up a controversy when he unveiled a painting of one hundred cans of Campbell's soup. They look so real that we might think they came right off the supermarket shelf, but many viewers asked, "Why would anyone want to paint cans of soup?"

A recent play named, simply, *Art* concerns a man who pays an exorbitant sum for a stark, white canvas with nothing depicted on it. One friend, a cynic, decides he has gone mad. The purchaser is secretly not confident he has made a wise decision but vehemently defends the painting. In a gripping climactic scene, he gives the cynic a Magic Marker and dares him to put something on the canvas he seems to think is so worthless. Without changing his evaluation of the painting, the cynic is nonetheless intimidated and at first hesitates to deface it. Is it the price tag that stops him? Is it the possibility that maybe it *is* art? Whatever the considerations, the cynic has his honor to defend and draws a stick figure skiing down a mountain. The whiteness becomes snow, becomes a recognizable *thing*. The play ends in a minor key. What is art after all?

Art is what the artist does.
—**Robert Thiele**

This chapter offers a brief introduction to the visual arts: painting, sculpture, and architecture. We encourage you to approach the chapter without bias, without defined expectations. Be open to what may at first seem unfamiliar and, in some cases, downright crazy. Above all, do not expect a basic definition of visual art that can apply to every work by every artist. The world of art should be entered with open-ended expectations and an understanding that not every work will look like something recognizable. Consider, instead, the artist's intention. If you can do that, you have made a connection between the artist and yourself. Anyone seeking clear guidelines of taste can find them in any number of excellent resource books. Since the present text aims at offering insight into the use of the humanities as a means of enhancing the quality of life, the emphasis will be on looking into the wondrous variety of things that art can do for us.

The Need to Imitate

Astonishing cave paintings dating back to the days of primitive cultures teach us that even the earliest humans expressed themselves through art. While the artistic technique is hardly polished, we can recognize the subject—usually animals, such as a wild horse, familiar to the cave dwellers. The exact motivation of the artists cannot be known, but one thing about the work speaks for itself: *the early artists developed a technique for imitating what they saw.* Some of the paintings seem to express feelings as well: perhaps fear of the animal's power, or perhaps a sense of mastery over that power. A good bet, however, is that early artists enjoyed imitation, because they had an instinctive knowledge of how to do it. *They liked to transfer to a two-dimensional surface what they saw in their three-dimensional world.* All visual art is imitation. Some of it—and *only* some of it—strives for a **likeness** of the world out there—the familiar world. Some of it imitates the world of imagination inside the artist, and often it is rejected because it is *not* familiar.

Imitation is also a key factor in music and dramatic art. Music can imitate the sound of birds chirping, the wind whistling through a forest, or waves crashing against a shore, though we know that these effects are created by instruments. Aristotle called the art of acting *mimesis*—or imitation—even though Greek actors wearing masks and walking on stilts could not have *looked* like real people. The actor's art of imitation, from the Greeks to the present, involves the truth, not necessarily the appearance, of human beings.

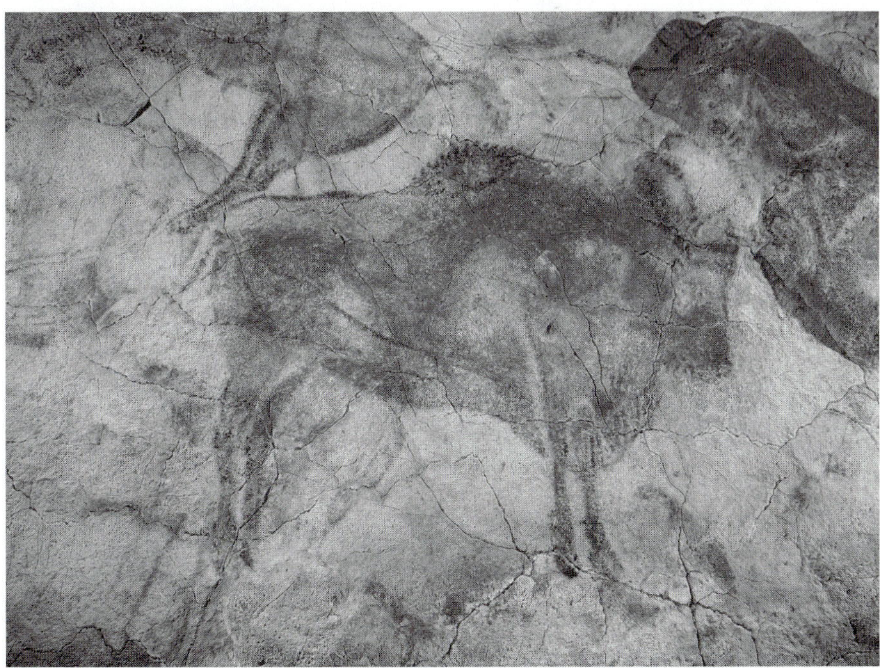

Very early cave drawings show a basic need to imitate the three-dimensional world.
Source: Gianni Dagli Orti/Corbis.

A good spectator also creates.
—**Swiss proverb**

Imitation, therefore, needs to be broadly defined and understood. The term does not refer exclusively to what looks absolutely real and authentic. In the humanities, imitation means that the artist uses reality as a starting but not necessarily an ending point. Sometimes, though a work of art has the external appearance of reality, it may actually be making a comment about life. Yet we need to be cautious if we find we like a certain work because we know what it is saying.

The painting *The Bar at the Folies Bergère* by the French artist Édouard Manet (1832–1883), whom we discuss later in the chapter, does not represent photographic realism, but its likeness to reality is clear. The expression on the barmaid's face suggests either boredom with her necessary job or quiet despair over the disparity between her own circumstances and those of her affluent customers. One *could* therefore say that the painting is making a social comment, but that is probably not the intent of this artist, who was primarily interested in imitating the shapes, colors, and the light of the world around him. At any rate, social commentary is unlikely to be the reason for the work's enduring fame.

Sometimes artists want to reproduce the sort of scene that catches the fancy of others. They enjoy meeting the challenge of making a two-dimensional canvas look three-dimensional. Sometimes the sheer difficulty of making the canvas seem to have depth, rather than the scene itself, is what motivates the artist. Imitating is such a universal human need that, when it is done well, critical viewers admire without demanding more.

In the 1874 painting *The Ball on Shipboard* by French artist James Tissot (1836–1902), the photographic likeness was probably a strong reason for its appeal. Tissot spent much of his life in England, and in this work he depicts a group of upper-class Victorians on a yachting pleasure cruise. The work is

Social commentary is probably not the primary interest of the artist in this work.

Source: Edouard Manet, *The Bar at the Folies Bergères*. Credit: Fotomarburg/Art Resource, NY.

a meticulous imitation of reality, filled with many details, including the intricate designs on the flags. The painter gives the illusion that he has just happened along at a particular moment and caught the scene with an instantaneous click of his camera. Photography was in its infancy at the time, and the pictures taken may not have been much sharper than the artist's brushwork. At any rate, the painting is so true to life we can almost believe we are standing on that deck, observing those people.

A painting so true to life that we can believe we are stanting on that deck, observing those people.

Source: James Tissot, *The Ball on Shipboard*, Tate Gallery, London. Credit: Art Resource, NY.

Those who insist on assigning specific meaning to works of art might see a critical attitude on the part of the artist toward the leisurely idleness of Victorian society, but, even if such an attitude existed, it would hardly account for the picture's success. The technique of the artist does that.

On the other hand, we miss out on a great deal if we demand strict realism in every work we view. The artist may be imitating things we have never seen and never will see except on that canvas or in a bronze shape. Visual art, as Ralph Waldo Emerson said of poetry, "adorns nature with a new thing." In all its myriad forms, realistic or not, art enhances our world.

Let Me See!

It's dangerous to generalize, but it's a safe assumption that most people who are born to be artists felt the urge to imitate. An artist's need to imitate grows out of a particular way of seeing: seeing intensely, noticing details, shapes, and colors. Unfortunately, most of us tend to see selectively, except in isolated moments when a landscape or a sunset calls us sharply to attention. Children tend to see as the artist sees, and perhaps that is why Picasso urged people not to grow up, to come to the world each day as the child does.

The poet Walt Whitman captures the child's—and we could add the young artist's—relationship to the world in these lines:

> *There was a child went forth every day,*
> *And the first object he look'd upon, that object he became,*
> *And that object became part of him for the day or a certain part of the day,*
> *Or for many years or stretching cycles of years.*[1]

Why do children in cars, buses, or trains demand to sit by the window? For that matter, why do they make this demand on planes, when there is often nothing to look at but clouds? What is out there doesn't matter. Children are new to the world, and instinctively they want to see everything, if only clouds. Older people confined in apartments along crowded streets like to look out the window for hours on end. Integral to the experience of being alive is looking at things. Those without sight substitute touching or close listening, but they will frequently describe these actions as "seeing." The point is that we spend much of our lives just looking around for no practical reason, except one: *we have to.*

Every child is an artist. The problem is how to remain an artist once he grows up.

—**Pablo Picasso**

Though we saw more intensely as children than as adults, most of us probably did not imitate what we looked at—at least not very accurately. Remember what you did when the elementary school teacher asked you to draw a house? Unless you were an instinctive artist, you were content to make the generic two-dimensional house (three rectangles and a triangle), just as you made stick figures to represent people. You made the *symbol* of a house because by now you were acquiring language, and the inner world of symbolism was taking over your life.

If asked to draw the sunrise, the true artist will imitate what he or she has seen many times: a sun that has radiance, depth, and color shadings. The rest of us draw something that could just as easily be a porcupine peeking from behind a fence.

The generic house and the stick figure got the job done for most of us. We assumed everyone knew what we meant when we drew that skeleton of a house, but we were drawing the *idea* of the house. We couldn't be bothered to imitate a real house. Isn't that what cameras are for?

The artist bent on directly imitating something can produce an astonishing likeness of the original. The Dutch masters of the seventeenth century were so good at faithful rendering that many artists who came later decided it was unwise to compete and began to experiment with other techniques and other goals.

What are such goals? One is the imitation of inner reality. Just think of your dreams. Every object, every location is made up of bits and pieces of other things. If you could hold onto a moment of a dream long enough to draw it, you would be, at least for a time, a modern artist. In a sense, the imitation factor is still there, except that a strange new world is being imitated. When the artist's production offers unfamiliar stimuli to us, we need to look at it non-judgmentally, trying to absorb all that is there to behold.

The artist who emerges from the childlike wonder at seeing is, ultimately, a creator, not a copy machine. Even the most rigorous attempt to create an absolute likeness is selective. For example, when painting a portrait, the artist may ask the subject to look serious, or perhaps to adopt a coy smile because this is more indicative of the subject's personality. Yet any portrait presents only one, often posed and artificial, reality. We know Leonardo da Vinci's Mona Lisa through her mysterious smile, but we will never know her fully as she was.

The treasure of art, however, is that *its* reality lives on after its subjects change or die. The final product is an addition to reality, not simply a way of reproducing it. The artist always contributes something new, something that never before was put together in precisely that way. Leonardo's *Mona Lisa* is not Mona Lisa. The latter left the earth long ago; the former will never die. Even though it seems to be slowly fading, it is still there, awaiting only a painstaking restoration.

Styles and Media

Now that we know all visual art is imitation but that imitation does not always mean creating a direct likeness, we can talk about the varied styles and methods—or **media**—of imitation.

Imagine a school where everyone else is drawing rectangles and stick figures, except for one pupil who wants to be different, to make a drawing that looks like the real thing. Already we have a *style* decision. The young artist feels confined by the sheet of paper handed out for the assignment. A two-dimensional surface does not offer enough freedom or originality, so the artist brings a bar of soap to school and proceeds to carve a tiny three-dimensional model of a real house. Not only is this a departure from the *style* of the others, but soap is a different *medium* from paper. The medium of imitation can be just as exciting as the act of imitating itself. Standing close to Michelangelo's statue of David or Moses, we are astounded at how lifelike the artist was able to make the marble seem. A painting of David is not the same as the statue, even though we might recognize that both imitate the same character. The medium enters strongly into the experience of art.

If the basic urge of the artist is to imitate the appearance of people, places, and things, the basic style is therefore *art as likeness*: The intention of the artist is to reproduce the appearance of the real world, though artists differ widely on how they define and create that world. Though a myriad of artists claim to be reproducing reality, we nonetheless find in their work a variety of styles and approaches.

Creating Likeness in Different Styles

There may be as many styles of art as there are artists. After all, we are told that no two thumbprints are exactly alike. Such an approach to an introductory study of the visual arts, however, could never establish broad enough categories to explain major developments or to recognize what different styles or "schools" of art are attempting to do. General principles or characteristics that identify a number of artists as belonging to a school or style are valuable tools of learning, even though any given artist can be an exception to the very rules that make such a thing as art history possible.

Even when the ultimate aim is to create something that looks very much like the real thing, artists can greatly differ in the kind of likeness transferred from the external world to a medium, especially if they are widely separated in time or come from very different cultures. The head of a man sculpted in marble by an Athenian artist of the fifth century B.C.E. might in no way resemble the head of a man molded in clay by a contemporary artist living in Fiji. But we would be able to recognize that both artists were creating the likeness of a man. The key is the word "likeness" itself and the myriad ways in which its meaning is understood.

Artwork in earlier civilizations was both decorative and imitative of the real world. Statues of the Egyptian pharaohs were intended to reproduce their appearance as a way of making them immortal. The decorative scrollwork on Greek columns sprang from the artist's imagination and was thus another form of imitation. In London's Westminster Abbey, the tops of stone sepulchers have faithful renderings of the persons entombed below, but the stained-glass windows of the abbey can also be considered art, even though they do not imitate the external world.

Without attempting to comprehend the intricacies of art history, we can, however, begin with the broad generalization that for thousands of years, beginning with the earliest known artistic products (such as cave drawings), a major purpose of art was *indeed* to transfer the real world to a given medium. In this section we investigate Art as Likeness, looking at major achievements and styles in its long history. We shall then be prepared to understand when and why artists began to consider other possibilities of artistic expression.

Art is essentially the affirmation, the blessing, and the deification of existence.

—Friedrich Nietzsche

Classical Art

Early in the history of Art as Likeness is the **classicism** of Greece and Rome. But first, let us look again at the term "classic," as defined in Chapter 4, and then consider *classicism* as the style of a specific era in the history of the humanities.

A classic is a work of literature, drama, film, or song that continues to be read, performed, seen, or sung long after its creation. Critics will sometimes become so enthusiastic about a new work that they label it an "instant classic." The implication is usually that the work will endure, will still be relevant many years from now. Of course, when that label is given to a recent work, no one can really know how long it will survive. Generally it is safer, before applying the label "classic," to glance backward and make sure that a given work has indeed outlived its time. The irony is that the creators of acknowledged classics seldom knew their works would live on. History is also filled with would-be artists who were confident they had created a "classic," only to have their work forgotten.

In Western civilization the phrase "classical music" refers primarily to works composed in the West from the middle of the seventeenth to near the end of the eighteenth century. Sometimes the phrase is loosely, if confusingly, applied to *all* concert music composed before the twentieth century, or even more confusingly, to any music heard in concert halls as opposed to that heard on pop radio stations. Chapter 6 discusses classical music in the primary sense of the term. It is associated with the musical style of composers like Haydn and the early Mozart.

In the visual arts, classical refers to a historical period when a culture's distinct artistic styles and media first flowered. Because cultures evolve on their own timelines, their classical periods date to different historical eras. Classical Islamic art, for example, generally dates from the time of the prophet Mohammed (570–612 C.E.) through the eleventh century. It is highly abstract and geometrical in nature, imitative not of the familiar world but of the artist's vision of the spiritual world. Art was used primarily to decorate tapestries, rugs, holy buildings, and the residences of high-ranking persons.

Classical art of India roughly spans the sixth through second centuries B.C.E. Some of it is, like Islamic art, abstract, but much Indian art is amazingly lifelike. Sculptures of nude males show painstaking effort to duplicate in stone the soft textures and muscles of the human body.

Classical Chinese art dates from around 500 B.C.E. to the fall of the Han empire in 220 C.E. Ancient pottery displays lifelike figures of men and animals, similar to those in the cave drawings, suggesting the central importance of the successful hunt. There are also many fantastic masks meant to depict the faces of gods, who of course could not resemble human beings.

Ancient Japanese art has the oldest history, for there is evidence of human settlements in Japan 30,000 years ago. Pottery and household utensils unearthed by archeologists cannot be precisely dated but are assumed to be older than almost any other comparable artifacts. Findings suggest that ceramic art was highly advanced, combining form and function. Jugs and plates served not only for practical household needs but for aesthetic pleasure as well. They tend to have unusual shapes and are often elaborately decorated with abstract designs, indicative of a style of living that required the beautiful as well as the useful.

In Western culture, classical art means the sculpture, wall carvings, **frescoes** (wall paintings), mosaics, and architecture of Greece and Rome. It spans the sixth century B.C.E. through the fifth century C.E. Although the statues and buildings of many tourist-visited ruins are white or gray, the popular image of this art is of stone shapes that lack color. In fact, classical artists were fond of color and had methods for making paints, which have, unfortunately, faded over the centuries. Most of the gleaming white columns found on the Acropolis of Athens, for example, were originally painted in bright colors.

This statue of Poseidon, god of the sea, shows a deity as the perfection of a human being.

Source: Poseidon of Artemision. Credit: Foto Marburg/Art Resource, NY.

Stone and marble were abundant in this classical world, and artists made generous use of these media. The artists responsible for decorating the city of Athens in the fifth century B.C.E. liked to work in marble, but they left it for the most part in an unpolished state. The Romans, who incorporated Athens into their empire in 146 B.C.E., were intent on rivaling or, if possible, eclipsing that city's monumental achievements in art. Hence Roman sculptors vigorously polished their marble, establishing the process that has been followed ever since.

Much Greek art, including the Parthenon, has been attributed to Phidias, a painter, sculptor, and architect greatly admired during the fifth century. The ruler Pericles hired Phidias as superintendent of public works, commissioning him to create monumental buildings and works of art that would glorify Athens, ensure its immortality, and remind the world that the Athenians were descendants of the gods.

Classical Athenian buildings were designed and constructed with mathematical precision, in keeping with the Greek love of numerical and geometric harmony. The statues were mainly depictions of gods and goddesses cast in human forms. They were likenesses of noble, heroic beings, larger than life and thus not direct likenesses of particular human beings. In this sense they represented the perfection of *humanness*, which the artists apparently considered the appropriate way to imitate the appearance of the divine. By depicting their deities as human beings, the artists were also elevating humanity to a godlike level.

Most of the statuary art survives in fragments: torsos, arms, legs, and heads. The faces share a generic look; almost all wear a smile of inner satisfaction. There are probably two reasons for this sameness of expression. One is that divine beings were expected to be happy. The other is that the Athenians, in seeking to tie themselves to the gods, believed that the goal of life was to achieve physical and moral perfection, which entitled them to wear a smile of contentment.

The best preserved of all the statues from the fifth century is *The Charioteer*. Cast in bronze, it shows that classical Greek artists could also imitate real people. The likeness is that of a young man, a chariot driver, who was certainly not a god. Yet his features are without flaw. His face is noble. He could well be a god, even as the Poseidon of Artemision could well be a perfect human.

This best preserved of all fifth-century Athenian statues shows us that classical artists knew how to imitate real people.

Source: The Charioteer. Credit: Nimatallah/Art Resource, NY.

The idealization is of course deliberate, but by studying this work, we can tell that *The Charioteer* is the work of a sculptor who knew anatomy. The veins of the young man's right arm (the left is missing) as well as his feet are rendered with painstaking fidelity to life, and the folds of his garment are so believable that they suggest the genius of Renaissance artists.

Beginning in the fourth century B.C.E. there was a movement in Greek art toward greater realism and less idealization. Whereas the chariot driver is an ordinary mortal with the appearance of a god, many of the new period's statues depict gods with the more defining features of mortals. There is less geometry and more genuine likeness, suggesting that actual models may have been used. By the third century, classicism gave way to even more ambitious attempts at realism.

Man is the measure of all things.
—Protagoras

The new artists chose subjects that were far less serene than those of their predecessors, more dynamic, with strong appeal to the passions. They often captured moments of sensuality and the agony of death throes for a new kind of public, one that demanded excitement from art. The *Laocoön* is a first-century sculpture, depicting in graphic detail the anguish of a father and his two sons as they are being strangled by sea serpents. The figures are not idealized, unless we were to say that their agony represents the "perfection" of pain! The Romans would imitate the quieter classicism of the fifth century, but they were also heavily influenced by the vivid realism of the later periods.

Greek and Roman art, however, leaves the general impression of a civilization that valued balance and harmony, and for many people "classicism" will continue to mean *that which reflects the love of order*. In fact, the classical music that emerged in the seventeenth century was linked to a revival of interest in that aspect of the classical world demonstrating such order.

The statue of the *Laocoön*, a father and his sons battling serpents, is a fine example of late classical art. Note that the serene formalism of the earlier period is gone.

Source: Nimatallah/Art Resource, NY.

The classical world is typified by the Parthenon, built as a temple for the goddess Athena. But it also represents the Athenians' passion for the ordered world of mathematics. The floor of the Parthenon was for a long time believed to embody a particular formula discovered and expressed mathematically by Euclid (c. 300 B.C.E.), one of the early founders of geometry. Legend has it that Euclid was fond of handing friends a stick and asking them to indicate where they would divide it that was aesthetically satisfying to them. He found that nearly everybody divided the stick in about the same place, which was not the center. So he began to measure the ratio between the two sections and discovered that it tended to be 1 to 1.68. Expressed verbally, Euclid's law states that the most pleasing relationship between two connecting sections is such that the smaller is to the larger what the larger is to the sum of the two. Euclid called it the law of the **Golden Section**. Fascinated by the theory, mathematicians and art historians have sought—and claim to have found—the Golden Section in a variety of places, including, in addition to the floor of the Parthenon, the foundations of many Roman ruins, the floor plan of medieval cathedrals, the pages of medieval illuminated manuscripts, and in much Renaissance art and architecture. There is some doubt that the exact Euclidean ratio exists in all the places claimed for it, but researchers say many come astoundingly close.

The ratio of the Golden Section, found all over the world, is 1 to 1.68. No one knows how it originated beyond the fact that Euclid was fond of asking people to divide a stick at the most pleasing point and the relationship of the two divisions was often 1 to 1.68.

The floor of this great symbol of Athenian glory seems to exemplify the Golden Section: a ratio of 1 to 1.68 between the shorter and longer sides.

Source: The Parthenon. Credit: Bettmann/Corbis.

Medieval Art

Christianity, which dominated Western civilization from the fifth to the fifteenth centuries, turned its back on what it considered the pagan world of classical art. Visual art mainly had one purpose: to remind the faithful of the life and death of Jesus, Mary, the saints, and the disciples. Artists who were selected by the church devoted their talents to the sacred adornment of church interiors. With a limited number of available paints (often made from the juice of berries), they created art on wood, in stained glass, and on church walls. Sculptors made marble statues of saints and members of the Holy Family. Like the Greeks and Romans centuries before them, medieval artists imagined spiritual beings in human terms, though their work is not completely lifelike. Medieval art generally presents the *idea*, not a faithful imitation, of its subjects. Some of it, however, such as the famous Bayeux tapestry of the eleventh century, does indeed indicate that, when dealing with earthbound subjects, medieval artists attempted to be realistic.

Nearly all of the professional art was done by males. One exception was the art of embroidery, which flourished in both France and England during the period. The Bayeux tapestry is not really a tapestry at all but a series of panels embroidered in colored yarn on a linen background. It stretches 203 feet and tells the story of the Battle of Hastings in 1066, in which Normans under William the Conqueror defeated the Saxon army of King Harold. The tapestry is believed to have been commissioned by William's half-brother and was once attributed to Queen

A panel from the 1886 English replica of the medieval Bayeux tapestry, an example of medieval art made by women.

Source: Nick Wheeler, Corbis.

Portrait of the Madonna, once attributed to St. Luke, but probably painted during the twelfth century. Note how mature the child looks.

Source: Alinari/Art Resource, NY.

Matilda, William's wife. But it was more likely made years later by English embroiderers.

In the twelfth-century painting of the Madonna reproduced here, the artist has made an effort to duplicate the look of a real woman, but the nose is improbably extended, and there is a definite masculinity about the face. The face of the baby Jesus in no way suggests that of an actual infant. It belongs to an adolescent, as it does in nearly all such paintings. Medieval artists thought of the infant Jesus as being already wise. We see the *idea* of the divine child, not the appearance of a real-life baby.

Classicism was, however, by no means completely dormant during the Middle Ages. Medieval cathedrals, generally built during the eleventh and twelfth centuries, utilized classical principles of mathematical order. They were, of course, strongly reflective of the Christian religion, and their floor plan—a central aisle called the *nave* and a smaller chapel on each side—was shaped like the cross. They are considered the finest examples of the **Gothic** style. A sixteenth-century Italian art historian named the style after the "barbarian" Goths, the Teutonic invaders who had conquered Rome. The label was meant to connote a barbaric departure from classicism, perhaps because of the demonic looking gargoyles, statues of ugly, evil monsters designed to frighten away malevolent spirits. But there was nothing barbaric about the plan of construction. With their soaring towers reaching up to heaven and their stone buttresses, the cathedrals were so finely engineered that no mortar was originally used to attach the stones to each other.

Entrance to the cathedral of Notre Dame in Paris, constructed beginning in the twelfth century. If you look carefully, you can see the gargoyles squatting on the ledge beneath the two towers.

Source: David Sailors/Corbis.

Giotto

The work of a thirteenth-century Florentine artist, Giotto di Bondone (1266/67–1337), introduced revolutionary new techniques and prepared the way for the greater artistic realism of the Renaissance. Along with a number of colleagues, Giotto sought to bring new life to what had become the workmanlike craft of decorating church interiors.

Artists of the Renaissance, influenced by Giotto, experimented with an imitation of how the eye actually sees.

St. Francis of Assisi had been canonized in 1228, just two years after his death, and even though he had taken a vow of poverty and urged his followers to divest themselves of worldly possessions, the decision was made to honor him by erecting a great church. For a number of years after its completion, it lacked interior decorations, but finally Giotto and his assistants were commissioned to do a series of wall paintings depicting incidents in the life of the saint.

As did many Greek and Roman artists, Giotto experimented with *fresco*, an art that would not be perfected until a century after his death. Art scholar William Fleming explains the nature of the art:

> *The artist must first make his drawing on the dry plaster of the wall. Then, taking an area he can finish in a single day, he spreads a thin coat of wet plaster over the dry, making it necessary to retrace the lines underneath. Earth pigments are then mixed with water, combined with white of egg as a binder, and applied directly to the fresh plaster—hence the term* fresco. *The pigments and wet plaster combine chemically to produce a surface as permanent as that of any medium in painting.*[2]

Fresco illustrating the later style of Giotto, when he had begun to master the art of perspective.

Source: Giotto, *Death of St. Francis*, Cappella Bardi, S. Croce, Florence, Italy. Credit: Scala/Art Resource, NY.

What gives us surer knowledge than our senses? With what else can we better distinguish the true from the false?

—Lucretius

The fresco *Death of St. Francis* (c. 1320), reproduced here, was not part of the St. Francis cycle painted for the church in Assisi, but is possibly by young artists influenced by the master. This fresco can be found in the cathedral of Santa Croce in Florence and bears the unmistakable mark of Giotto's later style, which had evolved from earlier, more naive attempts at realism. In this work we see a greater mastery of **perspective**, a technique that was just beginning to emerge, with Giotto leading the way.

Artists of the early Italian **Renaissance** were beginning to experiment with efforts to transfer to their medium an imitation of how the eye actually sees. They recognized that if art were to attain true likeness, it would have to seem three-dimensional. Perspective in art is now taken for granted, and viewers new to the work of Giotto may fail to appreciate how revolutionary this technique was. If you look back at the painting of the medieval Madonna on page 128, you will note that the infant Jesus, besides having an improbably mature face, is also much larger than we would expect. Perspective is the art of varying the size of figures and objects to approximate how we see. The priests on either side of the saint's bier in the Giotto fresco are larger than the figures standing behind it. The brain then supplies the knowledge that the room has depth.

As a medieval artist, Giotto was still interested in the religious ideas embodied in his work, but as an artist of the emerging Renaissance, he was also interested in fidelity to real life.

Renaissance Art

The *Renaissance*, meaning "rebirth," began in Italy as early as the fourteenth century, then spread throughout western Europe, finally reaching the British Isles late in the sixteenth century. At first an art movement, it led to a political and social revolution against the tight controls of religion. It deemphasized the next world as the sole concern of human beings and began to focus on leading the good life in *this* world. It reinstated science as a legitimate source of knowledge and held a greater respect for individual achievement. In the humanities, the term *renaissance* signifies a renewed interest in the knowledge and art of the classical world—in part because that world had been ignored for so many centuries, but also because classical artists and thinkers were concerned with making sense of and bringing beauty to the only life they believed they were given to live. Renaissance artists combined classical discipline with something new: the demand for freedom of individual expression. The Renaissance constitutes the greatest single revolution in the history of Western art and thought, though centuries earlier the Arab world had kept alive the teachings of Greek philosophy, especially those of Aristotle, with his desire to analyze the human condition and his anticipation of the scientific method.

At first the artistic revolution was a quiet one: artists experimenting with more lifelike representations of the human form. As the years went by, however, the revolutionary fires grew more intense. Artists began to react boldly against religious traditionalism and demand the right to practice their craft without constraints and fear of censorship.

Fillippo Lippi (1406?–1469) typifies the Renaissance spirit. Forced into monastic orders at the age of eight, he had a hard time suppressing his desire to escape from the confines of his cell. Finally he lost the battle and begin to sneak out at night, roaming the countryside, drawing people and objects that caught his eye.

A forerunner of the great Italian Renaissance artists of the sixteenth century, Lippi (better known as Fra Lippo Lippi) was recognized for his genius at a very young age and commissioned to paint biblical scenes in the chapel. So astonishingly real were his figures that he was accused of using forbidden human models. There were even rumors that he hired prostitutes to pose for his depiction of the Virgin Mary.

Of particular interest to the artists of the Italian Renaissance was that in classicism the human body was often depicted in the nude—something prohibited by the church. True, the nude human form as displayed in ancient times had customarily been geometrically perfect and thus not truly lifelike, but classical art set in motion the interest of the new artists in realistic anatomy.

One theory of the near-perfect classicism of Michelangelo's *David* is that the young artist had only classical statues to work from and knew little about the actual human body. *David* is a work in the purely classical style, depicting a human being in heroic, godlike terms, physically perfect in every respect. A widespread belief is that there must have been a model for the sculpture, but even if the suspicion is well founded, Michelangelo still idealized his model in classical style. Eventually, however, he and many of his colleagues *would* work directly and realistically from models, causing considerable scandal among the clergy and political conservatives.

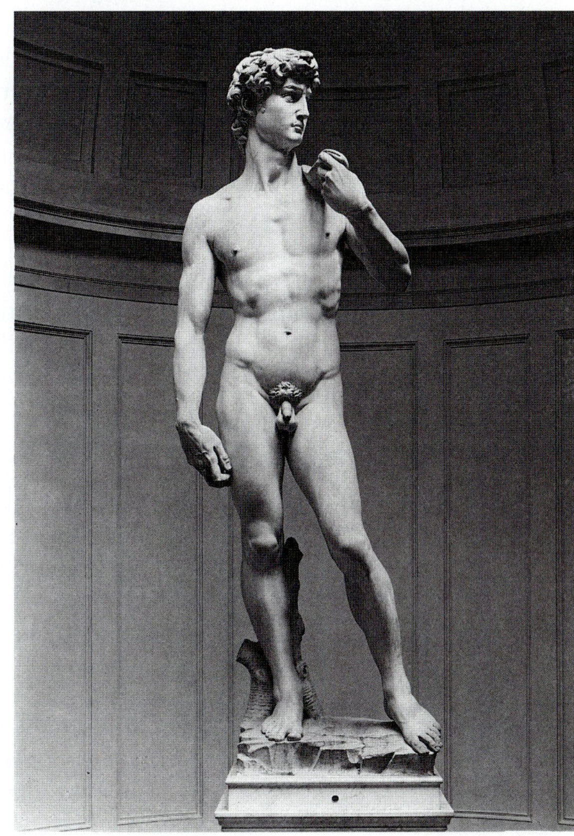

(a) Donatello's Dionysian David, showing the Renaissance desire to create lifelike, individualized works of art. (b) By contrast, the Apollonian David of the young Michelangelo is a classical idealization of the human body.

Source: (Right and left) Alinari/Art Resource, NY.

The new art had two dominant characteristics. First, continuing in Giotto's tradition, it tried to make the eye of the viewer see things and people as they appeared in real life, continuing to use perspective to achieve the illusion of three dimensions. Second, it invited an *emotional response* from the viewer. Compare the *David* of Michelangelo, which is the epitome of the Apollonian in art, to the *David* of Italian Renaissance artist Donatello (1386?–1466), which depicts, in Dionysian style, a young man who is surely not idealized, a young man who typifies the respect for individualism and personal differences that would be fundamental in the Renaissance. The sensuality of Donatello, who died a century before Michelangelo, anticipates a new emotional style that is a long way from suggesting classical repose. Yet despite the classicism of Michelangelo's *David*, the Florentines did, after all, react emotionally to it. It is Renaissance in subject if not in form. The subject—the boy about to take on the giant Goliath—was not only biblical but also contemporary and political. The townspeople saw David as a symbol of relatively tiny Florence challenging mightier Italian cities such as Venice or Rome for supremacy in religion, art, and urban sophistication, and perhaps challenging the Vatican itself in the name of individual freedom.

The obsession of Renaissance artists with imitating life as precisely as possible owes something to the general spirit of the age. The new realism, with its charged emotions, its sense of the dramatic, and its introduction of new ways of seeing and imitating life, brought together an astonishing array of great artists, most of them located in or near Florence. Many of these artists have achieved places of honor in the history of the humanities, but Leonardo, Michelangelo, and Raphael were accorded almost instant immortality. Each is generally referred to by his first name only, an honor bestowed on them in their lifetime and retained ever since.

Leonardo

Iron rusts from disuse; stagnant water loses its purity and in cold weather becomes frozen; even so does inaction sap the vigor of the mind.

—**Leonardo**

The oldest of the three, Leonardo, came to Florence from the nearby town of Vinci. He excelled in so many fields—as a painter, sculptor, architect, inventor, and at least *conceiver* of such astounding marvels as the submarine and the airplane—that he richly deserves the label "Renaissance man," which is an integral part of the human vocabulary, still used as a reference to those who achieve excellence in many fields of study, such as Einstein, who was not only the greatest scientist of the twentieth century but a writer and accomplished violinist as well.

At least two of Leonardo's works stand out as definitive examples of their respective genres: the mural *The Last Supper* (Color Plate 6), and the portrait *Mona Lisa* (Color Plate 1). Commissioned in 1494 as a sacred fresco for the refectory (dining hall) of Santa Maria del Grazie in Milan, *The Last Supper*, which shows the final gathering of Jesus and his twelve disciples before his arrest and crucifixion, took three years to complete. *The Last Supper* is celebrated for a number of reasons. First, it is a triumph of perspective. Designed to occupy the entire far wall of the dining room, the mural presents to the astonished spectator the illusion that the room actually extends into the painting, continuing on into the natural world glimpsed through the windows behind Jesus and the disciples.

Second, Leonardo introduced a technique known as **chiaroscuro**, in which the contrast between light and shadow deepens the imitation of how people and things look to us in the real world. The technique of blending light and shadow was quickly copied by other artists, but except for Rembrandt, the great seventeenth-century Dutch master, Leonardo's handling of the technique has not been equaled or surpassed. The artist wanted his two-dimensional canvases to come closer to representing how the eye actually sees. Perspective contributed to the illusion of reality, but the interplay of dark and light was necessary for a totally authentic experience of vision. The chiaroscuro effect in *The Last Supper* is among the most dramatic ever captured by an artist, for the shadows in the foreground are in striking contrast to the light coming from the windows, perhaps suggesting the difference between the human world of betrayal and sorrow and a heavenly world of eternal peace.

Archetypes in This Chapter

Judas	has become a generic term for "betrayer," especially among close acquaintances when one suspects that the other has betrayed a confidence.
Medieval	adjective for someone or something that is out of date, such as a person with old-fashioned views or a regulation considered outmoded.
Renaissance man	a person of extraordinary accomplishments in many fields, such as Leonardo da Vinci or Albert Einstein.
Starving artist	stereotype of an artist who lives in a garret, with little money or food, but willing to give up everything for art.
Surreal	adjective for a person, object, or event that seems too weird to be part of the familiar world.

Third, the mural is a notable example of Leonardo's genius for capturing the endless complexity of human beings, reproducing not just physical but *psychological* likeness. Jesus has just said: "One of you which eateth with me shall betray me" (Mark: 14:18). While he remains the calm center of the group, his pronouncement creates an emotional storm among the others. Most of the disciples are desperate to know if they are the betrayer. Most of the faces show also elements of anger—that one of them might commit so hideous a crime—and fear—that any one of them might be guilty. Only one knows that the betrayal has already taken place.

Does the painting show which one is Judas, the betrayer? Look carefully. From the viewer's perspective, Judas is third to the left of Jesus, his arm leaning on the table, and he appears to be holding the bag of coins he has received for pointing Jesus out to the Romans. The magic of Leonardo is nowhere better illustrated than in the fact that we do not need to see the bag to identify Judas. He is not looking directly toward Jesus.

The figure to the immediate left became the center of a huge controversy ever since the 2002 publication of Dan Brown's bestseller *The Da Vinci Code*, in which the suggestion is made (actually it is stated as a fact) that this person is Mary Magdalene, the only female disciple. In any case, this person is also not looking at Jesus, but the difference is that this person is in deep sorrow.

Leonardo is also master of subtext, a way of showing what may be happening behind a human face, though just what it is can be debated.

Leonardo is like a stage director. By his placement of the characters and the direction of their eyes, he controls the manner in which the viewer watches the scene. And *watch* is a more appropriate word than *see*, because though a painting is a static object, depicting a moment frozen in time, *The Last Supper* unfolds as a drama being witnessed on a stage. It overcomes the limitation of having no real movement or sound. Also in the style of the stage director, Leonardo lights the scene, using the chiaroscuro effect to highlight the unspoken drama transpiring between Jesus and Judas.

Leonardo's complex faces, especially that of Jesus, are the parallel in visual art to what the modern theater calls *subtext*, a technique whereby the playwright lets the audience know what is happening below the surface by having a character remain silent or else speak a very few words. Great performers on the stage can provoke thoughts and pique the curiosity by a slight glance or by the silences that precede or follow their words. Similarly, a great artist like Leonardo is able somehow to show what is happening inside a subject. Leonardo is almost without peer in the ability to capture emotional complexity behind a face that shows little of it. In Christ's face we can read sorrow, because he knows who the betrayer is and knows that the deed cannot be undone. There is resignation to his imminent death on the cross. And, astonishingly, we see understanding and forgiveness too.

Through both the placement of his figures—Judas and Jesus, for example—and his ability to suggest the inner life, Leonardo greatly influenced the development of dramatic art. Max Reinhardt, one of the great theater directors of the last century, counseled his students and apprentices to study Leonardo if they wanted to learn how best to stage a scene. Stanislavsky, who founded the modern school of truthful acting, was known to have spent many hours in his classes analyzing the dramatic qualities in works like *The Last Supper*.

To better appreciate Leonardo's use of subtext in painting, compare the face of Christ in his version of the Last Supper with that in a modern version (1927) by Gustave van der Woestyne (Color Plate 7). The latter painting, while striking, uses the well-known scene for the purpose of demonstrating a bold new technique. The artist does not attempt to improve upon Leonardo's subtlety. Rather, he appears to want to shock the viewer with strongly outlined faces of both Christ and the disciples that belong to the world of modern art, not that of Renaissance realism. He offers far less subtext for the viewer to ponder. There are probably good reasons for the difference. One is that the modern artist needs to recreate the occasion in his own style. Another is that the artist obviously believes that a real Christ would not have been able to conceal the knowledge of the painful death he was about to endure. Van der Woestyne's *Last Supper* is in keeping with the modern tendency to depict Christ as a human being tragically betrayed.

Leonardo also goes far beyond surface realism in another masterpiece, the *Mona Lisa* (1503–1505). The work has become the most famous single work of art in the world, still attracting huge numbers of visitors each day to the Louvre Museum in Paris (Color Plate 1).

What is all the fuss about? How do we account for the extraordinary stature of this relatively small canvas in the world of the humanities? A reason, of course, may be that widely discussed mysterious smile. One does not find many complexities in portrait paintings, because artists customarily are hired to render both a realistic likeness *and* an idealization in the classical mode. Her famous, and still mysterious, smile particularizes Mona Lisa Gioconda, whom Leonardo was commissioned to paint. She is not only idealized in the traditional manner of portraiture, but she is also an individual woman captured in a particular inner action at a particular time.

A close look at the painting, however, reveals that the mouth is shown with only the faintest trace of a smile. Just as interesting is the fact that Signora Gioconda is looking at something not shown in the painting—just *what* we can never know. But this adds to the mystery.

The following experiment, suggested by one art critic, can be performed right at this moment. Cover the left side of Mona Lisa's face, using your hand or an index card. Presumably you will see a warm, sensuous woman, gazing provocatively—at *you*! Now cover the right side, and presumably you will see an aristocrat who finds something (not you, of course) mildly amusing. Many have said that Leonardo in this work has revealed the essential ambiguity of all human faces and personalities. If we agree, then we could say that the *Mona Lisa* accomplishes a goal many artists rarely achieve: its creator has both particularized and generalized his subject. What should stand out in our mind, however, is that the portrait is a supreme example of the Renaissance movement toward individualism, an organic part of the rebellion against the medieval emphasis on the oneness of all people in the eyes of heaven and the promise of everlasting life in the hereafter rather than on the rich diversity of life in this world.

Michelangelo

What Shakespeare is to theater and Beethoven is to music, Michelangelo is to sculpture. Before he came upon the scene, sculpture was thought to be a skill at best, ordinary decoration at its least. Michelangelo helped to change the reputation of sculpture, making it an art form of the highest order. He did it through an effort of will and physical strength that is almost unimaginable.

No one has mastery before he is at the end of his art and his life.

—Michelangelo

As a youth, Michelangelo learned from masters of the classical style, but the artist soon realized he wanted more than what they were teaching. He wanted to create figures that were totally his, that bore his unmistakable mark. In fact, he was so confident that no one would confuse his style with another artist's that he signed his name to a work only once—and that was the *Pietà* in St. Peter's at the Vatican, created when he was just twenty-two and perhaps somewhat less self-assured than he would become in a short time.

(a) In contrast to his later work, this sculpture by Michelangelo has an uplifting serenity about it: clearly the work of a youthful genius who has not yet experienced the pain of living. (b) A very different version by Michelangelo of the *Pietà*.

Source: Left: Michelangelo, *Pietá*. Credit: Scala/Art Resource, NY. Right: Castello Sforesco, Milan, Italy. Credit: Scala/Art Resource, NY.

. . .we must recognize the emergence of Michelangelo as one of the great events in the history of man.

—Sir Kenneth Clark

As Michelangelo matured, his work shows a tension between classicism and the expression of passion. The Vatican *Pietà*, however, viewed by the thousands who daily visit St. Peter's, shows the crucified son, lying across the lap of his grieving mother. Since its creator had come so recently from the studio where he first learned his craft, a craft that was essentially classical, the sculpture, as we should expect, contains more of the *idea* of pain than the *essence* of it. There is a serenity about the work that is uplifting indeed, but a little removed from an effort to capture in marble a most extreme human emotion.

In contrast is the *Pietà Rondanini*, created when the artist was in his eighties. The sculptor attempted to destroy the work before anyone could see it, so convinced was he that it was unworthy of his most severe critic, whom he believed to be God. Presumably it was originally intended for his own tomb, but now we are left with only fragments. Most clearly seen is the face of Mary, on which Michelangelo indelibly chiseled the pain missing in the youthful work. This is intensely personal art, a personal statement by a genius who is not happy with what he has done, a genius who has felt the sorrow unknown to most human beings: the sorrow of having not quite ascended to the very highest level possible for a mortal. Of course, the judgment of the ages has been that Michelangelo did indeed attain this level, but he never enjoyed the knowledge of what he had achieved. A story repeated over and over in the humanities!

That in thy holy footsteps I may tread:
The fetters of my tongue do thou unwind,
That I may have the power to sing of thee,
And sound thy praises everlastingly!

—Michelangelo

Michelangelo's restless, unceasing quest for perfection helps explain why he was not content to stay only with the art of sculpture. He also aspired to be the greatest painter the world had ever known. His biggest challenge—even greater than that of the seventeen-foot block of marble that became *David*—was a task given him by Pope Julius II: to paint the ceiling of the Sistine Chapel inside the Vatican. Michelangelo's imagination was immediately stirred. There was the height itself, as close to heaven as his art was ever likely to take him. There was the huge expanse of the ceiling, allowing for a series of paintings on religious themes that would at the same time present to the viewer a totally unified effect. And there was the challenge that fresco posed, for the plaster had to be applied to the ceiling and painted before it was completely dry. Legend has it that the artist worked almost single-handedly for four long years, lying on his back for hours at a time while plaster continually dripped down on his face. But Michelangelo was both passionate and businesslike in his work. He had assistants, and the project was carefully planned—and kept secret even from the pope until the gasp-filled unveiling. Never for a moment did the artist fear that the pontiff would be disappointed, but Michelangelo may still have harbored the gnawing belief that God was not satisfied.

I'm sure marble puts up a good fight too. It's dead, and it resents being hammered into life.

—Henrik ibsen

That Michelangelo not only sought perfection but did so in such challenging media as marble and fresco tells us why he has come to symbolize the Renaissance itself. The unending—and apparently unsatisfied—quest for greatness is surely a sign of an enormous human ego, quite consistent with the period's stress on individualism and human achievement. At the same time, to offer up that ego in the service of God was to renounce the self and worldly fame.

Sometimes losing the struggle against ego added further to his anguish. He was adored by a huge public. Prospective patrons offered incredible sums for his services. How could he not have felt a measure of pride when he saw on all sides confirmation of his greatness? His letters reveal someone who was always at odds with himself, always fighting to suppress his ego. On the other hand, some critics have suggested that to believe God was the only audience suitable for one's work constitutes arrogance of cosmic scope.

His style—sometimes referred to by the word *terribilità*, which means "awfulness" in its fundamental sense of "awesomeness"—reflects the need to challenge the medium in the way that the matador challenges the bull. But Michelangelo cannot be the only artist whose creative process was inspired by the difficulty of the medium. All artists—to *be* artists—have overcome obstacles that would stop most of us in our tracks. The medium cannot surrender willingly; otherwise it is not worth conquering. Referring to the permissiveness in modern poetry and modern theater, where great liberties are allowed in language and structure, one critic has made the telling observation: *Where everything is possible, nothing matters.*

Yet great art must hide the effort that goes into it. Try never to sit in the front row at a ballet. You should not hear the heavy breathing or see the drops of perspiration falling to the stage. Likewise, the blank screen on the computer dares the would-be writer to find just the right words in the right order. And ivory keys coldly reflect overhead stage lights—so still, and offering no help at all to the pianist. Still, we have to know that the passionate striving is there, underneath it all. We've said it before, but it bears repeating: *Art is the illusion that there is no art.*

Raphael

The youngest of the three great artists of the Florentine Renaissance, Raphael died only a year after Leonardo and nearly half a century before Michelangelo. This fact is important to remember, for when we consider how much Raphael achieved in a relatively short lifespan, we can only speculate on what he might have done had he lived longer. Raphael had the advantage of observing the techniques of his two predecessors, and his work clearly shows their influence. Moving to Florence in 1504, when both artists were already being celebrated, he observed Leonardo's characteristic interplay of light and shadow, a technique he borrowed for the *Alba Madonna* of 1510.

I know an artist who spent a dreadful morning comparing himself to Raphael.
—**Bertrand Russell**

The painting illustrates how far the techniques of realism and perspective had progressed from the time of Giotto. The hills in the distance, painted near the top, are much smaller than the figures of the infant Jesus and his playmate. Moreover, the Virgin Mary looks like a real woman, while the playmates look reasonably as children should. The divine nature of mother and child is suggested by the adoring, almost worshipful look on the face of the other child; otherwise this could be a moment in real life.

The chiaroscuro effect comes from the light Raphael gives to his sky and from the dark interior of the cloak from which the Virgin Mary's arm extends, as well as her right sleeve. The background also shows a contrast between light and shadow, and there is shade in the very foreground, suggesting that the figures may be near a tree.

In 1508 Raphael, already famous, had been called to Rome by Pope Julius II, who commissioned him to paint four frescoes for the Vatican Palace, illustrating theology, philosophy, poetry, and justice. The most famous of these is the fresco celebrating philosophy, *The School of Athens* (Color Plate 9). In the painting we see, again, a highly sophisticated use of perspective, with the many, many figures all painted in accurate proportion relative to the two arches in the background and the two statues that tower over the participants. In addition, each figure is painstakingly detailed, despite the fact that, in order to recreate so large a scene, the artist had to paint with extremely minute strokes on the wet plaster.

The work of Raphael and the other great artists of the Italian Renaissance has made Florence and Rome places in which millions, through the magic of the Internet, can observe the humanities coming to vibrant life. These cities provide a good introduction to Internet art tours, and from there you can visit the scores of other

In contrast to the medieval Madonna on page 128, this Virgin Mary looks more like a real woman and the children more lifelike.

Source: Raphael, *The Alba Madonna*, © 1999 Board of Trustees, National Gallery of Art, Washington DC.

magnificent locations in which yesterday is hard to distinguish from today. Eventually you will want to see the originals up close. Life offers few comparable experiences.

Two Women of the Post-Renaissance

Overlooked in art histories for centuries, the works of Sophonisba Anguissola and Artimisia Gentileschi are now being recognized, not just because they were done by women, but because of their brilliance.

Until relatively modern times—say, the last hundred years—women were largely excluded from artistic production by the societies in which they lived. Unfortunately, this was true during both the Renaissance and the *post-Renaissance*, a term sometimes used to describe the art of the late sixteenth century. A few women, however, defied the conventions of their time and managed to produce great art. Two of the most renowned of these women are Sophonisba Anguissola and Artemisia Gentileschi.

Sophonisba Anguissola (c. 1532–1626) and her five sisters were all trained artists, but she was the first female to achieve an international reputation for her art. So precocious was her talent for realistic portraiture that the great Michelangelo agreed to teach her and later expressed admiration for her work.

Georgio Vasari, the first major critic and art historian of the Italian Renaissance, author of the male-oriented *Lives of the Artists*, credited Anguissola with having produced "rare and beautiful" work and placed her above all other female artists. This tells us that she not only held her own in a field dominated by men but that she was probably one of many women who practiced the art of painting.

Several generations younger was Artemisia Gentileschi (1592–1652), whose reputation has eclipsed Anguissola's. Art historians now consider her the most important female artist of the post-Renaissance. She was quite prolific, though only thirty-four of her works have survived. In her time, however, she was scorned by both critics and male colleagues as too aggressive—that is, "unfeminine"—in promoting her work. As a youth she showed as much promise as Anguissola had shown years earlier, but she was denied the chance to study with an established painter.

Art does not reproduce the visible; rather, it makes visible.

—**Paul Klee**

Scorn for her spread to the public sector when she was involved in a sex scandal that became the topic of gossip in Florence. She accused a fellow artist, Agostino Tassi, of raping her and demanded that he be arrested and brought to justice. The trial lasted seven months, during which several of Tassi's male friends testified that she was generally known as promiscuous. Another witness saved the day by testifying that Tassi had, in his presence, openly boasted of the rape. Her reputation somewhat restored (though still a bit tarnished from all the negative publicity), Gentileschi nonetheless persevered. Feminists and art historians have debated the effect of the trial on her paintings, citing in particular their frequently violent themes. One of her most acclaimed works, *Judith Slaying Holofernes* (Color Plate 10), depicts the biblical heroine Judith, who seduced the Assyrian general Holofernes, then beheaded him with his own sword in order to protect her community from invasion.

Rembrandt: The Perfection of Likeness

From Leonardo on, the demand for portraiture increased in Europe. As years passed, rich and powerful households began to decorate their halls with the watchful eyes of departed ancestors. Perfect likenesses, which might also doctor up an unattractive wrinkle here or a weak chin there, brought newfound riches to artists who could master the skill of faithful—or nearly so—imitation.

The master painters of the **Dutch school** of the seventeenth century were able to reproduce faces, figures, and landscapes with the greatest accuracy possible until the invention of photography two centuries later. In fact, many casual and infrequent visitors to museums still respond most favorably to their work, because of its startling realism. A Dutch **still life**—such as apples, pears, a loaf of bread, and a bottle of wine on a table—can look so real you might imagine all you had to do was reach inside the frame for food and drink.

Of all the Dutch masters, none surpassed Rembrandt Harmenszoon van Rijn (1606–1669) in either quality or quantity of work. Like the great Italian masters, history has accorded Rembrandt the honor of being known by his first name. In a lifetime much shorter than that of Michelangelo, he was able to produce so many works of art that a precise count has yet to be made. While he can be said to have mastered the art of perfect likenesses, he was also, like Leonardo, interested in what we may call **psychological realism**. Like many artists, Rembrandt often worked on commission, but he almost always looked for the challenge in his subject: the character behind the face, the pain suffered (even if he didn't know the cause), the longing for something else that might have compensated for a disappointing life. He was fond of

Rembrandt's many self-portraits give us an autobiography without words.

Source: Rembrandt van Rijn, *Self Portrait*, © 1999 Board of Trustees, National Gallery of Art, Washington, DC.

painting old people, whose faces bore the marks and burdens of many years of hardship and loss.

In seeking ways to further the technique of intense inner realism, Rembrandt was aided by the chiaroscuro effect that Leonardo had used so eloquently. So painstakingly did Rembrandt practice the effect that he, rather than Leonardo, has come to be identified with it. In the *Self-Portrait* reproduced here, only the face matters, bathed in light, while almost nothing else about the figure is visible, except for the hand, which is partially in darkness. To look at many paintings by Rembrandt is to see such a contrast between light and darkness that it is tempting to believe the source of light must be external to the painting. Though the amazing light dominates this picture, we must not suppose that the darkness is unimportant to the total effect; for the artist uses it to enhance the aura of quiet wisdom that age and experience in life have given.

A visit to a major museum will afford you the opportunity to look at many conventional portraits, which have their nearly perfect likenesses, but *only* of surface realism. Expressions seem devoid of emotion. They offer not a sign of what sort of life the person has led. It is not an exaggeration to say that Rembrandt's series of self-portraits, painted at various ages and points in his career, give us an autobiography without words.

A Rebellion against Perfect Likeness

The art world was well aware that the Dutch masters had taken the imitative aspect of visual art about as far as it could go. So, as one would expect, new generations of artists would attempt to emulate their work. Well into the eighteenth century, on both sides of the Atlantic, landscape and portrait painting tended to be technically proficient—and, with rare exception, generally unexciting. One of the chief characteristics of art, however, is novelty, so sooner or later this trend had to run its course. Someone was bound to come along and rebel against the tradition of perfect likeness. Could art be anything more than expensive decoration? Francisco Goya (1746–1828), Spain's major artist of the late eighteenth century, answered a resounding Yes! and set about to lead a decisive rebellion.

Goya

His early work, it is true, is characterized by realistic landscapes depicting the natural beauty of the Aragon countryside in which he was nurtured, as well as portraits of considerable vitality, with finely detailed, nearly photographic likenesses of his

Plate 16 Vincent van Gogh, *The Starry Night* (1889).
The Museum of Modern Art, New York. Acquired through the Lillie P. Bliss Bequest, [472.19]. Credit: Digital Image © The Museum of Modern Art/Licensed by SCALA/Art Resource, NY.

The artist's most famous work, illustrating his love of color and his fierce, stabbing brushstrokes. Van Gogh is often called a post-Impressionist. Looking at this painting, can you think of any reason why it does not fit within the Impressionist school? (See page 146 for more on van Gogh.)

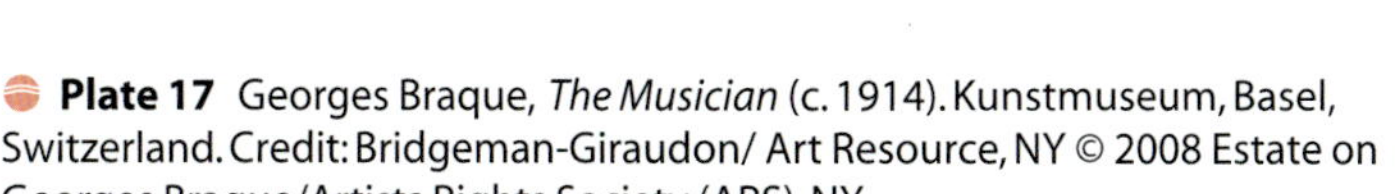

Plate 17 Georges Braque, *The Musician* (c. 1914). Kunstmuseum, Basel, Switzerland. Credit: Bridgeman-Giraudon/ Art Resource, NY © 2008 Estate on Georges Braque/Artists Rights Society (ARS), NY.

The Cubist equivalent of the unfamiliar in modern music. (See pages 150 and 179 for more on Braque.)

Plate 18 Pablo Picasso, Seated Bather (1930). The Museum of Modern Art, New York. Mrs. Simon Guggenheim Fund, [82.50]. Credit: © 2005 Estate of Pablo Picasso/Artists Rights Society (ARS), New York/Digital Image © The Museum of Modern Art/Licensed by SCALA/Art Resource, NY.

A prime example of Cubism. The figure is somewhat recognizable, but Picasso composed it out of geometric blocks. (See page 150 for more on Picasso.)

Plate 19 Salvador Dalí, *Invention of the Monsters* (1937). Art Institute of Chicago. Credit: Salvador Dalí, Spanish, 1904–1989, *Inventions of the Monsters,* 1937, oil on canvas, 51.2 x 78.4 cm, Joseph Winterbotham Collection, 1943.798 Reproduction, The Art Institute of Chicago. © 2008 Gala-Salvador Dali Foundation/Artists Rights Society (ARS), NY.

Freudian elements in a surrealist painting suggesting wicked thoughts and death longings repressed and filed away in the unconscious. (See page 154 for more on Dalí.)

Plate 20 (Left) African mask, Lega culture. Democratic Republic of the Congo. Credit: University of Iowa Museum of Art, Stanley Collection. (Right) Pablo Picasso, *Les Demoiselles d'Avignon*, June-July 1907. Credit: Acquired through the Lille P. Bliss Bequest, The Museum of Modern Art, New York, NY. Digital Image © The Museum of Modern Art/Licensed by SCALA/Art Resource, NY. © 1999 Estate of Pablo Picasso/Artists Rights Society (ARS), New York.

When you look at the mask and at Picasso's famous painting side by side, you can see a major influence on the development of the artist's work. (See page 150 for more on Picasso.)

Plate 21 Ogata Korin, *Azaleas* (late seventeenth century). Credit: The Hatakeyama Memorial Museum of Fine Art, Tokyo.

Korin's work exemplifies the simplicity of Japanese and Chinese art that so intrigued Western artists such as Georgia O'Keeffe. (See page 156 for more on Korin.)

Plate 22 Georgia O'Keeffe, *Purple Petunias* (1925). Credit: Collection of the Newark Museum, New Jersey. Bequest of Miss Cora Louise Hartshorn, 1958. [Inv.58.167]. Copyright © 2003 The Georgia O'Keeffe Foundation/Artists Rights Society [ARS], New York. Photo: Copyright The Newark Museum/Art Resource, NY.

Like the Japanese artist Korin, O'Keeffe simplified the natural world by focusing on the beauty of a single subject. (See page 156 for more on O'Keeffe.)

Plate 23 R.C.Gorman, *Navajo Dawn* (1989). Credit: R.C. Gorman's Navajo Gallery.

Gorman, an artist of the Southwest, who may have been influenced by O'Keeffe, simplifies this desert scene to a point of near abstraction. (See page 156 for more on Gorman.)

Plate 24 Maggie Taylor, *The Philosopher's Daughter* (2000). Credit: Courtesy of Maggie Taylor.

Computer art using images from scanners and cameras to create an entirely imagined scene. (See page 160 for more on Taylor.)

Plate 25 Andy Warhol, *Marilyn Monroe* (1962).
Credit: Phillips, The International Fine Art Auctioneers, UK.Copyright © 2003 Andy Warhol Foundation for the Visual Arts/Artists Rights Society [ARS], New York. TM 2002 Marilyn Monroe LLC by CMG Worldwide Inc. http://www.MarilynMonroe.com. Photo: Bridgeman Art Library.

Warhol's celebrity portraits, such as this one of the screen goddess Marilyn Monroe, suggest tacky movie magazines, but they are more than that. They make serious comments on our culture, Hollywood celebrities and their fans, and the individuals they depict. (See page 161 for more on Warhol.)

Plate 26 Sydney Opera House. Credit: © L. Clarke/Corbis.

Like many architectural works, the Sydney Opera House is meant to provide aesthetic pleasure as well as to fill citizens with pride. Now a favorite landmark, the opera house was not warmly embraced by all citizens when first completed in 1973. (See page 166 for more on the Sydney Opera house and other architectural achievements.)

Plate 27 Finale from *A Chorus Line* (1975). Credit: Everett Collection.

This photograph depicts the musical's famous finale, in which those driven and skilled enough to make the show's final cut lose their individuality and meld into " One," a chorus line. (See page 290 for more on *A Chorus Line* and other Broadway musicals.)

Plate 28 Scene from *The Godfather* (1973). Credit: Photofest, Inc.

A scene from the famous wedding sequence that opens Francis Ford Coppola's film. On the surface, *The Godfather* is an intimate exploration of honor, revenge, and betrayal in the Mafia. The film's deeper themes, however, point to the relationship of crime, power, and the American Dream. (See page 341 for more on *The Godfather*.)

Plate 29 Chagall, *Job in Despair.* Credit: Image courtesy of goldmarkart.com. © 2008 Estate of Marc Chagall, Artists Rights Society (ARS), NY.

The Book of Job faces one of the most challenging questions for religious writers: why do disasters befall the innocent? (See page 370 for more on *The Book of Job*.)

subjects. The young Goya proved he could do what the Dutch had done—well, almost. Though he was little known when he came to Madrid, the cultural center of Spain, he quickly became a star, gaining great favor among the aristocracy because of his talent for portraiture.

Then something happened he had not counted on: The lifestyle of Madrid's fashionable elite became unbearable to him. He was appalled by the greed, hypocrisy, and constant jockeying for social position, realizing that, if his success were to continue, he would have to race through life churning out portraits for the aristocracy. Fortunately for posterity, the demands of artistic integrity were too great for Goya. Instead of doing the hack work of a money-grubbing portrait painter, he wanted to paint what he *felt* about this society. He wanted to put his negative feelings on canvas, often in a style that mocked the pretentiousness of the lazy, unproductive, yet arrogant aristocracy. The negativity may have been partly influenced by a serious illness which left him totally deaf in 1792.

The artist became a thorough-going cynic, developing a hatred for privileged upper classes and the things they did to hold their power. His "portrait" of royalty, *The Family of Charles IV* (Color Plate 11), completed in 1800, is outrageously satiric in nature and intent. Instead of surface or psychological realism, it is something approaching caricature.

The family is shown standing in a gallery: the king, the queen, and the rest, of varying ages and sizes. In Rembrandtian style, there is light coming into the gallery from some undefined source beyond the canvas, just enough light to illuminate the faces. They are far from the idealization of royalty that artists were normally paid to create. The youngest children have bizarre, almost paranoid expressions. Perhaps for the very first time an artist captured the less-than-enviable lives of children who are not so much spoiled and pampered as enslaved to certain behaviors. The queen seems insensitive to them—and indeed, to just about everything. She is posing foolishly, as though she has a naive conception of what regal bearing is all about. The king is just as silly-looking, but there is also a trace of sadness in his face, a fleeting memory of happy times long ago? We know that the children will grow up to be like their parents.

The fact that the royal family must have been pleased with the portrait—after all, they did accept it and did not throw the artist out of the palace—remains one of the ironies of art history. Were the king and queen so vain or so blind to reality that they never noticed Goya's insulting approach? If so, then Goya was probably right in his assessment of the Madrid court. At any rate, his style became even darker, more pessimistic.

The invasion of Spain by Napoleon during the first decade of the nineteenth century did not help Goya's disposition. The ravages of war, the inhumanities human beings were capable of inflicting on each other, depressed him further. In two of his masterpieces, *The Second of May* and *The Third of May*, Goya used art to make an intense statement about social and political issues by dramatizing the theme of war's cruelty. In the latter work, reproduced here, we see the execution of several Spaniards by Napoleon's firing squad. The artist's focus is on the pleading looks in the faces of the condemned and frightened men. Nothing in the painting detracts from its bitter theme. Anger at the inhumanity of a species that once prided itself on its benevolence and rationality has usurped the desire for perfect likeness. The figures are recognizable as men, but the artist's powerful statement is what we remember. Notice, too, Goya's superb handling of chiaroscuro.

Anger has overcome realism in this famous work from the older, cynical Goya.
Source: Goya, *The Third of May*. Credit: A.K.G., Berlin/Superstock.

A modern perspective is that art by virtue of its activity is beautiful, no matter what the subject matter or technique.

Many of Goya's later works, especially *Saturn Devouring His Children* (Color Plate 12), completed when he was seventy-seven, seem downright unpleasant, if not hideous, to many viewers. They raise even now, as they surely did then, questions about the legitimacy of art that is intended to disturb, to externalize its creator's dismal view of existence—art that seems anything but aesthetic, and provokes feelings of outrage and horror.

Contemporary art that intentionally disturbs the viewer is so commonplace that many of Goya's descendants would regard as impertinent the question of whether art always has to be beautiful. Or they would contend that art by virtue of its artistry always *is* beautiful regardless of subject matter. If one of the criteria for determining that a given work should be labeled as "art" is that the artist has conquered a challenging medium, breaking through steel-like limitations, then Goya's astonishing feat of capturing humanity's elusive passions must be called beautiful.

Impressionism

While Goya opened the door for the intensely personal in art, realistic landscapes and portraits continued to be popular. Although in some countries there were rumblings among younger artists that the days of perfect likeness had run their course, in art meccas such as France and England, art had come to mean "the imitation of likeness in fine detail." Would-be artists were judged on how proficiently they abided by the rules. In Paris, particularly, new artists aspired to have their work exhibited at the annual Salon, a vast exhibition held at the Champs-Élysées Palace. The jurors who selected the works to be shown were by and large drawn from the ranks of so-called experts who had governed popular taste for decades. Paintings in unfamiliar styles were seldom welcome, and the few that slipped by were generally crucified by the critics.

One such regularly rejected artist was Édouard Manet (1832–1883), who was intent on painting in a style that was wholly his own, not following the strict guidelines established by the panel of experts who selected the pieces for Salon showing. Accustomed to rejection, Manet nonetheless went ahead, convinced that eventually his methods would be recognized as legitimate. In 1862 he submitted the work that is now acknowledged as an early masterpiece of the Impressionist movement but was at the time the subject of scorn and derision: *Le Déjeuner sur l'Herbe* (*Picnic on the Lawn*), which features three figures seated on grass: two well-dressed men and a nude woman (Color Plate 42).

Manet advanced a comprehensive rationale for a wholly new style. A painting, he said, should not imitate the superficial appearance of things. Nor should it be valued because it makes a statement. Instead, a painting should be an event, equal to nothing but itself, existing for itself—not for an issue and not as a souvenir of how someone looked. It should be an experience of color and light. The familiar world is the starting point for Manet, as it would be for many who followed in his footsteps, but it becomes a world transformed by some of the most brilliant colors ever applied to canvas, a world in which the outlines of human beings and natural shapes are softened, less boldly distinguished one from the other, but each playing an integral part in the total unity that is a subjective vision of the world at each moment.

Right now a moment of time is fleeting by! Capture its reality in paint! To do that we must put all else out of our minds. We must become the moment.

—**Paul Cézanne**

Those who were affected by Manet's rationale were also greatly influenced by the science of optics, which had originated during the Middle Ages in Islamic countries, notably Egypt, investigating the phenomenon of sight. The new artists wanted to go further than their Renaissance predecessors in the attempt to recreate true visual experience. They wanted to experiment with how color strikes the eye. Philosophers were beginning to ask questions like "Is color inherent in objects, or is it something that happens within the viewer?" Such questions parallel the traditional "Is beauty in the eye of the beholder?"

The artist, for example, sees a family enjoying a picnic by a lake and decides to paint the event. But what is seen and must therefore be duplicated on canvas is a rush of light falling upon the eye in various hues and shadings, blending in with each other, and with brightness blending in with shadows. Rembrandt and Leonardo had done wonders with the effect of light on their subjects, but their technique was a way of giving drama to those subjects. For the French artists, light *itself* should now be central to art: the colors of the world carried to the marveling eyes of an artist by the amazing phenomenon of light. It would be many years before physicists would discover that light was made up of tiny particles call photons, but Impressionism revolutionized art by instinctively perceiving that light wasn't just *there*: it was somehow a physical thing. Like all physical things, it affected each person differently.

The new style found its name in a haphazard manner. Claude Monet (1840–1926), whose name was often confused with that of Manet, had also been rejected for years by the experts, but he began to sell after many of his contemporaries, working in similar styles, gained recognition. Edmond Renoir, son of another Impressionist, Auguste Renoir, was in Monet's studio one day, browsing through some of Monet's new works, when he came upon an intriguing scene of

It is for the artist...in portrait painting to put on canvas something more than the face the model wears for that one day.
—James McNeill Whistler

fishing boats in the harbor at Le Havre. What attracted him was the vibrant color of sunrise flooding the canvas and the hazy indistinctness of the boats, the entire scene forming a subjective experience capturing a glorious moment in time. He asked Monet what he was going to title the painting. The artist merely shrugged and said, "Oh, you can just call it *Impression*." Renoir, thinking the work deserved a less generic label, wrote *Impression: Sunrise* (Color Plate 13). From then on, Monet and all of his close allies were identified (and not always with a positive connotation) as the *Impressionists.*

The Impressionist revolution in visual art fostered the careers of two major female artists of the nineteenth century: Berthe Morisot (1841–1895), Manet's sister-in-law, and the American Mary Cassatt (1845–1926). Morisot was the first woman admitted to the tight circle of French Impressionists, and her work, like theirs, shows an intense concern with the way light is seen. But, like Manet, she is also interested in creating true likenesses and remained throughout her life on the outer rim of the circle. In *The Psyche* (Color Plate 14), the figure of the woman dominates the work. Morisot takes great care to transfer to the canvas a faithful depiction of the woman and her reflection in the mirror. At the same time, muted light and shadow give the painting the soft glow characteristic of Impressionism. Morisot combines domestic realism with Impressionist techniques.

Though the artist is adroit at imitating likeness, the figures in this painting are part of the entire design.

Source: Mary Cassatt, American, 1844–1926. *The Childs Bath*, 1893, oil on canvas, 39½ × 26 in. Robert A. Waller Fund, 1910. 2. Photograph © 1999 The Art Institute of Chicago. All rights reserved.

Impressionism in America

Mary Cassatt was influenced by the Impressionist use of light and by the Impressionist philosophy that, in painting, content is subordinate to the artist's technique. Because of her affluence, she was instrumental in keeping the movement alive and gaining acceptance for it in the United States. Her father, a wealthy businessman of French ancestry, who recognized his daughter's artistic talent, sent her to the Pennsylvania Academy of Fine Art and, after graduation, to live in Paris. There the young woman met many of the important artists of the Impressionist movement and fell under their influence.

In the softness of its colors and its handling of light, her work, on the whole, is tied to that movement, but Cassatt had an agenda of her own. Unlike most of her French colleagues, she was more interested in domestic than in natural scenes as the starting point for a painting. The majority of her paintings focus on people—in particular, mothers and children in close, loving relationships. *The Bath*, shown here, depicts a mother bathing a young girl, and though love and tenderness are masterfully captured by the artist, the figures and their relationship form part of a total design and total effect. All of the details are equally important: the furniture in the background, the mother's dress, the towel wrapped around the child, the bowl of water, the pitcher, and finally, the rug. The Dutch portrait painters of the seventeenth century focused on reproducing an exact likeness of the subject's face. Cassatt is adroit at likeness, but the figures also form part of the entire design. In times past, the details in the room would have formed a visual framework for the subjects. They would have *accentuated* the subject. Here, the figures and their surroundings form a continuous flow of experience. In real life, all of us are linked to our surroundings in this way, but we seldom know it unless an Impressionist happens to be standing by.

For *The Bath*, Cassatt paints from a vantage point above the scene, instead of directly in front of it. Perhaps her wish is to disengage the viewer from the normal way of seeing. She forces viewers to look with their right brains (the right brain sees things as they are, without interpretation, while the left brain sees selectively, processing and making sense out of what is seen). From this elevated perspective all of the objects in the scene acquire a visual meaningfulness they might not have in direct head-on observation, which is the normal way of visually connecting with our world. Since most people see selectively, head-on observation tends to invite abstracting—*really* seeing what seems most important—in this case, only the human figures.

The title of the work, *The Bath*, does not indicate whether the woman is the mother or the maid, nor does it prompt us to ask: "What is the artist trying to communicate about these people?" The appropriate questions are: "What happens on the canvas?" and "What is the effect, and how does the artist achieve it?"

Cassatt's *Mother and Child against a Green Background* (Color Plate 15) spells out the relationship in the title, and here the vantage point is direct. But the title also includes the word "background," the color of which seems to matter more than any specific details. This particular piece shows the French influence on Cassatt: the figures flow into streams of color and light. At the same time, the mother-child relationship is clearly evident, a signature characteristic of Cassatt's work.

For us artists there waits the joyous compromise through art with all that wounded us in daily life.

—**Lawrence Durrell**

Another American exponent of Impressionism was James McNeill Whistler (1834–1903), who painted the famous portrait of his mother in 1871. Though the work is universally admired for the subject matter, and though reproductions have sold in the millions, many are unaware that the painting is NOT called "Whistler's Mother" but *Arrangement in Black and Gray*, and the title indicates the artist's purpose. Whistler uses his mother as a woman in a particular moment of time, in a complex of light and shadow which evokes feelings that cannot be quite named. The way she sits, the expression on her face, the folds of her garment—all come together as a total visual experience that says more than "This is my mother." In fact, the portrait, in which the subject is sitting sideways instead of facing forward, is a reminder that Impressionism seeks to imitate visual consciousness, not to abstract from an event a meaning such as "motherhood."

Not just a portrait of Whistler's mother, but a unified duplication of a total visual design in which the seated woman is just a component.

Source: Musée d'Orsay, Paris, France. Credit: Reunion des Musees Nationaux/Art Resource, NY.

Post-Impressionism

The Impressionist movement took hold so strongly on both sides of the Atlantic that it eventually became as authoritative as the traditions it replaced. Newer artists emerged who began to resist slavish imitation and go their own ways. The label **post-impressionism** has been coined by art historians as a convenient way to refer to the work of the artists who came after the heyday of Impressionism and whose work, though influenced by it, does not clearly belong to the earlier school. Of this group, Vincent van Gogh (1853–1890) was surely the most original and the most intense. He differs from the Impressionists in a major respect. He had no real theory of art. He simply loved color, especially yellow. He had no interest in consulting the science of optics so that he could accurately imitate the experience of seeing. For him, imitating the bright colors of the world was his way of expressing the uninhibited feelings of pleasure they aroused in him. And if he were painting a scene that had less yellow than he liked, he would splash yellow onto the canvas without restraint. No one gives us as much yellow in a starry night as van Gogh does.

Van Gogh is the prototype of the artist who creates entirely for himself. His style was so strange in its time that the few critics who ever took notice of his work were generally baffled, having nothing with which to compare it. If his devoted brother Theo had not handled most of his expenses, chances are he would have been hungry and homeless most of the time. But Theo believed in his genius and stood by him even when his paintings were denounced and ridiculed. Only one of the artist's paintings was sold during his lifetime. Tragically, he committed suicide before he reached the age of thirty-eight.

Van Gogh's life reinforces the romantic concept of the starving artist for whom art is the last outpost of being. Totally alienated, totally misunderstood by almost everyone except his brother, rejected twice as a suitor (once with a vehement cry of "No, never, never!"), hovering much of the time on the thin borderline between functional rationality and insanity (eventually to cross the border, never to return), he survived as long as he did only because of an often childlike delight in his private way of seeing and imitating the world. What obligation did the artist feel to communicate with an everyday world through which he passed as a stranger?

Flowers bursting with energy against a background of van Gogh's favorite color.

Source: Vincent van Gogh, *Sunflowers*. Credit: Art Resource, NY.

Works such as *Sunflowers, The Potato Eaters*, and *The Starry Night* (Color Plate 16) have become priceless since van Gogh's death. (His work can bring $30 million or more.) These and his many other paintings show a brushstroke method that has become utterly identified with its creator: a short, stabbing technique, as opposed to a flowing line, that makes the entire canvas seem to be throbbing with energy. Despite the indifference of the art world, van Gogh abandoned himself to the sensuous impact of life's forms and colors, absorbing them fully and converting them into a heightened reality—an explosion of pure feeling transferred to color, shapes, and paint textures. Van Gogh's lines and bright colors virtually scream from the canvas.

Van Gogh, unappreciated in his lifetime, nonetheless continued to paint in the style that must have seemed the true expression of his inner being. As we move into our own time, we find less innocence and more conscious, calculated insistence from artists that they be granted license to express themselves in any way they deem fit, to use any medium that suits their purpose, and to be recognized on their own ground. Van Gogh in retrospect is seen to have defied tradition, but he did not do so loudly and rebelliously or with a planned rationale. The twentieth century of the visual arts is one of "artist's rights," a worldwide movement that sometimes has met with bewilderment, confusion, critical scorn, critical praise, even angry denunciation from hostile governments and censors—but also much cheering on the part of humanists who believe that the artist is an endangered species, to be treasured and supported at all costs.

Art as Alteration

Neither van Gogh nor the Impressionists rendered perfect likenesses, nor were they trying to. Unlike Rembrandt, who even with his psychological probing felt responsible to imitate a world the viewer would recognize, they were compelled to transfer to canvas the world as *they* saw it. They never denied that their subjects were themselves, their subjective experience of color and form. Even so, their work does not represent so startling a departure that we cannot recognize on their canvases any trace of the familiar world. What we see is that world drastically changed. Looking at van Gogh's *The Starry Night*, we *still* recognize a sky. At the same time, his work is moving in the direction of what has come to be called **modernism**. Many schools, movements, and techniques dating from about the last quarter of the nineteenth century to roughly the last quarter of the twentieth century have been linked by critics and art historians under that broad term. The style of the literature and visual arts from the late twentieth century to the present is often called **postmodernism**. What unifies modern and postmodern artists and makes them different from, say, van Gogh is *intention*.

Art comes to you proposing frankly to give nothing but the highest quality to your moments as they pass.

—**Walter Pater**

Both van Gogh and the Impressionists start with the familiar world and then paint it as they wish. They give us the familiar world as altered by the emotions and the subjective experiences of light, color, and form. But when we speak of the later art as **alteration**, we are speaking of artists *who do not even start with the familiar world*. They want to impose something new on that world, some secret part of themselves. With such an intent, they have no reason to be bound by an artistic tradition unless it suits their personality, unless it can be adapted to their imagination.

Entering the world of modern art can be confusing at first. There may seem to be no rationale at all, no clear overall purpose, no rules. All of this is at least partially true. Rationales, if they are expressed at all, belong to the individual artist, who may deny having any purpose other than to do something on canvas or in stone. When Marcel Duchamp bought a urinal and submitted it, untouched, for an exhibition in 1917, he challenged all definitions of art. Critics of such **found art** ask: "How much work does an artist have to do? What is off-limits for an artist?" Modern artists impose their own rules upon their own work. They may even be the least forgiving of their critics. After all, they are out there creating new traditions, and most of the time they feel alone. Small wonder that they sometimes, like Duchamp, develop a sense of humor.

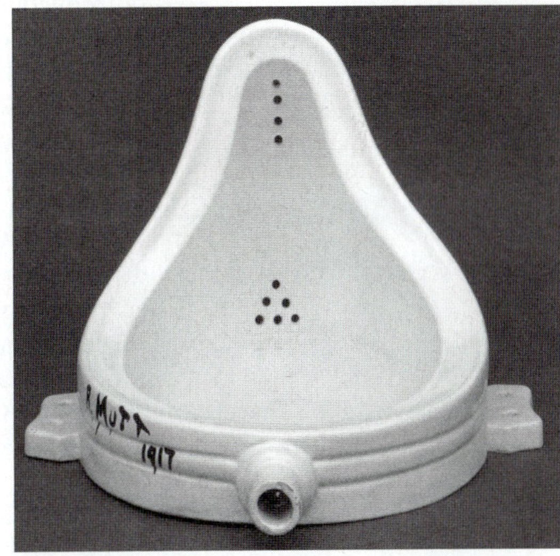

Famous urinal submitted in 1917 to an exhibition sponsored by the American Society of Independent Artists. The artist did not sign his own name but one that closely resembled that of the manufacturer.

Source: Marcel Duchamp, *Fountain*. Credit: © 2005 Artists Rights Society (ARS), New York/ADAGP, Paris/Succession Marcel Duchamp. Tate Gallery, London/Art Resource, NY.

Some modern art—in fact, a good deal of it—does in fact resemble people, places, and things. But that is usually where its traditionalism ends. Francis Bacon (1909–1992), for example, offers canvases with recognizable reality, but that reality might be somebody sitting on the toilet, or a slab of meat bleeding. You know what it *represents*, but you may ask: "Why would anybody want to paint *that*?" The gap between the artist's need for freedom of expression and the public's ideas about proper subjects for art will be further discussed in Chapter 15.

The Sixty-ninth Regiment Armory Show, 1913

Some people want to know when modern art actually began. Are we talking about last week or a hundred years ago? Assigning approximate dates also depends on geography. New stirrings in the art world were happening in Europe before the dawn of the twentieth century, long before word reached this side of the Atlantic, much in the same way that the Renaissance was happening in Florence long before it traveled to northern Europe.

Modern art made its way to the United States at the tail end of the *Gilded Age*, a name given to the last two decades of the nineteenth century. Some Americans who had made their fortunes in railroads, coal, or steel, for example, were becoming intensely art conscious. This was the time of elaborate mansions, incredibly luxurious ocean voyages, and the accumulation of what became priceless art collections. New York in particular had a burning need to be respected as a hub of modernism in art. It wanted to see all that was new and exciting. It had already opened its arms to the Impressionists, long before they were fully respected in Europe.

The true function of art is to edit nature and so make it coherent and lovely. The artist is an impassioned proofreader.

—**H. L. Mencken**

In 1913, the Sixty-ninth Regiment Armory in Manhattan was the site of an exhibition of new works by European artists that is still considered the most important single art show ever held in this country. Many American viewers saw for the first time the startling paintings of van Gogh, as well as the work of other artists whose styles seemed downright puzzling, if not laughable.

One of these artists was Wassily Kandinsky (1866–1944), whom we mentioned at the beginning of this chapter and whose work provides an excellent introduction to modern art. Though as a young artist he achieved technical competence in drawing the human figure, he set his eyes on other goals. Kandinsky came to believe that what mattered in a work of art was *form*: a pleasing arrangement of lines and color, existing for no purpose other than aesthetic experience. In other words, a painting should provide an experience of the beautiful. Kandinsky delved into his imagination, found a new world of pure shapes and forms, and imitated those in a style that came to be known as **abstract art**. However, "What's that supposed to be?" is often the first question viewers ask. (Remember the two viewers who turned a Kandinsky into two light bulbs.)

Having abandoned the study of law for that of art, the young Kandinsky came under the heavy influence of van Gogh and his friend Paul Gauguin (1848–1903), who had made his reputation by painting the lush vegetation and exotic natives of Tahiti. But Gauguin unknowingly took some steps toward abstractionism in that his work presents a few key shapes in bold outline and bold colors (with no pretense at an illusion of depth in them) while eliminating minute, realistic details. When van Gogh turns the familiar world into throbbing symphonies of bold brush strokes and riots of color, his work also leans more toward the abstract than the real. Both of these artists seemed to belong with Kandinsky in the Armory show.

Like many other modern artists, Kandinsky distinguished between beauty and anything else one might see in a painting such as his *Black Lines*: "He argued that in order to speak directly to the soul and avoid materialistic distractions, it was preferable to use an art based solely on the language of color. Free from references to a specific reality, color could become like music, beautiful for its interrelationships of tones and intensities."[3]

Kandinsky's rationale made perfect sense to him, as well as to other exhibited artists, but not to all of the art critics and potential collectors who came to the Armory show in droves, hoping to pick up some real bargains. In fact, not much of the show was received with open arms by either critics or public. The shock of so much alteration was simply too devastating, confined as it was to one building. Canvases by Picasso, who would become the century's most celebrated artist, were widely denounced. The room in which they were displayed was nicknamed the Chamber of Horrors.

The work that caused the biggest uproar and controversy, however, bringing instant notoriety to its creator, was Duchamp's *Nude Descending a Staircase*. One critic called him "the biggest transgressor" in modern art. Duchamp could not have expected to be warmly welcomed after a newspaper published his observation that "the only works of art America has given are her plumbing and her bridges."

For this painting Duchamp had developed his own brand of abstractionism by which he moved from an actual model through successive stages of reduction until all that was left from reality was the sense of descending movement and the hint of a human figure. Duchamp, in other words, abstracted from a real scene only those elements that interested him as an artist, excluding everything else because he had signed away his responsibility and obligation to make his work resemble something a viewer could instantly recognize. The controversy might have been less heated had the painting's title not promised disappointed viewers an interesting reality that was virtually invisible. Abstract art remains a popular form of expression among contemporary artists. Sometimes we can gain subject matter clues from the title, but more often the artist will be altogether casual and call the painting or sculpture *Study*, or *Untitled*, or *Line and Color*.

Piet Mondrian (1872–1944), a Dutch artist who helped establish abstractionism, was already at the peak of his career at the time of the Armory show. His work departs from reality much more radically than does Duchamp's. In it there is not even the suggestion of the familiar world. *Composition*, with its characteristically bland title, is a painting of austere and absolute simplicity in which all dynamic motion is absent; colors, shapes, and lines sit serenely in geometric relationships that defy all need to interpret them. Mondrian can be called a

Art Movements and Styles

Cubism — movement in modern art, epitomized by Picasso, in which the artist breaks down the field of vision into discontinuous segments or in which the artist shows a number of visual events taking place simultaneously (as in *Guernica*).

Dutch school — group of painters producing intensely realistic art, centered in Holland during the seventeenth century, with Rembrandt the outstanding example.

Impressionism — mid-nineteenth-century art movement wherein the attempt to be realistic is abandoned, and instead, the artist projects onto the canvas a subjective experience of the world as color and light. In Impressionist art, forms tend to be less sharply divided from each other than they are in, say, landscape painting.

Gothic — an architectural style of the late Middle Ages, featuring high pointed spires and pointed arches; label coined by a critic of the style who called it barbaric "like the Goths who destroyed the Roman Empire."

performance art — art as an event that generally exists only for the time it takes for the presentation or installation. The wrapped buildings, surrounded islands, and other installations of Christo may be kept for longer periods of time, but not indefinitely.

Pop Art — style of mid-twentieth-century art influenced by comic books, movies, television commercials, and billboard advertising; can be just plain fun or satiric.

post-impressionism — broad term used by art historians for art of the late nineteenth and early twentieth centuries that resembles but is not strict Impressionism; it is neither realistic nor abstract. The work of van Gogh belongs to this category.

superrealism — modern style made famous by sculptures of Duane Hanson that are so lifelike they seem about to move; this art form also can make biting social commentary.

surrealism — modern style associated with work of Salvador Dalí, among others, in which recognizable objects are put together in bizarre contexts that seem like visualizations of dreams.

"classic abstractionist" in that his beautifully ordered designs are meant to evoke the same sort of serenity found in classical art.

Cubism: Picasso and Braque

The enduring fame of the Armory show owes much to its having introduced America to the work of the most baffling, the most controversial, yet easily the most innovative of all modern artists. His work, displayed in the "Chamber of Horrors," drew thousands who came to laugh, but many came away in admiration. He exercised more influence on a whole century of artists than any other we can think of, and he transcended his age so completely that some art historians rank him among the three or four greatest artists of all time.

Pablo Picasso (1881–1973) lived the entire length of the modernist movement in art. Anyone seeing only his work and none by his contemporaries would nonetheless know what modernism is all about. In his youth, he came under the heavy influence of the Impressionists and their decision that, with the emergence of photography, imitative realism was dead. During the incredible span of his artistic existence, he worked steadily and impeccably in more modern styles than any other artist of his time. Classically trained, he could bring to the canvas a lifelike portrait, but he could also duplicate subjective visual experience, or create a wholly new style that was neither realistic nor abstract (in the sense that Mondrian and Kandinsky are abstract) but derived from yet another way of seeing the world. This style, which Picasso invented with strong help from a fellow artist named Georges Braque, was **Cubism.**

Painting isn't an aesthetic operation; it's a form of magic designed as a mediator between this strange hostile world and us; a way of seizing the power by giving form to our terrors as well as our desires.
—Pablo Picasso

Picasso, whose father taught painting, grew up surrounded by art. He was just nineteen when he visited Paris for the first time and there saw and marveled at the colors of the Impressionists. He was particularly drawn to the color blue (as van Gogh was to yellow) and quickly developed extraordinary skill at both imitation and alteration by painting mostly indigent types—such as prostitutes and homeless wanderers—all in distinctly blue tones.

From the outset, Picasso wanted to show more than a "mere" talent for perfect likeness, which he possessed in abundance. As he intended to mark the world with the stamp of his unique genius, so too did Picasso want to alter its reality. And indeed he did, working not only on two-dimensional flat surfaces but in sculpture, architecture, and scenic design for the theater. (He also wrote poems and plays in his spare time!)

His joy in using colors has something of the child about it, the child who refuses to grow up; as a matter of fact, as he aged, he was fond of advising young artists to do everything possible to avoid growing up. Retain your childlike delight in all things, he would say. Don't be suffocated by the adult world of rules and regulations, of schedules and timelines, to the point where you stop hearing the voice of your intuition, where you stop feeling the compulsion to try new things that will shock the society of dull, convention-bound folk.

The child in Picasso led him into an obsession with the circus, where—still in his twenties—he embarked on a new period dominated by pink, orange, yellow, and gray and did portraits of clowns, trapeze artists, and other performers—portraits lifelike enough to be recognizable, but beginning to show the distortions of real forms that would characterize most of his mature work.

At an exhibition of African masks in Paris, he became excited by their colors and distortions of the human face. The influence of these masks was overpowering and immediate, leading him to his first major triumph, *Les Demoiselles d'Avignon* (1907), a portrait of five young women in which features and body parts form a geometric design. Early viewers found the painting startling if not amusing, because while pure geometric design might have been a *little* acceptable, designs made from figures that were *supposed* to look like people would have been not only radical but smile provoking (Color Plate 20).

Art is meant to disturb. Science reassures.

—**Georges Braque**

Picasso, in fact, began his career showing intense interest in the art of portraiture. Despite the innovative techniques of the Impressionists and post-impressionists, the assumption still held that making a living as an artist required big commissions from patrons who wanted their likenesses to survive them. At the same time the new discipline known as psychology was making its presence felt, though many refused to call it a science. Picasso was fascinated by descriptions of the unconscious mind and the often huge difference between what people looked like on the outside and what they were really like on the inside. So even when he worked on portraits, distortions began to invade his canvas—sometimes close to caricature. In this he was a descendant of his countryman, Goya. As his new style evolved, his distortions turned into a total revision of reality, while he and Georges Braque created the theory behind Cubism.

Braque (1882–1963), a year younger than Picasso, saw *Les Demoiselles* in its initial showing and admitted that it changed his life and his artistic plans for the future. He made it his business to meet the genius who had opened his eyes to a wholly new way not only of painting but of *seeing*. Acting on advice from his "older" mentor, Braque began working in a new style. He would look at a scene that appealed to him for some reason, then leave it, allowing himself to forget

Supreme example of Cubism, turning the bombing victims into fragmentary and horrifying images of atrocities.

Source: Pablo Picasso, *Guernica*. Credit: © 1999 Estate of Pablo Picasso/Artists Rights Society (ARS), New York.

the realistic details until he was ready to *deconstruct* it in his memory and then *reconstruct* it on the canvas as geometric blocks in bold, unshaded colors. He did a series of landscapes in this style, causing one critic to complain that Braque had taken beautiful subjects and reduced them "to cubes." After the critical article appeared, the label *Cubism* was applied to the work of both Braque and Picasso. In 1909 the two artists formed a close association and consciously devised a Cubism movement, providing for it a clearly articulated rationale.

In thinking critically about their art, the two friends discovered that nobody ever really sees an object or a figure. Rather, what is seen is an event extending over a period of time, no matter how rapidly. The eye, moreover, is in continual motion and observes from continually shifting viewpoints. From where we sit or stand, we *think* we are looking from a particular and fixed vantage point. Both realistic paintings and photographs foster the misconception that such a thing exists as an observer with a stable field of vision. Our language suggests that we see reality, but in truth what we really see is fragments, reassembled by the mind.

Looking at Braque's *The Musician* (1917) (Color Plate 17), we would need to know the title of the painting to have a clue as to the artist's subject. We can make out what looks vaguely like a hand holding a cigarette, and across from it a shape that suggests a musical instrument.

The cubist wished to present the total reality of forms in space, and since objects appear not only as they are seen from one viewpoint at a time, it became necessary to introduce multiple angles of vision and simultaneous presentation of discontinuous planes. This of course shatters the old continuity of composition imposed by the Renaissance single viewpoint.

—**Helen Gardner**

Picasso and Braque did not turn away from realism just to be rebels; they believed **realism**—that is, art as likeness—could not show the world as it is. The world is made up of shapes and colors that swirl before our consciousness as if seen in a kaleidoscope, and if we could slow down our vision, the world would actually look like one of their paintings. We would see pieces of things and pieces of people (as in Picasso's *Seated Bather*, Color Plate 18).

In 1937 Picasso was invited to do a large mural for the Spanish Pavilion at the Paris World's Fair. Instead of choosing a visual event and breaking it into geometric shapes in his customary style, which was based on an intellectual theory of vision and was on the whole non-emotional, the artist used his style to make an impassioned statement against war. *Guernica* (page 151) is now considered not only Picasso's masterpiece but one of the great artworks of all time. Among other things, it silenced critics who were saying that modern artists were too wrapped up in their technique and their innovations to pay attention to what was happening in the world.

With Cubism, Picasso was able to deliver a message with one swift visual impact, a message that required thousands of words from reporters and innumerable pictures from photographers. The mural describes an event that caused worldwide revulsion: the German air force's infamous saturation bombing of Guernica, the cultural center of the Basque region in northern Spain and a stronghold of the Republican Army fighting against insurgent forces, who would ultimately win the Spanish Civil War. Francisco Franco, leader of the antigovernment army, had appealed to both Germany and Italy for support. The United States backed the Republican government that had been duly elected, while Hitler sided with Franco. The bombing of Guernica was also a way for Germany to demonstrate its military strength to the world.

The bombing took place on April 26, 1937, and numbered among its casualties not only hundreds of Republican soldiers but 2,500 civilians, including hundreds of children. Newspapers around the world published graphic images of the dead. Picasso, who had been undecided about whether he wanted to do a mural for the Spanish Pavilion, saw the pictures and was so moved that he rushed home and immediately began sketching out what would become his masterpiece.

When it was unveiled at the World's Fair, *Guernica* received nearly unanimous critical acclaim and established Picasso's supremacy among living artists. There were, of course, detractors. The Marxist government in Russia said that only realistic art could bring about significant social change, and the Nazi regime, as expected, denounced it as "degenerate art" (discussed in Chapter 15).

Without Cubism, a style that can present simultaneously things that happen over a period of time, how could an artist have captured such a scene of total devastation? Few artists have attempted anything of the scope Picasso was able to achieve, for most paintings are essentially static, freezing a single moment in time. What Cubism does in *Guernica* is to place on a two-dimensional plane the dynamic motion generally found only in films.

Like a true masterpiece, *Guernica* continues to be frighteningly relevant. Wars like those in Vietnam and Iraq, which also scarred national and world consciousness, come to mind whenever one looks closely at Picasso's mural. It is not a historical record of an event long past, but a living conscience. As such, it continues to generate profound emotional responses. The United Nations headquarters in Manhattan has on display a tapestry reproduction of the mural. When in 2003 Colin Powell, then the U.S. secretary of state, addressed the UN Security Council to advocate military action against Iraq, the tapestry, which would have been in full view, was covered.

Picasso's work became simpler in his later years, reflecting a childlike innocence that makes as strong a statement in its own way as *Guernica* does. This is a statement of hope for the future in a world tamed by peace and love, a statement that will be needed as long as the horrors of a Guernica repeat themselves. The artist painted childlike doves on the ceiling of a tiny chapel in the southern French town of Valauris, near his home in Nice. With his friend and neighbor Henri Matisse, he developed **collage** into an art form, spending hundreds of hours cutting out tiny designs and pasting them onto large and colorful backgrounds. The ninety-year-old Picasso was not "losing it"—as has been suggested by a few cynics—but was showing that he had managed to do what few of us can: he had kept alive the child inside him. The art of being human needs the spirit of children.

Unreal Realism

One reason for any artist's huge critical reputation is the degree to which the work influences other artists. Future artists viewed Picasso as a revolutionary leader, encouraging others to follow their own bent, regardless of how the public might react. In this section we look at the work of several other modern artists who carry banners of revolution, however different each flag may be.

Surrealism, a popular style during the first half of the twentieth century, employs recognizable shapes and forms put together in unrecognizable contexts. The best way to define it is to say that it claims to imitate the world of dreams and the unconscious mind. It owes much to the psychological studies of Freud and Jung. Their explorations into the strange regions below consciousness excited visual artists, writers, and philosophers. Inner space was proving to be just as fascinating as recent discoveries regarding the physical universe.

Dalì question: was the artist painting from a deeply disordered mind or giving the public the Freudian subjects it wanted?

The surrealists wanted to imitate the geography of inner space, to make the unconscious mind a tangible part of the external world. At least this was the stated purpose of the movement, the major exponent of which was the Spanish painter Salvador Dalí (1904–1989). Unlike Picasso, who gives us fragments of things, Dalí creates a dream world made up of recognizable images that do not fit rationally together.

Dalí became as famous for his neurotic behavior as for the bizarre world of his canvas. His paintings are objects of fascination for psychiatrists and art critics who interpret an artist's work in terms of psychological disorders. Some cite the artist's maladjusted childhood as responsible for both his behavior and his art. Some call him as mad an artist as ever lived, but add that madness is often the price of genius. This observation may well be made of van Gogh, and future generations of critics may confirm that it applies to Dalí. Yet many will argue that surrealism as practiced by Dalí was a highly commercial, carefully calculated artistic oddity, designed from the outset to capitalize on the popularity of Freud, to make the artist a center of widely publicized controversy, and thus to increase the price of his paintings.

If nothing else, we can say that there is little subtlety in Dalí's style, which is sometimes so obviously Freudian that students of Psychology 101 would have no trouble with it. Dalí seems especially obsessed with the popular Freudian belief that many of our actions are a result of two drives: the constant need for sex, which we are forced to hide, and the death wish, which comes from the pain of our neuroses. A good example is his *Inventions of the Monsters* (Color Plate 19), with its naked upper torso, its disembodied bare buttocks, and its skeletal death figures, all suggesting wicked thoughts and death longings that have been repressed and filed away, thus rekindling the neuroses which caused the misery in the first place.

Was Dalí lost in the maze of the subconscious—or was he giving the public what it wanted?

Source: Salvador Dalí. (Spanish, 1904–1989). *The Persistence of Memory*. 1931. Oil on canvas, 9½ × 13" (24.1 × 33 cm). The Museum of Modern Art, New York. Given anonymously.

Dalí's most famous work is *The Persistence of Memory* (1931), a completely Freudian title. It shows a tree branch over which hangs a wristwatch distorted because it is made of a soft, rubbery material. Another rubbery watch hangs limply from a table on which rests a pocket watch that is not rubbery. Yet another limp watch is draped over what ought to be, but is not, a wrist. Those who insist on a Freudian interpretation, as Dalí perhaps hoped they would, may recognize the limp watches as symbols of unresponsive male sex organs, and the non-distorted pocket watch as a symbol of a happier sexual past. Was the artist forced to hide his sexual attitudes? Or was he deliberately giving his public the controversy he thought it wanted?

Even if we grant the possibility that Dalí was giving the public what it wanted—*shock*—and doing it for the money, we still have to ask ourselves where his strange images, figures, and landscapes *came* from if not from his innermost self. And granting that they are emanations from the artist's true unconscious, do they make us aware of anything except the artist's suppressed self? Do they adorn the world with a new kind of beauty?

The paintings of Georgia O'Keeffe (1887–1986) present another form of unreal realism: likeness that is also abstraction. The artist appears to have worked from deep impulses inside her which led her to reinterpret the familiar world. When asked what she was intending to show in her paintings, she answered, "Do you think I know what art is?" Nor was she one bit apologetic. She added, "Do you think I'd care what anybody thought?" Her attitude typifies that of the modern artist insisting on the right to follow the demands of intuition. She maintained resolutely that all art can be analyzed only in terms of what is happening on the canvas, of what the artist is *doing*, not saying.

Where I was born, and where and how I lived is unimportant. It is what I have done and where I have been that should be of interest.

—Georgia O'Keeffe

What O'Keeffe *does*, then, is usually to imitate one or two striking and colorful forms in the familiar world and transfer them to canvas with many details left out. O'Keeffe sees the world not as the Cubists did—broken down into geometric shapes—but as a place in which certain shapes leap out at the artist for whatever reason: the colors, the aesthetic appeal of the form itself, the textures, or as some critics have said, the unconscious significance to the artist of the form—what it *looks* like or *suggests*.

It has been said that O'Keeffe, like many other women conditioned in youth to be proper Victorian wives, was obsessed with sex and often turned real shapes into sexual organs—somewhat akin to Dalí, except that O'Keeffe's images are not placed together in bizarre contexts. She is neither a realist—though she works from real things—nor an abstractionist—though she simplifies reality. She is her own style.

In 1905, eighteen years of age, O'Keeffe left her home in Sun Prairie, Wisconsin, to study at the famous Art Institute of Chicago. Like other young artists at the turn of a new century, she was brimming with exciting ideas about what constitutes art and what an artist has the right to do. Today young people from a later generation of artists may be standing exactly where O'Keeffe stood. Perhaps one or two of them will be thinking it is time to rebel against "traditionalists" like O'Keeffe.

"She brought to the big city her love for simple shapes and extremely bright colors," one biographer notes; "she recalls seeing light on a red, white, and black patterned quilt before she could walk, and, as a toddler, the soft, smooth shapes made by buggy wheels in the dust—they looked good enough to eat!"[4] When she was twenty, O'Keeffe moved to New York. There she met the most fashionable artists of the day, whose work was shown in the studio of photographer Alfred Stieglitz, whom she was eventually to marry. But Stieglitz and his sophisticated circle were not able to influence the maturing artist as much as did the simplicity and sensuous beauty of Asian art.

In Asian art O'Keeffe found a style she could immediately understand, respond to, and imitate. The simplicity of a painting such as *Azaleas* (Color Plate 21) by the Japanese artist Ogata Korin (1658–1716) appealed to her love of color and shapes that convey an instantaneous image. Asian influence is clearly evident in *Purple Petunias* (Color Plate 22). Later, when her aesthetic and emotional differences with Stieglitz made their marriage seem less idyllic than it had once been, O'Keeffe moved to New Mexico, a land of bright color and bold shape. In the undulating hills, the orange craggy rocks, the snow-tipped mountains, and the exotic flowers, she found a constant visual stimulation she had never experienced in drab (by comparison) New York.

Her most famous works date from after this move, as she developed her unique style: flowers bursting from their stems; mountains, canyons, the infinite sky with its continually changing colors; the bleached skull of a dead animal. All of these forms she transferred to canvases that were first painted stark white so that the electric colors and the proud shapes would stand out in sharp relief. As colorful as the Southwest surely is, O'Keeffe altered the landscape, giving it an electric vibrancy, giving as much as she took from this land, something all artists claim the right to do.

Pronounced though the Asian influence is on her work, it is hard to imagine that O'Keeffe could have been indifferent to the Native American art of the Southwest, especially that of the most famous Navajo artist, R. C. Gorman (b.1931). He is more interested in depicting human figures than O'Keeffe is, but his work is like hers in its simplicity. Navajo women were among his favorite subjects. If you look at his *Navajo Dawn* (Color Plate 23), you will see the recognizable form of a woman, but the desert scene in which she is placed is simplified to a point of near abstraction. Except for the mountains in the background, the landscape is stark save for one small flowering plant. Gorman's strength is his colors: the dark and light shades of sky and the superb chiaroscuro effect in the handling of the mountains. This is clearly a landscape and a treatment of it that O'Keeffe would have appreciated.

Another contemporary of O'Keeffe and exponent of a simplified realism that leaves out unimportant details was Edward Hopper (1882–1967), who emerged out of the Great Depression of the 1930s. Hopper, like so many artists and writers, could not help being touched by the belief among American artists that art should not only appeal to the aesthetic sense but be a strong social commentary as well.

Hopper's forms come from the streets of urban America and the forlorn, despairing souls who walk them: the homeless, the abandoned, the chronic poor, the newly poor, the alienated drifters who move from one place to another, seeking not only decent jobs but meaningful communication with someone else, and people who we suspect came from good backgrounds and now find themselves displaced. Among his lonely, unhappy Americans are the three hunched figures sitting in a late-night diner in one of his best known paintings: *Nighthawks* (see page 449, Chapter 12).

Running through most of his works are the common threads of alienation, despair, and the faint rays of hope perhaps misplaced, stamping him as an artist through whose eyes we experience a sense of the Great Depression. In a few bold details Hopper shows us what American writers have devoted hundreds of pages to describing: American loneliness. Hopper does not give us a perfect likeness of a diner in *Nighthawks*, but the few figures are all he needs to tell his sad stories.

While Dalí, O'Keeffe, and Hopper were honing their craft, a young African American artist named Aaron Douglas (1899–1988) was traveling from Kansas

City for a stopover in New York before heading to Paris. During the 1920s and 1930s the French capital was a magnet, luring artists from every country in the world and with every imaginable style. Ever since the heyday of Impressionism it was recognized as *the* place to be for those intending to make a name for themselves in the art world. However, the stopover took far longer than he expected, for while Douglas was in New York, he discovered Harlem.

Chapter 4 described the achievements of Charles S. Johnson and others who created the Harlem Renaissance and insisted that white America listen to artistic voices that had gone unheeded for too long. Johnson's group was also to discover the electric talent of Douglas and draft him for the Harlem movement.

Douglas, born in Kansas of middle-class stock, and a visual arts graduate of the University of Nebraska, at first lacked a sense of connection to African roots. The eventual discovery of an African heritage made a deep impression on a young artist looking for a style and a statement. What Douglas responded to in Africa was something he had not found in the quiet, uneventful life of midwestern America: a sense of being able to express emotion without restraint, whether it was joy and exaltation or bitterness and sorrow. All around him Harlem voices were giving vent to their feelings in poetry, jazz, dance, and drama. Some were seeking an appropriate visual arts language and encouraged Douglas to join them.

Aaron Douglas created his own style, aiming to go beyond the mere appearance of things.

Source: General Research & Reference Division Schomburg Center for Research in Black Culture, The New York Public Library, Astor, Lenox and Tilden Foundations.

Douglas knew he wanted to go beyond art as strict likeness, but he hadn't an idea of *where* he wanted to go—and why. In Harlem and Cubism he found that idea. Douglas liked the fact that Cubist paintings forced the viewer to reconsider how reality was viewed. He also knew that he did not agree with those African American leaders who urged artists and writers to use their talents to make protest statements. He believed passionately that African American art should be its own movement and stand on its own merit. It too could show the world a new way to see.

The art of ancient Egypt gave Douglas his first encounter with Africa. What both shocked and excited him was that ancient Egyptian artists stylized the human figure in a way that he knew Picasso would understand. In the pen-and-ink drawing *Invincible Music, the Spirit of Africa*, an illustration for the February 1926 issue of *Crisis* magazine, an African drummer expresses himself ecstatically; but the figure is drawn in what Douglas called "Egyptian form." The right eye is unnaturally shown in its entirety, not the way it would be seen in real life. In fact, there is far too much of the man's face for the position of the body, while the left hand is disproportionately larger than the right. Douglas explains that if he drew the hand the way you would see it in real life, "you wouldn't understand that that was a hand. It's only when it's done this way, when the fingers spread out that you understand. So you see that I spread the hand out with the fingers out. . . . I used that hand all the time . . . got it from the Egyptians."[5]

Douglas's style is the result of a philosophy, a deep-rooted belief that in trying to imitate the actual world, art as likeness was really falsifying the way we see that world. Figures such as the drummer enabled him to transfer to visual art the excitement he found in the African American spirit, an excitement that was part of the way he saw things. Thus he was an imitator of both reality and his own emotions.

Superrealism

Hanson's superrealism does not exist just to astonish us with its lifelike appearance, but to make a definite statement about our society.

During the last half of the twentieth century, a sculptor named Duane Hanson (1925–1996) took the banner of revolution and turned his back on modernists who had forsaken realism. What he gave the world was **superrealism**—a method of creating life-size figures that look so real you would expect them to answer if you talked to them. Some critics have compared his sculptures to the figures in Madame Tussaud's famous Wax Museum, a comparison that always infuriated the artist.

For one thing, Hanson's "people" are far more lifelike than the wax replicas of famous personalities at Madame Tussaud's. Yet the artist's aim is not solely to render a likeness so perfect it shocks us; he also insists on our seeing the violent, sordid, and comic elements of our society. Hanson is a commentator on what he believes we have become as a nation. His figures are not celebrities we would recognize. They are social (and very often *antisocial*) types. (Look, for example, at his *Supermarket Lady*.) They are super real in order to help us see more clearly, not just to make us marvel at the artist's skill.

Superrealism making a biting commentary about middle-class society.

Source: Duane Hanson, *Supermarket Lady*. Credit: Art © Estate of Duane Hanson/Licensed by VAGA, New York, NY.

Hanson burst upon the art scene several decades ago with a show that almost redefined sculpture. Neither classical nor abstract, his figures offered the somewhat frightened (and relatively few) visitors to his first studio—an old garage—their startling first experience with superrealistic three-dimensional art. Entering the studio through a rusty and squeaking door, which only added to the ghoulish scene inside, the visitor was greeted by the life-size figure of a young woman hanging from a cross, the victim of a savage rape. In an adjoining alcove one gasped at the horrifying sight of a young woman lying nude on a bed, pairs of blood-stained scissors thrust into her stomach, her open eyes still showing the terror she experienced before death came. Across from this sculpture lay the bloody figure of a dead young man, the twisted wreckage of his motorcycle beside him. As if believing the shock of the exhibit was not yet strong enough, Hanson capped off the evening with the piece that brought him to the attention of the Whitney Museum, New York's premier showcase for what is new, controversial, but significant in contemporary art: bloody corpses of young soldiers strewn across a Vietnamese battlefield. A visitor was heard to whisper: "The technique is marvelous, but would you want this in your *house*?" It was clear from the outset that the sculptor was not primarily interested in selling to private collectors. His fame has come from exhibitions the world over.

With Hanson's statement about violence and America, notoriety was instantaneous, and the artist, perhaps believing no more need be said on the subject, embarked on a second phase in which his sculptures were superrealistic but not as frightening—at least not overtly so. The new figures, like the lady in the supermarket, bring us face to face with the dismal life of the American middle class, accurate down to the last detail. Hanson also is thinking of the soulless accuracy with which human-looking robots are constructed in the Disney theme parks, figures that smile vacuously at us and deliver electronic life-affirming platitudes with all the warmth of the computerized phone voice that says, "Sorry, but I did not understand you. Press or say 'one' again."

While O'Keeffe, Gorman, and Hopper simplify reality, Hanson's details tend to overwhelm, as in the real hair curlers, the dangling cigarette, and most of all, the riot of items flung into the shopping cart: the sack of dog food; the frozen dinners (evidence of what has happened to the art of dining); the bargain packages of teabags and toilet paper: startlingly real, yet there for a purpose other than the likenesses themselves. The sculpture encourages the question of whether this is how life should be. Something seems wrong, but what? Art that makes viewers question the life all of us may come dangerously close to living needs no further justification.

While there is a province in which the photographer can tell us nothing more than what we see with our own eyes, there is another in which it proves to us how little our eyes permit us to see.

—Dorothea Lange

In order to achieve such likeness, Hanson covered a live model with wire to form a "dummy," which he then immersed in plaster of Paris, allowing it to harden enough for him to sculpt the lifelike details and apply the many necessary paints. He finished the process by coating the statue with "fixative," a substance that makes paint or dye permanent. Fixative, highly toxic if breathed in an enclosed space, eventually proved fatal to the artist. He was in the process of changing his style and his medium when his life ended, and we can only speculate on the further riches his legacy might have contained.

Alfred Stieglitz, in this portrait of his wife, Georgia O'Keeffe, showed that in-depth portraiture was not the sole province of the painter.

Source: Private Collection/Archives Charmet/The Bridgeman Art Library. © 2008 Estate of Alfred Stieglitz/Artists Rights Society (ARS), NY.

Camera and Computer Art

With the increasing popularity of photography since its invention in the nineteenth century, the roles of portrait painting and realistic landscape art, beginning in the early twentieth century, were diminished. People argued that if they wanted something that looked like the real thing, why not go to a medium that could better provide it? We should not, however, overlook the fact that creative artists, fascinated by the new invention, would begin to experiment with and greatly expand its possibilities.

One of the finest photographers working in the twentieth century was Alfred Stieglitz (1864–1946), who was obsessed with the desire to establish photography as a distinctly American art form. Some of his most famous works are camera images of his wife, Georgia O'Keeffe. He became famous both for his portraits, in which he was bent on proving that the camera could capture the inner person as well as, if not better than, the eye of the painter, and scenes of big-city life. Although photographic art at the time was far less sophisticated than it is now, Stieglitz nonetheless was able to use camera imagery to affect us emotionally, as well as to make a statement about life in New York, already showing signs of the congestion and frenetic pace that would become signature characteristics. In 1902 he founded *Camera Notes*, the first periodical devoted to studying the art and science of photography.

It's admirable, I think, to be open to the new, and willing to learn; I submit, however, that once one has adjusted to the new, it must give pleasure or it will not be art.

—**Richard Wilbur**

Jerry Uelsmann (b. 1934) makes full use of new camera technologies that allow the artist to take multiple images, then link them together in the darkroom to create a world akin to surrealism on canvas. Reproduced here is *Homage to Duchamp* (2000), in which two images of the French artist overlap in a frame that overwhelms the strange room in which it is placed. This is truly photography as alteration.

Computer art is a medium that goes far beyond the "Graphics" menu on a toolbar. Maggie Taylor (b. 1961), for example, conjures up images from a variety ofsources, including photos from digital and regular cameras and pictures scanned from newspaper and magazine clippings. Sometimes the result is a computerized collage, and sometimes Taylor creates a surreal picture, like *The Philosopher's Daughter* (Color Plate 24), that could easily have been painted but, astonishingly, is not.

There is also fax art, which can be an ordinary photocopied reproduction of something, acquiring the label of art only after it has gone through the shading process of a fax machine. We are probably not far from "video cellphone art," in which the receiver of a call will not see the person calling but, instead, a surreal person in a non-existent room. Perhaps that genre is already here. And perhaps you can think of other, newer, more dazzling art forms related to today's electronic devices.

Pop Art

Influenced by comic books, movies, television, commercials, and billboard advertising, **Pop Art** arose as a phenomenon of the mid-twentieth century that brought

Using photography to create a surreal world.

Source: Jerry Uelsmann, *Homage to Duchamp*. Credit: Courtesy Jerry Uelsmann.

fame to a few artists. It has been described as "fun" art, for its exponents all seem to have a sense of humor about much of what they do. They are sometimes, like Hanson, making a statement about the endless fads and superficiality of American culture. It has a link with the second phase of Hanson's art in its focus on ordinary objects and sometimes the sly suggestion that American life has nothing more important to offer.

Claes Oldenburg (b. 1929), a Swedish-born, naturalized American exponent of Pop Art, finished a cardboard and wood mural in 1961 called *The Street*, showing people, buildings, automobiles, and other objects seen in everyday life, but drawn in comic-book style, which is his artistic domain. The following year he achieved notoriety with *Giant Ice-Cream Cone* and the first of his soft vinyl sculptures, *Giant Hamburger*. These were followed by *Giant Tooth Brush*, *Soft Toilet*, and *Giant Ice Bag*, which was made for the Osaka World's Fair, a sculpture that inflates and deflates as the viewer watches. With *Soft Toilet*, reproduced on page 161, he may have been thinking whimsically of Duchamp's still notorious urinal.

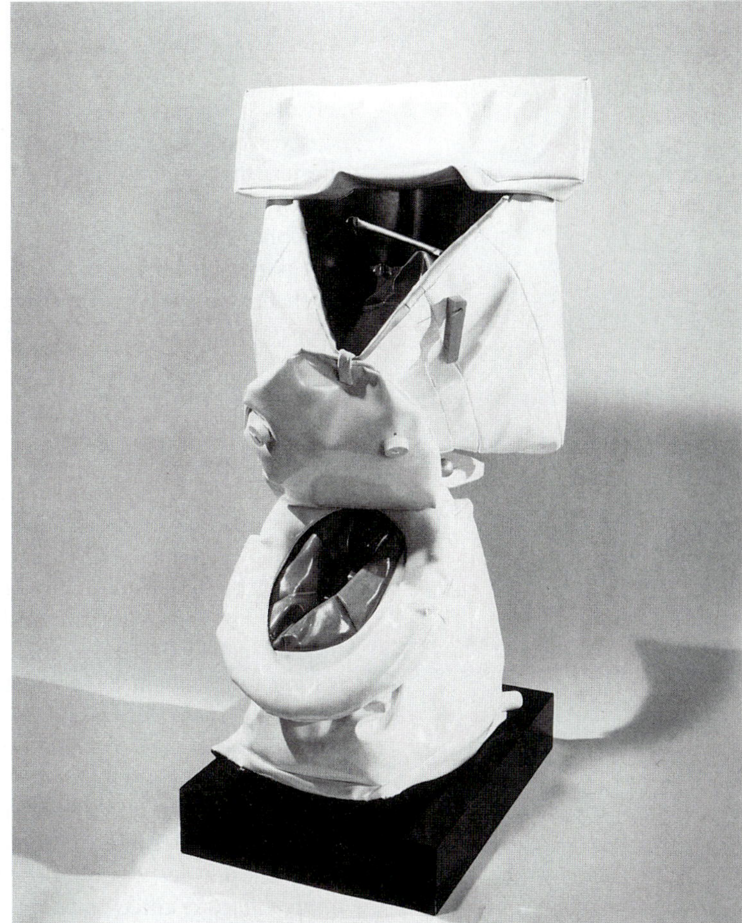

Sculpture showing Oldenburg's love of turning commonplace objects into museum pieces.

Source: Claes Oldenburg, *Soft Toilet*, (1996). Wood, vinyl, kapok, wire, plexiglass; on metal stand and painted wood base. $57\,^{1}/_{16} \times 27\,^{5}/_{8} \times 28\,^{1}/_{16}$ in. (144.9 × 70.2 × 71.3 cm) Whitney Museum of American Art, New York. COPYRIGHT Claes Oldenburg and Coosje van Bruggen.

Probably the biggest name in Pop Art is Andy Warhol (1928–1987), who earned his reputation with a painting mentioned earlier: *100 Cans*, containing stark likenesses of row upon row of Campbell's beef noodle soup. The inspiration for this kind of art is clearly the popular ad, but the excessive repetition of the can is both amusing and frightening. Is Warhol ridiculing the stultifying conformism in American culture and its lack of imagination?

Yet Warhol is also in *love* with our tawdry culture, as we can see from his portrait of glamorous movie star Marilyn Monroe (Color Plate 25), a heightening of what used to grace the covers of tacky movie magazines. The colors are brilliant, suggesting the unreality of "tinsel town." But the artist, like so many others, was unable to resist the flashy sensuality that turned Monroe—once an unremarkable young woman named Norma Jean Baker—into a modern Aphrodite. Yes, Warhol knows that the star was a studio-manufactured product, but he himself was a filmmaker who manufactured a whole bevy of unreal types for his bizarre movies, including a fleshy transvestite named Divine and an entourage that was a walking Pop Art statement.

Warhol's films were central to his art, and *Chelsea Girls* (1966) ushered in a new cinematic phenomenon, the "underground film," popular for a time with young people who opposed almost anything connected with established American culture. The film lasted more than three hours and was shown on two screens that seemed unconnected with each other. The "plot" comprised disconnected, fragmentary sequences but also strangely haunting images. In one five-minute sequence a young woman is shown standing in front of a mirror, cutting her hair. Nothing else happens, yet the intense camera focus on her face and the sound of scissors create a mesmerizing effect.

Warhol's films are occasionally shown on special nights in "art houses"—theaters that cater to "alternative tastes." Most of his film art, however, is hard to track down. Even so, it remains an important link between what we might call "stationary" art that is available in museums and galleries and "impermanent" art that is not meant to last, that occupies a brief moment in time—a new kind of art that may have been an inevitable development in America, a land of short attention spans and people always on the move.

Performance Art

Performance art is art as event. Perhaps performance artists are looking for ways to be different in an art world that changes all the time, a very tall order indeed. Or perhaps they believe that art is more beautiful to the extent that it doesn't stay around very long. Performance artists ignore the goal of one day having their work part of a permanent collection in a prestigious museum; they prefer to do something that will create a momentary stir, even a storm of controversy, and then be seen or heard no more. They may also perform pranks or engineer hoaxes just meant for themselves and a closed circle of friends.

Prank artists often cite Orson Welles, the great film director (more fully discussed in Chapter 9), as the founder of their movement. In the 1930s, Welles and his Mercury Theatre Company performed a radio adaptation of a famous science fiction novel, *The War of the Worlds*, about an army of Martians who invade the United States. Because the radio play was written in the style of a news program, many people—especially those tuning in late—believed the invasion was the real thing. Chaos erupted as people ran from their homes, seeking safe hiding places. Welles insisted the program was not meant as a prank, but some performance artists insist that it *could* have been, and that even if it had been a prank, it would still count as legitimate art.

A great deal of prank art is intended for the sole pleasure of the artists themselves. One artist, for example, purchased a chicken from a supermarket, then brought it to a pet cemetery and conducted a full-scale funeral service. Another entered an alley cat in a prestigious show and, after the lowly entrant had won, greatly enjoyed laughing at the judges. One artist carried bags of horse droppings to Venice, scattering the contents all over the Piazza San Marco, and reported deriving aesthetic pleasure from watching the amazement of tourists, who knew that there were no horses in Venice. Those who refuse to apply the label "art" to such pranks might ask themselves whether art is not supposed to open us to new experiences, and was not the mysterious appearance of the horse droppings indeed a "new" experience? Is there a limit to what qualifies as a legitimate new experience?

A Massachusetts Institute of Technology student is reported to have spent her summer regularly sneaking into Soldiers Field, the Harvard football stadium, wearing a black-and-white striped shirt like that of a referee. On each visit, as she scattered birdseed over the field, she blew a whistle. At the opening football game of the season, when one of the real referees blew his whistle, hundreds of birds swooped into the stadium, ready to eat. Since prank art is necessarily private, the perpetrators might advertise their successes only later on the Internet.

Performance art can also contain social commentary. An instructor at Amherst College, for example, posted bogus signs all over campus, announcing that no more coffee would be sold because it was known to induce caffeine addiction. Then he and his colleagues spread the word that coffee was available from black-market vendors outside the campus. The pranksters posed at the vendors and reported brisk sales. Surely there is a moral here somewhere. During the 1970s at a Miami art gallery, a performance artist destroyed a piano with an axe while his assistant read the names of American soldiers killed in Vietnam.

Superrealist Edward Kienholz (1927–1993) created a computer-generated performance art piece called *Still Live*, which includes an armchair positioned in front of a black box said to contain "a live cartridge and a random timer triggered to fire once within the next 100 years." According to one art critic, "After eight years, it still hasn't gone off. Viewers foolish enough to want to sit in this 'hot seat' must sign a waiver. Kienholz told me, with some scorn and disbelief, that at the opening almost a dozen people did."[6]

No doubt many have sat in the armchair since the work's installation in 1974, but its title, *Still Live*, suggests a possible appeal to hidden Russian roulette impulses. If the artist had expected no one to sit there, why did he compose the piece at all? In any case, the performer here was not the artist, but the actual or potential viewer willing to risk all for a momentary thrill. Perhaps the work existed so that those who sat in the chair could look deep within themselves and ask why they came.

Christo Javacheff (b. 1935), who as an artist uses only his first name, does not imitate or perform; he literally alters the world briefly, creating a huge and highly publicized event. He claims the natural environment as his medium. Among his projects were wrapping over 1 million square feet of Australian coastline in plastic, installing a gigantic curtain between two mountains in Colorado, constructing a twenty-four-mile fence made of twenty-foot-high nylon panels across hills in northern California, and surrounding the islands in Biscayne Bay, Miami, with enormous sheets of flamingo-colored plastic, a feat that struck terror to the hearts of environmentalists, who attempted (unsuccessfully) to halt the proceedings.

Performance art was often considered radically new in the twentieth century, but it can be dated back as far as tribal rituals of many thousand years ago. During the Renaissance, some artists performed little acts to call attention to their work on display. And Will Kemp, the celebrated clown for whom Shakespeare wrote many parts, including the Fool in *King Lear*, was fond of adlibbing and extending a role far beyond what the script allowed, cheered on by his adoring fans.

Architecture as Art

Architecture in general is frozen music.

—**Friedrich von Schiller**

Performance art is transitory by nature, often limited to the time of presentation, and never seen or heard again. This final section is concerned with a more permanent component of society: architecture, which serves a dual purpose. It provides for our many human needs: shelter, work, play, religious worship, and so on. It also gives many of our cities their distinctive look; it adds an aesthetic dimension to life. At its best, architecture is an art form. Major architects Frank Lloyd Wright and Frank O. Gehry have approached the design of buildings as a painter or sculptor would contemplate beginning a new work: that is, as a contribution to the aesthetic well-being of society.

The fundamental issue in determining whether a given architectural work can be labeled "art" is the interplay of *form* and *function*. The function of a building is to accommodate the needs of the inhabitants. An office building should provide employees with pleasing surroundings that will make working less of a chore, and it should allow employees easy access to spaces they will have to visit throughout the day. It must make doing business there simple and enjoyable, and these days it must be wheelchair accessible. A religious edifice such as a cathedral or a temple should be imposing and awe-inspiring both inside and out, so worshippers or meditators can believe for a time that they have left the familiar world and entered a different, some might say higher, mode of consciousness.

The form of a building—the general impression that it makes as a pleasing presence in a certain space—can be as important as its function. If designed by an architect-as-artist, it can also make a personal statement: *This form is what I consider beautiful, and I offer it for your use and your aesthetic pleasure.* Like all visual artists, architects seek to project themselves into space. They want to know that, because of them, a public area has been altered in some way that reflects their identity and may ensure them lasting honor. They know that architecture is art that alters for very long periods of time, and in some cases forever. The Taj Mahal in India, Saint Peter's basilica in Rome, and the Hagia Sophia in Istanbul have endured for centuries and have become symbols of their culture.

The debate over which is more important, form or function, has continued for centuries and will probably never be resolved. Those who want architecture primarily to serve a useful purpose argue famously that *form follows function*. Others, often called architectural purists, elevate form and the aesthetic experience it provides over what they call "mere utility." Still others ask, "Why can't we have both?"

Religious Architecture

Buildings created for religious worship or meditation are among the finest achievements in world architecture. The Parthenon in Athens, built to honor the goddess Athena, is one of the world's oldest architectural marvels and remains for many the symbol of Western classical civilization (see photo page 126). Angkor Wat, the largest of seventy temples in a complex in Cambodia, is not only a place of meditation for thousands of Buddhists but, as one of the wonders of the world, the main tourist attraction in that nation. Each year many thousands come for inspiration and an aesthetic experience that has been described as nearly without parallel. Unlike St. Peter's, which was built to impress upon the visitor the glory of God and the supreme authority of the Roman Catholic church, Angkor Wat is intended as a place in which the visitor can be alone and at peace.

Not many edifices have been cornerstones of two religions, but Angkor Wat, still the world's largest religious building, has been home to both Hinduism and Buddhism. Built originally in honor of the Hindu god Vishnu (see Chapter 10), it became in 1177 C.E. a Buddhist shrine after the Cambodian king was converted to Buddhism. With five pineapple-shaped towers rising close to 200 feet against the sky, Angkor Wat became the most imposing temple in the holy city of Angkor, spread across 120 miles. The temple contains innumerable passageways and alcoves, the walls of which boast ornate facades depicting both mythic stories and scenes from everyday Cambodian life.

The former Hindu, now Buddhist temple Angkor Wat in Cambodia. It remains one of the world's architectural wonders.

Source: Mark Downey/Masterfile.

Few works of architecture have cast the same sort of spell as Angkor Wat. The English novelist W. Somerset Maugham once observed that the vast temple "needs the glow of sunset or the white brilliance of the moon to give it a loveliness that touches the heart." Many have noted that merely walking its nearly three-mile expanse is a transforming experience, leading to distinct (and for the better) changes in mood and attitude.

Modern cathedrals and other places of worship frequently break with tradition, and the results vary from praise in architectural journals to condemnations by the faithful. St. Louis Catholic Church in Miami looks like a flying saucer about to take off. The Crystal Cathedral in Garden Grove, California, has a neo-Gothic form, except that it is made entirely of glass and, according to some detractors, looks more like a luxury hotel than a church. A Lutheran church in Helsinki, Finland, was carved into the side of a hill and gives the illusion that one is entering a cave rather than a house of prayer.

Secular Architecture

Whenever the desire is to combine function with the form that only a great artist can bring to architecture, conflicts inevitably arise between those who create and those who pay for or use the structure. The architect-as-artist often runs into difficulties with both the general public and the specific person or group that has commissioned a given structure. The artist's irresistible urge to self-expression can be accused of subordinating a building's primary purpose. One notorious example is an office complex in Miami, Florida, built in the shape of a huge snail. Probably reflecting the designer's keen sense of humor, it has provoked much derision over the years.

We shape our buildings: thereafter they shape us.

—**Winston Churchill**

Even where architecture is viewed as a public art, those who finance it can only speculate on how to define the public interest. When a private corporation or city planners underwrite the erection of an expensive building such as a performing arts center, they will expect (for their millions of dollars) an edifice that satisfies both functional and aesthetic needs, but not exclusively the desires of the architect. They know their investment is going to result in an edifice that will be around for a long time, and they are in trouble if it meets with public disapproval! It is going to define their city—for better or worse—as Sydney, Australia, is identified by its daring but internationally admired opera house.

With its gleaming white, sharply pointed gables, looking like monks' hoods, the Sydney Opera House (Color Plate 26) opened in 1973 after sixteen years of construction. The design was to allow for excellent interior acoustics but also to create for the audience a pleasant environment that would heighten the pleasure of the music being heard. The building was also intended to symbolize the city, so that people on ships entering Sydney Harbor for the first time would know they were about to visit a progressive, young metropolitan area very much involved in the arts. An intense contest for the architectural commission resulted in the choice of a celebrated Danish architect, Jorn Utzon, who insisted on being able to express himself as an artist—to shape a certain space so as to embody his vision of the beautiful, not only to obey the functional requirements set forth by the city planners. The opera house, in short, was intended to be a meeting of the civic and the personal.

No house should ever be on any hill or anything. It should be of the hill, belonging to it, so hill and house can live together each the happier for the other.

—**Frank Lloyd Wright**

But not every taxpayer in Sydney agreed that the structure met either practical or aesthetic needs. As always happens when an environment is altered by a forward-looking artist who breaks with established tradition, there were many who decried his efforts and predicted that their city would be a laughingstock. World opinion, however, has been on the side of Utzon; now the Sydney Opera House is often singled out as one of the architectural achievements of the twentieth century, an edifice that perfectly marries form and function.

There is by now widespread agreement, however, over the innovations of a man considered the outstanding American architect of the twentieth century, Frank Lloyd Wright (1867–1959). He was born and raised in the relatively small Wisconsin town of Richmond Center. Accustomed to open spaces, air to breathe, and panoramic landscapes, he must have become aware of a growing urban America with huge buildings beginning to reach for the sky and densely crowded city neighborhoods where residents seldom interacted with nature. The writings of American philosopher Ralph Waldo Emerson and his vehemently anti-city friend Henry David Thoreau also had a strong impact on Wright's architectural vision. Early on, Wright developed a strong rationale for his work: to link the functional demands of large buildings with the environmental demands of his own heart. His mission would be to provide for the practical demands of big business without the claustrophobia of crowded industrial complexes.

At the outset of his career he designed what he called his "prairie house," a rambling one-story structure with plenty of windows and a low, overhanging roof. The idea was that it should blend into its surroundings, unlike the huge nineteenth-century mansions with their ornate external carvings, statues, and stained-glass windows, designed for the blatant display of wealth. Wright's aim was to create a balance among function, form, and the environment.

During the first decade of the twentieth century, Wright designed the Larkin Building in Buffalo, New York, and its distinctively sleek look brought him to the attention of European urban planners. By the 1930s the term "streamlined" became fashionable and international in its appeal, and Wright was the acknowledged exponent of the new style, with its use of glass, including glass brick, curved surfaces, spacious interiors, and absence of unnecessary, purely decorative frills. He believed strongly that form follows function. With Wright leading the way, many modern architects said that no building could be considered beautiful if its basic function was impaired by "artistic" aims—such as installing a fountain ringed by statues to block its entrance.

In 1936 Wright designed the administration building and in 1944 the research tower of the Johnson Wax Company in Racine, Wisconsin, an achievement hailed as a masterpieces of modern architecture. One architectural historian proclaimed it "the most profound work of art that America has ever produced."[7]

Money was never Wright's primary consideration. He wanted, first, to shield employees and visitors from the growing ugliness of the urban scene. Although he loved light and made extensive use of glass, he placed windows so that users of the buildings would not have to look out on parking lots and decaying streets. Instead they were enclosed by solid brick walls at street level while light was provided from overhead. He wanted users to feel as though they were "among the pine trees, breathing fresh air and sunlight." Wright was a visionary who helped create the modern world, and he was an archenemy of overbuilding in that world.

Wright's final work—and for many, his crowning achievement—is the Guggenheim Museum on Fifth Avenue in New York. It is admired by some as the best possible example of modern architecture, and scorned by others who say it looks like a parking garage. The building is a series of circular stone ramps, which ascend in great swirls and serve as a thick barrier to the noise of the city. There are

Sometimes scornfully compared to a parking garage, New York's Guggenheim was designed to shut out light and provide visitors with a peaceful environment for viewing art.

Source: Frank Lloyd Wright, Guggenheim Museum, New York. Credit: © Peter Mauss/Esto.

no windows this time. Instead, light enters through the small spaces between the ramps. Inside, art works are illuminated by soft indirect lighting. The artist's first thought was to shut out as much light as he could and provide visitors with a quiet oasis, another world of human creativity.

I don't think it's very useful to open wide the door for new artists; the ones who break down the door are more interesting.

—**Paul Schroeder**

Frank O. Gehry (b. 1929) has also taken modern American architecture to new levels. His work tends to put a great deal of emphasis on form without ignoring function. But from the beginning, he approached architectural design with an artist's eye, developing a style that is not only representatively modern but always characteristically *his*. For Gehry, form is paramount, yet his genius lies in the ability to make the form seem an inevitable result of function. Some of his critics call his style impractical, accusing him of subordinating function in the interest of artistic self-expression. A good many artists, however, defend his right to do just that.

Like many of his fellow southern Californians, Gehry enjoys the *funky* in modern art—those elements that incorporate whimsy into serious aims. He is fond of fish, for example, and is apt to put a fish sculpture where one would least expect it—in front of an elevator perhaps. He makes furniture out of corrugated boxes, and he uses chain-link fencing unsparingly and, again, unexpectedly. He will stretch a chain-link fence across a courtyard where it serves no useful purpose except to be an object of art, similar to what Christo might do, except that Gehry's installations are permanent. To those critics who call such installations "frivolous" and "ugly," he replies that he is not sure "what is ugly and what is beautiful." Such a retort, a denial of absolute aesthetic standards in architecture, defends the right of artists to make personal statements with their work.

Yet Gehry is as concerned as Wright about making a space enjoyable to its users. His California roots are evident in the brightness and spaciousness of his interiors. After all, southern California is a land of beaches, where stressed-out workers can go to unwind. In Gehry's buildings, the unwinding process has already begun.

By almost universal consent, Gehry's masterpiece is the Guggenheim Museum in Bilbao, Spain. Here he was commissioned by people who were already on the side of art, people who knew and loved the innovative, however daring and controversial, and people who wanted to call worldwide attention to the city they loved.

The structure stands as a giant work of art in itself, and then the visitor enters to find more and more art, in spacious galleries, lighted for the maximum enjoyment of each work on display. Even more imposing than the Sydney Opera House, the museum has boosted tourism in Bilbao. For those of us who love the humanities, such a financial success is gratifying indeed. And it proves that large segments of the public can respond to what is aesthetically pleasing, if given the chance.

We cannot close this section on architecture as an art form without giving some attention to the hotels that abound in metropolitan areas the world over. Here, the interplay of form and function is especially evident. The great hotels (for those who can afford them) are meant to fulfill every possible comfort need of the guest, but also to provide a pleasing aesthetic environment. In the nineteenth and early twentieth centuries, the greatest care and expense were often lavished on hotel lobbies; but of late the atrium has become a distinctive feature: open corridors built around a fountain or a swimming pool or even a rain forest, affording an instant view of something beautiful as soon as guests step out of their rooms.

The Guggenheim Museum, Bilbao, Spain, was designed not only to house great art but to be a work of art in itself.

Source: Frank O. Gehry, Guggenheim Museum, Bilbao, Spain. Credit: Ralph Richter/Esto/architekturphoto. All rights reserved.

One of the world's most spectacular new edifices is the Burj-al-Arab in Dubai, the capital of the United Arab Emirates. At one time the tallest structure in the world to function exclusively as a hotel, it required three years to build, at a staggering cost that reflects the vast oil wealth behind it. Shaped like a huge schooner mast, it is broad at the base, tapering to a conical tower, with a helipad for the arrival of important guests. The thousand-plus rooms open onto the world's tallest atrium and include a five-bedroom royal suite with a grand piano, a Jacuzzi on the spacious balcony, four bathrooms, and a dining-room table that can accommodate nearly one hundred guests. And it has a restaurant that can be accessed only by submarine!

The Burj-al-Arab Hotel in Dubai. Las Vegas tackiness or one of the world's architectural splendors?

Source: © George Hammerstein/Solus—Veer/Corbis.

While abundant praise has been showered on the building as a complex engineering feat, some critics have been put off by what the hotel symbolizes to them: money. One critic said it is a monument "to the triumph of money over practicality." After admitting that the structure was "fabulous," another critic venomously added that it was "the pinnacle of tackiness— like Vegas."

If you never visit Bilbao or spend a night in Burj-al-Arab, you may be fortunate enough to live in a city large enough to support a museum or gallery where traveling exhibits can be shown. Seize the opportunity whenever it presents itself. You will be delighted at how much your range of consciousness will expand and grow. If museums are not available, public libraries and the Internet have the astonishing capability of taking you to galleries and museums all over the world. You can relive the classical past in Greece and Rome, the magnificence of the Florentine Renaissance, the Holland of Rembrandt and other seventeenth-century artists who perfected the imitation of likeness, or visit the world of van Gogh and see the treasures he left for us. You can virtually travel to the Louvre in Paris with its multitude of antiquities, or to the Jeu de Paume with its priceless collection of Impressionist paintings. You can discover the rich legacy of American artists like Cassatt, Whistler, Douglas, O'Keeffe, and so many others. The world of art belongs to you, and it is our hope that this chapter has encouraged you to browse in it whenever your spirits need uplifting. Art never fails you if you come to it with an eager curiosity and a willingness to pause. The visual effects can be stunning. Look carefully.

Key Terms

abstract art art that takes from reality only what the artist wants or that renders a visual depiction of concepts in the artist's mind; a work of art that in no way resembles the real world.

alteration how the modern artist changes reality by adding to it shapes, lines, and even colors not found in nature.

chiaroscuro Italian term denoting a way of reproducing in a work of art the interplay of light and shadow in the real world.

classicism the balanced, harmonious, often mathematical characteristics of art and architecture in fifth-century Athens and those aspects of Roman art that were heavily influenced by artists of that period; also used for all subsequent art and architecture created in that style.

collage a work of art in which a variety of materials such as newsprint, magazine pictures, crepe paper, even glass and wood are glued together, forming a new whole, expressive of the artist.

fresco artwork painted on the walls of churches and public buildings, popular in the Renaissance, in which the artist applies paint to wet plaster.

Golden Section an aesthetically pleasing relationship between the two sides of a plane (like a rectangle), such that the shorter is to the longer as the longer is to the sum of both. The ratio is 1 to 1.68.

imitation the transference of what is experienced either outside or inside the artist to a medium of art; it can mean an idealized reproduction (as in classicism), a faithfully realistic one (as in the Dutch school of the seventeenth century), or an externalization of what exists in the artist's mind (as in abstract art).

likeness the reproduction by an artist of a person or landscape with the aim of being as close to reality as possible; popularity began to diminish with the invention of photography in the nineteenth century.

media the particular materials in which a given artist works, such as paint, acrylic, charcoal, stone, or even tires, mufflers, broken pieces of glass, etc.

modernism refers less to a particular art movement than to art produced in the late nineteenth to late twentieth centuries.

perspective technique of rendering, on a plane or curved surface, objects as they appear to natural vision; developed and refined during the early Italian Renaissance.

postmodernism art produced from the late twentieth century to the present; less a specific movement than a broad umbrella term for the many innovative techniques.

psychological realism the manner in which such artists as Leonardo and Rembrandt are able to convey the inner life of their figures.

realism as used in this chapter, art as likeness.

Renaissance the period of artistic, political, and social movement that began in fourteenth-century Italy, then spread throughout western Europe in the fifteenth and sixteenth centuries; characterized by renewed interest in the classical world, and also marking the end of medievalism and the emergence of the modern world.

still life genre of painting in which the artist reproduces the likeness of a particular arrangement of objects, such as a bowl of flowers or fruit or other kinds of food on a table.

Topics for
Writing and Discussion

1. In your own words, explain this statement as it applies to art in general: "Leonardo's *Mona Lisa* is not Mona Lisa."

2. Discuss why the term *terribilitá* (used to describe the passionate qualities in a Michelangelo scupture) is appropriate for Renaissance but not classical sculpture.

3. Go to an art gallery or museum in your area or on the Internet and carefully study a painting that attracts your eye. If none of these sources is available, select one of the illustrations in this chapter or the color inserts. Then describe orally or in writing how you would explain the value of the viewing experience to someone who tends to be uninterested in art.

4. Can you justify the fact that an enormous curtain, stretched by Christo between two mountains, has been called art by its creator and recognized as art by some critics?

5. Write a short paper based on either of the following sentences:
   a. "I would rather be a stable, moderately successful, happy, if obscure, person than a genius like van Gogh."
   b. "I would rather be a genius like van Gogh, even if the price were lack of recognition, than a moderately successful, happy, and obscure person."

6. You and a friend are standing in front of Duchamp's *Nude Descending a Staircase*. Your friend asks, "What is it supposed to be?" You reply that it doesn't matter. Your friend says, "Then how can it be any good?" What is your response?

7. Extravagant praise has been given to Picasso, including the view that he was not only one of the greatest artists who ever lived but one of the most important human beings. Do you find this view justifiable? Explain.

8. The architects studied in this chapter have been concerned with the aesthetic appeal of a building's exterior. The Miami office building that was built to look like a snail has incited both amused approval and critical scorn over the years. Committees have even been formed with the intent to have the building condemned, but so far without success. Other committees have worked diligently to preserve it. Which committee would you join? Explain.

9. At one time, national academies composed of government-subsidized critics and scholars had the power to decide what constituted art. They were like an aesthetic Supreme Court. The French panel keeping the Impressionists out of the prestigious annual Salon maintained they were preserving the integrity of France's artistic traditions.

   If a country refused to have such an academy, would there be any standards? Are standards important? If they don't come from an academy, where *do* they come from? Would it matter if everyone's opinion counted equally? Would it matter if everyone's opinion did *not* count equally? Would it matter if the traditionalists had been replaced by a liberal group who decided that anything anybody said was art could be exhibited?

   Write a short paper focusing on one aspect of this intriguing and ongoing debate.

10. So much of the past is known mainly from the artworks that were its silent witness. Describe the kind of silent witness you would like to leave behind so that people of the future would know what you were like.

6 Music

Overview

In a world of peace and love music would be the universal language.
—**Henry David Thoreau**

We live within an audio environment that is most of the time unplanned. That is, we hear what happens to be around, whether it is a jet taking off, the squeal of auto brakes, a hair dryer, or a train approaching a crossing. There's plenty of unwanted sound, but there is also music: our revenge on random noise. Even the unrelenting beat of the hardest rock music represents somebody's choice, a preference for one sound rather than another. The audio environment can be the sound of a stick being dragged along a wrought-iron fence or the bland tones of supermarket Musak; or it can be U2 at full steam two hours into a concert, or the upbeat country sounds of Martina McBride, or a Beethoven symphony.

Without music, we exist at the mercy of audio pollution as damaging to mental health as air and water pollution are damaging to physical health. Created by instruments or human voices, music can be defined as *the shaped sound between silences*: the better the shape, the richer and more pleasing the sound. Just as visual art offers a wide variety of shapes and forms to provide an enriched visual environment, music has many sounds: Bach, Mozart, Gershwin, Armstrong, Sinatra, the Beatles, Maroon 5. Limiting ourselves to one kind of music is as detrimental to our growth as if we were never to set foot outside our house and discover the unlimited life experiences waiting out there.

Perhaps it seems unnecessary to talk about variety in music. Yet many of us listen only to what we hear on mainstream radio and television stations or at movies, local music venues, and popular concerts. Exploring unfamiliar sounds, finding perhaps the one station (among fifty others) dedicated to music that is new to us, refusing to have our tastes dictated by promoters—these are actions we are free to perform. Yet too often we do not.

We may enjoy the popular music we find on the charts because we hear it all the time. Often we grow up with its sounds filling the house, and some of us come to think there are few musical options we might be overlooking. This is not so. Music has a long and continuing tradition not only in the West but in other parts of the world, dating back hundreds of years—music that is still being played. There are operas, chamber music, symphonies, concerti for

Source: Rome Milan Gallery.

orchestra and solo instruments, music to accompany ballets, and music created from non-Western scales.

The difference between the familiar and the unfamiliar in music is not necessarily qualitative. We may place greater value on the familiar music because we are accustomed to it and therefore comfortable with it. We may find lesser value in the unfamiliar because we are *not* comfortable with it, at least at first. This is not the best reason to avoid it. When Elvis Presley and Chuck Berry emerged on the musical scene in the mid-1950s, a good many listeners were horrified, not knowing that a new musical tradition—*rock 'n' roll*—was being born. Now we have rock groups experimenting with such unusual sounds that Elvis Presley and Chuck Berry seem old-fashioned. The purpose of this chapter is to encourage you to explore a wide range of musical sound. Some of it is recognized as part of the world's artistic heritage. Some of it is still very new and may achieve that distinction one day. (It's fun to predict what *will.*)

We will first separate music into its component elements, then talk about some of its major (and widely differing) forms, together with some suggested works from the past and present. We will look as well at music from other cultures that may offer us a richer musical life. As in any introductory text, the process is necessarily selective. We attempt to open the door of musical recognition a little wider.

The Basic Elements of Music

Most ancient cultures shared the belief that music was a vital component of the natural world, a gift from heavenly beings. One theory is that for very early people, natural sounds were the voices of the gods, and human song was developed to imitate their voices. We still often hear comments such as "She sings like an angel."

Credit for the development of formal music goes to the ancient Egyptians and their belief that the god Thoth gave humanity seven basic sounds, perhaps much like the seven-tone scale that would come later. Along with laying the foundations of Western thought, art, and literature, the Greeks also created a profound theory of music. The Greek term *armonia*, which became the English word **harmony**, indicates a connection between music and the structure of the universe. Religions of the world have long believed that through music we can achieve union with the divine. Ancient Chinese philosophers, for example, who believed all nature was ruled by a divine principle of order, saw music as the human connection to that order.

Even before it was thought to be the sound of the gods, music must already have existed. It may have originated in human imitation of pleasing sounds, such as birdsongs or raindrop patters or animal noises, in the same way that visual art may have begun as the human need to imitate the familiar world. Perhaps music began from the need for better communication, with rudimentary musical sounds an integral part of early language. Or there may have been a long ago moment when someone thought, *Why wait for the soothing call of a morning bird when I can make that sound myself?*

Tone

The basic element of music is the **tone**, or note, a sound produced by the human voice or by musical instrument that maintains the same frequency of vibration regardless of duration. Perhaps the imitation of a natural sound was then shaped to become pure and sweet. Or perhaps that pure and sweet tone just came from someone's imagination, and people nearby were astounded when they heard it. However it happened, the discovery of tones marked the beginning of the human victory over the unplanned audio environment. True music began when someone experimented with a variety of tones, some higher, some lower.

The Scale

People in the ancient world who discovered different tones could not have known that they were caused by the frequency of sound-wave vibrations: the higher the frequency, the higher the tone. After a time, someone must have happened upon a distinct progression of individual tones from low to high, and that was the beginning of music as *we* know it. This orderly progression of frequencies from low to high is the **scale.** All cultures that developed music used a scale, though they did not necessarily happen upon the same sequence of tones.

At first, the dominant scale in both non-Western and Western music consisted of five tones, known as a **pentatonic scale.** It remains the basis for most traditional Asian music. The Western scale was expanded to six tones by the sixth century C.E. and was first written down (or notated) by an Italian monk. With the later addition of a seventh tone, the Western **diatonic scale** was complete. Notes were also given letter designations—ABCDEFG—and each sequence of seven would constitute a scale. The addition of sharps and flats—or **half-tones**—expanded the number of scales possible. Over time, the first note of each scale became the identifying **key** in which a given piece of music was composed. The basic scale in Western music begins with the note C—hence CDEFGAB, and these notes acquired the names *do, re, mi, fa, so, la, ti.*

Imagine that you are sitting at a piano. Beginning with C, your finger travels up the seven-tone progression, using only the white keys. You are therefore in the key of C, which many singers find most comfortable. But there are also the five black keys, or half-tones, such as C-sharp and E-flat. When you play the white keys plus the black keys, you are now using the twelve-tone **chromatic scale.** To the list of musical keys we may thus include C-sharp, B-flat, and so on.

When we play or sing a seven whole-tone progression, except for that which starts with A, we are using a *major scale.* A *minor scale* is more complicated. The *natural* minor scale begins with A and goes up seven whole tones. The *melodic* minor scale substitutes G-sharp going up but the whole-tone G coming down. The *harmonic* minor scale substitutes G-sharp going up and also coming down. Though the verbal definitions are complex, music in minor keys is easily recognized. Many songs of heartbreak and loss are written in minor keys, as is instrumental music that seeks to create a somber mood.

> *I know that the twelve in each octave and the varieties of rhythm offer me opportunities that all human genius will never exhaust.*
> —**Igor Stravinsky**

Traditional symphonic music is usually identified in terms of the key and type of scale in which it begins (composers can change either or both within a given work) and the *opus* number (that is, where the piece occurs in the composer's repertoire). Thus one might see this on a program: Beethoven, Symphony No. 9 in D Minor, Op. 125.

Combined major and minor keys can be found in blues music (discussed later in the chapter). Composers of classic popular songs have had great success in switching from one scale to another as the lyrics dictate. For example, in the song "Every Time We Say Goodbye," the composer/lyricist Cole Porter enumerates the emotions he feels at parting from his beloved. In one line he says that, when she is gone, all the joy goes out of his life and "how strange the change from major to minor." The key changes to match the lyrics, creating an unusual and moving effect.

The music of most non-Western cultures is based on a scale of five tones that do not necessarily correspond to Western sounds. The Western preference for seven tones may have to do with the fact that Western listeners are accustomed to the narrower frequency intervals between the seven tones of the familiar scale. Hearing traditional Asian music for the first time and expecting the familiar scale, Western listeners are likely to find the sounds quite strange. But the music can be hypnotic. It places great reliance on the purity of musical line, made possible by the greater distinctness of the tones. There is often less complexity than in music composed using the seven-tone scale.

In contrast, Africa has a long musical tradition without a formalized scale at all. Tones were fundamental, as in other cultures, but these could change to suit the emotion of the musician or singer. Traditional African music has always made strong use of the human voice, and when the voice is the primary way of preserving melody, much variation is the rule. Musical notation is possible, but this doesn't mean performers feel obligated to repeat what others have played or sung. The music of Africa, brought to these shores by slaves and later by those who migrated here, has made possible the evolution of jazz and blues, two art forms that allow for maximum freedom of expression.

Rhythm

Early music throughout the world was probably monophonic: limited to just the melodic line and sung or played without harmony. But rhythmic accompaniment would have been provided when appropriate, such as at ritual events like a funeral or a rite of passage celebrating the arrival of puberty.

We know rhythm was the underlying factor in early Greek ceremonies because we have written accounts of it. Certain rhythms were held appropriate for inspirational ceremonies because of their uplifting effect on the soul, while other rhythms—certainly those involved in the orgies held annually in honor of Dionysus—were deemed conducive to uncontrolled, licentious behavior.

Formal music may have begun with the discovery of tones, but rhythm by itself might well have preceded tone, scale, and the earliest instruments. Most likely, a rat-a-tat pounding of sticks and stones was an early factor in human development, used to mark occasions of great joy or solemnity. The early instincts are still with us. We often see very young children rat-a-tatting with blocks or just with their hands, the beat becoming more pronounced and regular as they grow older. Rap and hip-hop forms of today clearly indicate that we are just as attracted to the hypnotic effect of steady rhythm as our ancestors were.

Moving to a beat—better known as dancing—may be even older than singing, though the two may spontaneously have erupted together on many occasions. Even without specific tones to sing, people must have found pleasure in letting out their feelings at the insistence of loud beats from any number and kinds of sources. Recall that Chapter 2 analyzed contrasting aspects of human culture and human personality: the Apollonian and the Dionysian. The Apollonian half of human beings enjoys order; the Dionysian half exults in unrestrained expressions of feeling. Neither side is sufficient by itself. Civilization advances with Apollonian order, but without Dionysian spontaneity, it can become rigid and uncreative. Dancing to Dionysian rhythms puts Apollonian control temporarily to sleep. Inspired by the rhythm, dancers can shut down their rational side and be driven by forces buried deep in the human unconscious.

Rhythm in music, as in poetry, is an alternation between stress and unstress. It acquires its different forms according to the pattern of alternation used. A familiar rhythm is that of the waltz, created from a stressed beat followed by two unstressed beats. Also described as a "stately" rhythm, it is far more Apollonian than it is Dionysian, and was thus suitable for the aristocrats of nineteenth-century ballrooms, though it had its Dionysian side in an era when touching the opposite sex in public was otherwise frowned upon. Popular among aristocrats of the eighteenth century, the minuet was also based on Apollonian (that is, rigid and repetitive) rhythms. So are the marches used for funeral and graduation processions. Plato approved of stately rhythms, which for him lent gravity to public occasions, affirming order in the state. He disapproved strongly of rhythms that were there only to excite the emotions.

People of today who enjoy letting go on a dance floor to the beat of rock bands evidently find Dionysian liberation a satisfying escape from the Apollonian demands of household duties, jobs, or schoolwork. The rhythms of rock and hip-hop probably date back to the dawn of humanity, and may well have bonded groups together in a collective, joyous release of pent-up energy. Dionysian rhythms have kept us in touch with our deeper self, our wild natures. If not expressed through art, they might find less appropriate means of escape.

In formal musical art, including concert pieces, standard popular songs, country, traditional dance music, and at least the beginning stages of rock, the rhythmic underpinning is often pronounced and unchanged either for the whole work or for specific portions of it. We can say that rhythm is the mortar that holds a work together, that gives coherence to a collection of sounds. A change in rhythm can be a major event, often very exciting to the listener. It opens up new possibilities, new directions, but then the new rhythm must continue the job of holding the piece together.

A conceivable theory of formal musical origins can be expressed as follows: When musical tones joined the ancient human passion for rhythm, a new force was born that provided a way for emotions to be expressed, released, and controlled. Once rhythm was discovered, it never left musical art. Even the plainsong, a chant sung by medieval monks and clerics, has a rhythm, though it is hard to detect because there are so many stressed tones, and those not stressed tend to be delicately sung. If we think the music of Impressionist composer Claude Debussy seems to be lacking in rhythm, perhaps our untrained ears cannot detect the subtle changes in stress marked by a subdued percussion section. In the famous *Bolero* by Debussy's

Archetypes in This Chapter

Blues more than just a musical genre, this term also refers to a feeling of sadness and frustration that accompanies life and especially love.

Hip originated before the popularity of hip-hop music; suggests people who shake their hips in a confident, carefree way and has come to mean that one is on top of things and very up to date.

Jazz has come to define much that is non-musical, as in "jazz it up," which means "give it style"; can also refer to "a whole bunch of stuff too complicated to go into at the moment," as in "all that jazz."

Rock can now mean anything from "We're going to win this game" to "We're going to make our presence felt at the zoning-board meeting."

Roll has the connotation of having things go smoothly, as in "on a roll," or springing into action, as in the military's "Let's roll!"

Scoundrel roguish male who embodies a Dionysian approach to life, forever seeking pleasure and shunning responsibility. Many contemporary rock and hip-hop musicians consciously or unconsciously emulate this archetype.

compatriot and fellow Impressionist Maurice Ravel, the underlying rhythm is so pronounced that it takes over the entire piece.

Desiring to free themselves from the restraints that traditional rhythms impose, some composers attempt to be totally arrhythmic; that is, they avoid all regular alternations of stress and unstress, seldom repeating a pattern. The listener is kept off guard, presumably on edge, and the piece aspires to create a mood of agitation and emotional instability. Whether this is done because the composer wishes to be "different" or to make some kind of statement through the music, the reality is that non-rhythm is a kind of rhythm. Even if every tone were stressed, the result would be a kind of rhythm.

Thus the issue is not what does or does not constitute rhythm but why music cannot exist without it. What is the magic that rhythm weaves inside us? We can speculate at great length, of course. Children are conceived in rhythm, born in rhythm; parents clap their hands in rhythm to keep children from crying. The universe itself throbs with rhythms: the rotation of the planet, the alternation of the seasons, incoming and outgoing tides, birth and death. How about order and disorder, Apollo and Dionysus, belief and doubt, joy and sorrow? Anthropologists studying early rituals have suggested that rhythmic effects were used to express the heartbeat of Mother Earth.

Rock percussionist Mickey Hart of the Grateful Dead once said, "Rhythm is at the very center of our lives." If you were to ask a number of people which musical element they could most easily dispense with, rhythm would most probably not be the answer.

Melody

The art of music began with differentiated tones played or sung in certain patterns that might or might not have been repeated. One might have flowed into another. These patterns were melodies. **Melody** is the part we remember of a song or a symphonic movement. If we remember nothing beyond a "babble" of instruments and a great deal of percussion, chances are many of us would ask, "What happened to the melody?"

Music was my refuge. I could crawl into the place between the notes and curl my back to loneliness.
—**Maya Angelou**

The discovery of tone made melody possible. Melody can be defined in two ways: one, most familiar to Western ears, as *a significant sequence of musical tones that form a unity, like a sentence of prose, and are usually repeated later in the exact order or as a recognizable variation of the original*; or two, as found in many non-Western cultures, *an arrangement of tones in a flowing sequence that may or may not have a definite end.* Certain melodies were used over and over because they were pleasing, and a method was needed for preserving them. Musical instruments may have been invented for this purpose.

Opera-goers listening to a new work in its premiere performance may at first find that "there are no melodies in it." Someone accustomed to only Western symphonic music may wonder why, at first hearing, there is no beautiful melody in sitar music from India, or may denounce a rock band for pounding out "just noise." But with any new work, we should try to hear what the composer wants us to hear, and *then* we can decide whether we want to hear it again.

Many are understandably drawn to what may be termed *romantic* melody, the melodic line that falls soothingly on the ears and is usually repeated. Much of its emotional impact has to do with the instruments that play it: often the violin, piano, guitar, and flute—instruments that produce delicate sounds. Romantic melody tends to be "gentle," befitting the tender emotions it calls up. It is almost always slow. Popular classics like "Smoke Gets in Your Eyes" and "Melancholy Baby" are said to be melodious for these reasons and, when sung today, are usually accompanied by delicate, as opposed to brassy and percussive, instruments.

A romantic musical style was dominant during the nineteenth and early twentieth centuries. Composers such as Brahms and Tchaikovsky provide lush sequences of tones that are easily recalled and that evoke emotions within the listener. Brahms's "Cradle Song," or "Lullaby," is known throughout the world and has become almost synonymous with treasured memories of an infant's earliest days. The main theme in Tchaikovsky's *Romeo and Juliet* overture reminds people of the joys of first love. Translated into a popular song called "Our Love," it contributed to Tchaikovsky's reputation as a king of melody.

Music is the arithmetic of sounds as optics is the geometry of light.
—**Claude Debussy**

Rhapsody on a Theme of Paganini by Sergei Rachmaninoff (1873–1943) offers excellent examples of romantic melody. The main theme is introduced at the beginning—a sprightly and graceful melody written by Nicolò Paganini, an Italian violinist and composer who lived a century earlier. Though Paganini's work has long been popular with violinists because of its intricate challenges to the instrument, Rachmaninoff's variations on the theme have become immensely more popular with audiences than the original—especially his Seventeenth Variation, in which, after a dramatic silence, the piano enters and plays a melody that is Paganini's lively theme turned around and performed at a much slower tempo. When the string section passionately repeats the theme, the listener cannot help experiencing a surge of emotion.

The world of art has its visual equivalents of familiar and unfamiliar melodies. It too experienced the romanticism of the nineteenth century, producing the calm of peaceful country scenes as well as the majesty of natural forces such as the ocean and towering mountains. Modern artists who wanted to break away from romanticism found support in new and unfamiliar styles of music, while their colleagues in the visual arts attempted to capture musical sound on canvas. Georges Braque, the Cubist painter discussed in Chapter 5, gave us *The Musician*, with Cubist images that parallel the breaking up of the romantic melodic line, as Cubism breaks up visual experience into fragments instead of continuous vision (Color Plate 17).

Among jazz musicians, melody usually means the theme that begins their performance and on which the remainder of it is based. By the conclusion of the piece, the original theme is usually different from the melody we heard at the outset —*very* different. Jazz is complex, requiring an initial willingness to devote the time needed to explore its many treasures. Many of us, at least in the beginning, become confused or bored when the melody disappears and is replaced by varied tones of varied instruments.

An effective way to increase your appreciation for what is often considered non-melody is to become a more attentive listener to jazz. In doing so, you will find variations on a melody performed by different instruments throughout a piece. From jazz move on to **chamber music** (concert music written for a few instruments rather than a symphony orchestra). Once again you will hear clearly defined themes that are then developed through variations into ever more complex patterns of sounds. By extending your definition of melody, you will find yourself enjoying a broader range of musical experience.

Sometimes melody is a sequence of tones that seems to go on indefinitely without repeating. During the rebellion of the 1960s against "the establishment," sitar music achieved popularity in the West, partly because of its extended melodic lines and its clearly non-Western sound. Some modern composers are drawn to non-Western sound in an effort to break away from the traditional. Philip Glass, a contemporary American composer, writes melodic lines that keep repeating a single pattern. Some have called his work monotonous and endlessly repetitive, while others find it pleasantly hypnotic. Director Martin Scorsese (to be discussed in Chapter 10) recruited Glass to write the Asian-sounding score for the film *Kundun* (1997), the story of the Dalai Lama. Although Glass is Western, the music was authentically Tibetan, and therefore unfamiliar to most Western ears. Listening to this music is a good way to explore alternative kinds of melody. We should remember that the so-called "beauty of melody" is a matter of historical period and cultural heritage. Not that all melody is beautiful—or that no melody is beautiful; rather, beauty in music has a lot to do with familiarity and the kind of instruments popular within a given cultural tradition.

Extreme departures from tradition have characterized modern Western music since the earliest years of the twentieth century, when composers reacted strongly against the romantic conception of melody. The aggressive **dissonance** in their music has had much to do with its deliberate lack of appeal to those who want music to sound romantic.

Throughout the twentieth century, composers kept experimenting with non-traditional scales and sounds. Sometimes they invented new kinds of musical notes that were not in any scale anyone knew but had to be half-sung and half-spoken. Sometimes composers even have long stretches of silence in their music. In recent years a significant number of composers have reacted against *modernism*, especially what they consider "noisy jangling and crashing," a fierce determination to sound like nothing that ever came before. The new music is called, like the new in visual art, *postmodern*. The most frequently performed works of this genre come from a group of composers calling themselves **minimalists**. Their goal is to divest music of modernism's unnecessary trappings and return to the basic elements, particularly rhythm. Minimalist music, such as that by Philip Glass and John Adams, is sometimes dismissed as coldly formal and unemotional, as well as monotonous, by unsympathetic listeners who also find it unmelodic. But like all unfamiliar music, minimalist compositions can reward those willing to take the time to listen.

It has been said that music is what emotion sounds like. And the emotional life of an individual is exceedingly complex. To insist that music sound only a certain way is like saying that people should feel only a certain way. We can turn away from strange-sounding music, just as we don't have to welcome any stranger we think we don't want to know. But we also have the freedom to make friends.

Harmony and the Orchestra

In Asian music, tones are usually played by themselves, that is, without *harmony*, which is the simultaneous production of tones by voices or instruments. So accustomed are Westerners to hearing simultaneous tones that they tend to take harmony for granted. But like melody, harmony has historical and cultural roots.

During the first millennium, Christian churches incorporated music into the private services of monks and priests as well as public masses. Emphasis was placed on song as a means of communicating with God. Greatly influenced by ancient Hebrew chants, these sung prayers became known as *plainsong*. They were performed in unison by clerics, acting as one voice praising God's glory and asking for mercy and forgiveness. Harmony created by units of voices singing different tones would have been out of place, a violation of the belief that all people were the same in the eyes of God.

Music provides a kind of pleasure which human nature cannot do without.

—**Confucius**

During the sixteenth century, as the Renaissance, with its rebirth of classical culture, moved from one European country to another, bringing with it a celebration of life on earth, music—secular music—was eagerly sought. Since the Renaissance emphasized enjoyment during one's brief stay on earth, music could fill leisure hours with many pleasures. The royal courts all had musicians on hand, and new instruments were invented to explore the richness and sensuality of secular music. In these venues scarcely an hour of the day went by without the sounds of lute, recorder, or oboe, playing sometimes alone but often in small groups. Renaissance composers explored the harmonious interweaving of instruments and voices, as if to say that music should be the contribution of a number of individuals, each adding to life's enjoyment, each with a musical statement to make.

The Renaissance also celebrated the uniqueness of each human being. No longer need music be limited to plainsong, delivered in unison to obscure the differences among the singers. Harmony allowed for a variety of interweaving musical themes, each with its own melody, played or sung by individualized instruments or voices. Eventually the development of harmony would lead to the complexities of the *baroque* style in music, art, and architecture, a style that flourished in Europe during the seventeenth century.

The invention of harmony also made possible an innovative art form known as *opera*, a collaboration of many distinct individuals: composers, orchestras, singers, poets who wrote the words, dancers, and that new species of artist, the scenic designer, the whole becoming a rich and complex visual tapestry and festival of sound, all working together to give added meaning to the concept of harmony. (A fuller discussion of opera is included in Chapter 8, The Musical Stage.)

Orchestras grew in size and complexity, and as they did, composers eagerly explored the range of the new instruments. By the eighteenth century the **symphony**, a musical form in separate units, or movements, became a concert staple. Major aggregations of musicians became known as symphony orchestras; these steadily increased in numbers as Haydn, Mozart, Beethoven, Brahms, and Mahler wrote works that required more and more instruments. One of Mahler's major works late in the nineteenth century is titled *The Symphony of a Thousand* because it involves literally that many musicians and singers. Tchaikovsky's *1812 Overture* needs, in addition to a massive orchestra, numerous cannons that are fired as the music reaches its climax. Beethoven's Ninth Symphony is now performed by an enormous orchestra of at least 150 musicians in addition to a chorus of perhaps 200 voices.

In 1990 Leonard Bernstein, an American composer and conductor, was invited to present the Ninth Symphony at the site of the newly fallen Berlin Wall, which had, since the ending of World War II, separated East and West Berlin. On this occasion *more* than 200 musicians and singers from the United States, the Soviet Union, Great Britain, and France participated. The theme of the final movement, a choral setting of the poet Schiller's "Ode to Joy," was an anthem heralding a new dawn of freedom and friendship between the previously separated citizens of Berlin, as well as the ringing hope that all oppressed peoples would triumph in their struggle against tyranny.

To open the 1998 winter Olympics in Nagano, Japan, conductor Seiji Ozawa performed the "Ode to Joy" using choruses from four locations around the globe, joined together by satellite. This time the music represented global unity, as athletes from diverse nations, unable to communicate with each other through words, could find in Beethoven's music a common bond.

Musical harmony, especially in the glorious complexities of the great symphony orchestras, has become a model of human society at its most ideal. It requires every musician to pull together for one common purpose. No one sound can be any more important than another, yet each one has its moment of prominence. If one tone is flat, the entire enterprise suffers. The ultimate product is a testimony to the genius of the individual.

Silence

After silence, that which comes nearest to expressing the inexpressible is music.

—**Aldous Huxley**

Silence is the unpublicized ingredient that makes music possible in the same way that the empty space around a sculpture makes the sculpture possible, or the judicious use of wall space can make or break an art exhibit. Just imagine twenty-five original van Goghs crammed together: "Where is *The Starry Night*? Oh, there it is. I almost missed it. Funny, but somehow it's not as exciting as I thought it would be." Fast-forwarding a DVD destroys all dramatic value. The acceleration erases the pauses, which are as significant as the words themselves. After all, if characters talk non-stop, how can a dramatic situation develop? In music, the spaces—or silences—between notes can be equally important.

To deepen an appreciation of music, it is necessary to hear and enjoy silence. Silence has been an integral part of many works. The pauses in the second movement, the "Funeral March," of Beethoven's Third Symphony are as famous as the themes that precede and follow them. They make possible the dramatic effect when the main theme of the movement returns for the last time. There is silence, then part of the theme, then more silence, then more of the theme. The effect reminds the listener of someone trying valiantly to hold back tears.

Think of the last time you were in the presence of someone struggling for self-control while overcome by a powerful surge of emotion. Weren't the silences full of meaning? Great composers handle silences in the same way that great artists like Leonardo da Vinci handle shadows. Great stage actors owe something of their greatness to the mastery they have achieved over the words that they do *not* speak and to the silences before and after the words they do speak.

A famous solo theme for French horn occurs soon after the opening of the fourth movement of Brahms's First Symphony. The moment is heralded by a timpani roll, which is followed by the introduction of the French horn theme. Some conductors, recognizing the musical benefits of silence, make the orchestra pause for several measures before the theme is heard. This silence dramatically intensifies the significance of what follows. The French horn enters like an actor at long last making an appearance for which the audience has been eagerly waiting. In some interpretations, however, there is almost no pause at all, perhaps losing an opportunity for creating a thrilling moment.

The composer John Cage (1912–1992) is famous for having incorporated silence into his work and making it as important as the actual notes he wrote down for musicians to play. One of his compositions, *4'33"*, named for the four and a half minutes it takes to perform it, asks the artist to sit at the piano for that length of time and, with his gestures, maintain the required tempo. Cage insisted that the "notes are silent," but that they are there all the same. One of his longer pieces for the piano combines both played and silent notes, and in yet another, the pianist performs a series of complex chords and difficult "runs" up and down the keyboard, and then sits perfectly still for about fifteen minutes. Audiences, according to one critic, seem "almost afraid to cough." A strong influence on Cage's work was Zen Buddhism (discussed in Chapter 10), an extremely austere and disciplined form of Buddhism, demanding long hours of meditation in absolute silence.

What ultimately distinguishes one musician from another is not only the ability to play the notes as written and at the proper tempo, but the musical intuition that manifests itself. One way the professional ear can detect the presence of this intuition, or this "feeling for the music," is to listen to how the performer manipulates the silences that surround the tones. Three world-class pianists might record Beethoven's *Pathetique Sonata*, each playing exactly the same notes and giving proper attention to the tempo indicated by the composer, but the interpretation by each will have subtle touches unique to that musician. In almost every instance the telling factor is the handling of silence. Here a pause is elongated, there foreshortened. As with the space surrounding a sculpture, silence in music helps to define, to single out, to create individuality.

The most evident gift from great music is its sound. The subtlest, least publicized gift is the very absence of sound. The definition in the Overview of this chapter was: *Music is the shaped sound between silences.*

The Varieties of Musical Experience

We would have to write a book several times this size to do justice to the multitude of musical experiences available in the humanities. There are so many styles, so many musical forms, that singling out a few is difficult indeed. Within those parameters, however, certain kinds of musical experience—musical genres of the past and present—illustrate what music has to offer and help to explain why the humanities are indispensable to a well-lived, happy life.

A Bach Fugue

Johann Sebastian Bach (1685–1750) was born in a Germany that did not regard music as an art form, that did not recognize what music could do for the human spirit, that viewed music either as court entertainment, composed and performed for upper-class amusement by hirelings paid to do a job, or else as a subordinate adjunct to religious services. The music with which Bach is associated, which indeed he came to epitomize, grew out of religion but went beyond religion in its impact and influence on the future of music as an art. It became the very epitome of the **baroque**, a highly complex style not only of music but of art and architecture as well. Historians of the humanities usually date the baroque period from the middle of the seventeenth century to 1750, which happens to be the very year in which Bach died.

Johann Sebastian Bach, considered a mere employee hired to play the church organ and compose a few hymns, ended up revolutionizing the art of music.

Source: The Granger Collection.

Classical music is stereotyped as an art of the dead, a repertory that begins with Bach and terminates with Mahler and Puccini. People are sometimes surprised to learn that composers are still writing at all.
—**Alex Ross**

The baroque period was characterized by architectural grandeur and an elaborate use of color and ornamentation. Civic buildings, such as those that still line the Ringstrasse, the main street of Vienna, were adorned with gilt, statuary, and other forms of embellishment, none of which was intended to be purely functional. The term *baroque* was taken from French and Portuguese words that meant "imperfect pearl" and applied to the new style, which was far from classical simplicity. Architecture made abundant use of curved rather than straight lines. And baroque music is exceptionally intricate.

Catholicism found in baroque architectural splendor one means of bringing people back to the fold. The German monk Martin Luther (1483–1546) had rebelled against Catholicism for what he considered its moral corruption, including the fact that the laws of celibacy were regularly broken, even by church leaders. With other reformers, he had started a revolutionary movement known as the Protestant Reformation, which aimed to divest religion of its Catholic sensuality. In sharp contrast to the stark, wooden churches of the Protestant Reformation, the Catholic baroque houses of worship, especially in Italy and Poland, reintroduced marble, brilliant colors, and statues, perhaps in an effort to encourage defectors to return to a reinvented religion with an appeal to both the spirit and the senses. These churches dating from the seventeenth century are adorned with flying angels suspended from brightly painted ceilings and smiling gold cherubs resting near the tops of marble columns. They were for their time the epitome of opulence, offering both dramatic and aesthetic appeal without apology.

Despite the many reforms instituted by Luther and his followers, Lutheranism remained closer to Catholicism than would be true of the multiple Protestant sects which were to develop. While Lutherans generally shunned the impetus toward elaborate visual ornamentation of the churches, they felt differently about ornamentation of their music. Music became especially important in the Lutheran service, for which Bach composed many of his works. As the era progressed, composers, both religious and secular, sought to outdo one another in the intricacy of their compositions. They made strong use of **counterpoint**, playing one melodic line against another, both melodic lines being given equal value and dominance.

Harmony, of course, had been standard in music since the early Renaissance, but Bach's counterpoint carried complexity a step further. Nonetheless, even though he had achieved considerable recognition for his music during his lifetime, after his death his church still considered him as primarily a great organist rather than a composer. When they first began to hear his compositions, congregations may have been slightly confused, if not overwhelmed by what they heard.

When Bach was hired to play the organ—and, if he wished, to compose little pieces to accompany the service—church music in early eighteenth-century Germany was hardly a recognized form of high art. Bach's appetite for experimenting with organ sound was insatiable. Seeking to expand his musical horizons, Bach took a leave of absence and went in 1705 to study with the famous Swedish organist and composer Dietrich Buxtehude, returning with new works of such intricacy and virtuosity that the church choir often could not sing them. By this time, however, word of the new music began to spread. Eventually he became musical director and choir director at St. Thomas's Church in Leipzig, where he remained for most of his productive life, scarcely traveling more than a few miles from the city.

His reputation expanded and blossomed, then began to fade as he grew older, even though the complexity of his work deepened. In some quarters he began to be called old-fashioned. He had almost single-handedly brought baroque music to its pinnacle and then was accused of not being modern enough. By midcentury Franz Josef Haydn (1732–1809) was learning his craft and soon would give birth to 104 symphonies, earning him the reputation he still enjoys as father of that musical genre. Haydn returned to the relative simplicity of classicism, and his tremendous influence helped to make baroque complexity obsolete. But even in Bach's declining years, younger composers were already experimenting with the style that Haydn would make famous.

Through the new works, German music was attaining stature as an art form, and thus the great repertoire of Bach—the cantatas, oratorios, and magnificent displays of counterpoint known as **fugues**—was considered dated even before it was ever really discovered. Bach's music would have to wait a full century before it would take its place among acknowledged masterworks.

Confined both geographically and professionally, Bach found liberation in exploring the possibilities of musical language. The baroque style required not only long, highly fluid melodies and countermelodies, but also **improvisation**—a spontaneous variation or set of variations on a given theme. Through improvisation he could take wings and soar into the endless skies of inner space.

Track 6

Music in the time of both Bach and Haydn was not expected to express a composer's innermost emotions; and indeed Bach's music is frequently labeled *intellectual.* It is, for example, greatly admired by mathematicians, who see in it a musical parallel to higher calculus. Nonetheless, there is indeed an emotional side to it. Bach's great Toccata and Fugue in D Minor draws the listener into a vortex of sensations that are almost indescribable. The ear discerns the many melodic strands that play against each other, and the inner eye translates the sounds into patterns of light and lines that crisscross, engulf each other, and continually change into shapes never before seen or imagined. Surrendering to this music, we find ourselves visiting strange inner landscapes flooded with both thoughts and feelings.

We need only listen to the D Minor performed on an organ to be astounded that one pair of hands could master so difficult a composition.

A **toccata** is a freestyle musical form designed to allow the performer to display virtuosity; it is frequently, as in the case of the D Minor work, followed by a fugue, which is more strictly controlled by established musical laws. In a toccata the composer or performer may improvise on the stated themes, taking them in a variety of directions.

This practice has definite counterparts in jazz. It is no coincidence that jazz players often acknowledge a strong debt to Bach, particularly for his genius at improvisation, and often include variations on Bach melodies in their repertoire. The fugue allows for the simultaneous hearing of different melodies played or sung; it is a swift-moving form, stabilized by the laws of counterpoint—the melodic lines heard simultaneously must complement, not conflict with, each other.

We need only listen to the D Minor performed on an organ to be astounded that one pair of hands could master so difficult a composition. The idea behind the fugue is to demonstrate that what for the average person would be an impossibility is indeed well within the capabilities of the performer. It allows both composer and performer to display their virtuosity. At the same time, the intricacies of the form require strong guidelines as well as enormous technical skills, developed over long years of practice. The result may sound as though the composer were allowing imagination free reign, but in actuality the music is rigorously disciplined. The major jazz composers and performers of our time are often highly trained musicians whose flights of improvisation follow definite rules, even as do the fugues of Bach.

The linear form of Bach's music allows us to experience its complexities little by little, note by note, rather than have them overwhelm us all at once, as baroque architectural interiors can do.

A Beethoven Symphony

Sometimes the history of the humanities lopes along for many years, even decades, without producing an artist who rises to the highest level of creative achievement. It can also happen that many artistic geniuses appear around the same time. The late fifteenth century in Italy, for example, produced three visual artists, acknowledged to be perhaps the world's greatest, all contemporary with each other: Leonardo, Michelangelo, and Raphael. Germany can boast that it gave the world Mozart and Beethoven during the late eighteenth century.

I heard one evening a symphony of Beethoven's. I thereupon fell ill of fever; and when recovered I was–a musician.

—**Richard Wagner**

In the baroque musical tradition, which Bach epitomized, composers worked in a limited range of musical forms to find their own way through the music. Bach achieved greatness by making the forms accommodate his tremendous musical intellect and imagination. Mozart (more fully discussed in Chapter 8) easily rivaled Bach with his phenomenal output—and in a much shorter lifespan (1756–1791)—composing not only operas but symphonies, chamber music for inexhaustible combinations of instruments, several huge masses, a long list of songs, and concerti for both violin and piano. Mozart expanded the capabilities of the symphony orchestra, thus preparing the way for Beethoven, who would take it to new heights. In order to provide emotional release from a tormented life in which he gradually lost his hearing, Beethoven composed in new or greatly expanded musical forms. It is not an exaggeration to say he reinvented the music of the West.

Ludwig van Beethoven expanded the range of many musical forms, including the symphony.

Source: Culver Pictures, Inc.

Whereas Bach was primarily a church composer/ performer, Beethoven composed for churches, concert halls, small salons, private performances, royal chambers, but above all for himself. When he lost his hearing during the peak of his musical career, Beethoven turned inward, and out of his complex and anguished soul came sounds no one had ever heard. Even today, more than a century and a half after the composer's death, when every note written by him has been played and interpreted by thousands upon thousands of musicians and heard by millions, new listeners and performers can find in the music some as yet undisclosed aspect of Beethoven's gigantic personality as well as some unexplored region of their own inner space.

Beethoven built on the new tradition in music established before him by Haydn and Mozart. This tradition combined secular, religious, and nationalistic trends into one. It declared that the music of northern Europe was every bit the equal of Italian music, which had been for centuries the dominant musical tradition of the West. In particular, it created and then quickly broadened the scope of the symphony, which became for Germany what the opera was for Italy.

The development of the symphony cannot be measured in terms of quantity alone. Haydn wrote 104 symphonies, Mozart forty-one, and Beethoven "just" nine. (Later, Johannes Brahms, intimidated by the majestic symphonic creations of Beethoven, would spend twenty years working on his first symphony and would ultimately leave the world "just" four!)

In 1804, after having given the world two symphonies in the tradition of Mozart (who had already stretched the limits of the form beyond anything yet known) Beethoven came forth with his Third or E-flat Major Symphony, which he named *Eroica* ("heroic"). The premiere proved to be an occasion for which the music world was still not completely prepared, even though the work had been preceded by Mozart's last symphony, the titanic *Jupiter*. After all, a symphony was originally a twenty-minute concert diversion, consisting of four movements: the first moderately paced, the second slow and lyrical, the third rapid and lighthearted, and the fourth rousing and climactic. The four movements were related only in terms of a composer's characteristic style; they were not expected to make a unified statement of any kind.

Beethoven is believed to have dedicated his Third Symphony to Napoleon, depicted in this famous portrait, then rescinded the dedication when word reached the composer that Napoleon had declared himself emperor.

Source: Jacques Louis David, *Napoleon Crossing the St. Bernard Pass*, 1800. Credit: © Erich Lessing/Art Resource, NY.

The *Eroica* was twice the length of the *Jupiter*. It was a work so huge in conception, so complex in execution, and so overwhelming in impact that by all rights it should have invited immediate comparison with Michelangelo's *David*, the Sistine Chapel ceiling, or the great tragedies of Shakespeare. Unfortunately, many of the first listeners could not accommodate the work's heroic dimensions or its daring innovations, particularly its heavy use of seventh chords, up to that time a musical taboo, considered barbarically dissonant, unfit for civilized ears.

In the opinion of music historians, the most astonishing aspect of the *Eroica* is that it is not just big for the sake of bigness. One critic sums up the matter: "We are used to the scale of the *Eroica*, but what is forever new is a musical substance which requires every second of the vast time expanse which Beethoven organized to contain it. In its size it is wholly efficient, as fine an example of economy of structure as any four-minute Bach fugue."[1] In the *Eroica*, not only do the four movements constitute a unity, but each succeeding movement sounds like a perfect complement to the one before it. It is clear that Beethoven did not finish one movement and then tack on another as though the preceding one had not existed.

The first movement is on a grand, heroic scale, an epic style with noble themes and huge orchestration to be rivaled only by the composer's own fifth and ninth symphonies. The story is that Beethoven, like a number of artists such as Jacques Louis David (1748–1825), was inspired by the heroic image of Napoleon as the liberator of Europe. He thus created, in the opening movement, music that paralleled his feelings and then dedicated the entire work to the man he perceived as savior of the free world. When word reached the composer that his hero had demanded to be crowned emperor, Beethoven apparently rescinded the dedication.

One is tempted to hear in the second movement a musical parallel to Beethoven's profound disillusionment with Napoleon.

The *Eroica*, for many, came to embody the "common man" movement, even if Napoleon did not. In fact, much of Beethoven's music has the same fist-shaking thunder we find in the work of Michelangelo. A musical rebel, defying all tradition, plagued by illness that would eventually rob him of his hearing, misunderstood and criticized by many, he could readily identify with revolutionary movements in his native Germany, as well as in America and France.

One is tempted to hear in the second movement a musical parallel to Beethoven's profound disillusionment with Napoleon. Profound sorrow is certainly there, as indicated by the tempo notation: *marcia funebre* (funeral march). It is the slowest of all slow movements, dirgelike and heartbroken. We have already spoken of it in the section on silence as a musical element. Whether Napoleon was the direct cause of the sorrow or whether Beethoven, having exhausted the range of noble emotions, found himself exploring the depths of sadness, we cannot know. But we can say that the first two movements of the *Eroica* strongly suggest an experience common to nearly everyone: the passage from heroic, idealistic youth to maturity and its awareness of tragedy.

The third movement, by contrast, is almost shocking, with its galloping pace and precise horns, all of it sounding like nothing so much as a hunting party. Out of place? Surely not. Listening carefully to every note of the funeral march shows that there is only so much emotional wrenching one can sustain. Life must go on. The depressed spirit must pull itself up from despair.

The finale begins with a graceful, dancelike melody suggestive of polite society: civilization restored, so to speak. This leads through an intricate development back into the same heroic mood that opened the symphony. We have passed from romantic illusion to the depths of tragedy and, through struggle, upward again to a more mature, sober, and deliberate affirmation. The composer of the *Eroica* captures the human soul in full range. It would not mark Beethoven's last glimpse of paradise.

Beethoven's Ninth Symphony was composed around 1818, when he was totally deaf. It is easily four times the length of a late Mozart symphony, and twice that of even the *Eroica*. Not the journey of a young man's soul coping with the sobering realities of life, the Ninth Symphony is rather the final statement of a gigantic mentality that has struggled for years with both physical and creative suffering—of a person who has labored to find and capture it all, as Michelangelo, two centuries earlier, had sought perfection in marble, and as Einstein, a century later, would seek the ultimate equation for unifying the interactions among all the forces in the universe.

During the first three movements of the Ninth, Beethoven gives us one haunting melody after another, complex rhythms, intricate harmonies, and bold dissonance. He seems to be striving to find a musical equivalent to every feeling that can be experienced. By the fourth movement he appears to have concluded that the orchestra alone was not enough to express the sounds he must have heard in the far recesses of his silent world. He needed human voices.

Other composers before him had written large choral works: Bach's *Passion According to Saint Matthew*, Haydn's *Creation*, and Mozart's *Requiem*, to name three supreme examples. But Beethoven pushes the human voice farther than many have believed possible.

There remains considerable controversy about the final movement of the Ninth. Some critics say it takes us as close to the gates of heaven as we can get in this earthly lifetime. Some have called it a musical embarrassment, totally unsingable. One soprano, after attempting it, vehemently declared that Beethoven had no respect whatever for the female voice. Others have suggested that in his deafness Beethoven heard extraordinary sounds that were not contained within the boundaries of music and for which there were no known instruments, not even the human voice. Perhaps such sentiments overromanticize the work. But perhaps not. No one will ever know what Beethoven was hearing.

The musical setting for Friedrich von Schiller's "Ode to Joy," the main theme of the fourth movement, has attained the stature of an international hymn. By far, the majority opinion about this music is that it transcends its own "unsingability" and any breach of musical taste it may commit. Asking whether one "likes it" seems beside the point. One can only feel humbled by its majesty. Listening to Beethoven's Ninth Symphony is discovering what human creativity really means.

The premiere performance of the work in Vienna, at that time the capital of European music, was attended by every Viennese musical luminary. By now fully convinced of the composer's genius, they were eager to discover what new sounds the great man could possibly bring forth from an inner world that was barred forever from the real sounds of humanity and nature. Beethoven was the co-conductor.

Witnesses to the event have left behind stories of the performance, especially of how the maestro conducted with sustained vigor, hearing his own orchestra no doubt, for when the "other" orchestra had finished the work and the enthusiastic applause began, Beethoven had not yet put down his baton. When at last he realized what was happening, he started to walk from the stage, perhaps feeling his music had not communicated. But the other conductor caught up with him and turned him around to see the people on their feet, shouting "Bravissimo!" Beethoven simply bowed his head. No one will ever know what it was he had heard, just as he could not have known what *they* had heard. Nonetheless, that moment lives on in the history of the humanities as a rare meeting of souls in that strange space where the spirit of art lives.

Art Songs

An art song is written as part of the concert repertoire of great singers.

So far we have discussed possible origins of music, the basic elements of music, and two major musical forms and composers who achieved distinction through making glorious musical history. For many of us, however, everyday musical experience comes from *songs*, much shorter compositions with easily remembered melodies and rhythms.

We had nursery songs to teach us and lullabies to soothe us. Most of us learned the alphabet by singing a song about the letters. Nonsense songs with refrains like *Nikkity Nakkity Noo Noo Noo* gave us an outlet for feelings we could not always understand or find words for. Some kind of song-making—if only the spontaneous chanting of a child—is innate to the growing-up process at every time and in every place. Like poetry and the other arts, song evolved into ever more sophisticated styles. Eventually it reached a point at which the composer's choices were rigidly defined by the rules of music.

The birth of song as art probably dates back to the classical period when epic poems like *The Iliad* (see Chapter 4) were sung by minstrels as a means of being more easily remembered. In the early Middle Ages monks sang their prayers as a regular part of the worship service. By the later Middle Ages, however, wealthy aristocrats demanded song as part of court entertainment, and the subject almost always was love. By the time of the great composers we have discussed, song was a recognized art form, expected in concert programs, and performed by highly trained professionals. These works have come to be known as art songs, as distinct from popular songs, which are not originally written as concert pieces.

Mozart and Beethoven wrote art songs in addition to their innumerable other works. Much of the time they supplied musical settings for the poetry of their day. With their prodigious genius they could create these shorter forms fast enough to fulfill the growing demand from well-known singers who needed to extend their repertoires. It was also a way to earn money.

Our sweetest songs are those that tell the saddest thoughts.

—**Percy Bysshe Shelley**

A genius of the art song was Franz Schubert, who in his tragically brief life (1797–1828) composed more than 600! He wrote painstakingly for both singer and accompanist, his musical settings precisely suiting the words and fitting the mood of a poem. An excellent introduction to Schubert is "The Trout," with its sprightly melodic line and rippling fishlike accompaniment, and also "Death and the Maiden," with its agitated melodies and strangely peaceful accompaniment. The maiden of the title sees Death, a savage-looking skeleton, approaching and pleads with him to pass by and not touch her. But Death turns out to be friendly and promises that she will sleep gently in his arms.

Among Schubert's most famous works is the musical setting he gave to "Ave Maria." There is a legend that the composer, chronically poor, wrote the piece rapidly on a napkin or tablecloth and sold it to someone for the equivalent of fifteen cents. True or not, the story does suggest what we know about Schubert: namely, that he was unsuccessful in his lifetime, though, unlike van Gogh, he had a small circle of friends who recognized his genius.

Folk Songs

Unlike many art forms that have established traditions within the humanities, the folk song has followed few aesthetic rules. Some folk songs originated centuries ago, perhaps as a way of spreading news in isolated areas, perhaps as musical improvisations by people who had little else to entertain them. Folk songs didn't require expert musical accompaniment or trained voices. They were likely to be handed down from generation to generation and changed every time they were sung. That's why you'll find many versions of the same song. Often the dedicated concert-goer considers folk music too haphazard in its origins and careless in its execution to warrant serious consideration. Folk songs, however, do indeed fulfill a major requirement of art: *they endure.*

Folk music in recent times has often attained the status of the art song, especially when sung by accomplished singers like Joan Baez, Joni Mitchell, Bob Dylan, Willie Nelson, Ani Difranco, and Ferraby Lionheart. Yet it can still be a participants' art, an affirmation of group identity. In certain parts of the country, let a fiddler introduce the first few notes of "Turkey in the Straw," and almost immediately people are clapping their hands or dancing. During the civil rights movement of the 1960s, the song "We Shall Overcome" created—and even now can create—instant bonding among people who may never have seen each other before. Surely there is a place in the humanities for music that can bring groups together as nothing else can.

Songs sung spontaneously at rallies or sporting events are not exactly folk music, but they fulfill a similar purpose in promoting group solidarity. For example, during the 1980s a widely popular rock group called *Queen* released an album containing the song "We Will Rock You" that is now sung by students all over the country, especially during football games.

The history of folk music includes the *commemorative song*, which derives from times before people had written records of important events. During the Middle Ages, for example, troubadours kept people informed of heroic actions in battles and skirmishes by traveling around and singing songs about them. Maritime lore abounds with songs commemorating events that took place at sea, such as atrocities committed by a pirate captain or the sinking of a ship to its lonely, watery grave. The narrator of the commemorative song is never identified. A typical opening line is: "My name is nothin' extra / So that I will not tell." One song winds up in this self-effacing manner: "Now to conclude and finish / Too far my lines have run." The group and the event are always more important than the singer/reporter.

The commemorative song does not belong just to the past. A modern American folk classic is Don McLean's "Bye, Bye, Miss American Pie," composed in 1971. Its mystifying refrain following the singing of the title, tells how the narrator drove his "Chevy to the levee / But the levee was dry." Like all folk music that continues to be sung, its tune is infectious, even though the meaning of the lyrics is not clear. A popular interpretation is that McLean wrote the song to commemorate the deaths of pop stars Buddy Holly and Richie Valens in a 1959 plane crash. That it does indeed make reference to a disaster is suggested by the final line, which speaks of "the day the music died."

The *work song* is also highly durable, for it is hard to imagine a time when work will not be central to most people's lives. In some cases the work song reflects great hardship and a state of tension between management and labor. Often, however, the music is jolly and full of bounce and joy, as though to help the original creator forget tired limbs and meager salary.

I've been workin' on the railroad
All the livelong day;
I've been workin' on the railroad
Just to pass the time away.

The nineteenth-century folk ballad "John Henry" reflects the conflict between worker and machine at a time when the steam drill was about to replace hammers swung by human arms. John Henry became a folk hero, mythologized as a superhuman individual who was stronger than a machine, at least for a while: in his effort to beat the steam drill through the mountain with his hammer and steel pike, John Henry's great heart finally failed him.

He hammered so hard
He burst his poor heart
And he laid down his hammer and he died.
Lord! Lord!
He laid down his hammer and he died.

In the past, management and labor disputes frequently erupted into violence before they could be settled by the two parties sitting around a table in the presence of a federal arbitrator. All too often workers had little power against corporate ownership. Songs memorializing those who had given their lives in the name of workers' rights no doubt kept up the spirits of many who might otherwise have resigned themselves to defeat.

One such worker was Joe Hill, a Swedish-born immigrant who, like so many others, came to the United States in the early twentieth century with dreams of success, only to be swallowed into a vast labor force, toiling for forty or more hours a week and trying to survive on a minimum wage. A born folk poet and singer, Hill began to compose songs about the hardships endured by the workers and the obstinate refusal of management to meet their demands or even to offer a compromise. He became a modern folk minstrel, and his songs—simple, easily sung and remembered—soon spread from union hall to union hall, adapted to many kinds of labor problems.

Action is the antidote to despair.
—**Joan Baez**

Hill was also an activist, traveling throughout the country, speaking to larger and larger gatherings of workers, and he inevitably acquired the reputation of troublemaker and rabble rouser. While he was in Salt Lake City to address a union meeting, a murder took place, and Hill was arrested and charged with the crime. In a still famous trial, the prosecution produced witnesses who placed Hill at the scene of the crime. After a short jury deliberation he was found guilty and sentenced to die by firing squad. Awaiting his execution, he wrote his final song, in which he said that some people could find justice in Salt Lake City "but not Joe Hill."

Joan Baez, a folk singer who epitomized the human rights movement of the 1960s and 1970s, wrote a commemorative ballad about Joe Hill, one that has already achieved the status of genuine folk art.

From San Diego up to Maine,
in every mine and mill,
where working-men defend their rights,
it's there you find Joe Hill,
it's there you find Joe Hill![2]

Whether written a century ago or just last week, folk music is easily recognized. It does not evolve in sophistication. It does not acquire subtle rhythms. Its rhymes are always simple, making the words easy to remember. Though "Joe Hill" was written by a seasoned professional who is a master of the guitar and possesses a voice of exquisite control, it has no professional "polish." It could have erupted spontaneously—always the mark of a real folk song.

The *accumulation song* is deliberately drawn out, with verse after verse and a refrain repeated after each one. Songs like "The Twelve Days of Christmas" and "Old MacDonald" start off with one detail (one gift, one animal) and then add more and more as the song continues. Accumulation songs extend group solidarity for longer periods, prolong the high spirits of the gathering, and keep loneliness at bay.

The *scoundrel song* celebrates the Dionysian personality—the perennial favorite of our hidden selves—the lawless, irresponsible, but charming rogue you couldn't trust or marry or put in charge of an important operation but who is always fun. An Irish favorite is "The Wild Rover," which upholds a life of drinking, carousing, gambling, and avoiding work. The narrator proudly sings that "if you don't like me, you can leave me alone." Who can argue with that premise? He intends to

eat when I'm hungry and drink when I'm dry,
And if moonshine don't kill me,
I'll live till I die.

To be sure, society would perish if it depended upon wild rovers. But the subject of a scoundrel song is usually a loner who could not, *would* not adapt easily to the demands of organized society and so could hardly be expected to celebrate the morally upright, the hard working, and the pious.

The *narrative song*, as its label implies, tells a tale, often at great length, answering, like the accumulation song, the need of listeners to stay together as long as possible. It was the folk version of the epic, usually filled with accounts of wondrous and miraculous events. The Scottish ballad "Binorie" recounts the sad story of a miraculous harp that was fashioned from the breastplate of a murdered young woman and that sings as it plays. The harp reveals the events leading up to the woman's murder, then comes to the shocking climax: "My sister it was who did me slay." Quite possibly the song, like many others, was based on an actual event.

Believe it or not, there are places in the world where music is important. There are places in the world where all the arts are a matter of national pride.

—**Frank Zappa**

Country and western music has carried on the narrative tradition of folk music, adding its own unique tales to the repertoire. During the late 1960s "Ode to Billy Joe" was popular as a crossover, topping country charts as well as the Top 40. Fans listened intently to the tragic story of a teenage boy who jumped to his death from the Tallahatchee Bridge. What was unique about the song was that it gave subtle suggestions about the "why" of the incident but never actually told us in so many words. Radio talk shows had hundreds of callers who gave their opinions, but the composer, Bobbie Gentry, refused to divulge the secret.

The 1960s, a period of widespread alienation in the United States, saw a significant revival of folk music. Young people, often far from home, got together for the night in hastily improvised camps or in communes with ever changing members and became instant—if temporary—friends through the common bond of singing. Joan Baez and Judy Collins attained huge popularity by reviving old songs, particularly those that still spoke to the rebellious spirit seeking freedom from restraint. But the main thrust of the folk revival was the tightness of the group. It could have a distinctly spiritual side. At concerts Judy Collins sang the old hymn "Amazing Grace" and soon had 10,000 voices joining in with hands interlocked in a show of community. The hymn, once revived, has remained an integral part of our culture; it was sung during the funeral of President Ronald Reagan at the National Cathedral in 2004.

Bob Dylan and John Lennon are two of the great folk minstrels to protest the war in Vietnam.

New folk minstrels emerged, using *protest songs* to make statements against war, pollution, inequality, and the corruption of the establishment. Bob Dylan's "A Hard Rain's Gonna Fall" and John Lennon's "Give Peace a Chance" were written and sung in protest, originally against the Vietnam War, but since then they have been used to protest other wars, or all wars. They are modern folk songs that attain the level of art. Lennon summed up the dream of a world without war, hunger, and hatred in what may be the most important folk song of the last century: "Imagine." Though composed and sung by a master musician, "Imagine" has all the simplicity and the passionate honesty of the folk tradition. These three songs will probably endure as long as there are troubled times.

A more recent folk minstrel is Ferraby Lionheart, who was raised in the Korea Town section of Nashville and whose songs, especially the words, show considerable Asian influence. Some of them faintly resemble haiku (discussed in Chapter 4) in their deceptive simplicity. "The Octopus and the Ambulance," for example, begins with the admonition to escape from worry and stress by riding in an ambulance and, while there, hear somebody tell a joke about an octopus that made "an awful mess." Listening to the joke, you can "give yourself a break and laugh a while."

These are not songs about the deterioration of nature or about war. They aren't protesting anything but seem to be saying love may be all we need—and maybe some laughter. Lionheart's sound is definitely unlike that of any other Western pop singer around. But as it becomes more well known, critics may label it *folk pop* or *folk rock*. His rhythms are steady and insistent, and he sometimes sings in falsetto. The difference between this and most rock music, however, is that for Lionheart, the words are as important as the rhythm. His lyrics are a blend of sophisticated poetry and what an idealistic schoolboy might write to the girl he loves.

The protest song, however, is very much alive, especially in the work of Ani Difranco, who began playing the guitar when she was nine years old. By the time she was twenty she had released her first CD, which instantly established her prominence in the field of folk rock. She has since sung in venues ranging from small clubs to Carnegie Hall. Difranco's songs are socially oriented and deal with a wide variety of issues, especially sexism, racism, domestic abuse, homophobia, the rights of people to determine whether they want to reproduce, the plight of the poor and homeless—and most particularly, the idiocy of fighting wars to solve problems. She has campaigned for independent presidential candidates, insisting that what America needs is a leader who is not tied to the philosophy of a particular party.

Difranco is a superb musician. Her guitar work is characterized by staccato rhythms, rapid fingerpicking, and constant changes in tuning. Her lyrics are those of a poet, using complex metaphors, alliteration, and irony. She delivers her words in a half-spoken intonation, with heavy rhythmic stress. With her, folk music has traveled a long road from its grass roots in work songs and nonsense songs intended for community bonding, yet Difranco never forgets that her sophistication ultimately springs from the same heart that produced "Joe Hill."

Ani Difranco and Ferraby Lionheart, two modern folk minstrels who also have rock credentials.

Source: Left: © Andrewe Goetz/Corbis. Right: Photo by R. E. Barbash.

Folk music has inspired concert composers of the past and present. Beethoven was charmed by the Gaelic folk tradition and composed song cycles based on both Irish and Scottish melodic patterns. The American composer Aaron Copland (1900–1990) was so delighted by the country's folk music, especially songs of the old West, that his music has come to define America in sound. *Billy the Kid*, one of Copland's many ballet scores, uses the folk song "Goodbye, Old Paint" (sung by a cowboy to his horse) in a stirring theme and variations. *Rodeo* interweaves themes and rhythms from Saturday-night barn dances. *El Salón México* is an orchestral suite woven out of traditional Mexican folk material and exuberant Latin rhythms, set against Copland's unique dissonance. Perhaps the composer's most famous score was written for the ballet *Appalachian Spring*, which employs a number of folk themes, notably the old Shaker hymn "Simple Gifts." The ballet itself celebrates time-honored rituals like the raising of a barn by everyone in the community.

American folk themes found their way into the concert hall in the symphonic music of Aaron Copland.

Folk themes such as those incorporated into this ballet often came from other cultures. Appalachian music, for example, has deep roots in the Gaelic folk music of Ireland and Scotland as well as the British folk tradition. The Israeli *hora* and the Italian *tarantella* are folk dances known throughout the world. *Polka* music was originally derived from Polish folk themes. We encourage you to pay attention to the many folk cultures brought to these shores from other countries and the rich musical experiences they provide.

The Spiritual

The spiritual had its beginnings in the need of African Americans to articulate and preserve, to give meaning to their suffering, and to demand a rightful place in society. Taken—stolen—away from their homeland as far back as the seventeenth century, with no future except slavery, pain, and death, they took comfort in their relationship with God and an ultimate reward in a paradise where everyone was free.

Deep river,
My home lies over Jordan.
Deep river,
I want to cross over into campground.

Spirituals emphasize God's personal concern for each person, however obscure that person may be in the eyes of other mortals. For instance:

I sing because I'm happy,
I sing because I'm free,
For His eye is on the sparrow,
And I know He watches me.

If all music does not have to express or appeal to the emotions, the spiritual is one kind that exists to make emotional release possible. We cannot imagine what life would have been like for slaves, or what it would be like today in the impoverished sections of inner cities, without this profound music of earthly sorrow and religious hope.

As the spiritual genre grew and developed, it was made more and more complex by church choirs and soloists, each of whom would add the mark of their individual interpretations. Often transported by religious ecstasy, they created the new genre of *gospel* music. Over the years this genre, while remaining as an indigenous part of church services, has also moved into the arena of popular music. It is characterized by giving the singer free reign to add enough notes to allow a fuller emotional expression.

Blues are songs of despair, but gospel songs are the songs of hope.
—**Mahalia Jackson**

Gospel singer Mahalia Jackson (1911–1972) became the best-known and highly influential exponent of the genre. Born in New Orleans, when that city was bursting at the seams with new music—ragtime, jazz, and blues—she grew up next door to a church in which music played a vital role. She heard traditional hymns played and sung with many rhythmic variations. In addition, the sounds of Mardi Gras music, street vendors, and the songs belted out from the barrooms with wide open doors and windows seeped into her blood. Devoutly religious, Jackson blended spirituals and aspects of the New Orleans secular style into religious songs that became nationally famous when she moved to Chicago and married a businessman who recognized her potential and launched her career. In 1954 Columbia Records signed her to a long-term contract, and gospel music was soon on the charts.

A civil rights activist, Jackson took part in the historic March on Washington in 1963, singing before thousands assembled on the Mall to hear Martin Luther King Jr.'s epoch-making "I Have a Dream" speech.

Ragtime

Ragtime dates back to the turn of the twentieth century, to a period when the legendary fortunes of the Rockefellers, Vanderbilts, Goulds, and Astors were being amassed and when the American moneyed aristocracy, their acquaintances, and all those who emulated their Victorian manners were entertaining guests with salon orchestras playing stately waltzes. Their aim was to establish European elegance on this side of the Atlantic.

Do not play this piece fast. It is never right to play Ragtime fast."
—**Scott Joplin**

Some of the less privileged were eager to take advantage of the freedom to pursue upward mobility. They wanted to gain the social recognition already enjoyed by wealthy families, and they wanted to show everyone they were capable of creating elegance of their own. Ragtime emerged from the African American community and its musical traditions, transformed by the influence of European styles. African American musicians wanted to do more than play the minstrel-show type music with which white audiences had come to identify them. Ragtime came along at just the right moment. The acknowledged master of the new genre was Scott Joplin (1868–1917), who began his career in backrooms and honky-tonks but became a national celebrity with the publication of "Maple Leaf Rag" in 1899.

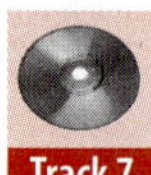
Track 7

Joplin heard the original ragtime tunes frequently played by small African American combos on riverboats. They may have been variations on old plantation songs, minstrel-show cakewalks, and banjo melodies, usually played at lively tempos. White audiences expected African American music to be high-spirited. The label **ragtime** was coined to identify the syncopation that was the trademark of the new genre. **Syncopation** occurs when the melodic line of a piece is played against, not with, the accented beats of the rhythm accompaniment. Syncopated pieces are usually difficult to play because the left hand and the right hand follow different beats. (For a perfect example of syncopation, listen to George Gershwin's "Fascinatin' Rhythm.")

Joplin was captivated by the new sounds, but he wanted to turn them into a legitimate, recognized genre that would be associated with African Americans but also prove the equal of the foreign imports. This meant imitating or at least coming close to European rhythm. Joplin slowed down the pace to make the music even more stately. On the sheet music of his "rags" he would write: "Do not play this piece fast. It is never right to play Ragtime fast."

The waltz is played in three-quarter time, a tempo that is never varied. Ragtime, played almost exclusively on the piano, is written in *two*-quarter time, its tempo also never changing. The primary influences on Joplin's music, in addition to riverboat songs, were the popular European marches as well as the waltz and the quadrille, a dignified French square dance.

The enormous popularity of "Maple Leaf Rag" and the other Joplin hits that quickly followed made African American musicians sit up and take notice, especially in New Orleans, which was a stronghold for the liberal acceptance of new music. Jelly Roll Morton (1885–1941) introduced Joplin's music to New Orleans but played it at a faster tempo, an innovation that would be integrated into yet another American musical genre.

Jazz

Jazz came to America 300 years ago in chains.

—Paul Whiteman

The musical roots of jazz were African, brought to this country by slaves, and the music was marked by what is known as a "call and response" pattern. Participants would sing or play a particular combination of tones, and this would be answered by singing or playing a variation on it. The original purpose was similar to that of the folk song: community bonding.

During the late nineteenth century, African American musicians went to New Orleans and studied European genres and rhythmic patterns. But they brought with them a knowledge of their own traditional sounds, derived from what were called "field hollers" as well as rhythmic songs sung by slaves as they rowed, and the spirituals that were a profound part of African American religious life.

The typical scale used in African music contains five tones instead of the European scale of seven. New Orleans musicians tried to combine the two without sacrificing the African scale. The result was that they added half-tones, called *blue notes*, to the five-tone scale. From ragtime, they borrowed syncopation. The synthesis of all these strains made possible the evolution of jazz.

As the decades of the twentieth century rolled by, the form attracted a range of musical geniuses, some self-taught, some classically trained. They had—and continue to have—one thing in common: knowing how to maintain a balance between control and the need for soaring release. The call and response form had required that the responders change the original theme, adding their own variation. Even when jazz became a sophisticated art form, improvisation continued to be its major characteristic.

Whatever their training, jazz instrumentalists and composers admire Bach because he more or less invented improvisation, the art of taking flight from a set theme. A typical jazz piece follows a disciplined pattern. The group, or the soloist backed by the group, will play the main theme once through, sometimes a well-known song, sometimes an original tune composed for the group. Then one instrument after another performs a variation of the theme.

Original jazz works have deliberately offbeat titles, like "Take the A Train," "One O'Clock Jump," and "Stompin' at the Savoy"—titles that generally do not relate to anything beyond themselves. Jazz often shapes and defines the "cool scene"—a late-night coming together of sophisticated people who want to lose themselves in the music and escape, if only briefly, from their problems, just as the performers seek to lose themselves in the music.

Duke Ellington did the most to bridge the gap between the concert hall and the intimate jazz club.

Following in the footsteps of Jelly Roll Morton, great jazz soloists like Charlie Parker and Louis Armstrong became famous for going off on lengthy variations, often improvising for ten or fifteen minutes before returning to the theme. One motive behind jazz improvisation was to explore the potential of one's instrument and take it to places that no one else had ever found. In a life tragically interrupted when he was only twenty-eight, a phenomenal cornet player named Bix Beiderbecke is said to have been obsessed with the desire to find the perfect note, beyond the normal range of other players. Presumably, he did not live long enough to reach his goal. Some who were fortunate enough to hear him report that, as he pushed his instrument beyond the ordinary limits of its capabilities, his face turned almost scarlet and all of his facial muscles threatened to break loose from his skin.

Musical histories that deal with jazz as a serious and major art form give preeminence to Edward Kennedy Ellington—known universally as Duke (1899–1974)—the person who did the most to bridge the gap between the concert hall and the intimate jazz club. A bandleader who had Manhattan society driving to the Cotton Club in Harlem during the late 1920s, Ellington sought to expand the range of jazz through continual experimentation "with what he called his 'jungle effects.' When the sounds of 'growling' trumpets and trombones, sinuous clarinets and eerie percussion were recorded, the originality of the orchestration was immediately grasped internationally by music critics and record buyers. . . . As a jazz arranger his great gift was in balancing orchestration and improvisation."[3]

Ellington brought jazz to Carnegie Hall, where it could be played and evaluated in a setting built for the performance of classical concert music. In so doing,

Duke Ellington brought jazz to Carnegie Hall, every piece carefully orchestrated.

Source: © Bettmann Archives/Corbis.

he wrote out elaborate and complex orchestrations—something no one had done before him. He did leave room for solo flights (or else it would not have been jazz), but his own compositions, like "Mood Indigo," "Satin Doll," and "Sophisticated Lady," display a classic sense of discipline and musicianship.

Another major American composer who brought jazz to Carnegie Hall in the early years was George Gershwin (1898–1937). He started his career as a Tin Pan Alley songwriter, then moved on to compose the scores for Broadway musicals of the 1920s and the opera *Porgy and Bess* (fully discussed in Chapter 8). Yet Gershwin, who had been classically trained and could have been a world-class concert pianist had he chosen that path, was hungry for greater things.

In 1924 he found his chance. Paul Whiteman, a bandleader also hungry for serious recognition, commissioned him to write a concert jazz piece. The result was *Rhapsody in Blue*, which combined the textures of romantic works for piano and symphony orchestra with the pulsations, dissonance, and syncopated rhythms of jazz. Gershwin put an American art form on the international musical map. *Rhapsody* became an overnight success and has sold millions of recordings. It remains in the standard concert repertoire of nearly every major orchestra.

George Gershwin's *Rhapsody in Blue* put jazz on the international musical map.

Source: Culver Pictures, Inc.

Jazz has remained a major art form, studied in every major music school and performed regularly in concert halls throughout the world as well as in annual festivals devoted exclusively to both jazz classics and the very newest styles and performers. The Newport Jazz Festival in Rhode Island and Jazz at Lincoln Center in New York are two notable examples. The genre has produced important artists who are at ease in both the classical and jazz scenes.

His [Gershwin's] genius, like all genius, was unique, but his all embracing artistic vision still resonates powerfully today in a world where music is sometimes the only benign avenue of communication between antagonists.

—Paul Simon

One such performer was trumpeter and pianist Miles Davis (1926–1991), whose versatility led him to the forefront of innovators in many subgenres of jazz, including *bebop* and *cool jazz*. By the time he was eighteen, Davis had shown so much talent that the Juilliard School offered him a scholarship, but he proved too impatient to wait for graduation. When he was nineteen, he made his first recording and joined the jazz quintet of Charlie Parker, the premier saxophonist of the period. Because of his youth and lack of professional experience, Davis was used as a *sideman*—a non-soloist who played backup to the stars. It was not very long before he stepped into the solo spotlight. In 1955 he created the Miles Davis Quintet, which took jazz to new heights.

In his earlier work, Davis experimented with bebop, which had become the rage in the 1940s. Bebop was almost totally improvised and therefore greatly favored by soloists who wanted music to serve their unique showcase needs. The more mature Davis of the Quintet gradually eased away from the eccentricities of bebop and moved toward what became known as cool jazz, more disciplined, more faithful to the music, and less given to wild flights of musical fancy. By the late 1950s Davis, who also played Carnegie Hall, was presenting jazz versions of concert music. One of his classic albums is *Sketches of Spain*, featuring works by Joaquin Rodrigo and Manuel de Falla.

Miles Davis, the preeminent creator of cool jazz.

Source: Hulton Archive/Getty Images.

Since the early 1980s, trumpeter Wynton Marsalis has distinguished himself as a performer and a composer, crossing over freely from jazz to symphonic music. Classically trained at the Juilliard School, he earned a reputation as its outstanding trumpeter. When he was barely seventeen, Marsalis was playing with the Jazz Messengers, a prestigious band that helped him develop his skills. He has released forty albums and won nine Grammy awards. In 1983 he won in both the symphonic and jazz categories, the first artist ever to do so. In 1997 he became the first jazz composer to win the Pulitzer Prize for music. The prize-winning work was *Blood on the Fields*, commissioned by Jazz at Lincoln Center, which has an international reputation as an outstanding venue in which the finest jazz musicians in the world perform. Marsalis is currently its artistic director.

Like many of the art forms we have studied thus far, jazz has evolved from humble beginnings to a position of glittering importance in the world of the humanities.

Blues

The term *blues* derives from the melancholy mood produced by music that made liberal use of the half-tones in the African American scale, the so-called blue notes. The genre has permeated our vocabulary to such an extent that "blue" seems always to have meant "down in the dumps." Many jazz tunes are bouncy and lively, uplifting the spirit, but the jazz repertoire includes its share of blues.

The genre had its origins, as did ragtime and jazz, in the songs sung by slaves after a grueling day in the fields. While they sometimes desired an upbeat mood, the workers must have, just as often, sought an outlet for depression. As the form became caught up in the entertainment industry of jazz, sophisticated composers and singers turned the old songs into haunting expressions of sadness that found ready listeners among audiences of varied backgrounds. The blue notes helped.

Track 8

Blues music is almost always about the empty aftermath of a once burning passion. The songs are written from either a male or a female point of view. Men sing of the faithlessness of woman, and women return the compliment about men. Probably the most famous of all the blues songs is "St. Louis Blues" by W. C. Handy (1873–1958), who also composed "Beale Street Blues." If jazz is strongly associated with New Orleans, the headquarters of blues was Memphis, and it was on Beale Street that many of the great blues clubs were located, attracting visitors from all over the world.

I've been told that nobody sings the word "hunger" like I do.

—**Billie Holliday**

Many of the soloists who elevated the form to a high status had tragic lives caused by bad relationships, social discrimination, or substance addiction—in some cases, all three. Outstanding was Bessie Smith (1894–1937), who many believe developed the blues style that was imitated by countless others. She has immortalized many lines from blues lyrics, including "If it wasn't for bad luck, I wouldn't have no luck at all." She achieved considerable renown before the automobile accident that claimed her life at the age of forty-three.

If it wasn't for bad luck, I wouldn't have no luck at all.

—**Bessie Smith**

Pop Music

The songs performed by contemporary singers such as Justin Timberlake, Kanye West, and Martina McBride are generally designated *pop music*. If they are still played and sung in the future, they may have attained the stature of popular classics, and a notable few have earned a place in the humanities.

During the 1930s through the early 1950s, big bands were all the fashion, each with at least one big-name singer who needed a constant supply of new songs to please a public eager to buy records and sheet music. Many, many of these songs have become classics, performed by stars such as Tony Bennett, Barbra Streisand, Barbara Cook, and Harry Connick Jr. Until he was close to eighty, vocal stylist Frank Sinatra attracted huge crowds with songs he helped become classics.

The big-band song had a very specific pattern. A song, usually around three minutes in length, would be played once by the orchestra; then a soloist—or a backup group—would sing it through once. The orchestra might or might not follow the vocal by playing another complete chorus. Thus the time allotted for each song was either six or nine minutes. The big-band orchestra played primarily so that couples could dance. Frequently the rhythm would change from song to song, going from a slow fox trot (which would draw most of the audience out to the floor) to a fast jitterbug number (older dancers would sit down) or a Latin American mambo or rumba (attracting the dancers who could execute the required steps in time to the demanding rhythm).

Bessie Smith, the great blues singer, sang deeply felt songs about the aftermath of once burning passion.

Source: The Granger Collection.

Though this pattern imposed stiff restraints upon lyricists, who had to develop and conclude an idea in a few minutes, the rules are no doubt responsible for the imaginative brilliance of the best songs, such as Jerome Kern's "Smoke Gets in Your Eyes." Otto Harbach, who wrote the lyrics to the song, really deserves the label *poet*. He develops a very common theme, dating at least as far back as Roman poetry: the theme of love lost. At first, the narrator of the song believes the beloved is faithful, though friends think otherwise, saying that when "your heart's on fire" you will realize that "smoke gets in your eyes." The narrator scoffs, only to discover in the next few lines that the beloved has gone. The friends are now the ones who scoff, but the narrator, in an absolutely brilliant repetition of the song title in a totally different context, points out that tears come when the flame of a beautiful romance is dying out and "smoke gets in your eyes."

Through songs we find out things about ourselves. We say, "Oh yeah. I've felt that way."

—**Lois Walder**

Irving Berlin (1888–1989), composer of "God Bless America," could not read a note of music but compiled perhaps the largest repertoire of any twentieth-century songwriter. All of his songs express simple, honest, and universal emotions. While Berlin could define the everlasting joys of love, he was at his best when providing the bittersweet happiness of nostalgia. It's all over, but one is left with fond memories all the same. And the nostalgia of the lyric "I'm dreaming of a white Christmas" elevated a popular song written for a sequence in a forgotten movie to the status of a Christmas carol. This and other songs of the period were treasured by millions, who could listen to the words, close their eyes, and relive their past.

In 1938 the popular singer Kate Smith asked Berlin to compose a patriotic song with which she could end her broadcast celebrating the twentieth anniversary of the armistice that ended World War I. After several attempts proved futile, he remembered a song he had written for an army camp show during that war, a song that was rejected for being "too jingoistic." He found "God Bless America" buried in an old trunk, polished it a bit, and then offered it to Smith. Its first performance on the broadcast of November 20, 1938, electrified both the studio and the vast national audience. The song contains ten short lines and probably takes less than three minutes to sing. No one has to be told about the song's impact in all times and on countless occasions since. When Jerome Kern was asked to indicate Berlin's place in American music, he answered tersely: "Irving Berlin *is* American music."

There is still an audience for the popular song that strikes at the heart, and perhaps that explains why a piece like Joni Mitchell's "Both Sides Now," first heard in the 1960s, is a continuing favorite. Mitchell (b. 1943), who writes both music and lyrics, is as adept at metaphor as the lyricist of "Smoke Gets in Your Eyes." In "Both Sides Now" she writes of coping with disillusionment, and she does so in a series of symbolic images. As a very young girl, she loved to lie back and look up at clouds, which she saw as "ice cream castles" and "feathered canyons." Now that she is an adult, she sees that clouds just "rain and snow on everyone." She has looked at clouds "from both sides now," but refuses to take on adult cynicism about life. She continues to cling to "clouds' illusions" just as she continues to believe in love's and finally *life's* illusions. The song parallels a listener's own process of maturation, and will probably be a favorite for as long as ideals are held and then shattered.

Frank Sinatra was responsible for turning many songs into enduring classics.

Source: © Hulton Archive/Corbis.

One of the great stylists of popular music was Frank Sinatra (1915–1998), who virtually owned the song of past love now sadly remembered. Composers and lyricists jumped at the chance to write for him, because he was without peer in delivering the song's message through his vocal flexibilities and his acting talent. Many of the songs with which he was associated are permanent classics. They crystallize emotions all of us share and give us comfort in knowing we are not alone.

A typical Sinatra classic is "One for My Baby," in which the narrator can be imagined as sitting at a bar very late at night, with no one around except a bartender who may or may not be listening as he pours out his heart. He has been abandoned by his one true love, though he does not deny having been responsible for the breakup; now there is only the effort to escape the pain through drink. The refrain to which he keeps returning asks the bartender to give him two more drinks: one "for my baby" and "one more for the road." As both songs and poems should do when they achieve art, this one captures a certain moment, an image in the flow of time: here, that of a loner in a bar late at night with no clear future and obviously no one to comfort him.

Rock

A pervasive phenomenon ever since it made the scene in the 1950s, rock music has become a major way of defining the present era in sound. **Rock** is a fusion of rhythm and blues, gospel, and country and western styles, and it has many complex facets, ranging from the conscious artistry of trained musicians to the out-of-control bellowing of unintelligible lyrics by performers prancing around a stage. But rock is first and foremost a celebration of the joy of life, sexual release, and often a total disregard for social rules.

. . .we note the glazed stares and numb, expressionless faces of youthful dancers at the great rock auditoriums where light shows, split screen movies, high decibel screams, shouts and moans. . . create a sensory environment characterized by. . . extreme unpredictability."

—Alvin Toffler

As a contemporary musical form, rock realizes its full potential in the rock concert, in a given totality of work presented in a unique program that is almost never repeated after a particular performance or tour. The most famous rock concert ever held took place in Woodstock, New York, in 1969, when bands and performers from all over the world gathered in one place to celebrate togetherness and protest the war in Vietnam. Monsoon rains found thousands of participants rolling around in mud, their enthusiasm undiminished by the hardships and indignities they endured. Not only was there memorable music performed, but the collective experience made the powerful statement that war as a means of settling human problems could no longer be tolerated. Generally speaking, in the history of the humanities there are few works that drive the audience into a frenzy the way a rock concert can. Concerts can take hold of thousands at the same moment, going beyond music altogether, to become a social event.

Rock has undergone many changes since 1955, the year in which the movie *Blackboard Jungle* leaped onto the screen in a flash of music titled "Rock around the Clock." With its overly pronounced and rapid beat, the music had film audiences jumping in the aisles and dancing—even as the rock concert would be doing in a few years. The band that arranged and played this piece was Bill Haley and the Comets, and to them is given the credit for popularizing the musical movement first called **rock 'n' roll**.

The incessant rhythmic beat of "Rock around the Clock" was derived from the rhythm and blues music of small African American dance clubs in the South. Because of their confined spaces, they could only accommodate small combos, which had to make a big sound to compensate. Besides, the polite dances of the big bands no longer suited a postwar generation bogged down in academic studies and office jobs and in need of weekend release. The beat of rock 'n' roll, accentuated by the strings of a twirling bass fiddle, met the new needs.

One year after "Rock around the Clock" spread the new sound nationwide, a young singer from Mississippi named Elvis Presley appeared on television's *Ed Sullivan Show*, the premier venue for showcasing new musical talent. Elvis (1935–1977) quickly became a cultural phenomenon, scandalizing older audiences with the gyrating of his pelvis while simultaneously making rock wildly popular with younger audiences. The immediate musical influence on Elvis was gospel, particularly its exuberance. He added the beat and chord progressions of the rhythm and blues being played in Memphis, where he had gotten his professional start. Finally, Elvis incorporated elements from country-western music, injecting them with a high-powered aggressiveness that remains the signature of rock. In some circles, his music became known as *country rock* or *rockabilly*.

Often hailed as the King of Rock, Elvis Presley fused musical elements from rhythm and blues, gospel, and country-western traditions to create his own brand of rock 'n' roll, a style that remains popular decades after his death.

Source: S.S. Archives/Shooting Star International.

In the opinion of rock historian Charlie Gillett, Elvis's peak as an artist was reached in the early days when his work related to the passionate themes of the country rock tradition—usually heartbreak with a strong rhythm, as in his first hit song "Heartbreak Hotel." In Gillett's opinion, becoming a superstar in record-breaking time was the worst thing that could have happened to Elvis. He signed a multimillion-dollar contract with RCA, which promptly put a high-powered gloss on the new music. The singer's former emotional directness became lost against a background of "vocal groups, heavily electrified guitars, and drums . . . more theatrical and self-conscious as he sought to contrive excitement and emotion," formerly generated "without any evident forethought."[4] Other singers and combos followed the trend, and the simple term *rock* was given to a variety of styles, many with the amplification of the later Presley work.

The excitement generated within audiences by rock had been foreshadowed in the frenetic energy of Little Richard, one of early rock's most outrageous performers, who set the style for later acts that would go even further in free-spiritedness. Rock historian Nik Cohn considers Little Richard to have been the true father of rock: "Dressed in shimmering suits with long drape jackets and baggy pants, his hair grown long and straight, white teeth and gold rings flashing in the spotlights, he stood up at, and sometimes on, the piano, hammering boogie chords as he screamed messages of celebration and self-centered pleasure."[5]

A hundred years from now, people will listen to the Beatles the same way we listen to Mozart.

—**Sir Paul McCartney**

By the early 1960s, rock 'n' roll had become popular throughout the Western world. It became so pervasive in England in particular that young musicians began imitating the music they were hearing from across the Atlantic. Ironically, what music historians and fans alike consider rock's most important band emerged not in the United States, where the genre was born, but in the economically depressed northern English port city of Liverpool. In 1964 the Beatles made an indelible mark on American consciousness the moment they were introduced on *The Ed Sullivan Show*, which had showcased Elvis Presley eight years earlier. Their name was whimsical and their hair longer than the short standards of the time. As their fame increased, so did the length of their hair, in what appeared to be defiance of convention. For some performances, they even wore eighteenth-century clothes, including knee breeches, doublets, and waistcoats. Older people shook their heads in despair over the decline of not only music but an entire generation. For it was the young who embraced the bizarre foursome, imitating their hair styles and turning John, Paul, George, and Ringo into icons of cultural revolution. The Beatles appealed to a rising subculture of "hippies," young people who championed freedom from all social and moral restraints. In all of its phases since the 1950s, rock has retained its revolutionary social battle cry, becoming the ultimate form of Dionysian music in our time.

The Beatles were admired for their honesty and a certain purity of heart. Their physical presence was so powerful that they would have attained enormous popularity even if their music had been second-rate. Of course, it was not. Paul McCartney and John Lennon created songs of such originality and beauty that some are considered among the best popular songs in Western culture. Songs like "Yesterday," "Eleanor Rigby" (also a model of syncopation), and "Michelle" have been performed by major symphony orchestras.

Both Lennon, whose life was cut short in 1980 by a deranged fan's bullet, and George Harrison, who played guitar for the group and who died in 2001, were strongly influenced by Indian culture and religion. All four of the Beatles briefly studied meditation at an ashram in India. Harrison studied the sitar, an ancient Indian instrument, with Ravi Shankar, a master Indian musician. Harrison's own

The Beatles—honesty and an off-center purity of heart.

Source: AP/Wide World Photos.

songs are less well-known than those of Lennon and McCartney, but many of them are deeply felt poems set to high spiritual music.

In 1965 another British combo, the Rolling Stones, came onto the scene, combining the exuberant defiance of the early Beatles with the free-spiritedness of a Little Richard. In the words of rock singer, critic, and poet Patti Smith: "By 1967 they all but eliminated the word guilt from our vocabulary . . . I never considered the Stones drug music . . . they were the drug itself . . . thru demon genius they hit that chord . . . as primitive as a western man could stand. Find the beat and you dance all night."[6]

To the Stones must go the credit for having originated the big-time rock concert, which could fill Yankee Stadium or the Los Angeles Coliseum. Enthusiastic fans were known to camp out for days in advance in order to buy tickets, and that ritual continues undiminished. The rock concert seemed to begin where "primitive" beings left off thousands of years ago. It cut through the many layers of civilized behavior that had evolved to put a lid on the untrammeled expression of freedom, and it demanded from the audience shouting, stamping, cries of ecstasy—a return to the enjoyment of the sheer act of living, unverbalized, unanalyzed, uncensored. Smith describes the historic Madison Square Garden concert of July 25, 1972, as a ritual "like any ancient ceremony," adding, "pass the sacred wafer."

In 1980 another of the great rock bands achieved world prominence with their debut album *Boy*. They were four musicians from Dublin who grew up nestled in the strong Celtic tradition in which people learned to sing when they were old enough to leave the cradle. In keeping with the customary practice of using offbeat names, they discarded their first two, Feedback and The Hype, before settling on U2, and the group arguably remains the premier rock band of the world. U2 became best known for their political and social themes, exemplified by their 2006 Grammy-winning album *How to Dismantle an Atomic Bomb*. For three

U2—rock music with Celtic roots and a peace-driven conscience.

Source: © Mike Blake/Reuters/Corbis.

decades now, the band has toured the world, driving home their pleas for peace, equality, and tolerance. The lead singer, Bono, has even been nominated for the Nobel Peace Prize.

Over the sixty years of its existence, rock has, understandably, gone through many changes. Progressive rock, now coming into its own, relies less on individual performances (such as those associated with the Stones' Mick Jagger) and more on the complexity and strength of the music. Many of the newer bands began as regional groups, and their music often reflects their cultural and gender background.

This diversification has given us many intriguing new sounds, including the contributions of female rock groups, which have survived and flourished despite early difficulties in being recognized as the equal of their male colleagues. The Temple of Rain, an all-female band, originated in lower Manhattan's small **avant-garde** clubs. The group, reflecting the sophistication of the New York scene, writes and performs songs protesting racism and gender discrimination.

Mama's Pit, an Italian rock band, combines the exuberant rhythms of folk dances with the darker themes of much progressive rock. Hubris originated in what they describe as Manila's "alternative scene." Like many of the newer ensembles, they write to express themselves, not to win over their audiences. In fact, they proclaim proudly that at first "we did not really catch on," though eventually "we were recognized for our instrumental prowess, challenging music, and thought-provoking lyrics."

Many progressive rock groups say they are happy they have not yet attained widespread recognition. They attract smaller legions of devoted fans, and they do not have to write for the sales charts, thus freeing themselves to go in many new directions.

Track 9

Miami has recently given rise to The Green Room, named for the topmost part of a wave that enfolds the surfer. Its founder and sole composer/performer is poet Jorge Mejia (b. 1973), whose songs, like a good deal of progressive rock, demand close listening. Mejia, classically trained, orchestrates his music, using a highly advanced synthesizer. Though he incorporates audience-pleasing rhythms, he can change tempo suddenly, darken his mood, and end a song on a note of melancholy alienation. Some of his songs reflect the serenity he says surfers feel when they suddenly find themselves gliding along through the protective green room.

Like Mejia's wave, rock continues to crest. There have already been highly successful rock operas, such as The Who's *Tommy*. The musical *Rent* (discussed in Chapter 2) is a rock updating of the opera *La Bohème*. There have been ballets set to rock beats. In all probability a rock symphony is on the way, perhaps even a rock cantata for a chorus of a hundred singers. The musical form that so many people predicted would soon die a natural death is very much alive and has already contributed much to the humanities.

Hip-Hop

While it is still too early to say whether hip-hop will last as long as rock has, the genre has become a significant part of contemporary society, especially among younger audiences, always seeking new ways to express their identity. **Hip-hop** is a broad term that defines an entire lifestyle, with different musical expressions as integral components. It "encompasses rap, baggy clothing, break-dancing, graffiti, vocabulary, and a general life style."[7] The latter can be described as free-wheeling and centered on the rights of individuals to declare their identity in any way they choose.

Rap, perhaps the most important contribution of the hip-hop culture thus far, is half-sung, half-spoken music with a pronounced and steady beat supporting rapid-fire rhyming words performed by singers with great verbal dexterity and often with extensive vocabularies. The subject matter is frequently social protest, but it can also range from philosophical cynicism about life to frank descriptions of sexual encounters.

We're all spokes in a wheel, going to the point, getting the ball rolling. Have you ever seen a wheel with one spoke? It's not a wheel. You got to come from different directions to get to the same point. And roll.

—**Ice Cube**

Rap had its origins in the urban setting of the Bronx in the late 1970s with toasts, dub talk, and improvisational poetry delivered over music at weddings, proms, and other celebrations. Reminiscent of the call-and-response characteristic of the plantation songs, it would begin with a DJ, band leader, or master of ceremonies shouting in rhythm something like "Now throw your hands in the air / And wave 'em like you just don't care / And if you got on clean underwear / Let me hear you say 'Oh yeah!'" The excited crowd would then scream: "Oh yeah!"[8] The first rap album, *Rapper's Delight*, performed by the Sugarhill Gang, appeared in 1979.

Rap has evolved into what many believe is an art form, and some of its leading exponents have been called modern folk poets. One such is Eminem (b. 1972), whose often cynical lyrics incite fierce controversy wherever they are heard, but they have also won thousands of loyal fans. One rock musician said of Eminem: "He's not a very nice person, but you can't deny the brilliance of his songs."

It is doubtful that rappers are asking to be considered nice. They believe they can best express themselves creatively through their chosen musical form. Rap has also been criticized for glorifying violence and drugs and expressing intolerance toward women and homosexuals. Defenders counter that these charges can also be leveled at some types of rock and that rap music does not promote antisocial values but instead honestly depicts the realities of urban life.

At its best, rap is virtuoso language and a spontaneous kind of poetry, an exercise in exciting creativity.

World Music

The diverse contemporary musical scene also includes contributions from many other cultures. A Chinese composer may be experimenting with new scales and new sounds on a synthesizer; a Cambodian equivalent of Celine Dión may be recording her first CD with a silky voice but in melodic terms that are not based on notes familiar to the West; an Islamic pop singer may be thrilling a cafe audience with a love song in a plaintive trembling vibrato to the accompaniment of an instrument that is akin to but not the same as a mandolin or guitar; a singing group in Zimbabwe may be swaying as they chant an updated version of a much older song of welcome. The majority of these non-Western sounds can be heard via the Internet, and because of today's rapid-fire communication, they will influence tomorrow's musical styles.

In China, music is no longer limited to the marches and patriotic songs approved by the communist government before it opened its doors to the outside world. Western musical influences were there during the earlier twentieth century, but some forms, including hard rock, judged a threat to government or society, were banned. A singer/composer named Cui Jian emerged during the student demonstrations of 1989 with daring lyrics denouncing government tyranny. Defecting to the West, where he found a strong welcome, he performed his new music before thousands in a 1999 Central Park concert. Almost as popular in both East and West is the Tang Dynasty, a Beijing rock band that blends the sounds of the Asian five-note scale with the more familiar diatonic, or seven-note, Western scale.

Traditional Chinese music is still prevalent, making liberal use of percussion, especially drums, timpani, gongs, cymbals, bells, xylophones, and triangles. Percussion has long been a major component of the classical Chinese style. String sections of traditional Chinese concert orchestras include the two-stringed violin, the dulcimer, the lute, and the harp. The woodwind section comprises flutes, pipes, and Chinese trumpets, which look but do not sound like oboes.

An afternoon can be well spent in the exploration of these sounds, now so profusely available on the Web.

Avant-Garde Music

I love the development of our music. How we've tried to develop, y'know? It grows. That is why everyday people come forward with new songs. Music goes on forever.
—**Bob Marley**

Like their counterparts in visual arts, innovators in concert music do not want to sound like anything or anyone that has gone before them; they do not wish to be confined by accepted conventions, but seek to forge new directions. The need to be free from restraints has been a key factor in past works of genius. Beethoven, for example, expanded the range of music in creating his Third Symphony, forcing the music to accommodate his mighty passions. Gershwin, commissioned to write a concert jazz piece, found he could not work within the traditional limits of either jazz or concert music. *Rhapsody in Blue* combined jazz and symphonic music as had never been done before, and there were probably many who doubted it could be done successfully. The Beatles knew the rock music that preceded them, but too many pieces were alike in rhythm and subject matter. Fans were not prepared for the style and the depth of musical expertise the Beatles brought to the form. The four young men with long hair probably did not suspect, at least in the beginning, that they were lifting rock to the level of art. All of these composers did what they had to do: *express themselves in ways congenial to their temperaments regardless of convention.*

Track 4

The need to rebel is felt not just in popular music circles. Today there are composers of concert music who denounce even the diatonic scale and most of the traditional instruments. They may belong to the West, but they do not want to sound connected to any national identity or style. Some have discovered in the synthesizer the key to uncharted inner worlds with sounds that no one has yet heard.

Igor Stravinsky (1882–1971) is for many the father of the modern avant-garde in music. His revolutionary score for the 1913 ballet *The Rite of Spring* introduced sounds so unfamiliar that they, combined with the daring movements of the dancers, sparked a riot at the Paris premiere (discussed more fully in Chapter 15). Denounced by audiences and critics alike, Stravinsky would win the day, and his **atonality**—music with less regard for key—encouraged composers who followed him to break away from bondage to familiar harmonies and structures.

Another modern music pioneer of the avant-garde was Arnold Schoenberg (1874–1951), born in Berlin and musically educated in Vienna. For his large-scale concert works, he is known to have reduced the size of the symphony orchestra to fifteen instruments, for which he provided dissonant, contrapuntal music and bizarre harmonic progressions. Embracing the Stravinsky atonality, he abandoned key altogether in many of his early works, such as *Pierrot Lunaire*, which was intended as a musical equivalent of mental disturbance. In this work Schoenberg also replaced musical notes with notations requiring the singers to speak, but not always in familiar prose. At times they sound like lost souls crying out for release from solitary confinement. In 1925 Schoenberg moved back to Berlin, where he came under the influence of the growing avant-garde movement in German art and music. It was there that he composed his opera *Moses and Aron*, in which the characters sing-speak of their inability to communicate with each other. Both of these works remain stern tests of one's willingness to entertain the very unfamiliar in sound.

Much of today's music, both popular and concert, comes from sounds created on the synthesizer. Leading the way in the concert use of electronic technology was the French avant-garde composer Edgard Varèse (1883–1965). Starting out as a student of mathematics but unable to resist the excitement of the new music, he utilized his training to study the science of sound. Armed with his experiments in producing unfamiliar sounds using both machines and traditional instruments (though seldom as they were intended to be played), Varèse declared boldly: "I refuse to submit to sounds that have already been heard." He added, "Rules do not make a work of art. You have the right to compose what you want to." Encouraged by his friend and admirer the Impressionist composer Claude Debussy, he explored non-Western music, eventually combining it with his own reconfiguration of Western scales and tonal patterns. In 1923 his work *Hyperprism* premiered, and like Stravinsky's *Rite of Spring*, it caused a riot in the theater. Some of the instruments he employed were sleigh bells, rattles, crash cymbals, an anvil, Chinese blocks, Indian drums, and a washtub with a hole in the bottom, which allowed the player to create the sound of a lion's roar.

When he was seventy-one, Varèse created *Deserts*, his response to atomic energy and the dangers it posed for the world. The piece, which used both taped and synthesized sounds, drove the audience into a frenzy and nearly led to another riot. One critic observed that Varèse deserved the electric chair for composing such noise.

Another dedicated user of the synthesizer to enhance the possibilities of musical sound is Karlheinz Stockhausen (b. 1928), noted for extremely long works, including an orchestral poem called *Light*, which celebrates the seven days of the week. If all seven movements were played non-stop, the audience would find themselves sitting in their chairs continuously for twenty-nine hours. One of his most remarkable—and *truly* avant-garde—achievements was his design of a sphere-shaped auditorium built for the 1970 World's Fair in Osaka, Japan. Within this sphere, an orchestra and chorus performed all of Stockhausen's works five and a half hours daily for 183 days.

Stockhausen is most identified with *serialism*, a musical technique by which the composer disregards all theories of pitch, harmony, and key, creating his own version of musical notes and writing them down in quite non-traditional ways. Those who specialize in the critical analysis of Stockhausen's work insist that his structures, while strange at first to the ear, are geometric and logical within their own set of rules.

Cathy Berberian, Joan La Barbara, and Greetje Bijma are highly productive in their unique innovative styles, much of their work created for female singers. Laurie Anderson and Meredith Monk have also achieved considerable renown. They and their sister composers, using a variety of electronic as well as traditional instruments, dispense not only with ordinary musical notes but, in their songs, with ordinary words. Often they are intent on converting into sound the experience of childbirth and the mother's bond with the newborn, employing a collage of baby talk, distorted nursery rhymes, and unexpected outbreaks of laughter, indicative of both the baby's and the mother's sudden spurts of joy.

In this chapter our goal has been to suggest how your life can be infinitely enriched if you are willing to listen—listen to the great classics of the past and the perhaps great-one-day experiments of the present. Don't forget, Beethoven was often considered too "modern" by some of his contemporaries.

But with all the sound that is there for you to hear, don't forget to spend a little time with your silences.

Key Terms

atonality a characteristic of much avant-garde music, composed without regard for key.

avant-garde art that defies traditional forms; contemporary avant-garde music uses much dissonance and atonality.

baroque label applied to the artistic style of the mid-seventeenth to mid-eighteenth centuries; marked by elaborate ornamentation and complexity; original meaning irregular pearl.

chamber music composition for small ensembles, such as a trio or quartet.

chromatic scale consists of twelve tones; if played on the piano, a consecutive run using both white and black keys.

counterpoint two melodic lines played against each other; characteristic of Bach's compositions.

diatonic scale consists of seven tones; white piano keys only; the fundamental but not the only scale of Western music.

dissonance in music, two or more uncongenial notes sounded or sung at the same time, producing an unfamiliar and, for some, unpleasant effect.

fugue lengthy musical composition, or section within a larger composition, in which two or more melodic lines are played against each other.

half-tone half of one interval between two notes in the diatonic scale; on a piano, half-tones are produced by the black keys.

harmony two or more tones, congenial or otherwise, sounded or sung at the same time.

hip-hop contemporary style of music that includes rap; a lifestyle marked by baggy clothes, idiomatic speech, graffiti, and break-dancing.

improvisation a spontaneous variation or set of variations on a stated musical theme; once performed, it may be written down and repeated by other performers.

key a particular scale that dominates in a musical composition; labeled according to the first note of that scale and whether it is major or minor: e.g., C major; F-sharp minor.

melody either any arrangement of tones in a flowing sequence, or a significant sequence of musical tones that form a unity and are usually meant to be distinguished from what comes before and what follows.

minimalism style of music that rebels against excesses such as overdone orchestrations or use of objects like washboards and garbage can lids; goal is a return to fundamental principles of composition.

pentatonic scale five-tone musical scale that preceded the familiar seven-tone scale dominant in the West; still the basic scale of much non-Western music.

ragtime musical genre, forerunner of jazz, invented in the late 1890s by African American composers, notably Scott Joplin; strongly influenced by slow and stately European dances.

rap major subgenre of hip-hop in which rhyming lyrics are half-sung, half-spoken rapidly.

rhythm alternation of stress and unstress in music, usually created by a percussion instrument.

rock generic name covering a variety of styles that have a loud and insistent beat.

rock 'n' roll style of music introduced in the 1950s and popularized by Elvis Presley; it grew out of a fusion of rhythm and blues, gospel, and country and western styles.

scale the orderly progression of sound-wave frequencies from low to high.

symphony a major orchestral form from the late eighteenth century to the present, usually consisting of four separate sections, or movements, with contrasting tempos, sometimes constituting a unity, often not.

syncopation a form in which the melodic line of a piece is played against, not with, the accented beats of the rhythm accompaniment, as in George Gershwin's "Fascinatin' Rhythm" and the Beatles' "Eleanor Rigby."

toccata musical form perfected by Johann Sebastian Bach, making liberal use of improvisation and allowing for an overpowering display of musical virtuosity by the performer.

tone a single sound produced by a human voice or a musical instrument; also called a note.

Topics for Writing and Discussion

1. "Background music" is not intended to encourage close attention. It's the music played in stores, restaurants, waiting rooms, and elevators. Become a "foreground" listener. Visit several places in which you expect to hear background music. Write a report on the kinds of music heard in different places. Speculate on why a particular style of music is chosen for a particular location.

2. Attend a concert of music often called "classical." There may be one on campus or in a concert hall conveniently located or on television (the public broadcasting stations have any number). Libraries usually have CDs and DVDs that you can borrow. In a report, describe the program. Indicate which selections pleased you the most, which the least. Explain your reasons for liking some and disliking others. Or even liking or disliking all of them.

3. Explore the connection between music and emotion in your own life. For example: what songs do you sing on long road trips? What music reminds you of incidents in your past? Do you tend to associate certain music with pleasant or unpleasant times? What do you play if you need to relax after a day of disappointment and frustration? What music can you hear over and over, without tiring of it? Can you say why?

4. Many people wear earphones on public transportation, while waiting on line, jogging, or just sitting on a park bench. Go to some place in which you expect to find people with earphones. As politely as possible, ask them what kind of music they are listening to and why. Make a report to the class in which you not only indicate which music you discovered was most popular with earphone people, but offer your opinion on whether earphone music is there for aesthetic reasons—or something else.

5. Write a report taking the form of an imaginary speech made to a friend in which you describe a concert you have just attended, one that featured five selections, all from different periods and representing very different styles of music. Make sure your vocabulary contains musical terms you have gleaned from this chapter.

6. Elvis Presley, Little Richard, and the Beatles represent classics of rock. Name a current hip-hop (including rap) performer or group you believe will achieve similar status. Explain why.

7. Find a CD containing ragtime music (libraries usually have a lot of Scott Joplin). Listen to a number of selections. Write a report presenting (and backing up) your opinion on why ragtime is no longer being written today.

8. Wynton Marsalis is the first composer to win a Pulitzer Prize for a jazz composition. He also serves as chief artistic director for the prestigious Jazz at Lincoln Center series. In your opinion, does jazz belong in a place like Lincoln Center, which also houses Avery Fisher Hall, home of the New York Philharmonic Orchestra and the Metropolitan Opera House? Explain.

9. Bach and Beethoven are frequently found at the top of World's Greatest Composers rankings. Since their time, many composers have attained considerable distinction, yet the two giants remain at the top. What did you learn about their musical accomplishments that might justify their hold on the title "the greatest"? If you think they no longer deserve the honor, explain why.

10. Female rock groups have had a tough time gaining recognition, except in certain places and among smaller contingents of loyal fans. Listen to the music of one such group and discuss the kind of music it plays. Extra credit: Explain why you think female rock bands are having trouble competing in what is still a male-dominated scene. Is it their brand of music? Or a form of sexism? Alternative extra credit: Ask a number of women who say they like rock whether they prefer male to female bands, or vice versa. Report to the class on reasons given.

MEDEE
THEATRE DE LA RENAISSANCE
SARAH BERNHARDT
Mucha
Imp. F. CHAMPENOIS
66, Boul.d St Michel, PARIS

7 Theater

Overview

Drama has always been a natural activity. Without being told to do so, children play-act, pretending to be people other than themselves. Often the players are divided into the totally good or totally bad, characters rarely found in real life. Yet drama *is* closely related to real life. It is a way of clarifying experience, a way of making sense out of life by imitating it; it is also a way of enhancing and intensifying certain occasions, as in a parade, a ceremony, or an imposing entrance to signal an important event. Drama gives shape to events, adds spice to life, quickens the pace. It is as though the dramatic instinct was invented to charge our lives with electricity and give us the need to project ourselves into make-believe action, as well as the wisdom to accept pretense as reality. To become involved in theater is to have a greater share of experience.

Theater, which exists in every culture, takes many different forms. Like visual art, drama does not always pretend to be an exact replica of real life. (In fact, realistic staging was absent throughout most of the history of theater.) One form of non-realistic theater with wide popular appeal is the musical, discussed in Chapter 8. This chapter focuses on various periods important to the study of Western theater, beginning with the major conventions of each. These are followed by an examination of the two major genres or forms of theater—**tragedy** and **comedy**—then other forms that have developed as audience tastes expanded, requiring greater variety in what could be offered. Our hope is that you will come to enjoy a variety of theatrical experiences.

Stylized poster by Alphonse Mucha for the 1898 Paris production of Euripides's *Medea*, showing the anguished protagonist after murdering her sons.
Source: © 2003 Artists Rights Society (ARS), New York/Paris. Courtesy of Park South Gallery at Carnegie Hall.

Conventions of the Theater

One way to begin is by ridding yourself of the desire to reject the unfamiliar. We therefore begin with an introduction to theatrical **conventions**, or *the conditions which the audience agrees to accept as real.* Ever since theater began, audiences have had to accept the conditions governing the staging and performance of every play. The stage may be totally bare, and the actors may look nothing like the characters they are portraying (for instance, King Lear played by a woman), yet habitual theater-goers cooperate by playing along, by *suspending their disbelief.* Conventions have changed throughout history, and modern directors often like to add flavor to a production by surprising audience expectations. Habitual theater-goers adjust immediately to the new rules. Indeed, doing so is part of the fun of going to plays.

The Classical Theater of Greece and Rome

Audiences attending the theater in ancient Athens would sit on stone benches in an outdoor stadium that accommodated 14,000 to 20,000 people. They would see plays shown only once during an annual three-day festival, part of a religious celebration sponsored by the state. In earlier times, the festival involved groups of masked men singing and dancing to hymns in praise of the gods, especially Dionysus, who provided the harvest. During the sixth century B.C.E., a soloist named Thespis stepped out of the **Chorus** and engaged in some form of sung dialogue with them. The songs began to tell stories of what could happen if the gods were not obeyed. Drama was born.

Classical conventions:
verse
masks
all-male cast
the messenger
the chorus
Unity of time, place, and action
Greek: *violence off-stage only*
Roman: *much on-stage violence*

By the fifth century, definite conventions for dramatizing the stories had been established. All parts were played by males; therefore, even the female characters would have male voices. The convention would not have bothered audiences, who expected nothing else, as audiences would not centuries later in the theater of Shakespeare. In Greek theater the convention of the mask, carried over from earlier times, made it possible for a few actors with strong voices to play more than one role. There was still a singing and dancing Chorus of either twelve or fifteen men, who observed but took no part in the action. The Chorus served to explain what had happened in the past, to speculate on the meaning of what was taking place in the present, and to make moral comments on the consequences of tragic mistakes made by the central character. In this sense they represented the public, the ordinary people watching the tragic downfall of the rich and powerful, showing compassion for their suffering but also pointing out the dangers of having too much power. In addition, the Chorus served as a bridge between scenes, possibly so that an actor could change his mask and play a different role. Often they danced and sang hymns, another convention surviving from pre-theater days.

Verse dialogue was half-spoken and half-sung, and gestures were not subtle. An amphitheater is not the place for subtle gestures. Actors used broad, sweeping movements to accompany their words, just as officials at an athletic event indicate penalties by using exaggerated hand gestures as they shout the nature of the offense that has been committed. The elevated verse language of the play was in keeping with the gravity of the issues involved and the moral implications of the actions.

Most classical tragedy revolves around a central character, or **protagonist**, in terms of whose fortunes we follow the story. Plays and movies of today continue to have this character, often called the *hero*, but this term can be misleading. *Hero* suggests a person of virtue and courage who usually triumphs over forces of evil. In the great tragedies, however, the protagonist seldom has these qualities. The flaw in his character leads to his tragic downfall.

Some of the plays had a character known as the **antagonist**, who initiates actions that oppose the protagonist. Later, he or she sometimes came to be known as the *villain*, a person of pure malice who tries to destroy the hero. Serious dramatists, screenwriters, and critics, however, avoid using the terms *hero* and *villain* when characters are too complex to be totally virtuous or totally bad.

In Greek theater, violence never occurred in front of the audience; rather, it was described, often in graphic detail, by a messenger. Because the Greek amphitheater was so large, actors had to wear stilts, making violent actions impossible. In contrast, theaters in ancient Rome were smaller, and audiences were closer to the stage. Roman actors wore masks but not stilts; this opened up the possibilities for action, and Roman plays often showed violent scenes, such as multiple stabbings, in full view of the audience. Sometimes slaves were substituted for actors at the last moment and actually killed.

The conventions of offstage violence and the messenger are illustrated in *Oedipus the King*, one of the masterpieces of Greek theater. The protagonist, after discovering the horrible truth of his past (we'll talk more about this later), tears his eyes from their sockets. We hear blood-curdling cries from offstage, then the messenger enters to describe the terrifying moment. So vivid is his telling of it that we feel we were actually *there*. In theater and films today, you can still find variations of the messenger convention.

In modern drama, *Greek element* means that an intensely dramatic moment is greatly underplayed, while *Roman element* means that such a moment is played full force, often with violence. Contemporary films are highly Romanized, with their car chases, realistic-looking fight scenes, and gory murders that leave nothing to the imagination.

The mythical basis for the tragedies was also a convention. Because they knew the myths, audiences had pre-knowledge of the action; they recognized names and basic events and could anticipate what was coming. They would have known, long before Oedipus does, that he has killed his father and unknowingly married his own mother. They would have waited in suspense for the climactic moment when the truth is revealed to him.

Pre-knowledge can still work to a playwright's advantage. It is the true basis of suspense. A sudden twist at the ending of a play or movie does not generate suspense, because it cannot be anticipated. So we would add *familiarity with the story* as an important convention of classical theater. Its modern counterpart would be foreshadowing, or the hints dropped by the playwright or screenwriter about what might happen. Surprise, shock, and suspense are not equivalents.

Another classical convention is *unity of time, place, and action*—or the **unities**. Unity of time means that everything happens in the course of a single day. Theater programs indicating "Two years later" or "A hotel in another part of the city" had yet to be invented, nor were they necessary. When a certain passage of time was essential to the plot, a choral interlude lasting three or four minutes represented perhaps one or two intervening hours. Unity of place means that all of the action occurs in one given locale. Unity of action means that the play consists of one story line only, without subplots revolving around minor characters. Audiences could concentrate on the single conflict unfolding before them, with no side issues.

Elizabethan Conventions

Elizabethan is the label attached to English history and culture during the sixteenth-century reign of Queen Elizabeth I. In theater history, it applies to the tragedies and comedies of William Shakespeare (1564–1616) and his contemporaries. Many scholars and historians believe that the period is unmatched for its drama.

London's new Globe Theatre, a 1997 replica of the original Elizabethan playhouse built circa 1598.

Source: Adams Pic Library 1/a apl/Alamy.

The major Elizabethan theater was the Globe, where most of Shakespeare's works were performed. It was an octagonal building, partly open at the top, because plays could be performed only in daylight. The stage, a platform bare of scenery, featured a long balcony as well as trapdoors for the entrance of hellish demons. Plots were no longer dependent on myths but in many cases were "borrowed" (there were no copyright laws at the time) from other works. The intention was not to provide the audience with the assurance of pre-knowledge but to show how much better the current version was over its predecessors. Few of Shakespeare's plots were entirely his own, but in every instance they surpassed the original.

Along with the entirely different-looking theater, Shakespeare and his contemporaries used a new set of conventions. Audiences, representing all levels of society, watched plays throughout the year, either standing or sitting, depending on their social status. Upper- and middle-class patrons were protected from inclement weather by a roof, while the lower classes, or *groundlings*, stood under the open sky, vulnerable to whatever the weather visited upon them.

Think, when we talk of horses, that you see them
Printing their proud hoofs i'the receiving earth;
For 'tis your thoughts that now must deck our kings,
Carry them here and there, jumping o'er times,
Turning the accomplishment of many years
Into an hour glass. . .

—**William Shakespeare**

In 1997 a new Globe Theater was erected on London's South Bank, reproducing the old Globe of Shakespeare's time. Modern audiences are now able to attend plays there in as authentic a setting as research allows. A theater-goer with tickets for the groundlings area once asked, "What do I do if it rains?" A retractable roof would of course not be authentic, so the reply was: "Get wet, or go home."

The actors in Elizabethan plays were all males. Boys played female characters using costumes, makeup, and wigs. There were few props and no scenery. This limitation was actually a plus, because Elizabethan playwrights were forced to set the scene with words alone, inspiring some of the loveliest poetry in the language.

In Shakespeare's *Henry V*, a narrator stands on a bare stage in daylight yet makes the audience believe they are watching a tense encampment of soldiers on the night before a great battle:

Now entertain conjecture of a time
When creeping murmur and the poring dark
Fills the wide vessel of the universe.
From camp to camp through the foul womb of night
The hum of either army stilly sounds.
That the fix'd sentinels almost receive
The secret whispers of each other's watch:
Fire answers fire, and through their paly flames
Each battle sees the others umber'd face. . . .
The poor condemned En'glish,
Like sacrifices, by their watchful fires
Sit patiently and inly ruminate
The morning's danger, and their gesture sad

Investing lank-lean cheeks and war-worn coats
Presenteth them unto the gazing moon
So many horrid ghosts.[1]

Because the audience was so close to the stage, they could see the faces of the actors and could also hear quiet speech. One of the foremost Elizabethan conventions is the **soliloquy**, in which an actor, alone on stage, speaks his or her thoughts aloud. The most famous soliloquy in all of drama is Hamlet's, which begins "To be or not to be."

Elizabethan conventions:
all-male cast
verse except for prose given to servants
the aside
the soliloquy
no scenery
unities discarded
subtext

Modern playwrights, often limited by the convention of making plays sound as much like real-life as possible, may wish the soliloquy were still acceptable to audiences. The one-person show, popular in theaters everywhere, usually recreates the story and thoughts of someone well known to the audience. These reenactments do not perform the same function as the Elizabethan soliloquy because the modern performer is alone throughout; in Elizabethan drama the actor performs with other actors as part of an ongoing story. Other characters might be on stage during a soliloquy, which the convention says they cannot hear.

Other modern playwrights use the convention of the **subtext**, through which characters reveal what is going on in their minds by speaking words that clearly mask their true feelings, or eloquently by silence. In *Twelfth Night*, written when Shakespeare was reaching the summit of his genius, a young woman named Viola, shipwrecked and cast upon a foreign land, disguises herself as a young man for safety. Hired as a page by a handsome duke, she falls madly in love with her master but cannot tell him directly. Instead she resorts to subtext as she describes the unrequited love of her "sister."

She never told her love,
But let concealment, like a worm i' the bud,
Feed on her damask cheek: she pined in thought,
And with a green and yellow melancholy
She sat like patience on a monument,
Smiling at grief. Was this not love indeed?[2]

Modern playwrights like the freedom subtext allows them to suggest complex thoughts without having to oververbalize. The best playwrights go in fear of having their characters put their emotions into words, preferring to let the audience understand without having to be told.

In contrast to the Elizabethan soliloquy, the **aside** is a remark made by an actor when other actors are present. The audience hears what is said, but other actors are not supposed to. Sometimes it is a shortened version of the soliloquy, as when Hamlet, after listening to his treacherous uncle's insincere rhetoric, comments to the audience, "A little more than kin, and less than kind." In ten words Shakespeare defines how Hamlet feels about his new stepfather, who married Hamlet's mother soon after his father's death. Serious drama stopped using the *aside* by the eighteenth century, but it was used in comedy well into the nineteenth century, and in musical comedy well into the twentieth.

Violent actions occurred on Shakespeare's stage, and even epic battles were fought. In front of the audience, eyes were gouged out, hands chopped off, poison administered, duels fought, and characters strangled, stabbed, or smothered. In the last scene of *Hamlet*, the Queen drinks poisoned wine, Laertes and Hamlet run each other through with poisoned swords, and the King dies from poisoned wine *and* being stabbed. Contemporary productions sometimes employ imaginative techniques to soften the Roman elements.

Elizabethan conventions allowed the wounded to make an eloquent speech before dying. Except for lower-class characters, who speak in prose, most of Shakespeare's characters speak in elaborate poetry, revealing deep feelings. No effort was made to have them speak the way ordinary people, including those in the audience, would actually speak. No one complains, "Haven't had a thing to eat since last night," or "This rain is a nuisance." Everyone has a speech appropriate to the situation. *That* is a timeless and universal convention. Only on a stage do people always have the right words when needed.

The verse is written in iambic pentameter (discussed in Chapter 4): a line of five feet, with rhythm sounding like this: da DAH, da DAH, da DAH, da DAH, da DAH. When skilled actors perform Shakespeare, the rhythm is often hard to detect. The rhythmic words fit the scene so precisely that audiences seldom know the rhythm is there. Except for the more obviously rhythmic ending of some scenes, the dialogue sounds like elegant prose. If it did not, just think how monotonous the play would be!

An amazing example of Shakespeare's genius for tying together iambic pentameter and the precise words for a dramatic situation is found in the final act of *Othello*. The protagonist of the title, maddened by suspicion that his wife is unfaithful, smothers her to death. Immediately after the deed, he hears a knocking on the door and an entreaty from the wife's attendant (Emilia) that she be allowed to enter. Othello shouts to Emilia that he will open the door soon, and then speaks to himself as the full horror of his deed becomes clear to him.

Yes: 'tis Emilia. By and by. She's dead:
'Tis like she comes to speak of Cassio's death,—

Laurence Fishburne and Kenneth Branagh in the 1995 film version of *Othello*, which offers a wonderful example of Shakespeare's genius for tying together iambic pentameter and the dramatic demands of a scene.

Source: The Everett Collection, Inc.

The noise was here. Ha! No more moving?
Still as the grave. Shall she come in? Were 't good?—
I think she stirs again:—no. What's best to do?
If she come in, she'll sure speak to my wife:
My wife! my wife! what wife? I have no wife.[3]

Part of Shakespeare's genius was his ability to write lines that scan almost perfectly but allow the actor to explore the full range of emotion.

The lines *scan* almost perfectly: that is, they can be read so as to exaggerate the iambic pentameter. The dramatic exception is the word "no" in the fifth line, which stands all by itself, demanding that the actor speak it between two pauses. Otherwise the line is exact iambic pentameter. Yet the entire passage compels the actor to hesitate wherever Othello's manic thought processes require it. Shakespeare's genius allows the actor to have it both ways: to have a rhythmic underpinning to the poetry as well as the freedom to explore the character's emotions.

The poetry is filled with **images**, as in this passage in which Hamlet reminds himself how his uncle, now the King, murdered his father:

He took my father grossly, full of bread,
With all his crimes broad blown, as flush as May,
And how his audit stands who knows save Heaven?[4]

The word *audit* is an image, suggesting an account sheet with good deeds on one side, sins on another.

When the Queen, having been roughly forced to confront her role in the crime, cries "O Hamlet, thou has cleft my heart in twain," Hamlet completes the image of a broken heart by telling her to "throw away the worser part of it, / And live the purer with the other half."

Shakespeare's verse also compels the actor to use *verbal dynamics*, moving from slow to fast, from soft to loud. Hamlet's famous speech to the actors who have come to perform at the castle indicates that Shakespeare was highly critical of the melodramatic acting styles of the period and sought a more natural kind of delivery. "Speak the speech I pray you, as I pronounced it to you, / trippingly on the tongue," Hamlet tells the players.

Nor do not saw the air too much
with your hand, thus, but use all gently; for in the very torrent,
tempest, and, as I may say, the whirlwind of passion, you must
acquire and beget a temperance that may give it smoothness.[5]

It is likely Shakespeare himself agreed with the advice. Still, it is a speech in a play, not in a handbook written for aspiring actors. So this speech, like those of many other characters, may not represent Shakespeare's own beliefs after all. He loved words, he loved ideas, and he seems to have enjoyed creating characters adept at both. Scholars have been tempted to discover a consistent Shakespearean philosophy that runs through all of his plays. Indeed many passages, especially in *Hamlet, King Lear*, and *Macbeth*, contain profound wisdom about the human condition, wisdom that will always stimulate thought, whether or not it represents Shakespeare's personal philosophy. Unlike Greek classical plays, Elizabethan drama was under no obligation to deal with universal themes. Shakespeare may have been primarily interested in giving his diverse public a rich, many-layered entertainment. The profundity of the major characters also suggests that he was fascinated by human psychology (though the word did not exist in his time) and the challenge, in Hamlet's words, to "hold . . . the mirror up to nature."

Another convention, that of the *narrator*—a character who stands outside the action but sets the scenes for the audience—is used sparingly by Shakespeare. A famous example, however, is the narrator in *Henry V*, a one-man Chorus, who begins the play by asking the audience to use their imaginations while watching simulated battle scenes. They would also need to be good listeners, for the only way to tell night from day was to hear what the actors said. Plays were performed in daylight, so "night" occurred when actors mentioned it. Audiences saw the Ghost of Hamlet's father wandering in the dark provided by their imaginations.

The classical unities of time, place, and action no longer applied. A play might begin at one specific time, and then have a delay of years or even a generation for the next scene. The Elizabethan theater was free from the burden of moving heavy scenery about, and playwrights realized that a bare stage could be any place as long as their words could describe it vividly. And Shakespeare did this better than his fellow dramatists. Scenes could move from indoors to outdoors or from garden to palace or the imaginary tomb in which Romeo and Juliet meet their deaths. Elizabethan audiences quickly adapted to the rules governing each play.

Neoclassic Conventions

In the years following the Elizabethan era, theatrical conventions changed once again. In the latter half of the seventeenth century, drama, poetry, painting, and architecture saw a general return to classical principles of order and balance. For a century and a half this period of the arts is appropriately called **neoclassicism.**

Neoclassic theater moved indoors. For the first time, plays no longer found themselves in a vast amphitheater or confined to a courtyard, depending on lighting from the sun. Instead, plays could be staged in elaborate rooms within a great house, and could be shown at night, through the use of lighting from elegant chandeliers.

Neoclassic conventions:
indoor theaters
chandelier lighting (candles)
upper-class audience
return of unities
artificial language in couplets
classical myths retold in terms of neoclassic behavioral codes
emotion described, not shown

Audiences changed, too. Instead of the many social levels that attended the Greek and Roman theaters and the Elizabethan playhouse, audiences were now made up of well-educated, beautifully dressed aristocrats, whose preferences had to be considered. The demand was strong for a return to a theater less violent than Shakespeare's and once again with subject matter based on myth, as it had been during the classical period—but the stories were altered to reflect the issues and moral values of the age. A non-classical element was the appearance for the first time of women playing female characters. The new convention allowed playwrights to focus on tragic myths about the effects of sexual passion and various destructive conflicts between men and women.

Playwrights returned as much as possible to the classical unities of time, place, and action. If the plot demanded scenes in different places, the problem was solved by having one lavish but neutral set, such as a large room that could represent a number of locales. Furniture and props were carried on and off by stagehands. Playwrights packed all the action into a single day or, if possible, into real time, the time that audiences were actually in the theater. The setting was likely to be an ornate French drawing room, and although the characters might have the Greek names from the original myths, they looked and sounded like seventeenth-century aristocrats. All realism vanished as characters crammed a lot of action into a short period of time: possibly a duel, expulsion from the country, heroism in battle, return for acclaim, forgiveness, and prospective marriage to the heroine.

Accomplishing all that is assisted by that handy holdover from the classical theater, the messenger, sometimes reporting offstage violence. If the aim had been realistic depiction of the delivery of terrible news, we might expect interruptions, sighs, sounds of horror or disbelief. But in the spirit of neoclassic tragedy, a messenger may coolly announce the unhappy news that the king's son has suffered "the unspeakable horror of being devoured by a sea monster."

In addition to the unities, neoclassical dramatists, like their ancient predecessors, employed a highly stylized, elevated stage poetry. The verse was farther removed from natural speech than the iambic pentameter of Shakespeare. Language was ornate, geared to aristocratic taste. The word "air," for example, was avoided in favor of "ozone," and "cat" became "feline creature."

In English neoclassical tragedy, characters speak in couplets: two consecutive rhyming lines, usually with a pause at the end of each one so that the rhymes stand out, as they do not in Shakespeare except in his scene-ending couplets. Neoclassical couplets, like all rhythmic lines, present a special challenge to actors, who must avoid the singsong delivery that would call undue attention to the rhymes.

Couplets can be found in comedy as well as tragedy. Here are lines (in a close translation by the poet Richard Wilbur) from the French satiric comedy *Tartuffe* by Molière (1622–1673). The speaker is Cléante, a voice of reason who has his doubts about the title character, a scoundrel who pretends to be an evangelist in order to take advantage of a very foolish man:

Brother, I don't pretend to be a sage,
Nor have I all the wisdom of the age.
There's just one insight I would dare to claim.
I know that true and false are not the same;
And just as there is nothing I more revere
Than a soul whose faith is steadfast and sincere,
Nothing that I more cherish and admire
Than honest zeal and true religious fire,
So there is nothing that I find more base
Than specious piety's dishonest face—
Whose impious mummeries and hollow shows
Exploit our love of heaven and make a jest
Of all that men think holiest and best.[6]

As we pointed out, the couplet usually has a pause between the rhyming lines, and this, of course, presented a challenge to the actor. Richard Wilbur, a major poet in his own right, softens the challenge by eliminating strong pauses. At the same time, the rhymes are unmistakably there. The critic John Simon calls Wilbur "easily one of the best translators of lyric poetry as well [as the rhymed couplet], but when it comes to Englishing French verse drama, he simply has no equal."[7] High praise indeed when one considers that the French language offers many more rhyming opportunities than does English.

The rhymed couplets of French neoclassic drama, so different from Shakespeare's blank verse, impressed neoclassic writers for the English stage. After all, Shakespeare had died in 1616, and although he had been admired during his lifetime, his work was not considered untouchable. Within half a century, efforts to improve him had already begun; indeed, audiences considered his emotional directness vulgar. Playwrights had no hesitation about rewriting his work. For example, John Dryden (1631–1700) turned *Antony and Cleopatra*, Shakespeare's tragedy of tempestuous middle-aged lovers who destroy each other, into *All for Love*, a "polite" tragedy of aristocrats who overstep the bounds of propriety. A neoclassical play, like a neoclassical building, exalts balance, harmony, and order, and it shuns out-of-control passion. Characters talk brilliantly—and in rhyme—about their emotions but do not *show* emotion except in death scenes.

Victorian Conventions

The lights go down and the pulse goes up.

—**Judith Anderson**

The *Victorian era* refers to the late nineteenth century, a period named for the queen who ruled England for most of the century. In Victorian theater, the audience sits in the dark and looks up at a lighted stage. People on the stage move and talk to each other without noticing that what they do is being seen and heard by a large number of eavesdroppers. Their job is to pretend the audience is not there, and the audience's job is to pretend they are not watching merely actors who move about a set made to look like a real interior. Instead, the audience suspends disbelief, so the actors walk up and down real stairs. They eat real food. Someone on the stage opens a door and walks through it, presumably to go outside. In reality, however, the actor is only going backstage, perhaps checking the script to make sure the next lines will be right, but the audience does not think about this. This is now the era of **verisimilitude**, the convention of making everything look and sound like the real world, of masking the fact that theater is an entertainment.

The front of the stage—or **proscenium**—is supposedly the *fourth wall* of the room in which the action takes place. Actors are not supposed to "break the fourth wall"—that is, to look at the audience. The play contains itself and only itself. But sometimes the actors cheat and partially face the fourth wall, speaking in tones much louder than people would normally use. The audience again pretends not to notice.

The audience is meant to believe not only in the reality of the set but in the authenticity of the dialogue. They think, "Yes, people sound like that. I have friends that have said words like that." Prose dialogue (poetry would sound too artificial) can be about the details of ordinary life. At last in the history of theater it is possible for characters to sound deceptively just like the people watching them.

Yet, when reading plays of the Victorian period, we are apt to wonder how on earth audiences of the time could have actually believed the dialogue was authentic. Up to a point it was—for a time when middle-class people observed the niceties of language that were stringently taught at home and in school. In today's theater and in films or on television, we still accept the "realities" of dialogue, except that by now actors often talk in short, sometimes incomplete sentences about food, trains, money, and sex. Much dialogue is not allowed to be more insightful or profound than ordinary conversation. Even at moments of great love or great loss, characters can be as inarticulate as anyone without a gifted scriptwriter to tell them what to say. Sometimes instead of words there are grunts and sighs. This too is authentic—up to a point.

Neoclassic theaters often employed small orchestras to play before, during, and after the performance. In the Victorian theater of verisimilitude there was generally no music, no sounds except those which would actually be heard in the circumstances of the play: the chiming of a clock, the tolling of a distant bell, a fog horn. Increasingly, sound effects become an important element in the theater, since there was no music to influence mood.

Time intervals were explained by a program handed to the audience. Lighting now indicated time of day or night. With the coming of electricity in the 1880s, actors were artificially lighted and their features heavily emphasized or even disguised by stage makeup. If a younger actor was cast as a middle-aged person, every effort was made to conceal the actor's youth. But as theater companies grew and spread about the country, actors began to be cast as they physically and vocally suited the part. Versatile actors, suitable for many roles, were able to demand high salaries.

The director became a major figure also. Before this period, plays were put together by the actors. Often the theater's manager would star in a production and instruct cast members to give him center stage at all times. In the theater of verisimilitude, however, movement and interpretation of lines were carefully supervised by a director.

The convention of verisimilitude gave rise to a new genre that continues to be a great audience pleaser: the tricky mystery play, in which the audience is kept in suspense about the identity of the murderer until a clever detective reveals surprises just before the final curtain. Phone lines have been cut, a raging storm prevents escape, everyone looks suspicious, with dubious movements and alibis for the time of the crime. The victim was disliked by any number of suspects. *Whodunit?* And *How?* Verisimilitude is the ideal convention for the puzzle play because, if the characters are trapped within a limited space, intensity builds quickly. Audiences also know that the murderer is one of the cast. Although a surprise ending is a must in this genre, verisimilitude prohibits improbability. The playwright is not supposed to introduce late in the play information that solves the puzzle. There can be no surprise wills or marriage licenses or incriminating letters. There should be just the audience and the playwright in a duel of wits. The solution in the very best mystery plays is arrived at through logic, not a chance happening. There have to be tiny details the audience is meant not to notice at the time, but they add up to a believable and clever revelation. The theater-goer thinks, "Oh. I should have known!" but is delighted at having been tricked. When there is no surprise, the experience is less satisfying.

The structure of a play is always the story of how the birds came home to roost.

—**Arthur Miller**

If theater of verisimilitude were completely true to the claim that it was mirroring real life in the most honest way possible, its stories would not be as tightly knit as they are. Something else was at work, popularized by French playwrights earlier in the century, something known as the **well-made play** structure. The realism of the set and the acting often disguised the fact that the play did not show what real life was actually like. In the well-made play, objects and people mentioned in Act 1 *must* be important later on. Guns are mentioned, and someone is shot. Someone who coughs slightly is revealed to have a fatal illness. The casual mention that a letter was mistakenly sent must make the viewer expect devastating consequences. Almost nothing is wasted as just about everything advances the plot or reveals character. Even the set has to observe the rules of this convention. Every chair on the set has to be occupied by one or another character at some point; a lamp must be lighted; a door must be opened; stairs have to be used.

If a gun is hanging on the wall in the first act, it must fire in the last.

—**Anton Chekhov**

Important to the well-made play was **exposition**, the revelation through dialogue of necessary background material, such as the past history and relationships among the characters. It remains vital to all realistic theater and has become a major problem for modern dramatists. In the hands of an inexperienced playwright attempting to sound realistic, exposition can sound silly. Families and friends in real life don't need to identify the people in a conversation. You already know that your best friend has a brother named Eddie who has been overseas in the army. You therefore would not dream of asking, "How's your brother Eddie, who's in the army?" Playwrights have to introduce information about the characters without sounding overly obvious, and they have to depend on appearance and dialogue alone—no narrator, no chorus, no soliloquy or asides to help explain.

Henrik Ibsen (1828–1906) revolutionized the theater of verisimilitude by writing plays about controversial social issues (discussed more fully later in the chapter). Here we see how adeptly and economically he handles exposition—in this case, the nature of the relationship between husband and wife in the 1879 work *A Doll's House*, which exposes the sham that was, for Ibsen, the Victorian marriage.

HELMER: *(from the study) Is that my little lark twittering out there?*

NORA: *(busy opening packages) Yes, it is.*

HELMER: *Is that my squirrel rummaging around?*

NORA: *Yes!*

HELMER: *When did my squirrel get in?*

NORA: *Just now. (Putting the macaroon bag in her pocket and wiping her mouth) Do come in, Torvald, and see what I've bought.*

HELMER: *Can't be disturbed. (After a moment he opens the door and peers in, pen in hand) Bought, you say? All that there? Has the little spendthrift been out throwing money around again?*

NORA: *Oh. But Torvald, this year we really should let ourselves go a bit. It's the first Christmas we haven't had to economize.*

HELMER: *But you know we can't go squandering.*

NORA: *Oh yes, Torvald, we can squander a little now. Can't we? Just a tiny, wee bit. Now that you've got a big salary and are going to make piles of money.*

HELMER: *Yes, starting New Year's. But then it's a full three months till the raise comes through.*[8]

Lark, squirrel, spendthrift, Christmas, a busy husband, a change in income in three months—we've learned a lot in those few lines of exposition. But this introduction also hints at the wife's revolt that is to come. In the hands of a great playwright, exposition not only provides background for the audience but, more important, promises what will eventually happen.

Victorian comic playwrights dealt with real issues as well, and they did so within the convention of verisimilitude, but their kind of dialogue, so witty and elegant, is rarely found except on the stage. In the plays of Oscar Wilde (whose scandalous trial will be discussed in Chapter 15), dialogue is an idealized version of how civilized people *should* talk. It is far from being a transcript of everyday speech, and when a play is as consistently witty as *The Importance of Being Earnest*, we are grateful. We can hear plenty of familiar speech *outside* the theater.

In the hands of a great playwright like Ibsen, exposition not only provides background for the audience, but, more important, promises what will eventually happen.

The sets for Victorian comedy, as for other plays of the period, were familiar to the audience: a well-appointed drawing room, a garden with landscaping and tables,

Jeff Quinn's realistic set for the 1980 revival of *A Doll's House* at the Green Room Theatre, Lancaster, Pennsylvania.

Source: Reprinted courtesy of the designer.

a bachelor's apartment. The one-set play, however, presented problems. Successful playwrights whose work was produced in theaters with money often required a change of scene. Wilde's *Earnest*, for example, has three sets, and each has to reflect an upper-middle-class lifestyle. Writers limited to one set were forced to invent reasons for having all of the necessary characters together in the same drawing room, and had to "cheat" about time intervals. A character leaves the stage saying "I'll be back in twenty minutes," but returns in five. An all-night conversation transpires in two hours. Modern playwrights inherited this problem, along with that of exposition.

Modern Conventions

The neatly plotted Victorian play, set in the well-furnished living room, inevitably struck younger writers as a cliché. Modern playwrights wanted to create theater that was not limited by the back-and-forth dialogue of fourth-wall drama and the pretense that the audience was not there. In the early twentieth century, German theater exerted universal influence with a new style known as *expressionism*. Sets were no longer realistic but symbolic. An American play called *The Adding Machine* (1923) had for a set a giant, early version of the calculator, on which the main character, named Mr. Zero, was eventually crucified.

Experiments in stage design as well as plot construction were many. *Theater-in-the-round*, in which the stage area may be completely surrounded by the audience, as in the still active Arena Stage in Washington, D.C., and the Circle-in-the-Square in New York, allowed audiences to feel closer to the actors and inspired playwrights to create works in which the visible presence of the audience was taken for granted. Stages were even bare, with no scenery, to encourage audience imagination, a component of theater that many believed had been lost in the

All the important modern dramatists saw no point in putting on plays that did not challenge, alienate, or push away their audiences. But they knew they needed their audiences to survive. They faced the classic problem. . . how do you offend people and keep them coming? And when they keep coming, how do you keep offending them?

—**Sarah Boxer**

Victorian era. In 1940 *Our Town* by Thornton Wilder (1897–1975) had a narrator walk out on an empty stage and, in the style of Shakespeare's *Henry V*, create a small New Hampshire village in the audience's mind. Like other modern playwrights, Wilder wanted to return to the fundamental premise that audiences will accept anything as long as the rules are clearly spelled out in the beginning.

In the late nineteenth and early twentieth centuries, stage sets were designed so as not to disguise their unreality, but often to convey a metaphor, representing society as a machine, a zoo, or a prison. Even in otherwise realistic drama, sets sometimes contained several rooms and levels all visible at the same time. Through increasingly sophisticated lighting techniques, audiences were trained to believe that, when a scene took place in a lighted part of the stage, the darkened part was not supposed to be there.

The theater introduced one innovation after another. American playwright Eugene O'Neill (1888–1953) wrote a modern tragedy called *Desire under the Elms* in which a dramatic encounter between a son and his stepmother is taking place in an upstairs bedroom while down below townspeople are doing a folk dance. So as not to detract from the intensity as the scene above nears its climax, the dancers are required to "freeze," though the audience is asked to assume the dancing is continuing. The climax of the scene shows the stepmother murdering the child sired by the stepson. Although the "frozen" dancers are in one sense not there, the still-visible figures serve as an ironic contrast: normal life goes about its business even as tragic lovers are committing an atrocity.

> *Masterpieces of the past are good for the past; they are not good for us. We have the right to say and even what has not been said in a way that belongs to us. . . corresponding to present modes of feeling. . .*
>
> —**Antonin Artaud**

O'Neill reinvented the Shakespearean soliloquy in *Strange Interlude*, a six-hour-long drama that meticulously and tirelessly dissects the complex thoughts of the characters. The play combines naturalistic dialogue, a realistic set, and monologues spoken directly to the audience. Even verse reappeared as playwrights sought ways to reach the heights achieved by the Greeks and Shakespeare. Except in a few instances, modern verse plays were ponderous and pretentious. Maxwell Anderson's *Winterset* (1935), for example, is about the son of an executed immigrant and his love for a young woman who lives in a tenement; both speak improbable poetry. The playwright was more successful with historical dramas like *Elizabeth the Queen* (1931) and *Mary of Scotland* (1936), characters for whom complex poetry was more believable.

The modern theater has created musicals, music-dramas, and operas reflecting modern times and modern issues. Some serious writers have found in music the means of conveying emotions that might in prose seem melodramatic.

That there are many new conventions does not mean that the older ones have been cast aside. Verisimilitude in setting, costumes, and makeup continues to dominate the professional theater. But *dialogue is ever more naturalistic* as writers and actors work to approximate the way people actually talk. There will always be an element of artificiality, however, since both drama and comedy are intensifications of reality. Also, *moments of silence* often replace lengthy conversations. Instead of telling each other how they feel, characters are made to be as inarticulate as most of us can be. For one reason or another, there are constraints on expressing our deepest thoughts and emotions, and many of the new writers have become adept at writing dialogue that isn't saying what characters are really talking about.

Stories can be told in reverse rather than chronological order. More common is the *flashback*, in which scenes from the past are dramatically enacted rather than merely spoken about as in the well-made play. With the emergence of style options, writers could have a set that resembles a real place but is lacking in just enough realistic detail to permit characters to move back and forth in time. Arthur Miller's *Death of a Salesman* (1949) makes brilliant use of the flashback. We first meet the two sons of the salesman Willy Loman as they are in present time, not having fulfilled the dreams their father had for them. Frequent flashbacks to earlier and happier times make the contrast painful to see, and they are necessary for Miller's intent.

A relatively new convention is *having two or three actors play all the parts*—perhaps the result of rising production costs and actors' salaries. Audiences are now willing to believe that Actor A is an old man in one scene and a teenager in the next or that Actor B is a man in one scene and a woman in the next.

A relatively new convention is having two or three actors play all the parts, as in the 2008 updating of Hitchcock's classic film The 39 Steps.

Such innovations can provide enormous pleasure. The audience may enjoy noting the skillful way the transformations take place (or be annoyed at the unnecessary confusion, believing that the decision to compress was a bad idea, possibly an ill-conceived effort to save money). Unconventional staging, cross-gendering, and "actor economy" may even give new life to a familiar plot customarily staged in a traditional style, although a playwright may resist a director's innovations, as Edward Albee (b. 1928) made clear in an interview:

> *After the movie of* Who's Afraid of Virginia Woolf? *came out, a critic, knowing I was gay, suggested that I was really writing about a gay relationship in the guise of a heterosexual relationship. It's just too preposterous—I mean I know a lot of gay relationships, and I haven't come across a hysterical pregnancy in one yet. But it led an awful lot of people to say, "Oh, let's do a production that way." And so I finally had to have it put in my contracts that my plays must be performed with accuracy as to the sex of the characters. To protect the play, not me. And protect the audiences. . . . I tell actors at the beginning of any new production, whether I'm directing or not: "Do whatever you want as long as you end up with exactly what I intended."*[9]

Some modern conventions:
bare stage
return of the narrator
contined use of verisimilitude
flashback
one actor in multiple parts
transgender casting

Experiments have not been limited to casting or even to those on stage. For example, the Living Theatre, based in New York, uses a hyper-realistic approach. Actors playing the poor and homeless might walk the aisles, begging for food. In other theaters, audiences have been blindfolded and led to where they must sit, while strange noises assailed their ears and they could imagine all manner of horrible ogres preparing to attack. There have even been plays performed with each scene at a different subway station.

Director Robert Wilson has led the way in creating **avant-garde** (ahead of their time) conventions. One of his works, *the CIVIL warS* (note the mandatory spelling), was presented on a mountain and took seven days. His production of Philip Glass's opera *Einstein on the Beach* (1993) was so long that audiences were encouraged to slip out for afternoon snacks. It didn't matter if they missed some of the action, because there were elaborate visual images but no discernible story line.

New York is not the only venue in which to find contemporary theatrical conventions. Small companies in almost every urban area as well as college town are taking advantage of freedom from the traditional staging that requires cash outlays they can ill afford. Frugality in production costs can motivate theater groups to compensate with imaginative techniques and superior acting. It also makes theater groups more willing to take risks on unusual works by unknown playwrights.

The chapter this far has been mainly concerned with staging in different periods of theater history, with the conventions that greet an audience even before the curtain is raised—if indeed there is a curtain. Now we turn for an in-depth-look at some of the major theatrical genres and major dramatists.

Tragedy

The good ended happily, and the bad unhappily. That is what fiction means.

—Oscar Wilde

The first known critical analysis and definition of tragedy came from ancient Greece, not from playwrights but from a philosophical spectator who observed the effect on the audience. Looking around the amphitheater, Aristotle (382–322 B.C.E.) wondered what moved people, *why* they were moved, what were the essential elements all tragedies must have, and finally, why some plays were more successful than others. This first critic of Western theater wrote his observations in *The Poetics*, which contains his famous essay on tragedy (and is believed to have included an essay on comedy, of which all but the first line has been lost).

Aristotle analyzes how experiencing a make-believe story could have the same effect as witnessing an actual tragic event. He realized spectators were identifying with the characters and feeling some of the pain that the actors pretended to be suffering. For this reason he decided that the ideal protagonist for a tragedy must be someone who is mainly virtuous (otherwise people wouldn't care what happened to the character) but is not totally innocent either. If a bad fate befell an innocent person, the audience would reject this outcome as being too cruel.

The lone surviving sentence of the essay on comedy is: *Tragedy is life seen close at hand; comedy is life seen from a distance.* We can infer from this that Aristotle believed comedy does not move people profoundly and does not expect audiences to identify with the characters and experience their pain.

Greek Tragedy

The bad ended unhappily, the good unluckily. That is what tragedy means.

—Tom Stoppard

Aristotle divided tragedy into six parts, arranged in order of importance: *plot, character, thought, poetry, spectacle*, and *song*. He then gave his famous definition of tragedy, which is "the imitation of a good action, which is complete and of a certain length, by means of language made pleasing for each part separately; it relies in its various elements not on narrative but on acting; through pity and fear it achieves the purgation of such emotions."[10]

By "acting" Aristotle is referring to the forward motion, or action, of the tragedy, which, through what the characters do, brings about a change of circumstances—a change for the worse—and thus the emotions of the audiences grow more intense as the play leads to inevitable catastrophe. The aim is to stimulate an emotional response not for the sake of the emotion, but for the aftermath of emotion: the feeling of calm that follows it.

This calm, called **catharsis**, can also come after undergoing other kinds of aesthetic experience: after listening to Beethoven's Third Symphony, for example. To the question "Why put oneself through such a wrenching ordeal?" the Aristotelian answer is that *we derive strength from reacting to make-believe pain as if it were real.* The spectator slowly returns to the life that was left outside the theater, but with the rational calm that would follow an actual catastrophe.

Aristotle's model of the perfect tragedy was the same play that Nietzsche used to explain his famous distinction between the Apollonian and the Dionysian (Chapter 1), a play based on a myth with which most of the audience would have been familiar: *Oedipus the King* by Sophocles (496–406 B.C.E.).

For Aristotle, tragedy was about the downfall of a human being of noble and virtuous qualities, except for one weakness: hubris, the misguided assumption that worldly power placed one on the level of the gods.

The play begins with relative peace, as tragedies often do—the calm before the storm. The state of Thebes is in good hands, or so it is believed. King Oedipus is powerful and wise, able to solve problems as no one else can. In the past he saved the citizens from being devoured by a horrible monster. Now, years later, Thebes faces another threat. There is a plague, and the Chorus, representing the people of Thebes, entreats the King to find out why. An oracle sends word that the plague will continue until the murderer of the previous king is found and brought to justice. Oedipus confidently agrees to solve the mystery, without realizing that he himself is the killer. A blind prophet tells him the truth, but Oedipus becomes enraged and denounces the man. He is the king, and cannot be a murderer. By the end of the play he is forced to recognize that the man he killed years before in an unplanned skirmish had been the king of Thebes—and his own father as well.

Disaster follows disaster. As if this news were not bad enough, Oedipus realizes that in marrying the deceased king's wife, Jocasta, he has actually married his mother, who has borne him four children. Horrified by his guilt, he blinds himself and goes into exile, fulfilling his promise to the people that he would find the murderer and send him from the land.

For the tragedy to affect audiences, according to Aristotle, the plight of Oedipus must involve them. They must experience empathy with him as he tries to solve the murder in order to save his kingdom, and then as he is devastated in the effort and has the courage to pronounce judgment on himself. In fifth-century Athens, a democratic society without kings but one that honored those who performed noble deeds, the audience would have recognized the nobility of Oedipus as well as the terrible price he had to pay. They would also have acknowledged his responsibility for the tragedy. True, he was doomed by fate to kill his father and marry his mother, but staring him in the face had been the prophet's revelation of the truth. He was free to believe or disbelieve, and his fatal error was choosing to accept only what suited him, to believe only in his own version of reality.

The play remains relevant. The flaw of Oedipus is called **hubris**, or arrogance. It is universal. Everyone knows people who insist that there is no other truth but theirs. Aristotle's analysis holds. Tragedy, he said, requires audience identification. Only then will the downfall of the protagonist be emotionally devastating, and no one can achieve catharsis who is not profoundly moved. Small wonder that playwrights have continued to reach for the heights of tragedy.

Dramatically underscoring the passing of the golden age of classical Greek tragedy were the deaths in the same year of Sophocles and another great classical playwright, Euripides (484–406 B.C.E.). Although the plays of Euripides seldom completely illustrate the principles set forth in Aristotle's *Poetics*, although they lack the concluding speech in which protagonists recognize their responsibility for the catastrophe, and although his plots generally lack the tight structure Aristotle so admired in *Oedipus*, Euripides was nevertheless called by Aristotle "the most tragic of all." Perhaps the philosopher meant that Euripides saw deeply into the pain of being alive. This pain is his subject. In fact, the *Medea* of Euripides has proved to be, for modern audiences, the most persistently stage-worthy of the Greek tragedies.

The plot structure of *Medea* is in fact uncharacteristically tight. The tragedy is driven by the terrifying inevitability of a jealous wife's seeking revenge on her husband by murdering their sons. Scene after scene shows the wife's hatred growing more bitter and her decision becoming more irreversible even as her maternal love intensifies. Euripides is more interested in the emotional and psychological turbulence that drives the work than in the moral and philosophical issues raised by a character's actions.

The play tells only the last part of Medea's story. We learn, though, that in the past Medea has used her magical powers to help her eventual husband, Jason, find the famous Golden Fleece and gain the stature of a hero. He has married her out of gratitude. As the play begins, Medea is living in Jason's country, finding herself among people with little regard for either foreigners or women. Jason tells Medea of his plans to marry a princess so that their sons will have the advantage of living in a royal household and be half-brothers to the royal children Jason will sire. He expects her to be pleased at the thought of their children's future. She is not, but pretends approval so that she can take revenge. After using her powers to design a poisonous gown that kills her rival, she is not yet satisfied that Jason has suffered enough. In one of the theater's most powerful scenes Medea struggles against what she knows would be the ultimate revenge: the death of Jason's sons.

As the innocent children play, their mother tries to stem the force that is driving her to do the unspeakable, but she cannot. She takes them inside and, after a terrifying moment of silence, we hear their agonized cries. Their throats have been cut.

The ending of the play lacks the moral completeness of *Oedipus*. For Sophocles, though the fate of Oedipus was prearranged, his blind arrogance was really a defiance of divine law. For this arrogance he pays a tragic price. The suffering of Medea, however, does not spring from a recognition that she has broken a moral law, but rather that as a loving mother she should not have been brought to such a state by an insensitive husband, and also that her passion for revenge has torn her apart. Nor does Medea go forth in ruins, as Oedipus does. With Jason grieving over the bodies of his slain children, Medea rides off in triumph on a chariot sent for her by a sympathetic neighboring king. Her last line as she looks up at the "unfriendly stars" is: "Not me they scorn." If she will feel the pangs of guilt for the rest of her life, her grief will be private and no business of the gods—if indeed there *are* gods.

Euripides gives every indication that he has abandoned the effort to find meaning in obedience to the laws of the gods. There is a pervading cynicism in his plays, a fear that humanity is abandoned in a godless universe, or at least one in which the gods, if they exist, are cruelly whimsical and justice is never carried out. As if to underscore his cynicism, many of his plays have contrived, unbelievable happy endings. He seems to be saying that in an amoral world, a happy ending is a random accident. In the world of Euripides, moral responsibility does not exist. Pain does.

Archetypes in This Chapter

Godot from Samuel Beckett's *Waiting for Godot*, an undefinable something we wait for or hope will happen.

Medea in Greek mythology, the lover and wife of Jason who helps the hero obtain the Golden Fleece and then later responds to his plans to marry another woman by poisoning her rival and murdering her own two sons by Jason. In our own times, a scorned woman who seeks vengeance.

Oedipus in Greek mythology, the king of Thebes who unwittingly murders his father and marries his mother. In modern times, Sigmund Freud used the myth of Oedipus to illustrate the unconscious sexual tensions between sons and their parents.

Rogue hero the charming scoundrel who breaks all the rules yet always wins our sympathy.

Romeo and Juliet the eternal icons of young, innocent love.

Shakespearean Tragedy

Because plays in ancient Greece were presented only once a year and in Elizabethan times were available all year long, audience tastes began to be important. By now there were theater companies competing with each other for those audiences, and playwrights had to satisfy their demands. Shakespeare gave them what they wanted. Although the Elizabethans on all levels of society were fascinated by poetry and intricate wordplay, they also adored action—lots of it—and the more violent the better. Shakespeare gave them unceasing action: simulated battles, sword fights, multiple stabbings, and poisonings. He was not afraid to inject scenes of low-life comedy, combined with sexual humor, in the midst of great tragic moments.

Speak the speech, I pray you, as I pronounced it to you, trippingly on the tongue; but if you mouth it, as many of your players do, I had as lief the town crier spoke my lines.

—Hamlet to the Players

Shakespeare's plays, on the whole, are less structurally tight than those of Sophocles. And they are not always faithful to the probabilities of human experience (though his insight into human nature has never been surpassed). An early work, *Romeo and Juliet* (1594), everyone's favorite love story, depends on a coincidence to justify the tragic deaths of the two protagonists. Nor is their tragedy brought about by flaws in their character. Aristotle would have said that their tragic fate is unacceptably cruel because it is totally undeserved.

In his greatest plays, however, character and thought are without equal in the entire realm of theater. His major characters go from the particular to the general, finding broad moral principles that offer profound insights into the meaning of human life. Many of his characters entertain a bleak vision of life. For example, Hamlet is challenged to a fencing match in which, unknown to him, his opponent's sword is dipped in poison. His friend Horatio has a grim foreboding and urges Hamlet to decline. Hamlet will not.

> *we defy augury: there's a special providence in the fall of*
> *a sparrow. If it be now, 'tis not to come; if it be not to come,*
> *it will be now; if it be not now, yet it will come: the readiness*
> *is all: since no man has aught of what he leaves, what is't*
> *to leave betimes?*[11]

Macbeth, whose kingdom lies in ruins and whose enemies are closing in on him, responds in this way to the news of his wife's death:

> *She should have died hereafter;*
> *There would have been a time for such a word*
> *To-morrow, and to-morrow, and to-morrow,*
> *Creeps in this petty pace from day to day*
> *To the last syllable of recorded time,*
> *And all our yesterdays have lighted fools*
> *The way to dusty death. Out, out, brief candle!*
> *Life's but a walking shadow, a poor player*
> *That struts and frets his hour upon the stage*
> *And then is heard no more; it is a tale*
> *Told by an idiot, full of sound and fury,*
> *Signifying nothing.*[12]

In medieval drama there is no tragedy, because the protagonists either repent their sins and God forgives them, or they do not repent and are thus damned. In Shakespeare's world, people are abandoned to themselves.

The Recognition Scene in Shakespeare

Tragedy rewards audiences willing to look beyond the action. The greatest tragedies have a **recognition scene**, a moment when the protagonist fully understands what has brought about the disaster. First, there is a search for the meaning of what has occurred. This may be followed by the attempt to justify the action, and finally, the acceptance of responsibility. Here is a famous recognition speech, delivered by Creon in Sophocles' *Antigone*. Having inherited the throne of Thebes after the downfall of Oedipus, Creon has become a powerful and arrogant ruler. In this speech, he realizes his arrogance has caused the deaths of those who were dearest to him and his life now lies in ruins. He cries:

Lead me away. I have been rash and foolish.
I have killed my son and my wife.
I look for comfort; my comfort lies here dead.
Whatever my hands have touched has come to nothing.
Fate has brought all my pride to a thought of dust.[13]

Playwrights of today, attempting tragedy, often have difficulty providing recognition scenes, because of a common belief that people are seldom fully responsible for their actions. Although Shakespeare rarely followed classical conventions, he understood that the speech of recognition was essential to a tragic effect. This one is from the final act of *Othello*, after the protagonist has realized that he was tricked into believing in his wife's infidelity and has murdered her without cause. At the point of his arrest he says to his captors:

Soft you; a word before you go.
I have done the state some service and they know't.
No more of that. I pray you, in your letters,
When you shall these unlucky deed relate,
Speak of me as I am; nothing extenuate,
Nor set down aught in malice. Then must you speak
Of one that lov'd not wisely but too well.[14]

Playwrights of today, attempting tragedy, often have difficulty providing recognition scenes, because of a common belief that people are seldom responsible for their actions.

At the conclusion of the speech, he removes a concealed dagger and stabs himself. The protagonist, having taken full responsibility, holds onto his dignity. Freedom to choose his own death is all that is left.

In *Othello*, as in all of the great Greek and Shakespearean tragedies, a moral order is reaffirmed. The audience has been emotionally devastated, but the evil elements in society—the twisted Iago and the tragic crime of Othello—are purged. The state will function once again as it should. Tragedy is like the diseased tissue that must be removed so that the body may regain its health. The restoration of order further allows the viewer to reach the catharsis that for Aristotle was the purpose of tragic theater.

In all theater there may be no scene to match the recognition scene in *King Lear*, when the king, close to death, finally understands the terrible mistake he has made by banishing his only loving daughter. Because of his prideful blindness to reality, he has supported his evil daughters, only to have them turn on him. When the innocent daughter is captured and executed, the old man, not always with full knowledge of who and where he is, fully comprehends what he has done and knows that he will never see his loving daughter again. The moment is unrivaled. Instead of vast eloquence, Shakespeare uses relatively few words—and silence.

Why should a dog, a horse, a rat, have life.
And thou no breath at all? Thou'lt come no more
Never, never, never, never, never.[15]

The last line is said to contain the five most tragic words in all of drama. Actors who perform Lear are often unable to say them all before dissolving into tears.

Neoclassical Tragedy

Phaedra (Phédre) by Jean Racine (1639–1699) was the major tragedy in England and France during the approximately hundred-year span of the neoclassical theater (1650–1750). The dialogue is elevated in accordance with the acceptable style, and characters speak elegantly of their intense emotions without actually demonstrating them, as we mentioned in the section on neoclassic conventions.

Phaedra, the protagonist, is married to the mythical hero Theseus but feels a burning lust for her stepson. She knows she must conceal that lust, but it builds to such intensity that the actress performing this challenging role is forced to find ways to externalize the torment she is suffering. Thus, *Phaedra* adds to the theater the element of the inner life.

Phaedra's tragic flaw is stepping over the bounds of appropriate behavior by revealing to her stepson how much she desires him.

Still, *Phaedra* was governed by the conventions of its time. All of it takes place in a civilized drawing room, and although the characters have Greek names, they look and sound like aristocratic contemporaries of the audience. Should Phaedra reveal to her stepson her burning desire for him? Of course not; it isn't done: strong feelings don't belong in public. But Phaedra steps over the bounds and tells her stepson that the only way she can bring herself to look at her husband is to see the facial resemblance to his son. She does the unthinkable by revealing her true feelings.

Her stepson's response would be more suited to a mild dispute about an assigned seat in a theater: "Madame, I fear there has been some mistake." He is of course playing the game. His manners are impeccable, but they set off lethal rage in Phaedra, who takes revenge for her humiliation by reversing the situation. She tells Theseus that she has been the victim of unwanted sexual advances by his son. Her husband impetuously pleads with one of the gods to whip up a storm and a sea monster along the shore and so have his son killed. That violent death is, of course, reported by a messenger.

Missing is a recognition speech in which the protagonist takes responsibility for her actions. There is no attempt to recapture Phaedra's lost nobility of character. In fact the audience doesn't even see her in what should be her supreme moment in the play. After hearing of her beloved stepson's death, she commits suicide offstage. The grieving father learns the truth from the note Phaedra has left behind, and he renounces her vigorously. Racine apparently believed that the audience would acknowledge this ending as proper. No matter how much pity they may have had for her, she *did* behave in a socially inappropriate way.

Modern Tragedy

Except for a few plays, Greek, Elizabethan, and neoclassical tragedies focus on fatal mistakes made by protagonists of high stature. The downfall of a non-aristocratic person was just not enough to lead the audience to an emotional catharsis. Beginning in the nineteenth century, a new kind of tragedy evolved, first in Europe and then in the United States. The majority of audience members were no longer well-educated aristocrats. A different sort of tragic protagonist was necessary,

Scene from a modern production of *Wozzeck*, an 1836 tragedy of a common man victimized by class distinction and his own irrationality.

Source: © Reuters.

along with a different philosophy about the cause of the downfall. Playwrights seeking tragic themes turned to people with ordinary occupations.

An early tragedy was *Wozzeck* (pronounced Voy-check), written in 1837 by Georg Büchner, and left incomplete when the playwright died at age twenty-four. The play revolves around a lowly worker and his obsessive love for a woman who has given him a son but whom he suspects of infidelity. In a violent confrontation, he plunges a knife into her throat; he later drowns when he attempts to retrieve the murder weapon. Büchner wanted to write for the theater but thrust aside all previous traditions, pioneering in the movement known as *expressionism*, which used non-realistic scenery and abandoned naturalistic dialogue.

The manuscript of *Wozzeck* was lost until the early twentieth century. Long after his death, Büchner influenced whole generations of tragic dramatists who share his view that the tragic protagonist does not have a flaw of character causing a catastrophe for which he or she is morally responsible. The real tragedy, for them, is that no moral order exists to be overthrown.

A century after Büchner, the American playwright Arthur Miller (1915–2005) attempted to elevate lower-middle-class characters to the stature of tragic protagonists in a true classical tradition. Miller's intent was to replace Aristotelian guidelines with new standards appropriate for his middle-class subject matter. He gained international recognition with *Death of a Salesman*, even the title of which suggests the ennoblement of a common man. Willy Loman, a "low man," not a king or prince, is a generally decent husband and father with a glaring weakness: he accepts the American Dream whole-heartedly and cannot face his own failure or that of his favorite son. Like a modern Oedipus, he insists on gilding reality with his own delusions; when they fail, he commits suicide, mistakenly believing that his son, a hopeless failure, will use the insurance money to become a financial success. While praising the work for its lyricism and dramatic intensity, many critics have insisted it falls short of tragedy because the protagonist remains deluded to the bitter end, never realizing his mistake.

> Death of a Salesman *is a play about a man who for years has misaken personality for merchandise. It stages the last crisis of his life, the day he realizes he no longer has a marketable product and decides to die.*
>
> —**Otto Reinert and Peter Arnott**

In 1955, however, Miller wrote *A View from the Bridge*, with a protagonist who does not fall from a position of great power but who nevertheless is aware of the mistake that has led to catastrophe. Without that awareness, the audience would not be able to share the character's pain and feel the intense pity that leads to catharsis.

Eddie Carbone, a middle-aged longshoreman, is fairly happy at the beginning of the play. He and his wife have an uneventful life, free of financial worries. But when his wife's attractive young niece moves in with them, Eddie is attracted to her, at first in a protective, fatherly way. When the young woman falls in love with an Italian immigrant smuggled illegally into the country and granted asylum by Eddie, the protagonist begins to be plagued by irrational fits of jealous rage. He monitors every move of the niece, paces the floor each night until she comes home, and angrily denounces her and her lover. Unable to bear the tension of living under Eddie's roof, the two lovers plan to run away. To stop them, Eddie informs the naturalization office of the immigrant's whereabouts. In retaliation the lover's best friend shoots him. As he lies dying, Eddie acknowledges his folly.

Miller created what he believed to be the ideal protagonist for modern tragedy. Not only can the audience identify with a hard-working, basically honest and charitable human being, but they can also understand his human weakness. If a modern tragedy is to succeed in the classical tradition, two factors must be involved. First, *we have to feel that the mistake could have been avoided.* Eddie is advised to curb his passions: gently by his understanding wife, and firmly by his lawyer, a character who serves a function similar to that of the Greek Chorus, counseling the protagonist. Eddie, in short, knows better. Second, *the mistake not avoided must have been caused by a believable character flaw.* Eddie is defensive about a sexual attraction which his conscious mind believes to be morally unacceptable. Consequently, he buries it deep inside, a suppression that only makes the situation worse.

The influence of Sigmund Freud is clearly evident in many modern tragedies. The father of psychoanalysis has given playwrights insight into the hidden sexual causes of anxiety and irrational behavior. Unsatisfied lust and unshakable feelings of guilt over forbidden sexual encounters are believable ways to explain character actions and motivations. Eddie's anger toward the young immigrant might also have been a sign of buried homosexual curiosity. Ultimately, then, the play is the tragedy of a decent man who refuses to acknowledge things about himself that he does not like and therefore denies.

Some critics have complained that both the wife and the lawyer go too far in attributing nobility of character to Eddie after his death, as though the author were overly intent on persuading the audience that he has indeed written a tragedy. Others have found the tributes moving and poetic, and the means by which Miller elevated the story to the level of classical drama.

Melodrama and Tragedy: A Contrast

Melodrama can be confused with tragedy, because it usually has scenes of suffering or death, such as a helpless heroine tied to a railroad track by a sinister villain, or poor people seeking shelter from the elements. In its basic form, it was highly popular with nineteenth-century theater audiences and early twentieth-century film-goers. It is still very much with us, though often in slicker forms, such as most "action" movies and movies made for television.

In tragedy, the protagonist, as noted by Aristotle, is mainly virtuous but not totally innocent. In nineteenth-century **melodrama**, the hero or heroine *is* innocent, and is beset by problems from external forces, never from an inner flaw that leads to destruction. Melodrama made no huge demands on the mind, and although it could be highly suspenseful, there was always the knowledge that everything would turn out as it should.

The characters in a melodrama are easily separated into the totally good and the totally bad. When the villain is punished, the audience cheers because "it served him right." Melodrama is not big on examining the motives of a character. The stereotypical nineteenth-century villain who threatened the virtue of a pure heroine was simply bad because, well, that's what he was. When the heroine was rescued by the equally pure hero, again there was no troubling ambiguity. Despite contemporary gloss, wide screens, crashing soundtracks, and the frequently tough vocabulary of hero and heroine, the underlying format remains the same.

Melodrama is the triumph of the righteous over the once powerful but finally defeated bad guys. It can also be lots of fun: a night out, popcorn, and going home untroubled by any new ideas.

In melodrama we do not have to confront unpleasant truths about humanity. True tragic elements are missing. Characterizations are thin, and the search for overarching meaning is unrewarding. When the villain has been arrested and the embattled lovers are finally able to embrace, the story is over. In addition, with its emphasis on superficial action, the language of melodrama deals only with the story, never the nature of human life and its struggles.

In melodrama . . . characterizations are thin, and the search for overarching meaning is unrewarding.

One element of melodrama really *is* a holdover from the Greeks: the **deus ex machina**—literally, the god from a machine. Not all the classical playwrights created characters like Oedipus, heading for an unavoidable doom because of a tragic flaw. Sometimes they wanted to provide a happier ending, so they invented the device of having a god descend onto the stage in a cart attached to a pulley, a god who would straighten everything out. The phrase *deus ex machina* is now used to describe any plot contrivance that violates the probabilities of human behavior and is introduced by the author for an expedient but implausible resolution: for example, the murderer, holding others at gunpoint, falls through an open window.

Audiences became so accustomed to the suspenseful thriller formula that they stopped caring whether the artificial separation of people into good and bad violated their sense of what was real. The melodrama lives on as a source of pure entertainment, enjoyed by those who want to escape from the storm and stress of the real in their lives. Aristotle would advise, however, that the cathartic effect of watching a profound tragedy is the best way to deal with storm and stress.

Comedy

At the opposite end of the theatrical spectrum from tragedy is comedy, which finds little audience identification with the protagonists, for otherwise how could we laugh at their foolishness? *We* are not foolish; *they* are. We must remain separate from them in order to enjoy the spectacle of their troubles, which are comparatively trivial and temporary.

The world is a comedy to those who think, a tragedy to those who feel.
—**Horace Walpole**

In addition to presenting three tragedies in a single afternoon, the Greeks invented the comic afterpiece, a fourth play designed to send the audience home in a happier state of mind. Instead of being based on myth, these plays made fun of greed and corruption in Athenian society itself. After a time they became so popular that audiences wanted to go to the theater only to laugh. Thus was born the still thriving institution of comic drama.

Recall the only surviving sentence from Aristotle's essay on comedy: *Tragedy is life seen close at hand; comedy is life seen from a distance.* It remains as valid as ever. Many disasters in *slapstick* comedy—someone falling through an open manhole; an arrogant man who has insulted the hero turning and suddenly tumbling down a flight of stairs—could turn dark if we were allowed to see the characters suffer; but we do not, and so we are able to enjoy ourselves at their expense. Our own lives don't seem so bad anymore.

Comedy has evolved into many forms. We will look at a few of them here: *farce, serious comedy, satire*, and the *comedy of character*.

Farce

Farce is a subgenre of comedy that draws laughter from outrageous physical actions and improbably chaotic situations. Its characters are two-dimensional stereotypes, easily described in a word or two. They are superficial, like dolls or animals in a cartoon. Many are derived from the **commedia dell'arte**, an Italian pantomime street theater originating in the middle of the sixteenth century. Its plays were usually improvised from bare plot outlines developed by the actors, each of whom was assigned to a certain character, often for life. Some of the comic types—or *stock characters*—were so universal they are still around, such as the doddering old man who really believes a beautiful woman loves *him*, not his money. Each age adds its own types: characters who are foolish because they do not fit the definition of a normal, rational human being.

Frivolity is the species' refusal to suffer.

—John Lahr

In the *commedia*, a central theme usually concerned the interaction of two young lovers trying to get together but thwarted by a miserly father, or by another characteristic type, the pretentious boor who used unnecessarily long words and thought himself a suitable mate for the young woman, only to have scheming servants aid the lovers. Actors wore costumes and masks that immediately identified the type portrayed. Audiences loved the repetition of familiar stories with minor variations and the pratfalls and physical abuse visited upon the fools, who were, after all, so silly that they could be safely laughed out of existence.

Here is a list of fools inspired by the *commedia*; they have peopled the farcical stage for centuries:

- the rich but stingy old man
- the old man who thinks a beautiful young woman is marrying him for love
- the pedant
- the bragging coward
- the clumsy, unpolished social climber
- the brat
- the completely self-absorbed actor
- the drunken, irresponsible husband
- the nagging wife
- the innocent "hick" or "rube"

We can add to the list any number of modern examples: nerds, jocks, airheads, people excessively concerned with their health and youth—there's almost no end to it, is there?

If it were not for the company of fools, a witty man would often be greatly at a loss.

—François de la Rochefoucauld

The *commedia* exerted strong influence on the work of the major neoclassical comic dramatist, Molière, mentioned earlier in the chapter, whose real name was Jean-Baptiste Poquelin. Monsieur Jourdain, the protagonist of one of his greatest comedies, *The Would-Be Gentleman*, is rich but still without the rank or social skills that would make him an acceptable guest at the court of King Louis XIV. His clumsy efforts to look like a titled gentleman and to learn fencing and the minuet provided a hilarious target of ridicule for aristocratic audiences. When he rejects the man his daughter loves as a prospective son-in-law, he is tricked into believing that the disguised suitor has a title and so delightedly allows the wedding to take place. As the curtain falls, everyone onstage and in the audience is aware of the

Scene from the 1958 Comédie Française film version of Molière's *The Would-Be Gentleman*, with Louis Seigner (seated left) as Monsieur Jourdain, a rich middle-class merchant totally lacking in social graces.

Source: The Everett Collection, Inc.

trick played on Jourdain, except the foolish social climber himself. In farce, there is no such thing as a recognition scene.

At about the time Molière's plays were appearing in France, the English stage entered a period labeled the Restoration, for it was in 1661 that the British monarchy was restored after twenty years of domination by austere Puritans who had taken over the government by force. Theaters, dubbed palaces of sin, had been closed. With the ascension of entertainment-loving Charles II, theaters were reopened for the pleasure of a more permissive society.

A British minister turned playwright, William Wycherley (1640–1716), was allegedly shocked by the new freedom of the stage and wrote a farce to make fun of it. *The Country Wife* was ironically a big hit, largely because it was as daring as the work it purported to condemn. *The Country Wife* depends for its comedy on a verbal technique that has endured through the centuries, *double entendre*, or "double meaning," whereby characters appear to be innocently talking of one thing, while audiences can infer less innocent goings-on from what they say. One of the most famous examples of the technique is the china scene, in which virtually all of the dialogue can be taken two ways, one of them so socially offensive that the play was banned in many places right up to the middle of the twentieth century!

The setting is the apartment of a scoundrel named Horner, a character with no moral scruples whatever but whose charm and cleverness delight the audiences. He is pretending to have become impotent, and has his servant spread the word, so that gullible husbands think their wives are safe with him. The pretense allows the wives to visit Horner without causing gossip. A group of these ladies have been given permission by their husbands to go shopping with Horner, who has been entertaining them in his own special way.

As the scene opens, Horner and Lady Fidget come out of a room, where Horner claims to keep a collection of china. When they emerge, Lady Fidget is holding a china teacup and thanking Horner for the gift. Mrs. Squeamish comes forward, urging Horner to allow her to go with him into the room: "O Lord," she says, "I'll have some china too. Good Mr. Horner, don't think to give other people china and me none; come in with me too."

He refuses, saying, "Upon my honor, I have none left now. . . . This lady had the last there." Lady Fidget agrees: "Yes indeed, madam, to my certain knowledge he has no more left."

When Mrs. Squeamish suggests that he may "have some you could not find," Lady Fidget retorts, "What; d'ye think if he had any left, I would not have had it too? For we women of quality never think we have china enough."

Husbands betrayed by their lusty wives were called cuckolds and treated as figures of fun. The Restoration period introduced any number of cuckolds, who took their place in the growing repertoire of comic types. Usually the cuckold was the subject of derision, whereas Horner and other characters like him were cheered. London upper-class audiences in the seventeenth century were quite sexually liberated. Because many women were sold into financially advantageous marriages with older, unromantic husbands, audiences could sympathize with Horner's female companions and the infidelities that they believed overbearing and stupid husbands deserved. (The clergy and some conservative audience members were less pleased, however, and eventually London plays had to pass the scrutiny of a censor.)

By 1700, a playwright named William Congreve (1670–1729) was apparently tired of the immorality and the superficiality of the London theaters. In that year he produced his masterwork *The Way of the World* (much more about this play in Chapter 13), which depends for its comedy on a complex plot of intrigue and chicanery, but more important, on the witty exchanges between Mirabell and Millamant, its central characters, who genuinely love each other but may not, in this society, say so directly. Consequently, *The Way of the World* has become a major example of theatrical subtext.

Serious Comedy

All the characters, including the cuckold, are treated much more sympathetically in *The Real Thing* (1982) by Tom Stoppard, a serious comedy that is anything but farce. The husband suspects that his wife has been unfaithful, but he is not like husbands in plays like *The Country Wife*, who are such absurd fools that they deserve our laughter. Nor is the wife a flirtatious, empty-headed deceiver who pretends innocence and is finally denounced, as happens in the broader style of comedy. Instead, they talk rationally about why she might be attracted to someone else—in this case a political activist just out of prison who has written a bad play about his cause. *The Real Thing* never lets you forget that you are watching characters with depth talk brilliantly. In a twist typical of Stoppard, the betrayed husband tells his wife that her real sin is not adultery, but loving a bad writer. "I don't think writers are important, but words are. They deserve respect. If you get the right word in the right order, you can nudge the world a little, or make a poem children will speak for you when you're dead."[16]

Two things people throughout history have had in common are hatred and humor. I am proud that, like Mark Twain, I have been able to use humor to lessen people's hatred.

—**Richard Pryor**

"Serious" comedy may sound like a contradiction in terms, but comic dramatists are not just deep thinkers; they are also wry observers of human folly as well. They vent their distress through dialogue that is sometimes witty, but sometimes deeply felt. All comedy, even farce, tells us we must be flexible, we must adapt to the changes life brings our way. To stay rigidly fixed in one mind-set is to go against nature and therefore to become laughable, as well as to be a continuing social menace. Unlike tragedy, comedy urges us to keep laughing, have perspective, and allow happiness to happen without rigid rules.

Satire

Experience is the name everyone gives to their mistakes.
—**Oscar Wilde**

The Greek tragic theater required playwrights to submit a comic afterpiece. It was known as the *satyr* play because it was performed by actors in costumes identifying them as the mythical creatures who were half-man and half-goat. In addition to having openly sexual plots, these plays made fun of the tragedies the audience had just seen and also social problems of the time. **Satire** has come to mean a species of comedy that ridicules such things as corruption in government, inequality, war as a solution, injustice, and hypocrisy. The satirist of the theater is both a comic writer, interested in getting audiences to laugh, and a reformer, dedicated to the betterment of society. Serious criticism of society can be communicated in other ways, such as newspaper editorials or sermons, but not everyone would get the message. People prefer to laugh, and the satirist obliges—but writes with a stiletto.

The Greek playwright Aristophanes (445–385 B.C.E.) skillfully used comedy to voice a plea for the improvement of the human condition. One of his enduring works is *Lysistrata*, with its perennially viable antiwar message and a basic situation that never fails to delight its audience. *Lysistrata* is set during the war between Athens and Sparta that lasted from 431 to 404 B.C.E. In the play, which was performed in 411 B.C.E., the women of both sides, tired of the senseless conflict and foolish loss of life, take matters into their own hands by uniting and establishing an all-female outpost on the Acropolis, the hill that dominates Athens. Not only are men barred from entering, but the women under the leadership of the title character go on strike. There will be no love-making until hostilities cease.

In addition to the foolishness of war, the play satirizes the frailties of human nature, in that the lovelorn men and women in both camps have difficulty living up to the terms of the oath they swore. The play is both comical and serious. One scene has a soldier disguising himself as a woman to be near his beloved. Another depicts a frustrated husband attempting to embrace his wife, who appears willing but keeps delaying until finally she retreats to the fortress on the Acropolis where she and the other women are in charge. Then she tells him that they can get together once the war is over.

An antiwar play performed in the midst of war? For the Athenians, it was no problem. Although some political leaders argued, "This is not the right time or place for such an unpatriotic attitude," most believed that the ability to express a point of view was more important than automatic obedience.

In another play, *The Clouds*, Aristophanes' satiric target was Socrates, the first major Greek philosopher. The dramatist portrays him as a foolish old man whose feet are never on the ground, insisting, for example, that rain is the result of natural forces rather than being sent by the Olympian gods. Since the prevailing view favored gods over meteorology, Socrates was depicted as an idiotic charlatan, running a school called The Thinkery, leading his pupils astray with ideas about natural causes and teaching them to debate so well they could win arguments against their own fathers. When the real-life Socrates was on trial for, among other things, corrupting the youth of Athens, it is possible that the unflattering characterization by Aristophanes may have influenced the votes of more than one juror who had seen the play. Considering his conviction and death sentence, Socrates could have seen that the satire by Aristophanes was not exclusively a laughing matter.

Satiric plays continue to be written, but their appeal is usually limited to an appreciative audience that already agrees with the author. A prospective producer concerned about box-office receipts is wary of writers who "preach to the choir." The genre finds a more comfortable home in popular media like comic strips (*Doonesbury*) or animated series on television. Satire is frequently found on late-night network shows (Jay Leno), on cable (Jon Stewart, Bill Maher, Carlos Mencia, and Dennis Miller), on *Saturday Night Live*, and on public radio's *A Prairie Home Companion*—all of which have followers who enjoy seeing prominent public figures reduced to the status of buffoons.

Parody is a form of satire that, at its best, is meant to be recognized as a serious attack on something the writer finds unacceptable. Parody can make fun of a particular work or genre of work—a film, song, painting, commercial—a work the author believes has been unjustifiably successful. The intention is for audiences to recognize the truth of the critical accusation being made when basic elements of the original are laughably exaggerated. The parodist pretends that his or her version of the object is the one under fire, but the version is so extreme that the audience (or reader) should see the absurdity of taking it seriously.

Tom Stoppard, author of *The Real Thing*, is also an inspired parodist. *The Real Inspector Hound* (1968) makes fun of the melodramatic thriller popular since the nineteenth century—and, he fears, still rather too popular. He employs an all-too-familiar plot of multiple murders in a remote English country house, complete with storms raging outside, a cast of suspicious characters, and plot entanglements impossible to understand.

What sets this work apart from the usual parody, however, is that Stoppard uses the tired old format to say something serious about the nature of reality. Two critics, sitting in a box and loudly denouncing the play, shatter the fourth-wall convention by climbing onto the stage when it appears the cast has deserted it. One critic answers the incessantly ringing telephone and thus becomes a character involved in the sinister proceedings. Soon he disappears, and the other critic is murdered. Meanwhile, two of the characters who have been previously killed, take their seats in the box and become the critics. Stoppard thus investigates the often nonexistent difference between illusion and reality.

Parody tends to be of only temporary interest, unless the target continues to be relevant. As long as people flock to creaky melodramas, *The Real Inspector Hound* will be funny. But more likely its serious theme of illusion versus reality will keep it alive. When watching a parody, we need to ask ourselves whether it offers something besides passing entertainment.

The Comedy of Character

Aristotle listed *character* as second in importance only to plot. It is not clear, however, that he and the Greek audience in general thought of *character* as we do today. He may have meant simply the actor playing a certain role, defined by certain traits. Thus Oedipus, for example, is a king, a man of power, arrogant about his power, and unyielding in his convictions. Today's writers have been strongly influenced by psychology, a pursuit unknown as such in Aristotle's day. A contemporary Oedipus might be shown as paranoid and defensive. His inner turmoil might be at least as important as the details of the story. Euripides, as we mentioned earlier, is probably the Greek tragic dramatist most accessible to modern audiences. In *Medea* he concentrates on the inner passions of his central character and thus develops something much closer in spirit to the modern concept of character as a component of theater.

Comedy is the clash of character. Eliminate character from comedy, and you get farce.
—**William Butler Yeats**

Thus we can say there is a big difference between character as a figure in a play and character as a combination of traits we remember about a person, traits that make that person unique. All plays have characters of the first kind. Not all plays have the second. Though the scientific study of the human mind that we call psychology was non-existent in Shakespeare's time, the playwright nonetheless created more in-depth characterizations than any writer before or since. Indeed, many of his works continue to hold the stage less for plot than for memorable characters, many of whom are the standout figures in his comedies.

One such character is Sir John Falstaff, whose comic portrait enlivens the history plays *Henry IV, Parts I and II*, and *Henry V*. Falstaff is a drunkard, a liar, and a con man, whose outrageous disregard for propriety makes Prince Hal—soon to become King Henry V—adore the company of this man who urges him to sow his wild oats as long as possible. Shakespeare gave him so many identifiable human weaknesses that his audience must have adored him as much as the prince, laughing *with*, not *at* him. Falstaff is not only a rogue but also the great philosopher of fun and corruption—the perfect Dionysian. He scandalously praises the sins of excess most of us commit but hate ourselves for. Nothing is worth repenting over, as far as he is concerned. Nothing is to be taken too seriously in this all-too-brief existence.

Falstaff not only consumes too much food and drink, without concern for a morning-after, but encourages the prince to do the same. Nor is he honest or patriotic. Given the assignment to buy uniforms for a group of recruits, he spends the allotment on himself. On the battlefield, when an enemy soldier expects to have hand-to-hand combat, Falstaff puts away his sword rather than fight, and delivers a famous speech on the dubious value of honor. He observes that it "hath no skill in surgery" and cannot be felt or heard by those living or dead. He may be dishonest in misappropriating public funds meant for uniforms, but he is certainly honest about his own disinclination to be a wartime casualty.

He is poignant, too, in his misunderstanding of what he thought was the prince's friendship for him. Pretending to be dead, Falstaff hears the prince deliver a "eulogy" by making unflattering comments about his size. Even worse, when the prince finally does become king, Falstaff tries to benefit from their old friendship, only to be totally rejected with these words:

> *I know thee not, old man; fall to thy prayers;*
> *How ill white hairs become a fool and jester!*
> *So surfeit-swell'd, so old and so profane;*
> *But, being awaked, I do despise my dream.*[17]

Do we then side with the new king and dismiss Falstaff? Literary scholar Harold Bloom, who has spent his life writing about and teaching Shakespeare, reports that one of his students denounced Falstaff by claiming that "the transformation of Prince Hal into King Henry V was exemplary . . . that Hal represented rule and that Falstaff was a lord of misrule, and I could not persuade her that Falstaff transcended her categories, as he transcends virtually all our categories of human sin and error."[18]

Bloom's admiration for Falstaff was so great that he briefly deserted the classroom to play the role in a stage production. He sees Falstaff as complex, not merely a coward or a jester. Bloom says that in his encounter with the king, he is courageous, aware that "Hal's ambivalence has resolved itself into a murderous negativity. . . . Time annihilates other Shakespearean protagonists, but not Falstaff."[19]

The debate goes on. Was Falstaff Prince Hal's rejected father-substitute or a dishonored mentor? In great drama, there is never a final answer.

In this analysis, Bloom is at odds with his student and with other critics who have argued endlessly about the relationship between Falstaff and the prince. Was he a rejected father-substitute or a dishonored mentor, as some have claimed? The critical fights continue, just as they have about countless other Shakespearean characters. To those who argue that "it's just a play" and wonder how there can be so much dispute about characters who never lived, theater lovers know: Shakespeare's characters do live. And they have helped elevate comedy to a stature equal to tragedy.

Theater of Ideas

Related to satire in terms of dealing with social issues, but generally presented in the convention of verisimilitude, *theater of ideas* came into prominence in the late Victorian period in the work of two playwrights who would use the stage to raise the consciousness of their audience. One was Henrik Ibsen of Norway, whose opening scene in *A Doll's House* was mentioned earlier as an example of adroit handling of exposition; the other was his Irish-born champion, George Bernard Shaw.

Ibsen

At first this journalist-turned playwright scandalized his staid Norwegian audiences with frank exposés of hypocrisy in all the major institutions of his time: marriage, business, government, the clergy, education. Although *A Doll's House* is now credited with having changed the whole course of Western theater, at the time of its writing it was considered shocking, even obscene. One critic commented: "No self-respecting man would take his wife to see this play."

The husband and wife of *A Doll's House* are Torvald, a recently promoted bank manager, and Nora, the "doll" of the title. The secret in Nora's past is her having forged her father's name on a promissory note in order to borrow money to take her sick husband to a warmer climate and thus save his life. Now an employee in her husband's bank has threatened to make her crime public unless she can persuade her husband to preserve his position at the bank.

So far this man fills the role of the villain in melodramas already familiar to audiences. The stereotypical villain, however, often wore a black cape and twirled his mustache as he uttered threats to the helpless heroine. But Ibsen is more subtle. His villain is a complex character with a need for love and acceptance.

Owen Teale as Torvald and Janet McTeer as Nora, a woman who has just discovered that her marriage is built on lies, in a 1997 revival of Ibsen's *A Doll's House*.

Source: © Joan Marcus.

Ignoring efforts to intervene, Torvald fires the man, an action that leads to a letter exposing her crime. Rather than rush to Nora's defense or take the blame himself (as she had assumed he would), Torvald denounces her, saying she is no longer a fit mother for their children.

One should never put on one's best trousers to go out to battle for freedom and truth.

—**Henrik Ibsen**

Meanwhile, the blackmailer has found a woman willing to marry and nurture him. His spirits uplifted, he returns the promissory note to Nora's angry spouse. In a moment that stirred up a huge controversy, Torvald cries joyfully, "Nora, I'm saved!" There is a profound silence, and then Nora asks quietly, "And what about me?" Eager to return the marriage to its former state, the husband tries to explain the rules of society: "No man sacrifices his honor for the one he loves." Nora's comeback shocked Ibsen's audience and remains one of the stirring lines in modern theater: "Millions of women have done so."

She has seen the truth, has seen the hypocrisy underlying their codified society, and now refuses to go back to where they were. Instead, she announces that she no longer consents to live a lie. Ignoring his protestations and promises to change the way he treats her, the newly liberated Nora quietly but resolutely informs him that she must first discover who she really is. She packs her bags, returns the wedding ring, and leaves, slamming the door behind her.

The slamming of that door is one of the most significant sounds in the history of Western theater. It caused a scandal so great that guests at dinner parties in respectable society were requested not to mention it. An actress playing Nora in Germany refused to play the final scene as written, so Ibsen wrote an alternate ending in which Nora realizes a mother cannot abandon her children.

A critic denounced Ghosts *as "an open garbage can."*

Encouraged by critical acclaim in more open societies, however, Ibsen was more resolved than ever to rip the mask from social respectability. In *Ghosts* (1885) he again horrified local audiences with a play that had venereal disease as a central issue, supported the idea of free love in preference to a marriage built on lies, and raised the question of whether euthanasia could be a valid solution to a hopeless medical condition. The "ghosts" of the title are secrets from the past which the respectable heroine has desperately sought to hide but which come back to haunt her in yet another now famous final scene when the curtain falls as she is facing the awful choice of whether to kill her son or allow him to live on in an unresponsive state. One of the critics who had denounced *A Doll's House* now called *Ghosts* "an open garbage can." While the critic's name is mercifully forgotten, Ibsen's powerful ideas have survived the hostility.

Shaw

Do not do unto others as you would that they should do to you. Their tastes may not be the same.

—George Bernard Shaw

Like Ibsen's, the plays of George Bernard Shaw (1856–1950) were aimed at shaking audiences loose from dangerous preconceived ideas. But for the most part, his vehicle was comedy. In *Pygmalion* (1912) he attacked the rigidity of the class system in Britain with an amusing story about the transformation of a Cockney flower seller into a well-dressed, well-spoken lady accepted at the very highest levels of British society. On the surface it is a Cinderella story: the poor grubby lass who can't speak English "properly" is eventually passed off as a highborn lady because she speaks so well.

Underneath the surface, the play criticizes just about every aspect of the sins committed by the British to preserve respectability. If Eliza Doolittle, it asks, can rise above her inherited lowly place in society by showing evidence of education, why are so many denied that privilege?

Eliza's father, a slacker with a love of alcohol and a phobia against gainful employment, suddenly comes into money. Yet he is shrewd enough to know that, if money determines a person's social standing, it says nothing about the moral principles of the one who possesses it. He also knows that belonging to a higher class incurs certain unpleasant obligations, such as the need to be respectably married, deprived of the pleasures that were his before anyone took notice of his existence. In *My Fair Lady* (1956), the Alan Jay Lerner and Frederick Loewe musical version of the play, Doolittle has two now classic songs: "With a Little Bit of Luck," a celebration of life without responsibility to uphold middle-class standards, and "Get Me to the Church on Time," in which he pleads for one more night on the town with his cronies before settling into a dull life of respectability.

Neither Shaw nor Ibsen belabored the same issue, nor did they have one speech per play which would have sent a too-explicit message to the audience. Plays designed as propaganda do that. Propaganda lacks subtlety and is less interested in character than in producing a desired action: to vote, to protest, to revolt. The playwright as propagandist belongs only nominally to the theater of ideas, but at its most extreme, the *agit-prop* (agitation propaganda) play can stir an audience to an emotional frenzy, as happened at the final curtain of Clifford Odets's *Waiting for Lefty* (1935), a play about the plight of underpaid cab drivers in New York. On opening night, as the actors made the crucial decision "Strike!"

the audience rose to its feet and echoed the call. Overcome with emotion, they rushed to the stage to embrace the actors.

In the more subtle theater of ideas, playwrights tend to present more than one side of an argument. Nora's final speech before slamming the door has been taken as a rallying cry for feminism, but does Ibsen really recommend abandoning marriage and children as the only possible solution? Some scholars who have studied the play maintain that it can be presented as the tragedy of a husband trapped in a social system that blinds him to the truth.

Naturalism

During the latter half of the nineteenth century, while Ibsen, Shaw, and their followers were forcing audiences to confront social problems once swept under the rug, other writers were experimenting with a new genre called **naturalism**. As its name implies, theatrical naturalism was an attempt to show life as it really was—without artificial-sounding stage dialogue or the well-made play structure.

Chekhov

In the creative process there is the father, the author of the play; the mother, the actor pregnant with the part; and the child, the role to be born.

—**Konstantin Stanislavsky**

The pioneer in naturalistic theater was the Russian playwright and former physician Anton Chekhov (1860–1904), who abandoned the play of one central figure in favor of the play that deals with a group of people, their actions, and interactions. Almost every character in a Chekhov drama is at one point or another an object of sympathetic understanding. The plays are plotless in the usual sense of the word, without carefully crafted exposition or a relentless drive toward a climax. They reflect a dedicated physician's insights from having observed and listened to many patients, and his unwillingness to make moral judgments.

Chekhov's works were discovered in the first decade of the twentieth century and staged by Konstantin Stanislavsky (1863–1938), founder of the Moscow Art Theater. The director noted that, since the plays lacked heroes and villains, there was no question of endorsing this character's behavior or condemning another's. It was really a matter of trying to understand why things happened. The author had spelled nothing out for the director. He seemed to have created certain individuals, set them in motion in certain situations, and allowed them to proceed according to mysterious laws of their own being. In order to present this new form of theater, Stanislavsky had to reinvent the art of acting, and his technique still pervades theater today.

Stanislavsky realized that an in-depth understanding of people in real life was the starting point. One had to know that, when people did anything, obvious reasons were not always accurate. Real people seldom behaved as one would expect, because all too often people were observed not as they were but in terms of preconceived notions. He came to see that Chekhov was being true to his own observations and knowledge of human nature, rather than to time-honored clichés that would be instantly understandable to theater audiences. If in real life a man were seen sitting by himself at a party, speaking to no one, someone might say of him, "He is antisocial." Someone else might observe, "Now there's an introvert" or "See that man? He feels guilty about something." Stanislavsky would say that the only way to come close to what was happening inside the man involved trying to experience reality through his eyes.

In developing his technique, Stanislavsky required his actors to use their imagination and project their characters into other times and places, determining what they would do or say under changing conditions. Gradually, he believed, they would put themselves inside the people they were playing, the only path to discovering the truth of a character. In rehearsal, Stanislavsky would ask his actors a question such as "Would a rejected suitor really say that line?" Then he would add, "But of course the author commands you to say it. Now find a way to say it that accords with probability." If the actor were to inquire, "How do I find the way?" Stanislavsky's typical response was, "Look into yourself." They would react to a given situation as if it were happening to them. The rehearsal process involved the actors' exploration of themselves—their past and present. In a very real sense, actors and playwrights were collaborators, and the director's function was to distinguish between what seemed truth and what did not. Hence the famous Stanislavsky definition of acting as *being truthful in imaginary circumstances.* The definition continues to be fundamental to dramatic training in many countries.

Acting is being truthful in imaginary circumstances.
—Konstantin Stanislavsky

Chekhov's characters are often trapped inside their own feelings and longings, and his plays often deal with the gap between human desires and what reality provides. For this reason he knew that, though enormous social changes were under way in his native Russia, they would have no effect on people's behavior or their search for happiness. Yet he is compassionate toward those who delude themselves into insisting that progress is inevitable and that life will get better.

Three Sisters (1901), believed by many to be his masterwork, is also the most complex of his plays. Each of the characters, who create a tight ensemble on the stage, is dependent on what the others say and do, yet each is an individual whose inner drives must be explored by the actor, believed in totally, *lived.* No two performances of *Three Sisters* are ever exactly the same, because, to play Chekhov, actors must continually seek new corners in their characters' inner lives.

The sisters in question are daughters of a deceased general and had once lived in Moscow, a place to which they long to return, a place where they are certain happiness lies. Unfortunately, lacking the money to move from the country, they must endure the monotony of their everyday existence, finding brief moments of joy only in thinking of Moscow.

The oldest sister, Olga, is an unmarried schoolteacher, who manages the household. She is afflicted with frequent headaches and fatigue from unrewarding work. Irina, the youngest sister, loves neither of the two men who want to marry her, but realizes she must settle for one of them and try to lead a life of useful work. The middle sister, Masha, is unhappily married to a dull and pedantic Latin teacher who probably would have been a good match for Olga. Their brother, at one time expected to have a brilliant career, has married a young woman from a lower-class family, who enjoys tyrannizing the household.

The arrival of a company of soldiers brings a brief excitement into their lives, until they depart. Other characters come and go. From time to time, small crises erupt: a fire, gambling debts, a duel in which one of the men who love Irina is slain. The brother's wife dismisses a beloved family servant and has an affair with a local official. Neither her husband nor his sisters know how to confront her. Their gentility has not taught them how to fight and win. Nor is Chekhov suggesting that they *should* know. They do what they must. Events are beyond their control. They react, they try, they cope. That is all anyone can do. Chekhov once remarked in a letter that it was a beautiful thing for people to hope that life will improve, but he knew it could not.

Drama is action, sir, action, and not confounded philosophy.
—Luigi Pirandello

In the hands of a romantic playwright, there might have been more overt drama, complete with impassioned speeches of love or denunciation. Far from romantic, Chekhov recorded reality as he found it, making riveting drama out of the everyday world.

The Family Theme

Chekhov's naturalism influenced many subsequent dramatists, especially in the focus on the tensions that trap people within a family. One who acknowledged this influence was Tennessee Williams (1914–1983), though his plays belong to the school of naturalism only in terms of their probing the psychological depths of their characters. Williams's dialogue is a blend of stark naturalism and poetic prose.

At the outset of the play that established his reputation, *The Glass Menagerie* (1945), the narrator, Tom, all but apologizes for the artless kind of experience about to unfold. He calls it a "memory play" and admits that in memory things are not seen exactly as they were. His play will consist of relatively few scenes, most of which develop some aspect of family conflict. The work makes us keenly aware that family ties, creating obstacles to happiness all but impossible to surmount, are the rightful descendants of Chekhovian drama. In the best of such plays there is never a happy, never a clear conclusion.

The family theme has led to tragedy of a high order that differs in kind, but not emotional intensity, from the plays of Aristotle's time. The intensity that can be achieved from the often bitter confrontation between parents and children or between siblings becomes more profound and moving as the playwright delves further and further into the past, into the darkness that threatens to engulf and bring down the characters involved.

Modern tragedies about how family bonds tear people apart are enduringly popular with audiences.

American playwright Eugene O'Neill (1888–1953) admitted that his play *Long Day's Journey into Night* (1941) was a personal document "born out of an old sorrow." The play tells the story of a family torn apart by the mother's drug addiction, the father's bitterness over the passing of his glory days as a famous Shakespearean actor, the older brother's alcoholic compensation for his failure to equal his father's success on the stage, and the younger brother's futile efforts to make the family understand he needs treatment for consumption. The play, in fact, is *about* how people who love each other do not and cannot help each other.

Though O'Neill relives his painful youth in the character of the consumptive Edmund Tyrone, he does not make himself the central character. In Chekhovian fashion, each member of the Tyrone family shares that honor. In the fourth act, the mother, upstairs in her bedroom, where she retreats from the world in morphine-induced fantasy, is heard walking back and forth. She will eventually surrender to her addiction and totally withdraw from all contact with reality. Downstairs, the men confront each other in one scene after another of unbearable intensity. The father, a lifelong miser, is now hopelessly drunk and insists Edmund does not need to go into an expensive sanatorium. The older brother, Jamie, comes home, also drunk, having spent all his money on prostitutes, hating himself for his wasted life, confessing how jealous he is of his younger brother's genius and his secret wish that he will fail as a writer. In a powerful speech, he shows us how closely connected are love and hate. "Never wanted you to succeed, and make me look worse by comparison. . . . Always jealous of you. Mama's baby. . . . And it was you being born that started Mama on dope. I know that's not your fault, but all the same, God damn you, I can't help hating your guts. . . . But don't get me wrong, kid. I love you more than I hate you. . . . you're all I got left."[20]

The play reaches its climax with the mother's sudden appearance, now lost in her fantasies, wearing her yellowed wedding gown, believing this is her happiest day. The three men look at her with infinite sadness. The curtain falls on the four members of the doomed family in what has been hailed as a work that scales the height of tragic drama, not equaled in its profound effect on audiences since the days of the Greek masters.

A Theatrical Century of Dynamic Change

During the twentieth century, rapid technological advances made warfare inevitable on a global scale. Economic ups and downs created social upheavals. These had a natural effect on the theater. Many new genres emerged as playwrights struggled to meet the challenges of a modern world, reducing it to the size of a stage and to a few hours' duration. For many of them, it became clear that the realistic theater of the previous century was too confining. They also had to contend with competition from the new entertainment form, cinema.

Naturalism, the theater of ideas, and both classical and neoclassical drama continued to be respected and performed, especially by repertory companies and on university campuses. But audiences, growing accustomed to the continued acceleration of change, were eager for fresh approaches. In addition, gradual changes in the fabric of society—minorities and women demanding equal recognition, for example—quickly made obsolete the kind of problems earlier writers had wrestled with. It was a totally new era, and the theater had to reflect it. The new playwrights realized that, if they wanted to use the theater as a platform for their ideas, they could no longer rely on the established traditions of Ibsen and Shaw.

The Modern Theater of Ideas

A German playwright who same to prominence in the 1920s, after his disillusioned nation had lost World War I and was drifting into chaos, Bertolt Brecht (1898–1956) had a lot to say to audiences about a social system he believed would stabilize his country. But he recognized that audiences can become so involved in a story being enacted that they overlook the ideas behind the story. His solution to the problem was **theater of alienation**, designed to wrap ideas in a sparkling package that often resembled musical comedy, a highly popular genre attracting huge audiences on both sides of the Atlantic. For example, his plays sometimes had musical and dance interludes that conveyed Brecht's activist ideas as much as the dramatic action did. Like Shaw, Brecht wanted to rid his audience of romantic preconceptions about what both the theater and life should be, but his techniques are radically different. Using these techniques, he believed he could prevent the viewer from identifying too strongly with the characters, thus missing the point being made. The undisguised unreality of the play would thus "alienate" the audience from the story and allow the playwright's message to be plainly heard.

Brecht. . . thought the greatest pleasure is to be found in "productive participation," which involves the active judgment of the spectator and his application of what he sees on the stage to conditions outside the theatre. To make him critical and capable of watching productively, the spectator must be "alienated" from the play's events.

—**Oscar G. Brockett**

In *The Caucasian Chalk Circle* (1944), written in America after Brecht had fled a Germany that he recognized as cruelly suppressing human rights, he creates

The History Boys *is modern Theater of Ideas, investigating whether education that seeks only to get applicants into the best schools has any real learning validity.*

a fairy tale about a fabled kingdom in which a servant girl saves and cares for the child of a ruler during an uprising. After the conflict is over, the child's birth mother returns, expecting to be reunited with her offspring. The servant, however, has become to all intents the true mother. To resolve the issue, a wise judge draws a chalk circle on the ground, places the child inside, then informs the onlookers that whichever woman is able to pull the child from the circle will be declared the official mother and granted full custody. Each takes one of the child's arms and begins to tug, causing the child excruciating pain. The servant loves the child too much to continue and allows the other woman to win. The judge surprises everyone by announcing that the loser in this case has the rightful claim and gives the child to her.

Brecht was drawing an allegorical parallel between the chalk circle test and socialism, an ideology in which he strongly believed. In his allegory the child symbolizes land—land that belongs to those who cultivate and care for it, not the absentee lords who happen to own it.

Playwrights continue to be driven by the need to communicate important ideas, but they are finding it increasingly difficult to attract producers and audiences, many of whom prefer a light musical to a play of ideas. Many musicals have catchy songs, sprightly dances, two-dimensional characters, and dialogue requiring little or no thought on the part of the audience. Some, however, embody profound ideas and reach the level of theatrical art. (A more complete discussion of musicals is provided in Chapter 8.)

As a metropolitan center for theater, London has a split personality. On the one hand, tourists flock to see musicals at West End theaters, and these sell out almost as soon as the first advertisement hits the newsstands. On the other hand, it has an enviable reputation for reviving the classics as well as presenting new plays that, when critically endorsed, make their way across the Atlantic.

One such play is *The History Boys* (2004) by English playwright Alan Bennett (b. 1934), originally produced by the National Theatre of Great Britain, a work that communicates complex ideas in memorable language galloping along at a dizzying pace, challenging audiences to perk up their ears and listen *very* closely. The central theme is education—or whether education still has any validity. The setting is an English prep school for boys whose families hope to have them accepted into either Oxford or Cambridge. The headmaster is also obsessed with that one goal and therefore runs a tight ship with rigid curriculum guidelines that, when followed, should result in the longed-for success.

To guarantee that the majority of his charges will pass the qualifying exam for the prestigious colleges, the headmaster turns to a teacher cleverly adept at teaching students how to write entertaining essays and give amusing answers on entrance applications. He admires the glibness and sophistry emphasized by this teacher and cares not at all that the boys will learn little else.

In stark contrast to the self-confident mentor who knows all the angles is the play's central character, Hector, an overweight homosexual literature teacher for whom closeness to the boys is his reason for living. He is extremely popular with them, but for reasons that are suspect. He doesn't exactly teach specifics and is so easygoing that his classes are always "fun." What he *thinks* he is teaching is respect for great language and thoughts. He hopes his boys will so admire the literary greats that they will become role models. Of course, the boys take advantage of his illusions. Some of them will get into the top schools, but how much will they really know—or care? Bennett is posing questions about education that apply to all countries that pretend to be providing a liberal education for every citizen.

The work has a kinship not only with Ibsen and Shaw but with Chekhov as well. The history boys, so-called because the qualifying exam is notoriously heavy on history questions, are not a generic group of two-dimensional characters who might be, in the hands of a lesser playwright, just The Class. Each student has a carefully developed persona and past that make him real to us. We come to like them as human beings, and by the end of the play we think they deserve much more from education. Then we ask: *But where are they going to get it?*

Richard Griffiths as the teacher in *The History Boys* who loves teaching but not school regulations.

Source: Sara Krulwich/*The New York Times Pictures*/Redux Pictures.

Theater of Cruelty

Closely related to Brecht's theater of alienation is the more recent **theater of cruelty**. Like Brecht, its playwrights want audiences to absorb the ideas they are setting forth, but they do it by pulverizing the viewer's emotions through shocking scenes. Unlike other innovative genres, theater of cruelty has grown in popularity, probably influenced by the violence in movies and on television and by conflicts the world over in which thousands of innocent people have died.

The genre appears to have a twofold purpose: one is to alienate the audience in Brechtian fashion; the other is to entertain audiences who have been weaned on violence in various media and who like to confront it in make-believe circumstances in which no real danger exists. In a certain sense, it is the modern equivalent of the tragic theater of Aristotle, providing its own brand of catharsis.

An early work in the genre has one of the longest titles in theater history: *The Persecution and Assassination of Jean-Paul Marat as Performed by the Inmates of the Charenton Asylum under the Direction of the Marquis de Sade*, written in 1964 by Peter Weiss and premiered by London's Royal Shakespeare Company. Audiences at the early showings of the play were jolted when they entered the theater to find all manner of apparently disturbed people behaving strangely on a set made to look like an asylum day room. From the outset, the whole enterprise seemed threatening—not your typical theatrical entertainment.

The Marquis de Sade is the author and director of the play-within-a-play about a French writer, Marat, whose inflammatory pamphlets helped initiate the reign of terror during the French Revolution. In the reenactment, Marat is stabbed to death in his bathtub by a woman who believes that Marat was acting out of self-interest, not for the ordinary people he said he was liberating. During the performance things get out of hand, and the inmate-actors become uncontrollable. The message being delivered to an audience meant to believe they may be in danger is that a change in a social system in no way changes people.

A mental institution, but this time with sympathies clearly on the side of inmates seeking freedom from oppressive authority, is the setting of Dale Wasserman's adaptation of Ken Kesey's 1962 novel *One Flew Over the Cuckoo's Nest*. It centers on the conflict between a power-hungry nurse and a young troublemaker who, though obviously not mentally ill, has been branded as an activist, dangerous to society. To the audience the man is a hero, rightfully angry at the cruel treatment of patients who get out of line. In the climactic scene he is given punitive shock treatment as a means of making him passive and controllable. The electric currents shooting through the head of the strapped-down victim make the audience think they are in a room watching an execution.

The Lieutenant of Inishmore *illustrates more Theater of Cruelty; its stage was drenched in six gallons of fake blood and littered with dismembered corpses.*

Theater of cruelty continues to attract audiences. It is an abundant element in the works of Martin McDonagh (b. 1970), a playwright who learned his art by buying a "How to Write for the Stage" book. Identifying with no previous theatrical tradition and highly influenced by film violence, he struck out boldly on his own, writing dark comedies about Irish men and women who refuse to suppress their wild Dionysian natures. *The Beauty Queen of Leenane* (1999) is a family-theme comedy about a cowering, unattractive daughter who finally works up the courage to murder her dominating mother as the audience cheers.

McDonagh's works have since become more "edgy," with blood and gore splashed all over the stage, causing some audience members to cringe and even cover their eyes. *The Lieutenant of Inishmore* (2001) is about a young terrorist thrown out of the Irish Republican Army because of his dangerous and irrational behavior. The only living creature he loves is his cat. Upon returning home, the former lieutenant is led to believe that the pet has been accidentally killed by his brother. This unhinges the man, who embarks upon a killing spree that is both horrifying and, because of its excesses, funny at the same time. (In the Broadway production the stage was drenched in six gallons of fake blood.) But yes, behind the blood and a stage littered with dismembered corpses there is a serious message: violence is absurd and irrational no matter how you try to justify it.

Racial Themes

The plague of racism is insidious, entering our minds as smoothly and quietly and invisibly as floating or airborne microbes enter into our bodies to find lifelong purchase in our bloodstreams.

—Maya Angelou

A groundbreaking play depicting the lives and experiences of African Americans is *A Raisin in the Sun* (1959) by Lorraine Hansberry (1930–1965). In it, a mother and her grown children argue over the best use of money received from an insurance policy. Both the son and daughter want to use the money to advance their own careers, but the mother insists on moving out of their crowded apartment and buying a house in a previously segregated white neighborhood. She strongly maintains her convictions against pressure from a white man who offers her money not to move into "his" neighborhood. Despite their earlier opposition, the children rally around her strength, and the family moves, ready to stand up to the hostility of their new neighbors.

In 1976, the South African playwright Athol Fugard (b. 1932) wrote *Sizwe Banze Is Dead*, an impassioned play condemning apartheid, the now outlawed segregation of the races. An illiterate man, seeking employment but finding he is unable to use the identity card issued in his own town, is persuaded by a friend to use one found on a dead man. Without a card he will be sent back to the township restricted to his tribe. In a powerful speech he demands the right to use his own name: "Am I not a man?" But his determination to cling to his own identity, a mark of personal dignity, is thwarted. By the end of the play he has been forced to accept the dead man's name. In return he is given a job and a little money to send home to his family. He will survive if he can continue to be deferential to white authorities. Though identity cards are no longer required of black South Africans, Fugard's play stands as a stern reminder of racial prejudice and its destructive effects.

A subtle question of identity for African Americans is posed in *Fences* (1987), which won the Pulitzer Prize for its author, August Wilson (1945–2005). This complex work touches on past and present racial inequities as well as the tangled relationships within a family. Wilson prefers not to deliver a direct message. Instead, he focuses on the psychology of his main character, who becomes a symbol of the African American lost in a changing society. Born into a sharecropper's family in the Deep South, victimized and forced to adjust to a white-dominated world as he grew up, he finds himself unprepared for a new world that demands liberation for everyone. He had found ways to survive prejudice, but now he feels lost. Wilson's theme is the tragedy of the semiliberated, the people who are tolerated without being welcome and who therefore suffer inwardly from a loss of identity—people who live behind the fences that separate them from each other and from themselves.

Gay Rights

Only in relatively recent times has theater addressed a subject that was once just whispered about. In the past, gay characters were not associated with the issue of rights but were more often given a comic treatment. Or, as in Tennessee Williams's *Cat on a Hot Tin Roof* (1955), homosexuality was made the unnamed source of failed marriages. The statement that homosexuality is tragic because of the suffering inflicted on gays by society had to wait for a changed social climate, a time when audiences were willing to confront once-taboo subject matter.

I cannot and will not cut my conscience to fit this year's fashion.
—Lillian Hellman

One early play that dealt seriously with homosexuality was *The Children's Hour* (1934) by Lillian Hellman (1905–1984), which dealt with a woman's slow realization of her passion for another woman. Audiences accepted the shocking theme, probably because the friend does not feel the same way, and thus the play treats the woman's "condition" as a pathological tragedy. The play makes no plea for acceptance of a homosexual lifestyle; rather, it shows the pernicious effects of scandal, as a malicious student deliberately spreads rumors about the women. The homosexual woman commits suicide, as would have been expected at the time; the heterosexual woman has the prospect of marrying the man she loves.

With the onset of the AIDS epidemic in the early 1980s, the subject of sexual preference began to be more openly debated. Some saw the disease as a punishment from God; some argued over whether homosexuality was preference or biological destiny; still others called for compassion and the total liberation of an oppressed group. Major themes in the 1990s were continued discrimination against gays (in housing and military service, for example) and the need for gay pride.

Far and away the most stirring work to emerge from the newly found freedom of the stage has been *Angels in America* by Tony Kushner (b. 1956), a seven-hour production, divided into two plays: *The Millennium Approaches* (1992) and *Perestroika* (1993). The first play was awarded the Pulitzer Prize before it ever opened in New York, and the second soon after its opening.

Subtitled "A Gay Fantasia on National Themes," *Angels* is a significant work of theatrical art both for its epic scope and its dazzling innovations in technique. Adopting a fast-moving, razzmatazz style, clearly influenced by the plays of Brecht, popular musical comedy, music videos, and the pacing of quick-action films, and requiring minimal scenery, the work is ultimately much more than a gay rights statement. The author touches on gay rights, of course, but also political and religious corruption, the decline of the family, deterioration of the environment, and the need for a true spiritual awakening.

Despite its grim subject matter, the work is not pessimistic. As the title suggests, a miraculous turn of events is on the way, and this is foreshadowed through

The Angel has a single line, the very final one, in *The Millennium Approaches*, Part One of *Angels in America*: "The great work begins." Ellen McLaughlin and Stephen Spinella in the 1993 Broadway production.

Source: Joan Marcus/Everett Collection.

The Millennium Approaches by feathers falling from the sky when least expected. At the conclusion of the play, the promised Angel finally appears, descending with white wings covering half the stage, and declares: "The great work begins."

Backstage

There is nothing disillusioning about looking backstage; rather, critical viewers discover a heightened sense of appreciation of theater there. They recognize that the most solid-looking stage set is made of muslin, the gown of a beautiful queen may contain a dozen snaps for a quick costume change, a glass of whiskey is cold tea, and a violent stabbing scene has been carefully rehearsed so that the victim knows exactly where and how to fall, then reappears for the curtain call having washed away the fake blood.

Knowing how illusions are achieved only enhances the pleasure of seeing the actual performance. Most audience members have not seen a work in progress during rehearsals. And although some have argued that looking for the director's mark on a production can detract from the enjoyment, knowing that different interpretations are possible adds richly to our ability to analyze and make critical observations. Seeing different productions of the same work offers the opportunity for enlightening comparisons, similar to hearing the same piece of music performed by different singers or musical groups.

Interpretation begins with the director. Even the greatest performer feels insecure on stage during rehearsals unless a trusted director sits out front, carefully scrutinizing every movement and listening to the interpretation of every line. After the performance, actors are applauded during curtain calls, but few would merit the applause without a director's guidance.

Long ago the director was the company manager and star, advising the others to keep out of his way. Now he is one member of a collaborative team.

The dependence on a director is relatively recent, considering the span of Western theater history, stretching back many thousands of years. It is unlikely that Greek actors were directed at all; Elizabethan and neoclassic theater companies had managers whose function was to arrange production details and then play leading roles themselves. They also saw to it that everyone kept out of their way and did not prevent them from attracting audience attention they believed was their due. During the time of Molière, in keeping with the rigid class system, the manager-lead played stage front all night long, while lesser members of the cast occupied stations farther upstage, according to the importance of their roles.

Nowadays the director is apt to guide the entire production, choosing the cast and working on interpretation with everyone involved, including set, lighting, sound, and costume designers. A basic responsibility is to indicate movement on the stage. Audiences tend to get restless if actors sit in one position and just talk for a long time. But the director must see that actors do not move aimlessly or just for the sake of changing their positions on stage—each movement must be purposeful. The director will ask actors to explain what motivates rising from a chair or walking over to a window, getting a drink, or pacing nervously about. A director who establishes unmotivated movement is likely to be regarded as a traffic cop. For this reason, modern directors spend a considerable amount of time on *table work*, on careful analysis with the cast of a play's theme, or spine, and how each character relates to it.

In turn, actors are expected to do their homework before the first rehearsal: to research the period, if the play is not set in the modern era, to develop a biography of their character, especially the *back story*—the events in their past that haveled them to where they are when the play's action begins, and to tell the director how and why what happens may cause them to change. Above all, both director and actors must finally agree on where the play is headed and what its climactic moment will be. The actors must also know why they enter and exit and what they are doing when they are not in a scene—and how every moment relates to the final scene.

Table work is absolutely essential before attempting Shakespeare. An age-old question about Hamlet, for example, is whether he really wants to avenge his father's murder by killing his uncle, the man his father's ghost tells him is responsible. When Hamlet believes he has evidence that the accusation is just and finds the king alone in the chapel, kneeling in prayer, does he feel the urge to stride toward the man, his sword drawn, and accomplish his mission? What holds him back? Does the actor believe Hamlet's reason for not doing so—namely, that if he were to slay the king when he is praying, would the king die without sin? Or is Hamlet justifying his inability to act? The words remain the same, but the actor, working with the director, can discover many options. Hamlet probably provides actors with more choices than any other character ever created, which may explain why playing the role is a challenge eagerly sought.

After table work is finished, the director calls a rehearsal, still around a table, in which the actors do a *cold reading*, the purpose of which is for the actors to become familiar or reacquainted with the story and for the director to make some preliminary interpretation comments.

Here is an example of how a director might approach a famous scene in Oscar Wilde's 1895 comic masterpiece *The Importance of Being Earnest*.[21] Earlier in the scene, the two heroines were discussing over tea the possibility that both are engaged to the same man. After they make their huffy exits, the suitors, Jack and Algernon, enter. Noting that refreshments are still on the table, Algernon avails himself of a buttered muffin.

JACK: *How you can sit there, calmly eating muffins when we are in this horrible trouble I can't make out. You seem to be perfectly heartless.*

ALGER: *Well, I can't eat muffins in an agitated manner. The butter would probably get on my cuffs. One should always eat muffins quite calmly.*

[*DIRECTOR:* Is Algernon really interested in the muffin, or is he playing a game with Jack; and if so, why?]

JACK: *I say it's perfectly heartless your eating muffins at all under the circumstances.*

ALGER: *When I am in trouble, eating is the only thing that consoles me. Indeed, when I am in really great trouble, as anyone who knows me intimately will tell you, I refuse everything except food and drink. . . .*

JACK: *Well, there is no reason why you should eat them all in that greedy way. (Takes muffins from Algernon.)*

[*DIRECTOR:* They are ignoring alleged trouble with their girlfriends and begin a physical dispute about ownership of the muffins. Does this tell us anything about these men? About the society to which they belong?]

For a play in a totally unfamiliar style with little or no traditional structure, directors are responsible for success or failure by coming to that first reading with a clear vision of the work and a plan of how they will communicate it to the cast. The 1956 American premiere of Samuel Beckett's *Waiting for Godot* was disastrous, with audiences feeling bewildered and cheated and many viewers walking out of the theater at intermission. The play, advertised as "the laugh sensation of two continents," starred two comic actors who had starred in popular films: Tom Ewell of *The Seven-Year Itch* and Bert Lahr, the Cowardly Lion of *The Wizard of Oz*.

The play deals with two tramps in a park; they do not enjoy being there but for some reason they cannot leave until they have seen a mysterious man named Godot. After the successful second American production, one critic observed that the play is about "the anguish of waiting," but actually it is the thing itself. They wait. Nothing really happens. One decides to hang himself, but all he can use is the rope that holds his trousers up. When he removes the rope, the trousers fall. The bit was common in vaudeville many years before, but in this play it is poignant, not funny. They decide that perhaps they can hang themselves tomorrow. And perhaps Godot will come tomorrow. And perhaps, if they finally get to meet Godot, they will understand why they have been waiting. Or perhaps not. Or perhaps they ought to leave right now. The final stage direction is: *They do not move*. Since the unsuccessful first production, *Godot* has been hailed as the greatest play of the twentieth century. The first director, Alan Schneider, saw the play as a profound treatment of the hopeless condition of humankind, always waiting for a better life, a better world that never comes, but was unable to connect with two actors who had made their reputation in light entertainment.

Waiting for Godot *is just about that: waiting. The two tramps know they must wait for the mysterious Godot but have no idea who he is or why they must wait. The play becomes a poweful metaphor for the confusion amid which we live.*

The conflict was especially bitter between Schneider and Lahr, whose son, theater critic John Lahr, writes: "Comedy without movement was impossible for Lahr. He balked at Schneider's dicta, at being asked to harness his energy. Lahr was suspicious and ignorant of the allegorical reasons at the basis of Schneider's demands. When the director would go on stage with masking tape and place strips where he was to stand, Lahr was shocked. 'I began to think to myself—this is all wrong. It's stark. It's dire; it's slow. There isn't any movement.' "[22]

The next production, with a different director and actors, was a huge critical success, ultimately becoming a milestone in theater history. Herbert Berghof recast it with non-comic actors, explaining to them that the spine of the play was a grim statement about how each of us is waiting but cannot define what we are waiting for any more than the tramps can define Godot. He also found the dark humor that makes the play both poignant and funny. He insisted on the basic humanity of the tramps, how they survive because they have nothing but each other.

Theater history is filled with examples of plays that were initially misinterpreted and then later resurrected successfully. Stanislavsky did not quite understand Chekhov's *The Seagull* when he gave the world its first production at the Moscow Art Theatre. He provided surface verisimilitude but none of the psychological complexity now associated with the Russian playwright. Only later, when rethinking the production and what went wrong, did he hit on a radical new definition of stage realism. In his revival of the play, he made the actors determine what traits the characters needed from them and where, in themselves, they could find them—and if they could not, what they could substitute from their own experience.

This introduction to one of the world's most enduring art forms may encourage you to seek the pleasure of watching drama wherever it is found. Broadway is not the only place to look. Schools and colleges revive classic works, present new plays, and compensate for their limited budgets with innovative approaches. Many important theatrical productions have been recorded on DVDs or shown on television. These media now offer a library of nearly all the modes and genres of theater discussed in this chapter, from tragedy and comedy to naturalism, the theater of ideas, the theater of cruelty, and avant-garde masterpieces like *Waiting for Godot*. You can readily become a critical viewer if you choose.

Key Terms

aside popular in Elizabethan drama, a remark made by an actor to the audience that other actors on the stage do not hear.

antagonist a character whose function in a play is to oppose the central character's actions; most often found in melodramas.

avant-garde French word meaning "vanguard or advance guard"; in the arts, a movement breaking with convention, experimenting with new forms.

catharsis according to Aristotle, the purging of pity and fear that comes from these emotional responses to a tragedy.

chorus in Greek tragedy, a group of masked actors who sing and dance and comment on the moral implications of the play; can be found in much contemporary theater in different forms and with different functions.

comedy one of two major genres to grow out of Greek theater; originally a short piece that followed a trilogy of tragic plays in order to lighten the mood of the audience; now, any theater work with the primary intent of promoting laughter.

commedia dell'arte professional acting and pantomime troupe that performed in Italian streets beginning in the Renaissance; famous for its stock repertoire of comic types, such as the doddering old man who pursues a beautiful young woman.

conventions rules governing a given style of theater, such as fourth-wall verisimilitude or bare stage. These rules should not be violated but often are, as when actors "break" the fourth wall by delivering a line directly to the audience.

deus ex machina in Greek theater, a god character who is lowered to the stage and resolves the action to audience's satisfaction; now, any contrived ending.

exposition dialogue in a play that gives the background of the story and the relevant history of the characters; problematic in the theater of verisimilitude, in which characters are supposed to talk as people do in real life, without statements like "As you know, dear, we have been married for twenty-five years."

expressionism form of avant-garde drama, introduced by German theaters during the 1920s, in which characters and sets are symbolic, as in the American play *The Adding Machine*, with a giant calculator for a set and a central character named Mr. Zero.

farce genre of comedy involving the actions of two-dimensional stock characters, improbable situations, slapstick, and improbable resolutions of plot complexities.

hubris Greek term meaning "arrogance," the common tragic flaw of protagonists in Greek tragedy.

image a technique, used to great effect by Shakespeare, in which something complex is communicated swiftly by being called something else that is easily understood and is usually visual as well.

melodrama form of theater that resembles but is not legitimate tragedy, dealing with a conflict between two-dimensional characters, often the very good and the very bad.

naturalism technique of acting and writing based on the imitation of people as they actually are and talk in real life; naturalistic plays, like those of Chekhov, often do not have well-structured plots, on the grounds that real life does not structure what happens.

neoclassicism in the arts, a style that reinvents the formalism of early Greece and Rome; abundant in the seventeenth century.

parody exaggeratedly funny imitation of a person (usually a public figure) or artistic work that, according to the parodist, deserves ridicule; often it masks serious criticism.

proscenium in modern theaters, the front of the stage, usually framed and sometimes containing a curtain that can be raised and lowered, or opened and closed.

protagonist central character in a literary work; the person in terms of whose fortune we view and respond to the action; not to be confused with the "hero," who generally is without flaws and who triumphs over bad people.

recognition scene moment in tragic drama, especially that of the Greeks and Shakespeare, when the doomed protagonist understands that he or she is responsible for the disaster; often lacking in modern tragedy.

satire comedy that ridicules such things as war, political corruption, and religious hypocrisy but tends to be less wildly exaggerated than parody.

soliloquy theatrical convention of Elizabethan drama, in which an actor, alone on stage, voices private thoughts.

subtext what is implied but not spoken in a dramatic line.

theater of alienation dramatic genre associated with the work of Bertolt Brecht; it highlights the artificiality of the theater to prevent the audience from becoming emotionally involved in the story and the characters instead of concentrating on the play's ideas.

theater of cruelty dramatic genre that affects the audience through emotional shock, in recent years overwhelming the audience with blood and gore.

tragedy one of the two major forms of drama, focusing on the downfall of a protagonist due to a serious character flaw. In Greek and Shakespearean tragic drama, the protagonist is a high-ranking noble person, but not so in modern tragedy.

unities convention of classical and neoclassical theater requiring the playwright to set the action in one place, have it occur during the time the audience is actually sitting in the theater, and limit the action to one central plot.

verisimilitude technique of making scenery and dialogue look and sound like real life; developed during the latter part of the nineteenth century but still dominant in today's theater.

well-made play also developed in the nineteenth century and using verisimilitude in scenery and dialogue, but the tight, carefully crafted plot structure does not resemble the flow of real life.

Topics for Writing and Discussion

1. Greek playwrights based their works on well-known myths. Discuss two famous events or persons of our time that you believe have acquired mythic status and would be appropriate subjects for a modern tragedy.
2. Of the six dramatic elements Aristotle discusses, he found plot most important. Explain what he means by *plot* and indicate why he believed it would be more important than even character, which he places second.
3. Both *Oedipus* and *Medea* are considered supreme examples of tragedy, but even though they have in common the survival of the main character, they are vastly different. Explain this difference, then tell why each is a tragedy.
4. "Comedy," wrote Aristotle in the only sentence surviving from his essay on the subject, "is life seen from a distance." Explain what this means relative to Molière's *The Would-Be Gentleman.*
5. Farce depends on stock or stereotyped characters whose foolish antics are laughable. Create three stereotypes from contemporary life and provide a brief summary of a play you could write about each one.
6. Try your hand at parody. Make fun of a recent work (stage, screen, or television) you think has been overpraised and should be held up to ridicule to protect the consumer. Remember: pretend your parody is the work itself.
7. The text provides three examples of plays within the theater of cruelty genre from different time periods. Do you see some sort of progression as we get closer to our own time—from *Marat/Sade* to *The Lieutenant of Inishmore*? If there is one, what do you think accounts for it? Predict a theater of cruelty play ten years from now.
8. Review briefly the works we discussed from the theater of ideas, both past and present. Single out the one with the ideas you believe are most relevant today, and explain why.
9. Television has adopted theater of alienation techniques. Discuss a particular series that you believe belongs to the genre. Describe a typical episode and indicate why it "alienates" the viewer. Is it doing so just to be different, or does it have a serious underlying idea the writers want to get across?
10. Shakespeare is frequently called the greatest writer in the English language. Review what you have learned about him from this chapter, then indicate why he does or does not deserve the honor.

8 The Musical Stage: Opera, Music Drama, Dance

Overview

This chapter discusses one of the most popular of all humanities disciplines: the musical stage. As two of the oldest forms of musical performance, opera and ballet have long histories and have achieved high stature in major cultural centers. Music drama, which includes musical comedy and that more recent phenomenon known as the musical play, have shorter histories but now rank among the world's favorite theatrical genres.

Theater and music have always been closely associated. It is hard to say which came first or whether they were inseparable from the start. A good guess is that theater history extends back to the rituals and ceremonies of very early cultures, which combined some form of dance and some kind of rhythmic accompaniment.

Perhaps we can imagine such a ritual: a group of people taking part in a prescribed series of movements and songs to mark an important occasion, such as the change of seasons. When people enter into a collective consciousness, focusing on movements, gestures, or some kind of chant, are they not in a sense *acting*? It is tempting to believe that musical theater was among the very earliest forms of human artistic expression.

Cultural anthropologists have dated musical rituals as far back as 30,000 B.C.E. Cave paintings of that long-ago time show human figures engaged in what has come to be known as the "buffalo dance." This dance was a symbolic reenactment of the hunt for the life-sustaining animal, and the "actors" would play the hunters and the hunted. The theory is that, by taking the part of the buffalo, hunters would be assured of the kill. Many thousands of years later, the Blackfoot nation of Montana still perform that particular ritual, which has become more structured and its musical accompaniment more sophisticated.[1]

Music, song, and dance combined to create the Dionysian festivals in early Greece. They were held annually in the spring to celebrate the return of Dionysus, the god of fertility, from the underworld (Chapter 7). A chorus of men, dressed in goat skins and wearing masks, would perform a series of elaborate and complex songs and dances, accompanied by music of some sort, though we do not know what this music sounded like. In *The Republic*

The rock score of *Spring Awakening* represents the suppressed emotions of students in an 1891 morally rigid society.

Source: Sara Krulwich/*The New York Times*/Redux Pictures.

Plato approved of music that aroused national spirit but did not exist solely to stir emotion. We suspect that the dancing in the Dionysian rites not only stirred emotion but perhaps even drove spectators into a frenzy—perhaps an ancient version of the rock concert!

We do not know when music drama began, because we do not know a time when man had no music drama.

—**John D. Drummond**

The time of Shakespeare—late sixteenth to early seventeenth centuries—represents the golden age of English theater. If the Bard did not write musical plays, he certainly wrote many plays *with* music. Romeo and Juliet meet at a party in which there is masked dancing, accompanied by a number of musical instruments. At the beginning of the memorable final scene in *Othello*, Desdemona has a premonition of impending doom while her maid is brushing her hair, and expresses it in the haunting and melancholy "Willow Song," for which both lyrics and music survive.

In Shakespeare's comedies, mirth and song abound. *Twelfth Night* in particular comes close to being a musical play. The songs have been printed and reprinted thousands of times and are in the repertoire of both folk singers and opera stars. Without music in the productions, Shakespeare's theater would be greatly diminished, though the poetry of the plays, when spoken by the best of actors, can be called unaccompanied music.

By the late seventeenth century, opera was already being developed in Italy. During the eighteenth century Italian opera became one of the world's premier art forms, and composers of other nationalities were forced to compose their operas in the Italian language if they ever hoped to get produced. From opera developed the musical play, the popularity of which seems to grow with each passing Broadway smash.

In this chapter we shall look at some major operas, the art of ballet past and present, the heyday of musical comedy, the gradual evolution of the musical play, and the many varieties of dance. Music alone is one of the great experiences offered by the humanities. Music as song and dance is a further enrichment.

Baroque, Classical, and Romantic Opera

The word **opera** is the Latin plural of *opus* ("work"), a label applied, during the Renaissance, to what was then a new musical art form, combining the work of a playwright (librettist), a composer, an orchestra, singers, and dancers. The growth of opera was an inevitable by-product of the Renaissance rediscovery of classical literature and art and the desire to create works that were elegant and noble enough to rival their ancient predecessors. The Renaissance, as indicated in Chapter 5, broke away from the medieval subjugation of humanity to heavenly beings and reaffirmed the glory of *human* beings. Opera fit nicely into the new strivings.

Monteverdi

Since the Renaissance began in late fourteenth-century Italy as an artistic and political movement, it was inevitable that Italy would create the first operas. Renaissance music gloried in the invention of new instruments, making possible new sounds, and in the harmonies of different vocal lines played or sung at the same time. Renaissance music tended to repeat musical themes over and over, possibly because melody, as we know it, was a novelty, and listeners did not tire of hearing the same sounds. Moreover, the constant repetition made the melodies easy to remember.

Renaissance composers were acutely aware of the public's hunger for melody, but librettists were supplying them with well-known classical myths that had to be told exactly as they were. Consequently, a problem arose: how to reconcile abundant use of melody with the need to move a dramatic plot forward. Events in a play, unlike melodic lines, are not repeated; and characters change as they are affected by experience. It seemed only logical that the music in these sung dramas should keep changing as well. But wouldn't that distress audiences who, having heard a beautiful melody, longed to hear it again—and yet again?

The baroque composer Claudio Monteverdi (1567–1643), born three years later than Shakespeare, laid the foundation for the glorious achievements to follow. Thanks to the pioneering efforts of Monteverdi, the opera of the seventeenth century found a way to move the story forward while keeping the audience interested in the music. Monteverdi developed a continuous musical line interrupted at regular intervals by a memorable aria. The breakthrough work was *La favola d'Orfeo* ("The Fable of Orpheus") in 1607, seven years later than Jacobo Peri's *Eurydice*, based on the same tale and credited with having been the world's first opera.

Monteverdi may be considered the true father of opera, having created the continuous musical line which is interrupted by memorable arias. Mozart, influenced by this invention, created the recitative, *or sung dialogue.*

In one version of the myth, Orpheus is the son of Apollo, the god of light, truth, order, and logic (as discussed in Chapter 1). In paintings, Apollo was often depicted accompanying himself with a lyre. It was only natural that Orpheus would have inherited musical tendencies and would one day attract composers of the new musical genre.

In the legend, whenever Orpheus played on his lyre, all those who heard him were struck dumb with wonder. Animals as well as humans would weep for joy at the sound. Even inanimate objects such as rocks would delight in the music. Orpheus became the very symbol of glorious sounds. How appropriate that his story would become the basis for the first major opera!

Orpheus falls in love with and marries Eurydice, who dies in the flower of youth and is transported down into the underworld. The abandoned lover plays such heart-breaking music on his lyre that Pluto, the god of the underworld, is moved to tears and promises to allow Orpheus to reclaim his wife and return to earth with her—on one condition. Eurydice is to follow behind him, but he must never turn around to see whether she is there. If he does, she will be lost to him forever. Midway through the journey, Orpheus, unable to bear the strain of not knowing, disobeys the order and looks back. True to his word, Pluto reclaims Eurydice.

Monteverdi's opera, however, provides a happy ending to the myth. Eurydice is not lost. Apollo descends from heaven in response to his son's grief and promises that husband and wife will eventually be reunited and live forever, for music cannot die.

To solve the problem of repetition versus dramatic line, Monteverdi uses recurrent themes to represent the characters. This form of repetition would be made famous by Richard Wagner (discussed later in the chapter), who called it the **leitmotif** (or "leading theme"). The *leitmotif* gave audiences melodic lines to remember and to recognize with pleasure when they heard them again. But since the theme was tied to character, and character changed with events, the theme could be both recognizable and yet somewhat altered.

Classical Opera

By the eighteenth century, European society settled into a time of polite behavior, elegance of dress, and the belief that excessive displays of emotion were vulgar. In the baroque musical style of *Orfeo*, Monteverdi develops the drama of his characters while striving to maintain a solid musical structure. Often, however, as in the music of Bach, Dionysian excitement threatens Apollonian structure. Early eighteenth-century opera, in contrast, is marked by greater restraint and can properly be labeled *classical*.

A prime example of this classicism is found in yet another version of the Orpheus myth, one that is more Apollonian than that of Monteverdi. In *Orfeo et Euridice* (1762) by German classical composer Christoph Glück (1714–1787), when Eurydice dies and is taken to the underworld, Orpheus is understandably grief stricken, and what could be more appropriate for an operatic aria than the sorrow of a young man robbed of his only love? His aria beginning "So I mourn her death" contains one of opera's most unforgettable melodies, but it is precise and carefully rhythmic, allowing little room for a tearful rendition. In fact, it could almost be played without words as an aristocratic minuet. Yet the lyrics express the hero's broken heart.

There is still some baroque complexity in the furious rhythms of the ballet danced by a chorus of Furies (the mythological demons tormenting the unworthy residents of the underworld). This is, however, immediately contrasted with the placid "Dance of the Blessed Spirits" and, later, with arias gently titled "These Meadows Are a Place of Blissful Peace" and "What a Clear Sky Decks This Place." The latter two arias represent a musical description that suggests the Christian concept of heaven, suited to the music of classical restraint.

Mozart gives us permission to live.
—**John Updike**

Mozart

The art of opera was fully developed—and perhaps never surpassed—in the work of Wolfgang Amadeus Mozart (1756–1791), often considered the most naturally gifted composer who ever lived. In his operas, as well as in his many other astonishing achievements, Mozart represents the major transition from the classical to the *romantic* style. In Chapter 6, romantic music was described as being extremely melodic with greatly expanded orchestrations and musical forms lengthened to accommodate the expressions of emotion. Yet Mozart's early training was at the hands of the greatest pure classicist of German music, Franz Josef Haydn (1732–1809). So we should expect Mozart operas to display a blending of graceful, symmetrical arias and interludes as well as swelling, romantic sounds.

By the time this prodigy reached the age of four, opera had taken its place among the world's premier arts. The great Italian opera centers—Rome, Florence, Venice, Milan, Bologna—beckoned wealthy tourists and aspiring composers. At the same time, other cities in Western Europe were developing their own singers and orchestras; other composers of opera were eager to be heard, though Italian remained the required language for libretti.

In Mozart's Austria, even small cities had their own versions of the opera house, which began to rival the town cathedral as the focal point of community pride. To the regional houses came the entire population, not just the upper classes and the aristocrats. In those days no one asked why all the dialogue had to be sung. Music drama was simply a given, and as long as it was Italian, audiences immediately accepted it. Later, the young Mozart would decide that he could do as well as the Italians. After all, he *had* written a kind of opera when he was four years old.

Music hath charms to soothe a savage breast,
To soften rocks or bend a knotted oak.

—**William Congreve**

Mozart was born in Salzburg, a city that boasted not only an opera house but a great musical environment in general. His father was an accomplished musician who quickly recognized his son's prodigious talents. By the time he was thirteen, Mozart had become concertmaster for the Archbishop of Salzburg and been decorated in Milan by the pope. Having been a truly *serious* composer from the age of six, when he wrote five pieces for the piano, he was probably not surprised that he was asked to write an opera for the Milanese audiences at the advanced age of fourteen. He not only composed but also directed *Mithridates, King of Pontus*, accomplishing this feat before his sixteenth birthday. For the next nine years, without the patronage of Emperor Franz Josef of Austria, he abandoned his country and struggled for financial security, nevertheless giving the world the most astonishing outpouring of great music ever received from one human being in so brief a time.

Opera intrigued him—the challenge of combining so many elements into one unified work. He mastered the complexities of orchestration and developed a distinctive style, which was at once personal and characteristic of his cultural heritage. His first major opera, *Idomeneo*, with an Italian text, was followed by *The Abduction from the Seraglio*, a delightfully complicated comic opera that has become famous for two reasons aside from its lilting and graceful music.

One reason is that it introduced the truly Mozartean operatic style: melodious arias alternating with dialogue, sometimes spoken, but mostly sung, the composer's solution to the problem of telling a dramatic story in song. Sung dialogue is called **recitative**. The combination of recitative and song is called **singspiel**. Some modern Broadway composers, such as Frank Loesser in *The Most Happy Fella* and Stephen Sondheim in *Sweeney Todd*, aspired to bring the musical closer to opera, leading them to revive the art of singspiel, not always to the pleasure of musical theater audiences who expect to hear one melodious song after another.

Track 13

Another reason for the fame of *The Abduction from the Seraglio* is that boldly—and shockingly to opera-goers of the time—the **libretto** was in German rather than in the standard Italian expected by the Viennese audience. Opera in German was revolutionary in 1782.

Opera. . . is one of the strangest inventions of Western man. It could not have been foreseen by any logical process.

—**Sir Kenneth Clarke**

In 1786 Mozart met a clergyman named Lorenzo da Ponte, who was also a poet and dramatist. Their collaboration resulted in three acknowledged masterpieces—*The Marriage of Figaro* (1786), *Don Giovanni* (1787), and *Cosi fan tutte* ("Thus are they all," sometimes translated as "Women are like that"; 1790). Together they produced three of the greatest operatic works of all time—in only four years! Of all the Mozart operas, *Figaro* has become one of the most popular. Yet the work was coolly received in Vienna and successful only in Prague. Why? There are several possible explanations.

One is that, while the opera was sung in the acceptable Italian, the composer was Austrian by birth. (What's that about a prophet without honor in his own country?) The official composer for the emperor's court was an Italian: Antonio Salieri. Though legend has it that Salieri was obsessively envious of Mozart and may even have poisoned him, the facts appear to tell a different story. Salieri had no reason to wish Mozart dead. He was far better known in the highest musical circles than was Mozart. Besides, Vienna preferred a real Italian to a local boy "borrowing" the language of opera.

Another reason is that it was probably a mistake to premiere the opera in Vienna. The story of how two lowly servants outwit the master of the house—the

Count—could not have pleased many of the aristocrats in the audience. The composer, an upstart from a little town of no consequence (at the time), already had a reputation for being a nonconformist. Nonetheless, as often happens in the history of the humanities, the future was on Mozart's side.

The glorious arias in *Figaro* have made it one of the world's favorite operas. In the recitative, Mozart has idealized human interaction. If Shakespeare's characters can talk to each other in verse, Mozart's characters can talk to each other in music. All theater, whether musical or not, depends on a contract between performers and audience. "We are going to do this and this," say the performers, and the audience replies, "We will believe you as long as you are consistent." In a Mozart opera, characters sing the dialogue between arias and duets throughout.

For his libretto, da Ponte adapted a French farce concerning the middle-aged Count who has grown tired of his wife and seeks fresh young conquests. According to custom, he has *le droit du seigneur*, the privilege of the master to enjoy the sexual favor of a servant on her wedding night—before the groom may do so! The young bride-to-be is engaged to marry Figaro, another servant. The Countess, weary of her husband's philandering, helps the unhappy pair outwit the *seigneur*, who denounces his profligate ways in time for a rousing and joyous finale.

Many elements justify the prominence now enjoyed by this opera in the standard repertoire. First, there is the genius of da Ponte, who, while retaining a lot of the farcical nonsense from the original, transforms the Countess into a character of depth: a lonely wife, facing the sorrow of aging and longing for the love she and

If Shakespeare's characters can talk to each other in verse, Mozart's characters can talk to each other in music.

Source: Northwestern University School of Music.

her husband had once shared. In the tradition of farce, the wife of a cheating husband is usually a nagging shrew, and the philandering husband, a charming rogue. Da Ponte gives the Countess almost tragic dimensions, and, even though the aristocratic opening-night audience did not shout its approval, there must surely have been among them many women who understood the Countess's sadness.

The libretto, with its unprecedented mixture of lively farce (the tricks played on the Count) and its unhappy Countess, with its parallel plots of happy young lovers and a troubled middle-aged marriage, gave the young Mozart a chance to reach into his amazing musical resources and put together a glorious score. What matter even long stretches of recitative when these are always followed by arias that are almost so beautiful that the listener *needs* some breathing space? Many other operas contain perhaps two or three famous arias for which the audience patiently waits. In *Figaro* the magic never stops.

For the Countess, a role to which sopranos always aspire, Mozart wrote two of the greatest arias in the history of opera. In the first, "Porgi, amor," she asks Love itself, which had once filled her life with joy, one final favor: restore her husband's affections or help her to find peace in death. In the second, "Dove sono" (so magnificent that critics have placed *the* before the title, an honor accorded to the major works such as the *Oedipus*, the *David*, and the *Mona Lisa*), she asks a question that people have been asking for centuries: Where have the golden moments fled? Why do happiness and love and youth slip through our fingers? Why can't they last?

The final act of *Figaro* has sometimes been hailed as the very summit of opera. The French original concludes with a farcical scene involving disguise, mistaken identity, and hiding behind bushes, a scene that da Ponte does copy faithfully. At first, everything seems to be rushed so that the curtain can ring down on happy people in a rousing finale, but then comes a moment when the injured wife forgives her husband. Da Ponte stays true to the spirit of farce, but Mozart transcends it with his music. The philandering husband falls to his knees and simply sings "I ask for your pardon," to which the Countess replies "I consent." However contrived this ending may sound, the music makes it thrilling.

We cannot know whether the composer ever predicted the immortality of his opera. Most likely he did not.

Mozart turns the moment into a soaring musical passage: an almost divine act of forgiveness from the soul of a woman who has long suffered neglect but has never lost her love and understanding. The stirring melody is then repeated by full chorus with the voice of the Countess heard above all the others, reaching ever higher and higher. The moment suddenly has attained all the majesty of a solemn requiem sung in an enormous cathedral, filled at last with the joy of redemption.

Listen to the Countess sing sweetly about events that usually provoke anger, and learn to forgive history. Listen to the Countess. . . She drinks "reality"–foul air–and transfigures it.
—Wayne Koestenbaum

We cannot know whether the composer ever predicted the immortality of his opera. Most likely, he did not. The lackluster reception of the premiere probably caused him to turn his attention elsewhere, little realizing the impact *Figaro* would have on the future of opera. That is often the price of genius.

As so often happens in the history of the humanities, the true genius of Mozart was not always apparent to his contemporaries. He composed forty-one symphonies, an enormous repertoire of chamber music and art songs, and massive choral works, but except for some success in his early years, he died at age thirty-five having been poor for much of his life. Mozart rests in an unmarked grave in Vienna.

Romantic Opera: Verdi

Though portions of Mozart's operas have the grace and balance of the classical style, most of the arias and duets, in keeping with the emerging romantic spirit, allow for a freer expression of emotion. The romantic movement—political, artistic, literary, and musical—protested against restraint: political and social restrictions on human behavior; Apollonian restrictions preventing poets, playwrights, and composers from being carried away emotionally. While French opera tended to be faithful to its classical roots, Italians and Germans embraced the new emotional freedom that Mozart had already shown.

The works of Giuseppe Verdi (1813–1901) offer major examples of the romantic style. They tend to contain many melodious arias and less sung dialogue. Two of his operas—*Rigoletto* in 1851 and *La Traviata* in 1852—are among the world's favorites. They became international successes almost at once, but they are forever associated with their original home: La Scala in Milan, still one of the world's great opera houses. Many notable singers have sung their first roles there.

Whenever I go to an opera, I leave my sense and reason at the door with my half-guinea, and deliver myself up to my eyes and my ears.
—**Lord Chesterfield**

A standing ovation at La Scala guarantees stardom, but success there is hard won. Italian audiences are notorious for their treatment of inadequate performances and judge newcomers by the most severe standards. Many a singer has been booed off the stage at La Scala, often for failing to sustain a high note for as long as the audience requires. On the other hand, audiences have been known to stand on their chairs screaming approval for fifteen minutes or even longer. It is particularly risky for a singer to debut at La Scala in an opera by Verdi, Italy's national treasure.

Without their music, Verdi's operas would have to be termed melodramas: the plots allow for many scenes of heartbreak and self-pity. Yet when these moments are combined with soaringly beautiful melodic lines, audiences are transported into a realm that only great art provides.

Rigoletto, like Mozart's *Figaro*, contains so many familiar arias that audiences feel toward it as they would to a dear friend. But the plot is typical of nineteenth-century melodrama. A court jester's daughter is seduced by her father's master. The angry father, hungry for revenge, plots to have the man killed. The daughter overhears the murder plot and deliberately walks into the trap, sacrificing herself to save the man she loves. The opera ends with the grieving father holding his dead daughter and singing one of Verdi's many glorious arias. We are so moved we forget the melodramatic story line.

Verdi insisted upon plots that would allow free reign to his genius for combining emotion and melody. In *La Traviata* (literally, "the strayed one") Verdi found a perfect vehicle. Based on a famous French novel, *La Dame aux Camélias* ("The Lady of the Camelias"), it is the story of a courtesan named Violetta, a woman living in luxury provided by wealthy male companions. Her beauty attracts a young man named Alfredo. Although she struggles against real love and insists on living a free life (expressed in the aria "Sempre Libera" (always free), the suitor overcomes her objections, and they begin living together in the country.

Alfredo's father visits and begs Violetta to renounce his son, whose affair would damage the family's reputation and prevent his daughter from marrying into a respectable family. Violetta tearfully agrees to leave her lover. In a note she tells Alfredo that she prefers her previous life in Paris.

In the final scene Alfredo returns to vow his love once more but finds that Violetta is dying of consumption. This turn of events allows Verdi to write some of his most memorable music. In true romantic fashion, love has been thwarted by social restrictions. This opera, however, transcends melodrama and approaches real tragedy because of the complex characterization of Violetta (another of the great roles for a soprano) and the believability of her doomed love for Alfredo.

Wagner

Romanticism also fostered nationalism, especially among countries that had not yet found a prominent place in the world. Germany in the nineteenth century was experiencing its first excitement of world recognition. German music had reached a position of supremacy with Beethoven and many others, including Mendelssohn and Brahms, who followed in his footsteps.

On the opera front, the showdown between Germany and Italy was inevitable. Mozart's great opera with a German libretto, *The Magic Flute*, still did not eclipse the composer's Italian-language works. Several decades later, the growing respect for a truly German opera can be largely attributed to the work of Richard Wagner (1813–1883), who was born in the same year as Verdi.

Wagner's works are enormous, epic, heroic, often noble and inspiring. Wagner made the German language as powerful on the stage as Italian. His masterpiece, *The Ring of the Nibelung*, is a four-opera saga based on stories from Germanic mythology, which was little known in the rest of the world. If performed as a whole, *The Ring* requires almost twenty hours. Its success made Germans proud that the world was now aware of a mythological heritage to rival that of the Greeks and the Romans.

Wagner went one step further than either Homer or Virgil. He added monumental symphonic music, demanding full orchestral accompaniment and singers of extraordinary vocal power. To this day the label "Wagnerian singer" carries with it prestige and critical respect. He added powerful dramatic confrontations and scenic effects, justifying his restoration of the label **music drama**. He made the most memorable use of *leitmotif*, giving all of the major characters a musical theme heard when they appeared and in variations in their arias or the symphonic introductions to scenes. The Wagnerian *leitmotifs*, running throughout the four operas, lend a unity to what might otherwise have been a sprawling musical narrative.

In his early adulthood, Wagner was fascinated by opera, and with his musical training he was able to secure jobs in various German opera houses, where he worked as vocal coach, chorus master, and music director. In these capacities he was involved in many productions of both classical and Italian romantic works. So obsessed was he to devote his life to opera that he spent five years preparing himself. The result of the careful thought he gave to the project was a book called *Opera and Drama*, which set forth his theories of what opera should be.

He wanted to liberate opera from both its classical restraints and its Italian melodrama. He wanted to create true music drama that would be critically placed beside the great works of Sophocles and Shakespeare. He wanted characters that were larger than life, characters that were heroic and noble and met tragic destinies with courage and honor. An opera historian writes: "Wagner's essential standpoint was that opera should not be mere entertainment, but (and he drew on Greek tragedy to support this) a fundamentally educative and ennobling experience."[2]

Whereas the Greek work of art expressed the spirit of a splendid nation, the work of art of the future is intended to express the spirit of a free people irrespective of national boundaries. The national element in it must be no more than an ornament, an added individual charm, and not a confining boundary.

—Richard Wagner

He believed Italian opera had made an aesthetic mistake in subordinating the drama to the music, beautiful as it might be; rather, he wanted to elevate drama to the position of dominance; otherwise, audiences would be there simply for a concert and would be denied the overwhelming emotional experience he knew opera was capable of providing. In order to do this, he realized, the composer must also write the libretto, thus assuring the creation of a solid unity never before seen.

Wagner turned first to the heroic figures of world mythology, to stories he thought worthy of his enormous talent. (Wagner was never modest about his genius.) As he was composing his first major opera, *The Flying Dutchman* (1841), he realized he was facing the same problem that both his classical predecessors and his Italian contemporaries had encountered: how to provide beautiful music and keep the flowing dramatic line from becoming uninteresting. In *Tannhaüser* (1845) and *Lohengrin* (1848) he found his answer. If the dramatic line were to be the dominating factor, the music that sustained it could never be less than glorious. He felt there was no choice but to conceive of an opera as a giant symphony, written for a full orchestra and singers with the vocal power to be heard soaring above the music. Orchestra and singers were to form a unity never before known.

Tannhaüser and *Lohengrin* drew on Christian and Arthurian legends. Now the time had come to base an opera on Teutonic mythology, which bore a close kinship with the old Norse stories of gods and mortal heroes. In Norse tales, the king of the gods is Odin; in German, Wotan. The hero of the *Ring* cycle is Siegfried, who appears in the Norse sagas as Sigurd. Wagner took the old myths and turned them into an epic tale about the downfall of those who struggle for the power that a magic ring bestows upon the wearer. In true romantic fashion, it is love that is ultimately greater than the lust for power.

In one of opera's most spectacular scenes, Brünnhilde rides her white horse onto the funeral pyre of her beloved Siegfried, dying for love and thus saving the world.

Source: Johan Elbers/Time and Life Pictures/Getty Images.

The Nibelung are a race of elves, or dwarfs, who control a huge store of treasure, including a wondrous lump of gold that, if made into a ring, would have the power to make the wearer the supreme ruler of the universe—as long as he remains chaste. Wotan, wanting no one to be his superior, steals the ring, which has been forged by a dwarf named Alberich, who places a curse on it. As a result, disaster after disaster occurs. Only genuine love will lift the curse. Until such time, which Alberich is confident will never come, people will destroy each other in the struggle for the power the ring holds.

The four-opera cycle reaches a stirring climax when Brünnhilde, one of Wotan's daughters, commits suicide by riding her horse into the funeral pyre on which the body of her beloved Siegfried is being burned. The fire is so spectacular that it consumes Valhalla, the palace of the gods, who are destroyed, after which the Rhine river overflows its banks to quench the flames. Here it is important to note that in addition to being a composer, Wagner was a political radical, very much involved with revolutionary ideologies sweeping Germany in the mid-nineteenth century. He took part in rallies and protest marches and translated into music his ideals of liberation. In the *Ring* cycle, the all-powerful gods are destroyed in the final act. The marathon cycle of operas comes to a magnificent close with a lyrical melody that represents the return of love to the world and the end of inhuman power.

The mythology of a magic ring is not limited to Norse and Germanic sagas or to Wagner's telling of the story. The fable of the ring of Gyges was originally found in Plato's *Republic* (Chapter 11), and *that* ring also bestowed magical powers upon the wearer, who could become invisible at will, causing no end of damage. Readers will certainly think of the modern version of the story, Oxford professor J. R. R. Tolkien's *The Lord of the Rings* trilogy, made into three epic films. In Tolkien, the magic ring is similar to that found by Plato's Gyges in that its power lies in allowing the wearer to become invisible and thus to rise above all human law. In Plato, Wagner, and Tolkien, the message is the same: power corrupts, and only selfless love can save the world.

Wagner's achievements illustrate an interesting facet of the humanities. While the writer Katherine Mansfield once said that a great poet must be a great poem, meaning that there should be no distinction between an artist's work and an artist's life, the fact is that in Wagner's case there was considerable disparity. He dwelt on themes of love and redemption in his work, but in his life, he was a total egotist, subjecting his acquaintances to lengthy readings of an opera newly finished, borrowing money he never paid back, and practicing infidelity. Theoretically liberal in his views, he was also strongly anti-Semitic. He was the center of his own universe, the diametric opposite of a Vincent van Gogh, who constantly reviled his own work. Genius, apparently, is unevenly distributed, but it cannot be ignored. We would be the poorer for having done so.

And we have all heard the anecdote of the composer who played his latest piece to his guests, after which they asked him what its meaning was. The composer sat down at the piano again and played the piece through once more.

—**Jacques Barzun**

Modern Opera and Operetta

Like all forms of music, not to mention the other arts, opera in the modern period has its own idioms and purposes. Italian is no longer the required language. Composers choose libretti written in their own tongue. If they do not, like Wagner, create their own libretti, they usually work closely with their authors. Wagner's ideal of opera as a unity of music and drama still applies, though by now the flow of the dramatic line is so completely dominant that audiences often long for outbursts of melody. More and more, the aria is replaced with a musical underscoring of dialogue. Often the question has been raised: "Why is this play set to music at all?"

Opera, among the summit achievements in the humanities, inspires modern composers to try reaching its heights. Similarly, modern playwrights often want to write tragedies that can rival those of the Greeks and Shakespeare. But the passage of time has affected musical styles. Melodious passages are considered dated and hackneyed by many young composers. Rarely do we hear a definite aria that stands out from the rest of a scene. To find one, we must often turn to the Broadway musical stage, to works like Leonard Bernstein's *West Side Story* or Stephen Sondheim's *Sweeney Todd*, which approach grand opera but keep their Broadway roots at the same time.

Modern operas are performed far less than enduring favorites such as *La Traviata*. Theaters are afraid to take chances. The cost of producing any opera is so high that, with the support of generous patrons, companies do well to break even. None can depend on ticket sales alone. Frequently patrons demand time-honored classics, but now and then a company dares to break with tradition and will commission a work by a composer whose credentials are above question.

Joplin's *Treemonisha*

A pioneer work in American opera was composed in 1911 by Scott Joplin, whose innovations in ragtime were discussed in Chapter 6. Titled *Treemonisha*, the first major opera by an African American composer was at first snubbed by the opera

A musician must make music, an artist must paint, a poet must write, if he is to be ultimately at peace with himself. What a man can be, he must be.

—**Abraham Maslow**

establishment, receiving generally unfavorable notices when it was finally produced in 1915.

Two possible reasons come to mind to explain the opera's failure. One may be that the opera world, almost exclusively a white institution up to that time, resented Joplin's effort to create grand opera rather than continue producing music "appropriate" for his cultural heritage. Another may be that audiences who knew and loved Joplin's music were expecting a ragtime opera, but Joplin wanted to go lightly in his use of the tempo that had served him so well. Although there is some ragtime in the score, the composer may have wanted to show that music transcended narrow racial ties.

As happens over and over in the history of the humanities, time has reversed the original criticism. *Treemonisha* is now widely accepted as the first truly American opera, using American subject matter and American folk themes. The symphonic score was inspired by Wagner, whom Joplin admired more than all other composers, even following in his footsteps by writing both libretto and music himself. The result is a work that combines nineteenth-century German musical romanticism with American themes.

Those themes spring from the heart of a rural America peopled by former slaves. The setting is a small Arkansas community in the late nineteenth century. The protagonist, for whom the opera is named, is a young woman, raised by a couple who had found her as an abandoned infant lying under a tree. The adoptive mother, Monisha, insisting that the child receive a proper education in order to have a better future than working in the fields, had enlisted the services of a white woman willing to teach the child to read. Now, at eighteen, Treemonisha sets her sights on ridding the community of illiteracy and ignorance.

One reason for the initial failure of Treemonisha may be that audiences were expecting–and did not get–a ragtime opera.

Joplin was also influenced by the melodramatic libretti of nineteenth-century Italian opera; there had to be villains who would thwart the heroine's idealistic goals. In this case they are fraudulent conjurors, evil men who exploit the town inhabitants, taking their money in exchange for "magic" that will presumably cure their ailments and eventually make them rich. Treemonisha takes them on, but before she can expose them, she is abducted and nearly murdered, saved at the last moment by her friend Remus. The finale is a syncopated rag in a much slower tempo than was customary for Joplin. Called "A Real Slow Drag," it is an affirmation of African American spirit and dignity, as Treemonisha and the chorus resolve to "march onward" to a brighter future.[3] *Treemonisha* was revived in 1975, receiving the acclaim that the composer, alas, had not lived to enjoy.

Showboat: An Operetta

The *operetta* was a nineteenth-century European invention, given worldwide fame by Austrian composers such as Johann Strauss (1825–1899), in which spoken dialogue moves the play forward but is continually interrupted by lengthy and melodious arias that are far more important than the drama itself. For many composers, the form solved the problem of how to keep the audience's attention during the spaces between songs: it shortened the spaces. In an operetta there are so *many* songs that audiences don't have long to wait for the next one. The story line is either silly and complicated but fast-moving or filled with tear-jerking sentimentality that never requires close listening. Characters in operetta tend to be two-dimensional with identifying traits that remain unchanged throughout the proceedings. The songs vaguely grow out of the context of a scene, but nobody complains if the two are not closely related. In any event, operetta lyrics are generally flowery or bombastic. There is a super-abundance of love songs and duets, meant to be self-sustaining outside the show for performance in clubs and cabarets, and later on radio.

The operetta genre, however, produced some memorable and important works. One of the best—also American—is *Showboat* (1927) with Jerome Kern music and Oscar Hammerstein II lyrics. It is important both for its songs, many of which remain popular to this day ("Ol' Man River," "Only Make-Believe," "Can't Help Lovin' That Man," "My Bill") and for the fact that it was really the first operetta to aim at a serious unification of music and story. Some historians of the musical stage have called *Showboat* the precursor of the musical play as well as a link between Broadway and opera.

Nonetheless, the story is embedded in nineteenth-century sentimental drama. The heroine is Magnolia, who falls madly in love with a Mississippi riverboat gambler improbably named Gaylord Ravenal. The handsome charmer sings divinely—and often—but we know that his addiction to gambling bodes no good. They marry, have a child, fight over his gambling, then separate. A reformed Gaylord eventually returns and has a tear-filled scene with his daughter, who doesn't know who he is, but that doesn't stop them from singing a duet. Ravenal is finally able to persuade Magnolia that he has changed for the better. The curtain falls on the required joyous finale.

Yet *Showboat* has darker undertones. "Ol' Man River," one of the classic songs of the American musical stage, is sung by an African American dock worker, with no future except for endless and exhausting toil. His few leisure moments are fraught with danger: If you get a little drunk, "you land in jail." He is "tired of livin', but feared of dyin'." *Showboat* dared to confront racism in America, as *Treemonisha* had done sixteen years earlier. But *Showboat* was a sensational hit, and its racial theme reached huge white audiences.

Porgy and Bess

George Gershwin, already discussed in Chapter 6 for his *Rhapsody in Blue*, shared the desire of many popular composers to reach the heights of grand opera. And why not? He had already proved that he was capable of writing rich symphonic scores. His brother Ira was a distinguished lyricist. All they needed was a subject that would allow them to keep their American roots and to create opera out of truly American sounds. They found the perfect subject in a novel called *Porgy* by DuBose Heyward, who was willing to write the libretto. So *Porgy and Bess* (1935) was born, a work that, like *Treemonisha* before it, met with critical coolness but has since been hailed as a supreme example of true American opera. From its beginnings, disguised as a Broadway musical to lure audiences, it has moved on and been performed at the world's major opera houses. Unfortunately, Gershwin, who died at thirty-eight, did not live to see *Porgy and Bess* hailed as a masterwork.

True music must repeat the thought and inspirations of the people and the time. My people are Americans. My time is today.

—George Gershwin

The setting for both the novel and the opera is a rundown section of Charleston called Catfish Row. Porgy, the unlikely hero, is crippled and gets around in a goat cart. He is high-spirited and optimistic despite his poverty. His first aria is the jaunty "I Got Plenty of Nuthin' and Nuthin's Plenty for Me." Bess, the heroine, is stunningly beautiful but shunned by the residents of "the Row" because of her lax morals. She lives with Crown, a violent lawbreaker who abuses her but whom Bess apparently finds irresistible. When Crown is forced to flee the law, Bess is

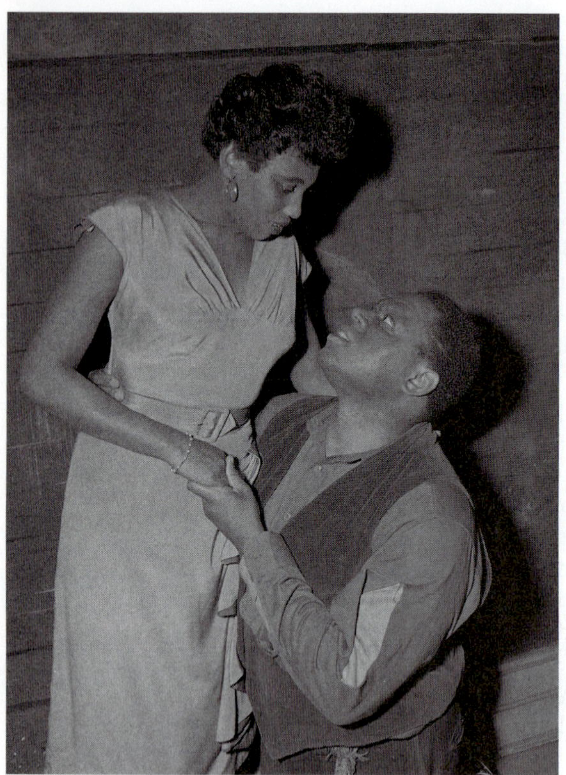

Leontyne Price and William Warfield in the love duet from *Porgy and Bess*, which moved from modest beginnings as a Broadway musical into the worldwide opera repertoire.

Source: © 2008 Associated Press.

abandoned and accepts Porgy's offer of a place to stay. Though at first Bess is just using Porgy until Crown returns, she becomes aware that the man in the goat cart loves her with all his soul. Little by little she responds to his gentle and affectionate kindness. "Bess, You Is My Woman Now," one of the glorious duets in modern opera, remains a concert favorite for singers and audiences, as does Bess's aria "I Loves You, Porgy," in which she pleads with her newfound love not to allow Crown to force her back.

Crown, however, does return and is killed by Porgy. The "Row" inhabitants—and the audience—believe the act is justifiable, and we are prepared for a happy ending. However, in the tradition of the greatest love stories, such as *Romeo and Juliet* and *La Traviata*, the curtain must fall on tragedy, this time brought about by Sportin' Life, a gambler, pimp, and drug dealer, dressed out in glittery, expensive clothes. Sportin' Life exudes Dionysian charm and almost wins the audience over, but then his true nature is revealed when he exploits Bess's weakness for drugs. He promises her a lifetime supply if she will just go with him to New York. She struggles briefly with the dilemma, but Sportin' Life wins out. Though abandoned, Porgy remains optimistic about finding his lost love. He doesn't know where New York is, except that it's "over that way." The opera ends with Porgy setting off in his goat cart as he and the chorus sing the rousing but ultimately sad "I'm on My Way."

The finale of *Porgy and Bess* is reminiscent of the closing chorus in *Treemonisha*, in which the heroine is similarly determined to find a better life. Joplin, however, seems more convinced of his character's success. The libretto of *Porgy* by DuBose Heyward clearly gives no such promise.

Other Modern Operas of Note

Though their contributions to modern opera have not yet achieved the international fame of *Porgy and Bess*, a number of modern composers of opera deserve to be included in a humanities text. Gian-Carlo Menotti and Leonard Bernstein, for example, have already left behind a considerable legacy of works in a number of musical genres, including opera. John Corigliano and Stephen Sondheim are among the others who can be expected to continue enriching our lives.

Italian-born Gian-Carlo Menotti (1911–2007) is assured of lasting musical fame, if only as the founder of one of the world's most prestigious music festivals held annually in Spoleto, Italy, with an American version in Charleston, South Carolina. New works are premiered in both places, along with performances of standard repertoire by outstanding musicians and conductors. Menotti has given the world perhaps the most prodigious offerings of the four composers discussed here, beginning with his 1951 Christmas opera *Amahl and the Night Visitors*, written for television when that medium was in its infancy and since performed hundreds, perhaps thousands, of times until it has been seen by more viewers than any opera in history.

The one-act opera concerns the night in which three kings, following the star of Bethlehem, stop at a humble dwelling in which lives Amahl, a crippled shepherd boy, and his mother. The kings tell the boy about their mission to follow the star until it leads them to the place where God's son is about to be born. Amahl, who is very poor, nonetheless gives the kings a humble gift for the child and is miraculously rewarded for so doing. The simplicity of the story and the extremely beautiful music make the work enduringly popular, even among those who profess no traditional faith.

Both Bernstein and Sondheim achieved success on the Broadway stage and both composed works that combined Broadway styles with genuine opera elements.

Leonard Bernstein (1918–1990), who will be discussed later in this chapter as the composer of *West Side Story*, one of the most revolutionary of Broadway musicals, also composed *Candide* (1956), an operatic adaptation of Voltaire's classic satire on idealism. Critics have debated whether the work is really an operetta, but labeling it seems beside the point. It has elements of both genres. With a libretto by Richard Wilbur, a major poet, *Candide* concerns a naive young man who has been led to believe by his tutor that "everything happens for the best in this best of all possible worlds." In the high comedy of pure satire, everything goes wrong in what turns out to be the worst of all possible worlds. The dialogue, combining the wit and wisdom of Voltaire and the poetic sounds of Wilbur, make the libretto of *Candide* far stronger than that of most operas.

Bernstein's music is every bit as strong and takes the work very close to the realm of opera. The aria "Glitter and Be Gay," sung by the heroine, who pretends she is faking enjoyment of her life as a prostitute but secretly loves it, is now in the repertoire of world-famous opera sopranos. The final chorus, "Make Our Garden Grow," is as rousing an ensemble piece as any opera has given us.

Stephen Sondheim (b. 1930) was still in his twenties when he wrote the lyrics for Bernstein's *West Side Story*. With songs such as "Maria," "Tonight," and "Somewhere," which have become classics, Sondheim quickly established a huge reputation for himself as a wordsmith. But he became the dominant force in the American musical theater during the last quarter of the twentieth century, composing *both* music and lyrics and working closely with his librettists to ensure the unity of every component. Up to this point, his masterpiece is a musical that is very close to being recognized as a genuine opera: *Sweeney Todd, the Demon Barber of Fleet Street* (1979), adapted from a creaky nineteenth-century melodramatic thriller. In the hands of Sondheim and Hugh Wheeler, the librettist, the melodrama disappears, replaced by a work of genuinely tragic dimensions, with a symphonic score of concert-hall importance.

Johnny Depp as the demon barber of Fleet Street in the 2007 film production of *Sweeney Todd*.

Source: © DreamWorks/The Everett Collection.

Sweeney Todd returns to his home and business in London after being freed from a jail term imposed by a judge who lusted for and then raped his wife. In his obsession with revenge against the entire judicial profession, Todd rents rooms upstairs from Mrs. Loveit, a pie-maker whose business is faltering because she makes, as a song suggests, "The Worst Pies in London." He opens a barbershop, and when a customer turns out to be a judge, he slashes the man's throat with a razor, sending the body down a chute to the waiting Mrs. Loveit, who then dismembers and bakes it into a pie. Her business skyrockets, and she becomes famous for serving up the best pies in London. Todd, of course, awaits the day when the villainous judge who destroyed his wife will come in for a shave.

The development of Sweeney from a wronged husband to a cold-blooded killer is carried out with meticulous and chilling precision by Sondheim and Wheeler. The barber's burning desire for revenge is thwarted when the judge escapes his grasp, a turn of fate that drives Sweeney into total madness and random killings. In the final scene, the work approaches tragic heights when the crazed barber murders a prostitute, only to discover that she is his wife. His blood-curdling cry of "*No!*", accompanied by crashing chords from the orchestra, rivals the cries of despair often heard at the climax of great tragedies.

Though there are memorable songs along the way—notably "Joanna," "Green Finch and Linnet Bird," "Not While I'm Around," and the grimly hilarious "A Little Priest," a duet in which Todd and Mrs. Loveit sing about the various professions to be found in her pies—the emphasis is on the onrushing flow of the drama. Sondheim sacrifices opportunities for hit songs in the interest of the plot. Much of the dialogue is sung—an updated version of the Mozartean recitative.

Unlike Bernstein and Sondheim, John Corigliano (b. 1938) has never written a Broadway musical, but he did win the Academy Award for scoring the 1997 dramatic documentary *The Red Violin* about the 300-year-old history of an instrument that affects many lives in many different ways. He is also known for having written several important symphonies and an award-winning opera, *The Ghosts of Versailles* (1991), about what the ravages of the French Revolution did to genteel eighteenth-century French society, of which the Palace of Versailles still stands as a symbol. Like most contemporary works based on historical incidents, however, the opera is really about the recurring human tragedy of war.

The Broadway Musical

Those in the free seats are the first to hiss.

—**Chinese proverb**

If ragtime, blues, and jazz are said to be American contributions to the humanities, the same holds true for the Broadway musical, still popular after a century and a half, still dominant at the box office, and perhaps more widely performed throughout the world than any other theatrical genre. The genre has undergone a number of changes throughout its history. First there was **musical comedy**, typically characterized by ridiculous plot lines but ever more sophisticated music by noted composers and lyricists. Then came the **musical play**, which combined serious plot, stronger dialogue, characters with a certain amount of depth, and often complex dances, as well as music and lyrics designed more to serve the story and less to be performed and sold as musical hits.

The heyday of the American musical comedy was in the decades from World War I to the early 1950s, though the form is far from obsolete, with many of the classic shows enjoying continual revivals. It appealed to a public hungry to forget the devastation of war, and then later, to a public wanting to forget both the financial distress of the Great Depression and anxiety over another approaching global catastrophe. And finally, it appealed to a public in the mood to celebrate newly won (if short-lived) world peace.

The typical plot was threadbare, the characters two-dimensional, the dialogue unbelievable, but all of these elements simply existed for the songs that were for the most part so bouncy that audiences tapped their feet in accompaniment. Every now and then the pace slowed, and the audience was treated to a song with a beautiful melody and simple, easily remembered lyrics. The sheet music of a show's hits was for sale in the lobby so the songs could be played in parlors throughout the country. If one could not play well enough, there were also piano rolls, inserted into pianolas (player pianos), which made the keys move as if by magic. The song hits from musical comedies were parallel to the romantic operatic arias that stood out from their context, and there was never a problem of how to keep the dramatic line going. The whirlwind pace of the show did that.

The musical comedy era between the wars ushered in the prodigious talents of Cole Porter, who wrote his own brilliant lyrics, Jerome Kern, Irving Berlin, and the collaborative team of Richard Rodgers and Lorenz Hart as well as that of the Gershwin brothers, George and Ira. In this golden age of musical comedy, lyrics assumed a life of their own. Because musical comedy plots were usually foolish, nobody cared if a song's lyrics were not tightly bound to a scene. The two-dimensional characters were often "adjusted" to fit the songs. Some lyrics of the period can be read apart from the music as serious poems or humorous verse. Cole Porter was a master lyricist as well as musician. Songs like "Anything Goes," "Begin the Beguine," and the amusing "Brush Up Your Shakespeare" and "Let's Do It" have long since outlived the plots that gave birth to them.

Your audience gives you everything you need. They tell you. There is no director who can direct you like an audience.

—Fanny Brice

Of Thee I Sing

An outstanding musical comedy of the period, *Of Thee I Sing* (1932) was the work of the Gershwins. It elevated the stature of musical comedy by winning the Pulitzer Prize, usually reserved for serious, non-musical work. *Of Thee I Sing* is anything but serious. It is a swiftly moving satire on presidential politics that is often revived in theaters throughout the country in time for presidential elections. So consistently hilarious yet right on target did the show prove to be that some critics compared it to the comic operas of Gilbert and Sullivan, which had taken London by storm during the last quarter of the nineteenth century.

Manhattan crowds,
With their turbulent musical chorus!
Manhattan faces and eyes forever for me.

—Walt Whitman

The theme of the show is that candidates will do just about anything to win the presidency—anything, that is, beside having a serious, profoundly considered agenda. The "hero," Wintergreen, is chosen as a candidate by the power brokers because of his innocent and appealing nature. That he has little brain power appears not to be a problem. For his running mate, the party bosses corral a dolt named Throcklebottom, whose name they never can remember. The only problem is that Wintergreen has no wife, so the party conducts a widely publicized beauty pageant to find "Miss White House."

The winner of the pageant is Diana Deveraux, empty headed and gorgeous. But our hero has already fallen in love and proposed marriage to Mary, a young woman who lacks glamour but has common sense. Not only that, but she can bake corn muffins. When the jilted beauty queen sues the candidate, the Supreme Court decides the country needs the muffins (which Mary promises to bake in abundance in order to feed the homeless). A grateful country elects Wintergreen.

The Supreme Court is called back into session to debate the sex of the "First Baby," which turns out to be boy/girl twins, showing that the Court is not always on top of things. There is an impeachment hearing, prompted by the rival party's efforts to use the jilting of Diana to its own advantage. The problem is resolved when Wintergreen's bosses force Diana to marry Throcklebottom, the vice president, who has nothing else to do and cannot even find the Capitol. The curtain falls on a rousing finale that has everyone joyously united either in marriage or in political unity.

After it is expertly done, can you draw sweet water from a foul well?
—**Brooks Atkinson**

Pal Joey

An important "transition" work of the Broadway theater is *Pal Joey* (1940), with music by Richard Rodgers and lyrics by Lorenz Hart. Still very much in the musical comedy tradition with peppy songs, tap dances, and ear-caressing ballads, *Pal Joey* deepened the Broadway musical and deserves to be considered a pioneer musical play, casting some dark shadows on the traditionally sunny landscape of the musical stage and providing the audience with a very *un*traditional hero who could sing and dance but was ultimately not very likeable.

The authors were already established as major collaborators whose names alone guaranteed the success of any venture, thus minimizing any risk to the backers. In addition, the libretto was written by John O'Hara, one of America's leading authors of serious fiction, known for his novels, Hollywood screenplays, and *New Yorker* short stories. Although *Showboat* had been adapted from a best-selling novel (by Edna Ferber), the author did not write the book for the operetta. In the case of *Pal Joey*, a celebrated author adapted his own work for the stage.

It all happened by chance. O'Hara, who was tired of the compromises a screenwriter was forced to make in order to satisfy studio executives, was determined to earn a living by selling stories to the *New Yorker*. Unfortunately the editor of the magazine rejected his work, declaring that he would never publish another John O'Hara story unless he could understand it. Feeling sorry for himself, O'Hara went on a drunken binge; when he recovered, he began writing a story about a ruthless and decidedly unpleasant master of ceremonies in a seedy nightclub. The character, Joey Evans, suited O'Hara's bleak mood. At first he had no idea where the piece was going, but "the more I wrote about the slob, the more I got to like him."[4]

There is a traditional trick that theatre people have played as long as I can remember. A veteran member of a company will order a gullible newcomer to find the key to the curtain. Naturally the joke is that there is no such thing. . . but all my life I've been searching for that key.
—**Richard Rodgers**

The story became a whole series of stories. A close friend read them, fell in love with this charming scoundrel, and suggested that O'Hara write a play about him. O'Hara liked the idea but thought it should be a musical because of its nightclub setting and Joey's profession as a showman. Rodgers and Hart, who were looking for more challenging subject matter, became O'Hara's collaborators.

The work did not erupt overnight into a theatrical masterpiece. O'Hara's first draft was called "disorganized" by George Abbott, hired to direct the show. The main problem seemed to be Joey, who, it was feared, might alienate the audience. The final story line, however, arrived at after numerous rewrites and even with Abbott's attempt to turn it into traditional musical comedy fare, did not fit the mold.

A spoiled socialite ventures into Joey's club, seeking escape from her dull and loveless existence. She meets Joey, and though she sees through him instantly, she is unable to resist his charms and sexuality. Rodgers and Hart gave her one of their greatest tunes—"Bewitched, Bothered, and Bewildered"—which has become an anthem for all those who are obsessed with absolutely the wrong people. Of course, the affair ends unhappily. Joey will never change, and she will always love him anyway. Despite being well rid of Joey, she will never find anyone who can measure up to him. O'Hara refused to twist the plot so that the audience could go home happy.

Both Rodgers and Hart had trouble with O'Hara, fearing that the character and the story itself would upstage *their* work. Insisting on retaining some musical comedy lightheartedness, they decided to exploit the nightclub for all it was worth, introducing a chorus of broken-down, no-talent singers and dancers who, according to reports, kept the audience in an uproar. The biggest *coup* was finding just the

Gene Kelly as the antihero of *Pal Joey*, a dark musical by an author who didn't care whether the audience went home happy.

Source: Photofest.

right person to play Joey. It was Gene Kelly, who later became a Hollywood legend as one of the greatest dancers ever to hit the screen. Not only could he overwhelm audiences with his complex choreography, but he had a velvet singing voice and an outgoing personality filled with the desperately needed charm without which the show could not have succeeded.

Joey Evans was and remains an antihero. Critics were split down the middle. Some were delighted with a story and a protagonist that broke the mold and avoided the stereotypes of musical predecessors. Others were put off by the cruel streak beneath Joey's surface likeability. Audiences, however, kept filling the theater, and the box-office success would encourage others to keep striving for greater depth in the genre. Despite the efforts of the collaborators to keep the show well within the parameters of musical comedy, they could not resist the tide of change. As William Hyland writes: "Although the excellent music . . . was integral to the spirit of the play, for once Rodgers was overshadowed by the character, the lyrics, and the play itself. Because of the harsh and realistic story and the biting lyrics, the show became a landmark . . . a milestone in the liberation of the musical from the stale forms of the 1920s and 1930s."[5]

Every once in a while a theatre-goer needs a shot of Rodgers and Hammerstein to make the world seem a better place or allow newbies to gain an appreciation of what musical theatre is all about.

—**Roy Berko**

Oklahoma! *was so poorly reviewed in its Boston tryout that it almost never made it to Broadway.*

Oklahoma!

The advent of World War II made the country eager for escapist entertainment, though the desire to have shows with strong libretti was still there. In 1942, Richard Rodgers teamed up with Oscar Hammerstein II, whose libretto and lyrics for *Showboat* and other hit shows were already famous. Both were looking for something new and different. Hammerstein came from a tradition that in no way resembled Lorenz Hart's Manhattan sophistication. The lyrics for *Showboat* had proved him to be a poet, but he was not of the modern school. By temperament he was a romantic.

In 1933 Rodgers had seen a folk play called *Green Grow the Lilacs*, about the rivalry between two cowboys for a sweet and innocent young woman. One was handsome and honorable, the other villainous, placing the heroine in grave danger. On the face of it, it was a tired old plot, reminiscent of nineteenth-century melodramas. Rodgers, however, thought it would make a successful musical. He had tried to interest Hart in the project, but the latter considered the story unsuited for his brand of worldly wise lyrics. Hammerstein *was* interested.

Both men knew that writing realistically about the present meant writing about the war, and perhaps Broadway audiences were in the mood for a return to less troubled times. *Green Grow the Lilacs* was set in the late nineteenth-century Midwest, when tension could arise over which young man would bid highest for a girl's picnic basket and win the right to be her companion for the day.

The first version of the musical was given a tryout in Boston, as was customary in those days. Called *Away We Go!*, it received such poor critical notices that the producers feared they couldn't raise enough money to bring the show into New York. They did, however, find someone willing to invest $50,000 to keep the show going during the extensive revisions needed. Rodgers and Hammerstein and the director spent long nights in a Boston hotel, reworking every scene while trying to retain the show's down-to-earth honesty and simplicity. Yet they also knew that it needed one rousing choral number, without which a show could not survive, a number that would explode on the stage and send the audience out singing and relishing the memory of it. Since the setting was the Oklahoma territory just prior to its achieving statehood, the collaborators realized they had not yet given prominence to the event. What better way to end the show than singing of the promise that statehood brings, the promise of a better life in a better world?

They named both the number *and* the show *Oklahoma!* and brought it into New York to ecstatic reviews and the largest post-opening box office any show had ever known up to that time. Ticket scalpers were charging up to fifty dollars—at a time when three and a half dollars was the reigning box-office price for orchestra seats. On a radio sitcom, one character promised his beloved tickets to *Oklahoma!* if she would marry him. Her answer was: "And where would you get them?"

From the moment the curtain rose, audiences were seeing something completely different on the musical stage. Instead of a chorus singing a traditional opening, they saw an elderly farm woman, alone on stage, churning butter and listening to an offstage cowboy, singing "Oh, What a Beautiful Mornin'." The cowboy enters, concludes the song, and talks about his love for the woman's niece, who soon appears and seems annoyed at the cowboy's attentions. He returns her jibes. Then they sing the required romantic duet, but instead of the usual love-at-first-sight sentiments, each demands that the other refrain from showing any sign of affection in front of others, because "People Will Say We're in Love." Their underlying bond is quite evident, but the sparring breathed new life into a cliché.

Everything about the story works to musical advantage. The settlers in the territory make up the chorus. A picnic auction allows for folk dances. Interaction between believable characters motivates the songs. The crux of the drama comes when Laurie, the heroine, has to decide between the handsome Curley and the farmhand Judd. The conflict is dramatized in a spectacular dream ballet called *Laurie Makes Up Her Mind*, for which the choreographer Agnes de Mille cast highly trained dancers, performing against surrealistic backgrounds rich with Freudian symbolism. The dance sequence started a trend that lasted for decades. Musicals *had* to tell part of their story in ballet form.

Oklahoma! was followed by one huge success after another for Rodgers and Hammerstein: *Carousel* (1945), *South Pacific* (1949), *The King and I* (1951), and *The Sound of Music* (1959). The death of Hammerstein in 1960 brought an end to one of the most productive collaborations in musical theater history. Rodgers would work with other lyricists and librettists, but none was able to equal Hammerstein's skill in combining all of a musical's elements into a tight unity. He is credited with having fully developed the genre of the musical play.

West Side Story

Given the increased use of dance elements in musicals since *Oklahoma!*, the arrival of *West Side Story* in 1958 was inevitable. *West Side Story* is a musical play dominated by intricate ballets, modern dances, and a symphonic score that has since become standard in the repertoire of great orchestras. As an updated version of *Romeo and Juliet*, it also relies heavily on the drama of the doomed love affair. Because of the show's Shakespearean origins, the audience readily accepted the tragic ending.

West Side Story is a product of upscale collaboration. The idea of making *Romeo and Juliet* into a tale of two lovers caught in the feud between rival New York street gangs belonged to Jerome Robbins (1918–1998), a choreographer well known in the world of serious modern dance. Leonard Bernstein (1918–1990), the composer of the score, had been classically trained at Harvard and was destined to become one of the world's leading conductors as well as composers.

Bernstein and Robbins had collaborated in 1944 on a sprightly musical comedy called *On the Town*, which chronicled, mainly in dance, the adventures of three sailors on a twenty-four-hour leave in New York City. The new project resulted in what some critics called "a dance opera," but its underlying drama was never subordinated to the other components, because the libretto was written by Arthur Laurents, a recognized playwright. The work is so versatile and so rich in every element that it is still performed as both a Broadway musical and as an opera. The dance sequences have been taken out of their dramatic context and performed by international ballet companies. Theater companies have even performed love scenes from Shakespeare interspersed with Bernstein's songs. The pairing creates a flowing unity.

The third member of this extraordinary collaboration was the young lyricist Stephen Sondheim (b. 1930), a trained composer in his own right. The lyrics have a simplicity that is not characteristic of Sondheim's later work but are eminently suited to this tragedy.

In *West Side Story*, Romeo becomes Tony, of Polish descent and a reluctant member of the Jets, who respect his sensitivity and idealism but nonetheless expect him to fight when they say the need arises. Their archrivals are the Sharks, young Puerto Ricans battling to own the neighborhood turf and rid their streets of non-Hispanics. The gang members were all played by seasoned ballet dancers, but Robbins's choreography was so filled with athletic leaps and carefully staged fierce encounters that audiences soon forgot that the "gangs" were not really endangering the streets of New York.

Juliet becomes Maria, sister to the leader of the Sharks and therefore sworn to be an archenemy of the Jets. She and Tony meet at a school dance, even as Romeo and Juliet meet at a masquerade ball. The famous Balcony Scene of Shakespeare is transformed into the duet "Tonight," sung by Maria on her fire escape to a lovesick Tony in the alley below. Meanwhile, the Sharks invite the Jets to take part in a "rumble," an all-out street fight, with the victor laying claim to the "turf." Tony is reluctant, aware that the Sharks' leader is Maria's brother. But gang loyalty forces him to take part in the rumble, during which Bernardo keeps baiting Tony, daring him to strike the first blow. Tony holds back, but when Bernardo kills Riff, the Jets' leader and Tony's best friend, the anguished hero kills Bernardo in revenge, even as Romeo slays Juliet's cousin Tybalt in a sword fight.

In Shakespeare, the tragic climax is brought about by a quarantine preventing Romeo from getting a letter assuring him that Juliet is alive and waiting for him. In the dance opera, Tony is deceived into believing that Maria has been killed by her jealous boyfriend. Bereft of all hope, he rushes into a darkened street, pleading with one of the Sharks to end his life. Hearing his voice, Maria rushes joyfully to meet him, but he is shot just before she can reach him. She cradles the dying Tony in her arms as a police siren is heard, too late to prevent the tragedy.

Many of the songs from *West Side Story* have become classics of popular music. In addition to the duet "Tonight," they include the jazzy "Jet Song," the haunting ballad "Maria," and the main theme of the dream ballet, "Somewhere," which tells of a happy land where there is "a place for us" with "peace and quiet and open air." Barbra Streisand chose this song to close her final public concert in 2000.

The Lion King

No one needs to be told about the twentieth-century phenomenon that was Walt Disney (1901–1966). From the first pen-and-ink drawings of Mickey Mouse to theme parks throughout the world, the Disney empire is responsible for the creation of an imaginary reality that has become fundamental for millions. Disney and his successors have created a whole gallery of characters, animal and human, as well as elaborate fantasies based on fairy tales and myths that are indigenous to human society. They have represented the ultimate in escapism for nearly three-quarters of a century. Historians and critics of the humanities may overlook these achievements, or at least to relegate them to a niche in the "popular arts." Indeed, the Disney animated features have all been popular, but this should not be held against them. As early as 1937, with the release of *Snow White and the Seven Dwarfs*, the world's first full-length animated film, the Disney staff of painstaking illustrators gave every indication that they were developing an art form.

Always seeking new worlds to conquer, the Disney empire inevitably turned its eyes to Broadway. Animated creatures on a screen had one kind of reality, but surely live actors embodying them on a stage would add another dimension to its imaginary universe. A musical adaptation of *Beauty and the Beast* opened in 1994 and has had thousands of performances in many different languages. The corporation, with great wealth amassed from films, books, television channels, theme parks, and millions of toys, was able to afford special effects that Broadway had never before seen.

In 1997 the Disney corporation transferred the hugely successful animated film *The Lion King* to the stage, outdoing every Disney venture up to that point. The show gives every indication that it will be a near permanent fixture of the musical stage, a theatrical version of a theme park to which adults return again and again, and for which new generations of enthralled children keep appearing year after year.

The Lion King combines numerous theatrical elements into a unified whole. The eclectic score combines mellow rock music by Elton John with authentic African chants and drumming. A multicultural cast provides a mix of modern and ritualistic dance. The libretto by Roger Allers and Irene Mecchi has a fairy-tale simplicity that echoes Shakespeare's *Hamlet* in its basic story of a young lion prince, Simba, who must find a way to reclaim the throne wrongfully taken by his evil uncle named Scar.

Shakespeare's Hamlet is visited by the ghost of his murdered father and made to promise that he will avenge the king's death. By the middle of the play, since the promise has not been fulfilled, the ghost returns to restate his demand. In the Disney version, director Julie Taymor (b. 1952) assembles all of the singers and dancers into a production number taking place on a series of platforms rising vertically from the stage floor. Gradually appearing is the head of the dead king, who has come back from the grave to urge Simba on.

When first hired to direct *The Lion King*, Taymor faced a daunting task no director had ever been asked to undertake: finding a way to put African savannahs and hordes of animals into a space obviously limited by its physical dimensions, *plus* finding a way to have live actors singing and dancing as animals of many different species. Yes, there had been precedents. Actors had dressed up as bears or horses to make brief comic appearances; but here the animals were the *only* characters in a story that would require nearly three hours to unfold.

Taymor studied Far East puppetry and discovered that Asian audiences were accustomed to the convention of seeing puppeteers on stage, manipulating their figures. Why should not Western audiences also accept such a simple solution? The director decided to use both puppets and live actors only partially clothed as animals, so that no attempt would be made to deceive viewers into believing that the animals were real. Besides, she knew that in the world of fantasy, there is no limit to what the human imagination will accept.

Children quickly adapt to the new rules, and adult audience members are charmed by the game-playing in

Archetypes in This Chapter

Icons and Symbols in Musical Theater

The antihero major modern archetype, found on stage, screen, and television; descendant of the rogue hero (discussed in Chapter 7).

The beauty a woman of extraordinary physical attributes, the implication being that she needs no other qualities to win people over.

The couple the inevitable romantic pairing of a man and a woman.

The prince male equivalent of the beauty: a handsome, rich young man, supposedly the object of every woman's dreams.

The Lion King is the Broadway musical at its most spectacular, as shown in this assemblage of a mask to form the ghost of the hero's murdered father.

Source: © Joan Marcus.

full view. The conventions in *The Lion King* are centuries old but represent a radically different experience for Westerners unfamiliar with the theater of the East and the ancient music of Africa. *The Lion King* is a multicultural opera that goes beyond just casting actors of varying ethnicities: it makes profound use of the arts in which those ethnicities excel.

Spring Awakening

The rock musical and the rock opera have become increasingly ensconced in the Broadway scene. *Rent*, already mentioned in Chapter 1 as a rock adaptation of Puccini's opera *La Bohème*, inhabited a 42nd Street theater for more than a dozen years, testifying to the power of rock to communicate stories of love found and lost or to celebrate the joy of life.

Spring Awakening *is set in 1891, the time period of the German expressionist tragedy on which it is based; but it makes an unusual use of a rock score to represent the submerged feelings of the oppressed students in a rigidly moral school.*

Spring Awakening (2007), however, may be regarded by historians of the musical stage as the consummate achievement in rock musicals to date. It is not a rock adaptation of another kind of musical experience. Its source is a darkly tragic 1891 German play of the same name by Frank Wedekind (1864–1918), a dramatist and poet who, in this work, exposed middle-class moral rigidity, as Ibsen had done in Norway. Unlike *Rent, Spring Awakening* adheres closely to its roots, changing very little of the story and, of special importance, not providing an unbelievable happy ending. This is a tragic rock musical play. There would have been no way to alter Wedekind's original intent without destroying a work that many consider a masterpiece in its own right. Adaptation to the musical stage was risky, and even more so because of the rock score. The time is still 1891. So what is rock music doing in a German prep school of more than a century ago?

The music, so completely out of place for the time and the setting, is an externalization of the suppressed emotions, especially sexual desires, of a teenage student body that has been raised with no knowledge of where babies come from and no one to tell them that their hormonal awakening is natural and not to be denied. In this society, parents never discuss sex, either pro *or* con, with their children; as a result, the children grow up obsessed with the subject and filled with wrong information passed from one student to another in fearful whispers.

Melchior, the hero, is academically gifted and intent on probing the mystery of life, hiding forbidden books under his mattress and reading them late at night. Gradually he achieves an understanding of sexual intimacy as a natural rite of passage, dangerous if suppressed (much as Sigmund Freud theorized, shocking that same society). The result of his awakening is to write an essay explaining the sexual process in considerable detail and distributing it among the student body. He is painfully aware that his close friend Moritz had been so obsessed with misunderstood sexual urges that, unable to study, he failed his exams and committed suicide rather than face his family.

Melchior's girlfriend is the innocent Wendla, who at first resists his protestations of passionate love and his assurance that their sexual coupling would be both natural and beautiful. But Wendla is also a victim of sexual denial that makes her unable to think of anything except being alone with Melchior. They sing one of the show's memorable songs, a slow rock duet called "The Word of Your Body," and are finally able to enjoy intimacy.

Their joy does not last very long. The authorities discover that Melchior has written the shocking essay. He is sentenced to solitary confinement in a reform school. Wendla becomes pregnant, though she does not understand what is happening inside her, and her desperate parents bungle the explanation. Instead, they send her to a doctor who specializes in "handling" these delicate matters, diagnosing her pregnancy as a disease and applying a fatal overdose of medicine.

Perhaps now we can understand how the rock score functions in what would otherwise be a bitterly tragic evening of theater. The chorus of students can both sing and dance, and they break into rock affirmations of sexual attraction and rebellious denunciations of society's repressiveness. These are message pieces, but they are filled with rock's celebration of the Dionysian side of life.

One may well ask whether an 1891 play, however updated by its rock score, has any relevance to our own society. After all, except in some morally conservative areas, a permissive atmosphere prevails. And perhaps therein lies the significance of *Spring Awakening* (though the strength of the drama and the excitement of the music are reasons enough to justify a trip to the theater). The performance may leave critical viewers discussing whether overpermissiveness may not be nearly as harmful as overrepressiveness was in Wedekind's version of middle-class society. Or discussing whether the need to succumb to peer pressure and be part of the group does not constitute its own brand of repression. Like many important works in the humanities, this one awakens not only spring but thought.

Dance

Movements are as eloquent as words.

—**Isadora Duncan**

Pianist Leon Fleisher, discussing the elements of music, puts rhythm first, followed by harmony and then melody. His rationale appears to be that although music can and indeed does exist without either harmony or melody, it has to have a rhythmic underpinning or else it becomes random sound. Many music historians have theorized that rhythm came first, probably as accompaniment to rituals of birth, coming of age, planting and harvest times, death, and burial. These rituals were an early form of dance. Some anthropologists believe that dancing was "invented" even before the emergence of human beings. They point out that chimpanzees, for example, engage in group movements that have a kind of rhythm. At the beginning of this chapter you learned that the ritual known as the Buffalo Dance can be traced back 30,000 years.

The Egyptians are known to have taken part in highly elaborate dance ceremonies in which they imitated the movements of heavenly bodies. Pharaohs required slaves to entertain them with dances that involved unusual gyrations and acrobatic skills. Set around the same period, the Hebrew Bible refers to dance as an expression of joy, as when Miriam, the sister of Moses and Aaron, dances in celebration of the Red Sea escape from Pharaoh's soldiers.

In Greece, beginning around the sixth century B.C.E., the art of the dance became an official form of public entertainment. Dancing became a respected profession, and those with sufficient strength and suppleness of limbs were trained from an early age. During the Middle Ages, dancing was banned by the church, probably because it was associated with pagan rituals and religions. Folk dancing, however, was practiced despite the ban, and remnants of it survive to the present time. A dance still performed in May in many parts of the world has medieval origins. Circling a pole decked out in crepe paper of varied colors and chanting traditional words, the dancers probably do not realize that their joyful activity dates back to an annual but forbidden spring mating ritual. The May dance is a symbolic rite of passage, as the following chant exemplifies:

Weave, weave, weave me a rainbow
Out of the falling rain,
Weave me the hope of a new tomorrow,
Fill my cup again.

During the plague of 1348 known as "the Black Death," the terrified populations of Western Europe released their fears by performing the "dance of death," usually led by a dancer dressed as a skeleton. Children danced in a circle to this chant still heard on streets and in playgrounds.

Ring around the rosey,
A pocketful of posey,
Ashes! Ashes!
All fall down!

Few who perform the chant today think about the original meaning of "rosey"—a reference to the reddish boils on the skin of those afflicted with buboes (hence "bubonic" plague). Today's young dancers fall on the ground probably giggling in excitement, unaware that they are reenacting a musical drama, told mainly through movement.

In the thirteenth century, an Islamic spiritual leader named Mevlana Rumi established a religious sect, the *Mevlevi Order*, whose members took part in a ritual still practiced today. Known as whirling dervishes, they turned ever faster and faster until they achieved a trancelike state, which they believed liberated their souls from earthly bondage and allowed direct union with Allah.

In the later Middle Ages, as major cities grew in size and sophistication, dance became a highly refined art for which only the graceful few were suited. Mimes, such as those in Italy's celebrated *commedia dell'arte* (Chapter 7), studied dance to give their bodies the flexibility required to execute any sort of movement, including the pratfall (a sudden collapse onto the buttocks that seems both unexpected and painful but is in reality a skillfully rehearsed and executed movement, and still a mainstay of the circus clown).

In the early eighteenth century, the *kathak* dance was integral to the entertainment at the royal court of Lucknow, a cultural center of northern India. Originating as a stylized method of telling stories and educating viewers about their mythological past, it became a highly professional art form with its elegantly swirling movements, lightning-quick pirouettes, sudden poses, rapid stamping of feet, and subtle gestures capable of expressing the fullest possible range of emotions. Dancing had long been indigenous to Indian culture, as it was to other cultures separated by time and geography.

There is much evidence to support the contention that dance is a universal human need and that it may have been one of the earliest art forms to demand professional skill. While folk dancing also has ancient roots, enjoyed by all people as a joyous celebration of community, viewers must have been content at times to remain seated while professionals whirled about, executing highly complicated steps. The seated audience probably swayed or tapped their feet in rhythm. Dance is an art form that readily invites empathy. When you unconsciously move your feet as you watch others dance, you become a participant. Watching dance awakens the sleeping spirit in all of us, a spirit that longs to be free.

Ballet

Two principal dancers in a statuesque moment.

Source: Digital Vision/Alamy.

Acknowledged by many critics, historians, and viewers to be the premier form of dance art, ballet developed from Italian street mime cultivated into a court entertainment for the aristocracy. Ballet is fundamentally a series of controlled body positions and movements that require years of training to be perfected, yet must seem effortless to an audience. Ballet dancers appear to float across the stage, and viewers forget the unnaturalness of the motion. Ballet forces the body to do things the body is not basically equipped to do. In training, for example, a fundamental position is to have the feet turned outward with the heels touching. Most of us can form a "V" with our feet, but ballet dancers, after touching their heels, can form a straight horizontal line with their feet!

Female dancers must learn how to stand on their toes for unnaturally long periods. Male dancers must be strong enough to hold a ballerina, sometimes with one hand. They must be muscular and lithe at the same time, their bodies resembling classical statues. To the French and the Russians in the nineteenth century must go the credit for having formalized the *art* of ballet. French ballet schools developed the basic positions and movements that are still taught, and they all have French names. A **plié** is a lowering of the torso while keeping the feet turned outward, as described above. A **jeté** is a leap, executed so lightly that the landing makes almost no sound. A **pirouette** is performed while standing on the toes of one foot as the body spins round and round, faster and faster. If the *pirouette* is observed closely, the viewer will see that the dancer does in fact put the other foot on the floor every so often in order to maintain balance, but the greatest dancers whirl so rapidly that they almost become a blur and the foot "rest" goes unnoticed.

I put my dancing feet before my allegiances to friends and lovers, even husbands: before my home. . . . I gave one hundred percent of myself to my art, and my art has repaid me.

—**Alexandra Danilova**

Classical ballets usually tell a story, but viewers generally don't come for plots. They come to see exquisite movements and the statuesque use of the human body. Classical ballets follow a traditional format. There is an ensemble of male dancers and ballerinas as well as a male and female soloist. The ensemble performs intricate movements perfectly synchronized. The solo ballerina then does an elaborate routine on her toes (**en pointe**), with many pirouettes. She exits rapidly as the male soloist leaps onto the stage, also with many pirouettes, but adds athletic jumps and body spins in the air. The great dancers—such as Nijinsky, Nureyev, and Baryshnikov—are famous for the amazing heights they could reach in their spins. Finally, the ballerina returns, holds out her arm to her partner, and the two perform an exquisite duet (**pas de deux**) to a slow, melodious accompaniment.

French Ballet: *Giselle*

Since ballet terms are all French, we should expect the art form to have originated, or at least developed early, in France. By the late seventeenth century, French operas included a ballet, whether relevant to the story or not. By the eighteenth century, French ballet had become an internationally recognized institution. The delicacy of movement and the statuesqueness of the dancers appealed to the French love of classical beauty.

In the nineteenth century, the spirit of romanticism, with its less restrained emotionalism, became popular in France, which gave the ballet world one of its most romantic and enduringly popular works, *Giselle* (1841), with music by Adolphe Adam (1801–1856). The ballet has an unusually appealing story line, as well as traditional components such as the *pas de deux* and a chorus of beautiful young women executing complex movements *en pointe*. The story centers on the love of a maiden named Giselle for an aristocrat named Albrecht, who has courted her, disguised as a suitor on her own social level. Eventually betrayed by him, Giselle dies from a broken heart and is destined to join the ranks of the Wilis (*Willies*), the souls of young women jilted before they reached the altar. The mission of the Wilis is to torment the men responsible. In true romantic fashion, however, Albrecht has a change of heart and, while mourning at Giselle's grave, is visited by her spirit. Instead of tormenting Albrecht, she joins him in one last pas de deux. We know their love will last forever.

Russian Ballet: Tchaikovsky and Diaghilev

Russia has proclaimed itself the dominant force in ballet since the nineteenth century for a number of very good reasons. The first is that Tchaikovsky, discussed in Chapter 6 as a master of romantic melody, wrote some of the greatest scores in the ballet world. Largely because of his music, three ballets—*Swan Lake* (1875), *Sleeping Beauty* (1890), and *The Nutcracker* (1891)—are famous all over the world and have been seen by millions.

These three full-length works all follow the simple story lines of fairy tales and involve magical spells. In *Swan Lake* a prince, melancholy at being forced to select a bride from among the eligible young ladies provided by his parents, goes out to hunt swans. As he is about to shoot one of the birds with his arrow, the Swan Queen intervenes, informing him that she and the other swans are young women transformed by an evil sorcerer. He falls in love with her and promises marriage. During a ball sequence at the palace, the sorcerer enters with his beautiful daughter, who has been made to look like the Swan Queen. The prince announces she is to be his bride, but he catches sight of the real Swan Queen outside the window. Rushing to the lake, he arrives just in time to hold her, dying of grief, in his arms. The story is typical of nineteenth-century sentimental melodrama, but the music and the dazzling choreography, always evident in major productions, more than compensate.

Sleeping Beauty is based on the popular tale of a child who is cursed by a witch, angry at not being invited to her christening, and fated to die when she is sixteen. The evil prophecy comes to pass, but because of the young woman's beauty, her parents refuse to bury her. When a handsome prince hears of her, he journeys to the castle, falls in love, and kisses her lips. The kiss breaks the spell, and they live happily ever after.

The Nutcracker, performed during the Christmas season in hundreds of theaters, often gives children their first exposure to ballet, and adults, perhaps having shared the same experience in *their* childhood, continue to watch it year after year. A little girl is given many expensive Christmas gifts, but the one she loves most is a Nutcracker doll. Late at night, when she sneaks into the parlor to play with her doll, she is suddenly threatened by an army of aggressive mice. The Nutcracker springs to life and, with the assistance of toy soldiers, challenges the mice in battle. The Mouse King corners the Nutcracker and is about to slay him when the girl intervenes and pulls off the mouse's tail. The deed breaks a magic spell, and the Nutcracker turns into a handsome prince, who becomes her guide as she watches a variety of dances from around the world. Eventually she must wake up, but then she, like the viewer, has memories of a wondrous dream.

I don't want people who want to dance. I want people who have to dance.

—**George Balanchine**

Orchestral suites based on themes from these three ballets belong to the repertoire of every major symphony orchestra. And if there were just these and no others, classical ballet would remain a living art form. Having produced many of the world's favorite ballets, Russian companies became internationally famous. *Ballets Russes de Monte Carlo* was founded in 1909 by Sergei Diaghilev (1872–1929), influencing not only the dance world but the entire cultural life of Europe. Diaghilev was a brilliant choreographer with a multitude of skills and interests, but it was in ballet that he found the most intense challenge, combining as it did dance, drama, visual art, and symphonic music.

Next to being the impresario of what was the world's leading ballet company, Diaghilev is famous for having fostered the career of a revolutionary dancer, one whose creative imagination and athletic agility has influenced male dancing ever since. In the opinion of many, Vaslav Nijinsky (1889–1950) was the greatest male dancer of all time. In 1913 Nijinsky choreographed and starred in *The Rite of Spring* (Chapter 6), a work that alternately bewildered and scandalized viewers accustomed to the prettiness of classical dance.

The Nijinsky choreography, with graphic depictions of mating rituals, and the dissonant score by Stravinsky proved far too sensational for the opening-night audience. That dance, however, would change the direction of ballet, even as the score would change the direction of music. But the transition took a while. Male dancers would have to train hard to come close to Nijinsky's high-flying leaps and spins. As time passed, Nijinsky's athletic style exerted great influence on midcentury artists like Rudolf Nureyev, who, as a star of Britain's Royal Ballet, was adept at both classical ballet and modern dance. Audiences would throng not only to see whether Nureyev could leap as high as Nijinsky, but also to watch in wonder as he performed the prince in *Swan Lake* to Margot Fonteyn's Swan Queen.

The man who brought Russian ballet to the West was George Balanchine (1904–1983). In the late 1900s he founded the New York City Ballet, and in 1934 the School of American Ballet, dedicated to the training of American dancers so that companies on this side of the Atlantic would not have to import their stars from Russia. Balanchine married the great ballerina Maria Tallchief, who had been born on an Oklahoma reservation. He ultimately became one of the world's finest dancers, who could choreograph *Swan Lake* with the best of them, but he declined to play the role of classical snob. He used jazz motifs in his dances, and even teamed up with Rodgers and Hart for the musical comedy *On Your Toes*, choreographing an elaborate ballet, *Slaughter on Tenth Avenue*, which was called groundbreaking by dance critics because it used intricate and highly athletic dance combinations to tell a story of passion and murder in a Manhattan saloon.

Modern Dance

Modern dance is not so called just because of its roots in the modern world. It is a definite style of serious dance that consciously has broken with the classical tradition and demands equal respect as an art form in its own right with its own label. Its ancestor was *The Rite of Spring*, which gave dancers freedom of movement and body positions.

Art is the only way to run away without leaving home.
—Twyla Tharp

Modern dance begins with classical positions and movements, then adds complex variations: leaping; catching and being caught; falling to the floor, rolling, and then springing up effortlessly; much physical contact with other dancers. In early modern dance, for example, a male dancer might lift a female dancer, hold her aloft with one hand, then suddenly release her as the audience gasps and she slides down and around the body of the male, reaching the floor with a leg extension that can reach to his neck.

Dancers in the modern school undergo double training. They must spend years mastering the basic positions and movements of French ballet. In addition, they must do arduous exercises and weightlifting in order to perform athletic movements in the style of Nijinsky and Nureyev. One of the star dancers in Balanchine's company was Edward Villella (b. 1936), who started out as a boxer, then brought his muscular physique and dazzling footwork to the world of dance. Equally at home in classical ballet, Villella created a number of works that combine traditional movements with the extreme athleticism and agility demanded by modern dance. In 1988 he founded the Miami City Ballet, which rapidly gained international recognition.

A dancer who has risen to the top of his profession in both ballet and modern is Mikhail Baryshnikov, born in Latvia in 1948. His athleticism and super-conditioning even at the age of fifteen made him a star with the famed Kirov company of Leningrad in only a few years. Dissatisfied with being limited to standard ballet repertoire, Baryshnikov immigrated to the United States because he wanted to perform in musical theater as well. Probably more than any other dancer today, he has created legions of new fans for modern dance. Audiences packed theaters to see his breathtaking leaps, which often exceeded those of Nijinksy in height. He is also famous for the longest midair spins, from which he would recover in a graceful leap and go immediately into a pirouette, spinning so fast that he was almost invisible.

One of the pioneers in modern dance was Martha Graham (1894–1991), who continued to create new works until she was well into her eighties. American-born, Graham introduced strenuous movements into her narrative dances. Whereas in classical ballet the body is held rigid for long periods, Graham trained her dancers to be flexible and loose of limb and able to contract themselves inwardly as well as extend outwardly. There are much lifting and rolling of shoulders in Graham, and much floor work. Her style requires dancers to express emotion with their bodies, and therefore their bodies have to be as free as possible. Freedom of movement may sound simple, but it also takes years to achieve.

Graham was deeply rooted in America and its traditions. She studied many kinds of folk dancing and used them for her masterwork, *Appalachian Spring* (1947), with its great symphonic score by Aaron Copland (Chapter 6). But these are stylized folk dances, some in unexpectedly slow tempos. Rhythmically the work is profoundly complex. Instead of adhering to customary combinations in which dancers count from one to eight in time to the music, Graham allowed the music and the story to dictate what the count should be. Watching a Graham work, you would not always be aware that there *is* underlying rhythm, so completely fused are the dramatic moment, the music, and the movements.

Graham, along with Agnes de Mille, the choreographer of *Oklahoma!*, greatly influenced the Broadway stage. Both found the means of telling a story without sacrificing the grace and beauty of the dance. In 1975 a show called *A Chorus Line*, with choreography by Michael Bennett, dispensed with the traditional hero and heroine who were destined to become "a couple" in the classic musical comedy plot. Instead, it focused on a group of dancers auditioning for a Broadway show. The story of each dancer was told in a brief vignette, and parts of an elaborate

Mikhail Baryshnikov has bridged the gap between the worlds of ballet, modern dance, and popular musicals.

Source: Andrea Comas/Corbis.

production number were worked in as audition pieces. The dancers were dressed in rehearsal clothes—mostly shorts, T-shirts, and sweatpants. In the show's famous finale (Color Plate 27), the entire ensemble suddenly reappeared in white and gold suits, top hats, and canes, and performed the full number in perfect rhythm. Everyone in the finale moved as one ("One" also happened to be the name of the song), but the audience came away having made the acquaintance of distinct individuals who had endured arduous training and bitter rejections in order to *be* that "one." The struggle had been worth it after all, for now they had their moment as part of the magical world of dance.

Modern dance enjoys equal status with classical ballet in the repertoire of major companies. Throughout the twentieth century, far-seeing choreographers kept adding new kinds of movement, making possible more and more complex narratives told through dance. One such choreographer was José Limón (1908–1972), who formulated a new aesthetic rationale, based on the dancer's relationship to gravity. Dancers first develop a sense of weight and methods for translating weight into energy. He also taught techniques of breathing so as to distribute energy throughout the body. His most famous work is *The Moor's Pavanne*, a retelling in dance of Shakespeare's *Othello*.

Ailey's early work benefited greatly from African dance and music traditions, introducing dazzling movements that were new to modern dance. At performances of Revelations, a gospel musical, audiences have been known to dance in the aisles.

Also of great importance were the contributions of Alvin Ailey (1931–1989), founder in 1958 of the dance company that still bears his name. When he was a teenager, he became interested in dance, but although he studied with Lester Horton, a major choreographer, he believed professional opportunities would be limited because he was African American. At the time, most dance companies were not racially mixed. In 1953, however, Ailey's debut performance was a thunderous success. After the death of Horton in that same year, he became manager of the company. In 1958, encouraged by his further studies with Martha Graham and Doris Humphrey, he founded the Alvin Ailey Dance Theater, which has won worldwide acclaim and continues long after his untimely death to train young dancers, create major new works, and tour in America and abroad.

Ailey's early work benefited greatly from African dance and music traditions, introducing dazzling movements that were new to modern dance. His 1958 *Blues Suite*, with its heavy percussion, New Orleans blues themes, and barrelhouse setting, gave audiences not only electrifying dance patterns but also a sobering confrontation with the realities of a poverty-stricken class in the South. But Ailey was also steeped in classical training. The dance included traditional male and female partnering as well as folk and jazz dancing. The hallmark of the company continues to be its eclectic mixture of strains from different ethnic backgrounds and from ballet and modern dance.

One of the favorite works in the company's repertoire is *Revelations*, based on gospel and spiritual music, depicting Sunday church worship, a baptism ritual, a quiet solo of personal union with God, and a rousing finale in which the ensemble joyously celebrates togetherness. Audiences of all ethnicities regularly clap their hands to the music, and some have even been known to dance in the aisles.

Ailey's company won many major awards from the start but in some quarters was criticized for not opening its doors to performers of all races. In 1963, Ailey integrated the company and incorporated styles and techniques from Japanese and Native American dance traditions that he had learned while studying with Horton. The varied, international repertoire of Ailey's dancers led to an invitation from the Soviet Union. They became the first American troupe to tour that nation in half a century.

Paul Taylor (b. 1930) sees dance as the human form engaged in ever changing patterns and astonishing athleticism. Most of his work is non-narrative and uses a wide range of music, from Bach to popular standards. He has taken many pop dance forms, such as the jitterbug, and translated them into high art performed by rigorously trained dancers. Like most choreographers, Taylor has notated his works carefully and made them available for restaging by other companies. A frequent critical objection, however, is that unless a company is highly trained in the Taylor technique, the works are not shown at their best.

Twyla Tharp (b. 1941) is a choreographer who combines elements of classical and modern dance with jazz and pop music. Originally a member of the Paul Taylor company, she went on to develop her own style. Her loose-limbed dancers, exhibiting freedom of the body attained through years of disciplined exercises, adapt readily to many kinds of music often thought unsuitable for dance. For example, she created a piece set to the songs of Frank Sinatra, which change

The Alvin Ailey Dance Theater combines classically disciplined movement with modern freedom of expression.

Source: Julie Lemberger/Corbis.

rhythm frequently. She also brings humor into the world of dance in such works as *Push Comes to Shove*, created for Mikhail Baryshnikov.

Like Alvin Ailey, Tharp emerged from rigorous classical dance training to become highly individualized in her approach, combining ballet, modern, jazz, and tap—accompanied by as broad a range of music as the world of dance has heard. In 1973 her ballet *Deuce Coupe* juxtaposed classical formations with a soundtrack by the Beach Boys. *Push Comes to Shove* has Mozart interspersed with Scott Joplin rags.

In 2002 she joined forces with singer/composer Billy Joel to create an all-dance musical called *Movin' Out* based on over twenty of Joel's classic songs. The meaning of each piece is translated into movement of varying styles and rhythms. Together they tell the story of six young men and women through the decades of the 1960s and 1970s. The dancers—and consequently their dance styles—change from youthful exuberance to the slower tempos of separation from loved ones and anxieties caused by the war in Vietnam to the sobering return of hardened veterans facing the challenge of a changing nation and their own vanished youth. All of this is presented through song lyrics and dance patterns. *Movin' Out* represents another step forward in the evolution of modern dance: telling a complete story without dramatic dialogue, allowing song and dance to communicate theme and meaning.

Today both classical ballet and the many varieties of modern dance can be offered by the same company on any given night. New electronic sound technology can substitute for live orchestras, allowing regional companies to have repertoires as large and exciting as those of dance theaters in metropolitan areas. Whether or not you live in or near a big city, chances are that a dance company is not too far away, and you can thus treat yourself to the experience of watching the perfection of form and movement.

Folkloric Dance

Folk dancing, like folk singing, is rooted in the ancient customs and values of a given culture, differing from formal dance art in that it requires little or no training and can be performed at any time, in any place. Yet some folk dancing has evolved into high art.

Native American dance varies from one tribal nation to another. Each member of the nation grows up knowing how to execute dances appropriate to a given occasion. In Alaska and Canada, for example, the dead are remembered and honored in frequently performed drum dances involving everyone. Participants wear masks and elaborate costumes. Visitors come from all over to witness the dances and are usually given gifts as a show of hospitality.

In the Northwest there is a Native American tradition known as **potlatch**, a coming together of community members to a feast and dance that celebrate a significant occasion, such as a marriage or a new birth. At one point in the dance, the younger members of the community take over and create their own steps to show the continuity as well as the evolving nature of the people.

Native Americans have had a long unbroken relationship to the earth, and their dance reflects the reliance on and the glorification of nature as provider. The Bear Dance, performed by nations of the American Far West, is a reenactment of a very ancient ceremony ritualizing the hunt and the gathering of enough food to sustain the community, especially through the winter.

In the Plains, the tradition of the **powwow** dance is very strong. It is a component of a tribal reunion and an example of how a folk dance becomes an art form. Throughout its evolution the powwow has developed a codified sequence that is strictly observed. It begins with the pageantry of the Grand Entry, in which young and old participants perform a rhythmic march to a regular drumbeat. This is followed by the group's singing of the tribe's anthem and then a series of dances celebrating activities such as planting, harvesting, courtship, and marriage. Non-natives who are frequent visitors may be invited to join in the dances, but only if they can be trusted to follow the strict guidelines.

A dance form with roots in the folk traditions of various cultures is the **flamenco**, identified with Spain, or more specifically, with the province of Andalusia. It emerged, however, from the contributions of gypsy songs thought to be from India, Hebrew incantations, Moorish (Arab) rhythms, and Andalusian folk songs. Of all the folkloric arts, flamenco is probably the one characterized by the strictest possible rules. It involves guitar playing, singing, and a dance with foot-stamping rhythm, accompanied by hand-clapping (which has become an art form in itself and must be rigorously practiced before it can be performed in public).

Its first professional embodiment occurred in 1842 as part of café entertainment. Within two decades the flamenco had spread to Madrid and other parts of

Spain. Its typical perfomance involved four female and two male dancers, two guitars, and two singers. As a result of the rapidly growing popularity of the dance, the guitar became the leading Spanish instrument, eventually developing into its own art form. Today flamenco guitar solos can be heard in concert halls all over the world.

Flamenco dancers demonstrating the strict guidelines that must be followed.

Source: Denkou Images/Alamy.

Of all the folkloric art forms, none has amassed more international renown than the Ballet Folklorico de Mexico, which has evolved from folk roots into a number of dance companies that perform in many venues, showcasing professional dancers as highly trained as any to be found in other professional companies such as the Alvin Ailey Dance Theater or the New York City Ballet. Under the guidance of Amalia Hernández, the Ballet Folklorico originated in Mexico City in 1952. This remains the most important and honored of all the companies, but all major Mexican cities have their own folklorico, performing certain dances in common with other companies but also specializing in pieces reflecting local mythology and rituals. The mission of each one is to preserve the traditional culture, which has always been rich in dance, and to educate outsiders about the Mexican heritage. Depending on the financial resources of the area, the folklorico presentations can have elaborate costumes and stage sets, or be more sparsely but no less artistically performed.

While the repertoire is constantly changing, certain set pieces form the basis of a performance. The "Stag Dance," for example, is a traditional work in which a male dancer wearing a stag's head is chased by hunters, eluding them cleverly until the very end, when he succumbs to a wound from a huntsman's arrow. In this respect it bears some relationship to the ancient Buffalo Dance mentioned earlier. Other traditional folkloric dances celebrate love, marriage, and the cycle of life. The mood is generally one of joy and pride in an artistic legacy.

The Ballet Folklorico has a well-established dance school in Mexico City and other venues throughout Mexico as well as the United States. The earliest schools were in the Southwest, but folkloric training can now be found in many universities, such as Dartmouth and Princeton. A study of the techniques and contents of the dances is part of many high school and college curricula.

Various companies regularly tour, performing not only in recital halls but in schools as part of the institution's cultural mission. Before her death in 2001, Amalia Hernández carefully supervised the mission, which continues to expand its reach. The Ballet Folklorico de Mexico is a prime example of the humanities as ambassador of good will and cultural enrichment.

Also dedicated to the preservation of a cultural art are those who perform the ancient Buddhist dances of Tibet and Nepal. In the Tibetan city of Karnataka there is a college that offers training to Buddhist monks. The curriculum includes traditional dances performed as religious ceremonies. All of the dancers are monks, and the audience is limited to the students. Hence there is no intent to win wider approval. But a ritual as ancient as this has surely achieved the status of art.

In the first dance, the participants wear black metal caps adorned with peacock feathers. The group enters in a solemn line, making graceful gestures with their hands and moving their feet slowly to the accompaniment of deep-throated

In Tibetan Buddhist dance movements are monotonous, suggesting the void that is life.

Buddhist chants. (You can get some idea of this sound in Philip Glass's music for the film *Kundun*, discussed in Chapter 9.) The dance is intentionally monotonous, because it is a form of meditation. Buddhist meditation (discussed in Chapter 10) is meant to still the emotions and bring about a serene acceptance of existence without the illusions created by ego. Of all the dance traditions in the world, Buddhist dance is the least likely to arouse in the viewer a state of excitement.

In the next dance, colorful silk garments are worn, perhaps because of the Tibetan Buddhist belief that color can enhance, if only briefly, the void that is life. It is understood that a colorful experience is only transitory and, like everything else, soon vanishes. (In Japanese Zen Buddhism, on the other hand, black is the preferred color for all human surroundings, because the addition of color will only foster the illusion that there *is* no void, that life may have a meaning.) But movements are equally monotonous in this dance, as if to counteract the slight heightening of emotion that color will bring.

The final dance is held in the monastery courtyard, and both ordained and student monks participate, wearing white robes and moving in a solemn circle around a fire that symbolizes the brevity of all existence as well as indifference to worldly possessions.

In the Kathmandu Valley of Nepal, by a lake in which a disciple of the Buddha saw what he called a divine light, is a monastery that was built to commemorate the vision. Here the monks practice *Tantric* Buddhism, which involves long hours of meditation until a profound state of total wakefulness, unfettered by the emotions, is achieved. Tantric dances, similar to those practiced in the Tibetan monastery, are regular components of meditation here. The accompaniment, however, is a song rather than a guttural chant, but it has the same purpose: to aid the practitioner in the quest for wakeful detachment from all worldly involvement. Unlike the Tibetan ceremonies, those in Nepal have been videotaped and made accessible to a wider audience.

In this chapter we have explored the many varieties of dance in the human experience. Clearly, movement to rhythmic accompaniment is a universal need both for the dancers and those who watch. Dance can stir the emotions of both viewer and participant, bringing about the catharsis, or purgation of emotions, discussed in Chapter 7 as central to Aristotle's theory of tragedy. Or it can, as in Buddhist dance styles, serve to calm us into a state of detachment from inner emotional stress. Dance, like all of the other disciplines of the humanities, is of vital importance to our lives.

Key Terms

en pointe term used in ballet to indicate standing on one's toes.

flamenco type of dance originating in Andalusia, Spain, involving very precise foot movements and hand-clapping, accompanied by a guitar.

jeté a leap in ballet.

leitmotif a musical theme associated with a particular character or a force, such as fate or a curse, and repeated throughout the work.

libretto the dialogue and lyrics of an opera or musical; also called the book or script.

music drama a musical work in which the libretto is as strong as the music, and the equivalent of a great stage drama.

musical comedy a genre of the musical stressing the songs, which are sometimes easily removed from what is usually a silly plot that may nonetheless have serious undertones, as in *Of Thee I Sing*.

musical play a genre of the musical with a strong plot, much dialogue, developed characters, and songs that flow from the dramatic situation, as in *Pal Joey* and *Oklahoma!*

opera the plural of *opus*, Latin for "work"; a genre of music with sung dialogue that is interspersed with melodic arias and duets.

operetta a lighter version of opera, featuring melodic arias and duets that have little to do with the scene, and with a melodramatic and sentimental libretto that is usually an excuse for having the music.

pas de deux French phrase meaning "step of two"; a dance duet, usually slow, set to melodious accompaniment.

pirouette a spinning movement, executed by the dancer balancing on one foot while the body spins around rapidly.

plié ballet training movement in which the feet are extended horizontally with heels touching, and the torso is slowly lowered into a squat position.

potlatch a Native American community gathering to celebrate significant occasions such as marriage or birth.

powwow a dance performed by Native Americans of the Plains as a means of community unification.

recitative dialogue in an opera that is sung; distinct from the aria or duet, which is more melodic.

singspiel German term for dialogue in an opera that is half-sung and half-spoken.

Topics for Writing and Discussion

1. As early as the seventeenth century, opera composers such as Monteverdi faced a problem with maintaining audience interest in the story. What was that problem, and how did they solve it?
2. Have some fun with opera. Take a familiar fairy tale, updated of course, and write a very short opera libretto for it.
3. *Of Thee I Sing* rose above run-of-the-mill musical comedies because of its libretto and its hilarious satire on politics. Outline your own book for a contemporary musical comedy that does for the present time what the Gershwins did for the 1930s.
4. Study the lyrics to three songs from musicals. Compare them side by side. Which would most easily stand on its own as a poem? Be prepared to read your selection to the class and explain why you think it is a legitimate poem.
5. Dance has been around for thousands of years, but the formal arts of ballet and the various genres of modern dance are relatively recent. What were the origins of formal dance art? Give two or three examples of how this art has changed over the years.
6. If you are fortunate enough to have a heritage that includes dance rituals for special occasions, share a description of one of these with the class. (It's a plus if you are able to provide a little demonstration.)
7. Until late in the twentieth century, couples who went out dancing had a variety of steps and patterns to perform. Analyze present-day dance fads. Are there definite steps and patterns, as was the case with the waltz and the fox trot? Describe one particular dance that is popular today and has a name.
8. Although *Sweeney Todd, the Demon Barber of Fleet Street* is a musical version of a creaky nineteenth-century thriller, it reaches tragic heights. You learned something about tragedy in Chapter 7. Study the plot summary of *Sweeney Todd* and explain why this version, in your opinion, is or is not a tragedy.
9. In this chapter you were introduced to the *antihero* through a description of the musical *Pal Joey*. Explain how this character came to be, at a time when most musicals had the traditional hero and heroine pairings.
10. Reread the plot summary of the musical *Spring Awakening*. Remember that it is based on an 1891 play. What current social issues is it relevant to? Suggest at least one other way in which the updated version is indeed updated.

9 Cinema

Overview

The motion picture, like other arts, is a vehicle of creative expression, and no study of the humanities is complete without including it. Even though it is a most collaborative art form, involving many contributors (think of those closing credits!), genius can be found throughout its history.

After each weekend, the box-office rankings of current films are reported in newspapers and on television, information seldom given concerning art gallery openings or the premiere performance of a new musical composition. Further evidence of public attachment to film can be found each year when nominations and awards are announced. At the Academy Awards telecast, the public is aware at least for one night that film is indeed the most collaborative of all the arts. When all of the participants somehow blend their talents, the result may be a film classic, with a wide following for years to come.

Through the many extra features of a DVD version, we can follow scene by scene the choices made by directors in achieving an effect. We are thus able to understand the reasoning behind camera angles, music or its lack, and the compromises between the final product as shown on the screen and what the director may have originally intended. Documentaries about the making of a film encourage critical analysis, allowing viewers behind the scenes, becoming part of the creative process itself.

This chapter begins with a discussion of the various elements, or *conventions*, of the cinema, for only by understanding their function can we view a film more critically and, if all goes well, with greater enjoyment. Next come milestones in early film history, followed by an analysis of some popular film *genres*, and finally some prominent directors whose work is so completely identified with their personalities and philosophy that they can be called *auteurs*: that is, authors of the film.

The hard-to-please food critic in *Ratatouille*, an animated film for both children and adults, centering on the mature subject of what constitutes critical taste.
Source: The Everett Collection.

Conventions of Film

In film, as on the stage, **conventions** are the conditions of a genre that audiences agree to accept. They include the rules or the grammar of seeing a film.

Beginning readers learn the rules for print—left to right, top to bottom, capital letters, periods, etc. Rules for film begin with a darkened theater, a screen, and a projector causing light to appear on the screen.

The *camera* is a major convention of film, though audiences don't always "see" it there. But the critical viewer is acutely aware at all times of what the camera is up to. The objects on the screen appear distant or close because the camera can change their size at will. Looking at a **close-up**, we take for granted that the face on the screen will not always be that large. The expression on the face will not always be crucial to the action taking place. Sometimes the camera will focus on a letter lying on a desk, and the close-up signals that this item is going to play an important part in what is to come. In the early days of film, when cameras were much less sophisticated than they are now and directors may have had only one camera to work with, a film was often like a photographed play, lacking in close-ups. This lack was also a convention of its time. Nowadays a director who chooses not to employ close-ups would be considered highly experimental.

To be an artist means never to avert one's eyes.

—Akira Kurosawa

Cinematography is the appropriate term for the camera work. Though we are meant to forget the unseen presence of those doing the filming, the critical viewer can find much pleasure in observing whether the camera work adds to film artistry or is simply using tried-and-true techniques, such as the intercut, which is quick back-and-forth images of characters confronting each other, or the **establishing shot**, a scene that identifies where the action is to take place.

Color—or the lack of it—is an important element in cinematography. Before 1936, when the first major Technicolor movie appeared (*The Trail of the Lonesome Pine*), all films were shot in black and white, a convention that is not necessarily an old-fashioned relic to be patiently endured when you are watching an older movie. Some of the best films ever made, such as *Citizen Kane* in 1941, analyzed later in the chapter, derive much of their power from the contrast between light and shadow that black-and-white film makes possible. Although some contemporary filmmakers might still prefer to film in black and white, they rarely do so, because color is demanded by audiences and those purchasing television rights to a film. When a film classic such as *Casablanca* is colorized, however, there is generally an outcry from loyal fans, as if an artist's original had been defaced.

Before the introduction of sound in the talkies, there were silent pictures, with printed cards inserted to indicate necessary dialogue or information. But many of the early films could be understood without such aids. The fact that sound was not possible led to the development of wonderful screen pantomime, such as that epitomized in the work of Buster Keaton or Charlie Chaplin, also discussed later in the chapter.

Background music guided audience reactions in the days of silent films. Rescuers on horseback required one kind of music, a tender love scene another. Music continues to be a major convention of film. Like the camera, it is always there, and we are meant to forget that in real life music does not suddenly come out of nowhere. Pounding rock music adds excitement to scenes of brutality among criminals on city streets. The Simon and Garfunkel song "The Sounds of Silence" underscored the bewildered search of the alienated young hero of Mike Nichols's *The Graduate* (1968). Sometimes music is used as ironic counterpoint to what is being shown, as in Oliver Stone's 1978 antiwar film *Platoon*, in which a scene of violence and atrocities is played against the slow and melodious sounds of Samuel Barber's "Adagio for Strings." The actual sound of silence is so unnatural to a movie audience accustomed to music that it calls attention to itself and seems experimental.

As with the convention of the close-up, the director who chooses not to use music may limit to a smaller audience the appeal of the resulting film.

Point of view is the way the camera is positioned in any given scene so it is clear which character or which mind is experiencing the action. In a murder mystery, for example, the detective's consciousness may be pivotal, and scenes are shot from his or her viewpoint. If all of the other characters are suspects, we should not be allowed to see things from their perspective. On the other hand, if the central character is a clever thief whom we really don't want to see caught, the camera might keep us in that character's mind.

Sometimes the point of view is that of the omniscient director, and the camera will focus on first one, then another character, according to the core of a given scene, but we are not asked to follow the fortunes of one particular character. A sign that the director is shifting into a character's point of view is a close-up of that character.

The same scene can be shown from more than one point of view. In Akira Kurosawa's *Rashomon* (1950), each witness to a crime describes the events in a different way. A film may also begin with confusing dialogue and action that seem to spring from no point of view. The Mexican film *Amores Perros* (2000) begins with a car chase and frantic dialogue by the occupants of one car about the effort to stop the bleeding of a dog. The audience doesn't know the identity of the occupants or why they are being chased. Then there is a crash, and the first of three stories begins, each from a different point of view, showing the varied impact of the crash on the lives of the characters. By the end of the film, the three stories come together, and the importance of the accident is revealed in the line "God laughs at those who make plans." We finally understand why there is no focus on one character throughout the film. The director has become a philosophical observer.

The convention of *time* is as flexible as the director chooses to make it. An action meant to last a minute can be prolonged on screen for several minutes, as the camera focuses on separate objects or people and returns to them again and again. A 1925 film about a massacre, Sergei Eisenstein's *The Battleship Potemkin*, shows the brutality of soldiers firing on civilians. Details—a horrified face, a baby carriage careening out of control, shattered eyeglasses—are shown more than once in a scene lasting far longer than its action in real time. Eisenstein is credited with pioneering in the convention of the **elongated moment**, or the slowing down of time.

D. W. Griffith (1875–1948), often considered the first giant of film art, created a new convention called the **lingering take** for his three-hour epic *The Birth of a Nation* (1915). This kind of shot remains on the screen for a longer interval than the plot requires. It is still used in cinema and television when the director wants to arouse the audience's curiosity. In a mystery, for example, the camera may move, or **pan**, from one suspect to another, pausing on one of them to make the audience think they have seen the guilty person. Usually they haven't.

The opposite is the convention of *compressed time*. In some early movies, the passage of time could be shown by the riffling of calendar pages, or even an insert card with the words "That evening" or simply "Later." A common time-compression device is to show, for example, a tree with bare branches, which then dissolves into a tree covered with blossoms, and the audience knows at once that the season has changed. A more sophisticated technique is to use a close-up of an object in the hands of a child, for example, and then the camera pulls back to show that the object is now in the hands of a different actor playing the same character as an adult. In Joseph Strick's *A Portrait of the Artist as a Young Man* (1977), a pair of eyeglasses worn by one character serves this purpose.

A **dissolve** occurs when one scene fades into another, a technique that replaced the older fading to black to mark the end of a scene. The dissolve often marks a transition in time or place. One scene is fading out as another is superimposed. In one of the cinema masterpieces of the twentieth century, *Casablanca* (discussed later in the chapter), the protagonist, Rick, sits alone in his café late at night while the room in back of him slowly changes into a scene in Paris, the subject of his thoughts.

Deliberately *slowing down* the film signals a lyrical, dreamlike scene, perhaps a beautiful memory or fantasy. Shutting it down completely results in a series of still photographs or **freeze frames**, a technique used by François Truffaut at the beginning of *Jules and Jim* (1961) and later by Martin Scorsese in his gangster film *Goodfellas* (1990).

Deliberately *speeding up* the film makes the characters either comical, like Mack Sennett's Keystone Cops of the 1920s, or surreal and mechanical, like the thugs in *A Clockwork Orange* (1971) fighting each other in fast, jerky movements—all to the music of the equally fast Rossini overture to *The Thieving Magpie*. The unnatural speed produces a sense of machines rather than human beings, with no more lasting effects than the violence in an animated cartoon.

Just as time can expand or contract, so too can space. An example of the **tracking shot** is found in the 1939 *Gone with the Wind*, when Scarlett O'Hara (Vivien Leigh) rushes wildly into the street to find the family doctor. Blundering onto a scene of unburied corpses, and in her dazed condition at first unaware of where she is, Scarlett slowly perceives she is in the midst of death on a scale she has never dreamed of. As the camera slowly backs away, the scene opens wider and wider to reveal hundreds upon hundreds of bodies. The tracking shot is achieved by placing the camera on rollers or a slowly moving platform so that it can track inward or outward, or even complete a circle around characters, as in the famous kissing scene in the 1959 film *On the Beach*, which also involved the elongation of real time. Tracking involves the continuous movement of the camera, without pausing for individual shots. Robert Altman's film *about* film, *The Player* (1992), opens with an eight-minute tracking shot that moves through a film studio and introduces the main characters in the various buildings on the lot, with one of them mentioning the very tracking shot as it is taking place.

The **cut** may be the most familiar convention. In this context, the word has two meanings. As a command from the director, it means "stop." As a technical term, it signifies the movement of the camera from one character or scene to another. If the director does not fade the camera from one scene to the next, he or she will use the cut, sometimes a *quick cut*, so the audience finds itself in another place before it even realizes that the preceding scene is over. The quick cut accelerates the rhythm of a fast-action film. On rare occasions in film, but more frequently on television, the **flip** changes the scene as rapidly as one can turn a coin from one side to another.

Film monsters have frightened audiences ever since the giant ape King Kong overwhelmed the comparatively tiny human object of his love. Building the figure of Kong and manipulating his movements in the jungle and on the side of the Empire State Building required ingenious use of animation techniques. Modern filmmakers can use computers to whip up a storm or devise a creature threatening the planet. We are living at a time when filmmakers are like guests at a buffet table filled with a wide array of *special effects*.

These conventions of film are so familiar that to audiences caught up in the story, there might seem to be no other way to tell it. Yet they have been challenged by a manifesto called "Dogma 9" written by Danish film director Lars von Trier, that demands "pure cinema" from directors who agree to make pictures look and sound as natural as possible. Films are to be photographed with handheld cameras, without using artificial light, optical effects, filters, special effects, or speeding up or slowing down of the camera to alter time. The length of each film is the time needed for the events to take place, as was the case in von Trier's *The Celebration* (1998), about adult children marking the birthday of their father and revealing some unpleasant secrets as they do.

More recently, in *Dogville* (2003), von Trier used even more experimental techniques to tell an even more unpleasant story. Ridding the film of all artificial aids, in a manner reminiscent of Thornton Wilder's play *Our Town* (discussed in Chapter 7), von Trier shot the film within an almost bare studio, with a minimum of props and with actors using pantomime to tell the story of a refuge-seeking woman (played by Nicole Kidman) who agrees to work for her benefactors but who then becomes the victim of their greed and sadism. Von Trier insists on making films that are the opposite of escapist, and to do so, he doesn't mind doing away with the conventions audiences have come to expect.

Photography is truth. And cinema is truth twenty-four times a second.
—Jean-Luc Godard

Some Early Milestones

The origin of motion pictures can be traced as far back as 1824, when Peter Mark Roget, creator of the popular *Thesaurus*, formulated a theory called "The Persistence of Vision with Regard to Moving Objects." Roget gave some thought to something we all do thousands of times every day: *We blink our eyes.* He realized that when the eyes are momentarily covered as we blink, vision should be interrupted by intervals of blackness, but vision is continuous. The reason, he determined, is the eye's ability to retain an image for a split second after vision is stopped: that is, during the time it takes for the eyelid to close and reopen. Though the eyes keep blinking, the images retained keep overlapping each other, producing an *illusion* of continuous vision. If the object of vision is in motion, the eye is actually absorbing a series of individual "frames," though it sees fluid movement.

Soon after the publication of Roget's theory, entertainers developed the trick of showing an audience drawings of a figure in successive states of motion. The individual drawings were stacked together and held firmly so that the pages could be flipped through rapidly. The figure actually appeared to move. During the mid-nineteenth century, the development of photography made people hungry for tricks in which pictures of actual people replaced drawings. Inventors on both sides of the Atlantic began to develop mechanisms to move the pictures faster and create an ever better illusion of motion. One such mechanism was a circular drum with slits through which the eye peered. Inside the drum, still images were fastened, and when the contraption spun around, the eye saw fluid motion.

Thomas Edison invented the movie projector, but it was his assistant who made the first movie, which lasted ten seconds.

The invention of the motion picture camera and projector is attributed to Thomas Edison (1847–1931), who had made the first "peep show," a machine with a slot to look through and a crank handle for turning the pictures inside. This led to the building of penny arcades, where the public could play with the new technology. But Edison, at first more concerned with reproducing sound, concentrated on the earliest phonograph, and he put aside his work on simulated motion. One day in 1889, his assistant amazed him by putting sound and sight together in a ten-second movie of a person who seemed actually to move and speak.

By 1896 projection technology had advanced to a point at which people could go to the movies to watch extremely brief films presenting one action, such as someone swimming, running, or starting to sneeze. These novelties were presented as interludes in the more important entertainment of the time, live singing and dancing on the vaudeville stage. Full-length films appeared soon after the turn of the century.

Art and Propaganda I: D. W. Griffith

Griffith has been called the father of film because he consolidated and expanded many of the techniques invented by his predecessors and was the first to go beyond gimmickry into the realm of art.
—**Louis Giannetti**

In 1915, when the elegant and huge Strand Theatre opened on Broadway, the director D. W. Griffith gave *The Birth of a Nation*—all three hours of it—to an adoring and dazzled public. This was the same year in which Louis B. Mayer started the company that was to become M.G.M. In that brief span from 1899 to 1915, movies had arrived as a mature form of entertainment, crafted by skilled artists like Griffith.

The film, which dealt with the American Civil War and the Reconstruction period, established movies as a mass medium. Griffith imposed his own point of view on history, one that was sympathetic even to the attacks of the Ku Klux Klan on carpetbaggers, the money-seeking politicians and scam artists from the North who came to the South with false promises of rebuilding shattered homes and cities. Many critics praised the marvelous cinematography and the film's epic sweep, hailing Griffith as the first genius of the new art form, but others denounced the director as a racist who used movies as propaganda. At any rate, the film had everyone talking, and the more intense the controversy, the longer the lines in front of the theater.

The Birth of a Nation was the first film to exhibit a definite directing style. Griffith's camera moves in for a close-up at a climactic moment, then cuts to a scene that moves at a different tempo. His work has been called rhythmic, because of the editing, which does not simply tell a story but controls the pace at which the story is experienced by the audience.

The film also introduced the lingering take, which became Griffith's trademark. During one famous moment, a young Confederate soldier, rushing across a battlefield, stops at the sight of a corpse lying on the ground. He recognizes that this Union soldier had been his closest friend before the war. The grief is short-lived, for he is suddenly pierced by a bullet and falls across his friend's body. Instead of dissolving the scene, Griffith allows the camera to hold the moment silently. There they are, two friends, both dead, two young lives never to realize their human potential.

In summing up the contribution of Griffith to the history of movies, one critic, Gerald Mast, wrote, "The film remains solid as human drama and cinematic excitement, flimsy as social theory."[1]

Art and Propaganda II: Sergei Eisenstein

Propaganda in a different style was offered in 1925 by the Soviet director Sergei Eisenstein (1898–1948). When the Bolsheviks gained power after the overthrow of the Russian czar in 1917, the first leader of the Soviet Union, Vladimir Lenin, recognized the power of film to instruct the public with a message favorable to the

One of the most famous scenes ever filmed, Eisenstein's Odessa steps sequence set a new standard for screen editing technique.

Source: Museum of Modern Art, Film Stills Archive.

state. Eisenstein was chosen to commemorate an unsuccessful Bolshevik uprising against the czarist regime in 1905 in his film *The Battleship Potemkin*. The film features a now famous episode that supposedly recreates a horrifying event in which soldiers loyal to the czar massacre hundreds of innocent civilians on the town steps in the city of Odessa. The massacre apparently never happened, but the film is widely admired for its editing techniques, especially in the famous Odessa steps scene, and is still required viewing in all film schools.

Eisenstein's Odessa Steps sequence in Potemkin *revolutionized the art of film editing.*

The film was shot on location, using a flight of steps deemed appropriate for the action. The sequence, six and three-quarter minutes long, depicted a minute or two of real time and required the splicing of 157 shots. The sequence begins with 57 shots that show an assortment of happy and unconcerned townspeople on the steps. Most significant of all is a young mother wheeling her baby in a carriage.

Then the soldiers on horseback come thundering to the top of the steps, splattering carnage as they ride. A little boy is separated from his mother and crushed to death in the stampede. The mother, finding her son's body, lifts him as an appeal to the soldiers, who respond by gunning her down. Back to the baby carriage sequence. The mother who had been wheeling the baby carriage is mangled by Cossack sabers. Now there is a close-up of the abandoned carriage, rocking back and forth dangerously on the edge of the steps, pushed ironically over the brink as the mother, bleeding to death, leans against it for support. A close-up

Film is strongest when it makes greatest use of what is peculiarly its own–the ability to record time and space, slice them up into fragments, and glue them together in a new relationship.

—**John Bigby**

shows the innocent child inside the careening vehicle, which is hurtling down the steps, over and around hundreds of corpses. Another character is an apparently cultured woman wearing fragile reading glasses. Throughout the massacre the director returns to her, and each time she is splattered with blood. Finally we see a Cossack rider slashing at something out of our view, followed by a rapid cut to the woman's face. She has been mortally struck in the eye, but we do not actually see the saber strike her. Eisenstein instead gives us a close-up of the glasses lying on the steps, broken.

Although Eisenstein was a loyal Communist Party member and was committed to the Soviet doctrine of art as Communist instruction for the masses, he was also an artist and used film in an innovative way that went far beyond mere propaganda. While using film for Soviet propaganda, Eisenstein nevertheless could not ignore the artist within him.

Major Film Genres

Hollywood's a place where they'll pay you a thousand dollars for a kiss and fifty cents for your soul.

—**Marilyn Monroe**

Film genres—for example, a farce or a three-hankie sentimental melodrama—were born almost as soon as movies moved beyond short sequences and began to tell stories. By the mid-1920s, the tastes and preferences of the movie-going public controlled what studios could present. Up until the mid-1930s, when films began to reflect serious social issues brought on by the Great Depression, demand was greatest for formula plots and big-name stars performing in a number of different genres. Popular were westerns and gangster films, with mainly predictable stories designed for quick and easy production to take advantage of public hunger for entertainment. But there was also an audience for language-oriented plays about the marriage problems of those affluent enough to have escaped the widespread poverty of the Depression. This was a genre that can be called the *filmed play*. Directors used stage-trained diction coaches to turn film stars into replicas of British actors, carefully articulating each word and projecting their voices in a manner more suitable for the stage than for screen close-ups. Most of these filmed plays are of interest mainly to film historians, as are the films of one-time screen idols Rudolph Valentino, Clara Bow, and Theda Bara, which seem excessively emotional today, with their broad gestures and exaggerated facial expressions.

In this section we analyze several screen genres that are still prevalent, however much they have changed with the times.

Slapstick Comedy: Sennett and Chaplin

The director Mack Sennett (1884–1960) was known for films filled with **slapstick**, rapid and violent comic action in which people completely lost their dignity, got struck in the face with pies, crashed their cars into each other, and wound up getting doused with water. Sennett's world is one of total chaos, kept in disorder by a band of idiotic, incompetent, bungling policemen known as the Keystone Cops.

Today we tend to think that the speeded-up, jerky movements of the Sennett films were unplanned consequences of early technology. Nothing could be further from the truth! Sennett became obsessed with the sight gag and the potentially unlimited resources of film to provide it. He photographed action at an average of ten frames per second, but he ran the film through the projector at an average of eighteen frames per second—almost twice as fast as it really occurred in the studio. The effect was to dehumanize the characters so that the violent catastrophes—Sennett's stock in trade—could not be taken seriously.

While working for Sennett, an aspiring young comic named Charles Chaplin (1889–1977) happened to put together a funny costume to wear in a crowd scene, probably as a means of getting a little attention. That costume became his signature outfit and would be worn again and again. In baggy trousers and shoes much too big for him, Chaplin became the Little Tramp, the prototype of the social misfit. Chaplin's developing interest in character, not sight gags, as the main source of comedy led him to leave Sennett and strike out on his own. The result: Charlie Chaplin became the first truly big and international star.

The Little Tramp becomes part of the machinery in *Modern Times*, a film showing Chaplin's sensitivity to social issues.

Source: S.S. Archives/Shooting Star.

The Little Tramp is an incongruity—always out of place wherever he is. Yet he is not completely ridiculous; what humanizes him is the attempt at dignity implicit in both his costume and face. He is also a survivor. In a cruel world he manages to get by. Even though he is thin and weak-looking, he is always able to outwit the villains and bullies who threaten. The ongoing myth in Chaplin films is the eternal triumph of the underdog, a myth with universal appeal.

Chaplin won his reputation during the era of silent films, both short and feature length. Even after the introduction of sound, his films depended largely on his ability to tell a story through mimed actions. He almost always depicted the awkward, inept, and yet lovable underdog who somehow manages to emerge victorious even though the situation nearly overwhelms him. In *The Gold Rush* (1925), the Tramp becomes so hungry he cooks his shoes and eats the shoelaces like spaghetti, delicately twirling them on a fork and dabbing at his mouth to wipe away the imaginary gravy. Though far from nutritious, the shoelaces keep him alive. When his tiny Alaskan cabin is blown to the edge of a cliff during a blizzard, he unknowingly exits through the door—nearly to his doom. Teetering and tottering, he always manages to avoid certain disaster.

a tramp, a gentleman, a poet, a dreamer, a lonely fellow, always gallant, always hopeful of romance

Yet his film *Modern Times* (1936) shows Chaplin to have been sensitive to social issues. It is the story of Depression-era society, of a host of workers either being replaced by a machine or treated like one. In the opening shot, the screen is filled with sheep all headed in the same direction. The next shot is of a horde of people coming out of the subway, looking like a herd of human sheep. In a large factory, Chaplin's character works on an assembly line, where his job requires him to tighten the screws on a product ever more quickly, as the boss keeps increasing the speed of the conveyor belt. In an effort to cut time from the workers' lunch break, the boss considers installing an automatic feeding machine so that each worker can keep his hands free. In the most famous scene, Charlie is caught in the gears and becomes part of the machinery. As usual, there is a woman who loves him, as well as an idyllic dream sequence showing how life ought to be, with simplicity, love, and respect for each individual. And as usual, Charlie is ever gallant in ill-fitting but clean clothes.

Farce: The Marx Brothers

The Marx Brothers—Groucho, Chico, and Harpo—dominated the comic scene during the 1930s into the war years of the early 1940s. Usually on the wrong side of rules and regulations, they managed never to be caught, thus delighting those who cheered for the underdog. Whether it was their inability to pay a huge hotel bill or stowing away on ocean liners, they never played it safe, never walked the straight and narrow. Yet audiences always knew that the rules they broke were somehow unfair, or else codes of behavior that only snooty aristocrats would approve.

Their masterpiece, one of the screen's most memorable comedies, is *A Night at the Opera* (1935), where the three try to help a pair of young lovers succeed in the opera world. In an early scene, Groucho, always the suave con man, and Chico, always the seemingly dumb but really clever purveyor of his own brand of common sense, are negotiating a legal contract for the services of an unemployed tenor. The scene is a hilarious satire on legalese language. The two tricksters keep tearing out of the contract whatever they don't understand, until there is nothing left.

One of the most famous scenes takes place in the tiny stateroom in which the three brothers and the tenor, now smuggled on board, are supposed to be living. Into the narrow space pour repairmen as well as maids who are supposed to be making up beds. In addition to the outlandish number of people, there are several huge trunks. Finally, a chambermaid appears and tells Groucho, "I've come to mop up," to which he replies, "You'll have to start on the ceiling." Then someone opens the door from the outside and everyone cascades into the hallway.

The climactic episode of *A Night at the Opera* is the most uproarious in the film. At a performance of Verdi's *Il Trovatore*, both the tenor and the soprano have been unfairly excluded, according to the brothers, who wreak havoc on the opera with their antics. Harpo (a classic mime, never speaking in any of their films) inserts the music of "Take Me out to the Ball Game" as part of the overture, dutifully played by the orchestra. As detectives and police raid the back of the theater, Harpo evades them by climbing up the ropes that change the backdrops. The tenor on stage continues his aria as inappropriate scenes appear and disappear. The villain of the movie is knocked out. The tenor refuses to continue, so the two lovers finish the opera and all ends happily, something that can happen only in a farce.

An all-time classic scene, the packed room in a Marx Brothers farce, about to explode.

Source: The Everett Collection.

Though elements of slapstick and farce can be found sporadically in contemporary films, the age of the great comics seems to have passed—or at least to be on hold. Film historians disagree on the cause. Perhaps escapism now takes so many forms—graphic violence, overwhelming special effects, sophisticated editing techniques that make films roar by at dizzying speed—that today's audiences can't be satisfied by the relatively slower pace of the classic comedies.

Enduring Appeal of the Animated Film

By the early 1930s, the movie-going public was treated to a lengthy evening of film: in addition to an A movie, or feature, and a B or minor movie, there would be a newsreel and a cartoon. Early animated films were black-and-white, carefully drawn cartoons of mischievous animals with high-pitched voices. Invariably, the smaller animals outwitted their larger predators, who met unlikely disasters. In this manner, Disney's Mickey Mouse and Donald Duck achieved international fame. But with Disney's *Snow White and the Seven Dwarfs* (1936), fans were lining up at the box office to see the first full-length animated feature, with color and artwork never before seen, and an unforgettable musical score.

Animation technology has become so sophisticated that the simplicity of *Snow White* makes it appear dated, but the everlasting charm of the story still delights youngsters and gives older adults a brief excursion back to their youth. The Disney group and others who now employ top-notch artists and computer geniuses have developed the means of populating animated films with both human and animal figures that seem almost three-dimensional. The new world of animated film is a virtual universe with its own reality. Contemporary cartoons use dialogue that is frequently sophisticated enough for adults who accompany their small children. In the 1988 film *Who Framed Roger Rabbit?*, for example, the animated seductress calls attention to her own lack of reality by remarking in a sultry voice, "I'm not really bad; I'm just drawn that way."

The new technology has resulted in works that adults can enjoy, with or without children. One such film is Disney's *Ratatouille* (2006), the story of Remy, a gourmet rat who saves the reputation of a fine restaurant and instructs fellow rats to care about what they eat (which should be more than fuel, please, and certainly not garbage). In the process he overcomes his father's opposition and wins the approval of an inordinately hard-to-please food critic.

Remy has read in a cookbook that the right ingredients must be combined, cooked, and then described with just the right words. He becomes the mentor of a young human named Linguine. By hiding under the latter's hat, Remy is able to supervise the composition of dinners that have patrons and eventually the finicky critic clamoring for more. When the human cooks abandon the kitchen, Remy invites his family to help him prepare an exquisite meal. The happy ending finds (as expected) greater understanding between father and son, a budding romance between the inept Linguine and the female chef he has shyly and distantly adored, and the now satisfied food critic remembering with delight the way Remy's food, particularly the vegetable stew of the title, reminds him of his mother's cooking.

Ratatouille enraptured children with its adorable cartoon rodents, but it also pleased adult critical viewers with its theme of what constitutes good taste—rare for any film and heretofore non-existent in an animated one. The work marks a further development of animation as an art form, with a screenplay in which the realistic three-dimensionality of the characters is matched by the intelligence of subject and language.

Film Noir

During the 1920s, after Congress passed legislation prohibiting the sale and consumption of alcohol, illegal drinking establishments called "speakeasies" were supplied by bootleggers with liquor from abroad or else an infamous and potent local concoction referred to as "bathtub gin." The underworld liquor traffic

Archetypes in This Chapter

Cowboy the archetypal American hero throughout much of the twentieth century; protagonist of hundreds of Western novels and films. Initially a figure characterized by rugged individualism, honor, and forthrightness. Later, after the history of the American frontier became more widely known, the cowboy was looked on with greater skepticism, even cynicism.

Gangster the subject of hundreds of pulp novels and noir movies. The gangster can range from a somewhat benign or even Robin Hood–like rogue figure to something much darker and crueler, the worst embodiment of American capitalism.

Loner a person not committed to anyone or any cause, alienated from society.

Underdog a person weaker than opponents, or poor and scorned, or otherwise considered an unworthy protagonist but who miraculously manages to wind up on top, e.g., Chaplin's Little Tramp.

triggered the rise of organized crime and in film led to the archetype of the gangster, a cynical antihero who justified his contempt for the law with a belief in a generally corrupt world in which those who followed the rules deserved no mercy.

As appealing as the gangster was the private eye, a pay-for-hire investigator, sometimes a former gangster himself, who knew every dark corner of the city and every murderer lurking in the shadows—someone who shot just as straight as the criminals themselves and who, like them, could kill without a moment's reflection. He operated just outside the law, but was forgiven, even admired, by the audience because he never killed for personal reasons. Identifying with him was easy and unambiguous. He was hired to find the bad guys, and did so, even if his methods were straight out of the gangster's handbook.

Like his gangster counterpart, the private eye projected a deep-rooted cynicism about the corrupt world. Both knew that ruthlessness was necessary for survival. He paved the way for what French critics called **film noir** (literally, "black film"), a new genre "characterized by its dark, somber tone and cynical, pessimistic mood." The term was also used "to describe those Hollywood films of the 40s and early 50s which portrayed the dark and gloomy underworld of crime and corruption, films whose heroes as well as villains are cynical, disillusioned, and often insecure loners." Film noir "characteristically abounds with night scenes . . . with sets that suggest dingy realism, and with lighting that emphasizes deep shadows and accents the mood of fatalism."[2]

> *Film noir makes use of dark, shadowy camerawork to evoke a menacing hostile universe in which nothing is as it appears.*
>
> —**Geoff Andrew**

The private eye proved an apt hero for *film noir*. He usually worked alone or with one partner, had no family ties, and was good at his trade, operating on the fringes of society, he knew the underworld and could easily pass for a gangster. At the head of the class in this genre stands John Huston's *The Maltese Falcon* (1941), which created the powerful screen persona of Humphrey Bogart (1899–1957). In earlier films, Bogart had often played ruthless gangsters. In *The Maltese Falcon* he was given the opportunity to add a moral streak to his tough-minded realism, and this addition gave depth to his most memorable screen creations.

Here, Bogart plays Sam Spade, who shoots to kill if he has to and has no illusions about the world or the people who inhabit it. Yet he has his own principles, his own code of ethics, even if others have none. The death of his partner involves him in a labyrinth of dangerous intrigue, murder, and deceit as he seeks to solve the murder: "When your partner is killed, you're supposed to do something about it."

> *. . . Rather than amorality...[it was] honor among detectives. Find your partner's killer even if it meant breaking your heart. Spade has done the Right Thing and ends up the ultimate cynic.*
>
> —**A.M. Sperber and Eric Lax**

Throughout the film, Spade is in trouble with both the police and a conspiracy of international crooks who are seeking the expensive, jeweled bird of the title. Like a warrior of old, Spade is equal to any task, despite being threatened, deceived, cheated, and knocked unconscious. But he has something else: vulnerability. He becomes romantically involved with an attractive woman, a client, who may or may not be worthy of his trust. Yet, love notwithstanding, he never allows emotion to override either his reason or his ethics; instead, he remains a principled realist to the end. In a world like this, he seems to say, you cannot afford to be anything else.

In *Double Indemnity* (1944), by writer-director Billy Wilder, the protagonist (Fred MacMurray) is not a private eye but an insurance investigator, persuaded by a beautiful woman (Barbara Stanwyck) to murder her rich husband and help her collect on a huge policy. The woman pretends to have emotions but is unable to feel either genuine love for the investigator or remorse for the crime they commit. The investigator, recognizing that the woman is not what he had thought, becomes cynical and hard-boiled, the two requirements for a film noir hero. He has seen human nature, including his own, at its worst, but he too achieves a moral vision, confessing to the crime and admitting his corruption.

In film noir, women do not often reach such a vision, nor do the villains ever pretend what they do is morally right—it's only "necessary." Usually absent from the genre are sincere smiles and long discussions of feelings. Typically the point of view is first person, forcing the audience to identify with the hero's dark view of the world.

The genre caught the imagination of European directors such as François Truffaut (1932–1984), whose *Shoot the Piano Player* (1961) was in part a film *about* film, an homage to Alfred Hitchcock (discussed later in this chapter), to the Bogart **persona**, and in particular to film noir. Truffaut was a conscious artist, intrigued by the theme of alienation, strongly suggested by the cynicism of American noir heroes. In *Shoot the Piano Player* the theme of alienation is established in the opening scene. On a shadowy street, one man runs away from another, whom we don't see. He falls and is helped to his feet by a stranger. During their brief walk together, the stranger tells the other man about how he met his wife, about the birth of their first child, how love developed slowly. Will there be a relationship between the two? In other films, the answer is always yes, of course. Here, the two men shake hands and separate. The stranger never appears again. In film noir, that is how the world is.

In another scene, Charlie, the protagonist of the title (Charles Aznavour), hesitates at the door of an impresario who is waiting to hear him audition. Then the door opens and a young woman carrying a violin walks out. There is only the slightest meeting of their eyes, something that in most films suggests that more will come of this encounter. Instead, the camera follows the violinist down a long hallway, down the stairs, and into the street. We never see her again, either.

Resistance to human contact is the core of Charlie's character. He really wants to be left alone to play a tinny piano in a bar and not become involved with the people who need him: his brothers, who are smalltime crooks, the men who are chasing his brothers, and the women who keep being attracted to him. Cynical, philosophical, Charlie remains untouched, almost numb. And yet, before the film is over, he has been forced by circumstances to take part in extortion, kidnapping, suicide, and murder. Like Bogart's character in *The Maltese Falcon*, he cannot remain uninvolved with others. Life doesn't let the loner remain alone, but it doesn't give him much in return.

Romantic Comedy

A movie theater used to be the perfect place for romance, on screen and off, perfect for a Saturday-night date, when couples sitting in the dark could look at other couples on the screen, secure in the knowledge that, no matter what has kept them apart for most of the film, they will surely end in each other's arms.

The man and woman on the screen were apt to be better looking, better dressed, and richer than the couple on a date. For Depression-era audiences, looking at the luxury in a film offered welcome, if temporary, escape. The sets were authentic recreations of Art Deco, and the costumes worn by the actresses were products of world-famous designers. The characters—often a man and woman who love each other—become enmeshed in a ridiculous disarray of circumstances that very nearly but not quite terminate the relationship. After all, if boy meets girl and soon boy gets girl, the film would not be feature length. Instead, boy loses girl through misunderstandings, jumping to conclusions, refusing to listen to facts. Wisecracks substitute for sentimental admissions of affection. True love is hidden rather than spoken, until the end. Audiences knew the admission was coming, even if it didn't turn out that way in real life. But then, who needed a reminder of what real life was like in those hard times?

A classic romantic comedy, *It Happened One Night* (1934) concerns an extraordinarily wealthy young woman (Claudette Colbert) and her attempts to find true love. At the beginning of the picture, the audience knows immediately that she is making a mistake in her choice of mates, but the runaway heiress is so determined to marry a fortune-hunting playboy against her father's wishes that she escapes from the family yacht by swimming to shore. She avoids her father's detectives by taking a bus on which, in the destined-for-each-other world of romantic comedy, she meets a charismatic reporter (played by Clark Gable, the reigning matinee idol of the period), who will, of course, be the true love for which she longs.

As a formerly spoiled and protected but now penniless heiress, she lacks survival skills, but these are quickly furnished by the hero, who intervenes to protect her from a lecherous man in the adjoining seat and offers her the seat next to his. As is customary in the genre, the heroine at first resents the help offered by the reporter.

After a flash flood stops the bus, the heiress and reporter are forced to share the last remaining motel room. The hero, bound by the motion picture moral code of the period, constructs a clothesline with a blanket thrown over it to separate the twin beds, dubbing the divider "the Walls of Jericho." At breakfast he shows her how to dunk a doughnut, a talent her upbringing has never before required. When bus travel is no longer possible, he attempts to explain the technique of hitchhiking. In the film's most famous scene, her provocatively lifted skirt and revelation of a shapely leg prove more effective than the reporter's confident waving of his thumb. In fact, the heiress gradually proves to be the reporter's equal. The romantic comedy heralded the liberation of film women from earlier stereotyping.

A classic romantic comedy of the 1930s, *It Happened One Night* delivered the popular message that love is more important than money.

Source: Photofest, Inc.

The heiress and reporter of course fall in love, and of course are driven apart by circumstances. The heiress seems destined for the playboy. In the romantic comedies of the Great Depression, audiences loved to be reminded that money cannot buy happiness. As the heiress and her father are walking down the aisle toward the altar at her wedding ceremony, her father tells her she is marrying the wrong groom. At the crucial "Do you take this man?" question, the heroine flees the church and dashes to a car conveniently waiting outside—a motif repeated in other films.

The finale, naturally, has to be the return of the heiress and the reporter, now married, to the same motel room, but this time the blanket on the clothesline will come down like the biblical

"Walls of Jericho." The reporter has been so sincerely in love, he has been able to bridge class differences and earn the right to marry the rich man's daughter, to the delight of the audience who may have decided the moral of the film was *love is greater than money*. In point of fact, however, the woman remains an heiress, and her approving father will always be there.

As the shadow of war became more ominous and the effects of the Depression lingered in many segments of the country, the movies continued to provide much needed escape. The difference is that audience tastes had grown more sophisticated. In George Cukor's *The Philadelphia Story* (1939), romantic comedy borrowed elements of the *comedy of manners* from the stages of Broadway and London. With elegant and witty dialogue, the genre purported to show the audience how truly educated and articulate people spoke and behaved. But behavior was often scandalous, a clear violation of manners, and therefore hilarious.

In *The Philadelphia Story*, the heroine (played by Katharine Hepburn, an icon of good breeding and intelligence), engaged to marry a wealthy, respectable, and dull second husband, is still in love with her divorced husband (played by Cary Grant, the most dapper leading man in Hollywood), who shows up at the coming nuptials. Class difference, a common theme in comedy of manners, is evident in the film. The heroine's choice of second husband is a self-made man. Obviously proud to be forming an alliance with Old Money, he believes the marriage will advance his career in business and politics. But he doesn't fit in (as her first husband had indeed). Brash and nouveau riche, he doesn't realize, for example, that his brand-new riding clothes mark him as a newcomer, uncomfortable around horses. Nor does he see anything wrong with the newspaper attention and photographs that will accompany his union with a publicity-hating bride-to-be. He is stuffy, overly earnest, and ill at ease as he tries too hard in an alien world. Worst of all, he lacks wit, a cardinal sin in this genre.

Screen writers had to invent dialogue that was rich and colorful, pungent and amusing, but also stripped of inessentials.

—**Arthur Knight**

The clever lines belong to Hepburn and Grant. They argue throughout the film (which opens with a famous scene in which she breaks his expensive golf club over her knee, after which he reciprocates by pushing her backwards to the floor) and say unpleasant things to each other, but their obvious elegance, pitted against the boorishness of the would-be-groom, inevitably wins the day. They were born for each other. In comedy of manners, the "right" people always triumph.

The heyday of brilliant dialogue and romantic sparring continued into the postwar years when parents of baby boomers, facing inevitable domestic complexities, flocked to movie houses to watch the problems of other married couples that were inevitably resolved satisfyingly. George Cukor's *Adam's Rib* (1949) starred the now legendary Hepburn with the sparring partner with whom she would make eight films, Spencer Tracy. Less overtly comedic than Grant, Tracy usually projected an inner wisdom that Hepburn's characters always recognized and could never resist. Not that they didn't bicker as expected. In the film, Hepburn and Tracy are two attorneys married to each other. Hepburn is defending an abused wife who has shot and seriously wounded her husband, whom she discovered in the arms of another woman. The plot gains its sparkle from the fact that Tracy is the prosecuting attorney.

What sets *Adam's Rib* apart from other romantic comedies is that, despite the undercurrent of true love that persists behind the often bitter clash of wills and opinions, there is a strong theme of gender discrimination, which threatens to tear the lawyers' marriage apart. Hepburn argues that the law has always been tilted in favor of men and unfair to women who refuse to play meek, subservient roles. Her courtroom speeches cause her to realize that in her own marriage she has been expected to bow before her husband's superior knowledge of the law.

The abused wife is exonerated after Hepburn nearly reduces the jury to tears, but Tracy is furious, accusing her of making a mockery of the law. He then reverts to crocodile tears in an effort to win her sympathy—and is successful at it. The traditional happy ending is there, of course. The marriage is saved, but the film leaves us with much to think about. How deeply rooted are gender roles? Doesn't everyone at one time or another make use of them for personal gain? Will there ever be true equality?

Thus far, in this section, we have seen the evolution of a major film genre from breezy, witty entertainment to comedy with a serious undercurrent. The romantic comedy has proved to be an enduringly popular genre, always changing to meet the challenge of new times. By the late 1980s, the movement encouraging sexual equality was in full swing. Both men and women found themselves trying to cope with shifting gender roles. But changes in both society and romantic comedy were on the horizon.

By the 1980s romantic comedy was beginning to reflect the change in gender roles. In 1934, Claudette Colbert willingly surrendered her independence to masculine Clark Gable. In 1989, Meg Ryan is self-assured and can get along without male guidance.

In the groundbreaking *When Harry Met Sally* (1989), independent woman Meg Ryan encounters traditionally disposed man Billy Crystal. Although they barely know each other, the plot sends them driving together cross-country. Along the way, casual conversation turns to sharp repartee, a battle of wits between a woman who believes a non-sexual, friendly relationship can exist between two people and a man who argues that sex will always be the main issue, whether talked about or not. She adds that women aren't nearly as interested in sex as he believes but often pretend to be enjoying it, which she demonstrates by imitating the sounds of orgasm while they sit in a restaurant. Through their developing relationship, the film shows two equal partners.

In the two decades following *When Harry Met Sally*, according to some film historians, gender equality in films began to erode. Women continued to make strides in society, often occupying positions of authority over male workers. The male, in films and on television, was frequently depicted as hapless and very much in need of female guidance. It became difficult to find those elements that made earlier romantic comedies so appealing. In a *New Yorker* article, film critic David Denby analyzes possible reasons. Using the 2007 comedy *Knocked Up* as a contemporary example, he contrasts the squabbling lovers in the old films with their modern-day counterparts and finds that today's are no longer equal partners. "There they are, the young man and young woman of the dominant romantic comedy trend of the past several years—the slovenly hipster and the female straight arrow. The movies form a genre of sorts: the slacker-striver romance. . . . For almost a decade, Hollywood has pulled jokes and romance out of the struggle between male infantilism and female ambition."[3]

Where the genre is headed is as yet unclear. The slacker-achiever couple may prove to be a passing trend. Will there ever be another Hepburn-Tracy partnership? Will witty repartee once again replace run-of-the-mill dialogue? One trend that deserves to be mentioned is the recent emergence of romantic comedies that end in *bittersweet compromise* between the traditional happy ending after a long verbal battle and something that perhaps comes closer to reality.

In the aptly titled *As Good as It Gets* (1997), Helen Hunt plays a struggling single mother working as a waitress trying to bring up an asthmatic son. She attracts the attention of a cranky older man played by Jack Nicholson. The Nicholson character, a successful writer, is extremely demanding, with excessive compulsions about order and neatness. The couple has little in common. Still, he is able to get good medical help for her son, and he does modify his behavior enough to become a little more romantic. When he proposes marriage, the heroine's mother reminds her that this is "as good as it gets," and the embrace in the final scene suggests that a workable compromise has been reached. Neither character has changed all that much. People usually don't, says the film, but isn't it better to be with someone who has come to understand you than to spend your life dreaming of a perfect relationship?

In *Monsoon Wedding* (2001), a romantic comedy from India, the heroine is a young woman whose parents have arranged a marriage for her. With the approval of both families, the groom is due to arrive soon for an elaborate Punjabi wedding. But the heroine must first determine what her former lover, a married man, plans to do about their secret affair. The questions are old and familiar: Will he divorce his wife? Will the affair continue? Will the bride call off the wedding? Will the groom reject the bride when he learns the truth?

The new romantic comedy of bittersweet compromise, showing that a less than perfect relationship may be as good as it gets.

Source: Mirabli Films/Delhi Dot Com/The Kobal Collection.

Old-fashioned melodramas would have had loud denunciations and possible disaster. But *Monsoon Wedding* is far more modern than that. When the heroine recognizes that nothing about her affair will change and that the man she is slated to marry is at least a suitable mate, she tells him about her affair. Sobered by the confession but respectful of his bride's honesty, the groom proves to be understanding as they move toward a new definition of love. The result is a film filled with color—the saris, the henna-painted skin, the captivating music—all underscoring a marriage seemingly destined for happiness by blending the modern and the traditional. Again, we are shown a world that's "as good as it gets."

Tokyo is the setting for Sofia Coppola's *Lost in Translation* (2003) starring Bill Murray as an aging actor, Bob Harris, reduced to shooting a whisky commercial in a city filled with bewildering sights and sounds. Staying in the same hotel is Charlotte, a bored young wife (Scarlett Johannsen) whose photographer husband is often absent on business. She and the Bill Murray character meet and share their loneliness. A critic describes their growing intimacy as they explore karaoke bars, talk, and come close to each other before going their separate ways: "In the early hours of the morning, Harris puts his suit jacket around Charlotte's shoulders. The tails reach her knees; the sleeves submerge her hands. The odd couple wander back through the alien city streets. . . . The moment marks a change in their relationship, as it shifts from friendship into an emotional bond. The sight of Charlotte's figure drowned by the jacket is as painful (their relationship is a nonstarter) as it is heart-warming."[4]

Murray, whose career is built on comedy, makes disillusion and apathy as believable as his attraction to the young woman who obviously cares for him. But the ending is realistic and right. They do not have enough in common to sustain a lasting relationship. Perhaps not enough people really do. Yet the need for contact, if only fleeting, is always there. The comedies of compromise refuse to perpetuate mythology.

I just put my feet in the air and move them around.

—**Fred Astaire**

The Screen Musical

The stories in musical films, hugely popular in the 1930s into the 1950s, were often similar to those in romantic comedies of the period. The couple was kept apart until the final embrace, except when they sang and danced together. This formula was especially true for Fred Astaire and Ginger Rogers, who essentially played the same people from one film to the next. The clothing and sets in Astaire-Rogers films were lavish. Impeccably garbed Fred, with top hat and tails, and satin-gowned Ginger, with sequins and feathers, dance up and down stairs, on table tops, and even on miraculously cleared dance floors in intricately choreographed routines, even though the script may indicate they have just met and obviously had no time to rehearse. No matter what minor misunderstanding may have separated them, when the band begins to play, the logic of the story disappears as they tapdance, waltz, swirl, and introduce new rhythms.

Dancing at any moment was a convention of musical film, as was singing that could occur anywhere: on the deck of a ship or in a moonlit garden. Anytime a lover wanted to woo, romantic feelings could be described in song. An unseen orchestra offered accompaniment, as the singing and dancing that brought them together offered a preview of a future of harmony. Opera had long had sung dialogue and orchestral accompaniment, but musical comedy songs offered more spoken dialogue and songs that could be sung by the untrained voices of a public expected to buy the records.

In what has been called the greatest movie musical ever made, there are joyous singing, dancing, and a believable plot.

Source: The Everett Collection, Inc.

The major choreographer of Hollywood musicals in the 1930s was Busby Berkeley (1895–1976), who placed beautiful women in designs that would have been impossible on the stage. Audiences loved synchronized dancing, like that of Radio City Music Hall's high-kicking, long-legged Rockettes (still packing them in), a tradition carried on by the top-hatted ensemble in the finale of *A Chorus Line* and the Irish Step Dancers of *Riverdance*. The screen musical provided effects Broadway could not match. Berkeley was able to arrange his dancers in intricate configurations, photographed from above, with some of them in the dark and others in the light as they swirled into kaleidoscopic patterns.

Singin' in the Rain (1952), directed by Stanley Donen and Gene Kelly, is generally considered the greatest musical Hollywood has ever made. For a change, the plot is believable and deals not with the usual banter between hero and heroine but with what really happened when movies first acquired sound. Gene Kelly, who also stars in the film, dances in joyous abandon on every kind of surface, including a rain-soaked street. In the famous title number, Kelly sings about the happiness of being in love, as he splashes and dances through puddles, umbrella in hand—a scene that can be separated from the story and viewed with delight as an expression of pure joy. *Singin' in the Rain* was glorious escapist entertainment for the public without sacrificing integrity of plot and characterization.

As films became more special-effects oriented during the 1980s, the screen musical tried, usually without success, to adapt to the changing fashions by venturing into unexplored territory. *Dirty Dancing*, in 1987, however, was a huge success, largely because it featured spectacular dance routines and the disappearance of by now hackneyed elements. There isn't even any singing by the characters in the film, and we never hear an orchestra suddenly and mysteriously present as a lead-in to a romantic duet.

The female protagonist, Baby, is a young woman who is insecure and seems to have two left feet. She is of course drawn to the male protagonist, a dance instructor at the lake resort where she is staying with her family. Through a plot twist, Baby must learn how to do a professional-level dance routine, and as she rehearses with the dance instructor, they grow romantically involved. He is accused of fraternizing with a guest and of stealing but redeems himself, then rescues the hotel from the lackluster entertainment it has been providing. In the thirty-minute finale not only the performers but the guests do the "dirty dancing" of the title, with its lifts, leaps, bends, and embraces. The resort owner is delighted to see his guests so happy, and he knows they will return the following year, thus saving the enterprise from bankruptcy. Baby's parents, who had opposed her relationship with the seemingly irresponsible dance instructor, are delighted to see that their daughter has so much dancing talent. In fact, *everyone* is delighted, including the filmmakers, who created a modest musical with no special effects that has become a film classic.

Characters and plot are even more believable in the Japanese film *Shall We Dance?* (Masayuki Suo, 1996) in which an affluent businessman, mired in a boring routine life, happens to look out of a commuter train window and see into a room where an attractive woman is giving dance lessons. Acting uncharacteristically, on impulse, he signs up for lessons and finds that learning dance steps shakes him out of the predictability of his life. The core of the film, however, revolves around the intricacies and shifting dynamics of real human relationships, explored in ways rarely found in musicals of yesterday.

In some respects, Rob Marshall's 2002 Oscar-winning *Chicago* is like earlier musicals in its lavish, glitzy production numbers, but unlike them in the seriousness of its cynical satire on ambition, crime, tabloid journalism, and public celebrity worship that exceeds all bounds of reason. It also follows in the wake of Baz Luhrmann's *Moulin Rouge* in its use of what has been described as "pure cinema," using the quick cut in ways undreamed of in years past.

The show-stopper here is the soft-shoe dance by the attorney (Richard Gere), who is defending an accused and apparently guilty murderess (Renée Zellweger). He musically describes how clever lawyers hoodwink and outthink gullible juries. "Give 'em the old razzle-dazzle," he sings. As he goes into his dance, the camera keeps cutting to scenes of an actual court trial, then back to Gere's glittering showmanship. Both *Moulin Rouge* and *Chicago* epitomize the *new* musical, combining traditional elements, dazzling camera work, and serious themes.

The Western

No film genre is more historically associated with Hollywood than the western tale of good and evil. In one film after another, bad guys menace the decent folks in a town that is often the same studio back-lot set, complete with horses, a stagecoach, the jail, the general store, the saloon, and a dusty main street, scene of a thousand shootouts. Actors embody the time-honored personae of cowboys, sheriffs, outlaws, schoolmarms, and dance-hall girls, to the delight of loyal fans. Some of the characters had recognizable historical names, such as Wyatt Earp, Doc Holliday, Jesse and Frank James, and Billy the Kid. Others were purely fictional. All became part of an American morality myth, so much so that children continue to play the parts and tourists continue to visit the Ghost Towns where scenes from a basic western are reenacted in an authentic setting.

In 1939, as Americans were heatedly debating how much the country should be involved in the war that had already begun in Europe, *Destry Rides Again* was a satiric version of the traditional western. In the film, the popular actor James Stewart plays a newly appointed sheriff who refuses to carry a gun! The bad guys are the usual ones who drive law-abiding farmers from their lands, after which they gamble and drink at the local saloon, where the main entertainment is provided by the husky-voiced, scantily clad Frenchy (Marlene Dietrich), the ungenteel costume always a sign that this woman will not win the heart of the good guy, even though she has the traditional heart of gold.

Two other important characters, indispensable in the western, are the good woman, in this case a teacher who is worthy of Destry's affections, and the sheriff's sidekick, a lovable drunk whose irresponsibility immediately wins the audience's affection. The non-violent sheriff manages to maintain order until the lovable sidekick is shot and dies in his arms. At this point, he stands up, straps on his gunbelt (to the cheers of the audience), and goes off to avenge the death and clear the town of evil. During the gun battle in the classic western finale, Frenchy deliberately sacrifices herself by shielding Destry and taking the bullet meant for him. The heart of gold comes through but is not allowed—ever—to end happily.

With decency restored, the farmers can safely return home and Destry can marry his refined lady. Students of contemporary history will find a possible connection between the 1939 date of the film and Destry's realization that pacifism in the long run is ineffective against strong opponents.

Talk low, talk slow, and don't say too much.

—**John Wayne**

In Fred Zinnemann's *High Noon* (1952), Will Kane (Gary Cooper) is retiring from the office of marshal, with his replacement due to arrive the following day. Kane plans to leave the town and open a store with his bride (Grace Kelly), whose Quaker religion opposes the use of firearms. But on Kane's last day, the town is facing the reappearance of a deranged killer who, with his brothers, has vowed revenge against the marshal responsible for his prison sentence. The film examines a legitimate moral dilemma. Kane must decide whether to stay and defend both himself and the law-abiding citizens of the town, who will be in danger should the menacing gang triumph, or to accompany his wife away from violence, to a life of peace. The French film *Shoot the Piano Player*, already discussed, would have a similar theme: is it possible to detach oneself from involvement in violence and moral corruption?

The plot continues to darken in this complex—and, to many, greatest ever—western. As the clock approaches high noon, when the train carrying the villains is due to arrive, Kane seeks help from the townsfolk. Though the town has seemed united in its moral denunciation of the bad men, no one else is willing to fight. After all, it isn't their problem. Kane's pacifist wife begs him to leave, with an ultimatum threatening their brief marriage, but his integrity and loyalty to his duty as marshal cause him to stay. He is left alone to decide whether to fight against overwhelming odds or flee, knowing none would blame him.

The film has been called the *Hamlet* of the western genre. Like Shakespeare's Prince of Denmark, Will Kane continually asks himself why he should be the one to carry out a dreadful task (in Hamlet's case, the murder of his uncle), why he should have to die for a town that has betrayed him. Yet the film was obliged to abide by *some* of the rules governing the western. The noble marshal simply could not be allowed to die. On the other hand, the creators of this film were not about to turn their believable protagonist into an improbable superman.

In the famous climactic shootout, Kane manages to do away with two of the four villains. As one of the remaining killers is about to blast the unsuspecting Kane, a shot is fired by an unseen gun and the villain falls. The camera then shows us Kane's Quaker wife, who had picked up a gun and sent the killer to his death, but she is then taken captive by the last vengeance-seeking killer. Both Kane and his wife survive and the villain is killed. But the couple now feel alienated from the townsfolk.

Much has been made of the fact that the appearance of *High Noon* coincided with the start of the Korean War. Is this film also saying that pacifism is not a valid position? At the eleventh hour, doesn't the wife recognize that preserving justice at all costs is everyone's obligation? In the tradition of much high art, *High Noon* is content to remain ambiguous, perhaps understanding that it has posed questions for which there are no easy answers. If nothing else, in the manner of the very best myths, it tells us that, when a hero is needed, a hero will be there, because *somebody has to be there.* It doesn't guarantee that "being there" is necessarily its own reward. In the famous last scene, as the townspeople suddenly reappear to congratulate him, Kane bitterly removes his badge and drops it in the dust.

One popular 1969 western boasted two heroes who were on the wrong side of the law. They were a charming pair of bank robbers (Paul Newman and Robert Redford) whose names gave the film its title, *Butch Cassidy and the Sundance Kid.* Throughout George Roy Hill's brand of western, the rogue protagonists commit one crime after another, almost always managing to escape—and, in the true tradition of the rogue hero, with audience approval. (It is much easier to identify with a handsome, smart-talking Dionysian duo than with their humorless pursuers.)

Chased to the edge of a very high cliff, Butch (Newman) urges Sundance (Redford) to jump into the river below, only to learn that his partner can't swim. After he encourages his friend by telling him the fall will probably kill them, they do jump. Hill makes use of the *freeze frame*, at the time a new convention in which the camera stops an action suddenly. The lovable crooks are stranded in midair, bringing unexpected whimsy into a story that is moving toward an inevitable tragic ending. Yet the director's smile never entirely disappears, even when Butch and Sundance are ultimately riddled with bullets by Bolivian police. They die without a shred of remorse or self-pity.

The Old West has been the setting for more recent films, but the old mythology is no longer there. These are not black-and-white tales of good and evil. A significant modern western is Kevin Costner's 1990 *Dances with Wolves*, in which Native Americans are treated more sympathetically than when they were shown as stereotyped menaces to white settlers, who killed them one by one as audiences cheered. *Dances with Wolves* views Native Americans as victims of white oppression, and clearly belongs to the serious tradition of film as something more than popular entertainment. It is also a classic example of revisiting a film genre in a new context.

It is easy enough to guess why American presidents like [High Noon] *so much. The man with the nuclear gun who thinks to himself that he often must do the hard thing, the unpopular thing, would also like to think of himself as spiritually resembling Gary Cooper.*

—Paul Buhle and David Wagner

Horror and Suspense Films

Even though the sights and sounds of screened horror may cause some to close their eyes and cover their ears, audiences keep coming back for more. The desire to be thrilled in the theater is very old. Long before the invention of motion pictures, audiences watched terrible things happen to actors on stage, safe in the realization that the mutilations and executions were make believe. Shakespeare and his contemporaries showed scenes of eye gouging, amputations, and other forms of torture, sometimes right in front of the audience. In Greek tragedy, horror and violence happened offstage but was reported in often frightening detail by an onstage messenger, whose job was to make audiences shudder as their imaginations filled in the details.

Films can show the gory details magnified, and creepy background music makes certain that viewers are kept on the edge of their seats. Look! There goes the innocent victim down the dark street where the killer waits. Suspense builds as the camera zooms in on an ominous object, such as a pair of shoes walking along a deserted pavement. Or just the fierce eyes of an obsessed murderer—even better, a mask.

In 1929, Spanish director Luis Buñuel captured a horrifying moment, what seemed to be the slitting of an eyeball, in *Un Chien Andalou*. It remains shocking today, as this and other special effects allow us to see blood-spattered mutilations, or smooth, youthful skin peeled from a face that suddenly becomes too horrifying to look at. (Of course, we *do*!)

Social Issues

Beginning with Mr. Deeds Goes to Town. . .*with Gary Cooper as the small-town man who triumphs over city slickers, Capra's work emphasized the common-sense skills and leadership qualities of little people.*

—**Robert Sklar**

From its beginning, some directors recognized the power of film as a medium for social criticism. Such works make a statement about institutions and economic policies that are the root causes of human problems. A very early (1909) one-reel silent movie, *A Corner in Wheat*, took on the stock market and the tragic results of human greed. Like most early films, it exaggerated its case. The discrepancy between the haves and have-nots could not be missed. In one scene, newly made millionaires lift champagne glasses in celebration; a quick cut shows miserable-looking crowds on a bread line.

During the Depression of the 1930s, issue-oriented films became more sophisticated and were almost as popular as the escapist musicals and romantic comedies. Audiences who shared the deprivations experienced by the characters easily identified with real social problems and derived a measure of comfort by realizing that many others were in the same predicaments. Movie screens offered a balance between stories set in elegant drawing rooms and stories set in ill-heated shacks. And though audiences were not afraid to confront grim realities, some films were successful because they combined social realism with contrived happy endings.

Frank Capra (1897–1991) created films about bigotry, political corruption, and the abuse of workers' rights, with attractive, plain-talking heroes. An immigrant himself, the son of a fruit-picker, he had firsthand knowledge of poverty, but he also had profound respect for America, the land of opportunity. The optimism with which he ended his films worked box-office magic, although he has been criticized for providing easy solutions that could never happen in reality.

In *Mr. Deeds Goes to Town* (1936), Gary Cooper (the ideal Capra down-to-earth hero) tries to distribute an inheritance of $20 million to the poor and, as a result, must fight a legal battle to prove his sanity. Goodness once again prevails, and the Depression is over for a lucky few. In the 1939 *Mr. Smith Goes to Washington*, the hero, played by James Stewart, another Capra stalwart, is an idealistic junior senator, unaware that a political machine has sponsored him because of his boyish appeal to voters. Gradually learning that his sponsors are ruthless and willing to do anything to control him, he engages in a marathon filibuster to block the passage of a bill he was supposed to support. Capra provides a by-now-expected happy conclusion in which the forces of righteousness, led by his appealingly innocent hero, are eventually (temporarily?) triumphant.

In Capra's most popular film, *It's a Wonderful Life* (1947), a desperate, bankrupt hero (James Stewart again) is saved at the last minute (and, not coincidentally, on Christmas Eve) by the contributions of grateful townspeople whose homes were spared by his bank. He had contemplated suicide, believing that he was a total failure in life. The film's message—that people's worth is measured by the amount of good they do—has elevated the movie to almost mythic status. Alternately condemned as unabashed sentimentality and praised as a welcome addition to the Christmas spirit, *It's a Wonderful Life* is revived every year during the holiday season.

John Ford (1895–1973), like Capra the son of immigrants, was another director who grew up knowing the underprivileged side of life. He developed a special fondness for that American symbol of rugged individualism, the cowboy. When he became a film director (as early as 1917), he was attracted to scripts about the struggles of the poor to retain their integrity against the encroachments of the wealthy and powerful. The central characters in *The Grapes of Wrath* (1940), adapted from the John Steinbeck novel mentioned in Chapter 4, are the poor Joad family, forced to leave their farm after a bank foreclosure.

The land, unable to sustain them, has become part of the Dust Bowl, and the only opportunity appears to be in California, where they have heard fruit pickers are desperately needed. Ma Joad (Jane Darwell in an Oscar-winning performance) is a resource of quiet wisdom. Her son Tom (Henry Fonda, who brought naturalistic acting to a new level) is an impatient rebel. When they manage to drive their rickety old car to California, they learn that the rule of supply and demand is in full force. So many would-be farm workers have arrived that the advertised wages have been slashed. Tom Joad sees that the struggle for justice must transcend his own family and his own self-interest. He will dedicate his life to the cause of saving all of humanity.

A very different approach to the plight of the poor in the Depression was taken by Preston Sturges (1898–1959) in *Sullivan's Travels* (1941). Sturges, usually a writer-director of lighthearted, clever romantic comedies, seems to have questioned the tired formula that made him a success. His new film was a clearly personal one about a writer-director who decides to abandon comedy and deal with the problems of the poor and homeless. Disguising himself as a vagrant and living under bridges in squatters' camps, he is horrified when he unexpectedly finds himself a real victim of inequality. He is thrown in jail for a crime he didn't commit and sentenced to hard labor on a chain gang. The experience sobers him, but his confrontation with reality leads to an unexpected conclusion. The hero realizes that people need the gift of comedy more than they need to be reminded that they are poor. There is no $20 million to give away—only what Sturges himself possessed in abundance: humor plus a keen awareness of social realities.

The contemporary writer-director Spike Lee (b. 1957) is in the tradition of those who, like Ford, use the medium of film to confront real social problems. Early on, he decided he would devote his life to making films about oppressed minorities and enrolled at NYU. One of Lee's first assignments was to make a short film. His was short enough—ten minutes—but its subject matter was startling. Lee ridiculed the stereotypes of African Americans found in films like *The Birth of a Nation*, substituting *white* stereotypes.

Lee survived criticism of his irreverent school exercise, but the desire to shock by shaking up cherished beliefs has not left him. He has remained socially oriented, tackling such themes as racial and ethnic prejudice (*Do the Right Thing*, 1989), interracial romance (*Jungle Fever*, 1991), the seemingly irreversible poverty of African Americans (*Tales from the Hood*, 1995), and the biography of *Malcolm X* (1992), considered by many critics to be his finest film so far.

Lee has never been afraid to take a stand, both on and off screen. In making *Malcolm X*, he battled against a studio decision to allow a white director to make a film about the hero, and when he was finally given the job, he refused to be constrained by what he regarded as an inadequate budget. Instead he went out and raised private funds. In *Do the Right Thing*, he won critical acclaim for his use of an unusual film convention—a revival of the Greek Chorus—in this case a group of men sitting on the front steps of a house and commenting on what is happening in the neighborhood. Lee remains controversial, a director whose films continue to stimulate debate about whether he exaggerates or is delivering a needed message; whether audiences will imitate violence seen on the screen, and whether he himself is using damaging stereotypes.

There will never be an end of social problems, and films about social issues will always be produced, not only in the United States but all over the world. German director Florian Henckel von Donnersmarck's *The Lives of Others* won the Academy Award for best foreign film of 2006. Though it deals with the government-backed eavesdropping on private citizens that was prevalent in East Berlin before the destruction of the wall separating it from West Berlin, the film has obvious relevance to similar practices in other places and more recent times.

Government-backed spying on the lives of others in a 2007 German thriller with a strong social conscience.

Source: © Lara Tomlin. Originally published in *The New Yorker*.

In the film, Captain Gerd Wiesler, with the East German spy organization Stasi, a master of surveillance and interrogation techniques, is assigned to test the loyalty of a gifted playwright and pianist Georg Dreyman. So above-board is Dreyman's behavior that Wiesler believes something must be wrong. He is "too good to be true" and therefore must be investigated.

The artist's apartment is subjected to thorough wire-tapping. In shifts, the captain and a subordinate eavesdrop on every conversation, knowing every detail of the subject's parties, his music, and even his lovemaking. The contrast between the artist and the captain becomes increasingly clear, and is the central core of the film. As he eavesdrops, he hears music unfamiliar to him, and as he searches the apartment, he finds poetry he has never read.

A crisis is reached when Dreyman's girlfriend, also a spy, discovers where he has hidden papers that are contrary to the official policies of the regime in power. Yet the conscience of Wiesler is troubled. Should he advance his own career by using the newfound information to indict Dreyman or allow a genuine artist the freedom to be himself? By the end of the film, the Wall has been destroyed, but so has Wiesler. *The Lives of Others* has its share of thrills, stalking, suspense, and betrayal. Unlike most spy films, however, it delivers a subject central to the humanities: the suppression of artistic freedom. We have much more to say on this matter in Chapter 15.

Documentaries and Docudramas

Nonfiction films, or **documentaries**, are often respected for their efforts to tell the truth about an important issue or segment of the population. At the same time, films claiming to be documentaries have aroused opposition because of the possibility that truth has been doctored in order to make a case.

A film is a petrified fountain of thought.

—**Jean Cocteau**

One of the outstanding and influential exponents of this genre is Frederick Wiseman (b. 1938), who specializes in showing familiar institutions in unique ways. Over the years he has made films whose titles hint at their content: *Hospital, Welfare, Racetrack, The Store, High School, Meat.* Unlike some documentary makers who add biting social and political commentaries to their work, Wiseman refrains from making comments or using interviews. He allows what is being filmed to speak for itself.

His best known work, *Titicut Follies* (1967), exposes the brutal treatment of inmates in a Massachusetts hospital for people labeled "criminally insane." The work was banned in that state until just recently. *High School* (1968) uncovers what really happens on a typical day: the bells, the regimentation, the strict enforcement of institutional rules. "Where's your pass?" snaps a hall monitor to a student. A dean is overheard telling another student, "We are out to establish that you are a man and that you can take orders."

An extraordinarily beautiful documentary with minimal narration is *Winged Migration* (2001), photographed by five film crews under the direction of Jacques Perrin. It shows birds—all kinds of birds—in flight, in long journeys marking the seasons as they search for food and nesting places. The film is totally descriptive and impartial. The screen is simply filled with birds endlessly moving, accompanied by music, but with rare commentary demanding any certain response from the viewer beyond recognition of rhythmic beauty. At one point, as a ship containing caged exotic birds makes its way up the Amazon River, one parrot thrusts its head through the bars and reaches down to lift the latch locking the cage. When the wooden door opens and the bird escapes, viewers are tempted to applaud, just as they wince at the sight of birds being shot down by hunters. But the main reaction is probably amazement that filmmakers were able to get so close to their subjects at the right time.

The documentaries of Michael Moore (b. 1954) leave no doubt about his sympathies. His *Roger and Me* (1989) attacked the closing of Flint, Michigan's main industry when General Motors moved its factories out of the country. The "Roger" of the title was the CEO whom Moore pursued throughout the film in an effort to get answers about the corporate decision. *Bowling for Columbine* (2002), about the murderous rampage of two Colorado high school students in 1994, made a plea for tough gun control laws. *Fahrenheit 9/11* (2004), which was selected as the best film shown at the Cannes Film Festival in that year, gathered an enormous amount of footage to demonstrate what Moore considered the government's lax handling of the World Trade Center attacks as well as the wars in Afghanistan and Iraq. In 2007, *Sicko* investigated health care in the United States and other countries. As always, Moore's narrative voice guides the way audiences are meant to view the film.

A compromise between documentary and drama is the **docudrama**, which provides narration in addition to Wiseman-style objectivity. It generally focuses on a sympathetic protagonist, who is faced with very real problems. But instead of simply being shown the facts or being guided toward a particular point of view, audiences identify with and root for an oppressed individual, whose misfortunes represent a much larger social problem. Directors of docudramas have built modest careers on the desire to tell a story that would otherwise be overlooked in an industry aiming for blockbuster thrills.

One such director is Ken Loach (b. 1936), who, in *Ladybird, Ladybird*, tells the true story of a woman whose children are taken away after authorities decide she is an unfit mother. They contend that she has never married, that each of her children has a different father, and that she sometimes leaves them alone to go to bars, at one point abandoning them in an apartment that caught fire. When she and a man who wants to marry her try to regain custody rights, they encounter hostility from officials claiming it would not be in the best interests of the children.

Loach's film does not tack on a happy ending. Instead, audiences have an opportunity to meet a woman they would otherwise not know and to decide for themselves whether her suffering was reason enough to claim the children. At its best, docudrama is as inconclusive as reality—and as provocative.

One very successful documentary in recent years has been Al Gore's *An Inconvenient Truth* (2006), a film about global warming that aims to stir audiences up to demand action from governments and industries. Gore's thesis is stated simply but toughly: "Humanity is sitting on a time bomb." The movie won the Academy Award in 2006 for Best Documentary, and in 2007 Gore shared the Nobel Peace Prize for his untiring efforts on behalf of the environment, which the Nobel committee said were directly related to peace in the world. They argued that if Gore's thesis is as accurate as both he and many scientists believe, and if nothing is done to control the warming of Earth and the melting of the ice caps, there will be unceasing violence and warfare as nations struggle for food and water.

Humanity is sitting on a time bomb.

—**Al Gore**

Like most works with explosive, disturbing themes, *An Inconvenient Truth* has its share of foes. A judge in Great Britain ruled that scientists in his country had found nine errors in Gore's reasoning. He condemned the apocalyptic alarmism of the film and ruled that it could not be shown in British schools. Other detractors accused Gore of forsaking pure science for partisan politics. But any work that arouses such a storm of controversy, say others, should not be dismissed lightly.

Fictionalized Biography

Films that claim to be about actual people do not always stay close to the facts, and ironically, many of the films that bend the truth are about people with famous names. Fictionalized biographies often seem to do whatever they like with their subjects, and audiences are often misled. The very quality that makes film unique—its ability to put striking images on the screen—is also the quality that can make a film biography lack a major element: fidelity to the facts. Producers of biographical cinema have to make sure their products will sell. They want screenwriters and directors to focus on exciting moments in a real person's life and generally don't mind if these moments never happened or are highly exaggerated.

Historical accuracy has seldom been the goal of the fictionalized biography. If the subject's life is not as interesting or dramatic as filmmakers would like, they go ahead and change it.

Lincoln, Gandhi, Lawrence of Arabia, Richard Nixon, Queen Victoria, Thomas Jefferson, John F. Kennedy, not to mention Chopin, Beethoven, van Gogh, and many others, have all been subjects of full-length screen biographies. When people attend these films, what do they expect to see? Do they want to come away with actual knowledge of these personalities? Or do they want to see an absorbing film? Filmmakers have no desire to present a history lesson about important legislation, so when they make a film about an American president, for example, they want to show him as a hero or a lover or, in the case of Nixon, as a fascinating psychological study. Lincoln's log cabin is part of his myth, as is the rail-splitting, the lanky, bearded figure with the sad eyes, who was assassinated while watching a comedy at Ford's Theater. In filmed biographies of him, these elements are usually given greater prominence than his wrestling with the overwhelming complexities of trying to govern a bitterly divided nation.

Omissions and even distortions affect audience perceptions and often create highly inaccurate national memories. One critic, commenting on a 1991 "filmography" of the late President John F. Kennedy, writes rather scathingly: "More than a century before the advent of the Hollywood pseudodocumentary Karl Marx suggested that all great events and personalities in world history happen twice: 'the first time as tragedy, the second as farce.' Oliver Stone's film *JFK* is a case in point."[5] Challenged later about the accuracy of his film, Stone responded with the recommendation that people who want to know what really happened should go to the library and do some research.

Films about artists encounter another problem: how to make the creation of a painting, a novel, or a musical composition as interesting as the wild antics of the creator who lives on the edge of normal behavior. To the credit of writers and directors of the past, some of the films about visual artists have actually left audiences with memories of the art as well as the artist's temper tantrums and mental illness.

Michelangelo, Vincent van Gogh, and Paul Gauguin have all become known to a wider public because of film biographies. In *The Agony and the Ecstasy* (1965), audiences saw Michelangelo cramped and strained as he heroically paints the ceiling of the Sistine Chapel (in fact, the artist had a number of assistants who did their share of the work). They also saw fictionalized bitter and tension-filled confrontations between Michelangelo and Pope Julius II.

In *Lust for Life* (1956), they saw van Gogh and Gauguin arguing violently in the tiny house they shared, so violently that, on one occasion, van Gogh is shown rushing upstairs to cut off his ear (a response with no basis in fact). All the while they are fighting, the two men continue to generate great paintings. Despite some overacting in the scenes depicting the madness that led van Gogh to suicide, the final moments of the film are impressive indeed as the camera slowly pans along a wall on which hang the artist's greatest works. For many, this art show may have been an extraordinary introduction to the genius of a tragic artist—and more than enough justification for the filmography genre.

Composers have suffered their share of inaccuracies. The Mozart in the movie version of Peter Shaffer's play *Amadeus* (1984) was flamboyantly portrayed as a giggling, childlike man given to bawdy jokes, uncouth gestures, and continual flirtations. How he found time to compose was a mystery. The film also dramatized the totally unfounded legend that Mozart was poisoned by Antonio Salieri, a court composer who is supposed to have been obsessed with jealousy. According to the script, Salieri paid Mozart to compose a Requiem Mass he intended to pass off as his own work after the poison took effect. In real life, someone else commissioned Mozart to write the Requiem, and the composer died before completing it, possibly from typhoid fever. Less dramatic than attempting to appropriate another man's work after poisoning him is the question of the real-life Salieri's relations with Mozart. The film shows him burning with hatred of his rival. History shows him as an admired musician willing to help the younger man.

Lovers of Edith Piaf's songs have no doubt been delighted to see *La Vie en Rose* (2006), the film based on her life of both success and inner pain. The soundtrack features old favorites such as the title song as well as the passionate and highly personal "Non, Je Ne Regrette Rien" (No, I regret nothing), and Marion Cotillard (winner of the Best Actress Oscar for her performance in the film) convincingly portrays the singer as tormented. Yet those who thrilled to the music may still be wondering whether Piaf was really abandoned by a parent, lived on the street, or had a child out of wedlock. Those who head for the library can at least still have the wonderful music to remember.

Loosely Based on the Original: Film Adaptations

A film made from a popular literary work is under no obligation to follow the book, though sometimes controversies arise concerning the advisability of transferring a work to a different medium. Early on, Hollywood snapped up the work of important writers, promising more money than they hoped to earn from publishing alone.

The Hemingway short story "The Killers," hailed by some literary critics as a nearly perfect example of the genre, became a two-hour routine 1946 gangster movie that bore little relationship to the original. The original was about the sudden appearance of two hit-men in a sleepy middle American town that has been remote from any real contact with evil. Their mission is to kill a fighter who did not "throw" a championship match. Hemingway knew that for most ordinary people, direct confrontation with genuine evil is unthinkable. Nick Adams, the coming-of-age protagonist from whose point of view we perceive the story, has never experienced such a confrontation. When he does, all he can say is, "It's awful." The older and wiser man who owns the diner in which Nick works, responds, in typically laconic Hemingway fashion: "Well, you'd better not think about it." We are never told whether the fighter is eventually killed. It doesn't matter. What does matter is that most of us are powerless to do much about evil in the world. Whether not thinking about it is the best course to take is, of course, open to question. But great literature does nothing if not make us ask questions. In the film, Nick Adams is relegated to a minor role as the movie focuses on the prize fighter and his impressive biceps, displayed prominently enough to make a star of Burt Lancaster. In the story, the fighter never appears. It is all about what it means to come of age.

Even when some fidelity to the original is attempted, Hollywood has often tacked on an ending totally at odds with the author's obvious intention. In Thomas Hardy's novel *Tess of the D'Urbervilles* the protagonist, having killed the man who seduced and deserted her, is sent to the gallows without mercy, an ending consistent with the author's generally pessimistic view of life. In an early film version, the filmmakers, believing the public needed a happy ending, twisted the plot so that Tess could be rescued. Hardy, outraged at what had been done to his work, sadly observed, "I am an old man and have no defense against this sort of thing."

In *The Player* (1992), Robert Altman satirized the sugarcoating of serious works in a story about a director who had insisted on preserving the integrity of a novel but who submits to pressure and allows a ludicrous, last-minute happy ending. The director is rewarded with a beautiful wife as well as limitless wealth.

Troy (2004), starring Brad Pitt as Achilles in a film "loosely based" on Homer's *The Iliad*, has been praised for its realistic war scenes, but there were major changes in plot, theme, and important details that seem to go beyond artistic license. Agamemnon is depicted as a liar, really after power though he uses the abduction of Helen as a pretext for war. In the film, he is killed before the end of the war, thus making it impossible for him to return home to face the revenge of his wife and her lover—an outcome well-known to students of mythology as well as the thousands familiar with *The Oresteia* of Aeschylus, one of the landmarks in the history of theater.

Critic Edward Rothstein comments on what he calls director Wolfgang Petersen's "spear and sandal epic" with an imposed theme and overly obvious nod to the growing public disapproval of the war in Iraq: "A latent antiwar message also peeks through, here and there, with a directorial wink. 'If we leave now,' the wise general Nestor says in the film after a few days of fighting, 'we lose all credibility.' This is not quite what Homer had in mind."[6]

Two American Film Classics

On almost everyone's list of classic American films are two masterpieces that appeared within a year of each other: *Citizen Kane* (1941) and *Casablanca* (1942). The history of the humanities is filled with such chronologies. Masterpieces, as well as the artists who produced them, have a way of appearing close together. Perhaps creativity is highly contagious. Remember that three of the greatest artists of all time—Leonardo, Michelangelo, and Raphael—all lived and worked at the same time in Florence.

Citizen Kane

Here was a relatively low-budget film, consigned to an amazing twenty-six-year-old named Orson Welles. Several years before, he had done the radio adaptation of H. G. Wells's *The War of the Worlds* that created panic throughout the United States. After the furor and subsequent notoriety for Welles, Hollywood gave him free reign within the confines of a modest budget. The resulting film, *Citizen Kane*, was far from a box-office sensation, but its reputation as screen art has grown steadily with each passing decade. Like many another artist, Welles died without ever quite knowing the full extent of his achievements. During his lifetime, he was admired for his courage to do what his taste compelled him to do, but studios feared him as one who could be counted on to lose their money.

I don't say we all ought to behave, but we ought to look as if we could.

—Orson Welles

To be acclaimed "the best" is to challenge other aspirants to the title. Why *Kane*? Why not any one of the other films that have lasted long enough to deserve to be called classics? Is it one of the film's major themes—the question of whether money can buy happiness? Then again, other films have dealt with that theme. We don't really attend movies in order to learn lessons about happiness, or pride, or whether crime "pays." It must be something else—something bigger. In its exposure of the hollowness of the American Dream, it has been compared to Fitzgerald's masterpiece, *The Great Gatsby* (Chapter 4).

The plot, which centers on one reporter's attempt to unravel the mystery of Kane's unexplained dying word, "Rosebud," unfolds in a technique innovative for its time and part of the reason for the film's acclaim. The story is told from several points of view. One is the director's objective presentation of the facts, such as the opening: Charles Foster Kane, a man who has interested the public for decades, is on his death bed in his legendary mansion, Xanadu. We hear the unseen protagonist whisper his final word, then we see his hand drop to the side of the bed.

Citizen Kane *was not a box-office sensation when it opened; its techniques were too unfamiliar for too many viewers.*

The retrospective of Kane's life begins as a voice-over narration by the reporter who is investigating the meaning of the word. Knowing that the camera cannot photograph what is inside a human being and that the audience can only guess at what lies hidden, Welles makes the investigating reporter the central character. The camera becomes his (and our) eyes.

Testimony comes from several sources, as the reporter interviews everyone who knew Kane. In the shadowy catacombs of the public library, he studies old newspapers in an attempt to recreate every incident in the life of a famous and incredibly wealthy man who starting out as a carefree little boy inherits a great

Citizen Kane reveals the hollowness of the American Dream, much like *The Great Gatsby*, with which it has been compared.

Source: Museum of Modern Art/Film Stills Archive.

deal of money and must leave home to collect his fortune. The investigation centers on documents and eyewitness accounts that can assist the search. One sequence is told from the point of view of the man who knew Kane as a boy, one from a longtime associate in the newspaper business, another from his best friend who became disillusioned by Kane's unethical behavior, and the last sequence by the woman who became Kane's mistress and then his second wife. Some incidents appear more than once, but they are told in different versions.

As the reporter pieces together the fragments, we follow the success of Kane's first newspaper venture, the opening of his vast chain, his increasingly gaudy lifestyle, his developing megalomania—the total self-absorption of someone who has everything but is never satisfied. Kane wants to be governor, then perhaps president, but with enough money and power one can become almost royal. His political progress is stopped by scandal when, as a married man, he is shown to be having an affair with a young woman. He then employs his great wealth and influence in an unsuccessful attempt to make his mistress into a star of Grand Opera. Eventually, he and the woman retreat to a mansion surrounded by statues and other art objects Kane has imported. The woman, bored, does jigsaw puzzles, complains, and abandons him. Kane dies, alone.

In Citizen Kane *Orson Welles did not romanticize the American Dream. His film ultimately reveals the hollowness behind the dream and the tragedy of those whose only concerns are money and power.*

Individual scenes are as compelling as the innovative structure. In one, the disintegration of Kane's first marriage is indicated in a rapid montage of the couple at the breakfast table, at first sitting next to each other, then sitting farther and farther apart until, in a few seconds of screen time, the wife is shown at the opposite end of a very long table reading a newspaper published by Kane's rival. In another scene, Kane's second wife Susan, the would-be opera star, is shown on the stage, shrieking an aria for the small audience of Kane's friends and employees. As she trills on, the camera slowly ascends from stage level, up through the massive riggings that raise and lower the backdrops, finally coming to rest on a gridwalk hundreds of feet above the appalling recital below. As one stagehand looks on in amusement, the other pinches his nose with two fingers to signify his critique of the performance. The scene is now studied in film schools as a supreme example of the tracking shot.

Another shot illustrates an innovative technique known as *depth focus*, made possible by the wizardry of Welles's cinematographer Greg Toland, who subsequently became a star in his own field. In the scene, Kane's friend Jed, the music critic for Kane's paper, is sitting at his typewriter, finishing a scathing review of the performance. He is shown in the foreground as Kane enters the large room and stands in the background. An obvious rift is implied by the relationship of the figures. Kane is kept in the background so that we can only guess at what he is thinking.

The final scene of Citizen Kane *reverses the famous tracking shot of the train station in* Gone with the Wind. *The camera starts wide, without focus, then finally comes to rest on a trivial object: Rosebud.*

The passion that once drew him to Susan wanes. He continues to purchase more treasures to fill the vast salons of the mansion, ultimately not able to find room for any more. They must remain in their crates. He is a lonely, lost old man, dying with none by his side. The mystery of "Rosebud" is finally understood by the audience in the famous final sequence, which opens with an epic-scale image of thousands of boxes containing Kane's treasures, using an innovative twist on the tracking shot. Instead of widening the shot so that the huge material empire is slowly revealed, the camera shows the whole thing at once, then slowly tracks in toward a distant flickering light, which is discovered to be a furnace into which a workman is tossing the "junk" nobody wants—and, finally, the camera zeros in for a close-up of a seemingly worthless remnant of Kane's lost childhood, a small sled containing the word "Rosebud." Even so, neither we nor the reporter ever learns the complete truth about the man. The film captures the ambiguities in human nature and offers as profound an analysis of power-seeking as Hollywood has ever achieved.

Citizen Kane was widely believed to be based on the career of the real-life William Randolph Hearst, a newspaper publisher famous for manipulating the news and sensationalizing events that might otherwise have gone unnoticed. Hearst even tried to prevent the studio from advertising and distributing the work. The character of Susan was said to be based on Hearst's long affair with movie actress Marion Davies. Yet Hearst's California mansion in San Simeon, although filled with treasures like Kane's Xanadu, was also filled with interesting guests who reported that Hearst's hospitality was genuine and knew no bounds. Unlike Susan, Marion Davies remained faithful to the end and seems not to have needed to depend on jigsaw puzzles to pass the time. Reality, however, would have suited Orson Welles much less than the opportunity to create a film of vast, shadowy complexity that continues to fascinate. What he created was not at all the same as a deliberate distortion of historical fact, nor a Hollywoodized decimation of a great literary work. It is a great work of cinema, standing entirely on its own.

Casablanca

Casablanca (1942) became immortal almost in spite of itself. Each day the scriptwriters would give revised scenes to the cast. None of them knew how the film would end, and almost everyone thought it would be a disastrous failure. The United States had just entered World War II, the outcome of which was by no means certain. War movies abounded in Hollywood, most of them filled with multiple scenes of artillery fire, bombings, and mine explosions. Audiences were given Allied successes on the battlefield and reason to cheer. Yet *Casablanca*, despite its wartime background, lacked the expected kind of action scenes. Somehow, through revision after revision, it became a powerful story about ordinary people's ethical dilemmas at a time of conflicting moral values.

Today young people, who may lack full knowledge of the period, are attracted to the film for its powerful love story, but there have been other powerful love stories. Chances are the appeal of *Casablanca* springs from its film noir hero, the hard-boiled but idealistic Rick Blaine, who transcends the stereotype, becoming a three-dimensional, fully realized human being who learns to conceal a broken heart with a facade of toughness that ensures he will never be hurt again. The song from the film, "As Time Goes By," has become a classic in its own right, as has the image of Sam, sitting at the piano, being commanded to "Play it." One of the immortal lines in screen history is Bogart's trademark, "Here's looking at you, kid"—a line that seems to express love quite as much as Romeo's great speeches do. If Juliet is the "sun," Rick's lost love is the "kid."

Because the Hollywood studio system of the 1930s and 1940s had the big stars tied up with long-term contracts, film executives had to commission screenplays tailor-made for the stars' on-camera personalities. Humphrey Bogart became such a star after *The Maltese Falcon*. He was perceived as specializing in the film noir hero: a tough, unflinching man of steel with a susceptible heart and an uncanny ability to survive both danger and personal tragedy.

The studio thought it had found just what it was looking for in the story of an expatriate American who operates an illegal gambling casino in the capital of

French Morocco, neutral territory during World War II. French and German police prowled the streets on the lookout for people trying to buy exit visas, which would allow them to escape. The basically tender-hearted Rick helped them—by letting them gamble for the money. Yet there was always a gun in his pocket, just in case his business was threatened.

As the rewriting continued, Bogart's character apparently took center stage. He is shown as an unemotional realist, at heart concerned about the refugees, but unwilling to become involved in their lives. He cannot afford to. With the apparent blessing of Louis, the police chief who would like nothing better than to crack his veneer, he maintains a well-run establishment in the well-ordered world he has created for himself. Basic to his philosophy of uninvolvement—his defense against the hurt he experienced in Paris when the love of his life left him—is his refusal to take sides in the war, despite the fact that his country is fighting against the Nazis. He shares nothing with anyone about his private life. When the police chief attempts coyly to find out what he is doing in Casablanca, Rick answers in his typical deadpan that he came for the waters. Reminded that they are in a desert and there are no waters in Casablanca, he replies calmly, "I was misinformed."

In one early scene his tough exterior softens just a bit when he counsels a desperate young wife who has come to him for advice. The police chief has offered her enough money for a letter of transit if she agrees to sleep with him. She doesn't want to be disloyal to her husband, but does Rick think she would be wrong to accept the offer? He advises her, instead, to gamble at the roulette wheel and covertly directs the croupier to let her win. The police chief knows what has happened and smilingly accuses Rick of being "a sentimentalist" at heart. But Rick is careful not to show this side of him. He is a loner, just supervising the club, refusing to drink or make friends with the patrons.

The world's favorite Hollywood love story is all the more romantic because it doesn't exalt romantic love above all.

—Stephen D. Greydanes

Inevitably his armor is pierced. The lost love, Ilse, walks in one night with her husband, Victor Laszlo, a leading Resistance fighter against the Nazis and, for them, the top of the Most Wanted list. Later, after everyone else has left, Rick sits at a table with a drink and a cigarette. The shape of the doorway in back of the room dissolves into a similar shape, that of the Arc de Triomphe in Paris, as the flashback shows him remembering the joy of his passionate love affair with Ilse and their mutual determination to escape the approaching German troops. Ilse has agreed to leave with him on the last train, but he waits at the railway station in vain. Only when she reenters his life does he learn that she was married all the time they were together in Paris but that she had believed that she was a widow. When she discovered at the last minute that her husband was alive, she decided she had to return to him rather than leave with Rick.

Now Rick, still hurt and angry, is nevertheless forced to abandon his neutral stand. When Ilse's husband asks the club's orchestra to play the French national anthem to drown out the singing of Nazi soldiers at a nearby table, the orchestra leader looks to Rick for permission. He nods. The refugees stand, joining Laszlo in an emotional singing of *La Marseillaise*. From that point on, it will be difficult for Rick to remain uninvolved.

The Nazi major seems ready to capture Laszlo, who knows he and Ilse must find a way to escape from Casablanca. Ilse confronts Rick with a gun to get the exit visas, but she cannot shoot. The flame of passion has reignited. He will get the visas for Lazlo if she will stay behind with him. Unable to resist for a second time, she agrees. A plane to freedom awaits at the airport, a plane that Laszlo and Ilse are

The climax of *Casablanca* contains one of the most famous decisions in the history of film.

Source: The Museum of Modern Art, Film Stills Archive, New York.

supposed to board. Laszlo does not know that Ilse has agreed to stay with Rick. Legend has it that the scriptwriters did not know what they were going to do with the scene. Through the mysterious, often chaotic labyrinth known as the creative process, their dilemma suddenly turned into Rick's famous moral choice.

After Rick kills the Nazi commander, the French captain shields him by ordering his men to "round up the usual suspects."

The choice in that scene (which should be obvious from what we have told you about Rick), a scene that was not written until the final day of shooting, has made film history. Call him a "sentimentalist." Say that what he chose no red-blooded man would ever choose in real life. Or call him a moral role model for all time. Like all great films, *Casablanca* offers its audiences a very complex set of options.

Citizen Kane and *Casablanca* have much in common. Both begin with exposition provided by a news broadcast. Both films employ dialogue sparingly. Neither central character reveals himself through what he says. Both use the screen medium to create a complex reality that we must interpret because neither makes a direct, easily phrased statement about people or existence. Yet the two films are different in that *Citizen Kane* was consciously designed to be a quality film made by an independent young director with no ties to Hollywood, while *Casablanca* was the product of a studio paying high prices to its stars and directed by a man who specialized in action adventure movies rather than artistic masterpieces. Two opposite roads led to the same destination: a secure niche in the history of classic films.

The Film Auteur

> *Write what you feel, not what you think the audience wants.*
>
> —**Stephen Sondheim**

The French word **auteur**, or "author," has been applied to the most significant directors, those whose special style and themes are so evident that their work is instantly recognizable. "A film by . . ." usually means the director rather than the scriptwriter (unless they are the same person). The work of the auteur bears signs of individual technique—like an author's unique way of using language or an artist's unique brushstrokes. It can be recognized in camera angles, overlapping dialogue, swift transitions, and a personal view of reality.

Directors who attain auteur status choose the material, write the script or collaborate with the screenwriter, and have total control over the plot and characters. Their situation is unlike that of most of the directors in the old studio system who were simply handed a script that their contracts called for them to accept without question. *Final cut*, that is, the right to decide when the work was indeed completed, was a rare privilege for them. Response cards from preview audiences were read carefully, and contract directors often were forced to make unwanted changes based on those responses. Or an all-powerful producer might decide he didn't like what he saw and demand that the film not be released until it met with his satisfaction. Response cards and powerful producers are still around. Even today, when some directors are honored as never before, the Academy Award for Best Picture is handed to a producer. But it is the great director who is most likely to be remembered, not the producer. This section describes the work of some prominent auteurs.

Ingmar Bergman

Swedish director Ingmar Bergman (1918–2007) did not come to film because of its glamour and the promise of quick wealth. He was a serious theater director intent on creating art, and he saw in film a challenging medium offering him great freedom to explore his subjects. For a decade he studied the techniques of cinema, and by the mid-1950s he had made Sweden very nearly the art film capital of the world. Two of his masterworks, *The Seventh Seal* (1956) and *Wild Strawberries* (1957), are so typically Bergman that they could not have been made by anyone else. Both films are intensely philosophical, concerned about the human place in existence. Both have central characters who wonder whether they are in this world for some reason. They feel themselves alienated from others, meaningless entities walking around on the earth for a few years and then vanishing into endless night.

The Seventh Seal is a medieval fable about a knight who has survived the Crusades, then ironically finds Death waiting for him when he returns home. He challenges the Grim Reaper to a game of chess, the contract being that he can stay alive until Death achieves victory. The knight is determined to delay the inevitable until he discovers the meaning of his life. While the fantasy game proceeds, the knight is also journeying about the countryside in search of something—a person, a cause, a religion—that will convince him that existence has not been an absurd waste of time. The knight's quest very likely paralleled Bergman's own philosophical journey.

In the great tradition of the mythic journey (Chapter 3), the knight has many adventures and interacts with many people along the way, including his former teacher, a brutal hypocrite who had urged him to join the Crusades, and a young woman being tortured and finally burned at the stake as a witch.

In Bergman's great film *The Seventh Seal*, Max von Sydow, left, is the knight who challenges Death to a game of chess in order to gain enough time to seek the meaning of life.

Source: Topham/The Image Works.

Various penitents thrash each other and themselves as signs of penance for sin and as a means of getting rid of a virulent plague. Organized religion, he finds, does not make existence seem valuable. He discovers the fullness of life only when he meets a young married couple named Joseph and Mary who have one child. In the loving warmth of the family circle, where members support and nurture each other, life begins to make sense. Contrasted with one dark scene after another is the scene in which he and the family share strawberries and fresh milk in the sunlight. Not to have known love and joy is, he realizes, not to have lived.

Bergman's message is simple but not simplistic. He finds it only after struggling with utter nihilism (the belief that all comes to nothing in the end). With the knight's help, the young family escapes Death. Though he himself will die, his final vision is a joyous one, and the film ends with the happy family standing by the sea as the knight joins a joyful procession silhouetted against the sky and led by the figure of Death. There is nothing mournful here. Death is not to be feared if one has lived for something.

In *Wild Strawberries* Bergman shapes an identical vision in contemporary terms. It is the story of an aging doctor facing death, not in allegorical but in a very real, biological way. The film blends reality, dreams, and memories of the past with sophisticated editing techniques, taking advantage of the storytelling economy allowed by the medium. As in *The Seventh Seal*, the author-director uses a journey for his plot structure. Isak Borg must travel to a great university in order to receive an award for distinguished scientific achievement. While he is traveling, he looks closely at his life and asks whether it has really amounted to something. Unlike the knight in *The Seventh Seal*, who has no family in the beginning, Isak Borg has a son and daughter-in-law with whom he shares only a strained relationship lacking in warmth and spontaneity.

The Knight, challenging Death to a chess match in The Seventh Seal, *learns that death is nothing to fear if one has found meaning in life.*

The travelers stop to pick up some hitchhikers, two young men and a woman, cheerful, casually dressed, and quite different from the stiff academics he has always known. The young woman looks exactly like the sweetheart Borg loved long ago and begins now to remember, the same actress playing both roles. Though he has no intellectual rapport with his passengers, they help to free him from the emotional repression that has destroyed his family. Gradually he relives the summers in the country when he was a free-spirited youth, long before he became a victim of the codified adult world—a time when he was as spontaneous as he now feels when he stops with the hitchhikers to pick and eat wild strawberries by the roadside. (The fruit becomes symbolic in both films of the sweetness of present existence, all we can know for sure.) Bergman asks why ruin existence with rigid norms of civilized behavior and high intellectual standards that imprison the multidimensional human being within each of us? *Wild Strawberries* is a timeless, poetic plea for humanity to hold fast to youth, to love, and to caring—treasures the world will always need.

Federico Fellini

The young Federico Fellini (1920–1993) learned his craft from the Italian neorealistic directors who, in the aftermath of World War II, had little money to work with and often used untrained actors to tell stories of ordinary people amid the streets and buildings bombed out during that war. Fellini, however, dissatisfied with the limitations of using the camera to photograph only external reality as it unfolded, saw other possibilities. He wanted to be a true artist, using the camera for the haunting imagery it could film. He sought to combine realism with poetry. To retain control of his vision, he became his own screenwriter and, eventually, an *auteur*.

In *La Strada* (1955) Fellini tells the story of Gelsomina, a simple-minded young woman (Giulietta Massina) working in a traveling carnival as assistant to Zampano (Anthony Quinn), billed as the world's strongest man. Secretly in love with him, she becomes his virtual slave, although his enormous ego doesn't allow him to treat her like a fellow human being. He rebukes her for every little mistake and eventually deserts her altogether, leaving her penniless in a world she can never hope to comprehend. The only tenderness she is ever shown comes from a musician, also a victim of Zampano's brutality, who teaches her to play a simple tune on a trumpet. In the final scene, as Zampano sits on the sand near the water and recognizes that for all his strength he is nothing, he begins to recall Gelsomina's devoted smile and the sound of her music. He weeps.

There was in Fellini a joy in images, a sad flavor of life, a something of Cervantes and Rabelais that somehow makes us finally shout "Yes but" to all criticism.
—**Donald Lyons**

La Dolce Vita (The Good Life), which appeared in 1959, was a three-hour film, shot in color, about the moral decadence of postwar Rome, a gathering place for the rich and the bored. It established Fellini's worldwide reputation among audiences seeking an artistic alternative to commercial movies. The images and camera wizardry are unforgettable. The opening shot has become classic in film history, an example of what would be Fellini's trademark: the bold, fantastic, and symbolic image that stimulates both the eye and the mind. A helicopter is carrying a statue of Jesus to a new location. As it flies over a city of shiny modern hotels and aqua-blue swimming pools, over bikini-clad bathers and merry-makers clinking glasses in sidewalk cafes, the shadow of Jesus is unnoticed by the self-centered, vain, bored, hopelessly materialistic people below.

Fellini's symbolism is not as easy to fathom as one might think. The helicopter image could be interpreted as the need for Christian belief, but it could also be saying something about the decline of the church, powerless against the forces of moral decay in the "new" Italy. The film's climactic image is even more ambiguous. As an assortment of scantily clad sunbathers lazily stretch out on the beach, a huge, unidentifiable dead fish is washed ashore, its still-open eye terrifyingly staring. Is this a message from an angry God? Or is Fellini saying that God is dead, that there is little hope for the redemption of this "good life" because there is no redeemer?

Even *La Strada* had left an ambiguous message. Is love the answer? To what question? The young woman's love for Zampano bore no fruit, and the strongman is left with no one to love him. Is love just another illusion, sweet and poetic but, sadly, non-existent?

As he continued to experiment, Fellini became more and more complex. He turned inward upon himself and concentrated on the often tragic waning of the artist's creativity (perhaps fearing that it was happening to him?). In what many consider Fellini's masterpiece, *8 1/2* (1963), the protagonist is a film director who, like Fellini, has made eight films and is now seeking to finish his ninth, except that he never quite gets there. Early commercial success, fame, a restless sexual appetite, and the continual pressures exerted by Hollywood-influenced studio executives all conspire to keep him from focusing sharply on his goal.

Again the opening shot is memorable. The protagonist is inside an automobile on a ferry, windows shut tightly so that sounds of reveling passengers cannot be heard. It is the artist alienated within his environment. Yet there is no comfort in that inner space, only more confusion. Fellini in a few breathtaking seconds has summed up the plight of the artist in an indifferent world. The fantastic final scene, in which various kinds of artists are shown dancing in a ring, gives hope that somehow the creative imagination will survive, but it might also mean that true art is simply going in circles within itself unable to reach an audience.

Some have said that Fellini would have reached more people if he had used his genius to good commercial effect, but it is his very need to use film as a vehicle of self-expression that makes him an auteur, one who had to tell his own story whether anyone liked it or not.

Alfred Hitchcock

Unlike Orson Welles, who came to Hollywood determined to create film art, British-born Alfred Hitchcock (1899–1980) was imported to make scary melodramas and only gradually acquired the critical reputation his work continues to merit. Known first as a man who made thrillers about spies and murders among highly civilized people, he was dubbed the "master of suspense" in the late 1930s. The plots in his films were filled with unexpected twists, and always there was a breathtaking and surprising finale with an always new and ingenious kind of danger, as in the 1942 spy film *Saboteur*, when hero and villain have their showdown fight to the death on the torch of the Statue of Liberty.

Drama is life with the dull bits cut out.

—**Alfred Hitchcock**

Hitchcock, however, soon tired of exploiting in obvious ways the audience's love of terror. His work acquired greater subtlety. His evildoers were generally suave, sophisticated beings on the surface, but underneath they were inhuman, disordered, and dangerously antisocial. In films like *Shadow of a Doubt* (1943) and *Strangers on a Train* (1951), evil enters the lives of ordinary, decent people, whom we get to know and like, and only then does Hitchcock, the master craftsman, put them in danger, causing the viewer's heart to pound a little faster.

His greatest early success was the 1946 *Notorious*. In a South American country, a Nazi spy lives in luxurious surroundings with his beautiful wife, who has been manipulated into the marriage by a handsome U.S. intelligence agent seeking to trap the husband. The agent is played by the dapper Cary Grant, whom we have met before, and the wife by Ingrid Bergman, who had been Bogart's beloved Ilse in *Casablanca*. The wife, of course, loves the agent, but his feelings for her are ambiguous until he fully recognizes her perilous circumstances. Then it becomes a matter of rescuing her—certainly a Hollywood cliché. But in Hitchcock's hands, the tired old plot is revitalized, mainly because the director avoids obvious devices, once again imposing evil on an otherwise civilized and ordered world.

The most suspenseful moments in the film occur during an elegant party at the spy's mansion, when the agent and the wife, searching in the wine cellar for a vital message hidden there, are startled to hear the husband coming down the steps. They hide behind a row of shelves. While the husband quietly searches for a certain vintage, a bottle of wine on a shelf next to them perches dangerously on the edge. If it falls, the agent will be exposed, and both he and the wife may die. Without relying on creepy background music, Hitchcock instead gives us a close-up of the bottle. We keep expecting the bottle to crash and the deadly silence to be shattered. Hitchcock understood that real terror comes from what is imagined by the audience before anything is shown.

Of course, the spy is ultimately foiled, and the wife ends up in the arms of the agent. Hitchcock, with his cynical view of the world, also had a wonderful sense of humor. We can feel him smiling behind the fade-out. The director's personal philosophy, however, had no humor in it. He believed implicitly that we live in a fundamentally amoral universe in which good triumphs only by accident, in which, despite the civilized façade we erect, chaos is the law of nature.

In *The Birds* (1963) that chaos comes frighteningly to life in a formerly peaceful northern California village. Without warning and without any known motives, birds gang up on the town' inhabitants, killing some, injuring others. The most memorable scene is typically Hitchcock: the juxtaposition of danger and normal activity. A woman sits outside an elementary school, enjoying a cigarette as she waits, totally unmindful of a grim scene taking place behind her, where hundreds of blackbirds are massing in the schoolyard. From inside the schoolhouse comes the joyful sound of innocent young voices singing. Suddenly the calm erupts into a scene reminiscent of the elongated moment in Eisenstein's Odessa steps sequence in *The Battleship Potemkin*. The woman, the children, and the teacher are running down a steep hill, holding up their arms to shield themselves from the shrieking onslaught. Hitchcock cuts from one fleeing person to another in a montage so rapid that we actually *see* very little of the devastation but *think* we see it all.

Hitchcock had already used this technique in *Psycho* (1960), considered by many critics to be his masterwork. The film, which remains popular, is one of the scariest movies of all time. Here evil assumes the form of an apparently sweet, shy, and lonely young man who so yearns to be reunited with his dead mother that he sometimes wears her clothes and assumes her identity. In this guise he is capable of committing brutal acts without knowing what he is doing.

In *Psycho*, the Hitchcock vision of the world is fully realized. His philosophy of evil provides him with a signature technique for terrifying the audience. As usual, he places a twisted individual next to people who are unaware they are living in a dangerous world. An attractive young woman who has embezzled a huge sum of money is driving away from the scene of her crime but finds herself caught in a blinding rainstorm. Seeking shelter for the night in a motel where she is the only guest, she is relieved to be the recipient of warm hospitality by the shy young owner. As the woman prepares for bed, feeling snug and cozy and happy that she has evaded pursuit, she steps into an invitingly hot shower, apparently safe.

In the shower scene of Psycho *we think we are seeing every moment of gruesome horror, but in fact the scene moves so quickly that we actually see only a collage of camera shots. We have not witnessed the actual stabbing.*

The shower scene is one of the most admired ever filmed. We do not expect terrible things to happen in such a usually safe place. What surroundings could be more conventional and uncharacteristic of a horror film? As the woman lathers herself generously, washing away her guilt, enjoying the warm stream of water caressing her face, suddenly there appears a silhouette of someone who seems to be holding a knife. Against a score of violins imitating the sounds of a scream, the woman is repeatedly stabbed. We think we are seeing every moment of her agony, but in fact the scene moves so quickly that we are actually watching only a collage of camera shots: the water, the shower head, the woman's hands to her face, blood swirling into the drain; finally there is only an ominous silence as we are shown a close-up of a dead face, eyes still open in horror. We have not seen the murderer, nor have we seen any actual stabbing. The scene, which lasts only 45 seconds, was composed of 78 distinct shots, edited to move so rapidly through the projector that the effect is one of subliminal horror.

Hitchcock combined a civilized directing style with a zest for the bizarre and frightening. The real irony, of course, is that here was a screen auteur who believed that disorder and chaos were found in both human nature and the natural world, yet who communicated his belief in a very planned, meticulously ordered way, with the intricate details of every shot set down in writing before the camera was ever turned on. Perhaps Hitchcock is ultimately saying that art is the only compensation for evil.

Akira Kurosawa

Kurosawa is a man if all genres, all periods, bridging in his work the traditional and the modern, the old and the new, the cutures of the East and the West.

—**Ephraim Katz**

We have already mentioned the Japanese film *Rashomon* as an example of how the cinema is able to show the same scene from different points of view. That film catapulted its director, Akira Kurosawa (1910–1998), into the forefront of internationally recognized filmmakers and brought new audiences to an appreciation of the non-Western cinema. Though he had studied Western techniques very carefully, learning the wizardry of the camera, Kurosawa was also dedicated to recreating his country's past and bringing it to the attention of a worldwide audience. His masterpiece, *The Seven Samurai* (1954), introduced that audience to the

Kurosawa's masterpiece introduced Western audiences to Japan's noble warrior class.

Source: Courtesy Everett Collection.

code of feudal Japan's warrior class, their nobility, their sense of honor and decency, and their swordsmanship, which samurai were always prepared to demonstrate for a good cause. In some sense, the samurai were the equivalents of King Arthur's Round Table knights.

The Seven Samurai strengthened Kurosawa's already growing reputation and caught the attention of Hollywood, always eager to jump on a new bandwagon. In 1960 director John Sturges brought forth *The Magnificent Seven*, an unabashed westernization of feudal Japan, in which a band of roaming gunfighters with no allegiances fight against an army of bandits terrorizing the innocent inhabitants of a Mexican village. The blazing and dangerous shootout turns the previously lawless bunch into righteous crusaders. The film, which owes everything to Kurosawa, was hailed by critics as an ethical western with a solid sense of values.

Kurosawa always recognized his own debt to Western culture, and one of his most distinctive achievements was the Asianization of Shakespeare. *Throne of Blood* (1957) was his version of *Macbeth*, and *Ran* (1983) was his version of *King Lear*.

Like Chaplin before him, Kurosawa worked in black and white longer than Western directors did, preferring it for the *chiaroscuro* contrast between shadow and light that had distinguished *Citizen Kane* and the major film noir movies. In *Ran*, however, he capitulated to the public—both East and West—in their preference for Technicolor; the result was, in the opinion of many critics, color cinematography that rivals Impressionist art.

Kurosawa is also noted for his meticulous approach to filmmaking, often holding up production if something about the set was not quite right. On one occasion, during the filming of *The Seven Samurai*, he insisted that the painstakingly constructed sixteenth-century fortress—a set costing over a million dollars—be completely torn down and rebuilt because the carpenters had used steel nails that didn't exist at the time in which the film was set. When someone objected "Who'll know there are steel nails holding up the set?" he answered, "I will."

Ironically, as Kurosawa's reputation began to grow in the West, he steadily lost favor in Japan, especially among younger audiences and filmmakers, who thought his historical epics were too old-fashioned. Late in life he was reduced to begging for money to make a film. He even tried to commit suicide. The world of art was grateful that he failed.

Stanley Kubrick

An American director whose films were sometimes funny, even when his themes were death and the destruction of the planet and the cosmos, Stanley Kubrick (1928–1999), in the best tradition of satire, lashed out at self-deception and hypocrisy. He always did the unexpected, refusing to turn out formula work designed for the "blockbuster" market. He used a lot of music in his films, but never as an obvious parallel to emotion. He took many chances in an industry where risk-taking has become increasingly expensive. Very much in the tradition of Orson Welles, the earlier bad boy of Hollywood, Kubrick attained worldwide recognition as a true auteur.

I think clearly that there's a basic problem with people who are not paying attention with their eyes. They're listening. And they don't get much from listening. . .

—**Stanley Kubrick**

Paths of Glory (1957) is an early, straightforward narrative film based on an incident that struck Kubrick as too bitter for satire. It denounces officials who save themselves at the expense of those serving under them. In World War I an ethical French Army colonel (Kirk Douglas) finds himself at odds with some generals who he believes are attempting to conceal their responsibility for a mistaken strategy that has resulted in unnecessary bloodshed. In an effort to prevent the remaining soldiers from resisting their next order, the generals have decided to make an example of three soldiers chosen at random and convicted of cowardice. They are to be given a speedy trial with a foregone conclusion—conviction and death by firing squad.

The colonel is assigned to defend them but refuses to just go through the motions and play the generals' game. Instead, he investigates and learns the truth, including the fact that a lieutenant chose one of the men for death not randomly, but for personal reasons.

Despite the eloquence of the colonel in defending them, the men, as expected, are condemned to die. On the night before the execution, they face the prospect in different ways. One becomes so hysterical he needs to be drugged into insensibility. When another points out that a cockroach in the cell will continue to live after they have died, the third man matter-of-factly steps on it and remarks, "Now he won't." The third condemned man has suffered so many injuries during the fighting that he cannot walk. Nevertheless, at dawn he is carried outside on a stretcher that is placed upright in range of the firing squad.

After the execution is duly carried out, the colonel is congratulated for dispatching his assignment so well. He knows that if he remains silent about the costly errors of the generals, he is sure to earn a promotion. To their astonishment, he insists on telling the truth, then walks out of the meeting after hearing that the next morning the troops will once again be commanded to suffer more bloodshed in a hopeless cause. In a moving final scene, he passes a tavern where a young German woman, a prisoner of war, is singing a plaintive song for the entertainment of happily drunken soldiers. He decides to delay telling them the grim news about what awaits them the next day. Released during the Korean War that many were protesting as immoral, *Paths of Glory* was readily seen as its own kind of protest, from a director who was not afraid to use the film medium as an agent of change.

Dr. Strangelove, or How I Learned to Stop Worrying and Love the Bomb (1963) continued Kubrick's interest in antiwar, antihypocrisy themes, but in a blatantly satiric style. It was made just when America was becoming involved in Vietnam and some legislators as well as many in the Pentagon were considering an all-out nuclear war against the communist world.

The film concerns the effort of a general named Jack D. Ripper to start a war by ordering American pilots to drop a nuclear bomb on the Soviet Union. When word reaches the Pentagon, the president and his staff are able to rescind the order, but one bomber crew continues flying. Kubrick parodies World War II movies by making the bomber crew the customary cross-section of geographic and ethnic backgrounds. The music accompanying the bomber as it flies over Soviet territory is the Civil War song "When Johnny Comes Marching Home Again." The pilot, wearing a ten-gallon hat, discovers that the bomb bay door will not open; undaunted, he climbs on the bomb himself and, uttering a triumphant "Yee-haw," rides it gleefully to the destruction of both himself and thousands of civilians below.

The president of the United States puts in a call to the leader of the Soviet Union. In an effort to be fair, he suggests that, since an American plane has bombed Soviet territory, perhaps the Soviet leader would like to retaliate by bombing "only" one place in America. But that solution would not work. He learns that a Doomsday Machine designed by the Soviets to rid the planet of all life for the next ninety-nine years has started its countdown. Nothing can stop it. As politicians and military strategists on both sides prepare to take shelter deep underground (accompanied by lovely young women who will breed future generations), they look forward to a time when their descendants will be able to continue the hostilities, once Earth has breathable air again. The final scene shows an airplane being refueled by another plane in midair, to the tune of "We'll Meet Again."

Kubrick showed himself consistently concerned about cruelty, whether it stems from corruption in high places or the dehumanizing effects of technology, or—as in *A Clockwork Orange* (1971)—from a ruthless penal system that tames a violent central character, using methods that are as sadistic as he is. The film's protagonist is Alex, a violent criminal so passionately in love with Beethoven's Ninth Symphony that his sexuality becomes uncontrollably stimulated when he hears it and he commits one violent rape after another. When he is finally captured and sent to prison, Alex is offered a chance for early parole, but only if he is willing to submit to behavior modification to ensure that he will never commit another crime. He agrees and is strapped to a machine, his eyes taped open, while being forced to look at films of brutality. Simultaneously, he is given sickening drugs and forced to listen to the final movement of the Ninth Symphony. This aversive conditioning will, according to the theory, safeguard society. From that time forward, the music as well as thoughts of crime will cause Alex excruciating pain. In this sci-fi treatment of a serious theme, Kubrick continued his imaginative examination of contemporary problems for which we human beings as yet have found no solution. In this case, the problem was the question of whether "justice" may be as bad as the crimes it seeks to punish.

Riding the atom bomb happily to the earth in Kubrick's vicious satire on presidential and military mentality, *Dr. Strangelove*.

Source: The Everett Collection.

Francis Ford Coppola

If Francis Ford Coppola (b. 1939) had directed only *The Godfather* trilogy beginning in 1972, he might still lay claim to being an acknowledged American film auteur. He took the popular theme of rival Mafia families and, especially in the first two films of the trilogy, transcended Hollywood formula to achieve works of Greek-like tragic dimensions, the dream of many an artist working in both theater and film.

In Mario Puzo's powerful novel of a Mafia empire and its ruling patriarch, respectfully known as "godfather" to the extended Mafia family (Color Plate 28), Coppola saw the stuff of which great tragedy is made: a proud family dynasty in which the sins of the father condemn the next generations to repeat the same crimes of extortion and brutal murder and to suffer the vengeance of their enemies. The protagonist of the saga is the eldest son of the patriarch, a young man of basic moral decency who, like Hamlet, is forced into upholding his murdered father's honor, though he lacks the tough-mindedness for the job.

A belief in a supernatural source of evil is not necessary; man alone is quite capable of every wickedness.

—**Joseph Conrad**

Coppola brought other riches to the project besides co-authorship of the screenplay and a director's keen sense of rhythm. He possessed the stage director's ability to extract performances of sustained psychological realism and subtlety (still rare in the film medium) and the film director's ability to tell a story in image, sound, and quick cuts, always in control of a pace that kept audiences on the edge of their seats. In one memorable and representative scene, the idyll of a Sicilian wedding, filmed against a glorious background of mountains, olive trees, and azure sky, with a lilting Italian melody playing off in the distance, is abruptly interrupted by a car bombing. *The Godfather* renders themes of family tragedy, violence, and betrayal with a haunting visual lyricism never before achieved in a gangster film.

Like many others who score a tremendous box-office success, win awards, and earn lavish praise from critics and peers, Coppola seemed to believe he had been handed a blank check and could proceed to go his independent way. He established his own company and embarked on projects that took no notice of current public tastes. In 1979 he engineered one of the most controversial film projects of all time: *Apocalypse Now*, loosely based on Joseph Conrad's great novel *Heart of Darkness*, which dealt with the search through a dense jungle for a missing white trader, finally discovered to be a mad tyrant ruling an African tribe.

Coppola's film sets the story in Cambodia during the Vietnam War, and it involves the search for a missing U.S. military officer, who is eventually revealed as a cruel overlord. A box-office disappointment in 1975, it was released in a restored version in 2001, but critical reaction has always been decidedly mixed. Many critics place it up there with *Citizen Kane*; others see it as an ambitious failure. Keep in mind, however, that even the failures of an artist are worth our time.

Martin Scorsese

Let me put it this way: I'm always questioning...You save a man on one corner and on the next corner a man dies...It begs the question, the constant question of what our existence is, the 'Who-are-we? Why are we here?' kind of thing.

—**Martin Scorsese**

Unlike other auteurs who announced early on that they were walking a different path, Martin Scorsese (b. 1942) reached his present status after initially turning out low-grade formula stuff. Perhaps the reason was that this son of Sicilian immigrants, raised on the crime-ridden streets of New York City, was a product of a professional school of film from which he earned two degrees and at which he wrote and directed several prize-winning short films, leading almost automatically to a job in Hollywood. He paid his dues by working on projects that did nothing for his artistic reputation but caused studio bigwigs to take notice of a talented young filmmaker eager to operate within the system.

Scorsese, armed with studio backing, wasted no time creating a major effort: *Mean Streets* (1973) set in the Little Italy of his adolescent years. It was a moody piece about a young man (the director himself?) alienated from and bitter within a bad environment. The handheld camera, moving along actual locations, made the film seem almost like a home movie and lent further authenticity to it. Whether entertaining or not, it dazzled may critics with its honesty and its performances that in no way resembled traditional acting. Much of the public, however, stayed away.

Scorsese bounced back with a feminist film, *Alice Doesn't Live Here Anymore* (1975), which appeared at just the right time, when critics and public alike were clamoring for movies with strong heroines. The success of *Alice* enabled him to go off on his own once again, and the result was *Taxi Driver* (1976), in which he returned to his favorite subject: the dangerous streets of New York and the angry sensibilities of those who are trapped there. The protagonist is a Vietnam veteran, already scarred psychologically by the war, now driving a cab and turning nearly psychotic from the environment and the frantic pace of city life. The film won the Grand Prize at the Cannes Film Festival, and its star, Robert De Niro, would begin a long partnership with Scorsese. The team paired again in *Raging Bull* (1980), a biography of one-time boxing champion Jake La Motta. Unlike some other filmographies, this portrait, shot in black and white, is brutally realistic and, according to reliable reports, psychologically accurate. There's no denying that Scorsese has been heavily influenced by the film noir tradition, and once again we observe that this genre often transcends escapist formula and becomes screen art.

Emboldened by awards and critical praise, Scorsese, like most auteurs, took a bold chance. In 1988 he filmed an adaptation of Nikos Kazantzakis's highly controversial novel *The Last Temptation of Christ*, seeking to show Jesus as a human being with human doubts and fears. The film was condemned not only by many religious groups, but also by the very critics who had praised Scorsese's earlier work. Some complained that the director soft-pedaled much of the psychological torment Jesus undergoes in the novel.

Changing course again, Scorsese made an uncharacteristically genteel film, *The Age of Innocence*, in 1993. Scorsese seems to have wanted to show what he could do in an entirely unexpected style. The movie, based on Edith Wharton's classic American novel about the moneyed aristocracy of a century ago and its rigid code of manners, moves slowly, relying on many close-ups of expressionless faces, belonging to characters unable to express their true feelings. The plot centers on the love of a married man for a wealthy widow at a time when upper-class marriages did *not* end in divorce. All three characters in the triangle are unhappy: the widow, because she knows she will never have the man she loves; the husband, who knows he must, with feelings of guilt, endure a loveless marriage to a woman who has done him no wrong; and the wife, who knows her husband's anguish but is powerless to help. Very possibly Scorsese was drawn to Wharton's novel because he was looking for a different kind of dramatic tension, one that could not be verbalized by the characters. The material provided a stirring context for a drama of exquisite subtlety.

The Age of Innocence is worth revisiting if only for its lush set decorations, for its gracious music, for its costumes, and for the high style with which the actors move and speak. It features one memorable camera sequence in which a host of New York businessmen in their bowler hats are shown walking briskly along Madison Avenue, while in the background we hear the traditional ballad *I Dreamt I Dwelt in Marble Halls*—cinematic irony at its very best. The slow and melodious music played against the rapid strides of the hundreds of extras makes a powerful statement about corporate culture.

Having become a Hollywood icon, Scorsese somehow never won an Academy Award for Best Picture, until *The Departed* in 2006. Some critics maintained that the celebrated director and acknowledged auteur had sold out to studio bosses who wanted him to take advantage of the public's craving for extreme violence and bloodshed. But others found in this movie, about an Irish mob boss and his two young protégés who are working on both sides of the law (one has infiltrated the police department, and the other is actually an undercover police officer spying on the mob boss), a reaffirmation of Scorsese's patented cynicism, working now with all of his camera skills and mastery of pacing. The finale, in which all three of its stars, Leonardo Di Caprio, Matt Damon, and Jack Nicholson, die in graphic shootouts, has caused many film-goers to turn away from the screen. *The Departed* is a triumph of film realism, if nothing else. Whether one prefers the more subtle Scorsese of *The Age of Innocence* is a matter of taste.

With *The Departed*, Scorsese uses all of his directing skills to create his most violent film, reaffirming the cynicism in much of his work.

Source: The Everett Collection.

Pedro Almodóvar

A master of startling narratives and a unique cinematic style, Spanish film director Pedro Almodóvar (b. 1949) creates films with the recurrent themes of loneliness and the need people have to connect with each other. The work that helped establish his fame with

American audiences was *To sobre mi madre* (*All About My Mother*, 1999), which won the Academy Award for Best Foreign Language film. The plot centers on a single mother in Madrid who sees her teenage son killed by a speeding car and her subsequent journey to Barcelona in quest of the father, a transvestite who has had no previous knowledge of the son's existence. The son's death is used as a device to bring the mother to a city foreign to her and to show her interactions with a variety of striking and memorable characters, including yet another transvestite and a pregnant nun, whom she takes care of. Each character, in typically Almodóvar fashion, needs a human connection and understanding, sometimes there, sometimes not there. The uniqueness of his work, however, is the result not so much of his themes but of his characters, none of whom is stereotyped, all of whom are three-dimensional human beings with different behavioral characteristics.

Hable con ella (*Talk to Her*, 2002) has been hailed by critics in many countries as a masterpiece. A technicality kept it from Oscar consideration, though it was allowed to be cited for its screenplay. The film's central location is a hospital, one of Almodóvar's favorite settings, for a hospital is a place in which the need for connection is acute. In the film, two men visit two comatose women and talk to them, returning again and again in hopes of waking them from what they fear will be a permanent sleep. One of the comatose patients had been a dancer, and her devoted bedside companion becomes the film's hero, a hospital worker who has had no previous encounters with her.

Lonely, as is usual in an Almodóvar film, and desperate for love (also usual), Benigno tries to inhabit the dancer's life by visiting her favorite haunts: a dance studio; a movie house that shows only subtle, uncommercial films; and a theater where he watches ballets and dance revues. The dancer has been in a deep coma for four years. Benigno understands that she will probably never recover, but going through a day in her life is the only way this poignant and pathetically comic individual can make the connection.

The other man, Marco, has found love with a former female bullfighter plunged into a coma after being gored nearly to death. Since she too is unresponsive as he talks to her, and since he therefore shares the same feelings as Benigno, the two men form their own connection, one that subtly suggests the possibility of homosexual attraction, except that nothing comes of it. But that is very much at the core of Almodóvar's work. Often the chance for a deeper connection suddenly appears, only to remain unacknowledged.

Audiences who hunger for challenging screen fare rallied around *Talk to Her*. It is a film without closure, without a climax in any traditional sense. Yet it is not slice-of-life either. Almodóvar uses flashbacks and fantasy, often slipping inside the mind of a character without warning. He will even change the style abruptly, as when he introduces a seven-minute, silent-film sequence in the middle of *Talk to Her* that only in retrospect seems to have a connection with the theme of lost and unfound human connections.

Quite clearly, Pedro Almodóvar doesn't mind mystifying audiences and making them lean into a film that they must watch with an intense focus not usually demanded in a movie theater. His work cannot be viewed passively or for brief relaxation. You can't get up to visit the refreshment counter—at least not without becoming disoriented when you return. It is pure cinema that makes no compromises. And if it doesn't necessarily gel into a neatly shaped whole, the strange journey is eminently worth the time to broaden your toleration and eventual enjoyment of the unfamiliar and the unexpected.

Notes on Critical Viewing

Throughout this book so far, we have stressed the primacy of critical thinking in your life and the role played by the humanities in helping you to develop the skill. The critical viewing of films is a way to bring the pleasure of movie-going to a new and higher level. Recognizing the choices made by filmmakers is akin to learning more about the craft of a poem or a painting. Films come in a variety of themes and styles. Here are some criteria that will help you determine the merit of a film:

Use of a style unique to cinema. No other medium can so skillfully show quick cuts, overlapping dialogue, in contrast to the long speeches of many stage plays, and powerful imagery that needs no words. (In Buñuel's *Viridiana*, an imperious employer reaches out to seduce a frightened servant. Instead of showing the human attack, the camera shifts to a cat pouncing on a mouse.)

Characters with complex inner lives. The best films, like the best novels and plays, reward close attention of viewers willing to listen carefully and concentrate. (There is nothing wrong with casual entertainment, but you tend to forget it once you leave the theater.) For example, Rick Blaine in *Casablanca* is both the hard-boiled realist of film noir and a tender-hearted romantic who would like the world to be a better place.

Relevance to the times. Both documentary and fictional films are sometimes responses to social conditions in need of reform. Ford's *The Grapes of Wrath*, which dealt with displaced farmers forced to become ill-paid migrant workers, and Chaplin's *Modern Times*, which showed the dehumanization of the working class during the Depression, are good examples.

Integrity. Films that present serious problems should respect their audiences enough not to hand them unbelievable solutions. The hero of Coppola's *Godfather* films would rather not become a ruthless killer expected to vindicate the family honor. Coppola might have distorted Mario Puzo's novel by having the hero's moral sense triumph, but he did not. He remained faithful to the novel's recognition that, in Mafia culture, family honor supersedes all else.

Avoidance of stereotypes. Films, past or present, that depict minorities as adorable but unsophisticated, and foreign characters as people wearing strange clothes and following strange customs, may seek to entertain but do little to widen our perspective. For example, both *The Godfather* films and *The Departed* have three-dimensional characters who may be law-defying but are not portrayed as being rotten and soulless and nothing more.

Gravity of theme. If a film deals with a timeless subject, it is usually a sign that the writer or director is reaching for art. *Citizen Kane* concerns the moral decline of a person who values wealth and fame above all else. Both *Wild Strawberries* and *The Seventh Seal* are concerned with the search for the meaning and purpose of life. But a big theme does not guarantee an artistic result. Two-dimensional characters and stilted dialogue can doom even the most high-minded film.

No violations of probability. Distortion of the events in the biography of a public figure is inexcusable, as are tacked-on happy endings not justified by the events leading up to them. Cinema announced early in its history that anything could be fair game when pleasing an audience was at stake, and Hollywood has always been cynical about audience willingness to face reality. In the 1940 stage play *Our Town*, the heroine dies in childbirth, and the implied statement is that birth and death are natural to the life cycle; people have to live with that. It would have been dishonest for the playwright, Thornton Wilder, to ignore death, nor should death have come only to old people. Wilder knows that life does not follow an expected scenario. In the screen version, however, the heroine is brought back from near death, apparently through the strength of love. The film distorted the author's intention. It lied about life. To lie when a film promises to be true to life is to cheat those in the audience who appreciate screen art and do not require a sugar-coated myth.

Realistic depiction of gender. In many films the stereotypical woman has been a decorative "handmaiden" whose happiness depends on victory in the mating game. Typically she is well groomed and well dressed (though never seen at an ironing board) and will encounter a powerful man who by the end of the picture will be convinced that happiness for him will mean marriage to her. Being blonde was helpful, as was living in a society with lots of discretionary income to lavish on jewels and other gifts, supposedly what women really want. Fortunately, Hollywood has broken the mold in the past (Ma Joad was poor but strong-willed and independent) and continues to do so. Films from abroad, especially countries with serious problems of gender inequality, are giving audiences realistic, often painful, insights into women's lives. And many Hollywood and independent films now offer women as capable, multifaceted protagonists, like Frances McDormand's pregnant police chief in *Fargo* (1996).

This chapter has discussed many films, and if you have viewed the ones we singled out for praise, you may disagree with our assessment. Nothing could be more harmonious with the spirit of the humanities than disputes among critical thinkers giving serious consideration to a work that aspires to be art. Often the dispute itself is more important than the work. If you disagree, you are expressing your precious rights of free thought and free speech. What is crucial is the willingness to consider, the openness to possibility, the intelligence to choose.

Key Terms

auteur French term for "author," used in reference to certain film directors whose imprint is found in almost every film they make, because of recognizable camera styles, rhythms, themes, and symbols.

cinematography the way the camera tells a story.

close-up film technique in which the camera moves in to enlarge the image of one character or object on the screen.

conventions elements of filmmaking often unnoticed by audiences, e.g., the presence of the camera and its variety of shots.

cut film technique in which the camera moves from one character to another or from one scene to another; also, a director's command that the shooting of a scene must stop.

dissolve film technique in which one scene fades out, to be replaced by another, or the camera superimposes the next scene on the present one, which then gradually fades out.

docudrama nonfiction film that has not only a narrator but characters, either real people or actors, and a story line.

documentary nonfiction film that usually has a narrator but not a structured story line.

elongated moment film technique associated with Eisenstein, in which an action that may be brief in real time is broken into component details and thus lasts longer in screen time.

establishing shot camera shot used to identify the location of a scene, such as the exterior of a house, which is then followed by an interior scene; sometimes dialogue from the interior scene is heard behind the establishing shot, before we see who is talking.

film noir a genre of film known for dark settings, cynicism, and emphasis on the seamy side of human nature; the story usually centers on crime in the city, investigated by an alienated hero.

flip a cut in which a screen image is turned over quickly like a coin, becoming something else; may still be found in comedies.

freeze frame film technique in which the camera suddenly stops the action and the image becomes a photograph.

genre a category of film, such as romantic comedy, western, or film noir; recognizing genre helps film-goers know what to expect about style and content.

lingering take film technique associated with Griffith, in which the camera lingers on a face or an object to underscore a dramatic effect or a significant moment.

pan film technique in which the camera travels from one character to another, or from one object in a room to another, without pausing on anyone or anything.

persona a characterization identified with a certain actor, such as Humphrey Bogart, often to the point where the public comes to believe the actor and the character are the same person.

point of view the vantage from which the camera is filming a scene so the audience knows whether it is supposed to be inside a character's consciousness or sharing the director's objectivity.

slapstick an enduring comic style in which characters are totally dehumanized, fall down, get hit repeatedly, or flattened against a wall when a door violently opens; the term comes from the sound made by two sticks being slapped together, a sound often used in old films and plays to make a slap or a punch in the nose seem more violent.

tracking shot film technique in which the camera, on rollers or rails, moves in for a close-up or moves outward to display a wider area, such as the gradual revelation of the hundreds of dead in the railway depot scene from *Gone with the Wind.*

Topics for Writing and Discussion

1. Some of the films mentioned in the chapter—*Citizen Kane*, for example—did not fare well at the box office, though they were critically acclaimed. Others were poorly reviewed yet showed soaring box-office receipts. Some critics look with disfavor on the blockbuster, implying that a broad segment of the public is lacking in taste and patronizes bad films. Identify a film you have seen recently that did well at the box office but not with critics and that you consider cinema art. Or identify a film you have seen recently that did not fare well at the box office but that you consider a work of art. Explain why in either case.
2. Write a short paper on a director not mentioned in the chapter whom you consider a film auteur.
3. Chaplin and Bogart were discussed in the chapter as having a screen persona. Write a short paper on a contemporary screen figure who, in your opinion, projects a specific persona, playing the same sort of role in every film. Give specific examples.
4. Does it make any difference that the famous Odessa steps incident depicted in Eisenstein's *Battleship Potemkin* may never have happened? In other words, if a film pretends to be history, is it able to stray from the facts? Does historical accuracy add to a film's value as entertainment?
5. Women and minorities did not fare well in many earlier films. Has the situation improved? Does more need to be done? If so, suggest some remedies.
6. Almost every film today is shot in color. Earlier masterpieces such as *Citizen Kane* and *Casablanca* are in black and white. In the case of both of these films, color was available but not chosen. Why do you think the directors preferred black and white?
7. Reread the section on Alfred Hitchcock's techniques for creating horror scenes. (Or better still, rent *Psycho.*) Compare these techniques with those found in a contemporary horror film. Which do you prefer—the old or the new? Why?
8. Special effects, such as those in the *Spiderman* mega-hits, are hugely popular with audiences. What is *your* opinion? Do you prefer a lot of special effects, or a straightforward story with no special effects? Explain.
9. Look over the section on Major Genres of Film. Which are rarely seen anymore? Why do you think this is the case? Which remain popular? Again, why do you think so?
10. Discuss a film genre that has been overhauled, restyled to fit contemporary tastes. Cite an example of a recent film in the genre and compare it with one you learned about in the chapter.

PART

III

Themes of the Humanities

10 Religion

Overview

Religion is integral to daily life for billions of people around the world. They read books, wear sacred symbols, eat or don't eat certain foods in holiday observances, and are born, married, and laid to rest in accordance with the requirements of a given faith. Because religion is so prevalent and because religious themes appear so frequently in the arts, philosophy, and literature, recognition of the enormous influence of this powerful force is indispensable to a study of the humanities. Among the sacred books of the world are the Hebrew and Christian Bibles, the Qur'an (Koran) of Islam, the Vedas of India, the Buddhist scriptures, and the *Tao Te Ching* (*The Way of Life*) of China, books that offer information about the past and guidelines for living in the present.

Artists and sculptors have for thousands of years depicted the appearance of God, the gods, the afterworld, and innumerable supernatural beings, both demonic and angelic. Religion and religious questions underlie great works of literature such as Dante's *Divine Comedy*, with its descriptions of Hell, Purgatory, and Heaven, and Milton's *Paradise Lost*, with its interpretation of the Adam and Eve story from Genesis and its solution to the age-old dilemma of how to account for evil in a world created by a benevolent God.

Questioning of traditional belief is found in works such as the novels of Fyodor Dostoevski (1821–1888), who eventually decided, after much soul-searching, that Christianity is the answer to the world's troubles. The final sentence of *Tess of the d'Urbervilles* by Thomas Hardy (1840–1928) clearly makes a negative statement about religion; after the execution of the heroine for having murdered her seducer, the narrator comments: "The President of the Immortals had ended his sport with Tess."

This micrograph of Moses revealing that he has received the Ten Commandments is the work of Australian artist Menachem Boas (b. 1949). Micrography is a uniquely Jewish art form, using Hebrew letters to create visual images. *Source:* © Menachem Boas.

Debates over religious doctrines have been widespread in Western humanities for many centuries, but far less among Eastern writers. Western minds have long been accustomed to inquiry and analysis. Even as far back as Augustine, as we shall see later in this chapter, a profound questioning of belief preceded the philosopher's final acceptance of it.

Religion has aroused a great deal of discussion and has even led to devastating wars. It continues to spur heated debates between those who believe in the literal interpretation of a sacred text and those who view the writings as allegorical and metaphoric and therefore not literally true; between those who believe the religion they follow is fixed for all time and those who are flexible, willing to explore and discuss. Others find themselves somewhere in the middle, or else they ignore religion altogether—until it is the center of an issue such as tax support for sectarian schools, public prayer, or a family member's unexpected choice of marriage partner.

This chapter considers some of the many ways in which religion affects us and the humanities. Religion is presented here as a phenomenon found in all cultures and all periods of time, as a recognition of the need to believe in a higher order, and as an investigation into various pathways to divinity.

We have divided the chapter into studies of religions that believe in more than one god; those that see deity as a universal, spiritual order, but not a person; and those that believe in one god only. We conclude with a sampling of religious themes in the humanities.

The Belief in Many Gods

Religion is something infinitely simple, ingenuous. It is not knowledge nor content of feeling. . . it is not duty and not renunciation, it is not restriction, but in the infinite extent of the universe, it is the direction of the heart.
—**Rainier Maria Rilke**

Early religions practiced **polytheism**, with ceremonial rituals honoring different gods. The concept of **monotheism**, the worship of a single deity responsible for the creation and governance of the universe, dates back only a few thousand years to the time of the Egyptian pharaoh Amenhotep IV (c. 1410–1375 B.C.E.), when it replaced traditional polytheism for just a short time. A considerable body of mythology was created around the many gods of early religions. Some gods, like Thor, the iron-fisted ruler of the Norse otherworld, were fierce and terrifying, wielding enormous power over the human race. The Greek goddess Aphrodite, on the other hand, brought love to the world, and the Greek god Apollo brought enlightenment.

Egypt

Beginning at least 7,000 years ago, religion and daily life were inseparable in Egypt. Kings were to be worshipped as gods, and for them great cities and monuments were built. Ordinary people were surrounded with reminders of their god-rulers. Religion thus fostered an extraordinary early civilization. Giant statues, stone busts, heads made of precious metals, temples adorned with elaborate stone carvings, and of course, the pyramids and tombs, built to provide a luxurious afterlife for the pharaohs—all came into existence because the principle of the king-as-god demanded it. Little remains of the cities, but because the great tombs, containing so much artwork and so many artifacts, have stood supremely independent of time, we can piece together an understanding of what ancient Egypt was like.

The walls of the tombs are inscribed with hieroglyphics—carved pictures and symbols representing words and ideas, functioning, as far as we know, as the Egyptian alphabet; and from deciphering them, we have learned that Egyptians thought of life as a continuous, orderly process, governed by a succession of king-gods, who passed their divinity to the next generations. The period of time in which a given family held power was known as a *dynasty*.

The history of Egyptian art is divided into dynasties. While each dynasty has its particular art style, for thousands of years pharaohs were depicted in similar ways, as idealized versions of human beings. Traditional Egyptian art probably influenced the techniques used by Greek and Roman artists to create visual images of their own gods. Since the pharaohs were deities who would live forever in their tombs, there could be nothing "simply" human about the way they looked in stone or metal.

This image of Akhenaton shows a movement away from the traditionally idealized depiction of kings as god in Egyptian art.

Source: (late fourteenth century B.C.E.). Credit: © Giraudon/Art Resource, NY.

In the late fourteenth century B.C.E. a change took place. Amenhotep IV declared that the universe was ruled by one supreme god, Aton, whose visible appearance was the sun's disk, and he changed his name from Amenhotep to Akhenaton, or son of Aton. He said that pharaohs were the earthly representatives of this god and still commanded adoration and worship, though they were no longer to be regarded as gods. After their deaths, kings would enjoy the pleasure of eternal existence. Their tombs were to be built and decorated as before.

The style of Egyptian art, however, was altered during the reign of Akhenaton, as the photograph reproduced here of a *bas-relief* (a stone wall carving) clearly shows. Akhenaton's profile is far from idealized. The features are coarse and the jaw so prominent that it could almost be a caricature.

Akhenaton was succeeded by his son-in-law, Tutankhamen (exact dates unknown), who died at eighteen but still managed to overturn the monotheism of his predecessor. Presumably, as king, he considered himself a god. Preparations for his departure from the world must have begun as soon as he came to the throne, because his tomb, discovered in 1922, is filled with some of the world's greatest art treasures. The pharaoh has become immortalized as "King Tut," a name sometimes used to mean an incredibly wealthy man who flaunts his ownership of every possible material possession.

During the 1970s the Egyptian government sent an exhibition of the tomb's contents around the world. Thousands of people crowded into major museums and marveled at the magnificent pottery, the still intact carvings, and above all, the solid gold casket with its reclining statue of Tutankhamen, arms crossed, each hand holding the scepters of kingly power.

The wonders of Egyptian art arose from the need of powerful men to be enshrined and adored, and this need in turn arose from a religion that conferred godhead to a continuous line of god-rulers.

Hinduism

The origins of the Hindu religion in India are lost in the mists of history. Though the term itself did not appear in the West until the nineteenth century, **Hinduism** is believed to have evolved from around 1500 B.C.E. As it did so, it incorporated into itself many religious practices and writings. We use the term here as an all-inclusive generic word for the religious tradition of India and its practitioners. Within India, however, there have been many historical factions and much disagreement about the interpretation of sacred writings and the role played by the many gods in the lives of human beings.

During the third millennium B.C.E., the land of India was invaded and occupied by numerous armies and cultures, all bringing their own gods, rituals, and practices. Scholars have assigned the date of 1500 B.C.E. as the beginning of the long Hindu tradition because it was around this time that the Aryans (the word *aryan* means "noble") took over, bringing the Sanskrit alphabet and establishing a national religion.

He who hath no understanding, whose mind is always unrestrained, his senses are out of conrol, as wicked horses are for a charioteer.
—Katha Upanishad

Diyaus Pita is the Aryan equivalent of Zeus, the main god in Greek polytheism (Roman name, Jupiter). Prithivi is the earth mother; Indra is the god of storms and war; and Varuna is the god of the sky, responsible for the order in the universe. One of the principal rituals was that of sacrifice (probably human in its earliest phases), for the belief was that the gods would come to earth to help those who had performed the sacrifice. In almost every early religion the gods had to be appeased continually; otherwise, mortals would suffer terrible consequences.

The sacred documents are the *Vedas*, of which the *Rig-Veda* is considered the most important. It contains poems and hymns used in rituals as well as the names of the various gods to whom the rituals were directed. The Vedas are the sacred words revealed to mortals. In this respect they are similar to the Hebrew Bible and the Islamic Qur'an. Closely related to them are *The Upanishads*—not revealed religious truths, but rather, philosophical dialogues between holy men and their students. But they contain strict guidelines for living and are therefore also considered sacred. One of the most beloved texts is *The Bhagavad-Gita* ("Song of the Lord"), a still widely read epic poem, which, like *The Upanishads*, offers philosophical views on both human and divine existence. In addition to these writings are literary works that depict the heroic deeds of ancestors as well as more philosophical arguments about the meaning of life and the responsibilities of human beings toward the gods.

The earliest of these texts is *The Mahabharata*, or "The Epic of the Bharata War." The Bharata was one of the Aryan tribes, and the epic—the longest poem in the history of the world, running to more than 100,000 stanzas—provided descendants with a proud history, much as did the Roman epic *The Aeneid* of Virgil, discussed in Chapter 4. The hero of the Hindu text is Krishna, a god who could also become mortal and assist in a just cause.

Not as long but equally cherished is *The Ramayana*, describing the heroic exploits of Rama, another mortal who is also a deity—in this case the god Vishnu. In addition to the heroic acts, the poem contains passages of advice to mortal beings on how to lead a happy life despite the pain and suffering that abound in the world. The work continues to be held in the highest esteem, and its teachings are still followed by the devout Hindu.

As time passed and cultural strains crisscrossed, the religious tradition of India underwent many changes. Coming to the fore was the familiar threesome of deities: **Brahma**, the creator of all that exists in the visible universe; **Shiva**, the destroyer, who makes sure everything eventually passes out of existence, making way for the new; and **Vishnu**, the preserver, who balances the two forces of creation and destruction so that the continuity of existence is assured. As time passed, Shiva and Vishnu assumed greater and greater prominence in the pantheon of gods.

Vishnu is especially important as the bringer of stability. In the Hindu view of life, the individual, on a day-by-day basis, is aware of continual change, but change is only an illusion. The failure to see the eternal nature of existence is the cause of human suffering.

Shiva is the god of change. He is often shown in Hindu statues and paintings doing an elaborate dance with his multiple arms and legs. The dance represents the continual movement and changing nature of the visible world, and learning to accept it without being overwhelmed is one of the fundamental goals, according to Indian thought.

Shiva, second in the Hindu trinity, shown here as Lord of the Dance, responsible for continual change.

Source: © Scala/Art Resource, NY.

Beyond the constant dance of life, the comings and goings, the daily commerce of the marketplace; beyond wealth, poverty, hard work, love won and lost; beyond pain and death—beyond all these is a universal, unchanging soul, **brahman**, of which everything and everyone are parts. The three gods Brahma, Vishnu, and Shiva are the embodiments of this universal, unchanging soul. They define its workings: creation, destruction, stability. Brahman transcended the separate gods, but it could be known only through them.

Western philosophers and artists have been influenced by this concept of a unifying spirit behind the universe and have given it various names. The German poet Johann Wolfgang von Goethe (1749–1832) called it the "world-soul." The American philosopher Ralph Waldo Emerson called it the "over-soul" and wrote a famous essay by that title. In John Steinbeck's *The Grapes of Wrath*, a novel discussed in Chapter 4, the hero, Tom Joad, explains to his mother that he cannot remain with the family, working only for their survival, when so many others are hungry and homeless. He believes all people are part of "one big soul," and now that he has realized this truth, he has no choice but to work for others, even if it means sacrificing his own safety and the possibility of a happier future.

Walt Whitman, an American poet greatly influenced by the religious thought of India, entitled his most famous work *Leaves of Grass*. Grass, like brahman, is a totality that exists only through its individual leaves. If you have one leaf, thought Whitman, you have grass. If you have one drop of water, you have water. If only one person is left on Earth, humanity has survived. Any individual is as important as all others, and no one individual is more important than the rest. Whitman's famous opening lines should not be interpreted as egotism.

I celebrate myself, and sing myself,
And what I assume you shall assume,
For every atom belonging to me as good belongs to you.[1]

On the other hand, one solitary leaf would be lost in the universe, and so would one lone individual isolated from the human family. Whitman's idea of

The smallest sprout shows there is really no death,
And if ever there was it led forward life, and does not wait at the end to arrest it,
And ceas'd the moment life appeared.

—Walt Whitman

democracy and the relationship between the private citizen and the whole population is a political extension of an ancient religious philosophy.

Whitman, a proponent of human rights, was against all totalitarian governments and against bureaucracy in his own country. Indian religion is egalitarian, at least in principle. As brahman is the big soul, so too in each of us is the individual soul called **atman**. One is the equal of the other. Religious scholar John A. Hutchinson tells us that in the Hindu mind "there is a complete identity between the absolute or universal reality underlying the objective world and that which every man may find at the foundation of his subjecthood. These are two paths to the same Supreme Reality. Of this Reality each human soul is a broken fragment. Hence man's highest destiny is to realize this fact and so to realize the great identity or unity which is fulfillment, salvation, and blessedness."[2]

Greek and Roman Polytheism

We have already talked about some of the many gods in Greek religion, which generally lacked a belief in a universal soul. Instead, the Greek gods and their Roman counterparts were larger-than-life versions of human beings. Zeus and his wife Hera, or the Roman Jupiter and his wife Juno, squabbled continually and constantly meddled in the affairs of people, not always to their benefit. But both the Greeks and Romans respected human rationality and had deities that governed this precious commodity: Athena (Minerva) and Apollo (Roman as well as Greek) were bringers of truth and wisdom to those who performed sacrifices in their honor.

Greece and Rome were divided, however, in their view of humanity's relationship to the gods. Greek mythology is filled with stories of individuals and families doomed because this or that god or goddess was offended by an action or a remark. The sins of a father or mother were always being visited upon the children. Some writers, such as Sophocles, saw life as an unending and in the long run futile struggle to avoid fate. They stressed the anger of the gods and the tragic disobedience of humanity. Others, like Euripides, were either non-believers or else considered the gods on the whole to be whimsical, unpredictable, and unfair to mortals—hardly worth worshipping.

For the Romans the gods were idealized versions of themselves. They incorporated some of the Greek myths into their own literature, but the emphasis was clearly on the godlike qualities of Roman mortals, capable of conquering and ruling the world. Fate existed as a divine force that was taking Roman civilization to every corner of the known world. Greek polytheism had tragic consequences. Roman polytheism offered a vision of Roman superiority.

Native American Religions

Native American cultures and the various religions practiced within them are as diversified as any in the world. People who live near reservations and areas dominated by a particular Native American population may be accustomed to attending exhibitions of arts and crafts as well as ceremonies and rituals that are open to the public. Yet confining one's knowledge of Native Americans to often necessary profit-making events is to deny oneself a deeper understanding of extraordinarily complex civilizations that may be much older than those of the West, which are too often regarded as the very beginning of significant human achievement. "The culture, values and traditions of native people amount to more than crafts and carvings. Their respect for the wisdom of their elders, their concept of family responsibilities extending beyond the nuclear family to embrace a whole village, their respect for the environment, their willingness to share—all of these values persist within their own culture even though they have been under unremitting pressure to abandon them."[3]

Mi taku oyasin.
We are all related.

Source: Lakota pipe-smoking ceremony.

Some anthropologists believe that various Native American groups can be traced back to migrations from northern Asia over 10,000 years ago, when it would have been possible to walk from Siberia to Alaska. But some Native American tribes maintain that their culture has always existed in the Americas, having originally emerged from beneath the earth. Some believe that human beings came first and that many then became animals, a kind of reverse Darwinism that helps to explain, at least partly, the long-standing bond between these cultures and the animal world.

Whatever their beginnings, Native Americans long ago divided into groups, migrating throughout both American continents, establishing early civilizations wherever they settled, developing their own languages, and practicing their own religions. Cultural anthropologists who have made a careful study of the many groups found certain common beliefs and values as well as many differences.

An overarching common belief is a polytheistic one. However, like the Greeks and Romans who were to come, the various groups tended to think of the gods and their world as an extension of this world. Just as some mortals were better hunters than others, so too were there gods and goddesses who controlled the hunt, rewarding those who led exemplary lives, which included performing charitable acts such as sharing food, and punishing those who didn't by making game scarce for them.

The Inuits of Alaska, depended on the sea for their bounty, worshipped a goddess named Sedna, who was part human and part fish and lived underwater. She kept a watchful eye on the daily lives of her people, allowing the good to haul in as many fish as they needed. Among cultures that depended on the land for survival, gods and goddesses were connected to agriculture. In this respect, they shared the same kind of rituals practiced all over the globe by those who feared drought and freezing cold and rejoiced in spring and summer rains.

The arrival of Christianity in or about the sixteenth century created massive changes in belief, lifestyle, and religious practice. In many cases, there was a blending of the old and the new. "God the Father" of the Christians sometimes became the Great Spirit who controlled the entire world, but he had many helpers overseeing the hunt, the planting, and the harvest; thus, religious worship became divided into a number of rituals performed in honor of both the Great Spirit and the other gods and goddesses.

Transitions did not come easily. Often there were terrible clashes between Christian settlers and Native American peoples who were often looked upon as savages, children of the devil. There were frequent massacres, leaving tribes no choice but to retaliate, thus intensifying their reputations as uncontrolled warriors who needed to be slaughtered or converted for their own good. Eventually reservations were established, and many still remain. Assimilation into mainstream culture has of course taken place, but great numbers continue to cherish and practice their traditional customs and modes of worship.

Some Native Americans argue that no such thing as "Native American religion" exists at all, that what some have considered religious practice is in reality the daily mode of existence among a people with close ties to the earth, the sea, and the sky. The contention is that, unlike other cultures with religious observances limited to certain days of the week or certain hours of the day, Native Americans are continually aware of the forces that govern them.

Belief in an Impersonal Divinity

For some Native Americans the Great Spirit is a personal god in human form. Recall that the Native American version of the Twenty-third Psalm, cited in Chapter 4, describes the next world as a tepee in which sits a council of the wise, presided over by a supreme chieftain. Many others, however, view the Great Spirit as the force behind nature on which the survival of humanity depends.

How Hinduism Led to Buddhism

Hinduism, with its principle of the universal soul, does not include a belief in a personal god promising freedom from pain. True, it gives a name to the universal soul: *brahman*. But brahman is not a conscious being. Brahman is universal order. Brahman is what believers mean by "it" in the sentence "It is raining." Rain is in the nature of things, and brahman *is* the nature of things.

Are suffering and pain also part of that nature? Or are they, too, like change, an illusion? The devout in India believe that suffering, if not intentional on the part of some god, must be part of the universal order. Somehow there must be a reason for it, or at least the hope of tolerating it. *The Upanishads* ask the question of whether life is worth living. The answer is in the affirmative, and this fact means that eventually there will be emancipation from pain.

We live very close together. So our prime purpose in this life is to help others. And if you can't help them, at least do them no harm.

—**The Dalai Lama**

This condition was at first called **moksha**, and later, in Buddhism, **nirvana**, a state of bliss that is freedom from the pain and stress of life. Without pain there could be no such thing as bliss. How could anyone recognize bliss if it were attained without a struggle? Reaching moksha is extremely difficult for the average person. Pain must be the result of unfulfilled desire, so clearly desires are bad. Transcending desire must therefore be the primary human goal, even if one is poor and desires a better life. But freedom from desire cannot be accomplished overnight. For some, it can take centuries? But how is that possible?

Feeling constant anger over life's tribulations can easily lead to wrongful deeds, such as stealing, robbing another to satisfy one's own needs, or lying and cheating, even killing. Wrongful deeds result in further misfortune for the individual, because punishment for immoral behavior is also in the nature of things. **Karma** is the name given to the cumulative moral consequences of actions. *Good* karma means an accumulation of good deeds; *bad* karma is the accumulation of sins. At the end of one's life comes the summing up. A preponderance of bad karma results in having to be reborn into a lower social class and attempting once again to lead a virtuous life regardless of suffering. Good karma results in reincarnation in a higher social class with better living conditions and less suffering.

Still, the temptations of this world are great, so the cycle of death and rebirth can be expected to continue for a very long time. Eventually, however—perhaps after many thousands of years—one might attain moksha, the reward of eternal release from pain—not heaven, just peace at last. Within such a state, it was promised, the rightful order of the universe would be understood. One would achieve **enlightenment**, the total union of atman and brahman, and the cycle ends.

The sacred books, however, say that once in a very long time, a person will lead a perfect life and achieve enlightenment without ever having to be reborn. This person is called a **buddha** (meaning "enlightened one"). The coming of a buddha occurs perhaps every 25,000 years. But that belief changed for a small group of people more than 2,000 years ago, a group that would be the ancestors of what is now one of the major religions of the world. One person, after undergoing much pain and suffering to reach enlightenment, was hailed as the promised Buddha and, inadvertently, became founder of a new religion, one that at first held an impersonal view of divinity—until the Buddha came to be looked upon as a god.

Buddhism

The one who was called the Buddha has become, for millions of Buddhists, a godlike figure, though he would not have thought of himself in that fashion. Nonetheless, hailed by his followers as Jesus would be hailed by his, he was originally an unlikely candidate for the honor. Siddhartha Gautama (564?–483 B.C.E.?) was born a prince in India, surrounded by luxuries beyond imagining. He married a beautiful woman, who bore him a handsome son. The family lived in the gorgeous palace he inherited from his father. He was the envy of all who knew him. Yet he became restless and unhappy. Something kept telling him he did not belong where he was, leading a life that was filled with sensuous pleasure but was essentially meaningless. If he continued in this way, he would die leaving behind mementos of a wasted life.

One day, according to legend, Siddhartha went for a walk through his village and encountered three things that were new to him. The first was *poverty*. Everywhere he looked he saw beggars reaching out their bony hands for alms. The second was *sickness*. He saw people who could no longer sit up and beg but could only lie wasting away from malnutrition and disease. Finally, he saw *death*. A man in the prime of life had just died, and his relatives were preparing the body for cremation right there on the street. Siddhartha was appalled by the fact that for the poor people outside the privileged confines of his palace, life amounted to nothing more than a desperate attempt to survive, and the "reward" for the struggle was death and rebirth into perhaps an even more wretched existence.

Sculpture showing the Buddha after he had undergone lengthy fasting. Ultimately he rejected extreme asceticism and adopted the Middle Way.

Source: The Seattle Art Museum, Eugene Fuller Memorial Collection.

Siddhartha is reputed to have experienced a sudden revelation, like Saint Paul, the Emperor Constantine, and Mohammed after him. Legend has it that on that very day he went home, threw off his royal apparel, dressed himself in cast-off garments and rags, bade farewell to his wife and son, and, abandoning the comforts of the palace forever, set out on a quest for another way to live.

Like the beggars he had seen, he sank into abject poverty. One story is that he denied himself food, except for one sesame seed a day, until he grew so weak that he knew he would die before he discovered the secret of a truly meaningful and virtuous life. He was so obsessed with the search for the exact opposite of his former life that he was killing himself in the process. One day he said: "If the string is too tight, it will snap."

Finally, in a state of near total exhaustion, he found a large *bodhi* (or rose apple) tree and flung himself down under it. He sat there in a cross-legged position, not resting against the trunk, because he found that, by sitting perfectly upright, with his back straight, he was wide awake, and in that state he suddenly began to see everything and everyone around him with a clarity he had never known. No doubt in the beginning his inner thoughts collided with his observations of the outside world, but as time went by he must have become less and less aware of his inner life, of being an isolated self and more and more a part of what he was observing. Putting his ego to rest, Siddhartha engaged in the first recorded instance of the **meditation** practice that Buddhists call, simply, "sitting."

Buddhist scripture tells us that there were howling storms, even floods, during the long sitting, which was said to have lasted for forty days and forty nights. Those who gathered around were amazed that Siddhartha never moved or reacted in any way to the pounding of the elements. The scripture also reports that evil demons attempted to distract him, sometimes disguised as beautiful women holding out large baskets of food, but Siddhartha was not to be swayed. At length the storms and demons went away, and there was peace, not only there but all over the world. "Mandarava flowers and lotus blossoms, and also water lilies made of gold and beryl, fell from the sky onto the ground near the Shakya sage . . . so that it looked like a place in the world of the gods. At that moment no one anywhere was angry, ill, or sad; no one was evil; none was proud; the world became quite quiet, as though it had reached full perfection."[4]

Siddhartha had attained enlightenment, an important step on the way to nirvana. In the West, enlightenment means cognitive understanding. In **Buddhism**, an enlightened person loses all consciousness of ego. Utterly detached from participation in the stream of life, he or she sees everything as it is and, gaining total objectivity, begins to understand everyone's thoughts, motives, joys, and sorrows. Since it is freedom from the emotional strain of living within one's ego, enlightenment in Buddhism is the gateway to achieving total peace—nirvana, which is not death but peace without end. In nirvana, atman, the individual soul, is reunited with brahman, the universal soul.

After forty days, according to legend, Siddhartha finally rose from his meditation and decided that he had a greater mission than to remain in the blissful state of enlightenment. He would first advise those who would listen that they must find a Middle Way between the extremes of total self-denial (as when he had denied himself food and money) and a total mystical withdrawal from life. One should conduct oneself like a string that is neither too tight nor too loose. In many statues of Buddha, the fingertips are lightly touching, perhaps suggesting the analogy with the string.

As he walked through the villages of India, Siddhartha would pause to speak to anyone who would listen. Gradually he attracted followers, who trudged beside him, and from time to time he would stop to share with them the insights that kept flooding his mind. The long meditation had sharpened his rationality. He arrived at what were to him the four basic truths of life. He called them the Four Noble Truths:

Life is filled with pain.

Pain is caused by unfulfilled desires.

There is a way out of pain.

The way is to follow the Eightfold Path.

The Eightfold Path has become the Buddhist guide to a life of peace and harmony, a life in tune with the Way, and a life that can, as death nears, be recalled happily, in the knowledge that one has brought goodness into the world. The Path consists of eight directives for living a "right" life. In this context, *right* means acting, reacting, and thinking relative to things as they are, not as we would like them to be or as we pretend to ourselves that they are. It means walking in a constant state of wakefulness so that all actions are appropriate and not based on narrow self-interest.

Right views are opinions based on a knowledge of things as they are.

Right intentions are decisions to act on such views.

Right speech is saying what is appropriate, guarding one's statements so that they do not provoke anger and defensive behavior in others, but it does not mean saying what is known to be false in order to avoid giving offense.

Right conduct is behaving toward and interacting with others in accordance with things as they are, not as you want them to be.

Right livelihood is earning what is needed to survive and help others to survive, but never earning for its own sake and for unnecessary possessions earning makes possible.

Right effort is striving to do what needs to be done, not to advance one's own cause or prestige.

Right mindfulness is maintaining the sitting or meditative attitude anywhere, whether in solitude or in society.

Right concentration is focusing unwaveringly on reality without the intrusion of ego and the idle chatter that floods the mind.

The Buddhism of Siddhartha was never intended to be a religion as such. Its practice was intensely personal. Instead of commandments, it offered advice for leading a life of goodness. As the centuries passed and followers numbered in the millions, Buddhism acquired many different aspects.

Hinduism, continuing to evolve, had followers who incorporated many of Siddhartha's teachings as well as features of the ancient Vedic religion of Brahma, Shiva, and Vishnu and the wisdom of the sacred texts. Statues of the Buddha can be found in India, where he is sometimes referred to as Lord Buddha. The meeting of Hinduism and Buddhism was not, however, always a peaceful one. One Hindu sect developed the legend that Krishna, the god-hero of *The Mahabharata*, came to earth in the guise of the Buddha for the purpose of leading bad people away from the Hindu faith, thus guaranteeing that they would be damned forever.

It is this fear of exposure, this denial of impermanence that imprisons us. It is only by acknowledging impermanence that there is a chance to die and the space to be reborn and the possibility of appreciating life as a creative process.

—**Chogyam Trungpa**

Zen is a way of liberation, concerned not with the discovery of what is good or bad or advantageous, but what is.
—**Alan Watts**

A major difference between Hinduism and the Buddhism of Siddhartha is the matter of attaining nirvana (or moksha) in one lifetime. Hinduism retains the belief that only the rare individual escapes having to be reborn. The concepts of karma and reincarnation continue to underlie the caste system.

Historically, **caste** was not a social class defined by economic resources and the lifestyle these made possible, with the hope of moving upward. The caste system rigidly confined the people born into it because it was tied to religion. Those born into dire poverty on the lowest rung of society were assumed to have had bad karma. The hapless beggars doomed to this miserable existence were called the *untouchables*. The polar opposite was the *Brahmin*, or priestly, caste. Its members were affluent and deserving of the respect of their inferiors, for it was believed they had lived over and over, gradually perfecting their lives so that, when they died, they would not have to come back. Though Indian society has become more flexible, some rigidity in social strata, related to religious tradition, still exists.

Zen Buddhism is that strain of the parent philosophy and practice that came to be closely associated with Japan. It was carried from India to China, however, before reaching Japan. The word *Zen* is a Japanese version of the Chinese word for meditation: *ch'an*. An austere, monastic form of Buddhism, Zen requires many years of practicing detachment and a continuing regimen of lengthy meditation sessions. The Zen tradition is traced to a Hindu monk named Bodhidharma. A thousand years after Siddhartha's enlightenment, he traveled to China with missionary zeal to win converts to Buddhist teachings. According to legend, this pious individual sat in cross-legged meditation on a mountain top for nine years until his legs fell off.

Zen is now practiced not only in Japan but in all Western countries. Zen novices enter a monastic facility called a *zendo* and are instructed in meditation technique by Zen masters, who are traditionally severe with their charges. They keep hawklike eyes on them during the meditation sessions and have been known to discourage sleeping by striking offenders between the shoulders with a thick wooden board.

Zen masters and their students engage in dialogues in which questions are asked that cannot be answered through logical reflection. Confused at first, the student gradually becomes adept at answering intuitively with what is called the *non-mind*. A typical exchange might be the following:

> *Master: How great is the merit due to me?*
> *Student: No merit at all.*
> *Master: What is the Noble Truth in its highest sense?*
> *Student: It is empty, no nobility whatever.*
> *Master: Who is it then that is facing me?*
> *Student: I do not know.*

The most famous Zen question—*What is the sound of one hand clapping?*—has been traced to the teachings of an eighteenth-century Zen monk named Hakuin Ekaku (1686–1769), who was also an artist. The aim of this question and response training is to clear the mind of the traditional reasoning process, which separates the individual from reality. In Zen Buddhism, reality has no words and thus cannot be understood rationally. The aim of meditation is to confront the void that is reality, thus losing ego and its fantasies.

Zen art has many facets, ranging from quick pen-and-ink drawings produced rapidly after a lengthy period of meditation, to sophisticated portraiture, such as the famous depiction of Bodhidharma by the fifteenth-century Zen master Tenyu Shokei reproduced here. The wide-open eyes suggest a state of total wakefulness, which is the goal of Zen, and the absence of eyelids is derived from the legend that Bodhidharma pulled them off in order to remain awake.

The portrait of Bodhidharma by the fifteenth-century Zen master Tenyu Shokei captures the aggressive wakefulness of Zen's founder.

Source: Tenyu Shokei (15th century), "Bodhidhama," Nanzenji Temple, Kyoto, Japan. Credit: Spencer Museum of Art, University of Kansas, Lawrence.

In modern Buddhist monasteries, Buddhist monks and nuns spend long hours in silent meditation. Interaction with the outside world is limited to purchasing necessities or tending to the poor and the sick. But many Buddhists paint or write poetry, stories, and music in their spare time. Or they record philosophical insights in journals they carry with them.

Though the schools of Buddhism are varied, the common thread is to trust the workings of the universe. Just as "it" knows when to rain, when to grow and yield the harvest, people must learn to walk in step with "it." If they do, they will behave righteously toward others, they will be treated righteously by others, and they will be at peace. Hinduism, Buddhism, and Taoism, a religious philosophy developed in China, share a belief in an intelligent (but not in the human sense) spirit that controls the operations of nature, which is its outer garment. If left alone, its workings ensure peace and harmony to all living creatures. Unfortunately some of these creatures seek to control it for their personal gain, thus destroying peace and harmony.

This intelligence is *brahma* in Hinduism, **dharma** in Buddhism, and the **Tao** (pronounced "dow") in Taoism. A common definition is "the Way." Morally right actions are aligned with the Way. The individual who follows the Way lives in harmony within society and the environment, and both of these live in harmony with the individual.

Taoism

Of Chinese origin, Taoism can be traced to the writings of Lao-tzu, who is believed to have lived some time during the sixth century B.C.E., but about whom little else is known. The name, simply meaning "the old one," may be purely legendary. The book attributed to "the old one" is called the *Tao Te Ching* (pronounced "dow day jing") or *The Way of Life*. Reprinted continually, it is a slender volume of short poems, often cryptic, seemingly simple, but at the same time extremely profound, containing the view that the Way is an impersonal divine order that rules the universe. Taoism is a religion only in the sense that its followers are obligated to live their lives in accordance with this order. It is expressed through the health of the body's system, the mind's harmonious processes, ethical dealings in all human interaction, respect for elders, and hospitality toward strangers. Those who do not follow the Way in every action or thought are considered nonfunctioning members of society and treated accordingly.

The philosophy grew out of a Chinese civilization that was rapidly advancing and was proud of its urban culture. In India at approximately the same time, in

The cosmic opposites in Taoism: yin, the passive element; yang, active energy. Though they are opposites, each is depicted as containing part of the other.

Source: New York Public Library.

the era of Siddhartha, there was a great disparity between the poor and the affluent. Siddhartha, a prince, saw no reason to be proud of luxury and left his place in society. Taoism, on the other hand, tells us we are all part of that society, with all of its prejudices and double-dealing, and teaches us to conduct ourselves honorably and ethically within it.

Fundamental to Taoism is the belief that the Tao operates through the continual interactions of opposites: joy and pain, birth and death, male and female, day and night, cold and heat, success and failure, and so on. We cannot embrace life without being prepared for death. The fear of death—or, for that matter, of anything opposite to what we hold dear—leads to suffering. If youth, vigor, and unwrinkled good looks are all-important, we must know that they cannot last and we must therefore feel no anguish with the onset of age. Success and failure are implicit in the way the world goes. Today's failure might be tomorrow's brilliant achiever.

The universe was created by the entwinement of the fundamental opposites: **yin**, the passive element, and **yang**, the active energy. In Chinese art, yin and yang are visually represented as a circle with a white crescent and a black crescent, each side containing a smaller circle of the other's color. The white crescent, yang, is the sun, the source of all life, and is traditionally known as the masculine principle. The black crescent, yin, is the moon, the passive and traditionally feminine principle. The passive yin requires the driving force of the active yang to bring forth the variety of things that go to make up the world. The two are equal partners. Without yin, the universe is cold and lifeless, a barren void. Without yang, yin cannot create.

All religions are the therapies for the sorrows and disorders of the soul.
—**Carl Jung**

Perhaps the wisest saying of Lao-tzu is the most deceptively simple: *Everything is what it is.* Before protesting "But that's so obvious," consider the statement carefully. We pick a maple leaf from a tree and know it is a maple leaf, not an oak leaf or an elm leaf. If some insect has nibbled away at it, we still know it is a maple leaf, but we say it has a hole in it. We do not gnash our teeth and bemoan the fact that the leaf is not what it should be. We understand that insects are what *they* are and will in the course of time nibble away on some of the leaves.

If we own such a tree and, returning home from a long journey, discover that a blight has struck and our tree has died, we are allowed to feel upset for a time. Our wonderful shade is gone. But the wise course, the Taoist says, is to recognize that blights happen and that is just the way "it" is. *Everything is what it is* helps us to comprehend the Tao. Events like the death of the tree are the way "it" goes. Accepting this is to live in harmony with the universe. But not all of us can do this. Some of us save our own trees at the expense of other parts of nature. Some of us would kill the insect. In Taoism, the death of an insect is as much a cause of sorrow as the death of a tree.

Other parts of nature are what they are and lack the human cleverness to pretend otherwise. Imagine a maple leaf masquerading as an orange blossom! Yet we human beings know how to deceive one another.

Taoism believes that the true nature of each person, what that person is to be, assuming all factors are in their right place, is in harmony with the Way. But things happen, of course. A potentially good member of society can be tarnished by anger or envy or the obsessive desire to win at all cost. Instead of saying about someone, "What a disagreeable, thoroughly obnoxious person," the ideal Taoist might say, "How sad that something so terrible has happened to that person." After all, if people we love become very ill, we do not hate *them*; we hate the disease; we hate their suffering. Naturally we find it difficult to forgive what seems like malicious intent on someone's part, and there are those who will probably never change, never make society better, never perform a good deed. Yet anger and hatred on our part do not solve anyone's problems and can only weaken us.

Central to Taoist teachings is the concept of **wu wei**. Perhaps the closest definition is: *to do without doing*. Exponents of Taoism experience difficulty explaining to the Western mind what they mean by *doing*. One possibility is that *doing* in this sense is *attempting to manipulate the reality in which we find ourselves*—to alter it in accordance with the way we want it to be. This involves manipulating the thought and behavior of the people with whom we have to deal, even to lie and cheat to do so. On the other hand, if we allow the Tao to work freely, then we are not *doing*.

If you do without doing, you are following your true nature, and you will be successful no matter how insignificant your accomplishments may seem to others. Every true person contributes to the richness of the Tao, and the Tao enfolds that person in its protective arms.

Does *wu wei* mean that we should remain passive while others manipulate us? Does it mean that our goal is to sit back while others suffer pain or injustice? Not at all. Lao-tzu also says: "*The Tao does not do, but nothing is not done.*" Taoism teaches that we must take appropriate action whenever necessary and possible. The Tao is ethical in all things, and your true nature is ethical as well. If you become aware that a close friend is guilty of wrongdoing, it is your obligation not to turn away or say "I really don't want to become involved." You must act to prevent the wrong from happening, or if it has already happened, to see that the action does not go unreported. Putting friendship before ethical responsibility may be deeply rooted in our natures, but these "natures" are distortions of the Tao, acquired from a long history of living within complex society and adopting its values.

Taoism has readily found its way into the rest of the world. It has been warmly greeted, especially in the West, where the *Tao Te Ching* of Lao-tzu can be found abundantly in bookstores and libraries. It appeals to those who are tired of the ceaseless quest for money and fame, but also of the need to comprehend and then alter the way the universe works. "Leave it alone!" is the motto of Western Taoists. "Leave it alone, and it will run as it should." They want forests, for example, to be left as nature intended, but they may also recommend cutting undergrowth to diminish the danger of wildfires, though they realize some fires can be nature's way of cleansing itself. Echoing Taoist sentiments, environmentalists believe in working in close cooperation with nature. Opponents believe that human reason can and should bend nature to its will.

Some Western scientists find Taoist philosophy profoundly meaningful and hardly limited to Chinese culture. In 1976, for example, Fritjof Capra published *The Tao of Physics*, in which he shows parallels between the Taoist concept of yin and yang and the basic forces in nature that involve the interaction of opposites, as in the magnetic force that binds protons and electrons to form the nucleus of the atom.

Taoism has found its way into Western literature in the not-only-for-children books of British author A. A. Milne (1882–1956) about the little bear Winnie-the-Pooh and his friends. In *The Tao of Pooh* (1982) Benjamin Hoff gives us an imaginative introduction to Taoist philosophy, using characters and incidents from the Milne stories. The innocent and childlike Pooh seems a perfect spokesperson for Lao-tzu. Pooh is open to experience; he is close to every moment as it passes. He is never confused by the need to make sense of things, nor is he ever driven by self-interest. Unlike his friend Piglet, Pooh has no sense of self.

In the first book of Milne's Pooh series, the 1926 *Winnie-the-Pooh*, all the animals are excited because Eeyore the donkey is about to have a birthday. Each of them wants to give Eeyore a present, but Piglet, seeking the gratification that Eeyore's effusive thank-you will bring, wants to be the first to present a gift. But the Tao takes care of him!

> *Piglet had gone back to his own house to get Eeyore's balloon. He held it very tightly against himself, so that it shouldn't blow away, and he ran as fast as he could so as to get to Eeyore before Pooh did; for he thought that he would be the first one to give a present, just as if he had thought of it without being told by anybody. And running along, and thinking how pleased Eeyore would be, he didn't look where he was going . . . and suddenly he put his foot in a rabbit hole, and fell down flat on his face.*[5]

Does Piglet learn from this experience? No. He interprets it in a way that shows his continuing preoccupation with self.

> *Piglet lay there, wondering what had happened. At first he thought that the whole world had blown up; and then he thought that perhaps only the Forest part of it had; and then he thought that perhaps only he had, and he was now alone in the moon or somewhere, and would never see Christopher Robin or Pooh or Eeyore again.*[6]

Hoff's study of Taoism in the Pooh stories does not necessarily mean that Milne was consciously imbuing his work with ancient Chinese wisdom. Minds widely separated in time and place can, after all, arrive at the same ideas, testifying to their strength and durability. In any case, Milne made a sizable contribution to the humanities. His books are very wise indeed, proving that sometimes the most complicated things are best explained in simple, not complex intellectual, terms. Certainly *wu wei* can defeat the efforts of learned philosophers, but it can be intuitively accepted with the innocence of a small bear "without a large brain," whose only bout with self-interest revolves around his pot of honey, which he quite naturally hides because that is what bears are supposed to eat according to their true nature.

There are some actual references to Chinese philosophy in the Pooh stories, not to the Taoists directly but to the followers of Confucius (557?–479 B.C.E.), a Chinese master whose wisdom is preserved in a work called *The Analects* (*Sayings*). Confucius negated Taoism, telling his followers that Taoists were out of touch with reality. He did not believe that ethical actions came naturally to us. They had to be taught, and to this end he opened a school dedicated to the teaching of ethics in government, in the family circle, and in all social dealings. But Pooh calls the followers "Confusionists," perhaps thinking of the legend that Confucius died unhappy because he could not establish his ideal society.

Socrates and Plato

The great Athenian civilization of the fifth century B.C.E. witnessed a surge of philosophy, including that of Socrates and Plato, that did not further the cause of polytheism in Greece. Socrates (469–399 B.C.E.) specialized in the **dialectic**, an analytical method of thinking. Instead of merely presenting an idea, he arrives at it by revealing the flaws of its opposite. Though his contributions to human thought are recorded in no writings of his own, his esteemed follower Plato (427–347 B.C.E.) did leave behind some of the greatest works of the humanities, most of them written as dialogues in which Socrates debates with his students on philosophical matters. One of these is *The Republic*, which offers a profound vision of the ideal society.

Socrates was arrested on charges of preaching atheism and corrupting the youth of Athens. Historians of philosophy, however, believe that the true "crime" that condemned him to imprisonment and execution was that he taught his young followers to think for themselves, a goal that makes many governments uneasy. Socrates even referred to himself as "gadfly to the state," and he said it with pride.

According to Plato, Socrates refers both to "gods" and "a god," and it is not clear whether he is making metaphoric use of the terms. In his famous speech to the assembly of citizens who have just condemned him to death, a speech Plato records in *The Apology of Socrates*, he tells them that he harbors no ill will toward them and that they are not to pity him. Rather, they should "be of good cheer about death, and know of a certainty that no evil can befall a good man, either in life or after death. He and his are not neglected by the gods; nor has his own approaching end happened by mere chance."[7]

Wisdom begins in wonder.
—Socrates

The polytheistic reference does not extend to the considerable body of Socratic thought written down by Plato and may simply have been intended to show the citizens that he was in the good hands of a higher authority; that they had not in fact won a victory over him. That authority was probably his own virtuous existence guided by the principle of reason. He concludes the speech by saying that the hour of departure has arrived, "and we go our ways—I to die, and you to live. Which is better God only knows."[8]

The singular "God" here should not be taken as a sign of an emerging monotheism. Nothing about the thought of Socrates and Plato suggests faith in any force except the inherent rationality of the universe and in the individual willing to think. Rationality was divinity to them. In *The Republic* they created a vision of the ideal state, governed by a philosopher-king, not a god-king like that of the Egyptians.

Aristotle's Unmoved Mover

Plato opened the first official university in the West, the *Academy*, named after the public groves of Academe, in which Socrates used to walk with his followers (see Color Plate 9). There he influenced his star pupil, Aristotle (384–322 B.C.E.), who would later open his own school, the Lyceum. Aristotle formalized logic as a method of thinking. In his metaphysics, he pondered the problem of how the universe got started. His conclusions came close to the monotheism of Judaism, and Christianity later embraced him as the pagan who anticipated Christian doctrine.

Aristotle believed that the universe, an orderly system of sun and planets, always existed, but in the beginning it was cold, lifeless, and without motion. Motion by definition always has a cause. Logic impelled him to conclude that the whole system must have been *set* in motion, far back in the past, by something that was not in motion itself. If it were, we would then have to determine the cause of *its* motion, and so on into infinity.

The result was the principle of the **Unmoved Mover**, to be thought of as a cause that led to the first effect, which was motion, but not as a causer. This distinction is all-important. Causers can become personalized, and that is precisely what happened later. For Aristotle, the cold and lifeless universe was not created. It just *was*. But his system required a mover, one that was a principle of motion—a *potentiality* for motion that was always there. He could not fathom how what existed could ever have been non-existent. "For if it had ever come into existence, we should have to suppose an original constitutive element 'already there' for it to come out of. But this character of being 'a subject already there as a basis of change' is precisely the thing we have been inquiring about; hence, if the matter of what changes were itself to change, it would have to exist before its own coming into existence."[9]

The three religions that were to dominate the Western and Middle Eastern worlds would make a separation between what creates (God) and what is created (the universe). Lacking a theory of "God the Creator," Aristotle had to explain just what the Unmoved Mover was and where it was found.

He envisioned the universe as a sphere. The outer two rims were the circle of the sun and the planets and the circle he called the Prime Mover. Beyond this sphere was the *Empyrean*, the abode of the Unmoved Mover. Whether he knew it or not, Aristotle was getting close to monotheism, or at least a philosophical foundation that would support monotheism.

The Belief in One God

Monotheism is a powerful religious concept, central to three major religions in the world today: Judaism, Christianity, and Islam. It can be traced back over 3,000 years to the short reign of the pharaoh Akhenaton, but his idea of one god did little to eclipse the overwhelming polytheism of early cultures. The monotheism that would eventually dominate Western religious thought had many obstacles to overcome. Judaism, the religion of early Semitic tribes who traced their ancestry to the patriarch Abraham, introduced the first powerful vision of one almighty deity, a vision later shared by Christianity and Islam.

Judaism

The earliest of the three major monotheistic religions of the world, *Judaism*, derives its name from Judah, a son of Jacob. Of the original twelve Hebrew tribes, the one descended from Judah became dominant. Its monotheistic religion may have existed in many forms before the time of Siddhartha, Lao-tzu, and Confucius.

The Hebrew Bible is presumed to have been collaboratively written over a period of many centuries, some time after the exodus of Hebrew slaves from Egypt in the thirteenth century B.C.E. Much later, it is believed, Hebrew scholars, desiring to gather together the history and literature of their people, organized and wrote an early version of their sacred book.

The Hebrew Bible remains the foundation of Judaism. Because the text has been subjected to so much scrutiny and so many interpretations, almost any statement about evidence or meaning can be open to debate. There is disagreement about the origin of the book, whether the writers were putting down the literal word of God, about how certain words should be translated, and whether the book is to be read as history, legend, or literature. At one extreme are fundamentalists who continue to seek evidence of biblical truth, such as a piece of wood from Noah's Ark. Others, concerned with how biblical stories and characters can be applied to today's world, concentrate on a psychological approach. Still others prefer an anthropological investigation into what the development of the Bible tells us about the changing nature of divinity. For some people, regardless of their beliefs about the ultimate, the Hebrew Bible is a source of solace and wisdom.

From listening comes wisdom and from speaking, repentance.
—**Jewish proverb**

The first five books of this Bible, traditionally attributed to Moses, are known as the **Torah** or Pentateuch. The Torah begins with Genesis, which traces, in compact prose, the early history of the Hebrews. One of the most remarkable documents in the history of the humanities, it contains stories and characters familiar throughout the world. Genesis begins with an account of how the universe was created and how Adam and Eve, the first human beings, were expelled from Eden for disobedience. It tells of the covenant (or pact) between God and Abraham and the Promised Land given as a reward for obedience. It can stand on its own as an epic, rivaling *The Iliad* and *The Aeneid.*

Episodes recounted in Genesis have inspired poets and artists through the centuries. In Color Plate 30, you will find Rembrandt's famous painting *Joseph Accused by Potiphar's Wife*. Joseph, a son of Jacob, hence grandson of Abraham, the first of the Hebrew patriarchs, was his father's favorite, having been a child of Jacob's old age. This made his brothers jealous, especially after Jacob gave him a present of a many-colored coat that was the envy of all who saw it. The brothers cast him into a pit without water, assuming he would die and they would not be blamed. But Joseph was rescued by some traders who took him into Egypt, where he became a trusted servant of Potiphar, the pharaoh's chief officer. Potiphar's wife, attracted to the young man, pleads with him "Lie with me." Joseph refuses, saying he could not betray his master nor give offense to God. Furious, Potiphar's wife accuses him of making improper advances, whereupon Potiphar has him thrown into prison. But God protects him, and Joseph soon wins the protection of the pharaoh because of his ability to interpret dreams. The parable illustrates the Hebrew view of a God who can be wrathful and vengeful toward those who disobey him but also merciful toward the righteous.

The second book of the Torah, Exodus, tells the story of the liberation of Hebrew slaves and their flight from Egypt into the desert under the leadership of Moses, who receives the Ten Commandments on Mount Sinai. The third book, Leviticus, contains priestly laws about temple rituals. The fourth book, Numbers, contains a census of the Hebrew population and the story of an attempted rebellion against Moses. The final book, Deuteronomy, describes how Moses received the Ten Commandments on Mount Sinai and recounts the farewell speech of Moses, who dies before reaching the Promised Land.

Other books of the Bible tell stories of kings, generals, judges, and prophets; of war and treachery, family betrayals, and reconciliations. The central figures are human rather than idealized as they struggle to learn about God and to maintain their communities.

In biblical texts beginning in the tenth century B.C.E., there are indications of changing attitudes about the nature of God, who is perceived not only as the supreme ruler but as a father and comforter. In the Book of Psalms, containing lyrical poems attributed to David, the second king of Israel, who succeeded

Saul around 1000 B.C.E., we find contrasting views of divinity. Some of the psalms are pleas for God to strike down an enemy, and some reflect a gentle, loving God, who cares for his people—or his "flock," as in the well-known 23rd Psalm.

During the sixth or seventh century B.C.E., the age of the Hebrew prophets began, and the books of specific prophets were added to the Bible, some responding to actual events, such as the fall of Jerusalem, others as tales with a philosophical and moral purpose. Judaism underwent a profound change, becoming more complex, more concerned with justice for the widowed, the poor, and the helpless. This emphasis on social action remains an important tenet of modern Judaism. But later works modify the Hebrew laws as set forth in earlier books.

What we find in the later biblical period is a God who can be both awesome and merciful. He has set down absolute laws for human conduct and severely punishes those who violate them. He is a shepherd who restores the soul, but who also controls all the forces of nature, which he can unleash upon humanity. This dual nature of the deity led to the famous question that theologians and the devout of many faiths and sects still ask: *If God is good, why is there so much evil in the world?* The answer that evil is punishment does not satisfy everyone, nor does the question of whether God is all-powerful.

The agonizing puzzle of God's true nature is examined in the Book of Job, considered by many to be the masterpiece of the later period. The work of a profound and gifted writer, it not only tackles perhaps the most important question raised by monotheism, but it also supplies an answer that has resonated through the ages.

In Oedipus at Colonus *the aged king is still in exile...But his destiny has taken him beyond tragedy, and his death is a holy mystery. Our questions of divine justice are not answered, but they are silenced...before the absolute, pride and power and virtue are equally helpless.*

—Peter Arnott

The book rivals the greatest works in the Greek tragic theater, particularly the *Oedipus at Colonus* of Sophocles, in which the protagonist, having exiled himself to a life of blindness and wandering in the desert as a penance for his sins of pride and incest, sees a blinding light as death nears. He walks toward it, his face at last radiant with an understanding of the complex ways of the gods. The burning philosophical question raised by the *Oedipus* plays is: Why did Oedipus have to do penance for a sin decreed by fate? Though that fate was the working out of a curse on the descendants of Cadmus, a man who tried to be the equal of the gods, the question remained of why the innocent descendants had to suffer.

Track 15

The Book of Job, thought to have been written around the time of Sophocles, also faces the challenging question of why disasters befall an innocent person. What Job does not know is that the disasters he endures—the death of his sons, his servants, and his sheep, as well as physical disfigurement—were the result of a challenge given to God by Satan. God has singled out Job as the very model of a good and pious man, but Satan argues that Job's piety comes from the fact that God has never allowed anything bad to happen to him. "But put forth thy hand now, and touch all that he hath, and he will curse thee to thy face" (Job 1:11).

At first Job is resolute in his faith. He "sinned not, nor charged God foolishly." After God allows Satan to cover Job with painful boils, Job's wife chides him for retaining his integrity, urging him to curse God. The afflicted man will not curse God, but he does curse the day he was ever born. He grieves over his lost sons and wonders why he was created with intelligence, only to be torn apart by questions he cannot answer. "Why is light given to a man whose way is hid, and whom God hath hedged in?" (Job 3:23).

A famous debate follows between Job and his friends, reminiscent of dialogues between Socrates and his followers. They question everything, and Job refuses to yield up his faith, though holding onto it has become increasingly difficult:

"Touching the Almighty, we cannot find him out." Whereupon a mighty whirlwind comes upon them, and God speaks to Job, reminding him of the fact that, since he did not create the universe, he must accept God's justice in all things. "Where wast thou when I laid the foundations of the earth? Declare, if thou hast understanding" (Job 38:4). As a reward for his patience, piety, and refusal to curse his fate, Job receives, in addition to herds of livestock, a new family of "seven sons and three daughters," and lives long enough (140 years) to enjoy great age and prosperity.

Still, both the wager with Satan and Job's "compensation" of a new family seem naive to some scholars, unlike the main body of the story. Rabbi Joseph Telushkin comments: "The angel Satan makes his only appearance in the Hebrew Bible, and God is cast in the morally dubious role of wreaking havoc on Job's life just to show off to Satan." But, he adds, the ending of the story does not overshadow the stature of the work as a great allegory "about the problem of God and evil."[10]

Archetypes in This Chapter

Angel a higher being who serves God in heaven; an iconic label also commonly used to describe a good child, loved one, or person who behaves with great compassion or high ethical standards.

Devil a being who resides in hell and perpetrates evil; a name also used to describe a mischievous child or person suspected of malicious intentions.

Messiah in Judaism, the person who will be sent by God to redeem the Jews and Israel; in numerous religions, a Promised One; also used as a term of praise for someone who arrives in the nick of time to solve a problem or effect a rescue.

Nirvana in Buddhism, a state of supreme spiritual liberation; also used to describe any state of bliss or freedom from anxiety.

Prophet literally, "foreteller"; a divine interpreter who offers people messages from God or the gods through inspired speech or visions; also a label commonly used to describe anyone whose predictions turn out to be accurate.

Unifying Force the cosmic principle underlying the universe; known as brahman in Hinduism, dharma in Buddhism, and the Tao (Way) in Taoism; in modern physics, a term used to identify an as yet unknown equation that can unify all natural laws.

The books that follow Job contain prophecies, philosophy, and lament for the destruction of the Temple and for the exile that followed. The major work of the post-biblical period is the **Talmud** (*talmud* means "learning"). The document continues to be studied as an interpretation of the Torah. The Talmud includes minute discussions of biblical laws, such as rules for payment of laborers, care for orphans, and ways of establishing ownership. The new writings had to take into account conditions of living in foreign lands and responding to the treatment given to Hebrews by the host countries, at times as welcoming as Spain under the Muslims during the tenth to twelfth centuries, and at other times as intolerant as much of Europe during crusades and pogroms. The religion of Judaism continues to evolve, with the examination and modification of the old texts and the development of new texts about a God thought to be involved in the lives of human beings.

Perhaps no other single work in history has had as much influence on art, literature, thought, drama, and popular idiom as the Hebrew Bible. Here are a few examples of Bible-derived contributions to human culture.

> "*Am I my brother's keeper?*" from the story of Cain and Abel in the Book of Genesis, asks a fundamental question about how much responsibility one person has for another.
>
> "*Spare the rod and spoil the child*" is one of many proverbs offering advice on the best way to raise children.
>
> "*A coat of many colors,*" from the story of Joseph and his brothers, has become part of the popular idiom as a way of describing privilege and favor. The story is the basis of the enduringly popular Andrew Lloyd Webber musical *Joseph and the Amazing Technicolor Dreamcoat.*
>
> "*To everything, there is a season.*" The modern folk song "Turn, Turn,

Turn" is a setting of a famous passage from Ecclesiastes that recounts the cycle of life and death, telling us that everything happens at its proper time, that there is "a time to every purpose under heaven." The song, composed by folksinger and political activist Pete Seeger, delivers a strong antiwar message, using Ecclesiastes as a comforting reminder that, if there is war, there will also be peace.

The Golden Calf, fashioned by his impatient followers while Moses was receiving the Ten Commandments on Mount Sinai, has become a synonym for excessive materialism.

The Ten Commandments have formed the basis for civil and criminal laws, including those forbidding theft, murder, and perjury.

Many titles have been derived from biblical sources: for example, *Paradise Lost, The Grapes of Wrath, Earth Abides, Adam's Rib*, and *East of Eden*. Biblical names for children—David, Sarah, Samuel, Joshua—though at times considered old-fashioned, have nonetheless managed to retain their popularity through the years. For art lovers, no matter what their religious affiliation, a knowledge of biblical persons and events adds to the enjoyment of a Rembrandt painting or a Michelangelo sculpture, as well as countless other masterpieces.

Who is truly repentant? The one who, when temptation to sin is repeated, refrains from sinning.

—**The Talmud**

Many composers have been inspired by biblical themes. Mendelssohn's nineteenth-century *Elijah* is one notable example, as is Leonard Bernstein's twentieth-century *Lamentations of Jeremiah*, based on the book that reflects deep despair over the fall of Jerusalem to an invading army, a fall permitted by God because "Jerusalem hath grievously sinned." Here God is regarded as the supreme ruler of the universe, the creator of that universe, the administrator of punishment to those who break his commandments. "The Lord hath done that which he had devised; he hath fulfilled his word that he had commanded in the days of old: he hath thrown down, and hath not pitied" (Lamentations 2:17).

The stories and characters in the Hebrew Bible have provided poets, philosophers, and artists with subject matter, plots, and profound questions for thousands of years. And as we can see from the examples above, its influence strongly continues.

Christianity

The cosmic religious experience is the strongest force and the noblest driving force behind scientific research.

—**Albert Einstein**

Even as the followers of Siddhartha believed he was the promised Buddha of the Hindu scriptures, so too did the followers of Jesus believe that he was the Messiah foretold in the Hebrew Bible by the prophet Isaiah. The prophet says: "Therefore the Lord himself shall give you a sign; Behold, a virgin shall conceive, and bear a son, and shall call his name Immanuel" (Isaiah 6:14). The prophecy is followed by predictions of dire catastrophes to be suffered by his people until they are saved by the birth of this child. "For unto us a child is born, unto us a son is given: and the government shall be upon his shoulder: and his name shall be called Wonderful, Counsellor, The Mighty God, The Everlasting Father, The Prince of Peace" (Isaiah 9:6).

The historical Jesus, walking among the Hebrews at a time when their region was occupied by the Roman Empire, was a source of controversy. Some hailed him as the Messiah, the Promised One of the prophecy, the bringer of a philosophy that would end oppression and bring peace to the world. Others refused to accept him as the Messiah. That difference caused the separation of Judaism and what became Christianity, a religion based on the teachings of Jesus and the belief that he was sent by God to save the world. Hebrews who did not accept his divinity and Romans who saw him as a fanatic, a troublemaker, both protested against him. After a trial officiated by Pontius Pilate, the Roman proconsul of Judea, he was crucified. But according to Christian belief, he rose from the dead and eventually ascended into heaven.

Most knowledge about Jesus is derived from the four gospels at the beginning of the Christian Bible. The gospels are attributed to four of the disciples of Jesus—Matthew, Mark, Luke, and John. Biblical scholars have long discussed the *synoptic problem*, noting that the four accounts offer different views of Jesus and report different acts and events. For example, the well-known nativity story is found in Luke but not the others. The Sermon on the Mount is told in Matthew only. This discrepancy suggests that the gospels were not eyewitness accounts; however, their influence cannot be minimized.

The Sermon on the Mount is a major source of the split between Christianity and Judaism. Jesus reviews the Ten Commandments approvingly but adds that they don't go far enough. They condemn wrongful action, but not wrongful intent. In Chapter 11, you will find a further discussion of differences between the commandments and the sermon.

The gospels all agree, however, that Jesus was the son of God. Christians point to the word "son" in the prophecy. But the son is also referred to as the "everlasting Father." Ultimately the Christian church adopted the belief that Jesus was both Father and Son, as well as a spiritual being they called the Holy Ghost. The Trinity—the idea that the one God exists as three divine persons—was hotly debated among Christians until it became mandatory for Christians to accept after a meeting of the Council of Nicaea in 325 C.E.

Christianity, which swept over the Western world after the fall of the Roman Empire in the fifth century C.E., eventually demanded absolute acceptance of its beliefs, and the church began to impose severe penalties on those who questioned church doctrine. In the early stages of the religion, however, Christian philosophers struggled to reconcile Christian mysticism with human logic.

For example, the idea of how the world was created, clearly stated in Genesis and adopted by Christianity, troubled some minds. "In the beginning God created the heaven and the earth. And the earth was without form, and void; and darkness was upon the face of the deep. And the Spirit of God moved upon the face of the waters. And God said, Let there be light: and there was light" (Genesis 1:1–3). This passage implies that God existed before there was a world and created that world out of nothing. In Christian philosophy, this concept is known by the Latin phrase ***creatio ex nihilo***.

Plato had taught that knowledge preexisted, and Aristotle that the Unmoved Mover must have preexisted in order to set everything else in motion. The concept of nothingness made classical thinkers uneasy. The Greeks, for example, had not recognized zero as a number. Yet the idea of *creatio ex nihilo* was obligatory among Christians, if the one and only God created everything. Aristotle's Mover only supplied motion, but everything that had to move was already there.

The *creatio* would not be the last monotheistic idea to cause consternation. This concept and others had to be taken on *faith* rather than accepted through *reason*. But it was difficult for Christian philosophers to abandon the right to question, especially in the centuries before official doctrine came into being. Here are some of the many problems they encountered.

> *Can this world have been the extent of God's creation?* If the ability to create matter out of nothing is intrinsic to God, then did creation stop with this one achievement?
>
> *Could God have had any purpose in creating the world?* How could an all-powerful God be so limited as to have had a purpose? Purpose implies *need.* What could God need?
>
> *Does God think?* If it is assumed that human beings engage in thought in order to know something that was not known before, what could a perfect God not know?
>
> *Does God feel?* Both Judaism and Christianity insist that human sinfulness offends God. The Hebrew Bible's stories of God's wrath against humanity, such as Noah and the terrible flood or the destruction of Sodom and Gomorrah, implied emotion. But emotion is a response to what is beyond control. Were there things God could not control?
>
> *If God does not think or feel, how can he respond to human need?* What was the use of praying to a God who neither thinks nor feels and therefore must be oblivious to us? Isn't it futile to believe that God will intervene in human affairs?

It is easy enough to be friendly to one's friends. But to befriend the one who regards himself as your enemy is the quintessence of true religion. The other is mere business.
—**Mahatma Gandhi**

As the centuries rolled on, questions increased. It did not take much for anyone to realize that the world was filled with corruption, depravity, and cruelty. If God knew in advance that these would come about, why did he not prevent them? Why did he not prevent maritime disasters or volcanic eruptions? Why did the good have to suffer?—an ominous question that had already been posed in the Book of Job. If God knew about catastrophes *before* they happened, did failure to prevent them indicate indifference? Callousness?

The major Christian philosopher of the early Middle Ages, Augustine (354–430), would ultimately conclude that philosophical questioning and analysis could not take Christians where they needed to go. Analysis could lead only to a weakening of belief and even to atheism. But before he found an answer that satisfied him, he had to wrestle with his own doubts.

Like Paul, who preceded him by several centuries, Augustine became a convert during his adulthood. As a young man without any religion, he lived for pleasure. His Christian mother despaired over her son's wanton ways and kept urging him to reform and find God. Though Augustine eventually renounced his life of sin and entered the Christian fold, he did not do so easily.

Augustine's *Confessions*, one of the most personal and candid works ever written by a philosopher, deals with the intellectual difficulties facing him upon his conversion. One of his first concerns was reason itself. Why was it given to us by God when it was of no use in trying to comprehend God or the universe? The doctrine of *creatio ex nihilo* puzzled him. In this passage, Augustine speaks directly to God: "Nor in the whole world didst Thou make the whole world; because there was no place to make it before it was made, that it might be. Nor didst Thou hold anything in Thy hand, whereof to make heaven and earth. For whence shouldest Thou have this, which Thou hadst not made, thereof to make anything? For what is, but because Thou art? Therefore Thou spakest, and they were made, and in Thy Word Thou madest them. But how didst Thou speak?"[11]

Good, Evil, and Augustine

Philosophy, ancient and modern, has had as a major concern the nature of the good. The hedonists of ancient Greece defined the good as a life filled with all possible pleasures (Chapter 12). Socrates and Plato use *good* in an ethical sense, referring to actions that are performed not for the sake of personal enjoyment or gain but for the sake of what reason decrees is right and just. *Evil* in ancient thought is the pain and suffering that are part of life, often rained down upon human beings by the gods or by the whimsies of fate. Socrates is famous for having said "No evil can befall a good man." The statement was made in his speech, already mentioned in this chapter, to the assembled citizens of Athens, who were to judge him guilty or innocent of corrupting their youth. What he meant by "evil" was the pain of death should the jury of citizens reach a guilty verdict. In other words, evil was a synonym for disaster, or what most people would consider disaster. It did not imply malicious intent.

The myth of Pandora, mentioned in Chapter 3, was one explanation for how evil came about. Locked in the box that Pandora (see Color Plate 4) was not supposed to open were war, plagues, and natural disasters like fire and floods. In this myth there is no implication that people are *born* evil. Evil is something that *happens* to them. Even the brutal killing of Hector by Achilles, as recounted in *The Iliad*, is less the action of a truly evil person than it is the fulfillment of a warrior's obligation to show his superiority in battle.

The Hebrew Bible gives a clear explanation of both good and evil. In Genesis, God creates Eve from Adam's rib and is satisfied that he has created two innocent human beings, whom he places in the Garden of Eden to be fruitful, to multiply, and to act as custodians of the earth. He warns them about the Tree of Knowledge (see Color Plate 5), the fruit of which they may not eat; if they do, they will learn the difference between good and evil, but it will be too late. They will be punished for disobeying God.

Adam and Eve are thus not born evil. They are born good: that is, without sin, the tendency to disobey God's commands. What changes them? A talking serpent that entices them to eat the forbidden fruit. At first they are afraid, because God has told them that, if they disobey him, they will surely die. The serpent tells them this is a lie. He gives this as the real reason for the command: "For God doth know that in the day ye eat thereof, then your eyes shall be opened, and ye shall be as gods, knowing good and evil" (Genesis 3:5).

Early Christianity accepted the Hebrew Bible as an accurate account of the beginnings of humankind, though it modified and expanded the range of the Ten Commandments. Christianity also transformed the serpent into the Devil, an embodiment of pure evil and one of the most influential of all archetypes. Pitting God against the Devil, Christianity thus created the concept of the eternal conflict between absolute good and absolute evil, a concept leading in turn to the agonizing question asked by early Christian philosophers and by Augustine: *If God is good and all-powerful, why does evil exist?*

In Genesis, the attitude of an angry God toward the sin of Adam and Eve is accepted as being appropriate for a supreme being. God curses the ground on which they walk and invents death for them, but only after Eve brings forth progeny in utmost pain. Things only get worse. By the time of Noah, God is so disgusted with the race he has created that he sends down a flood to destroy it—all except Noah and his family. Noah is the one good man, who pleases God with his piety and his burnt offerings: "And the Lord smelled a sweet savour; and the Lord said in his heart, I will not again curse the ground any more for man's sake; for the imagination of man's heart is evil from his youth; neither will I again smite any more every living thing, as I have done" (Genesis 8:21). Thus God became a supreme being and an angry father who was quickly offended by human sinfulness but pleased by piety and goodness.

Yet by the time of the early Christian philosophers, it was becoming difficult for those who questioned things to be content with the conflicting ideas that evil was inherent in humankind but that the choice of being good was always there, the choice of not being tempted to disobey. Did not God create the serpent? Had he done so deliberately to throw temptation into his children's path? Why would God do such a thing? Why not create a perfect race to begin with—without serpents?

By the time of Augustine, the problem of evil was well known and widely discussed. To the philosopher, it proved just as puzzling as that of creation. To a thinking person it seemed evident that evil happened *despite* God. Traditional Christian belief was that the universe was divided into two distinct substances: one, material; the other, immaterial. It was unthinkable to Augustine that evil should exist in the immaterial world. But God was also the creator of the material world, was he not? And the material world was the abode of evil. If one denied that God was responsible for evil but *was* responsible for the material world, then it followed that evil was neither material nor immaterial. Evil, then, could not exist!

Augustine reasoned that what we call evil must be *the absence of good* in the same way that disease is the absence of health. Evil was, then, moral disease. When a person sins, moral perfection departs. The world, like the human body, was perfect when created and returns to perfection when the disease is gone.

Yet why do people sin? If they were created perfect, where did moral disease come from? Here Augustine developed an idea that remains with us—not just in religion, but in philosophy and psychology as well. This idea was *freedom of the will*, and we shall be talking further about it in Chapter 16, which happens to be called Freedom. Augustine concluded that people sin because God allows them to choose between good and bad actions. He knew this had to be the case, because God exacted penance from sinners and doled out punishment to the unrepentant. The Tree of Knowledge was put in the Garden as a test, so freedom of choice made perfect sense.

Or did it? The matter of God's nature crossed Augustine's mind. An all-knowing God must be aware in advance of what our choices will be. Before we are tempted to appropriate the money carelessly left on a table by a departing guest, must not God know that we will or will not take it? In God's eyes, the deed has already taken place. Where then is the element of choice? And without choice, how can there be responsibility?

Augustine advanced the idea of **predestination**, which states that, before birth, the course of a human life is already determined. The philosopher believed that the concept of an all-powerful, all-knowing God made predestination mandatory for mortals to accept. There could be no argument about God's foreknowledge of human choice; at the same time, humanity could not be absolved of responsibility for sin. It was unthinkable that God should be blamed for human evil. Otherwise, what incentive was there to be good and to win God's approval?

Free will offered a way to make the two beliefs compatible. An all-powerful God could choose to bestow on humanity the *gift* of freedom. An all-knowing God could tell what our choices would be *without having willed those choices*. Thus freedom was real on the human level; predestination was real on the divine level.

If reason was too weak to reach these conclusions, then faith must be stronger than reason. How could humanity expect to understand God? Reason could take us to a certain point at which the paradox of fate and free will must be accepted. Faith, which was the answer in the Book of Job, stepped in to make acceptance possible. But again the matter did not end there. Some religious thinkers, in Judaism as well as Christianity, would not be satisfied with Augustine's conclusion that faith was all. Why did we have reason if we weren't supposed to use it? They would eventually say that reason *can* lead to an understanding of God, though critics of religious logic often point out that it only shows why a God must exist, not what *kind* of God.

Logical Proof

In the Book of Job, Judaism asks hard questions, and the answer is that the running of the universe is not humanity's business. Faith in God has to convince us that God has his reasons. In the twelfth century C.E. there emerged a rabbi who was also a profound philosopher and scholar, and he would show how logic and faith were not incompatible.

Do not imagine that character is determined at birth. We have been given free will...We ourselves decide whether to make ourselves learned or ignorant, compassionate or cruel, generous or miserly.

—**Moses Maimonides**

Moses Maimonides (1135–1204) was born in Spain of Hebrew ancestry. Because Jews there were threatened with persecution, he moved to Egypt, where he became physician to the Muslim ruler Saladin. Trained in medicine, he decided that philosophy and theology were of equal interest to healing the body. Besides, in the world of both Hebrew and Muslim scholars, if a man wished to be considered learned, he was expected to demonstrate knowledge in many areas.

At first Maimonides was appalled at the Muslims' acceptance of the philosophy of **materialism** that had been advanced centuries before Socrates and Plato—a belief that only matter existed and spiritual experiences were solely in the mind. A devout Jew, he maintained that the material world was created by God out of nothing, but he was enough of an Aristotelian to realize that he would have to use logic to defend his belief. Although many of his Hebrew contemporaries were content to accept the Bible as mystic revelation, Maimonides was also a scientist living among Muslims who had inherited and further developed the logical and mathematical theories of the classical world. They were fully acquainted with Aristotle, Euclid, and the work of mathematicians in India. His mission was to show his contemporaries that a belief in God was not only desirable but logically, not just mystically, inevitable.

Since he was familiar with Aristotle's theory of the Unmoved Mover, it made sense to him that nothing can be in motion uncaused by something else, but cause and effect cannot be traced back into infinity. Sooner or later there has to be a causer that is not in motion itself. What Maimonides did was to give the name of God to the Unmoved Mover. The perfection of God made the Unmoved Mover plausible. God was thus defined as *that which cannot be caused*; depending for his existence on a prior cause would make God imperfect. A perfect being cannot be dependent. If there *were* a prior cause which created God, then that cause would be God. No matter how far back you went, you would always find God waiting.

Some Hebrew scholars and theologians denounced the writings of Maimonides on the grounds that his so-called logic was founded on a strong belief in God to begin with and consequently was unnecessary—not only unnecessary, but an affront to the traditions of their forefathers for whom revelation was sufficient. Hadn't God told Job that it was not the place of humanity either to understand or to question the nature and ways of God? If you needed proof, you were not truly religious.

The world of Christian thought was also influenced by mathematics, stirrings in science, and the work of Aristotle. Thomas Aquinas (1225–1274) never doubted his own faith, but he was imbued with the spirit of inquiry that became widespread during the later Middle Ages. Educated by Benedictine monks and having become a Dominican, he moved to Paris, which was already an intellectual center, a place where bright young students met exciting teachers and where even the clergy were not afraid to question established beliefs.

Here Aquinas came into contact with Aristotelian logic and was responsible for creating a system of thought designed to persuade non-believers that God must exist. Once introduced, his theories gradually found their way into Christian tradition. Even today, students in Catholic seminaries are thoroughly trained in **Thomism**, the name given to the philosopher's logical methods of proving God's existence.

Aquinas gave five proofs of God's existence, all based, as were the theories of Maimonides, on Aristotle's Unmoved Mover. The first, *Argument from Motion*, is a restatement of that theory, as is the second, *Argument from Causation*. The third, *Argument from Being*, is cited by many philosophers as the strongest. Here is a paraphrased summary of that argument: "Though we have only to look around to see that things *are*, it is indeed possible to imagine that they should not be. On the other hand, though it is conceivable that nothing should be, it is clear that this is not the case. Hence there must be a principle of necessary being which cannot be imagined as not existing. Only God can be so imagined."

The fourth, *Argument from Gradation*, asserts that wherever we look we see greater or lesser amounts and qualities. We cannot conceive of "better," for example, unless we can also conceive of "best," for it stands to reason that we cannot go on into infinity, finding "better" things. Eventually there has to be a "best" beyond which the mind cannot go. God is therefore the fullest realization of "best."

Absence of evidence is not evidence of absence.

—**Carl Sagan**

The fifth, *Argument from Design*, is probably at once the most famous and the most hotly debated. It asserts that since there is clear evidence of order in the operation of the universe, it cannot have been put there by accident. If there is a design, it follows that there was a designer.

Countless millions continue to use this argument. To disprove it, one must say the universe is not governed by laws that have been experimentally verified. But whether natural law is equivalent to design is an issue over which there is no universal agreement.

Islam

The third of the great monotheistic religions, Islam was founded by the prophet Mohammed (571–632), an Arab who, before 610, was well respected, a husband and a father, successful in all respects. Like Siddhartha, he may have experienced the need for something more in his life. At any rate, while stopping in the city of Mecca, in what is now Saudi Arabia, he was visited by the angel Gabriel, sent by Allah (the word *Allah* means "the one God"), and commanded to deliver God's word and his laws to the world, even as Moses was told to deliver the Ten Commandments he received on Mount Sinai.

Mohammed listened but thought he must be going mad. He told his wife, who suggested he visit a wise relative and ask his opinion. This man assured Mohammed that he was blessed among all men and had been clearly chosen to restate the laws of God. The hearing of a divine voice convinced Mohammed that his relative had been right. The voice told him he must devote his life to teaching. Those who listened to his sermons wrote down what he said, and thus the Qur'an (Koran) came into existence. It is the sacred book of Islam, the central component of the religion.

Islam means "submission," and *Muslim* means "one who submits." Arab Muslims believe they are descended from Ishmael, the son of Abraham, who conceived him with Hagar, after Abraham's wife Sarah was found to be infertile. At first honored and groomed to succeed his father as patriarch of the Hebrew tribes, Ishmael lost this favored position when Sarah did in fact conceive a child, Isaac. Ishmael was cast out and became a wanderer in the desert, until, according to Islamic belief, he came to the city of Mecca, where Mohammed later founded the religion.

As Mohammed grew older, he wanted to do more than preach the word of God. He wanted to help fashion a society of brotherhood, peace, and ethical dealings—all based on Allah's laws. He became a political consultant and an agent for social reform, unlike Siddhartha, who taught the Eightfold Path and believed reform would come about by itself, as more and more followers heeded his message and incorporated it into their daily lives. Mohammed's vision of the ideal world is still the basis of government in Islamic nations: that is, the function of government is to implement the laws of God. Disagreements persist over how those laws should be interpreted.

As in all religions, Islam has its fundamentalists—believers in the very letter of the law—as well as those who support greater flexibility. The separation has grown stronger over the centuries. In the beginning, Mohammed as spiritual leader allowed Christians and Jews living in Islamic communities to practice their own faith openly and commanded his followers not to persecute or try to convert them. He told the people that Arabs, Jews, and Christians all prayed to the one God and that they were entitled to heed the word as passed down in their own sacred books.

The Qur'an bears striking similarities to those books. The commandments given to Mohammed by Allah are very much like those given to Moses and accepted, with modifications, by Jesus. In fact, Moses and Jesus were accorded much honor by Mohammed, who declared that they were pious and honorable men, much beloved by God, who had also spoken to them.

Who so has done an atom's weight of good shall see it; and who so has done an atom's weight of evil shall see it.

—The Qur'an

There are, however, significant differences among the three religions. Judaism was at least a thousand years old by the time of Mohammed, and though it had a number of prophets after Moses, the latter was regarded as of prime importance. Judaism saw in Jesus a latter-day prophet but not the son of God, not the promised Messiah. Islam, recognizing the historical importance of Moses and Jesus, nonetheless saw in Mohammed the one true prophet. If he were not, why should God have felt the need to have his commandments restated?

Like Christianity, Islam believes there will be an inevitable ending of the world, followed by a Judgment Day, in which the good will be rewarded with eternal life in heaven, and the bad will suffer the torments of hell. Heaven and hell are vividly described in the Qur'an.

Devout Muslims, firm believers in a blissful eternity beyond this life, follow a rigid pattern of worship. The Qur'an demands the observance of five activities: *confession, prayer* (at least five times a day), *fasting, charity, and pilgrimage.*

Confession is not made to a priest, as in the Catholic faith, but directly to God. Worshippers speak their daily prayers sometimes alone but, as often as possible, in groups, reflecting Mohammed's insistence on community. Fasting builds discipline, necessary if one is to resist the temptations of the world. During the sacred month of Ramadan, Muslims are required to fast each day and to refrain from all sexual activity from sunrise to sunset. Ramadan commemorates the communication of the Qur'an to Mohammed. It occurs during the ninth month of the Muslim calendar, which is based on the revolution of the moon, and advances ten days each year according to the Western calendar.

Strict Islamic law forbids gambling and drinking alcohol. Instead of stressing redemption, the forgiveness of sin, Islam seeks to make its followers morally perfect. Redemption is thus unnecessary.

Like Judaism and Christianity, Islam produced its questioners. One in particular, al-Ghazzali (1058–1111), was trained in both law and theology. He taught at the University of Baghdad and was eventually caught between worldly matters and the austere discipline of the Muslim faith. He had problems with both extremes.

The Arab world was becoming a center of culture and erudition, rivaling those of the great Western cities such as Paris and Bologna. There were many temptations that could easily lead one to forego, for example, daily prayers or fasting. Al-Ghazzali realized he had to make a choice: either total immersion in the pursuits of the material world or total submission to the will of Allah.

He also found Islamic tradition too demanding for its followers, with its emphasis on discipline, and too remote from God. Wherever he looked, he could see people disobeying the laws set forth in the Qur'an. He realized that, if he were to practice total submission, he could not do so and lead a secular existence as well. Then he discovered the *Sufi*, Islamic mystics who practiced meditation in their efforts to achieve total unity with God. In this they resembled some of the monastic orders of Christianity and the Hasidic branch of Judaism, whose members gave free reign to song and dance as means of transcending cold reason. After his conversion to Sufism, he again took up his teaching duties, but this time he taught his students that God must be an active force in their lives, not a distant figure in whose name they went without emotion through their daily practices.

After the death of Mohammed, there was considerable disruption in Islam, a profound division between those who believed Muslim leadership belonged to Mohammed's father-in-law Abu Bakr and those who wanted Mohammed's cousin and son-in-law Ali. Abu Bakr emerged victorious after a long struggle between the two parties, but followers of Ali insisted that the command had been wrongfully taken from him. At length, those loyal to Abu Bakr became the Sunni Muslims, while those loyal to Ali became the Shiites. The followers of each form continue to believe that control of the Islamic faith is rightfully theirs.

The Protestant Reformation

As Christianity spread and gained millions of converts during the Middle Ages, it became Catholicism (meaning "the one, true religion"). It was a powerful empire in itself and would command the faithful to refrain from sin or face the fires of hell. Among the greatest of sins was **heresy**, words or deeds interpreted as being anti-Christian. During the late Middle Ages a tribunal of church officials conducted the **Inquisition**, a high religious court in which heretics were tried and, if found guilty, imprisoned or even burnt at the stake.

There were rumblings of discontent. Dissidents in private complained about the growing wealth of the church as well as the continuing poverty of most worshippers. They also took exception to the church doctrine that salvation was impossible without the intervention of priests. They believed that God listened to each of his children, who could communicate with him privately. They called this principle "the priesthood of the true believer." They also condemned the church for its giant, expensive cathedrals (such as Notre Dame in Paris), with their artifacts of gold and silver, their expensive frescoes and statues. Such extravagant displays in the name of religion amounted to idolatry, which horrified them.

Ultimately the quiet questioning flared into open rebellion, led by Martin Luther (1483–1546), who made a list of ninety-five proposals for religious reform and nailed it to the door of the church at the University of Wittenberg. He hoped thereby to encourage open forums in which those who were protesting (Protestants) could confront church officials. The result was the great division in Christianity between the Protestants, who wanted to simplify religious worship and divest it of its bureaucracies and worldly power, and Catholics, who held tenaciously to the belief that the pope was the one true representative of God on earth and that priests were chosen to carry the word of God to the people and carry to God the prayers of the people. Lutheranism was thus the first Protestant sect. But Protestantism would eventually give rise to further disputes and the formulation of other sects.

The church must be reminded that it is not the master or the servant of the state, but rather the conscience of the state.

—Martin Luther King, Jr.

All of the religions discussed in this chapter are still very much with us. Some have strict rules that are binding on their followers, while others encourage the faithful to seek their own path to God, arguing that what matters in the long run is the development of a moral human being.

The Questioning of Belief

Time was when non-believers and those who dared to dispute the mandates of an organized religion could be imprisoned, tortured, or executed. There are still places in the world where the harshest penalties are imposed on those persons whose lifestyle and mode of dress deviate from prevailing religious requirements. The strict enforcement of religious law runs counter to widespread philosophical positions that question or openly deny the existence of God. As philosophy has been an instrument for the logical proof of God, so too has it been used for the opposite purpose.

Agnosticism

An **agnostic** (from a Greek word meaning "unknown or unknowable") is a person who does not patently disbelieve in God but who asserts that nothing about God, including his existence, can be known for certain. Agnostics are sometimes accused by the faithful of being too lazy to bother with religion. They are challenged to prove that God cannot be proven.

Yet agnosticism is a valid philosophical stance, often arrived at after much soul-searching. William James, a late nineteenth-century philosopher who will be discussed in the final chapter of this book, was an agnostic with compassion for those who relied on religion to see them through difficult times. James counseled innumerable people who were trying to make sense out of life, who had suffered grievous losses and were desperately seeking reasons. His advice was that, if religion is essential to happiness, who is to deny someone the right to believe? Carl Sagan, a widely read popularizer of modern science, once remarked, "Absence of evidence is not evidence of absence."

I have a conscience. It does not depend on religion.
—**Isaac Asimov**

In the arts one finds many who are "God obsessed," angry because reason prevents them from believing in God yet offers nothing to take God's place. The American poet Edwin Arlington Robinson (1869–1935) concludes his great work "The Man against the Sky" with these lines that attack the rational denial of faith.

If after all that we have lived and thought,
All comes to Nought,—
If there be nothing after Now,
And we be nothing anyhow,
And we know that,—why live?
'Twere sure but weaklings' vain distress
To suffer dungeons where so many doors
Will open on the cold eternal shores
That look sheer down
To the dark tideless floods of Nothingness
Where all who know may drown.[12]

For the confirmed agnostic, it makes sense not to burn bridges or to risk drowning in Robinson's "floods of Nothingness."

Atheism

Unlike the agnostic, the **atheist** takes a bold negative stand. Instead of shaking their heads and saying "I don't know," atheists challenge believers, especially those who use logic to prove God's existence. They sometimes take that very logic and use it to prove that the non-existence of God is logically necessary, but sometimes people who call themselves atheists do not do so on logical grounds.

One method, which can be called *informal* logic, is to point out that the very question "Does God exist?" is meaningless, since its subject has not been shown to have a valid identity. Consequently, all answers to that question have to be disregarded. Atheists are fond of the poem by Lewis Carroll (of *Alice in Wonderland* fame) called "The Hunting of the Snark," which concerns a dangerous sea voyage in search of the Snark, a creature no one has ever seen. The voyagers have been warned to be careful because there are rumors that the Snark may really be a Boojum. At length, in a hilarious conclusion, which could be a parody of *Moby Dick*, the Snark, finally encountered, destroys the ship, and we are left with the mournful final line: "The Snark was a Boojum after all."

A foremost American proponent of atheism was Charles Sanders Peirce (pronounced Purse, 1839–1914), who was deeply involved in a philosophical movement known as **pragmatism**. According to pragmatism, no philosophical question was important if it made no difference to the actual conduct of life. Like William James, Peirce realized, however, that religion did indeed make a great deal of difference to a good many people. In a pivotal essay called "How to Make Our Ideas Clear," he turns the notion of belief inside out. He analyzes it in terms of three properties: "First, it is something we are aware of; second, it appeases the irritation of doubt; and third, it involves the establishment in our nature of a rule of action, or say, for short, a *habit*."[13]

One difficulty with belief, Peirce argues, is that we are likely to seize on anything that will appease the "irritation of doubt." We cannot stand not to know or be able to explain, and for the majority of us, it is important that a belief be *good* rather than necessarily true. In his opinion, religious beliefs are notoriously successful in appeasing the irritation of doubt. Indeed they are held more often for this reason than for any other, no matter what claims for their logical necessity may be made. They are particularly difficult to dislodge from people's lives (or habits) because, if they cannot readily be proved, the believer is confident they cannot be disproved. "Thus if it be true that death is annihilation, then the man who believes that he will certainly go straight to heaven when he dies, provided he has fulfilled certain simple observations in this life, has a cheap pleasure which will not be followed by the least disappointment."[14]

If the premises are in fact not doubted at all, they cannot be more satisfactory than they are.

—Charles Sanders Peirce

The passage has become famous, not least because of its wit. Peirce is throwing down the gauntlet. He is saying: *if you don't believe me, prove that there's an afterlife*. Such reasoning employs the philosophical technique of *reductio ad absurdum*, by which you prove your point by postulating that its opposite leads to an absurdity. Thus, there can be no afterlife, because to say that there *is* such a thing is pointless and meaningless. The opposite of *There is no afterlife* is *There is an afterlife*. But the latter statement cannot possibly have any validity since no one has ever visited an afterlife. All one can say is "I believe there is an afterlife," but this automatically rules out logic.

The philosophy of Peirce is staunchly rooted in science. Nothing is true that cannot be observed or experimentally verified. In another famous passage he attacks the Catholic belief in *transubstantiation*, which holds that, through the mystical powers invested in the priest celebrating the mass, the communion wafer actually becomes the body of Jesus, and the communion wine, the blood of Jesus. However, "we can consequently mean nothing by wine but what has certain effects . . . upon our senses; and to talk of something as having all the sensible characters of wine, yet being in reality blood, is senseless jargon."[15]

Whether to accept this argument as a logical one is a personal decision, but if nothing else, it makes clear that the scientific and religious outlooks are on different wavelengths. The atheist is much closer to science, while the devout believer must be willing to accept even the miraculous on faith. Another American atheist, H. L. Mencken, defined faith as "an illogical belief in the occurrence of the improbable."

A number of other atheistic philosophies have become prominent. Friedrich Nietzsche, discussed in Chapter 1 in relation to Apollo and Dionysus, made the famous statement "God is dead"—that is, the very question of whether God exists or not is a dead issue. The implication is that religion had its day, but by the late nineteenth century, the time of Nietzsche, that day was over.

In the same time period, a number of writers and poets expressed disillusionment over what they considered the unfounded optimism of the late Victorian age, particularly the use of religion to justify the unstoppable accumulation of wealth and property. John D. Rockefeller, one of the world's richest men, wrote in his autobiography that his wealth showed he was favored by God.

Stephen Crane (1871–1900), who wrote *The Red Badge of Courage*, a biting antiwar novel, was also a poet, expressing not only stark pessimism about a world from which God was notably absent, but also a belief that humanity would somehow pull itself up from the dark pit of chaos. (His poem "I saw a man pursuing the horizon" closes this book.) In the following poem, Crane's pessimistic side turns grimly humorous.

God fashioned the ship of the world carefully,
With the infinite skill of an All-Master
Made He the hull and the sails,
Held He the rudder
Ready for adjustment.
Erect stood He, scanning His work proudly,
Then—at fateful time—a wrong called,
And God turned, heeding.
Lo, the ship, at this opportunity, slipped slyly,
Making cunning noiseless travel down the ways.
So that, forever rudderless, it went upon the seas
Going ridiculous voyages,
Making quaint progress,
Turning as with serious purpose
Before stupid winds.
And there were many in the sky
Who laughed at this thing.

Religion Versus . . .

Religion and science continue to cross swords, as do religion and the law. Murderers have told juries that God instructed them to kill their victims.

Religion and the rise of modern science collided head-on at the turn of the twentieth century, and the conflict has given rise to some impassioned novels, poetry, and dramas. In 1925 a Tennessee high school science teacher and football coach named John Scopes was tried on charges of illegally teaching evolution, found guilty, and fined $100. But slight as the penalty was, the trial was not dismissed as trivial. It became the cornerstone of a huge controversy that still rages, especially among populations with strong religious convictions. It became the subject of the 1950s play *Inherit the Wind*, in which the protagonist is a defense attorney, bearing a strong resemblance to the real-life staunch defender of the First Amendment: Clarence Darrow. Though he lost the case for his client, Darrow's speech to the court, paraphrased in the play, is one of the most important declarations of human rights ever articulated. His opponent in the play is based on the real-life prosecutor William Jennings Bryan, an avowed religious fundamentalist, whose argument against the defense is that Darwin's theory cannot be valid because evolution would have required millions of years, and all men of faith knew that creation took place in 4000 B.C.E.

Religion and science continue to cross swords, as do religion and the law. Murderers have told juries that God instructed them to kill their victims. Parents whose religion forbids medical intervention even in serious illness have been held for manslaughter when their children die. Opponents of gay rights legislation often argue that the Bible expressly forbids homosexuality and that marriage is specifically defined as a union of a man and a woman.

Americans live in a free society, for which all of us must be grateful. This also means that there will always be conflicting viewpoints, especially in religious matters, as people exercise their right to think and speak freely. Living with conflict seems a much saner alternative than having everyone forcibly subscribe to rules imposed by those in power, whose views can be neither overturned nor debated.

Religion and the Arts

The question of whether the world is ruled by one or more divine beings has always been of great interest to philosophers. Yet philosophy is only one discipline of the humanities. We must not forget that literature, the visual arts, music, theater, and cinema have been influenced by religion in so many ways that it would take a number of volumes this size to do justice to the subject. We cannot, however, close our discussion of religion without reference to how this huge component of human experience has been affected by those who believe, or at least explore the idea, that there is more to reality than the things in our immediate consciousness. The arts have been instrumental in bringing visions of higher realities to that consciousness.

Without religion, the visual arts would have a shorter history. Art and religion have maintained close relations since the beginning. The Egyptians saw painting and statuary as a means to immortality. Polytheism led the Greeks and Romans to erect masterpieces of art and architecture. In addition to the moral laws on which most societies, regardless of their religious orientation, are based, Judaism has given the world masterpieces of literature, poetry, and philosophers. The medieval church brought into the world countless paintings, statues, and frescoes in which heavenly beings and biblical incidents were visualized. The theater of the Western world had its beginnings in the medieval mass. Islam frowned upon the production of artificial images, but as we have seen, many of its buildings remain as very models of architectural grandeur.

Islam's influence on the art of Western civilization has been strong, largely because of the artistic bent of the Moors, a Muslim sect living in northwestern Africa, who invaded Spain during the eighth century C.E. In occupying much of Spain for a number of centuries, they were responsible for a good deal of Spanish architectural design, such as that of the Alhambra, pictured on the next page, built as a palace for Moorish kings during the thirteenth and fourteenth centuries and located outside the city of Granada. It is considered the epitome of Moorish art, with slender columns miraculously supporting complex arches, and a colorful interior of stucco and mosaic tiles in an infinite variety of patterns and designs. Visitors to the palace may feel as though they have been transported into an *Arabian Nights* fantasy. Though the building is a secular one, its architecture is an outgrowth of the richly designed and decorated mosques, which, like Christian cathedrals, are meant to bring the worshipper into closer touch with the next world.

Detail from the Alhambra, a Moorish palace in Granada, constructed between 1338 and 1390. The Moors, an Islamic people, ruled Spain during this period.

Source: © Dallas and John Heaton/Corbis.

The great artistic works of the Vatican, including Saint Peter's and the Sistine Chapel, were deliberately monumental, designed to overshadow and replace the polytheistic art that at one time had been pervasive throughout Rome. The art of Leonardo, Michelangelo, Raphael, and many others gave a vivid and visual reality to religious stories familiar to the public: Adam and Eve, Joseph and the wife of Potiphar, Moses, David, the Prodigal Son, the Virgin and Child, the Annunciation, the Crucifixion, the Resurrection, Judgment Day—the list is almost endless.

During the Protestant Reformation, beginning in the late fifteenth century, church architecture became simplified. But this change led indirectly to the flowering of baroque art and architecture in the seventeenth century. Baroque churches, as we saw in Chapter 6, were elaborately decorated in what may have been a strong effort to win back worshippers who felt that religion had lost its inspiring grandeur. The complex counterpoint of Bach was another great gift from the baroque period.

Some of the great works of Western literature are reaffirmations of religious teachings, such as Dante's *Divine Comedy* (fourteenth century) and Milton's *Paradise Lost* (1662), written to "justify the ways of God to man." Both works greatly influenced the way artists, other writers, and millions of worshippers think about God and the spiritual world beyond.

But writers and artists often have their own relationship to religion and give us unorthodox but no less uplifting visions. "Batter my heart," the sonnet by John Donne (1572–1631) analyzed in Chapter 4, speaks of religious ecstasy in highly sexual terms but strongly communicates the idea of submission to God's will in an unforgettable way.

During the Romantic movement in the last part of the eighteenth century and the first half of the nineteenth, Western artists and writers found a new kind of religious vision, founded on nature and the natural rights of all people. In his poem "The Divine Image," William Blake speaks of religion as a universal gift that unites everyone. Here Blake transcends all sectarian viewpoints, finding God in the human world.

To Mercy, Pity, Peace, and Love
All pray in their distress;
And to these virtues of delight
Return their thankfulness.

For Mercy, Pity, Peace, and Love
Is God, our father dear,
And Mercy, Pity, Peace, and Love
Is man, his child and care.

For Mercy has a human heart,
Pity a human face,
And Love, the human form divine,
And Peace, the human dress.

Then every man, of every clime,
That prays to his distress,
Prays to the human form divine,
Love, Mercy, Pity, Peace.

And all must love the human form,
In heathen, Turk, or Jew;
Where Mercy, Love and Pity dwell,
There God is dwelling too.

In Blake's poem, God is a force—imagination, creativity, and of course, the four cardinal gifts singled out by the poet, whose romanticism, not confined within the walls of a church, also finds divinity outside as he rejoices in the wonder of it all.

A major voice in romanticism is that of William Wordsworth (1770–1850), one of whose masterpieces is *Lines Composed a Few Miles above Tintern Abbey on the Banks of the Wye*. Here are two famous passages from the poem. It is indeed religious, but not in a traditional sense. For Wordsworth, God is the soul of nature, a belief that brings him close to Hinduism.

And I have felt
A presence that disturbs me with the joy
Of elevated thoughts; a sense sublime
Of something far more deeply interfused,
Whose dwelling is the light of setting suns,
And the round ocean and the living air,
And the blue sky, and in the mind of man;
A motion and a spirit, that impels
All thinking things, all objects of all thought,
And rolls through all things.

And this prayer I make
Knowing that Nature never did betray
The heart that loved her; 'tis her privilege
Through all the years of this our life, to lead
From joy to joy; for she can so inform
The mind that is within us, so impress
With quietness and beauty, and so feed
With lofty thoughts, that neither evil tongues,
Rash judgments, nor the sneers of selfish men,
Nor greetings where no kindness is, nor all
The dreary intercourse of daily life,
Shall e'er prevail against us, or disturb
Our cheerful faith, that all which we behold
Is full of blessings.

Every religion is true one way or another. It is true when understood metaphorically. But when it gets stuck in its own metaphors, interpreting them as facts, then you are in trouble.

—**Joseph Campbell**

The Romantic artist Eugene Delacroix (1799–1863) could almost have been illustrating Wordsworth's poem in his painting of a wild horse reproduced here. Today's environmental movement mourns the decline of the religious attitude toward nature shared by nineteenth-century poets and artists and, through their legacy, by many who feel as they did.

Religion cannot possibly be exhaustively treated in only one chapter of one text. We have presented an introductory outline of the major religions of the world and some consideration of the role played by religion in the humanities. As always, the purpose has been to stimulate your thoughts and encourage you to think about your own position relative to these matters.

Many people become uncomfortable when religion is analyzed as a human phenomenon, as if discussing it threatens sincerely held beliefs. Discussion should not have this effect. If engaged in intelligently and with an open mind, religious discussion can strengthen your beliefs. Knowing the *why* of belief is far better than expressing allegiance to it without understanding. All-important is full awareness of your commitment and your responsibilities after having *made* the commitment.

Despite the fear that Delacroix was capturing, both the horse and the background are magnificent in their power, illustrating the romantic sense of nature as the face of God.

Source: Eugene Delacroix, *Horse Frightened by Storm* (1828). Hungarian National Gallery, Budapest.

Key Terms

agnostic one who believes that we cannot know for sure whether God exists.

atheist one who believes that God cannot logically exist.

atman in Hinduism, the individual soul that is part of a universal soul.

Brahma in Hinduism, a godlike personification of the creative principle in the universe.

brahman in Hinduism, the name given to the spiritual force that governs the universe; the universal soul.

buddha Sanskrit term for "the awakened one"; used in Hindu prophecies as a reference to a special being who comes along once in 25,000 years and attains enlightenment without having to be reborn; the Buddha refers to Siddhartha Gautama, who taught that anyone is potentially able to do this.

Buddhism lifestyle, meditation practice, and religion based on the teachings of the Buddha.

caste in India, a social class; in Hindu belief, determined by the moral quality of your previous life.

creatio ex nihilo Latin phrase meaning "creation out of nothing"; used in Judaism, Christianity, and Islam to describe the universe that God made.

dharma in Hinduism, the moral structure underlying existence; in Buddhism, the equivalent of brahman, the universal soul; Chinese equivalent, Tao.

dialectic the philosophical method used by Socrates, involving question and answer.

enlightenment in Buddhism, the state achieved by the Buddha, total detachment, devoid of ego, in which one sees things as they really are.

heresy a belief held or statement made that challenged medieval Christian teachings.

Hinduism generic term for religion of India dating back to c. 1500 B.C.E., based on honoring numerous deities and a belief in reincarnation.

Inquisition high Christian court assembled beginning in the thirteenth century for the trial and sentencing of those convicted of heresy.

karma in Hinduism, a moral summing up of one's deeds that determines where one will be in the next lifetime.

materialism a philosophy that says only matter is real.

meditation in Buddhism, the practice of sitting until one achieves a state of detachment from ego.

moksha in Hinduism, Sanskrit term given to the state of eternal bliss achieved after having successfully gone through many rebirths.

monotheism religion based on one supreme god.

nirvana in Buddhism, a state of bliss attainable to those who devote their lives to meditation and a transcendence of ego; adapted into English to mean a totally stress-free condition.

polytheism religion based on more than one god.

pragmatism philosophy developed in America which holds that the truth of an idea is measurable by experiment and practical outcome.

predestination the belief stated by Augustine that one's entire life, including moral and immoral choices, is already determined before birth; in Calvinism, the belief that one is born either for salvation or damnation.

Shiva in Hinduism, a personification of the principle of change, of destroying what Brahma has created in order to make way for the new; the second god in the Hindu trinity.

Talmud a collection of writings that interpret the Torah and provide clarification of biblical laws.

Tao in Taoism, the moral order that rules the universe.

Thomism name given to the logical system developed by Aquinas, strongly influenced by Aristotle, to prove the existence of God.

Torah the first five books of the Hebrew Bible: Genesis, Exodus, Leviticus, Numbers, and Deuteronomy; attributed to Moses.

Unmoved Mover what Aristotle called the force that always existed and was responsible for setting the entire universe in motion but was not in itself set in motion by anything preceding it.

Vishnu in Hinduism, the principle that creates a balance between the need for permanance and the need for change.

wu wei phrase used in Taoism that translates as "to do without doing"; means that people who live their lives in tune with the moral order of the universe will always do the right thing.

yang in Taoism, the active component of existence, symbolized in art as the white crescent of a circle, which also contains a small black circle; the yang is balanced by and works with the yin.

yin in Taoism, the passive component of existence, symbolized in art as the black crescent of a circle, which also contains a small white circle; the yin is balanced by and works with the yang.

Zen austere and monastic form of Buddhism, centering on the highly disciplined practice of meditating for very long periods of time; from the Chinese *ch'an*, meaning "meditation."

Topics for Writing and Discussion

1. Some scholars of the humanities tell us there are *four* pathways to religion. One is *tradition*—belief because it is part of your culture and background; the second is *history*—belief because it is based on events that can be documented; the third is *philosophy*—belief through rational analysis. What do you think the fourth is? Explain your answer.
2. The Hebrew and Christian Bibles and the Islamic Qur'an all present the commandments of God. They are strikingly similar. Presumably all three religions pray to the same God. Briefly explain some of the disputes they have with each other.
3. What is the *synoptic problem*? Give one reason that it should not exist. Give your own explanation of what might account for it.
4. At the beginning of Whitman's *Leaves of Grass* is the line "For every atom belonging to me as good belongs

to you." This would at first appear not to have anything to do with religion, but as we point out in this chapter, Whitman was strongly influenced by a certain religion. What was it? What was the influence?

5. Augustine maintained that human beings are given free will by God and thus are responsible for their sins. At the same time, he said that God, being all-knowing, must see in advance everything that we are going to do. How did Augustine reconcile these two apparently opposing ideas? Do *you* think he succeeded?

6. One atheistic argument is based on a principle known as *reductio ad absurdum*, which means that you prove something by showing that its opposite leads to an absurd conclusion. For example, the opposite of "God does not exist" is "God exists," which is absurd because it cannot be proved. Its opposite does not have to be proved because it asserts nothing. Do you accept this argument? If not, what are your objections?

7. Faith is central in both Judaism and Christianity. Both maintain that the ways of God are too mysterious to be grasped by human reason. Non-believers find this argument unacceptable. Still, are not many things about living taken on faith? Suggest some.

8. Would the discovery of life on other planets strengthen or diminish the role of religion in modern society?

9. John Scopes, a high school biology teacher, was tried and convicted for teaching the theory of evolution. What, in your opinion, was the issue at the core of the trial? Has the issue been resolved once and for all? Explain your answer.

10. Can you have God without religion, or religion without God?

11 Morality

Overview

Because **moral** problems arise almost every day of our lives and because artists and philosophers are so often concerned with right and wrong, morality is a major theme in the humanities. It is strongly present in much fiction, poetry, drama, television, and film, and can be indirectly found in the visual arts and music. It is, of course, central in religious thought, philosophy, and law.

Morality can be defined as *the basis for a choice among significant options.* That definition eliminates a host of ordinary decisions and trivial differences of opinion. What is required is a "significant" option. This chapter is about significant moral problems that have concerned thoughtful people through the ages and continue to concern us today. These options can be put in the form of questions that seem universal, not tied to specific cultures or time. Here are five questions that have stirred debate among moral philosophers.

1. *Does the end ever justify the means?* If the goal is considered beneficial, is it morally right to do *anything*—including individual acts that on their own would be considered wrong or even criminal to achieve that goal? Machiavelli, one of the philosophers discussed in this chapter, would say yes. Others would say that any moral transgression, even telling a lie, is wrong under any circumstances.
2. *Are punishment and the fear of punishment the only things that keep a person from doing wrong?* The question of whether to obey the law when we can get away with breaking it is at the heart of a famous debate between Glaucon and Socrates in Plato's *Republic*, discussed in this chapter in the section on self-interest.
3. *Do the needs of society outweigh the needs of the individual?* Several philosophers have argued that the individual always come first. John Rawls, in the section on altruism, has a different idea.
4. *Should economic resources be owned and controlled by individuals or by communities?* Some political and economic leaders defend the free market, as described by Adam Smith, and others argue that the free market system does not work in quite the way

An American artist shows scorn for corrupt power. The police officer is being bribed in return for silence and protection. The title ironically echoes that of Kant's major work: *The Critique of Pure Reason*.

Source: Jack Levine, *Feast of Pure Reason* (1937). Credit: On extended loan from the United States WPA Art Program. Museum of Modern Art, NY. Reprinted with permission of VAGA, New York, NY.

Smith described. Some say that the perception of free enterprise as moral or not depends on whether one has an unlimited or rigidly fixed income.

5. *Are results all that matter, or do intentions also count?* The philosopher Jeremy Bentham favors results, but the philosopher Immanuel Kant and many religious thinkers believe it is important to consider motive as well as actions when deciding whether a certain action is or is not moral.

How We Arrive at Moral Decisions

Some philosophers argue that the knowledge of right and wrong is with us from birth. Others believe that we are *taught* the difference between the two. Sometimes we may know what is right, but we do the opposite and then try to justify our actions in some way. Sometimes we say we *used* to know what is right, but now experience has made us less certain. One way or another, we cannot escape *having* to choose.

Moral Systems

Elevation of morality over other goods in human life has been honored, wherever it has been achieved, as a tempering of the otherwise unquenchable human appetite for power, wealth, pleasure, and the rest.

—**Jack Miles**

Morals are an acquirement–like music, like a foreign language, like poetry, poker, piety, paralysis–no one is born with them.

—**Mark Twain**

A network of related values on which moral choices are based is called a **moral system**. Most religions, for example, share the belief that certain rules must be followed whether or not they interfere with an individual's personal desires, and often these rules are found in a sacred book. Accepting these rules thus involves (1) faith in the existence of the divinity making the rules, and (2) faith that the sacred book was written by those in a position to record correctly the words of that divinity.

Another moral system is based on reason. One does what is right because reason determines it to be right and therefore doing wrong is irrational. This view in turn depends on faith in reason as the ultimate decision maker in all matters.

Those who have a hard time making up their minds when faced with a difficult choice might wish to consult a moral authority, such as a well-known philosopher, a religious leader, or even a close friend with a reputation for making intelligent decisions. Yet another question immediately pops up: *In the event that two sources offer sharply divergent opinions—or absolute rules—about making a moral decision, which one do we follow?* Will we follow our gut feeling? Will the decision, in the end, come down to self-interest? Will we lack confidence in our own reasoning? Will it simply be easier to follow a moral authority than to wrestle with the problem and agonize over our decision?

You may have some thoughtful answers to moral questions. If so, and if you know the source of your answers, you may already understand a great deal of moral philosophy. By the end of this chapter you may not have definite answers to all of the questions, but you will have been introduced to some theories and some thinkers who have thought long and hard about them. Then it will be up to you to decide which to follow—or, if you prefer, which is right.

The words *should* and *should not* appearing in comments on morality seem appropriate for people who approach the subject with a desire to measure an action based on a particular text as interpreted by a specially trained or consecrated leader. Most religions are guided by commandments, but the *shoulds* and *should nots* can be found in rules of the military and other institutions as well.

People who feel uncomfortable with an absolute *should* are apt to reject the word in favor of *moral relativism* (discussed more fully later in the chapter). "Who's to say what's right?" "People are different. What's good for one may not be good for someone else." "Times change; there are no universals." All of us know of instances in which people who thought differently have been damaged by those who believed there was only one right way. Or one may reject *should* in favor of a simpler rule: "As long as no one is hurt, and if it makes you happy, do it."

Most of us derive some or all parts of a moral system from a variety of sources. Family, education, and society are all influential; so are fairy tales, literature, plays, movies, and television. No matter what the source, there are common taboos against killing, stealing, adultery, lying, and so on, and common beliefs about what constitutes praiseworthy behavior. Some people in totalitarian societies protest against the imposition of what seem to be arbitrary moral rules by a rigid governing body. Yet if you could travel from place to place, interviewing people at random, people not actively engaged in governing, you would probably discover a large body of moral principles that *are* universally accepted.

Conscience is the inner voice that tells us someone may be looking.
—H.L. Mencken

Nonetheless, sometimes these principles and their sources can be at odds with each other. Your rational assessment of a situation may lead you in one direction, religion in another, and family tradition in still another. Life pushes us into so many quandaries that doing the right thing in every instance is exceedingly difficult. That is why the humanities are sensitive to the pain and suffering that can be caused by moral dilemmas and the tragic results that often result from our choices. The humanities may also be the source of hidden moral beliefs and assumptions that underlie stories or characterizations. In the discussion of critical thinking in Chapter 2, we pointed out that the ability to discover hidden assumptions is an invaluable tool for the person who wishes to lead a rational life. Such a discovery is especially vital if we are to put our moral houses in order—if we are to take control of our lives and fully understand what makes us act as we do.

Morality in the Arts

If moral themes were removed from literature, what remained would be scanty indeed. Nathaniel Hawthorne's *The Scarlet Letter* (1850) ultimately wonders whether the individual citizen should be bound by the moral rules of the community. Hester Prynne, the protagonist, a member of Boston's austere Puritan community, is trapped in a loveless marriage. While her husband is away, she succumbs against her better judgment to her passion for a handsome young pastor who cares for her in a tender way she has never known. When a child is born and Hester refuses to name the father, the outraged community, led by the elders of the church, force her to wear a scarlet "A" (for adulteress) on her clothing and to endure the scorn of all the citizens. Though Hawthorne was raised as a strict Puritan, the democratic side of him began to see that an inflexible moral code, imposed by both religion and the community, was more sinful than the adulterous relationship, which had, after all, grown out of a sincere love. Even though *The Scarlet Letter* was written a century and a half ago, the question of whether genuine love supersedes a rigid moral code is still with us.

Hamlet deals with many issues, but perhaps most strongly with the question of whether the need to avenge the wrong done to one's father outweighs the need to follow one's own moral path. *The Godfather* restates the question in a tragic film. The issue of whether duty to one's family outweighs all other considerations, including personal preferences, remains as crucial today as it was in Shakespeare's time. By extension, we can add the conflict that erupts when the family disapproves of a son's or daughter's marital choice, and the inner turmoil when a son or daughter agonizes over whether to tell parents about a sexual preference they adamantly oppose.

Visual artists often concern themselves with moral wrongs. Picasso's *Guernica* remains one of the most potent statements ever made about the horror of attacking an enemy city and killing hundreds of innocent people. The atomic bombing of Hiroshima and Nagasaki, which destroyed thousands of civilians, the burning of Vietnamese villages (made unforgettable in Oliver Stone's 1978 film *Platoon*), and the deaths of non-combatants in the U.S.-led invasion of Iraq, which will inevitably be the subject of many novels and films . . . all of these descendants of *Guernica* keep the wheels of our mind spinning. Does even a just cause excuse acts of inhumanity? When is inhumanity humane?

Even music can be born from a moral stance. Music that is explicitly religious, such as Bach's *Passion According to Saint Matthew*, is a translation into sound of humanity's closeness to God. By contrast, a work such as Ravel's *La Valse* (The Waltz) has been interpreted as a musical vision of the chaos of Europe after the devastation of World War I. The work begins as a disciplined waltz, then gradually reflects chaos with crashing dissonance and electrifying rhythmic changes. It may be the product of an artist who mourns the passing of an age in which values were clear and straightforward. The moral dimension of a given work can lead to as much discussion and analysis as its form.

The relationship between morality and the law has raised problems that underlie many works of literature, stage, and screen. In the 1957 film *Twelve Angry Men*, eleven members of a sequestered jury are in favor of finding the defendant guilty of murder, but one person is not so sure and insists on closer analysis. As the intensity builds, we begin to see that some of the jurors simply want to go home and others had their minds made up from the beginning. The juror who opposes their decision finally wins them over, but we are left with an uncertainty. We don't know whether justice has been done.

The television series *Law and Order* frequently ends ambiguously, as police investigations followed by courtroom verdicts or plea-bargaining call into question the gulf between crime and punishment, let alone justice. The public remains fascinated, as shown by the continued popularity of the series and its spin-offs.

Shaw's play The Doctor's Dilemma *illustrates how painful a moral choice between two compelling options can be.*

The need to make a choice among significant options cannot be overstated. In George Bernard Shaw's play *The Doctor's Dilemma* (1906), an expensive cure for a previously fatal disease has been found, but it is so rare and so expensive that a physician in the play must choose between two applicants. One is a decent, hard-working doctor who has helped many patients; the other is an artist, a man of genius but a scoundrel, apparently interested only in himself and his work.

The play gives the audience a chance to debate the issue of how much selfishness or selflessness is involved in evaluating human life. The caring doctor, who devotes his entire life to others, ultimately is given the cure, while the artist must die. In his typically ironic ending, Shaw makes us realize that the self-interest of the artist has enriched the lives of thousands and we must be careful before we jump to hasty moral judgments.

Such dilemmas have inspired innumerable discussion groups, some of which, for example, have argued over which survivor of a shipwreck should be allowed into an overcrowded lifeboat that has space for only one more. In actual cases, medical transplant teams must choose between patients desperately in need of a scarce liver, kidney, or some other organ. Who goes to the head of the line while others wait their turn with the likelihood of more pain and death?

Shaw's play thus continues to have relevance. Consider the cost of health care in a large corporation. Management must choose an insurance plan with benefits that are either equal for all employees or different according to an employee's rank, usefulness to the organization, or citizenship. For example, would the dental care available to the company's chief executive officer be the same as that available to the cafeteria worker here on a temorary work visa? Minimum dental care is cheap: numb the area around the problem tooth and extract it. Making impressions of the area and fitting a crown in order to save the tooth can cost thousands of dollars. Does the morality of self-interest give management the right to make these distinctions? Yes, say many who argue that, in doing so, the company stays profitable, secure in the knowledge that an almost unlimited supply of applicants for the job of kitchen help is available.

There is really nothing more to say–except why. But since why is difficult to handle, one must take refuge in how.
—**Toni Morrison**

The Morality of Self-Interest

When young siblings angrily dispute who owns what, a parent will remind them not to fight. Instead, they are urged to share. In school, children are taught to obey rules, not to be selfish, and to cooperate with other members of a team. Public praise for philanthropists reminds us that charity is good, that acting out of self-interest is wrong (except when it was the way the donor's fortune was amassed). Yet free societies are also based on the principle that free enterprise, which benefits the entrepreneur first, also helps employees and their families. Getting ahead is a recognized goal, with its implied corollary that some must win while others lose.

The moral sentiment is the drop that balances the sea.
—**Ralph Waldo Emerson**

Is acting out of self-interest a bad thing? Is selflessness necessarily good? If everyone acted our of self-interest, would it breed a self-reliance that is better for society as a whole? During a sweeping nineteenth-century movement, self-interest came to the fore as the most desirable characteristic of a human being. The term was often preceded by the adjective *enlightened*. It was believed that self-reliant people, realizing their full potential as human beings, would enrich, not damage, society. Other theories, however, still popular today, tell us that, in a choice between self-interest and the general good, self-interest would prevail. That is the position taken by Glaucon in his classic debate with Socrates.

Glaucon versus Socrates

Early in *The Republic*, a series of philosophical dialogues between Socrates and his students, as chronicled by Plato, a confrontation occurs between Socrates, who is always on the side of reason, and Glaucon, a student described by Plato as "that most pugnacious of men" and a firm believer that everyone does the right thing out of motives that have nothing to do with reason or innate goodness. To strengthen his case, Glaucon tells the tale of a shepherd named Gyges, who discovers that a ring he has removed from a corpse has the power to make him invisible. (Think Frodo in *Lord of the Rings*.) Taking full advantage of his newfound power "he contrived to be chosen one of the messengers who were sent to the court; where as soon as he arrived he seduced the queen, and with her help conspired against the king and slew him, and took the kingdom."[1]

An argument then ensues in the class over whether a basically honest and just man would do the same thing. For all his "pugnaciousness," Glaucon is made to be ingenious as well. Glaucon continues: "Suppose now that there were two such magic rings, and the just [man] put on one of them and the unjust the other; no man can be imagined to be of such an iron nature that he would stand fast in justice. No man could keep his hands off what was not his own when he could safely take what he liked out of the market, or go into houses and lie with any one at his pleasure, or kill or release from prison whom he would, and in all respects be like a God among men."[2]

Socrates argues that, if the just man decided not to take advantage of the magic ring, he would die in peace, content that his had been a good life. Glaucon quickly counters by asking the group to suppose that somehow the just man had developed a reputation for being unjust, while the unjust man enjoyed the opposite reputation. Would the just man not decide he would be a fool not to use the powers of the ring? What would be the satisfaction of doing the right thing if nobody knew it? Furthermore, what if he was made to suffer excruciating torture because of his supposed lack of goodness? (Socrates, of course, is famous for teaching that nothing bad can happen to good people.) It will not be long, concludes Glaucon, before the just man realizes that the *appearance* of goodness is all that matters.

Having a reputation for being truthful, hence trustworthy, the unjust man goes on to enjoy all the benefits that come with social approval. "With his reputation of virtue, he will hold offices of state, ally himself by marriage to any family he may choose, become a partner in any business, and having no scruples about being dishonest, turn all these disadvantages to profit."[3] Society, so goes Glaucon's argument, expects virtue to be only an appearance. Virtue is the result of pressure brought to bear upon each of us, not of the human capacity to determine, through reason, what is right and what is wrong.

Truth has no special time of its own. Its hour is now–always.
—**Albert Schweitzer**

Yet reason is precisely what Socrates relies on, and his counterargument is one that has stirred up as much controversy as his opponent's. He maintains that the virtuous act is done *for its own sake*. Rational humans live according to the law, even if the law is harmful to them. Periclean democracy, or the direct rule of citizens, was still very new in the world, and Socrates firmly believed that rationality would give rise to laws that were fair, just, and moral. Plato attributes to Socrates one of the most ringing (and still controversial) declarations in all of philosophy: "To know the good is to do the good."

Socrates' meaning, which at first seems naive, is actually awesome in its simplicity and ultimately hard to refute. What he says is that people cannot claim to be deliberately choosing the wrong action despite knowing the right one. If you do the wrong thing, then that is what you know. *Acting is part of knowing*. In other words, anyone can pretend to know something, but the *only* possible proof of that knowledge is through actions. If your deeds are bad, then there is no evidence that you knew what was right. We may disagree, but the force of the argument is powerful.

Socrates paid with his life for his trust in reason. After being found guilty of trumped-up charges, he was sentenced to death. He refused to bargain for a lighter sentence, which would have required him to agree never to teach again. That would have meant no longer seeking the truth, and without possessing the truth, he would be no better than Glaucon's shepherd.

He does observe, however, that the opinion of others is important, but the opinion of good people *only*. Why should one care what bad people think? If one lives so as to win the respect of the good, then obviously one has led a good life. Then he gives one of his final lessons before drinking the hemlock that will end his days: "*not life, but a good life, is to be chiefly valued.*"

Nowadays it is not hard to find people who admire billionaire tycoons because they succeed so well without even the advantage of a magic ring. Their success is perhaps equivalent to Glaucon's idea of a good reputation, even though hordes of people know that the methods for achieving that success have not always been admirable. Also in the Glaucon camp are those who quote with admiration the cynical adage attributed to baseball manager Leo Durocher: "Nice guys finish last."

They deem him their worst enemy who tells them the truth.

—Plato

Yet, we may ask, what guided the Athenians who voted for the death sentence? Socrates was convicted not by a jury as we know it today, but rather, by an assembly of all the citizens. Reason may not, after all, have been *their* guiding principle. Political factors appear to have been involved. The philosopher's teachings sometimes challenged the state. Did the self-interest of the state finally triumph? And should it have? Even today, we might well inquire whether any governing body can totally sacrifice its well-being, its power, its political future in the name of reason alone.

Later in *The Republic*, Plato admits that the majority of people—both the governing and the governed—will generally be driven by self-interest unless both are held in check by one supreme ruler, a man like Socrates, motivated solely by what reason advises in every instance; a man not out for himself, ruling because he has a clear vision of a state in which justice prevails. He called this ruler the *philosopher-king*. Whether such a being has ever existed or *could* ever exist has long been debated. A number of rulers have made claims about their wisdom, and millions have had faith that their rulers were wise and good, but are such a claim and a people's faith the deciding factors?

Plato's plan has a major problem: who would decide on the identity of the philosopher-king? Reason says only the wisest would be qualified to make the decision. Since there can be only one "wisest person," who could decide that the right choice had been made? What would prevent *anyone* from claiming to be that person? Glaucon would probably say that the struggle for the power of being such a supreme ruler would result in all manner of underhanded magic-ring ploys on the part of ambitious people who would cheat, even kill, to win the position.

In the long history of the humanities, works abound that deal with the theme of self-interest, clearly a problem that has preyed on the conscience of a good many people. In the theater, a discipline that thrives on plots of conflict, the repertoire of important plays would be considerably shorter without that theme.

A play by the French existential philosopher Jean-Paul Sartre (1905–1980) examines the choice made by a young white woman whose testimony could save a black man from death. *The Respectful Prostitute* (1947) is based on an actual event involving two prostitutes who were urged by a judge and a sheriff to accuse two black men of rape, so that

Archetypes in This Chapter

Glaucon	a figure in Plato's *Republic* who has come to symbolize the hard-nosed realist always ready to challenge the lofty principles of idealists.
Greed	developed from various moral denunciations of hedonism and later of capitalist theories based on Adam Smith, but also praised as one of life's goods by supporters of the Smith theory that amassing wealth out of self-interest also benefits others.
Kindness	popular version of altruism, a quality we seek and admire whether we embody it or not.
Morals	for many, proper and acceptable conduct in all matters and not open to discussion; usually based on religious, family, and societal requirements that nonetheless can conflict with each other, causing much confusion.
Philosopher-king	the ideal of the totally rational ruler who puts aside all self-interest.
Puritan	broad term for a morally rigid person.
Ten Commandments	the archetypal set of moral laws for all cultures influenced by Judaism, Christianity, and Islam. Ingrained in most people born within such cultures whether or not they are religious.

the mob would feel justified in lynching them. One of the prostitutes agreed to lie. Sartre's drama focuses on just one prostitute, Lizzie. The play begins after the accusation of rape has been made. The men are being hunted by dozens of armed deputies and police bloodhounds. One of them seeks out Lizzie and begs her to tell police the truth. His passionate entreaties convince her that she cannot lie, not even in a racist community that wants to find and execute the fugitives. She resolves to save the men.

Later, however, she learns that one of her customers, a racist young man, is the son of a powerful senator. He and his father urge Lizzie to go ahead with the false accusation, because social stability requires certain sacrifices, one of which she must now make. Their argument is that the example of these two black men, if convicted, will guarantee that the area will be much safer in the future for decent, law-abiding citizens. Sartre's heroine experiences much inner torment before finally relenting and changing her story, inventing a harrowing account of how she was violently attacked. In a society clearly based on class and skin color, Sartre is saying, words like "reason," "virtue," and "the good" become subordinated to the majority will, and this becomes a major cause of injustice. Or rather, those words are used by the privileged class to justify their power. "Inferiors," or so they believe, could not be expected to understand the terms.

In real life we have all heard and read about the importance of testifying under oath to determine guilt or confirm an alibi. Perhaps lynch mobs are no longer prevalent, but threats to witnesses and the establishment of witness protection programs attest to the dangers that sometimes accompany telling the truth.

In Robert Bolt's 1960 Pulitzer Prize play *A Man for All Seasons*, the issue is religious conviction versus self-preservation. Based on historical events, the play concerns the dilemma and subsequent martyrdom faced by the writer and philosopher Thomas More. Widely admired in his native England and often honored by his once close friend King Henry VIII, More was eventually placed in a position of having to give his approval to the king's pending divorce or risk execution by upholding church doctrine. More, a faithful Catholic, believed so implicitly in the laws of the church that he could not do as the king demanded, not even to save his own life. In Socratic terms, More was objecting to Henry's efforts to rewrite church doctrine to suit his own needs, and thus assenting to the divorce would have amounted to a betrayal of reason. Although the king privately pleads with his friend not to die for his belief, More's obstinate refusal to sanction the divorce publicly leaves Henry no choice. More is beheaded. He was eventually canonized by the Catholic church.

The works of nineteenth-century novelists teem with male characters obsessed with moving to higher levels of society by making advantageous deals that injure the naive and benefit the shrewd, while poor but ambitious women use their charms to win proposals of marriage from good providers whom they do not and never will love. William Thackeray's Becky Sharp, heroine of the aptly titled *Vanity Fair*, is, like her American counterpart Scarlett O'Hara, the lasting symbol of the woman who uses her charm to get what she wants but inevitably finds herself alone and unloved.

In the short story "The Idealist," by Irish writer Frank O'Connor (1903–1966), a Protestant student in an Irish school is profoundly influenced by inspirational books about boys in such schools for whom honor and tradition are all-important. The student notes that, whenever Catholic classmates are late for school, they lie to the headmaster, saying they have been to Mass and thus escape punishment. The young hero, however, is so conditioned by his reading to believe in telling the truth at all costs that he is severely beaten every time he is late without offering an excuse. At length, broken in spirit (and nearly in body!), he lies like all the others. The story ends with the headmaster smiling to himself in triumph. The last holdout has finally come into the fold.

Frank O'Connor's short story "The Idealist" shows the terrible things that happen to a schoolboy who always believes in telling the truth.

There are also cynical writers who tell us that acting solely according to virtuous principles may *sound* praiseworthy but is in the end foolish and self-defeating. Often the cynicism is couched in humor. James Thurber, the *New Yorker* cartoonist and writer who specialized in making people laugh, dealt with righteousness as a futile enterprise in his *Fables for Our Time*. In these short stories, the humorist takes a second look at some time-honored tales and nursery rhymes that preach the value of honesty at all costs. One tells the story of a good, clean-living citizen whose life is one of strict moral and physical discipline, who is so predictable in all his opinions and actions that his wife knows she can take advantage of his clockwork bedtime habits by sneaking out to meet her lover. Then the pair decide to do away with him. Waiting until the appointed hour when the husband always falls asleep, the lover steals into the house and strangles him. Thurber concludes with an updated version of the old nursery rhyme, changing it to say that "early to rise, early to bed makes a man healthy, wealthy, and dead."

Following World War II, America emerged from the Great Depression and new moneyed classes came upon the scene. A good many people had amassed huge sums in the war effort and were often viewed with distrust. The evil of greed reared its head once more, supplying literature, drama, and cinema with abundant plot material. John Huston's *The Treasure of the Sierra Madre*, a 1948 film starring Humphrey Bogart in another of his memorable roles (see Chapter 9), was a cinematic updating of the classic fable about three partners who reap a great fortune—in this case, gold from an abandoned mine—only to destroy each other because each one wants the fortune for himself. In the humanities, extreme self-interest has seldom been applauded and is shown as the force that drives people to commit evil acts.

Enlightened Self-Interest

The end may justify the means as long as there's something that justifies the end.

—**Leon Trotsky**

The Renaissance philosopher Niccoló Machiavelli (1469–1527) argued in favor of political self-interest as the only possible means to a stable and harmonious society. His most famous work, *The Prince*, contains advice to all aspiring rulers. Effective leaders, he claims, must never assume their followers would seek a justice inconvenient to themselves. He therefore concludes that the wisest course for a true leader is to gain respect and obedience by creating a sense of awe. Leaders must present an intimidating appearance, letting the populace know that someone regal is in charge. They should dress well and be surrounded by signs of power, such as riding in magnificent carriages followed by a large retinue of influential friends, security personnel, and important local politicians. This advice has been followed by modern leaders, who fly from country to country in gigantic, official planes and are escorted to their destinations in stretch limousines, long motorcades, and a parade of bodyguards.

Machiavelli's political philosophy may well have been inspired by Plato and Aristotle, neither of whom accepted wholeheartedly the democratic state installed by Pericles. The latter believed that all laws and court decisions should be made by the private citizens (even though citizens constituted only about 5 percent of the total population, the other 95 percent being slaves and women). Plato and Aristotle did not trust even this small percentage to be rational enough to make fair decisions. Both demanded strong rule from the top in order to guarantee stability and justice. Plato created the philosopher-king; Aristotle advanced the theory that the ideal government had three major components: the king, the aristocrats, and groups of outstanding citizens known for their wisdom and fair dealings.

All three philosophers—Machiavelli, Plato, and Aristotle—were against ruthless, self-interested dictatorship and the whimsical rule of people whose wealth enabled them to buy their way to power. All three were concerned for the welfare of the total society, but they stopped short of recommending direct rule of the populace. Instead, wise rulers best served the interest of their country by imposing, for unselfish reasons, their own, carefully considered political philosophy. This idea can be called **enlightened self-interest**: serving the self in order to have an effective government that provides for people better than they could provide for themselves.

Machiavelli believed that, by acting in his own self-interest, the wise ruler was better for the state than one who was permissive.

The term **Machiavellian** has unfortunately become a reference to cynical individuals who exert power over others by manipulating them through duplicity. Literature offers a gallery of characters that critics have labeled—and always negatively—Machiavellian, such as Iago in Shakespeare's *Othello*. They are usually the villains, preying upon unsuspecting goodness. The true philosophy behind *The Prince* emerged from the Renaissance focus on individualism. In a sense, Machiavelli's ideal ruler typified the new age, for such a ruler was unencumbered by the restraints of the Christlike existence demanded of (but not necessarily realized by) rulers in the Middle Ages. The book was dedicated to Lorenzo de Medici, an aristocrat of Florence, a powerful political figure and patron of the arts, credited by Machiavelli with being the fully realized human being that was the Renaissance ideal, a man whose enlightened self-interest had helped make Florence a great city.

Thomas Hobbes (1588–1679) was a political philosopher who believed that tight autocratic control was necessary because the masses of people, *not* their rulers, were out for themselves. He believed that egoism was the natural condition of humanity. He described human beings as basically "nasty" and "brutish" and denied that such a thing as a noble purpose could exist. With this pessimistic view of the individual, Hobbes wrote *Leviathan* (1651), recommending a political system based on absolute monarchy. He employed the term *commonwealth* to describe the ideal state, one in which each subject must willingly turn over his rights to the sovereign for the mutual protection of all people from each other. He advised that "every man should say to every man, *I authorize and give up my right of governing myself, to this man* [i.e., the Leader], *or to this assembly of men, on this condition, that thou give up thy right to him, and authorize all his actions in like manner*."[4]

Although this may sound like a democratic kind of social contract whereby each person willingly gives up individual rights for the good of all, Hobbes makes no pretense of democracy. Reason told him that, once power is invested in the monarch, that ruler could not, by definition, be answerable to the people. If he were, he would not be feared, and if he were not feared, order would disintegrate. The monarch, backed by an invincible army, would protect his subjects from each other as well as from attacks from other nations. Hence the term *Leviathan*, which for Hobbes meant "*mortal god*, to which we owe under the *immortal God*, our peace and defense." The commonwealth would then flourish peacefully—an impossibility if each citizen were allowed to think and act for himself. Without the Leviathan, every person would distrust every other person, with the result that no person or property would be safe. Without the absolute strength of the leader, "every man has a right to every thing; even to one another's body. And therefore, as long as this natural right of every man endureth, there can be no security to any man."[5]

We can see that Hobbes and Machiavelli both favor non-democratic government as the only means to prevent self-interest from destroying society. Hobbes, further influenced by the rise of rational philosophy during the seventeenth century in reaction to the other-worldliness of the Middle Ages, maintained that reason alone, not a sentimental faith in human nature, could allow humanity to live in peace and harmony. Tough-minded as his political philosophy was, he insisted that it represented the only *rational* course if the human race were to survive its own cutthroat instincts.

Economics and Self-Interest

Adam Smith correctly observed that it is from the self-interest of the butcher, the baker and brewer that we expect our dinner, not from their benevolence.

—**Donald Livingston**

The economic philosopher Adam Smith (1723–1790) believed that the perfect society was one in which all people were free to pursue self-interest. Like Karl Marx, who would come later (see Chapter 16), he observed that economic well-being was the guiding force in human life. People were interested in making money, getting ahead, providing the most comfortable standard of living for themselves and their families. Greed itself was not necessarily a bad thing, as long as one did not break the law or harm others in the process of accumulating wealth. Greed in itself was thus not immoral. It was the natural condition of humanity.

Smith's theory that people should have the freedom to pursue wealth became the basis for the capitalist system of today. To those who argued that unlimited freedom of economic activity would yield a society of constant conflict and dangerous competition, Smith's answer was that *without* such freedom only those in power would enjoy the pleasures that rightfully belong to everyone.

His policy is called **laissez-faire** (a French phrase meaning "allow to do") and is based on the principle that businesses should be free to charge whatever they want for their goods and services. The public's response, not government controls, will regulate the process. Smith's ideal society has a built-in system of checks and balances that prevent the accumulation of wealth in just a few corporations.

Manufacturers, or *entrepreneurs*, as they are called in economic theory, perform a service for the public by seeking to make a profit for themselves. The salaries paid to employees increase the money supply, which keeps circulating throughout the economy, guaranteeing more employment for everyone. Without their being aware of it, says Smith, all people who live in a free-market system are joined together "as by an invisible hand."

It is in the best interest of the entrepreneur to manufacture products that people actually need. To continue to make an unneeded product would result in bankruptcy. (Once the automobile displaced the horse and carriage as the primary means of transportation, who would have wanted to buy buggy whips?)

Problems develop when entrepreneurs become *too* greedy. If a product is successful and large numbers of people buy it, chances are the price will go up. But, Smith adds, if costs get too high, people will stop buying; companies will be forced to lower prices—or go out of business. He is also in favor of unlimited, unrestricted competition as a market stabilizer. If one person charges too much, another will seize the chance to become rich by manufacturing the same product at a lower price. Demanding more and more money in exchange for goods is not immoral in

Smith's philosophy. The consumer inevitably benefits as public response exercises control over wanton enterprises.

Without civic morality communities perish; without personal morality their survival has no value.
—**Bertrand Russell**

Critics of Smith's version of **capitalism** sometimes point out that he lacked the foresight to see that entrepreneurs could collaborate and secretly agree not to undersell each other. In this way, prices remain stable, and everyone profits except the consumer. Smith also did not predict our present era of large aggregates, supercompanies formed from merger after merger until they all but monopolize the market for thousands of products under their control. One vestige of Smith's invisible hand (maybe one finger of it), however, remains strong, and that is the slowing down of sales when prices go too high. Yet, even at that, critics add, entrepreneurs can mutually agree to cut down on production in order to bolster prices, as the Organization of Petroleum Export Countries (OPEC) frequently does.

Smith's laissez-faire policy is predicated on the assumption that the laws of supply and demand will apply in every instance. The price goes up; nobody buys; the price goes down; the cycle repeats itself. When products are cheap, everyone starts buying them again, so the price goes up and the cycle repeats itself. But economists tell us that resources are not unlimited and may not always be available. Crude oil, for example, is non-renewable, no matter what OPEC does. The most pessimistic projections say that eventually there will be none left. The invisible hand in this case will totally vanish.

Nor could Smith have predicted the global economy that exists today, in which there are a few separate nations fending for themselves, but mainly an intricate network of mutual dependence. A bank collapse in a powerful country that previously attracted much foreign investment can cause chaos all over the world. Economists tend to agree that there is no such thing as a global self-regulating market. In any case, Smith's theory that self-interest is in the best interest of humanity continues to be debated. Recent world problems have only added to the controversy. We cannot make the blanket statement that economic self-interest is not moral. We still depend on a free market and faith in Adam Smith's theory of the invisible hand. But we have to admit that it poses problems that may never be resolved.

People create their own questions because they're afraid to look straight. All you have to do is look straight and see the road, and when you see it, don't sit looking at it–walk.
—**Ayn Rand**

For novelist Ayn Rand (1905–1982), however, capitalism was close to divine. She preached complete reliance on the free market, which she believed encourages the strong and self-reliant to make the most of their own talents, without having to spend a lifetime helping others, who would only grow weaker and lose the incentive to help themselves. Born in pre-revolutionary Russia, Rand as a teenager witnessed the sweeping changes and promise of a glorious future in a classless society. She resisted indoctrination after analyzing communist ideology, rejecting Karl Marx's claims about the benefits society would receive once the bourgeoisie had been eliminated.

Rand defected to the West and started writing. In the work that brought her fame in the United States, *The Fountainhead* (1943), she became a spokesperson for rugged, uncompromising individualism. The hero of the novel is a celebrated architect, known for his daring designs and fierce integrity, who refuses to lower his standards and turn out mediocre work for a muddled committee totally lacking in his vision and genius. Howard Roark is a descendant of the epic heroes of old, a strident loner, equal to any challenge.

In one of her famous essays, *The Virtue of Selfishness*, she says that people of foresight and vision should have unlimited opportunities to follow their own laws. In her version of the invisible hand, the strident loner does help others, but not out of the belief that it is moral and honorable to make sacrifices for them. Rand believed society profits because superior people such as Howard Roark build great cities and make the world a better place. But they must be left alone. Roark proudly asserts: "No man is worth five minutes of my time."

Rand's *Atlas Shrugged* (1957) presents a group of high-powered achievers who, tired of mass culture and socialist policies, create a utopian society high on a mountaintop, from which the lazy masses are excluded. At one point Rand makes a scathing denunciation of the Marxist dictum "From each according to his ability, to each according to his need." She has one of the characters, who had been a dedicated worker, finally express his disillusionment with socialist demands that he work for the desperately poor.

> *the harder you work the more is demanded of you, and you stand slinging buckets forty hours a week, then forty-eight, then fifty-six—for your neighbor's supper—for his wife's operation—for his child's measles—for his mother's wheel chair—for his uncle's shirt—for his nephew's schooling—for the baby next door—for the baby to be born—for anyone anywhere around you—it's theirs to receive, from diapers to dentures—and yours to work, from sunup to sundown*[6]

Ayn Rand believed society profits from the genius of strong people, who must be left alone.

Source: Warner Bros./The Kobal Collection.

Transcending Self-Interest: Altruism

When a blind man carries a lame man, both go forward.

—**Swedish proverb**

Self-interest is sometimes necessary. We recognize that in politics those who are called public servants serve their own interests, at least to an extent. Being elected to office brings fulfillment to their lives, as well as recognition and notoriety. Political self-interest can cause pessimists to assume that all politicians are out for wealth and power, that they take advantage of their position and cheat wherever possible. No one will deny that political corruption has always existed and will no doubt continue to exist, but American democracy is built on the principle of representative government. This means that we will always have to elect certain people willing to represent us. It would be depressing indeed to believe that in serving their own needs, the majority of them were not also serving *us*. Yet this brand of self-interest is not exactly the same thing as devoting one's life or risking all in the interest of others.

Can there be a place for **altruism**, or greater concern for the welfare of others more than for oneself? Some would say no, arguing that, even if reason in the Socratic sense requires us to place others before ourselves, what *appears* to be an altruistic, or selfless, act really springs from secret motives of self-interest.

To be sure, many examples of altruistic acts require no questioning of motives. During a shooting incident at an elementary school, for example, a teacher shielded the body of a child and received a fatal bullet instead. In such instances, the cynics are quiet, but they may later observe that the number of people willing to practice altruism is trivially small. The death of 300 firefighters in the disaster of September 11, 2001, may have changed many attitudes. Nor can we ever know how many of the thousands who perished that day did so because they stayed to help others.

Detractors might argue that the heroism displayed on September 11 was only a temporary interlude in the ongoing drama of self-interest. They might concede that at times of extreme disaster, the urge to suppress self-interest is strong, but they would argue that at most other times, altruism disappears.

To the good I would be good; to the not good I would also be good in order to make them good.

—**Lao-tzu**

In the everyday world, altruism *does* exist: in volunteers comforting the sick, youth groups devoted to getting rid of their town's litter, and in advocacy for any cause from which one stands to gain nothing tangible. Lifeguards swim out to answer a distress call without thinking twice. Passersby find lost wallets and mail them back untouched, without their own return address. In the Sudan, where millions of innocent women, men, and children were being slaughtered in acts of "ethnic cleansing" or were dying from malnutrition and disease, members of the group Doctors without Borders, humanitarian medical personnel, worked tirelessly to save as many lives as they could, even though they faced the possibility of being shot for their efforts or being infected with disease themselves.

In the corporate world of today, where workers may become aware of defective auto parts, unsanitary food preparations, or the deliberate advertising of products that are dangerous to health, cases of altruistic "whistle-blowing" exist. Michael Mann's 1999 film *The Insider*, based on an actual case, deals with a conflict between the need to transcend self-interest and the knowledge that doing so could result in not only the loss of a very comfortable income but even physical harm. It poses a question that all too frequently must be asked. Does an employee

Al Pacino, left, and Russell Crowe in *The Insider*. Crowe plays a man forced to decide between providing a comfortable life for his family and blowing the whistle on a tobacco company.

Source: The Everett Collection, Inc.

have a moral responsibility to blow the whistle when it is perceived that a product is harmful and often deadly?

In the film, a tobacco company scientist finally decides to appear on television to reveal information about chemical additives in cigarettes that he believes make smoking more addictive. The decision does not come easily. His contract with the tobacco company had specifically stated that he must never reveal the truth to the public, and he realizes his high income allows him to provide handsomely for his family in a well-appointed home. When he finally places moral responsibility before his own and his family's interest and agrees to testify in court, he is threatened, placed under surveillance, and grilled on the witness stand. His personal reputation and his marriage are destroyed.

Still he persists and agrees to appear on the television program *60 Minutes*, but the producers of the show are told by their superiors it would be best not to air the interview. The *Wall Street Journal*, however, prints the hero's story, and *60 Minutes* is finally willing to run it. There is a singular lack of triumph after the truth is revealed and the protagonist has acted righteously. He has indeed lost everything, and his future seems bleak. We are left to wonder whether his tragic losses are offset by the moral integrity of his actions. In the most notable works, there are no easy moral victories. If nothing else, we learn from them that doing the right thing takes not only courage but the willingness to stand quite alone.

People are naturally suspicious when they hear that someone has committed a purely altruistic act. Often they will seek out hidden motives of self-interest.

Though much literature reflects the belief that self-interest is stronger than altruism, many major works can be found in which characters perform noble deeds that in no way benefit themselves. A famous example is *A Tale of Two Cities* (1859) by Charles Dickens (1812–1870). The hero, Sydney Carton, is a well-educated but essentially unfulfilled gentleman, with little taste for causes and allegiances. And the woman he loves, Lucy, has married Charles Darnay, an expatriate French aristocrat who bears a strong resemblance to Carton. When the French Revolution breaks out, Darnay returns to Paris in order to save the life of one of his servants but is apprehended by the revolutionists and sentenced to die on the guillotine. Aware of the deep love between Lucy and Darnay, the heretofore detached Carton engineers a plot to smuggle Darnay out of the Bastille by taking his place. As he awaits the guillotine, Carton silently thinks, "This is a far far better thing I do than I have ever done. It's a far far better rest I go to than I have ever known." Millions of readers have wept over this ending, though some critics have dismissed the novel for being overly sentimental. Not only does nobility of purpose carry a high price, but it is frequently subject to critical scorn.

Altruism, the extreme opposite of self-interest, comes from the Latin *alter*, meaning "other." The word does not occur often in ordinary conversation. Hearing that an "altruist" has done something considered noble for others, we might look for a motive arising out of self-interest. Was the act truly unselfish, or was it done for the sake of a handsome tax reduction, favorable publicity, or even the pleasure of self-satisfaction? Was the self more involved than the "other"?

Yet the altruistic behavior of some people is above question. We've all heard inspiring declarations like "There is no greater love than to die for another." During times of war there are reports of soldiers who sacrifice themselves for others in their platoon. The stirring words of the seventeenth-century Anglican priest and poet John Donne (see Chapter 4) have become emblazoned in the history of the humanities: "No man is an island entire of itself; every man is a piece of the continent, a part of the main. If a clod be washed away by the sea, Europe is the less, as well as if a promontory were. . . . Any man's death diminishes me, because I am involved in mankind. And therefore never send to know for whom the bell tolls; it tolls for thee."[7] Ernest Hemingway took the title of his 1940 novel *For Whom the Bell Tolls* from this passage. The novel centers on an American who takes part in the Spanish Civil War and gives up his life to save others.

Steven Pinker, a Harvard psychology professor, writes that some moral philosophers and scientists are trying to validate what many still think may be the case—namely, that the moral instinct, the tendency to do what is right regardless of personal gain, is inborn in the species. "Though no one has identified genes for morality," he says, "there is circumstantial evidence they exist." Paraphrasing Richard Dawkins's contention that altruism has evolved in our species, Pinker explains: "Fairness is very close to what scientists call reciprocal altruism, where a willingness to be nice to others can evolve as long as the favor helps the recipient more than it costs the giver and the recipient returns the favor when fortunes reverse."[8]

Far from altruistic are the business executives involved in scandals, indictments, and imprisonments for dubious accounting practices, insider trading, and excessive bonuses unconnected to prudent business practices. The injured have included stockholders, employees, and the occasional whistle-blower who has notified the authorities about alleged crimes. Although three whistle-blowers were once honored by being pictured on the cover of a news magazine, most have not benefited in the least. Being known as the guardian of moral behavior does not enhance the résumé of a job-seeker!

Finding a job becomes even harder in these days of newer practices such as "outsourcing" that are said to benefit the disadvantaged in countries with lower standards of living than ours. When calling about a hotel room or how to solve a computer problem, one may be talking to someone in a far distant location, working for much less than employers would have to pay in America for the same job. Or one may be wearing a dress or shirt that has been manufactured in a factory thousands of miles away, in which workers toil for long hours and low pay in less than ideal conditions. Charity toward the underprivileged, or a new means of amassing huge profits? Would anyone step forward and refuse to work for an outsourcing company on the grounds that it is exploiting the downtrodden?

Moral Authorities

For centuries philosophers have been debating which source of moral values is most defensible, and as the world's population has increased along with a multiplicity of cultural and religious traditions, the need has arisen to find a stabilizing force acceptable to all. So far this force has not been discovered, at least to the satisfaction of everyone. In this section we will consider some of the major kinds of moral authorities that have put forth guidelines from which we can choose.

A Philosophical Defense of Altruism

American philosopher John Rawls (1921–2002), having thought deeply about whether altruism truly exists, agrees with Socrates that reason does not support self-interest. The way he does it is to propose that each of us pretend to be wearing a "Veil of Ignorance," which wipes out all awareness of who we are and where we came from. Starting from Square Zero, so to speak, we then list the requirements for an ideal society. That is, if you didn't *know* you were rich or would be someday or if you didn't *know* you came from a poor background, what would be on your list? Rawls lists two requirements he thinks everyone would cite:

1. Equal and maximum liberty (political, intellectual, and religious) for each person consistent with equal liberty for others.
2. Wealth and power to be distributed equally except where inequalities would work to the advantage of all and where there would be equal opportunity to achieve advantageous positions of equality.[9]

As we can see from this ingenious argument, the "Veil of Ignorance" puts everyone on an equal plane, and from this there would have to be general agreement about the just and fair society. What if you put "equal distribution of wealth" on your list and then found out you were going to be fabulously wealthy some day? You might then reconsider your choices. However, if you were honest, you would recognize that your self-interest was getting in the way of your reasoning. You would in fact be saying: "I believe in unequal distribution of wealth because I'm going to be rich." Similarly, if you discovered that you were poor and would always be so, you might change "equal distribution of wealth" to "tax the rich and give it to the poor." Rawls is not saying the reconsidered concepts are wrong. He is merely pointing out that self-interest usually colors our attitudes toward what is right or just.

The Moral Mathematics of Jeremy Bentham

The greatest happiness of the greatest number is the foundation of morals and legislation.

—**Jeremy Bentham**

Born into a well-established, conservative English family, Jeremy Bentham (1748–1832) was confirmed at the age of thirteen in the Episcopal (Church of England) faith. The ceremony required him to follow the absolute moral laws of his religion. As he matured and observed the world around him, he came to the conclusion that most people neither abided by these laws nor practiced any sort of other-directed morality. He saw humankind as a society of animals all driven by the need to gratify their basic (and often base) desires: in short, the need to serve only themselves.

On the other hand, he was unwilling to say that self-interest was wrong, though the pursuit of it might be contrary to the rigid morality taught to him as a child. Why must moral laws be so contrary to human nature? Accordingly, he became a philosopher and formulated the theory that, since self-serving pleasure was the natural condition sought by everyone, all people must have an equal chance of attaining it. He rebelled against the moral codes set forth by religion and traditional philosophy as well as those that became laws binding on an entire population. What, he asked, gave anyone the right to tell anyone else which pleasures to enjoy and which to avoid? But must there not be guidelines? Surely *everyone* could not wantonly pursue pleasure if this meant interfering with the right of others to do the same. *Unrestricted* self-interest made no sense to him.

As a philosopher he was attracted to science and mathematics, for these fields offered methods of achieving certainty. Accordingly, mathematics became the basis for a moral system that allowed self-interest to be both defended and restricted.

Numbers. Bentham declared that numbers were the key to moral certainty: finding a formula that would decide the right course of action in every instance. For him, the goal was a society in which the maximum number of people achieved the maximum amount of pleasure *without* impinging on the rights of others. He denied the validity of **moral absolutism**, defining the good as *the greatest good for the greatest number.*

In Bentham's system, before you decide upon an action with consequences that will affect others, you assign a plus or minus numerical value to the degree of pleasure or pain that action might cause for the most people. Let us say that, in a modern example, the question is whether to allow a giant resort complex to be built along a lakefront. So many plus points go to the builders, construction workers, and service personnel, all of whom stand to profit from the enterprise. Additional plus points are awarded to vacationers, who will surely benefit from having a place in which to relax and relieve stress. Minus points, however, come from environmentalists concerned about the inevitable pollution and the extermination of fish and waterfowl and from nearby residents who see the resort as destroying the neighborhood and bringing down the resale value of their property. The calculator (an invention Bentham would have loved) will tell the story. Plus points for those who benefit, minus points for those who don't. You do the simple arithmetic and get the moral answer.

Bentham's **moral mathematics** also adds or subtracts points based on "intensity" and "duration." In the example of the resort, we must consider the annoying sounds and air pollution of road expansion and the possibly permanent damage to wildlife. What do you think? Which side would get the most points? May points be determined strictly by the number of individuals involved? If so, the residents might outnumber the owners and the contractors. But what if the builders insist that the number of possible vacationers is almost infinite?

Results and Motives. For Bentham, measurable results tell all. The number of people benefiting is proof of moral rightness. But critics of Bentham's morality see many problems. Suppose the builder of the proposed resort has had a longstanding feud with the head of the environmental committee, a feud stemming from personal differences that have nothing to do with business or pollution. What if anger and revenge are his motives? He has proposed the entire scheme just to embarrass environmentalists in front of their supporters. The calculation yields only external results and pays no attention to motives *unless* there is the chance that a motive, once discovered, might cause pain to a lot of people, but that is unlikely to happen in this hypothetical case.

Another numerical question sidesteps motive. Is it better to give $10 to a cause because you believe it is the right thing to do or $1,000 to the same cause because you want to see your picture in the paper along with a caption praising your philanthropy? For Bentham (and probably for the fund-raisers) the larger amount would be preferable and morally approved.

What might be Bentham's mathematical calculations for a decision on abortion? Homosexuality? Abortion might be considered right or wrong depending on whether an underpopulated country needs more pregnancies carried to completion. As for homosexuality, the question would be whether it harms the general population. Would there be fewer babies born in a society that looked favorably on homosexual activity between consenting adults? Despite the fact that Bentham was essentially a political radical, he would have to approve of a ban on homosexuality if the greatest number in a given society decided that the practice would lessen the population and deprive the future of artists, philanthropists, scientists, and so on. In such a society homosexuality would be mathematically immoral, yet moral in a society that placed the highest priority on, for example, human rights.

In his famous essay satirizing the British treatment of the Irish poor, Jonathan Swift (1667–1745) almost seems to have had prophetic insight into Bentham's **utilitarianism**, which would emerge a century later. Swift launches his devastating attack on British arrogance by reducing the problem of the poor to a game of numbers in "A Modest Proposal," with the subtitle "For Preventing the Children of Poor People in Ireland from Becoming a Burden to Their Parents and Country and for Making Them Beneficial to the Public."

Adopting the persona of a country gentleman without personal knowledge of poverty, he begins by stating his concern about the number of beggars on the street, as well as mothers followed by "three, four or six children, *all in rags*." Instead of pleading for charity, Swift's narrator reverses the usual argument and takes the approach of a practical businessman, calculating the value of turning the youngest Irish children into dinner entrées for the wealthy: "I have been assured by a very knowing American of my acquaintance in London, that a young healthy child well nursed is at a year, delicious, nourishing and wholesome food, whether stewed, roasted, baked or boiled, and I make no doubt that it will equally serve in a fricassee or ragout."

Swift might almost be said to be anticipating making fun of Bentham's moral mathematics when he attacked the shocking treatment of the Irish poor by the British. He made it seem like a game of numbers devoid of humanity.

The narrator then calmly computes the figures: 20,000 for breeding, only one-fourth males, more than usual, he points out, than for "other livestock." The one-year-old child "will make two dishes as an entrée entertainment for friends, and when the family dines alone the fore or hind quarter will make a reasonable dish . . . seasoned with a little pepper or salt." The consequences of the new industry, in addition to reducing the number of poor children who die from malnutrition, will be that the breeders are rid of needless expenses; taverns will have a new dish, and "a skillful cook, who understands how to please his guests will contrive to make it as expensive as they please"; marriages will increase; and mothers will be treated more tenderly as they fatten up their children. Moreover, his proposal is not based on any desire for personal profit, because he has "no children by which I can propose to get a single penny, my youngest being nine years old and my wife past child-bearing."

As can be imagined, "A Modest Proposal" aroused indignation among readers who failed to understand Swift's purpose. Some literalists took him at his word, denouncing "his savagery," not recognizing that he was creating what remains as a masterfully vicious satire on cold calculations as a solution to human issues.

Bentham believed in various definitions of the good, depending on particular circumstances. The lakeside resort, for example, might bring wealth to the town nearby, but it might also draw tourists away from another resort twenty miles away. Back to the calculator. "The greatest good for the greatest number" may have to be redefined. What happens when mathematical calculations do not agree with each other? My pleasure, in other words, is your pain—and vice versa.

Bentham decided therefore that the government would have to step in and be responsible for providing the greatest good for the greatest number. He organized a political party called the Philosophical Radicals in order to campaign for moral reform based on his mathematical system. The name was eventually changed to the Utilitarian Party, suggesting a practical approach to moral philosophy, basically democratic in that it recognized the equality of all individuals in the matter of decision making, with majority rule holding sway.

Utilitarianism Modified: John Stuart Mill

Also designated as a Utilitarian, John Stuart Mill (1806–1873) came a half-century after Bentham. His father, James Mill, a close friend of Bentham, had assisted the philosopher in the development of his political party. James Mill was an elitist when it came to the education of his son, who was allowed to associate only with friends of whose intellectual capacities the father approved. But he was also taught a Socratic brand of rational liberalism: that is, almost unlimited freedom for those responsible enough to use it for purposes other than the gratification of selfish desires.

We can never be sure that the opinion we are endeavoring to stifle is a false opinion, and if we were sure, stifling it would be an evil still.
—**John Stuart Mill**

As Mill matured and became a philosopher and writer, he expressed approval of Bentham's views on government's responsibility to guard the rights of the private citizen, but he disagreed that majority rule is always the proper course. Bentham's mathematics had implied that decisions were quantifiable, but what about matters of taste? Followers of Mill continue to question the wisdom of the majority in all decisions. What if, for example, a proposal to erect a new museum or an opera house were put to a popular vote, and it had to compete with a new sports stadium? The "greatest number" might well opt for "low art" instead of "high art," thus depriving those with educated tastes of the pleasures that ought to be available to them. Imposing low art on everyone regardless of preference was, for Mill, as immoral as imposing absolute standards that had to apply in every situation. Mill questioned whether the rule of the majority may not in fact deprive many people of their own moral rights.

Our society's preoccupation with winners—with blockbusters, sports rankings, runs batted in, bestsellers, awards, scorekeeping of every kind—has caused regret in critics, concerned that numbers may overlook quality. Think back to the debate between the public building of a sports stadium or an opera house. A more subtle distinction has been made in a recent debate by two individuals who love opera but are divided on the question of whether the public should be asked to support it.

Mitchell Cohen is concerned about the availability of the art to the general public. If opera is not subsidized, will only the rich be able to enjoy it? "One consideration should surely be inequality in cultural opportunities . . . no important domain of culture should be accessible chiefly to social elites. So I offer a social democratic precept: in access to culture, no citizen should be more equal than others. Public funding for arts (opera among them) ought to help make varied forms of culture available in a fair manner to all citizens."[10]

Bruce Ackerman, on the other hand, argues that if society is neutral and fair, without preference for one form of art over another, and if we truly respect each other, we would recognize that "the Met merely provides another form of entertainment no different from skateboarding or hula-hooping. I myself do not hold this view—but for those who do, the case for selective subsidy vanishes immediately: why subsidize opera, and not skateboarding, if they are simply rival entertainments struggling for the consumer dollar?"[11]

Mill recognized that government was needed to balance irresponsibility on the part of the general population. But this did not give government the right to legislate morality for the responsible few. In the matter of the opera house, the equitable course would be for a committee of acknowledged patrons of the arts to decide that the aesthetic needs of society were more important than a sports stadium, and this committee would have the backing of the local government. In defending the rights of enlightened citizens, Mill proved to be more radical than Bentham.

One of Mill's most famous essays, *The Tyranny of the Majority*, maintains that letting the majority rule in all decisions is just as bad as the autocratic rule of monarchs in previous centuries. Mill writes that his objective "is to assert one very simple principle" regarding how societies may deal with an individual, "whether the means used be physical force in the form of legal penalties, or the moral coercion of public opinion." According to Mill, "the sole end for which mankind are warranted, individually or collectively, in interfering with the liberty of action of any of their number, is self-protection. That is, the only purpose for which power can be rightfully exercised over any member of a civilized community, against his will, is to prevent harm to others. His own good, either physical or moral, is not a sufficient warrant."[12] Mill's writings greatly influenced American democratic thought, especially that of Thomas Jefferson.

What is morality in any given time or place? It is what the majority then and there happen to like, and immorality is what they dislike.
—**Alfred North Whitehead**

The English artist William Hogarth (1697–1764), famous for paintings and engravings that poke fun at all levels of English society, gave us *The Enraged Musician*, showing both sides of the conflict. The musician in question sits by his open window, his work interrupted by an extremely noisy crowd. What if the musician were to call the police on the grounds that his right to work in privacy has been violated? What if the case ended up in court? Would the judge rule that the crowd has a right to cavort as it pleases as long as no one is being physically

Hogarth was probably the leading satiric artist of the eighteenth century in England. The question here is: what is Hogarth poking fun at?

Source: William Hogarth, *The Enraged Musician* (1741). Credit: Max A. Polster Archive.

harmed? Or that the musician is right in objecting to the crowd on the grounds that his work is more important than their fun? What do you think Mill would say?

A contemporary political scientist, Hans J. Morgenthau (1904–1980), echoes Mill's brand of liberalism: "Civilized man shares with the barbarian the faculty of making moral judgments, but excels over him in knowing why he makes them. He knows—as Socrates, the Greek tragedians . . . the Biblical prophets and the great moralists and tragedians of all ages know—what is meant by the sanctity of the moral law. The moral law is not made for the convenience of man, rather it is an indispensable precondition for his civilized existence."[13] The key word for both Mill and Morgenthau is "civilized." Both philosophers champion the maximum freedom for all persons of intelligence, good will, and objectivity, but they recognize that reason sometimes imposes limitations.

The Moral Imperative of Immanuel Kant

Born in East Prussia and a resident there for most of his life, the German philosopher Immanuel Kant (1724–1804) was, like Bentham, impressed with the certainties that science was able to achieve. As a member of the faculty at the University of Königsberg, he read insatiably in a number of fields, becoming so adept that he was given courses to teach in mathematics, physics, anthropology, logic, metaphysics, and ethics. This impressive background made Kant feel comfortable with both science and philosophy, and he would merge the two into one of the most influential systems of thought ever devised.

The various branches of his philosophy are like the spokes of a wheel, all radiating from a central belief, adopted from science, that truth is arrived at through experience. He differed, however, from kindred philosophers who took the extreme position that experience is strictly what our senses tell us.

Morality is not properly the doctrine of how we make ourselves happy, but how we make ourselves worthy of happiness.

—**Immanuel Kant**

Kant's view is that the input of the senses does not constitute experience until it is *interpreted* by our inborn rational capacity. He believes that we are born with mental **categories** into which sensory data are filed, much as a postal worker takes an armful of random mail and flips each letter into an appropriate box. We know, for example, that the chair is "next to" the table because we understand "nextness." If we did not, the spatial relationship would be meaningless. In such a case, if someone asked us to go fetch the chair next to the table, we would return a blank stare.

Kant then turns his attention to moral concerns. His theory is that the sense of right and wrong is also inborn. True, we come to understand "yes" or "no" from our parents, but no learning can take place unless we are able to attach approval and disapproval, first to specific actions, then to the abstract concepts of right and wrong. For Kant, the average person has no trouble reaching these abstractions because a moral sense, again inborn, gradually unfolds in the same way that a bud gradually opens into a flower. He calls this inborn faculty the **moral imperative**, or *sense of ought*: an intuitive classification of actions and choices as morally acceptable or unacceptable. Experience teaches us which specific actions are right and which are not, but "rightness" and "wrongness," like "nextness," cannot be taught.

Take, for example, the principle of honesty. Without a universal recognition of what it means, we could never ask "What time is it?" We rely on the honesty of the answer, or we would not have asked the question. People depend on a promise to keep an appointment or return borrowed money. If the promise is not kept, we say "That person has not been honest." If the breaker of the promise is not mentally disturbed, he or she would also recognize that the principle of honesty has been violated.

For Kant, slavery, which he was firmly against, was a particularly illuminating example. Kant argued that, regardless of the number of people who held slaves and justified their actions for a variety of reasons, even including religious ones, the fact remained that slavery was morally wrong. That slave-holders had to search around for justifications clearly indicated a secret knowledge that what they were doing was reprehensible. Socrates had said, "To know the good is to do the good." Kant did not believe this was necessarily true. Each of us is born with a knowledge of the good, whether or not we disregard it later. He admitted that self-interest all too often suppressed the moral imperative.

Kantian ethical philosophy has given us a powerful way of knowing in advance whether a proposed action is morally right. It does not depend upon consequences, and it is not relative to varying circumstances. It is a very simple procedure. All it demands is that we hesitate before we act and ask ourselves one vital question: *Would it be all right for everyone else to do this?*

A person temporarily poor sees a drunken man weaving his way down the street. A wallet falls out of the man's pocket without his noticing. He continues on his way. The poor observer immediately picks it up and sees that it contains a considerable amount of money. The drunken man cannot walk very fast, so it would be a simple matter to catch up with him and return the wallet.

The finder of the wallet is now like Glaucon's shepherd, invisible as far as the owner of the wallet is concerned. The temptation is great to wait until the owner is well out of sight and then to disappear with the money. Why not? Who would return the money under those circumstances? Suppose now that the finder of the wallet is convinced that the money is compensation for unjust treatment, and that people deserve what they can get. It's a dog-eat-dog world, is it not?

If faced with this example, Kant would surely not assume that this person, knowing deep down inside that keeping the wallet is wrong, would shout for the owner to stop so it could be returned. Keeping the wallet would in fact be making a definite choice between two options, deliberately choosing the immoral one.

But, you ask, how can we be certain that it *is* immoral? Just because the person has been taught that keeping what belongs to someone else is the same as stealing? Suppose the finder does not accept this view and believes that the world is really amoral, and so the wallet is not returned. And so no one is the wiser for it.

The story, however, does not end there. Having decided to use some of the money for a sumptuous dinner and later a comfortable hotel room, the finder is walking down a deserted street and is accosted by a thief who, brandishing a weapon, demands and gets money. The thief disappears, and the new victim is left once more homeless and hungry. Would the thought arise: "It serves you right"?

In Kantian terms, the latter response is indeed possible, but not very probable. The chances are good that the finder of the wallet would be exceedingly angry about the theft. Translating the anger into philosophical terms, the principle would be: *It was all right for me to keep the wallet, but wrong for the thief to steal it from me.*

If we agree that keeping the wallet is stealing, then what is the difference between the first and second thefts? The answer: NONE. Kant tells us that, before we commit any act, we should stop to ask ourselves: *Can we will that this act be universally acceptable?* Anyone who took the wallet but cannot do this, is actually saying: *It's all right for a particular person to steal, but not for everyone.* Such reasoning immediately strikes us as absurd. Accepting it is tantamount to saying that one person is the sole exception to a universal moral law. Stealing is universally wrong, except when I do it.

Kant's theory is ingenious, we must admit. In all probability none of us will lead morally perfect lives, but that does not excuse us from differentiating between the right and the wrong. It is a strong argument against a moral code that begins and ends with the self. His logic is impeccable, but one could only wish that every member of society were endowed with Kantian rationality.

Religion and Morality

Kant's parents were deeply religious, teaching that moral laws were set forth by God and could not be altered. As Kant grew older and learned about new theories in science and philosophy, he used reason rather than religion to justify absolute moral principles. For many however, religion itself remains a strong moral force. Though some of us may have subsequently entertained moral alternatives, we probably hear the whispers of those early teachings whenever we are faced with a moral evaluation of an action.

Remember, "action," either taken or avoided, is at the heart of significant moral choice, sometimes at odds with religious belief. A number of years ago the parents of an infant born with an abnormal heart were faced with an agonizing choice when a physician at Johns Hopkins University offered to perform the world's first heart surgery. Admittedly experimental at the time, the operation would, if successful, rescue a "blue baby" from respiratory problems that would surely result in imminent death. The parents had a short time to consider whether to allow the surgery. One argument against the surgery was the possible interpretation that "God's will" had created the baby with the disability and that it was meant to be. The doctor countered with another interpretation: it was "God's will" that he had been experimenting in the laboratory on a technique that would bypass the damaged artery and save the child. The parents gave their consent, the baby survived, and a medical breakthrough was hailed.

If the parents had followed a religion that strictly forbade tampering with God's will, their decision in favor of the doctor would have been against their moral code. Would their loved ones—the baby's siblings, aunts, and uncles—have been united in denouncing the successful surgery as immoral? Or would all of them ultimately decide that it was all right to question God's will under certain circumstances? Which ones? Does the list go on indefinitely? What then happens to the concept of God's will? Does it become meaningless?

Moral choices based on religious laws frequently clash with other options. Throughout history, religion has strongly influenced concepts not only of honoring the family but almost every kind of acceptable human behavior, often with harsh treatment for offenders.

The major world religions—Hinduism, Judaism, Christianity, and Islam—provide moral orientation for most of the world's population. They differ in many respects, and wars are still being fought in the name of some religious teachings.

Ritual is the basis of some of the conflict: dietary restrictions, clothing, methods and frequency of prayer, who belongs within a particular sect and who is outside it (and what to name the baby). Some conflict is theological: the true path to salvation, which leader warrants being called "divine," even the nature of deity itself. These concerns constitute traditions—often one opposed to another. They may include daily activities based on rankings within the family and what constitutes an appropriate role according to age and gender.

All of the major religions, however, show great similarities in their moral precepts. They share the belief that the world was not created for human beings to do with as they please. They all believe that human beings owe an obligation to either a personal God or to the moral order governing the universe. They believe no one is free to behave irresponsibly toward themselves (since *they* did not create themselves), toward others, or toward the earth (which they did not create either).

Good laws lead to the making of better ones; bad ones bring about worse.

—Jean-Jacques Rousseau

Basic moral codes for Western societies derive, wholly or partly, from the precepts expressed in the Ten Commandments, recorded in the Hebrew Bible as having been delivered by God to Moses after leading his people out of slavery in Egypt. These commandments

1. require people to recognize only one God.
2. forbid the making and worshiping of any graven image.
3. forbid the taking of the Lord's name in vain.
4. require that the Sabbath be kept holy.
5. require that people honor their parents.
6. forbid killing.
7. forbid adultery.
8. forbid stealing.
9. forbid the bearing of false witness against another.
10. forbid the coveting of another's wife and of another's goods.

Most of the commandments have parallels all over the world. Rules against killing and stealing are part of a universal criminal code. It is taken for granted that everyone tells lies for one reason or another, but it is hard to imagine any society in which lying is not condemned. Rules against adultery are either approved by the community or are legally enforced—sometimes with the death penalty.

The first four commandments will not be found in law books, although some communities have *blue laws* requiring businesses to be closed on Sunday, or at least preventing the sale of liquor on the morning when people are expected to worship. Nor are there universal rules for how to honor one's parents.

From its beginning, Hebrew moral law served to remind the powerful they were not exempt from obeying God's commands. Biblical prophets were not afraid to confront sinners no matter how exalted their rank, as when Nathan denounced King David for doing away with the husband of Bathsheba, whom David wished to marry. Biblical scholar Huston Smith describes the democratizing effect of the Ten Commandments:

> *Social as well as individual transgressions were denounced by the prophets. The prerequisite of political stability is social justice . . . Stated theologically the point reads: God has high standards. Divinity will not put up forever with exploitation, corruption, and mediocrity . . . One thing is common to all [the prophets]: the conviction that*

every human being, simply by virtue of his or her humanity, is a child of God and therefore in possession of rights that even kings must respect.[14]

Hebrew moral law is concerned primarily with actions based on principles. It places limitations, for example, on what an injured party may demand for revenge. "An eye for an eye and a tooth for a tooth" prevents restitution from being more than what was lost in the original crime. The Sermon on the Mount tells us: "Ye have heard that it hath been said, an eye for an eye and a tooth for a tooth: But I say unto you, That ye resist not evil: but whosoever shall smite thee on thy right cheek, turn to him the other also" (Matthew 5:38–39).

The commandment to turn the other cheek was already foreshadowed in the Buddhist moral treatise *Dhammapada*: " 'He abused me, he beat me, he defeated me, he robbed me'—in those who harbor such thoughts hatred will never cease. For hatred does not cease by hatred at any time; hatred ceases by love—this is an old rule."[15]

In general, Islam requires its followers to observe the biblical laws, for Mohammed declared that both Moses and Jesus were true prophets (see Chapter 10). He stressed especially the doctrines of brotherhood and placing the interests of others before one's own. But he also warned enemies of God not to attack or persecute the devout.

Punishment for disobedience to scriptural laws varies from religion to religion, as do promised rewards for leading a virtuous existence. Hebrew morality focuses on family and community. Disobedience can result in ostracism. Leading an exemplary life brings inner peace as well as good repute in the community. After death, the good person lives on in the happy memories of friends and family or, for some believers, in the world to come.

Islam fosters the belief that after death the virtuous children of Allah will be with him in paradise, a sentiment echoed in Christianity. Christian concepts of heaven for the blessed and hell for the damned evolved slowly. The Christian Bible's Gospel of Luke reports the dialogue between Jesus and one of the thieves who were also being crucified. The thief refers to the "kingdom" to which Jesus will go after death: "And he said unto Jesus, Lord, remember me when thou comest into thy kingdom. And Jesus said unto him, Verily I say unto thee, Today shalt thou be with me in paradise" (Luke 23:42–43).

"Paradise" is variously interpreted. Does it mean a state of freedom from pain, similar to the Hindu *moksha* and the Buddhist *nirvana*? The promise that the thief would be "with" Jesus, however, may indicate that the reference is to continuing life in a definite *place*. Both Christians and Muslims for the most part believe in an afterlife.

As Christianity developed and spread, the promise of joy for the virtuous in heaven and eternal torment in hell for the damned became increasingly ingrained in religious minds. The vivid images of heaven and hell in *The Divine Comedy* by Italian poet Dante Alighieri (1265–1321) have strongly influenced how many think of rewards and punishment after death. (The term *comedy* is used in the sense of "not tragic"; the work ends on a note of joy when the poet finally sees God.)

The vivid images of heaven and hell in Dante's Divine Comedy *have strongly influenced how many think of rewards and punishments after death.*

Dante pictures hell or the Inferno as a deep pit in which sinners endure degrees of endless pain, depending on the gravity of the offense. Punishment takes place on seven separate circles, not all of which are fiery. Though in the popular mind hell is associated with flames, in actuality the lowest circle of hell, home of Satan—the worst offender of all—is described by Dante as a lake of thick ice, representing a total lack of feeling and a total absence of love.

Purgatory is a mountain on which live those guilty of less grievous sins who will eventually ascend to paradise, the abode of God, the angels, and the souls of the righteous. Paradise consists of nine circles of heaven arranged in a hierarchy of blessedness—from ordinary good people to martyrs and saints. The abode of God is in a tenth heaven (10 being considered a perfect number), only briefly glimpsed by the poet, who is unable to describe in detail his mystic vision.

Naturally enough, the drama of sin, punishment, and redemption has inspired writers, artists, and philosophers for centuries. The thought of hell's torments has incited as much anger as fear and given rise to the age-old question of why humankind must be punished for sins that were predestined. In addition, the sinner has proved to be a more durable figure for writers than the virtuous person, even as in popular entertainment in film and television the characters who are bad tend to be more interesting than the characters who are good.

The classic example of moral ambiguity is the treatment of Lucifer in John Milton's epic poem *Paradise Lost* (1667). Milton declares at the outset that his purpose in writing the poem is to "justify the ways of God to men." Like Hawthorne after him, he was raised in the strict Puritan faith, which required a belief in predestination. The three main characters are Adam, Eve, and Lucifer. We learn that, before creation, Lucifer had been one of the angels closest in attendance to God, that he was jealous of God's power and organized an unsuccessful rebellion. He and his cohorts were banished from heaven and allowed to live in a dark palace called Pandemonium. There Lucifer becomes a powerful ruler, exulting in his authority and ostensibly embodying many admirable traits of the defiant individualist. Shaking his fist toward heaven, he cries out that he "would rather reign in Hell than serve in Heaven." Scholars and historians of the humanities have long debated the issue of whether Lucifer is really the hero of the poem.

The argument that Milton intended Lucifer to be despicable has not convinced everyone, even though, as the serpent in the garden, he eventually loses his heroic qualities. Nor is everyone convinced that the poet entirely makes his point when he tells us that God allowed Lucifer free access to human beings in order to tempt them. In the poem, God says he wants no more rebellion in heaven and so creates the race of mortals, capable of either sinning or choosing virtue. In this way only the good would be with God. Milton describes the fall of humankind as "fortunate," for the disobeying of divine law required the sacrifice of Jesus. Without sin, in other words, the path to redemption would never have been revealed.

The morality set forth by religion is exceedingly complex, open to much question, yet still a powerful force that helps us to understand many of the agonizing problems in the world today.

The Morality of Work

In the Western world, most of us are taught religious moral codes as we grow up; when we go to work for a living, we come under the influence of still other kinds of rules. By the time we leave school—or even before we do—we have learned the importance of work. Relatives ask, "What are you going to be when you grow up?" Before we know it, we *have* grown up to face the second question asked at introductions: "What do you do?" With rare exceptions, we tend to be defined according to the answer. Thus "good" and "bad" also have connotations of important versus unimportant jobs.

Western society accords honor to some and amusement toward other kinds of work, and scorn for no work. One of the most poignant reminders of work's fierce hold on us is contained in this passage from a 1987 novel, *Of Love and Shadows*, by Chilean author Isabel Allende (b. 1942): "He remembered his father's lesson: work as a source of pride. Idleness was foreign to the family. In the Leal household, holidays and even vacations were spent in some worthwhile undertaking. The family had had its difficult moments, but they had never dreamed of accepting charity, even from those who had previously helped."[16]

The viewpoint is that of Javier, a biologist who lost his job because of his political views and is trying to find any kind of work for fear of being disgraced. But the authorities block his efforts. Hours of waiting and frequent rejections result in humiliation and sleeplessness.

> *Without a job, he gradually lost his identity. He would have accepted any offers, however mean the pay, because he desperately needed to feel useful. As a man without employment, he was an outsider, anonymous, ignored by all because he was no longer productive, and that was the measure of a man in the world he lived in . . . The day his youngest son put on the kitchen table the few coins he had earned walking rich men's dogs, Javier cringed like a cornered animal. Since that moment he never looked anyone in the eyes; he sank into total despair.*[17]

The despair led to suicide.

A work life that denies our individuality, our creativity, our moral and aesthetic sensibility is one that denies our dignity as human beings.

—**Jerome M. Egal**

The workplace is for many people the means to the good life. As they describe their work, people reveal cherished values, which also become the basis for making decisions. In his book *Working* (1974), Studs Terkel (b. 1912) includes interviews with a variety of workers. The driver of a city garbage truck observes, "It's not like years ago, where people used everything. They're not too economy-wise today. They'll throw anything away." He speaks with approval of people who take care of their property and disapproval of those who throw garbage out the window. He doesn't approve of rules and the "spotters" who enforce them:

> *They'll turn you in for stopping for coffee. I can't see that. If you have a coffee break in the alley it's just using a little psychology. You'll get more out of them. But if you're watched continually, you're gonna lay down . . ." He is concerned with public disregard for his job, with jokes like "How's business, picking up?" and he knows, "My kids would just love to see me doing something else. I tell 'em, 'Honey, this is a good job. There's nothing to be ashamed of. We're not stealin' the money. You have everything you need.' "*[18]

A professional hockey player describes for Terkel the thrill of being on the ice when an audience of 20,000 gave the team an ovation, and the disappointment of being fired at age twenty-two. He describes how his teammates respond to injury:

> *"If you get hurt, the other players switch off. Nobody's sympathetic. When you get hurt, they don't look at you, even players on your own*

team. The curtain comes down 'cause it could have been me. . . . You don't want to think too much about it." He knows that to the team owners "You're a piece of property" and cynically observes that the team doctor says he is ready to play even though his shoulder has not yet healed. When the shoulder rips during play, the owner "shrugs his shoulders, walks away. He doesn't really hate me. He's impersonal."[19]

Yet the owners have not acted immorally according to the rules of that particular workplace.

All of the people interviewed for Terkel's book envision an ideal world of friendship, trust, and security—qualities associated with altruism. In an altruistic world, Isabel Allende's Javier would not be denied employment because of his politics; the sanitation truck driver would be credited with good judgment about when to stop for a break; hockey club owners would indicate genuine sympathy for the injuries of their players.

Firm believers in the morality of self-interest argue that economics is at the heart of all speculation about work. When unemployment is low, people are needed and are treated better because the law of supply and demand rules here as it does everywhere else. Others who look beyond self-interest would claim that respect, creativity, and idealism are not isolated examples but that they can be found in places never dreamed of by the realists—even in the workplace. Believers in altruism conceive of workers who take pride in doing the best possible job and in helping their fellow employees to do *their* best.

Be forewarned. Just as virtuous people are not always the most interesting to the makers of the humanities, so too people who love their jobs are usually not elevated to the status of heroes. In fiction and in film, a widespread assumption is that work is one thing and true freedom quite another. One of the themes in John Steinbeck's *The Grapes of Wrath* is the tragic separation of workers from the products of their labor. In following the misfortunes of the Joad family after they are dispossessed of their farm during the Great Depression, Steinbeck points out that, as long as they worked their land, they were content and had a sense of dignity. They lived the good life, being identified with their work, in the best sense. They were what they did. After they are forced to pack up their old truck and head into parts unknown in search of jobs, life holds no joy for them. They have lost their dignity.

Menial, routine, assembly-line jobs that require little or no thought are the subject of much literature, as well as visual art. *Bus Riders*, a 1962 sculpture by the American artist George Segal, shown here, clearly depicts a group of people who have become dehumanized by their work.

Much creative expression focuses on the tragedy of workers' loss of identity. What effect do you think the artist wanted this sculpture to have on viewers?

Source: George Segal, *Bus Riders* (1962). Credit: VAGA, New York, NY, Hirshorn Museum and Sculpture Garden.

Work is essential for most of us, and we defeat ourselves by starting out with the attitude that work is an unfortunate necessity that keeps us from what we *really* would like to do. The rules of any given workplace are external authorities in that they cannot accommodate the self-interest of each employee. Employee morale may improve if the Suggestion Box is more than a prop; nevertheless, a company can't function efficiently by allowing its workers unlimited freedom of when to show up, when to leave, and what needs to be accomplished each day. What would happen if someone, asked by a superior when a certain task would be completed, sat back in a chair, feet up on the desk, and said, "Whenever I feel like doing it"?

The moral authority in the workplace can be two-sided. Sometimes employees find company demands unreasonable. Differences can be resolved through negotiation, but often not until a lengthy strike has brought business to a halt. In rare cases they are never resolved, and the company has to shut down.

Moral Relativism

Morality consists of suspecting other people of not being legally married.
—**George Bernard Shaw**

If the opposite of "relative" is "absolute," it is easy to understand the appeal of the former, a term that promises flexibility and tolerance versus the latter, which connotes uncompromising rigidity. Moral relativists point out that prison, torture, war, and genocide have been inflicted by those certain there is only one truth and they know what it is. The temptation is great to reject all theories that place unwavering restrictions on us. According to **moral relativism**, beliefs about right and wrong have no universal meaning. It is therefore possible to make (and to hear) remarks like these:

> "Well, who has the right to tell another person what to do? A lot of trouble has been caused by people who were sure they were right."
>
> "It all depends . . ." (on the situation, the culture, the time a choice was made).
>
> "As long as they're happy" (a criterion that ignores those who aren't).

Many of the moral philosophers build a case for absolutism. After all, Socrates believed right and wrong were the same for all people, Kant believed in an inborn moral imperative, and Bentham said the right thing is that which provides the greatest good for the greatest number. Moral relativism, on the other hand, is the belief that right and wrong must be defined within a given context.

That context is not limited to the workplace. It can also be the culture, the community, the family, and religion. Each of these areas governing human behavior may impose absolute moral standards, but the standards are not always harmonious with each other. Bitter clashes result when two absolutes refuse to give ground: religious laws and those of the community, for example.

The Global View

A major factor in the rise of moral relativism is the globalized concept of human society. New communication technologies have made it easy for the world's various cultures to be in contact with each other, and exposure to the customs and values of different cultures has inevitably widened the issue of morality. Many cultural observers now argue that the appeal to absolute reason by Socrates and Kant, among others, was narrowly Western. It isn't that other cultures are thought of as not being rational; rather, it is the recognition that, while the capacity to reason may be universally shared, ideas and values arrived at rationally are influenced by culture, traditions, and circumstances.

Still, there are those who argue that aboriginal natives, for example, would be better off learning to succeed in the dominant culture, learning its ways and following its rules of behavior. The relativist, on the other hand, likes to point out that the imposition of dominant-culture values has caused breakdowns in both individuals and families. James Michener's 1959 novel *Hawaii* offered a fictionalized account of what happened when missionaries from the United States told native Polynesians their sexual morality was unacceptable to civilized people. In particular, they condemned the practice of marriage between siblings, assuring those who were "guilty" that they were damned. One "guilty" man felt such shame that he took his own life.

In 2000, a Cree Indian argued against what she considered cultural abuse in a church-run boarding school supported by the Canadian government. "The schools took us from our parents and taught us that the ways of our people were shameful and wrong," she said. She argued that efforts to make natives assimilate into "white" Canada were wrong, that being forced to learn English, adopt Christianity, and acquire "suitable" job skills led to "heavy drinking and domestic disharmony" and to the loss of her native tongue and traditions.[20]

Everybody always did our thinking for us.

—Winifred Jourdain

The problem offers no easy solutions. Some principles, taught in early childhood, are so deeply ingrained that they motivate actions throughout life and conflict with those of a different society. When an American living in Japan once held a birthday party for his five-year-old son, many of the invited children were Japanese. During a game of musical chairs, the father noticed that, when the music stopped, one of the Japanese children stood next to the chair but did not sit down.

> *So Gregory scrambled into her seat, and Chitose-chan beamed proudly at her own good manners. Then I walked over and told her that she had just lost the game and would have to sit out. She gazed up at me, her luminous eyes full of shocked disbelief, looking like Bambi might after a discussion of venison burgers. "You mean I lose because I'm polite?" Chitose-chan's eyes asked. "You mean the point of the game is to be rude? Well now that I think of it, I guess that is the point. American kids are taught to be winners, to seize their opportunities and maybe the next kid's as well. Japanese children are taught to be good citizens, to be team players, to obey rules, to be a mosaic tile in some larger design.*[21]

Sui Sin Far (1867–1914), a writer born to a Chinese mother and an English father, offers further evidence of how values are culturally created and how deep cultural misunderstandings are inevitable. In her story "The Americanizing of Pau Tsu," the difference in cultural practices ultimately leads to confusion in principles of etiquette, which are, after all, a form of morality—and relative at that, though not always acknowledged as such. The author describes how an eighteen-year-old Chinese bride is startled by the many new customs in her American husband's country.

> *It puzzled her to be always seeing this and hearing that—sights and sounds which as yet had no meaning for her. Why was it necessary to receive visitors nearly every evening?—visitors who could neither understand nor make themselves understood, by her, for all their curious smiles and stares . . . And why, oh! Why should she be constrained to eat her food with clumsy murderous looking American implements instead of with her own elegant and easily manipulated ivory chopsticks?*[22]

The young woman is particularly embarrassed when she becomes ill and is examined by an American doctor, a male, for she believes it is wrong for a man to look upon the flesh of any woman who is not his wife.

In a real-life incident, also involving the moral gulf between cultures, the mother of an Asian visual arts student in an American school of the arts refused to give permission for her son to attend a life-drawing class in which nude female models would pose. The department head later reported that he attempted to "reason" with the woman, who obstinately held her ground, insisting that her son was being unfairly forced to violate a strict moral principle. Given the ultimatum that her son take the required course or leave the school, she withdrew the boy and enrolled him the next day in a neighborhood school that offered no arts courses.

Another source of dispute has been school bans on students wearing head coverings that indicate religious affiliation. In order to have a cohesive student body, school officials in some European countries have forbidden the distinctive head coverings of certain religions but have often not been consistent about other religious symbols, such as those worn as jewelry. Immigrant students who abandon public school secularism for religious school may be encouraged to accept further separation from the dominant culture of the host country through a different set of heroes, villains, and causes of historical events. Objectivity is indeed an elusive goal.

Cultural traditions and generational differences uneasily exist side by side: an "assimilated" child impatient with a grandparent's old-world cooking; young people unwilling to accept traditional matchmaking; a religious teenager clashing with atheistic parents. Can the relativist position solve all conflicts by claiming that universal right and wrong are always outmoded concepts? Or are some issues simply a matter of taste, similar to one's preference for an ice cream flavor, while other things, like genocide, are to be considered absolutely wrong? Yet even genocide will be defended by those who commit atrocities in retaliation for past wrongs.

Almost every part of the world is now available to travelers and Internet users, and it seems inevitable that many will reject the idea that morality is the exclusive property of one group and all other traditions should be changed. An offshoot of cultural relativism, however, is that what used to be respect for the ideas of others can turn into the belief that no absolute values can ever exist. Or that there are no truths that can be accepted the world over. In our own lives, we can see how we view events differently as we age. What frightens children seems benign to adults, just as scandals seem harmless at a later date. If a good many moral viewpoints inevitably change, must we abandon the idea of universal, unchanging values?

Travelers may be delighted to observe cultures different from those in their home country. Seeing something truly different makes one more story to tell when they return home, whether it is the taste of an unfamiliar food or an exuberant wedding dance. One may be charmed by unexpected hospitality or by a gift offered by a merchant at a bazaar or by the appearance of a man accompanied by more than one wife. One is less charmed by the appearance of brutality and abuse, no matter how traditional the custom is said to be. Child prostitution, genital mutilation, and abandonment of unwanted family members are among the practices that horrify observers suddenly unwilling to be moral relativists.

An example of moral relativism in action is found in a prize-winning film from Iceland, *The Seagull's Laughter* (2003). The main character is Agga, a teenager and amateur sleuth who suspects that an abused wife has murdered her brutal husband, assisted in the crime by family members. Agga goes to the police and tells them about all of the clues she has gathered to confirm her suspicions. They agree to investigate. Agga then has a change of heart, realizing what would happen after the arrest. Money would be lost, a disabled family member would be institutionalized, there would be hardship all around. She returns to the police department and announces that she has made up the stories. In her case, the end—peace and prosperity in a poor household—justifies the means: letting the murderer get away with her crime. Bentham's judgment of "the greatest good for the greatest number" might also be applied here. The absolutist position is that justice must be served by punishment of all murderers regardless of extenuating circumstances.

Feminist Morality

Moral relativism of a different form has arisen during the past three decades from philosophers and cultural historians all over the world who point out that cultural, religious, and literary traditions have been dominated by the male viewpoint. In some cases, this coincides with the female viewpoint, but all too often it does not. The discrepancy, they say, is especially obvious in the formulation and application of moral principles—a consequence of the low esteem in which women have been held in many areas of the world. Restrictions on dress, education, travel, and even expression of personal feelings continue to exist in some areas, though old rules are gradually eroding in many cultures.

> *Women have served all these centuries as looking glasses possessing the magic and delicious power of reflecting the figure of man as twice its natural size.*
>
> —**Virginia Woolf**

Traditional philosophical debates over morality seem unsatisfactory to this relatively new branch of philosophy that has adopted the label *feminist ethics*, emphasizing the special circumstances surrounding half the world's population. The contemporary philosopher Rosemarie Tong (b. 1947) takes issue with schools of ethics that seek absolute moral principles. She is particularly critical of Kant's belief that we can test the validity (or lack of it) of a moral decision by deciding whether it would be right for everyone. Tong's contention is that, for Kant as well as many other male philosophers, "universal" means *men only*. Feminist ethics maintains that universal and impartial standards are difficult to apply when gender differences are ignored. Women's ways of feeling and women's needs may alter the moral nature of given circumstances.

Philosophers like Tong ask that we consider all relevant circumstances—especially the relevance of gender needs and differences—before we make a moral decision or evaluate somebody else's moral decision. A target of feminist criticism is the popular six-step approach to morality devised by developmental psychologist Lawrence Kohlberg, according to which the enlightened human being ascends from the most basic guidelines for behavior to the universal perspective found in Socrates and Kant:

Stage One: strict reward and punishment.

Stage Two: reciprocity (you hurt me, I hurt you).

Stage Three: the need for approval.

Stage Four: duty for the sake of social order.

Stage Five: the desire to avoid harming others.

Stage Six: universal ethics binding on all.

To test his theory, Kohlberg asked people how they would judge the case of a man, desperately in need of pain medicine for his terminally ill wife, who was being overcharged by the only pharmacist in his remote town. Should the man steal the medicine? If he did, would he be guilty of an immoral act or a justifiable one? If he did not steal the medicine, on the grounds that he could not will that stealing is universally acceptable, would he have reached Stage Six? One man answered that stealing would be morally permissible because the wife's need was greater than the pharmacist's (pure Bentham). A woman concentrated on the relationship between the man and the wife. She was concerned that, if the man were sent to jail, the wife's condition would worsen; hence, the man should somehow find the money and pay the exorbitant price. There is some Bentham in this view, but Rosemarie Tong points out that, because the woman questioned did not indicate how the husband could "somehow" find the money, she would not have fit into one of Kohlberg's levels. Yet her answer *was* a moral one, according to Tong, because feelings (fear that the wife's illness would take a turn for the worse) *are* crucial in moral evaluations.

Feminist philosophers are also suspicious of the absolutes in ethics derived from major religions on the grounds that they were set down by men without consulting women. To the objection that God communicated only to men, Elisabeth Schussler Fiorenza of the Harvard Divinity School faculty asks whether Jesus, who delivered the Beatitudes to a vast audience of oppressed people, would have been likely to ignore women, all of whom, the world over, occupied second-rate status.

She also finds that the "figure of Wisdom in the Hebrew Bible is almost always cast in female form or invoked with female imagery, and in the Gospels, Jesus too speaks with Wisdom's voice" In addition, "After the crucifixion, the women of Galilee helped hold together the Jesus movement in Jerusalem as other disciples fled. Women were the first to discover the empty tomb and the first to experience a vision of the resurrected Jesus."[23]

Paul, a Hebrew originally named Saul, who represents a bridge between Judaism and Christianity, wrote in one of his epistles that there "is neither Jew nor Greek, there is neither slave nor free, there is neither male nor female, for you are all one." Schussler Fiorenza contends that, following in Paul's footsteps, women were full participants in, and often leaders of, the early missionary movement.

Yet somehow women have been blamed for all the world's ills, have been stoned for immorality (despite the admonition of Christ, who prevented the crowd from stoning a prostitute), and have traditionally been told to "love, honor, and obey" their husbands, while men have been allowed plenty of license in their own conduct as long as they were caretakers of their wives. Women have traditionally found themselves forced into the worst types of employment. During the Industrial Revolution in America, poor women, often newly arrived immigrants who spoke very little English, were hardly recognized as human beings. Desperate for any job they could find, they were packed into sweatshops, toiling long hours over sewing machines or ironing boards in rooms without windows or any safety devices. Disasters like that at the Triangle Shirt Company—one of the most notorious sweatshops, which burst into flames trapping over 500 employees, most of them women and underage children—did lead to some improvement in working conditions but did little to improve the status of working-class women. As late as 1963, the United States had to pass a law to require that women and men be paid equally for doing the same job. Before the law passed (and unfortunately still in the minds of many employers), it was assumed that women should naturally make less money than men did—after all, they were *just* women. And women still fight to break through the "glass ceiling," which prevents them from attaining high-level positions in many sectors of the ecomony.

I have yet to hear a man ask for advice on how to combine marriage and a career.

—Gloria Steinem

Feminine ethicists of today believe serious injustices and inequalities persis. Advances in medical technology now allow for gender selection in fetuses. Protests have been raised that, if prospective parents can control the sex of their children, preference will be overwhelmingly in favor of boys, especially in those areas where males are needed for their physical prowess. The preferred sex is also apt to be male in countries where, as Matt Ridley, points out, "a rich son has a chance of having more than one wife or more than one sex partner, and a polygamous son can have more offspring than any daughter," and that "even in monogamous societies sons inherit wealth and status, but daughters leave home when they marry."[24]

Feminine ethicists worry that, if the dominant population is male, the plight of women can only worsen, and right and wrong will be subject more than ever to male definition. If Bentham's numbers are used to decide moral issues, will they be determined by "male math"? If morality is based on duty, may *duty* be defined as "obligation to abide by male standards"?

When a woman tells the truth she is creating the possibility for more truth around her.

—Adrienne Rich

Answers to these complex questions do not come easily. Yet feminist moral philosophy has already enhanced awareness that women's thoughts and feelings have been largely ignored over the centuries. Perhaps that philosophy will effect a change in universal moral standards.

We have said from the outset that being human is an art, and nowhere is that assumption more crucial than in moral matters. You can decide that you are a fully realized human being if you get everything you can from life regardless of how others are affected. You can also decide that moral integrity—doing what you know to be right regardless of profit—is the mark of a fully realized human being. There are risks involved, to be sure. The risk of running afoul of someone else's moral code, enforced by bully tactics, is and always has been there. But a ringing declaration in the humanities is that moral integrity is worth the risk. Gambling on integrity may be basic to the human condition in its finest hour.

Key Terms

altruism the quality of acting out of concern for the welfare of others rather than one's own.

capitalism economic system based on Adam Smith's philosophy that if people are allowed to make as much money as they can, others will profit also.

categories according to Immanuel Kant, mental "compartments" that we are born with, which allow us to interpret data from the senses; an inborn sense of reason allows us to understand spatial relationships ("nextness") as well as moral or immoral actions.

enlightened self-interest condition in which wise rulers impose, for unselfish reasons, their own political philosophy in order to have an effective government that provides for people better than those people could provide for themselves.

laissez-faire French phrase meaning "allow to do"; an economic policy of allowing businesses the freedom to operate with little or no government control.

Machiavellian pertains to the manipulation of others through duplicity; derived from Machiavelli's theory of government that advocates a powerful leader who exerts power over others.

moral an adjective indicating a choice between significant options, based on principles derived from reason, family teachings, education, religion, or law.

moral absolutism belief that a given set of moral standards, derived from reason, religion, or culture, is universally binding.

moral imperative in Kantian philosophy, the inborn capacity to understand what is right when we are faced with moral decisions; one of the Kantian categories, or mental "compartments."

moral mathematics a scientific system of making choices between options based on projected quantifiable positive or negative effects.

moral relativism the belief that moral standards are not universal but, rather, vary depending on time, culture, and situation.

moral system a network of beliefs that can form the basis on which a moral choice is made: e.g., religious laws or Socratic reasoning.

morality the study of moral systems by which significant choices are made; in popular usage, the user's sense of right conduct, so that a given person is said to be or not be "moral."

utilitarianism belief founded on Bentham's moral mathematics that, because moral choices have a scientific basis, they should not be made for the individual by any rulers espousing any particular moral system but should be the result of logical analysis of the number of people who could benefit from a given choice: "the greatest good for the greatest number."

Topics for Writing and Discussion

1. If morality begins in the home, what happens to someone who has been given a strong moral upbringing only to go out into the world and find that it is the clever, not the good, who generally succeed?
2. A dramatic example of the conflict between the law and differing moral systems is the issue of the death penalty. Write a short paper in which you: (1) summarize the rationale behind the death penalty as held by its proponents; (2) summarize a major argument that has been advanced in opposition to it; and (3) present as well as defend your own view.
3. After Socrates was sentenced to death, his followers told him how easy it would be to simply walk out of his minimum security prison and pleaded with him to do so. Pretend that he agonizes over the choice and asks first Bentham, then Kant for advice. Indicate what each philosopher would have recommended. Then present and defend your own view.
4. The arts were discussed as one of the sources of moral values. Cite a movie or television show you have seen recently that you believe suggests a recommended moral choice. How convincing do you think it was?
5. Reread the description of Shaw's play *The Doctor's Dilemma*. What *was* that dilemma? What was the doctor's decision? Was Shaw in support or opposition to the decision? What would *your* decision have been?
6. You are the mayor of a local government that has commissioners split evenly on the question of how a large amount of tax money should be spent. You listen

to the arguments of citizens who urge you to vote in favor of a new arts center, one with space for rehearsals and performances of dance, theater, and music of all kinds. Other citizens point to a survey which shows that the majority prefers a new sports arena. You have studied and been impressed by Mill's support of the rugged individualist. The commissioners are tied. You have the tie-breaking vote. What is it? Why?

7. Which character in which book said, "No man is worth five minutes of my time"? Why did the book's author consider that character heroic? How do you think that book should be received in today's world?

8. Look again at Hogarth's picture of *The Enraged Musician*. Why is it placed in this chapter? Whose side do you think Hogarth is on: the noisy crowd's or the musician's? Whose side would Bentham be on? John Stuart Mill? In each case, explain your answer.

9. You go to a supermarket with friends, who begin to remove the price labels fastened to the shelf under some items, replacing them with lower-priced labels taken from other items. They intend to tell the cashier that they want the price on the shelf, not in the computer, and urge you to help them. You are torn between group loyalty and the conviction that what they are doing is morally wrong. You have a hard time making up your mind, but fortunately you have read this chapter and know something about various options offered by moral philosophers. (1) What would Socrates do and why would he do it? (2) What would Glaucon do and why? (3) What would Rosemarie Tong do and why?

10. Imagine that a close friend is considering blowing the whistle on the manager of the drugstore in which she works part-time. Write a dialogue between the two of you in which (1) she explains what the manager is doing wrong; (2) she tells you the risks she would be taking, including jeopardizing her job; (3) you set forth the advice that you have for your friend; and (4) you present the final decision and the reason for it.

12 Happiness

Overview

The search for happiness is high up on the list of themes in the humanities. Consider how many novels and plays deal with unhappy people and either end sadly, all happiness denied, or somehow manage to conclude with a "happy ending." Think of how many poems, how many songs express the intricacies of joy or despair. Some of the world's greatest artworks capture human faces in moments made significant by what we take to be the presence or absence of happiness.

Small wonder that moral philosophy, in addition to its concerns for defining good and bad actions, also engages in exhaustive analysis of what makes life itself good and therefore happy. Few of us would deny that a good life is a happy one, for who would deliberately seek to be unhappy? So there would seem to be no need for analysis. What more is there to say? Happiness is good, and everyone wants it. But how easy is it to attain that thing called happiness? And what is it, anyway?

Happy, a word from our earliest memories, is written in cake frosting, shouted at midnight on New Year's Eve, and invoked by well-wishers during wedding receptions and ship sailings. It crops up automatically in everyday conversation. Good news is greeted with the congratulatory "I'm so happy for you." The word is even used to cover disappointment upon hearing of a friend's surprising decision to leave school in the middle of the semester, or to reject a long-awaited promotion, or to cancel a wedding even after the caterer has been chosen and the invitations mailed. We say, "Oh well, as long as she's happy." It's like breathing. We never think about it.

The need to find happiness becomes acute when it appears to have vanished. There is a sense of something missing, something lost, and then comes the desperate search for the elusive prize. People go to psychiatrists; they write or read any number of books on the subject of being happy.

Moral philosophy tells us that the problem becomes complex when we try to spell out what is meant by the good life. Is it one that is pleasurable, regardless of how pleasure is obtained? Is it one based on strict moral principles, obeyed even if it means a loss of pleasure? Or is that life happiest when it achieves something praised by others?

An Italian baroque artist visualizes the complexities of that thing we call happiness.

Source: Galleria e Museo Estense, Modena, Italy/The Bridgeman Art Library.

O happiness! Our being's end and aim!
Good, pleasure, ease, content! Whate'ver thy name:
That something still which prompts the eternal sigh,
For which we bear to live or dare to die.

—**Alexander Pope**

Joy is an emotion we have all experienced. Is joy equivalent to happiness? Most of us have experienced the release that comes from dancing—the easing of tension, the welcome break from worry, the relaxation of the thought process. No one would deny that letting oneself go in this manner is joyful. Yet we all know that joy is not an emotion we can feel continuously. Is joy an *ingredient* of happiness, or a by-product of it? Do we always feel joy when we think we are being happy? Can we be happy *without* joy? Is happiness a purely subjective state? Can our life be happy without our knowing it?

The humanities provide us with many interesting possibilities. As you study the subject, one of them may strike a responsive chord in you. You may even find you are happier than you knew.

Hedonism: Happiness as Pleasure

The Greek philosopher Aristippus (435–356 B.C.E.) declared happiness to be the *sum total of pleasures experienced during one's lifetime.* He thought of pleasure in purely physical terms: taste, sexual excitement, touch, and so on. He admits that a certain amount of satisfaction comes with the knowledge, for example, that one's country is faring well, but nothing mental compares with physical comfort. Bodily pain is far worse than mental pain, and therefore bodily pleasure is better than mental pleasure. People, he said, are by nature selfish animals, concerned solely with their own comforts. He asked the question that has been asked for centuries: *Is anything greater than being happy?* He said no, and added that, if it were not for pleasure, saying you were happy would mean nothing.

The writings of Aristippus have not survived, but a historian named Diogenes Laertius, living in the third century C.E., has provided a detailed summary of his philosophy of pleasure. He pointed out that Aristippus proved his argument by noting that, from the time they were capable of making choices between available options, people always selected what provided the most pleasure and the least amount of pain. Home and society might try to teach less selfish values, but instinct prevailed in the end.

Thus, if Aristippus is right, people prefer not to work, but do so only because what they earn will provide them with pleasure. There is no satisfaction in work for its own sake. As a matter of fact, Aristippus believed there was no satisfaction in even the memory or anticipation of pleasure. Nothing counted except what could be experienced at the moment.

Hedonism (from the Greek for "delight") is the name given to the philosophy that happiness is equivalent to physical pleasure and to the possession of things that provide us with pleasure. Hedonism has survived for thousands of years, substantially unchanged from its inception.

The artist Diego Velázquez (1599–1660) has given us one of the best visual representations of hedonism in *Los Borrachos* (The Drunkards), reproduced on the next page. The laughing figure on the left is Bacchus, the god of wine, whose associate is bestowing a garland of grape leaves on the kneeling figure. The work seems to give a comic reference to the traditional honoring of a hero with a laurel wreath. Velázquez may be spoofing the purely hedonistic life, but the painting allows viewers to place their own interpretation on the scene. To the dedicated hedonist, the

To the dedicated hedonist, the pleasure experienced by these drunken men may be all that is necessary for pure happiness.

Source: Diego Velázquez, *Los Borrachos* (1629). Credit: Alinari/Art Resource, NY.

pleasure obviously being experienced by the men may be all that is necessary for the highest state of happiness.

Regardless of time and place human beings cherish a common desire for happiness and a wish to avert suffering.

—The Dalai Lama

The Greek society in which Aristippus lived may have produced Socrates, Plato, and Aristotle, who spent their lives in thought, but it was also highly receptive to the idea that hedonism was basic to human nature. In fact, both Plato and Aristotle addressed themselves to the subject, disagreeing with the views of Aristippus but acknowledging the popular appeal of his ideas. In his famous analysis of love, Plato does not discredit the pleasures of sex but elevates nonphysical love to a position of greater importance. While Aristippus excludes the idea of intellectual pleasure, Plato and Aristotle believe it is one of the defining graces of a fully realized life. Aristotle developed a philosophy of happiness vastly different from that of Aristippus, as we shall see later in this chapter.

Between the austere Middle Ages and the time of the militantly rigid Puritans—both periods of strict moral codes—poets, including Shakespeare, celebrated the "eat, drink, and be merry" slogan of hedonism. One of the most famous declarations comes in this widely welcomed piece of poetic advice from Robert Herrick (1591–1674):

Gather ye rose-buds while ye may,
Old time is still a-flying:

And this same flower that smiles today
Tomorrow may be dying.

Another name given to this hedonist view is ***carpe diem*** (from the Latin "seize the day"). While this advice is rooted in Aristippus, it has had numerous applications through the ages. For some, it means doing the most with their potential; it means reaching for the stars. For others, such as Omar Khayyám in *The Rubáiyát* (see Chapter 14), it means, as it does in Herrick, have all you can during your brief lifetime.

A contemporary of Herrick, Andrew Marvell (1621–1678), makes a similar plea, this time to one special person in a poem called "To His Coy Mistress."

Had we but world enough, and time,
This coyness, lady, were no crime.
We would sit down, and think which way
To walk, and pass our long love's day.

If he had forever to woo her, the poet adds, he would spend a hundred years praising her eyes, two hundred for each breast and "thirty thousand to the rest."

But at my back I always hear
Time's winged chariot hurrying near:
And yonder all before us lie
Deserts of vast eternity.
Thy beauty shall no more be found,
Nor, in thy marble vault, shall sound
My echoing song: then worms shall try
That long preserv'd virginity:
And your quaint honour turn to dust,
And into ashes all my lust.
The grave's a fine and private place,
But none I think do there embrace.

Can it be that there was only one summer that I was ten?
—**May Swenson**

Many people are proud to call themselves hedonists. They openly boast of their income and possessions. They assert that with only one chance to live, they should deny themselves nothing and try to have it all. A bumper sticker proclaims: "He who dies with the most toys wins." Another boasts: "We're spending our grandchildren's inheritance." A current restatement of *carpe diem* is "Life is not a rehearsal. This is it!"

Still, hedonism does carry with it the reputation for reckless excess; therefore, many try to avoid applying the label to themselves. While they may admit they seek comfort and avoid discomfort as often as possible, they do not like to be considered selfish. Their priorities are giving and receiving love (sometimes more than in a physical sense), raising a family, finding an occupation both useful and satisfying, having security, pursuing intellectual stimulation, and expressing themselves creatively. Aristippus would contend that such persons are secret hedonists afraid to admit they are—but that they *ought* to! They seek pleasure but deny themselves too much. They sacrifice everything for their children, only to be confronted later with a thankless "What did you ever do for me?" They live frugally and work hard so their retirement years will be golden yet risk dying just before their pension comes due.

Hedonist Assumptions

For a hedonist, there never seems to be enough pleasurable moments in life. There seems to be so much undeserved pain. "Why me?" is a frequent question both openly and silently asked. When am I going to get *my* chance to be happy?"

So the first hedonist assumption is that *everyone deserves as much pleasure as possible.* A variant of this assumption is that *people never really get as much pleasure as they deserve.* Other people always appear to have more. Those believed to have more may communicate—even exaggerate—their pleasures, especially unexpected bonuses, which point out how truly deserving they really are. Those without bonuses perpetuate the myth that the undeserving are getting more from life.

A second assumption, vitally related to the first, is that *pleasure is automatically good.* In unprosperous times, when some are barely eating enough to get by, those who are able to eat anything they want are undoubtedly envied. No one feels sorry for the affluent people who might overeat and overdrink!

I fear not the uncleanness of meat but the uncleanness of desire.

—**Augustine**

Hedonists recognize that people cannot possibly have pleasure every moment of their lives, but still, they think they should. A third assumption, therefore, is that *no amount of pleasure is ever too much.* There may be a submerged feeling of guilt about gorging oneself in an "All U Can Eat" restaurant or downing one drink after another at somebody's open house, but the typical hedonist response is, "There will be time enough to cut down; don't bother me now." Besides, overindulgence in moments of plenty supposedly means making up for past disappointments.

A fourth hedonist assumption is that *the absence of pleasure is a misfortune for which compensation is due.* Many who attempt robbery believe they are only getting even with society. Those who carry the hedonist viewpoint through life find themselves plotting continually: "Just wait until *I* have the upper hand!" Since moments without definite feelings of pleasure are an abomination, they entertain themselves by thinking of the moment when they will finally gain "rightful" pleasures.

This particular mindset stems from the **big-earnings theory**. An *earning* is considered the pleasure owed to a deserving person for services rendered or unpleasant chores completed. In the ledger that many hedonists carry inside themselves, there is a strict accounting of pleasures owed them; eventually a vast number may accumulate. Unless something happens to change their philosophy of happiness, these hedonists may become obsessed with thinking about pleasures due. If they are paid off, life is good; if not, life is bad. Life is evaluated strictly in terms of total payments received. An excellent life is one in which no big earning is left unrewarded.

Hedonism Reconsidered

Since it is one of the oldest known theories of happiness, hedonism has been subjected to ongoing critical appraisal by philosophers and cultural historians alike. Hedonism has inspired three major critical questions: first, whether this philosophy is based on an accurate view of human nature; second, whether people are pleasure-loving at all times and in all places; and third, whether the idea that happiness is the sum total of all possible pleasures is self-defeating.

Too much of a good thing can be wonderful.

—**Mae West**

The crux of the arguments may be how limited or unlimited is our definition of *pleasure*. Fundamental hedonism is clear: pleasure is experienced through the five senses. People who spend time in thought are denying themselves that much pleasure and, we assume, that much happiness. People who devote their lives to working in a clinic a thousand miles from civilization, who expose themselves daily to the risk of disease without even the reward of outside recognition, are supposedly doing without pleasure. But how can we assume such people are deliberately perverting their own natures to follow a calling that requires them to labor in the interest of others? Are those whose happiness is not derived from hedonism wasting their time or being cheated of the pleasure they secretly desire?

In describing a conversation with noted writer Joseph Heller, the late novelist Kurt Vonnegut (1922–2007) reconsiders hedonism powerfully.

> *True story. Word of Honor.*
>
> *Joseph Heller, an important and funny writer now dead, and I were at a party given by a billionaire on Shelter Island. I said, "Joe, how does it make you feel to know that our host only yesterday may have made more money than your novel* Catch-22 *has earned in its entire history?"*
>
> *And Joe said, "I've got something he can never have."*
>
> *And I said, "What on earth could that be, Joe?"*
>
> *And Joe said, "The knowledge that I've got enough."*[1]

Buddhist monks sitting alone in silent meditation for hours, even days, at a time lose contact with the self in ways that the hedonist could never understand. Are they robbing themselves of the pleasure that their natures crave? Is it accurate to say that celibacy is necessarily a sublimation of normal sexual passion, as many contend? Or is human nature such that it cannot be narrowly defined? May sensory pleasure be all-sufficing for some and less fulfilling to others?

If, as existentialists (discussed in Chapter 16) maintain, no such thing as human nature exists at all and humanity is indeed a self-defining, self-determining species, then there is ample room for alternate ways of defining pleasure. In fact, those who choose to do so can relegate physical pleasure to a low priority without being unnatural.

Epicureanism: Happiness Is Avoiding Pain

In a musical comedy some years back, the heroine, trying to explain to the audience in song why she adores the hero, compares her love to a number of familiar pleasures. She includes the smell of bread baking and the feeling she has when a tooth stops hurting. In the first instance, she is a hedonist, directly sensuous in her values. In the second, however, she turns to a different philosophy of happiness: **epicureanism**. The sudden cessation of a toothache is not directly pleasurable in itself, but it *brings* happiness, according to that philosophy: the happiness of not being in pain.

Epicureanism is named for the Greek thinker Epicurus (c. 341–270 B.C.E.), who first formulated its precepts. Aware of Aristippus and his beliefs, Epicurus was highly critical of a philosophy he believed weak in logic and, more than that, impossible to follow.

Epicurean Assumptions

Epicurus indirectly accepted the initial premise of hedonism, that pleasure is a great good, but he added that it was not the *only* good. He refused to say with the hedonists that the more pleasure we have, the happier we are: "And since pleasure is the first good and natural to us, for this very reason we do not choose every pleasure, but sometimes we pass over many pleasures, when greater discomfort accrues to us as a result of them."[2]

Epicurus was particularly critical of those who recommended pleasures in excess, for these, he knew, would always be followed by both physical and moral pain. "For from prudence are sprung all the other virtues, and it teaches us that it is not possible to live pleasantly without living prudently and honourably and justly."[3]

Pleasure is the beginning and end of living happily.

—**Epicurus**

For Epicurus, hedonism was a time-conscious, death-ridden philosophy. If happiness increased with the quantity of physical pleasures, then logically no life could ever be long enough. We are here for an uncertain amount of time, true, but all of us are subject to the gradual infirmities that come with age—if indeed we do not burn ourselves out before age ever becomes a problem. Therefore hedonists are fundamentally insecure and unhappy, unable to accept the inevitability of age and death, always worried about the loss of pleasure. Thus the major assumption of epicureanism is that nothing lasts forever and we must accept this fact cheerfully. If we are to define the good life, it is the wiser course of action not to believe that it consists only of pleasure.

Archibald MacLeish, whose poem "Ars Poetica" we studied in Chapter 4, accuses the hedonist Andrew Marvell of being so obsessed with the brevity of life and the thought of death that he could not enjoy life while he had it. MacLeish's "You, Andrew Marvell" begins with these lines:

And here face down beneath the sun
And here upon earth's noonward height
To feel the always coming on
The always rising of the night.

Another epicurean assumption is that no one can sustain pleasure over prolonged periods of time. We cannot indefinitely gorge ourselves on delicious food, indulge in sex, stay drunk. Why, then, saddle ourselves with a philosophy of life that is so limiting from the very outset? Unable to satisfy our pleasure- seeking instincts perpetually, we do the next best thing: seek material possessions or fame, both of which symbolize happiness without *bringing* happiness. Money and fame are constantly in the hedonist's thoughts. They are the compensations for having to die. They are the only possible tangible embodiments of a successful life. When age makes physical pleasure less attainable, people turn to the accumulation of wealth. But Epicurus also recognized that the pursuit of wealth was self- defeating, futile. The same is true of insisting on fame. The wealthy or the famous person feels insecure and distrustful of others, certain that others are envious and scheming.

Why, asked Epicurus, burden ourselves with a philosophy with built-in disappointments, frustrations, and inevitable pain? Why not, rather, change the *requirements* for the good life? He assumed people of reason had free will and could control their desire for pleasure, and therefore they could reduce the amount of pain that always follows pleasure. Complete happiness is a moderate amount of pleasure with complete freedom from pain—an unlikely scenario for most people, but one that can be more nearly realized as we exert our will not to suffer. To those who would ask "Why may I not agree to the suffering as long as I have the pleasure?" epicureanism answers, "The anticipation of pain, if it is intense, detracts from the pleasure."

In "What Makes a Happy Life," Martial (c. 40–104 C.E.), a Roman poet born in Spain, offers epicurean advice:

What makes a happy life, dear friend,
If thou wouldst briefly learn, attend—
An income left, not earned by toil;
Some acres of a kindly soil;
The pot unfailing on the fire;
No lawsuits, seldom town attire;
Health, strength with grace; a peaceful mind;
Shrewdness with honesty combined;
Plain living, equal friends and free;
Evenings of temperate gaiety;
A wife discreet yet blithe and bright;
Sound slumber that lends wings to night.
With all thy heart embrace thy lot,
Wish not for death, and fear it not.

Hedonists might find that prescription lacking in excitement. They might say it is based on being satisfied with whatever one has, and they might ask: is ambition so bad? Health is fine, but who wants to go through life with just "plain living?" And what is "temperate gaiety"? Isn't it leaving the party just when the fun is getting started? What satisfaction would there be in that? Even the "pot unfailing on the fire," though probably filled with nourishing and sustaining food, cannot really compete with gourmet delights. Being able to afford nothing else is one thing, but that doesn't mean we wouldn't *long* for a better life.

A real obstacle to happiness is to expect too much happiness.
—**Fontenelle**

Insofar as it recognizes the importance of pleasure in our lives, epicureanism is not so much an all-out attack on hedonism as a modification of it. Unpleasantness is part of life, the epicurean admits and therefore plans strategies to ward it off as much as possible rather than march forward in the blind hope that things are going to be fine. The worst that can happen when you anticipate pain is that you will not be disappointed. But clearly, you have a good chance of doing something about much of life's pain before it occurs *if* you apply yourself conscientiously to the task.

Exerting control and enjoying pleasure in moderation, epicureans share with hedonists delight in the taste of exquisite food—but epicureans, anticipating the pain of overindulgence, stop themselves before reaching their limit. They will drink, but never to the point of drunkenness, and not at all if they are certain their health would suffer.

Hedonism is particularly hard to resist for people who become multimillionaires. They may become extravagant, self-indulgent, and for a time at least, totally hedonistic. Hollywood abounds with tragic stories of gifted actors, directors, and writers who were unable to resist the luxuries bought through stardom and found themselves suddenly out of popularity and out of work. Some, however, read the danger signs and left before being completely swept up in the excitement of possessing whatever they want. Ernest Hemingway sold many of his works to the movies for comfortable amounts that gave promise of an extravagant lifestyle. But unable to watch what had been done to them, he denounced Hollywood, its elaborate homes, its desperate thirst for celebrity, and its utter lack of interest in anything that could not make money.

At the peak of his career, however, Hemingway was as exciting and dramatic a figure as any of his heroes: the envy of men and the fantasy figure of women. Famous as a womanizer and a hard-drinker, he seems to have mellowed over the years and either adopted an epicurean outlook or at least admired those who did. A character in Hemingway's story "In Another Country" fully illustrates the epicurean outlook. Before going off to war, a major in the Italian army married a beautiful woman considerably younger than he. He discovers she was unfaithful while he was fighting. Now, injured and confined to a hospital, he learns his wife has died of pneumonia. "She had been sick only a few days. No one expected her to die." The lesson he gleans from the tragedy is a lesson about how best to live. A man, he explains, should not marry.

He should not place himself in a position to lose. He should find things he cannot lose.

—Ernest Hemingway

> *"He cannot marry. He cannot marry," he said angrily. "If he is to lose everything, he should not place himself in a position to lose that. He should not place himself in a position to lose. He should find things he cannot lose."*[4]

A hedonist reading this account might argue that it does not show epicurean control and discipline as much as a weary response to a world that has lost its luster, and this only proves that pleasure is the only thing worth living for. The question is worth pondering.

Confirmed epicureans avoid excess, seeking out many non-physical pleasures that are less likely to be affected by the aging process. They are lovers of art, theater, books, and music, perhaps realizing that the humanities represent treasures one "cannot lose." After all, intellectual and aesthetic pleasures seldom lead to pain. Epicureans are typically lean and trim, exercising their bodies to keep in the best possible shape. They are mentally agile and aware of the latest developments in many fields. They are good workers, and the one who finds a marital partner with a similar outlook is likely to build a reasonably happy relationship.

Epicureans are typically lean and trim, exercising their bodies to keep in the best possible shape. They are mentally agile and aware of the latest developments in many fields.

Pure hedonists, however, warn epicureans that they sell themselves too short and may often settle for less than they have a right to expect from life. The hedonist maintains that, unless you work aggressively at being happy, you will give up too easily, spending too much time running away from pain that might not be there. Why not go for all you can and take your chances? The pure epicurean, however, might well answer with an old French song that says "the joys of love are but a moment long; the pain of love endures forever."

Epicureanism Reconsidered

One objection that can be raised to epicureanism is that it is as firmly rooted in self-interest as the philosophy from which it departs. It has been accused of being hedonism in a disguised form. In seeking to avoid pain, it may be saying indirectly that pleasure really is the goal. Does it merely redefine pleasure? In addition to the good feeling one gets from the absence of pain, are not the pleasures of reading and spending one's life with the arts ultimately *selfish*?

Thus another objection is that epicureans are more interested in their own peace of mind than in social causes. If not wishing to lose means detaching oneself from life as much as possible, any form of activism becomes off limits. We may question how profound or lasting would be the peace of mind that comes from the careful control of one's own life if such were achieved at the cost of worrying about the pain of others. Concern for one's neighbor, stressed in all of the world's major religions, is generally absent from the traditional epicurean outlook. To be sure, Aristippus and Epicurus belonged to the classical world, and most classical theories of happiness focus on the individual, as though happiness *by definition* were a matter of how one's own life is faring.

In at least one of his novels, *For Whom the Bell Tolls* (1940), Hemingway does exhibit a strong social consciousness. The hero, Robert Jordan, is like the author, a rugged individualist who is used to dictating his own terms to life. But he becomes so involved with the anti-fascist cause in the Spanish Civil War of the 1930s that he gives up his life to save a band of guerrillas. Jordan is the complete opposite of Frederic Henry, the hero of Hemingway's youthful novel *A Farewell to Arms* (1929), who deserts the army and runs away with the woman he loves. Perhaps being unable to turn his back on a social cause became part of Hemingway's well-lighted place: self-satisfaction gained through self-sacrifice.

Wisdom consists of the anticipation of consequences.
—**Norman Cousins**

We cannot rule out the possibility that happiness can be achieved only by working to combat pain wherever it is found, and sometimes the battle incurs personal suffering, which is accepted as the high price of success. After all, there are people, seldom mentioned in history books, who have voluntarily spent their shortened lives nursing the sick in parts of the world ravaged by plagues of one kind or another. Maybe the new epicureanism seeks not only to avoid pain oneself but to do everything possible to help *others* avoid pain.

The disaster that befell New York and Washington on September 11, 2001, a cataclysmic event that took almost 3,000 lives, had an effect quite different from the total chaos the terrorists may have planned. Instead of scattering to the winds in a "Save yourself" mode, hundreds of police and firefighters gave up their own lives in an attempt to rescue as many victims as they could. It is now apparent from cellphone calls made to loved ones before the collapse of the towers that a number of those who might have escaped stayed to help others, forfeiting their lives to do so. There are further indications that some of the passengers aboard Flight 93, which crashed in a Pennsylvania meadow, may have overpowered the hijackers in order to save perhaps thousands who might have died had the deadly mission been completed. Who is to say that dedicated epicureans would not, in moments of extreme crisis, forgo self-interest? After all, if someone survived by not trying to save another, would that individual lead a peaceful and contented life from that day on? Would it be said that it was a good life, exemplifying happiness?

The cynic might say that social consciousness is only an extension of a principle stated by Epicurus: "The just man is most free from trouble." That is, happiness consists of an undisturbed conscience; if you want tranquility, you must sometimes labor in the interest of others. After all, can you sit down to relish a gourmet meal with three ragged and starving children pressing their noses against the restaurant window? But it seems unfair to assume that, given the dimensions of the September 11th catastrophe, all apparently selfless work is ultimately rooted in the effort to reach inner peace.

Stoicism: Happiness as a Strategy for Survival

A famous poster shows a cat holding tightly to the knotted end of a rope and just hanging there in empty black space. The caption reads: *When you come to the end of your rope, tie a knot and hang on.* This, in capsule form, is the philosophy of **stoicism**. It operates under even fewer illusions about life than does epicureanism. It tells us neither to plan ahead for a lifetime of unlimited pleasure nor to expect to avoid pain through discipline and moderation. Stoicism asserts pain is intrinsic to living. Even the most dedicated epicureans will feel a certain amount of frustration when their disciplined approach to living goes awry. The best possible course is to be prepared for the worst and to develop a technique for dealing with it. *Epicureans avoid; stoics cope.*

The art of life is more like the wrestler's art than the dancer's. It should stand ready and firm to meet onsets which are sudden and unexpected.

—**Marcus Aurelius**

Stoic Assumptions

Stoicism sees the will as the means through which each of us can control our response to external events. Despite the disasters that may befall us, stoics believe in human reason. They believe it is reasonable to know that disasters—natural, social, personal—inevitably happen. Life just occurs. We make our plans, but we cannot include life in those plans. As one philosopher put it: "Life is what happens to us while we are making other plans." But we shouldn't believe that all is chaos in the universe. If there is order within the human mind, there may be order in the universe as well, and the unpredictable things that happen may be *part* of that order. Understanding this, we can see to it that the will is in tune with events as they occur. The sometimes despairing question "How can terrible things be part of any order?" may be irrelevant. Stoics contend disasters are possible to accept without emotion.

Stoicism was born over 2,000 years ago. Like hedonism and its modified offspring epicureanism, it is the product of Greek intellect; it lays heavy stress on human reason and the belief that humankind is a superior form of animal life. The philosophy of Zeno, its first major advocate (335–264 B.C.E.), is therefore close in spirit to that of Plato and Aristotle.

The school founded by Zeno was located in a columned portico called a *stoa*—hence the name of the philosophy. Central to stoicism is the belief that true happiness is not a matter of circumstance, of good fortune, or of what happens to us, but rather a matter of *how we respond to what happens.* Happiness, like sorrow, is an idea, an attitude, not an object or an event. If no one welcomes the first day of spring, how can it be said that spring is a time of hope and joy? If in some remote civilization with unusual customs and mores the birth of a child were considered a dreadful curse, then the inability to produce offspring might be regarded as a happy stroke of luck.

To find the roots of unhappiness, we must look inward. Nothing is under our control except the way we think about things. Natural disasters, social upheavals, wars, revolutions, outbreaks of disease, rising crime rates—all happen as a result of either accidental or highly complicated causes. Our happiness should not depend on their *not* taking place. We cannot alter external circumstances, but we can decide not to feel negatively toward them.

"How do you expect me to feel?" is a common response when we are asked why we are so glum about a certain outcome—say, not being promoted to a higher position. Stoics cite habit as the guilty culprit, contending that people are conditioned by the values their society puts on what happens to or around them. This is acceptable; that is not. This is cause for joy; that is cause for tears. Reactions become automatic after a while. People come to *think* they are unhappy; hence they *are* unhappy. But typical responses can be altered. We can refuse to be affected in customary ways or as others tend to be affected.

True instruction is this: to learn to wish that each thing should come to pass as it does.

—**Epictetus**

One of the best-known stoic teachers was a Greek named Epictetus (50–130 C.E.), who was captured and enslaved by the Romans. His brilliance was eventually recognized, and he was allowed to conduct classes. But prior to that, Epictetus was tortured and oppressed in his captivity. On one occasion his leg was broken on a whim of his master's. During this period of extreme suffering, Epictetus was faced with the choice of surrendering to despair or finding some means of enduring. He chose the latter course, recognizing that nothing, not even torture, was unbearable unless one wished to find it so. After his liberation, he dedicated his life to spreading the stoic creed, which had preserved his spirit intact for so many years.

Stoicism later found ready acceptance among the Romans and became a sort of unofficial state philosophy. Its emphasis on reason and the control of negative emotions accorded well with the Roman ideal of the perfect human being. Besides, Rome was an empire-building civilization, requiring a superbly disciplined military machine to carry out its conquests. It therefore found a meaningful application of stoic teachings: the rigors of military training as well as the hardships of war itself must never depress the human spirit. Good soldiers, with feelings well under their control, must become indifferent to their own suffering.

When Christianity began to spread throughout the Roman Empire, many of the converts had, naturally enough, already been exposed to stoic beliefs. The by-then ancient and honorable philosophy accorded well with the outlook and needs of Christians. After all, they had to face untold sufferings—continual persecution, torture, flight, starvation, separation from loved ones. The stoic doctrine of inner control blended perfectly with the Christian belief that only the soul, not the body, mattered. One could endure all manner of pain and remain serene.

Christian martyrdom was deeply rooted in stoic principles. After all, the teachings of Jesus had strongly illustrated those principles, especially the directives to love one's enemies and to turn the other cheek. A famous martyrdom is that of Thomas á Becket (1118–1170), the archbishop of Canterbury and, as such, the pope's representative in England, sworn to carry out papal decrees and to uphold church dogma. By the twelfth century, however, England was becoming a major world power, and the English monarchy assumed more and more authority, even in matters of religion. King Henry II, once Becket's friend, had laws passed that were in direct violation of church canon. The pope was displeased, and Becket, of course, sided with him, causing a dangerous rift between monarch and prelate. Late in 1170 Becket urged the pope to dismiss several bishops known to be politically on the king's side. The king then sent four knights to Canterbury with the king's command for Becket to restore the deposed bishops, but Becket refused. Knowing that he had probably signed his own death warrant, the archbishop went into the cathedral to pray.

While he was there, the knights returned, this time with an armed band. Becket's attendants saw them coming, shut the heavy doors, and were about to lock them when the archbishop cried out: "God's house must be closed against no man." The assassins, thus given unchallenged entry, rushed to the altar, whereupon Becket made a ringing stoic declaration: "For the name of Jesus and for the defense of the Church I am ready to embrace death." They fell upon him with their swords, and he was murdered on the altar. The scene was memorably recorded in the verse play *Murder in the Cathedral* (1935) by the American poet T. S. Eliot and later in the film *Becket* (1964).

Whether religiously oriented or not, stoicism remains as pervasive as ever and offers to many a genuine alternative to hedonism. In a period of ever accelerating change, of being wary of possible violence as a condition of life, of the realization that prosperity may not last forever, it is small wonder that many are asking less for pleasure than for inner peace. Although weekly pilgrimages to analysts continue, some principles of stoicism may be at work here also. After all, self-knowledge is vital to psychoanalysis. Analysts contend that people will be able to transcend negative feelings once they understand what is making them unhappy or ineffective. This may be the same thing as saying that happiness is really within our own power to create and preserve. Not everyone agrees.

Success is getting what you want; happiness is wanting what you get.

—**Anonymous**

Stoicism Reconsidered

Stoicism in modern dress is, for its advocates, still a viable theory of happiness. Its basic assumption remains much the same as always: tranquility is worth any price. Stoicism has something to offer the chronically poor and dispossessed, who also suffer from low self-esteem and cannot see that they deserve any better fate. Even the most zealous social worker might agree that in some cases a stoic attitude is better than false hope for a better tomorrow.

The stoical scheme of supplying our wants by topping off our desires is like cutting off our feet when we want shoes.

—**Jonathan Swift**

One negative aspect of stoicism is its convenience. If you're down and out, abandoned by family and friends, with no prospects that things will turn around for you, why not become a stoic? Surely the distance is short from "Things are pretty bleak" to "There is no reason to believe things should be otherwise." Does this view mean simply coping but *doing* nothing?

Suppose, however, that the ad hoc stoic—the person who adopts this philosophy out of sheer desperation—suddenly experiences an unexpected reversal of fortune. Say he or she wins $5 million in the state lottery or, more modestly, finds a good-paying job. Or suppose, as actually happened in the wake of a TV newscaster's human-interest documentary about the homeless in New York, a couple randomly singled out for an interview found themselves swamped with offers of money, jobs, shelter—even a film contract! What happens to stoic doctrines then? Can one embrace stoicism one day and abandon it for hedonism the next?

Some might respond "Why not?" If adversity can be endured because the rational control of emotion makes endurance possible, dropping stoicism when it is no longer working or necessary is not necessarily *un*reasonable. Others could object to this line of thought, claiming that reason, which justified the initial adoption of the stoic philosophy during bad times, also requires us to believe that good fortune is not likely to be permanent.

There is an old fable about a tyrannical king who, finding himself plagued by bad fortune, kept asking various wise men to give him grounds for hope. If they could not, their heads were chopped off. Finally, one clever sage gave him a plaque to hang on his bedroom wall: *These Things Shall Pass*. The king, deriving much comfort from the plaque, rewarded the sage handsomely, until the king's fortunes took a turn for the better. The maxim, which had once buoyed up his spirits, now angered him, and he ordered the once-favored philosopher to be beheaded.

Joy is a net of love by which you can catch souls.

—**Mother Teresa**

A frequently raised objection to stoicism is that its advocates secretly want everyone else to be as miserable as they are, yet they don't realize it. Is adversity more bearable when no one around you is having a run of good luck? Loving the company of the miserable may be a fundamental human trait. Enjoying nothing so much as the sad tales of others may be as universal as secretly resenting a friend's prosperity. The German word **schadenfreude** describes the pleasure derived from the misfortunes of others. Radio and television programmers assume there's a smaller audience for good news than for accounts of grisly murders and natural disasters that kill thousands.

Yet another objection is that what passes for reason in stoicism should really be called rationalizing, a process by which we find satisfying rather than logical reasons for believing something. The possibility exists that control for the stoic actually means manipulating thoughts so that reality becomes bearable. When loved ones stop calling, do we endure the absence by admitting the possibility that they have transferred their affections or have ceased to be interested in us for this or that reason? Or do we more likely find reasons that make us feel good, such as the loved one's responding to a job interview? The interview may well turn out to be the actual reason, but the point is that we pick and choose among comfortable versions of reality. In this way, say the detractors, what masquerades as stoic acceptance is a false sense that reality is being fearlessly confronted. We accept what we *want* to accept, rejecting everything else. The trouble, they warn, is that rejected reality can strike back at any time, delivering a crushing blow.

Classical stoicism emerged from two cultures, the Greek and the Roman, with their strong belief in fate. The universe was run by all-powerful deities who intervened in human affairs whenever they chose. The gods and goddesses were capricious and unpredictable, but human reason could counteract heavenly whimsy by expecting ill times before they occurred. In other words, the universe of the Greeks and Romans was predictably full of disaster. But perhaps the universe really does not make even that much sense. Perhaps disasters are no less certain than continual success. A very strong criticism of stoicism is thus a recognition that it can inspire debilitating passivity. Expecting to fail has kept many a potential winner from even getting started.

There is also the passivity of the fortunate, especially when it comes to turning away from the fact that people the world over are suffering and that much could be done to help. "I'm a stoic and believe those who suffer from poverty or the ravages of war would be happier if they would only follow my example" can be an excuse for enjoying a comfortable existence without the nagging of conscience.

Harriet Beecher Stowe's novel *Uncle Tom's Cabin* (1852) opened the eyes of many who were unaware of the wretched poverty in which slaves were forced to live without hope of liberation. The title character, however, adopts a stoic acceptance of his lot and has since lent his name as the very icon of non-resistance. Looking at the novel from our century and a half remove, one might become infuriated by conditions that force those without hope to embrace stoicism. In contrast, one character, Eliza, also a slave, is indeed desperate enough to endanger her life in a flight from the plantation. Modern readers often criticize the passivity of Tom and praise the courage of Eliza.

Aristotelianism: Happiness as the Quality of a Whole Lifetime

For Aristotle, Plato's famous pupil and founder of the Lyceum, an early version of the liberal arts college, happiness is the purpose for which we live. In analyzing this most complex of phenomena, Aristotle concludes that happiness is not a moment-to-moment experience of pleasurable things but a way of characterizing how one's life is being conducted. Happiness is living and having lived a good life. It is not measured in momentary eruptions of joy. *Complete* happiness comes with the final summing up of one's life. But if we are leading a good life along the way, we can know that we are on the right path. Then the philosopher goes on to investigate what *makes* life good, therefore happy.

Pleasure a Limited Goal; Happiness a Complete Goal

In his great work on the conduct of living, *The Nicomachean Ethics* (named for his son Nichomachus), Aristotle makes a list of the things that can be said to make life good. What he wants to determine is the nature of the *highest* good, the one that is valued for its own sake, the one that, when (or if) reached, leaves nothing else to be desired.

When a small child...I thought success spelled happiness. I was wrong, happiness is like a butterfly which appears and delights us for one brief moment, but soon flies away.

—**Anna Pavlova**

If you asked passersby what makes them happy, you would probably hear "money," "health," "love," "a good job with a good future," "a house in a good neighborhood," and so on. No one can deny these are to be counted as among the goods that life can offer. As each one is named, you could continue, "Yes, and is that all?" Chances are that the other goods would be named in succession. That is, is money enough? Well no, not if my heath is bad. Is health then enough? Well, no, not if I hate my job. Is a good job enough? Well, no, not if I haven't found someone to share my life.

If someone were to ask you whether it would be enough if you were completely happy, you would have to think a minute, wouldn't you? You couldn't say, "Not if I didn't have money," because, logically, if money were important to your happiness and you didn't have any, you couldn't be *completely* happy then.

Aristotle concludes that the reason we want money, health, love, and all the other things that seem to be worth striving for is that they *provide* happiness. Therefore they cannot *be* happiness. The person who delivers your mail is not the mail. Individual goods, in other words, are means to the end, which is happiness. None of them can be the end in itself, though some people often make the mistake of believing that is possible. For example, a poor person might dream of someday winning the lottery and suddenly having millions. "If I had all that money, I wouldn't ask for anything more." Want to bet? In identifying happiness with any particular state or possession, we can *always* think of something else that would be better and therefore our life could be *more* happy at that moment. Just as Einstein told the world that at the speed of light time stops, so too can it be said that in a state of complete happiness, desire and need stop. But *only* then.

Aristotle believed happiness was not the same as goods we desire in hopes they will make us happy. It was a state, a condition, the satisfaction of knowing that one has lived a good life, dominated by reason and virtue.

Aristotle therefore defines happiness as the highest, or final, good. Since nearly all of us continually strive for greater goods than we have at any particular time, it follows that achieving complete happiness, reaching the final good, *must* be the goal, the purpose of life. It also follows that what affords us pleasure or joy at any given moment cannot be the same thing as happiness, because it is always possible to think of something that would be better. Winning gold medals in the Olympics leaves athletes in a state of extreme joy, often identified as *euphoria*, yet two medals are better than one, and three even better than that. Aristotle, who probably attended Olympic games too, might have told the rejoicing athletes that winning games is among the things that make life good, but when complete happiness is achieved, they would not need to compete ever again.

Aristotle's theory has enormous implications for how we can best live. It assures us that life can still be good without our having everything we thought we wanted. Every so often we can stop and take inventory and then decide how our life is going. Is it headed in a direction that can be summed up as "Yes, this is a good life—so far"?

Further, *do we want things that make happiness more difficult to attain than need be?* The answer, according to Aristotle, is staring us in the face: if happiness is the same as the good life, why not simply *live* the good life? He believed there was one good which stood out above all, one good that was better than all the others that promote happiness, and that was *reason*. If we allow reason to be our guide in making all decisions, we will always do the right thing. By doing the right thing in every circumstance—not the most profitable or immediately pleasurable—one can be sure that the summing up will be on the side of the good life.

Happiness arises from awareness of being.

—Trich Nhat Hahn

Aristotle, very much like Socrates before him, equated reason with virtue. The virtuous course is also the perfection of a particular action. To act out of self-interest, ignoring others, can never be excellence. Too many others can be hurt by the action, and pardoning oneself to avoid guilt means lying. Of what action is *lying* the perfection? Do we judge a lie to be a perfect action if nobody finds out? Or if we believe no one has been hurt? How can we know? And even if we could be assured that the lie is a harmless one, might we not be encouraged to choose lying over the truth in another, or perhaps even *every*, case? A life built on lies is bound to crumble like a house of cards.

Aristotle believed that the path to happiness was a life lived in accordance with reason and virtue. This cannot be said for a life that achieves only *some* of the goods that are possible: recognition without love, for example, or money without health, or health without fulfilling any other purpose. A life that has displayed reason and virtue in all actions and decisions can be one that is free of care, free of guilt, free from wishing that much more could have been done.

But it may *not* be. A person who has lived a totally virtuous life may, in the end, regret that all goals had not been reached: the promised pay hike never received; the novel never written; a reconciliation never reached. But—and this is crucial—such regret is not a sign that the life was not a good one. In other words, according to Aristotle's theory, life can be good even though you are not always aware of it. Of course, the secret is to *become* aware of it by asking every so often *What am I doing that makes my life good?* Not: what is missing in my life? If the "missing" is also the unattainable, then you have willfully blocked the road to happiness. Whatever happens, if you can look in the mirror and say you are a good person, and you are smart enough to know that everything cannot be attained, your life is proceeding happily.

Providing Happiness: A Government's Responsibility?

Aristotle proposed that the *only* purpose of a government was to see to it that the citizens were happy. Having deduced that the purpose of living is the attainment of the happy life, the philosopher believed that nothing should be allowed to hinder the quest. The institutions of society exist for no reason other than to promote the happiness of all and therefore the means to that end.

Law and order in the well-regulated state are necessary; otherwise the happiness of all cannot be guaranteed. People must be protected against their own baser natures, as well as against those who wish them harm, in order that their higher potential may be realized. For many critics of this theory, questions remain: How much power should the state be given before it contradicts its avowed purpose, which is to promote the happiness of all? Will not some harm inevitably be done to the innocent? In this age of DNA testing, many of those executed for high crimes have later been found not to have been guilty. The justification "Yes, but look how many killers the death penalty has kept off the streets" does not satisfy those who would support the view that the happiness—and therefore the rights—of all must come first. How, they ask, can happiness be guaranteed when freedom is denied?

Aristotle held fast to the belief that the road to happiness was through the exercise of virtue and reason and that the government must not stand in the way of reason. This would imply that the government itself should be a model of rationality. And therein lies the great dilemma. How can government *reasonably* protect the state if it sometimes has to use *un*reasonable methods?

There is a further dilemma. What happens when the ruler's rational view of happiness differs from the people's? In *The Republic* Plato reports a famous debate over whether the best interests of the government can coincide with the best interests of the governed. Socrates believed that there was only one rational course in every decision that had to be made and that, if the government truly followed reason, then it would automatically serve the interests of the people. That belief was the foundation of his decision not to escape from prison, though he had questioned the justice that brought him there. What he did *not* question was the logic of having law itself. He was found guilty, however unjustly, and therefore the law required a penalty, which in his case was death by drinking hemlock. He argued it was unreasonable to assume that everyone who thought he had been unjustly imprisoned had the right to escape if he could. Aristotle had less faith in the power of the ordinary citizen to be rational, but that only made him insist that those who governed *must* be capable of using reason at all times. Whether that has ever happened is open to endless debate.

Aristotle Reconsidered

There are always going to be limitations on happiness. Many millions have no choice but to wait and hope for a miraculous change of fortune: people who live under oppressive governments or in places where drought or other natural disasters create famine and the spread of fatal disease; people who cannot be said to have had or maybe never *will* have anything that can be called a good. It is almost impossible to tell them that their lives are good, that they are happy without knowing it. Aristotle would probably not have even tried. Recognizing when one is fortunate in comparison to many others can be a limitation on one's own progress toward happiness, and helping those in need might be the only way to find the path again. Until one does find it and until no further help is necessary (an unimaginable condition), complete happiness is unreachable.

No, no, we are not satisfied, and we will not be satisfied until justice rolls down like waters and righteousness like a mighty stream.
—Martin Luther King, Jr.

The economic disaster of the Great Depression was addressed by the administration of Franklin D. Roosevelt, which began in 1933, promising what it called a "New Deal." Based on the theories of John Maynard Keynes, an English economist, the New Deal was to stimulate economic growth—hence the expansion of the job market—through government spending on a vast array of new social programs. Financed by the government, the Works Projects Administration (WPA) and the Civilian Conservation Corps (CCC) put the unemployed to work building roads, laying railroad tracks, cleaning up the cities and the countryside, and building dams to supply electrical power for new homes and factories. The New Deal proclaimed that the government's responsibility was to look out for the welfare of all citizens. In theory, everyone capable of working would have a job; and also in theory, making a fair wage and putting food on the table equated with happiness.

Aristotle believed the function of government was to provide for the happiness of each citizen.

Aristotle's theory assumed an open society with citizens' welfare as the major concern of government. Since his time, it is clear, all societies have become much more complex and the role of government tangled in webs of red tape. Can anyone in any society rely solely on government to provide happiness? Is happiness unattainable under a *repressive* government? Does it follow that no one can ever be happy in Aristotle's sense of the word?

The Humanities and Unhappiness

Any theory of happiness is just that: a theory. People whose circumstances are deplorable, who live in fear, hunger, and ill health, whose lifespan is often considerably shorter than it could be, who can rightly say that they never did harm to another person yet they suffer, cannot be blamed for feeling they deserve a better fate. Misfortune is, unfortunately, inherent in this business of living. The amount of suffering in the world is for many a permanent roadblock to the happy life.

The humanities have not turned a deaf ear to human misery. The sometimes futile attempt to escape from poverty, for example, is the subject of much great art and literature. For example, Victor Hugo's *Les Misérables* (1862) called powerful attention to the plight of the poor in France. The hero, Jean Valjean, steals a loaf of bread for his hungry family, is sent to prison, and after his release gets into trouble again. He is then relentlessly pursued by Javert, a police inspector obsessed with punishing anyone who breaks a law regardless of the reason. The pursuit continues for hundreds of pages, resulting in Javert's suicide because he cannot capture Valjean and the latter's reunion with his family now as an old man near death—and all because of a loaf of bread!

The master novelist of the truly desperate is Charles Dickens (1812–1870), some of whose memorable characters are children near starvation and working for corrupt taskmasters. In a memorable scene from the novel *Oliver Twist*, the poor, starving orphan of the title holds out his little bowl and timidly asks the head of the wretched workhouse whether he could have a bit more gruel—a request which brings down as fearful a display of wrath as exists in all of literature. Later, Oliver is taken in by the villainous Fagin, who controls a band of boy pick-pockets. The "happy ending," in which Oliver is discovered to be the long-lost grandson of a wealthy man, was not available to Fagin's other slaves. Nor does it disguise Dickens's real subject: society's indifference to poverty.

I simplified the scene and made the restaurant bigger. I was painting the loneliness of a large city.

—Edward Hopper

In Dickens's popular seasonal treat *A Christmas Carol*, there is, again, a happy ending, this time with an entire family rescued from dire poverty by the once miserly skinflint Ebenezer Scrooge, whose supernatural visitors effect his change of heart. But happy endings were demanded by nineteenth-century readers, most of them members of the comfortable middle class, who didn't mind confronting the cold and hunger of the poor as long as they could anticipate joy on the final page, casting a golden glow of unreality over the truth. One suspects, however, that Dickens was confident discerning readers would see through the sham and recognize that real poverty wasn't going away.

Following the Depression years of the 1930s, American writers and artists were preoccupied with the bitter realism of characters suffering from hunger, disease, and isolation. Edward Hopper's art (discussed in Chapter 5) specialized in loneliness and the despair of life in urban America, just emerging from the

Edward Hopper specialized in painting lonely, despairing people and the limitations of the American Dream.

Source: Edward Hopper, American, 1882–1967, *Nighthawks*, 1942, oil on canvas, 84.1 × 152.4 cm. Friends of the American Art Collection/The Art Institute of Chicago.

most severe economic depression in its history. Hopper's works show the limitations of the American Dream, of believing that in a free society anybody can reach the top. How many people continue to base their idea of happiness on how successful they can be? How often do they make unrealistic lists of the goods they *must* have before they can even consider whether they are happy? The irony is that those who have almost nothing and have therefore shorter lists probably stand a better chance at happiness than the more fortunate and perennially dissatisfied.

Conditions in the modern world have not conspired to bring about rosier views in the literary depiction of life. The victims of desperate economic times and the daily threat of violence figure in the work of writers surrounded by bitterness and death in many parts of the world. A popular Egyptian novel in recent years, Alaa Al Aswany's *The Yacoubian Building* (2002), revolves around the tenants of an apartment house in Cairo. To one extent or another, all long for prosperity. The central character is Taha, son of the building's janitor, who has aspirations to become a policeman and then marry the woman he loves. When he is turned away from the police academy even after scoring high on the entrance examination, he enrolls in college, where he is snubbed by the wealthier, better-dressed students but welcomed by those as poor as he. They introduce Taha to a charismatic leader promising change and declaring the way to bring it about is to disrupt the status quo through well-placed bombs. What stands out in the novel is the fact that this solution is not described as a misfortune or the tragedy of modern times, but simply as a sad commentary on the way things are.

One might ask, how is it possible to be truly happy in a world where we are so often faced with the continued suffering of the less fortunate? Before we try to answer that question, let us look at a few inspiring examples of people whose lives—and, unfortunately, deaths—exemplify how life *can* be good even under the most trying of circumstances.

Models of the Happy Life

History is filled with remarkable examples of how good lives managed to overcome horrible barriers. Consider this remarkable passage by Austrian psychiatrist Viktor Frankl, held in a Nazi concentration camp. It illustrates how life can be good, even in the shadow of death.

> *The size of human suffering is absolutely relative. . . . It also follows that a very trifling thing can cause the greatest of joys. Take as an example something that happened on our journey from Auschwitz to the camp affiliated with Dachau. We had all been afraid that our transport was heading for the Mauthausen camp. We became more and more tense as we approached a certain bridge over the Danube which the train would have to cross in order to reach Mauthausen. . . . Those who have never seen anything similar cannot possibly imagine the dance of joy performed in the carriage by the prisoners when they saw that our transport was not crossing the bridge and was instead heading "only" for Dachau.*[5]

The Aristotelian moral of this story is that the rational course was for the prisoners to put themselves into the hands of a two-pronged fate: Mauthausen or Dachau—certain death or a chance to live, even if imprisoned. Knowing the two possibilities in advance, it was rational to be prepared for either eventuality, not to wish for luck. Had liberation been the only possible good that would have satisfied them, the fact that the transport did not cross the Danube would not have been enough to fill them with optimism. Instead, they made their own "luck."

Another inspiring example of Aristotelian happiness is that of Anne Frank (1929–1945), a Jewish girl who, with her parents and others, was hidden in the attic of an Amsterdam office building during the Nazi occupation. To occupy her time and possibly leave something of value behind, she began writing a diary of her thoughts and feelings, a work that was subsequently found, published, and read by millions.

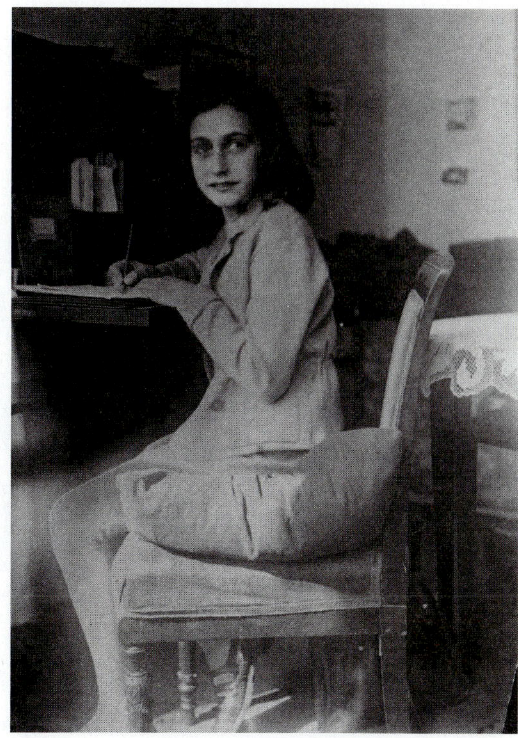

Anne Frank never knew she would become a legendary figure, an icon who continues to teach us the way to be happy under the most appalling circumstances.

Source: Handout/Reuters/Corbis.

Not the dewy-eyed idealist portrayed on stage, film, and television, Anne Frank was a girl with an adult mind that knew what it was doing at each moment. In 1944 she wrote: "I have made up my mind now to lead a different life from other girls and, later on, different from ordinary housewives." The "different life" was that of the calm, reflective writer. "I can shake off everything if I write, my sorrows disappear, my courage is reborn." After the war, she hoped to write and publish a work of great significance, but if this goal were denied, "my diary will be a great help."[6]

Remarkably able to transcend what would have been an understandable fear for her own safety and that of her family and friends, Frank takes the larger view, thinking sadly of those who have already been captured and sent to camps. "If it is as bad as this in Holland, whatever will it be like in the distant and barbarous regions they are sent to? We assume that most of them are murdered. The English radio speaks of their being gassed; perhaps that is the quickest way to die."[7]

Whosoever is happy will make others happy too.

—Anne Frank

Anne Frank's strength may have come from the fact that she knew herself to be innocent of any wrongdoing, and also from an acceptance of the conditions under which she and the others hiding in the attic had to live. She became the mainstay of the entire group. On the occasion of Hanukkah, she made presents for everyone out of old materials she found in the attic.

Her writing consistently reveals a person of resolve, one who has her emotions generally under control, and like the stoics, one whose spirit refuses to be broken. She admits to being afraid of death, but can that be called irrational? At the same time, she is not obsessed with fear. "When I sat in front of the window this morning I suddenly realized that we have had a great, great many compensations. I mean inward compensation."[8]

She proudly admits to believing nobody is all bad, despite the suffering she and her family have had to bear and the possibility of even more dreadful consequences to come. In the context of her brief but intensely rational life, her forgiving attitude seems more the triumph of the happy person (in Aristotle's sense) than the sentimentality of a young romantic. Observations like hers are not the result of a momentary, on-the-spot impulse, sudden flurries of passing joy unjustified by the circumstances; rather, they persist in one form or another

Aristotle would agree that Martin Luther King Jr. was a tragic victim, but would add that his was the very archetype of the happy life.

Source: Steve Schapiro/Corbis.

throughout the diary, evidence of a mature mind that knows intuitively what Aristotle had reasoned thousands of years ago: *life is good for one who is good.* Though Anne Frank was eventually captured and killed in a concentration camp, we can say, in Aristotelian terms, that hers was a happy life tragically foreshortened.

Martin Luther King Jr. (1929–1968), winner of the Nobel Peace Prize in 1964, devoted his own foreshortened life to non-violent protest against racism and the denial of civil rights to African Americans. An ordained Baptist minister, King was often in the midst of police brutality, urging victims to stay calm and not to reciprocate in kind when force was used. Considered by many as the greatest American orator since Abraham Lincoln, he gave hope with his stirring rhetoric to millions of the poor. He made numerous memorable speeches, but the most memorable of all was his "I Have a Dream" oration, delivered on the Washington Mall on August 28, 1963.

Considered by many to be the greatest orator since Abraham Lincoln, he gave hope to millions with his "I Have a Dream" speech on August 28, 1963.

In this oration, heard by the many thousands assembled for the March on Washington, King confronted the bitter truths of injustice, discrimination, school and housing segregation, and widespread joblessness. Without giving hollow protestations of hope, he gave what he surely must have considered rational reasons for hope, but always stressing non-violence.

> *Let us not seek to satisfy our thirst for freedom by drinking from the cup of bitterness and hatred. We must ever conduct our struggle on the high plane of dignity and discipline. We must not allow our creative protest to degenerate into physical violence. Again and again we must rise to the majestic heights of meeting physical force with soul force.*

Later in the speech, King introduced the now famous motif of "I have a dream," a statement that begins eight paragraphs. One is a poignant personal reference that is at the same time universal:

> *I have a dream that my four little children will one day live in a nation where they will not be judged by the color of their skin but by the content of their character.*

It is impossible to think that Dr. King was unaware of how dangerous it was to stand by his uncompromising principles and to take his powers of oratory into the most segregated parts of the country, knowing full well how many enemies were lying in wait. Five years after giving this speech that now belongs in the history of the humanities, he was assassinated by a man who spent the remainder of his life in prison, never admitting guilt or showing remorse.

Now, would Aristotle say Martin Luther King's life was a happy one? The answer is very probably *yes*. Aristotle would argue that he was a good man in the highest sense of that word, preaching a non-violent creed. His was a life extraordinarily characterized by virtue and reason, and although he was a tragic victim, his was the very archetype of a happy life.

Eastern Philosophy of Happiness

Learn to be calm and you will always be happy.

—**Paramhansa Yogananda**

In the West, as we have abundantly seen, happiness is often regarded as an entity, almost like an object that is to be sought, possessed, and cherished. To the non-Western mind what we call happiness is often called *bliss*, and it is a state, a condition. It is nothing that is ever owned. It is very like what is meant when someone remarks, "My head is in a good place today." It is somewhere to go, not something to hold. It is a place occupied sometimes, but not always. It is close to the stoicism of Western philosophy in that the state is one in which we cope with life's inevitable pain. For those who heed its call, bliss is the serenity that carries us through life.

Chapter 10 described the Eastern religions of Hinduism and Buddhism. Though they differ on many points, both stress the attainment of total release from suffering as the goal of living and the thing that makes life good—and, we would say, *happy*.

Gandhi

A sterling example of the Hindu path to bliss, or **moksha**, is provided by the life and death of Mohandas Gandhi (1869–1948), who spent his life preaching a gospel of non-violence. He attained a huge following, who anointed him with the title **Mahatma**, meaning "one who is wise and good." The word itself derives from two Sanskrit terms: *maha*, which means "great," and *atman*, which means "soul."

Like Siddhartha, Gandhi wanted to do more than simply save himself by becoming detached from all participation in the world. He wanted to save the world by persuading all those who would listen that a serene and therefore happy existence could come about only through non-violence and love.

Hindu doctrine teaches that the divine spirit dwells inside each person, that the soul of each person is part of *brahman*, the great soul, and therefore is fundamentally good. Unfortunately, the world is filled with luxuries, in plentiful supply to the rich, and with handsome and beautiful human beings who arouse sexual longings that must be fulfilled. The desire to possess both objects (including land) and other people leads to frustration and despair, because, as epicureans well know, there can never be enough pleasure if pleasure is the only goal. The thwarting of burning desire causes people to become violent, to seize what they want by any means.

Gandhi realized that when frustration was multiplied by the entire population of an oppressed land or by an ethnic group subjugated by a stronger power, then revolutionary uprisings were inevitable. The endless cycle of violence, war, and death (often of the most innocent) made life bitter. He knew that, for many, the only way to reach serenity was to back off and do nothing. But for himself, there could be no bliss, no serenity, in a world ruled by hate. Thus he became, as King would become, an activist, determined to make non-violence a potent counterforce.

As a native of India, Gandhi lived under British colonial rule and suffered the pain of discrimination. Speaking out against British imperialism, he acquired considerable notoriety and was frequently denounced in churches and meeting halls, but he also attracted many followers, including foreigners sympathetic to his cause. He carried his message to South Africa, where he found the same sort of prejudice and resistance to change. Exhausted and frequently ill from hunger strikes, he persisted, obsessed with the need to convince those who gathered to hear his speeches that there was only one way for people to live a good life in a good world: to lay down all weapons and talk to each other. He was convinced that through dialogue everyone would discover the basic oneness of all humanity. How could you hate someone who was really *you*?

Gandhi was painfully aware that the greatest threat to peace in India, even more than British sovereignty, was the irreconcilable divide between Hindus and Muslims—each practicing a different religion: the Hindus with their *brahman*, the soul of the world but not a personal god, and the Muslims with their father god, Allah. Hindus had no sacred books like the Qur'an, the word of God as delivered to the prophet Mohammed. To the Muslims, the Hindus were godless infidels. But often, the Hindus held the upper hand. This, after all, was their country.

Even under adversity, Mahatma Gandhi exemplified Aristotle's happy life.

Source: Bettman Corbis.

Gandhi stepped into this bitter conflict and sought to convince each side they could live in peace, that they must tolerate their differences and respect the rights of each to believe as they wished and practice religion as they saw fit. In 1947 India became an independent nation with self-rule, a tremendous step forward for which Gandhi was partly responsible. Yet he was not satisfied. The internal conflicts might never be resolved.

Gandhi's dream, like that of Martin Luther King Jr. decades later, would remain unrealized. On January 30, 1948, as he was about to enter a temple for a period of meditation, he was shot and killed by a Hindu fundamentalist, who apparently hated Muslims and could not tolerate the idea of universal love and peaceful coexistence.

Once again we have evidence that if perfect happiness is to be anything more than momentary joy, it has to be recognized as a distant goal that can probably never be reached but can be *approached* through unceasing effort. One can only conclude that Gandhi was one of the few really happy people. He may not have known he was or have even taken the time to think about the matter. If Aristotle's spirit had followed him about, much like a guardian angel, the Greek philosopher might have decided that his was a shining example of the happy life. He did not have health or wealth, two of the components of (but not the equivalents of) Aristotelian happiness, but he surely possessed the two most important ones: reason and virtue.

Gandhi's is an extreme, actually an archetypal, example of the good life. We should not expect it to demonstrate how the average citizen of India or any non-Western country views happiness, any more than we should expect the average citizen of the West to agree with Socrates or Epicurus or Epictetus. Perhaps happiness is a gossamer thing that we can ascribe to certain lives, while we wish that *ours* could be better.

Archetypes in This Chapter

Deserving	from earliest childhood we are conditioned to expect praise or material rewards; this has an impact later on our sense of how happy we are or are not.
Failure	inability to live up to standards imposed by society and its institutions, especially family, education, and workplace.
Happy	what we are brought up to believe we are supposed to be and, as we grow, what we deserve to be.
Ownership	one of the most important of all icons; what we learn to desire; what we come to think we deserve, the maximum of which we often equate with total happiness.
Peace	state or condition of being without personal stress; state of coexistence in which there is mutual understanding and no hostility, working toward which is the fundamental quality of the happy life for a good many persons, past and present.
Sad	exceedingly complex icon; a condition we are led to believe no one deserves and often assumed by those who enjoy self-pity or who desperately need compassion from others.
Success	often believed to be a tangible entity we must seek, or an inner self-congratulatory sensation, especially when it is achieved at the expense of someone else's failure.

Buddhist Paths to Happiness: Hinayana and Mahayana

For Buddhists, bliss, or **nirvana**, has a twofold nature. Historians of Buddhism explain that over the centuries the religion divided into two schools, both leading to nirvana. One is **Hinayana**, which means "little ferryboat." It developed first, and its job was to formulate the teachings of Siddhartha into a systematic use of the Four Noble Truths, which are: *life is filled with pain; the cause of pain is frustrated desire; there is a way out of pain; the way out is the Eightfold Path.* The latter has to do with how we think, speak, behave toward others, and above all, how we find peace through meditation (see Chapter 10).

While Hinayana Buddhism involves moral conduct, which is automatic if we follow all of the recommended steps, its practice was seen by those who came after Siddhartha as too narrow, too limited. It proved to be a wonderful means of self-help, of lifting the spirits of the depressed and the stressed-out people of the world (as it still is for the many who practice Buddhist meditation in Western societies), but not a way to assist others who may have lost their way.

We have no more right to consume happiness without producing it than to consume wealth without producing it.

—**George Bernard Shaw**

Gradually the school known as **Mahayana**, "big ferryboat," developed, adding a larger perspective and a more expansive concept of bliss. In Tibetan Buddhism, which continues the lineage of Siddhartha and teaches that nirvana is attainable in one lifetime by those who follow the rigorous discipline of the Eightfold Path, the fully enlightened person now becomes a buddha. In the company of other buddhas, he or she is ready to follow in the footsteps of Siddhartha: that is, renouncing bondage to the illusory pleasures of this world and doing whatever is necessary, wherever it may be. It can mean something as simple as collecting clothes, food, and other supplies for victims of a devastating fire, storm, or earthquake, or joining a corps of volunteers and helping to rebuild damaged homes. Or it can mean becoming a world-renowned person, carrying a message of peace and tolerance to millions. In Buddhism, both choices have equal importance.

There is nothing self-congratulatory about the Mahayana path. One does not pat oneself on the back and bask in the glow of satisfaction that comes from knowing one has done a good deed or made a tremendous sacrifice. Mahayana Buddhism says it is the logical next step after one has practiced the

Hinayana, or narrow, way. The idea is that, having reached enlightenment after long years of meditation, one has no choice but to live in and through others, just as Siddhartha, having reached enlightenment after forty days and forty nights of sitting under the *bodhi* tree, declined to enter nirvana, feeling he must share his bliss with everyone else: he must teach them how to be as serene as he has become.

Many thousands in the East and the West do not practice Buddhism as such, nor do they nor can they take the extreme steps of Gandhi or King, but they nonetheless care deeply about social issues, such as poverty or the environment. These people find they cannot be personally—or at least not entirely—happy in the midst of so much that is going wrong. Then there are people who, though comfortable in their own fortunate lives, feel guilty when they see photographs of hungry children in war-torn countries or the homeless in any major city anywhere. They can't shrug it off with a "Well, they're not people I know, and what can *I* do?" Whether they know it or not, they have already taken a few steps on the Mahayana, or wider, path.

In the time of Siddhartha the world had many troubles, but there were no global conflicts of today's dimensions, no continual outbreaks of terrorism, no everyday fears that disaster is omnipresent and waiting to happen anywhere, anytime, to anyone. Were he alive today, he would very likely have been at Ground Zero on September 12, 2001, asking what he could do to help. For most of the rest of us, doing what is necessary may have an understandably narrower definition. There are obligations to family, to work, to our circle of friends. There are children to meet at the corner where the school bus leaves them off, an aging parent or other relative to care for, and a host of personal tasks to be done, such as pursuing a degree, learning a trade or profession, supporting a family. Most of us cannot become buddhas or live as Siddhartha did, wandering from place to place without a family, eating very little, paying scant attention to our other wants. Yet Mahayana Buddhism does not expect quite this much. However far you go on the Path is better than not taking that first step. This is the Buddhist view of happiness.

The Dalai Lama

The Dalai Lama, the acknowledged leader of Tibetan Buddhism, is a role model for thousands who seek to emulate his serenity as well as his Mahayana efforts on behalf of world peace. Those who admire him and flock to his lectures often are curious about what it means to do without many of the pleasures that a others of his stature and following usually enjoy—particularly pleasures of the flesh.

> *I am sometimes asked whether this vow of celibacy is really desirable and indeed whether it is really possible. Suffice to say that its practice is not simply a matter of suppressing sexual desires. On the contrary, it is necessary to fully accept the existence of those desires and to transcend them by the power of reasoning. When successful, the result of the mind can be very beneficial. The trouble with sexual desire is that it is a blind desire and can only give temporary satisfaction. Thus, as Nagarjuna said: "When you*

> *have an itch, you scratch. But not to itch at all is better than any amount of scratching."*[9]

His writings are full of wise sayings and aphorisms in short entries that remind one of the *Tao Te Ching* of Lao-tzu. And with their publication and dissemination throughout the globe, the Dalai Lama must, of course, hope that he will lead thousands, even millions, to the path of serenity. Knowing how to live a serene existence would make a good many people desist from doing their utmost to spread terror and hatred and continually renew the cycle of war and broken peace accords. He cannot, however, wish that the peace (and hope for happiness) of the entire world would come about only when all sides are of one mind.

> *All the waters and rivers of different lands and climes have their ultimate meeting point in the ocean. So, too, the differing viewpoints on society, the variety of economic theories, and the means to their attainment benefit mankind itself. There is no point in indulging in dissension-creating discussions on differing ideologies. No positive result has accrued from attempting to convert all men of different temperaments and likings into one common ideology and mode of behavior.*[10]

In his view, serenity—or, as he calls it, tranquility—has to be achieved through acceptance of, not the burning need to change, everyone else.

If you want to be happy, be.
—Leo Tolstoy

> *The essence of all spiritual life is your emotion, your attitude toward others. Once you have pure and sincere motivation, all the rest follows. You can develop this right attitude toward others on the basis of kindness, love, and respect, and on the clear realization of the oneness of all human beings.*[11]

Whether we call it *bliss*, *moksha*, or *nirvana*, or go with the hedonists and insist that it is having as much as possible of life's pleasures—plenty of money, sex, fast cars, a showcase for a home—the nature of the good life remains open to debate. This chapter has not promised an easy resolution, a neat summing up. Happiness is but one of the colors we apply to the canvas of "human."

The terms *winner* and *loser* are strong in our vocabularies. Frequently they drive us to an either-or approach to living. Blithely we describe someone as a loser and resolve that only *winner* will ever apply to *us*. But if a loser is someone who fails at everything, must a winner be the exact opposite? Is it possible to win continually? Do we always know what it *means* to win? And what is *loss*? The absence of money, health, love? Can these be absent continually?

We do not wish to leave you with the impression that Aristippus, Epicurus, Aristotle, or Siddhartha discovered the best and only road to happiness. Our advice is to carefully map out your requirements for the good life, bearing in mind some of the options discussed in this chapter. Once you recognize that *you* are in control of defining happiness and can make it mean what is possible for you, not what you can never hope to achieve, then you may experience a measure of contentment.

Key Terms

big-earnings theory from the hedonist view that people who work hard or who make sacrifices for others deserve material rewards.

carpe diem Latin phrase meaning "seize the day"; a major hedonist creed which advises us to live for the moment and amass all the pleasures we can.

epicureanism based on teachings of Epicurus, the belief that happiness is freedom from pain.

hedonism from the Greek for "delight," the belief that happiness consists of the sum of all the pleasures we can experience.

Hinayana one of the two major schools of Buddhism; from the Sanskrit meaning "little ferryboat," also called the "narrow path," the personal attainment of serenity through meditation.

Mahatma from Sanskrit words meaning "great" and "soul," a title of love and respect for one who is known to be wise and good; applied to Gandhi.

Mahayana one of the two major schools of Buddhism; from Sanskrit meaning "big ferryboat," the wider path to happiness, attainable by helping others find the way.

moksha early Hindu term for the highest state of happiness possible, a condition of pure bliss in which one is free from all desire.

nirvana Buddhist term for the highest state of happiness possible, akin to the Hindu concept of *moksha*.

schadenfreude German term for the experience of joy in the misfortunes of others.

stoicism named for the *stoa* (porch) where Zeno taught the philosophy of curbing desire to cope with the inevitability of pain.

Topics for Writing and Discussion

1. If you had to choose one theory of happiness discussed in this chapter as dominant in our society, which would it be? Explain. Then indicate whether it represents your own view.
2. Create and then describe three television commercials for the same product, each directed toward a different audience: (a) a hedonist, (b) an epicurean, and (c) a Buddhist.
3. Choose one of the following options for discussion or a short paper:
   a. A gambler who has lost all evening makes one last bet with money that has been saved for the down payment on a house and wins back twice the sum. Could you justify the risk? Or take the gambler to task regardless of the win? Is life a matter of taking risks anyway? Is it worth playing close to the vest?
   b. In a children's game of musical chairs, one child is clearly the winner. Should the organizers of the game give each child the same prize in order not to hurt anyone's feelings? Or should children be taught at an early age how the world usually works? Which of these two approaches is likely to produce the happier child?
   c. The big-earnings theory, discussed in the chapter, maintains that people who work hard or sacrifice for each other deserve substantial rewards. Pretend you have found somebody's wallet containing $1,000 as well as the name and phone number of the owner. You return it and receive a "thank you very much" and that's all. You ask Aristippus, Epicurus, and Aristotle how you should feel. What do they answer?
4. Write a toast you would make for a newly married couple, as if you were (a) a stoic and then (b) the Dalai Lama.
5. Andrew Carnegie wrote: "While the law of competition may be sometimes hard for the individual, it is best for each race, because it insures the survival of the fittest. We accept and therefore welcome great inequality of environment, the concentration of business in the hands of a few, and the law of competition between them as being essential for the future progress of the race." On which theory of happiness is this idea based? Do you agree with it? Why or why not?
6. Which theory of happiness in your opinion is most helpful to the world and which the least? Explain your answers.
7. The mother in a very poor family once made fried dough with powdered sugar for Thanksgiving dinner

and told everyone they were going to have a real treat. Which philosophy of happiness would be most likely to say this was a lie? Which would be most likely to agree with the mother? Think carefully before you answer, then explain your choices.

8. Go back to the opening page of this chapter and look carefully at the illustration. The artist called it "Good Fortune." Do the people in the drawing exemplify that title? Is something else going on?

9. The English philosopher Bertrand Russell said work is a major component of happiness. Which kind of work do you anticipate doing? Which kind of work do you think offers the best chance of leading you to happiness? Are they the same?

10. A philosopher said, "Take care that your happiness does not depend on what happens to you." To which theory of happiness is this statement most closely related? Is it, in your opinion, a reasonable or even possible approach to living? What can be said in favor of and against it?

Plate 30 Rembrandt van Rijn, *Joseph accused by Potiphar's wife* (1655). Credit: Bildarchiv Preussischer Kulturbesitz/Art Resource, NY.

After becoming a trusted servant of Potiphar, Joseph is falsely accused of adultery by Poitphar's wife in an act of vengeance for his refusal of her. Joseph is thrown into prison, but God protects him, and he soon wins the protection of the pharaoh because of his ability to interpret dreams. (See page 369 for more on Joseph.)

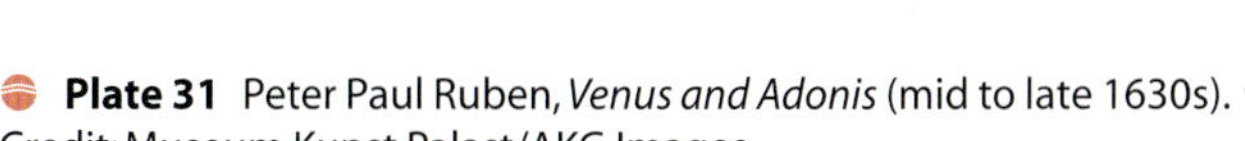

Plate 31 Peter Paul Ruben, *Venus and Adonis* (mid to late 1630s). Credit: Museum Kunst Palast/AKG Images.

In this Ruben's painting, the goddess Venus is entreating Adonis to hunt boar. His obstinacy kills him.

Plate 32 Georges Seurat, *A Sunday Afternoon on the Island of La Grande Jatte* (1884–1886). Art Institute of Chicago. Credit: Erich Lessing/Art Resource, NY.

Seurat's pointillest depiction of proper middle-class Victorian society.

Plate 33 Jan de Provoost *Death and the Miser.* Photographic Service City of Bruges, Jan Termont-Dirk Vander Borght. Groeninge Museum, Bruges, Belgium.

Popular image of Death as something that happens only to people who deserve it. (See page 496 for more on popular images of death.)

Plate 34 Krishna dancing in Paradise (eighteenth century).
Credit: British Library/The Art Archive.

Krishna, perhaps an incarnation of the god Vishnu, is here shown dancing in a geographical afterlife. Such belief is not widespread in Hinduism, which generally sees life after death as reincarnation in this world. (See page 509 for more on Krishna.)

Plate 35 Henry Tanner's *The Seine*.
Credit: Gift of the Avalon Foundation. Image courtesy of the Board of Trustees, National Gallery of Art, Washington, c. 1902, oil on canvas, .228 x 330 (1971.57.1).

The African-American artist Henry Tanner considered himself an Impressionist first and foremost, not an artist with a message. (See page 533 for more on Tanner.)

Plate 36 Christopher Ofili, *Holy Virgin Mary* (1999).
Credit: Courtesy Chris Ofili-Afroco and Victoria Miro Gallery, London/AP/World Wide Photos.

Ofili is a British artist who was born in Africa. His painting of the Virgin Mary, which uses both paint and elephant dung, shocked many viewers when it was exhibited in the United States. The artist insisted that elephant dung is highly valued in Africa as a symbol of the fertile earth, but his argument did not diffuse tension over the painting. Should art that offends people's religious faith be suppressed? (See page 535 for more on Ofili and the controversy over *Holy Virgin Mary*.)

Plate 37 Edouard Manet's Olympia. Musée d'Orsay, Paris. Credit: Réunion des Musées Nationaux/Art Resource, NY.

Now recognized as one of the great Impressionist painters in 19th century France, Manet was critically reviled for *Olympia*, a painting of a reclining nude woman. Not only was she obviously a courtesan, but her bold gaze seemed to stare shamelessly at the viewer. (See pages 143 and 538 for more on Manet.)

Plate 38 Emil Nolde (1867–1956), *The Last Supper.* Credit: Statens Museum fur Kunst, Denmark. © Nolde Foundation Stiftung Seebull.

Despite the artist's standing as an early member of the Nazi party, Expressionist works such as this were purged as a part of Hitler's campaign against "Degenerate art." (See page 544 for more on Nolde.)

Plate 39 Frida Kahlo, Self-Portrait on the Borderline Between Mexico and the United States (1932) Credit: Collection of Mr. and Mrs. Manual Reyero, New York. Instituto Nacional de Bellas Arty Literatura, Mexico / © 2005 Banco de Mexico Diego Rivera and Frida Kahlo Museums Trust Av. Cinco de Mayo No. 2, Col. Centro Del Cuauhtemoc 06059, Mexico, D.F./Image © Christie's Images/Corbis.

Frida Kahlo was at first exhibited as Mrs. Diego Rivera. One wonders what would have happened if the artist had not been married to a famous man. (See page 555 for more on Kahlo.)

Plate 40 Jan Brueghel, *The Garden of Eden* (1612). Credit: Victoria and Albert Museum, London/Art Resource, NY.

Landscapes became popular in the seventeenth century. Brueghel, in particular, popularized images of the paradise inhabited by Adam and Eve before their fall and subsequent expulsion. (See page 563 for more on Brueghel.)

Plate 41 Rembrandt van Rijn, *Sacrifice of Isaac* (1635).
Credit: Hermitage, St. Petersburg, Russia. Photo: Scala/Art Resource, NY.

One of the masterpieces of Dutch realism, this famous moment was used by Kierkegaard to symbolize the existential anguish of choice. (See page 139 for more on Rembrandt and page 580 for more on Kierkegaard.)

Plate 42 Edouard Manet, *Dejeuner Sur l'Herbe* (1863). Credit: Musée d'Orsay. Paris, France/Erich Lessing/Art Resource, NY.

Manet's *Déjeuner Sur l'Herbe* was originally met with scorn, then became one of the most famous of all Impressionist paintings. (See page 143 for more on Manet.)

13 Love

Overview

Love: any form of relationship between human beings when used in conjunction with the phrase "falling in love" or "being in love."
—**Morton M. Hunt**

We can scarcely overestimate the importance of love in our lives, in the world, and in the humanities. Without the theme of love, all of the arts would be diminished. Even the successive marriages of the frequently divorced (half of marriages now end that way) give evidence that people believe so strongly in love they keep looking for it, and that no matter what their other achievements, they probably believe they have wasted their lives if they cannot say they have loved and been loved at some point. In countless poems, novels, operas, films, and plays, love is shown as the source of both pleasure and pain, often at the same time.

Love is hard to describe scientifically; it may be solely the invention of the human imagination, without objective existence. Artists are not united in their depictions of love: some have glorified it; others have emphasized its pain; some have imagined a society whose leaders ban it entirely. This chapter offers an analysis of ways in which humanity has been affected by the myth or the mystery of love as it has been depicted in different cultures and their arts throughout the ages. Recognizing this obsession and its possible impact on our beliefs is crucial to the art of being human.

Body and Soul

A 1900 poster illustration showing an origin of romantic love in medieval stories of brave knights and their fair ladies. *Source:* Art.com.

Love has meant different things at different times and in particular places. Cultural anthropologists, for example, once discovered that people in a certain remote area of Africa had no word that translates as "love." As you may have guessed, their vocabulary was filled with words that relate to survival strategies, all with favorable connotations; however, they seemed to have little need for words that refer to tight family bonds and none for words indicating romance between adults.

Despite the sentiments in poems and songs that love is timeless, it must be considered in the context of history. Imagine the difficulty of having a meaningful discussion about love between people from totally different backgrounds—one, waiting for romance and passion, with a wide choice of partners, and the other, obediently preparing to marry a stranger in a match arranged by the parents of the couple. The Greeks made a famous distinction between **eros**, or love as physical lust, and **agape**, in which a spiritual and intellectual relationship is ultimately more important than a strictly physical one. Though the Romans are famous for their wine-filled orgies, they recognized the distinction as well, and that distinction is still with us.

Eros

Eros, in Greek mythology, is the god of erotic love; the Roman version is Cupid. In the classical world, passion was dangerous, responsible for endless misery. This poem by the Roman Petronius Gaius (c. 100 C.E.) offers a warning about lust and an invitation to something better:

Doing, a filthy pleasure is, and short;
And done, we straight repent us of the sport:
Let us not then rush blindly on unto it,
Like lustful beasts, that only know how to do it:
For lust will languish, and that heat decay.
But thus, thus, keeping endless holiday,
Let us together closely lie and kiss,
There is no labour, nor no shame in this;
This hath pleased, doth please, and long will please; never
Can this decay, but is beginning ever.[1]

The debate continues over whether what we call "love" can mean anything more than lust. A twenty-first-century writer and cultural satirist, Francine Prose, is convinced that lust is crucial to our survival. "Unlike the other deadly sins, lust and gluttony are allied with behaviors required for the survival of the individual and the species. One has to eat in order to live; presumably the race would die out if lust were never permitted to work its magic."[2]

Men have died from time to time and worms have eaten them, but not for love.
—**William Shakespeare**

The destructive, often tragic, effects of physical desire have been the source of some long-lasting stories emerging from classical mythology. Typical is the account of someone—mortal or divine—caught in the grip of uncontrollable passion. In Roman myth, the figure of Cupid, child of Venus, is often the mischief-maker, who aims his arrow at some unfortunate creature, rendering the person unable to think rationally.

One of Cupid's victims is his own mother, the goddess of love herself. Wounded by Cupid's arrow, Venus is overcome by attraction to a mortal, Adonis. After enjoying his moments of passion with a divine being, Adonis announces his intention to go hunting. Venus pleads with him not to go in search of dangerous game. Such advice being distinctly non-Roman, Adonis understandably ignores it and is promptly killed by a wild boar. To perpetuate his memory, Venus transforms his blood into a dark red flower called the anemone. But like passion itself, the anemone is short-lived. The wind blows the blossoms open, and all the petals suddenly are gone.

The story of Venus and Adonis lives on in powerful words and pictures. Many artists, especially the Flemish Peter Paul Rubens (1577–1640), have been inspired by the myth of an impossible love between a mortal and the immortal goddess who could not follow him to the grave (Color Plate 31). This story would not be the last to show not only that physical desire has a very brief existence but also that death alone can ensure what human beings dream of and sing about: love that never ends.

In classical mythology and literature, nothing good ever comes from love.

In Shakespeare's dramatic poem about the pair, Venus is very definitely the aggressor, pursuing and seducing the reluctant Adonis:

> *'Thrice-fairer than myself,' thus she began*
> *'The field's chief flower, sweet above compare,*
> *Stain to all nymphs, more lovely than a man,*
> *More white and red than doves or roses are;*
> *Nature that made thee, with herself at strife,*
> *Saith that the world hath ending with thy life. . .*

After the young man dies, the goddess puts a curse on love. Henceforth it shall never make anyone happy. Henceforth love shall be passion unfulfilled or passion turned bitter.

> *'It shall be fickle, false, and full of fraud,*
> *Bud and be blasted in a breathing-while;*
> *The bottom poison and the top o'erstrawed,*
> *With sweets that shall the truest sight beguile.*[3]

Love will be "cause of war and dire events." Fathers and sons will fight each other over the same woman. If any lovers are lucky enough to escape the decay of their passion for each other, that passion will nevertheless make them miserable. "They that love best their loves shall not enjoy." Shakespeare's comedies often end with joyful lovers falling into each other's arms, but sexual love is the driving force in some of the tragedies, such as *Romeo and Juliet*. The sonnets, however, indicate that sex would be just fine if disdainful ladies would only cooperate!

Adonis was not alone in being "radically" changed following an erotic misadventure. Other mythic mortals who attract the attention of Olympian gods and goddesses either die or are transformed into vegetation or heavenly bodies.

In classical mythology, human beings are not responsible for their tragic passions. Outside forces, personified as the gods, toy with them for their amusement or the satisfaction of their own physical needs. Occasionally, the afflicted mortal is rewarded for having been the target of a god's lust, but only after undergoing physical and mental torment. One myth inspired a masterpiece of visual art, *Jupiter and Io*, by the Italian artist Antonio Allegri da Correggio (1494–1536), known in art history by his last name only. Io is an innocent young woman who stirs the sexual longings of Jupiter, king of the gods, and is transformed into a heifer for her protection. Juno, the chronically jealous wife of Jupiter, does everything she can to rain destruction on Io but fails to kill her. One result of Jupiter and Io's coupling is a son, whose descendant was Hercules.

In Correggio's painting, Io is transformed back into a human being so that she can be enjoyed by Jupiter.

Source: Corregio, *Jupiter and Io*. Credit: Erich Lessing/Art Resource, NY.

Lust's passion will be served; it demands, it militates, it tyrannizes.
—**Marquis de Sade**

This tale is probably not making a statement that lust is guaranteed to have happy consequences. Rather, it suggests—as do many classical myths—that human beings are related to the gods and in many respects are more than their equals. This explains why the gods are jealous of mortals and often affect them tragically, even if Io's fate is better than that of most women who wander into a lustful god's field of vision.

Physical passion and its consummation in the pleasures of the flesh found their share of glorification in the ancient world. The Hebrew Bible, for example, contains the Song of Solomon (Song of Songs), which, though variously interpreted, appears to be a lyrical idealization of physical ecstasy. Its inclusion among sacred writings suggests that to the Hebrews, passion was a glorious experience, not at all inconsistent with the love of God. In this work the Lover speaks to his Beloved in sensuous terms. Her physical splendors fill him with joy. He compares her breasts to clusters of fruit and her breath to wine.

During the late Middle Ages, though Europe was strongly Christian, secular and erotic themes began to creep into poems and songs, often written by young men studying for the priesthood. If they did not turn from their faith, they could nonetheless be irreverent in their praise—or at least defense—of sexual pleasure. Groups of rebellious students known as **goliards** frequented the taverns in their leisure hours, singing the praises of secular life. The most famous of these songs is "Gaudeamus Igitur" (Let us rejoice while we are young), which is still played at countless college commencement ceremonies minus the lyrics that urge people to eat, drink, and be merry before the inevitable happens: "Then the dust shall claim us." Many of the goliard songs as well as others have been discovered within the past century, including "In Trutina" (I am suspended between chastity and lascivious love), which was given a modern setting by composer Carl Orff and recorded by innumerable artists, including Sarah Brightman and Barbra Streisand. The narrator of the poem is probably a novitiate about to take her final vows—and wishing she were not.

Some Cupid kills with arrows, some with traps.
—**William Shakespeare**

The most famous secular author of the fourteenth century was Geoffrey Chaucer (1340–1400), who, while reaffirming his devout faith, was fond of creating lusty stories and characters that shocked church authorities. In his masterpiece, *The Canterbury Tales*, he recognizes the weakness of the flesh, in both laypersons and clerics. Among the lust-driven men and women is his most unforgettable character: the Wife of Bath, married five times (but always "at church door") and as lusty a creature as can be found in the pages of literature. She sings the praises of youth and glorious sex, culminating with a misty-eyed recognition that, as we grow old and unattractive, we bid farewell to the joys that have made life rich and happy.

But lord Christ! When I remember
My youth and joyful times,
It tickles me to my heart's roots.
Even now it does my heart good
To know that I have had my world
In my own time.[4]

As the Middle Ages waned and the Renaissance began to spread over much of western Europe, bringing with it the lost glories of the classical world, the ancient theme of lust awakened a sympathetic response from writers who treated it compassionately as a human tragedy. And still others, like Shakespeare in his sonnets, ardently wished their lady friends would be a bit more obliging.

In what is probably the most popular love story ever written, *Romeo and Juliet*, it is quite clear that physical desire initially attracts the pair, a desire that makes Juliet fearful. Before encouraging Romeo's suit, she warns that such an attraction is "too like the lightning," because it "ceases to be ere one can say it lightens." Their sexual attraction causes them to forget family duty, forget the fact that Juliet is promised to someone else—in short, to commit themselves to each other with total abandon. Though their love is couched in the language of pure romance, they too are destroyed by the curse of Venus.

The darts of the mischievous Cupid are a popular plot device, whether for ill or good. And with or without him, we still have stories of people stricken with sudden, blinding passion—as if they *were* sporting arrows in their chest. Shakespeare saw the humorous side of the affliction in his comedy *A Midsummer Night's Dream* (1594), when Titania, queen of the fairies, finds herself irresistibly drawn to a man she would ordinarily never have looked at if she were in her right mind. But a magic love potion has caused her to desire the first creature she looks at—in this case, a bumbling, rustic, would-be actor wearing the head of a donkey and responding to the queen's passionate endearments with a typical donkey's bray, a sound that drives her into absolute sexual frenzy. This is the comic flip side of the "love coin" for Shakespeare. Whether you laugh or cry, passion doesn't bring much good fortune.

Shakespeare has fun with the absurdity of love at first sight in his play *A Midsummer Night's Dream.*

Source: James Cagney as Bottom and Anita Louise as Titania in Max Reinhardt's 1933 film version of *A Midsummer Nights Dream.* Credit: Underwood & Underwood/Corbis.

Nonetheless, Shakespeare's time was one in which passion took center stage. In England, the philosophy of hedonism (discussed in Chapter 12) enjoyed much favor. It urged people, as the songs of the medieval goliards had, to enjoy life to the fullest because who knew what lay beyond the grave? The time of Queen Elizabeth I, who reigned until the very beginning of the seventeenth century, was the heyday of celebrating the pleasures of the flesh, but usually with the darker implication that death can strike at any time. Remember that Epicurus denounced hedonism on the grounds that its underlying obsession with death was more than enough to offset the fleeting pleasures of loving.

Hedonism enjoyed much favor in Shakespeare's time, urging people to enjoy life to the fullest because who knew what lay beyond the grave?

The eighteenth century, on both sides of the channel, was a time of polite society. Manners were extremely important, but under the surface the lusty life continued to be celebrated. One historian of the period observed that, though the drawing room was elegant and proper in all respects, behind the gilded bedroom door the rules were abandoned. Infidelity was rampant. It was expected that every well-bred gentleman of means would keep at least one mistress. Though religion

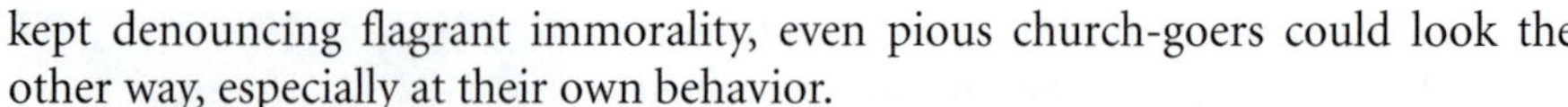

kept denouncing flagrant immorality, even pious church-goers could look the other way, especially at their own behavior.

By the nineteenth century, the middle class became dominant, and sexual morality became a serious business. Only in marriage could sex be tolerated—at least officially. But it is no coincidence that two of the most popular hedonistic works of all time were both translated in that period. One was *A Thousand and One Nights*; the other was *The Rubáiyát of Omar Khayyám* (also discussed in Chapter 14). Both reflect the exotic hedonism of foreign cultures and former times.

We are all like Scheherazade's husband, in that we want to know what happens next.
—**E.M. Forster**

A Thousand and One Nights is usually, and inaccurately, referred to simply as *The Arabian Nights*. This vast collection of more than 400 tales, put together from the ninth to the thirteenth centuries C.E., came from India and Persia as well as from Arabia, and so represents a blending of different cultures. In the decade of the 1880s the stories were translated into English by Richard Burton (1821–1890), an author and explorer, and the work has remained a classic ever since.

The central character is Scheherazade, the latest wife of a much married sultan who looks upon women as sexual playthings, with no other function than to be available at any time of the day or night. Because he is all-powerful and can have any woman he desires, he has each bride executed after the wedding night. Scheherazade faces the same fate as her predecessors unless she can find a way to entertain the sultan—other than through the customary lovemaking, which would guarantee her death. The resourceful heroine decides to start telling stories, and they prove so engrossing that she dazzles her husband for a thousand and one nights, by which time we can presume that the sultan begins to see her as a human being rather than as a temporary bed partner. We can never know whether the long book was hugely popular because the ending satisfied the moral standards of the time or because the ending was overlooked in favor of the exotic tales of harem intrigues. Perhaps it offered the perfect escape into a never-never land of brilliant colors, fragrant spices, scrumptious feasting, and nights of delirious sex.

The Rubáiyát (from a Persian word meaning quatrains, or four-line verses) was translated by the English scholar Edward Fitzgerald (1809–1883). Attributed to Omar, called Khayyám (tent-maker), a Persian poet and philosopher who lived around 1100 C.E., it is a collection of verses that celebrate both the glory and the short-lived pleasures of life, especially those of physical love. The poems tell us that this love is at once the thing that makes life exciting and the thing that, because it cannot endure, makes life ultimately a sad, futile enterprise.

Ah, Love! Could you and I with Him conspire
To grasp this sorry Scheme of Things entire,
Would we not shatter it to bits—and then
Re-mould it nearer to the Heart's desire.[5]

Though a philosopher, Omar appears to have abandoned the life of reason in favor of the life of the senses. Making love and drinking steadily were far more satisfying than spending sleepless nights trying to understand existence.

You know, my Friends, with what a brave Carouse
I made a Second Marriage in my house;

Divorced old barren Reason from my bed,
And took the Daughter of the Vine to Spouse.[6]

Bygone though these eras may have been, the fact remains that the theme of masculine domination and women-as-playthings—servants of Eros, if you will—has never gone entirely out of fashion. Two hugely popular operas by Mozart, *The Marriage of Figaro* (1786) and *Don Giovanni* (1787), center on roguish adulterers. The Countess in the *The Marriage of Figaro* (analyzed in Chapter 8) is the long-suffering wife of a philandering husband who tries to exercise his right to take to bed a female servant on her wedding night—*before* the husband does! The Countess is rewarded for her love and patience by getting to sing glorious musical laments.

Don Giovanni is a glorification of the most famous serial seducer of all time, the legendary figure Don Juan. One of his victims, Zerlina, is engaged to marry someone of her own station in life and has sworn fidelity to him, a fact that makes little difference to the Don—and presumably the audience. Though the legendary lover dies at the end and is consigned to hell, we cannot imagine that Mozart and the librettist Lorenzo da Ponte (both of whom were discussed in Chapter 8) intended to make a strong case against male promiscuity.

In some circles today, sexual encounters are assumed to be of brief duration, and relationships with numerous partners are accepted as the norm. The television series *Sex and the City* appears to give tacit approval to promiscuity, but in fact its central character, Carrie Bradshaw, longs for and continually seeks a permanent, stable domestic life with one person. One is tempted to conclude that, during the seventeenth and nineteenth centuries, tales of philandering outside of marriage were popular *because of* not despite the rigid moral codes prevailing. The relaxation of moral codes notwithstanding, physical passion and the pain of lost love remain dramatic subjects.

If love is often cruel or destructive, the reasons lie not in love itself, but in the inequality between people.
—**Anton Chekhov**

Agape

We should not think *love* in the humanities has always meant uncontrollable passion that makes people tragic victims or fools. In fact, the Greek word *agape* (pronounced ah-ga-pay) means simply "love." In the classical world, *eros*, or "lust," was not considered a form of love, but something else altogether. *Agape* is often called **Platonic love.** In popular usage today, the term *Platonic* not only means the opposite of lust but is a synonym for a totally non-physical relationship. But a truly Platonic friendship can involve much more than having a study companion.

The most famous discourse on the subject comes from Plato, whose ideal love may indeed include physical union with another, but the philosopher believed the pleasures of the body can never be the highest possible good. There is no reason to believe he did not enjoy those pleasures, only that he saw them as simply the first rung on what we may call a ladder to the ideal.

In Platonic philosophy, each of us is born with a soul, the rational capacity for comprehending all of the eternal truths. The soul eventually discovers that it is imprisoned in a body, which is subject to deterioration, pain, and death. The soul, however, is immortal and will find a new home after the present body dies. The constant longing of the soul is therefore to escape from the body.

In his 1629 play *The New Inn*, Ben Jonson (1572–1637) defined Platonic love as

> *A spiritual coupling of two souls*
> *So much more excellent, as it least relates*
> *Unto the body.*

Love must be as much a light as a flame.
—**Henry David Thoreau**

For Plato, a human being's attraction to another on a strictly physical level is at least a step in the right direction, because it represents a preoccupation with something other than the self, which, being short-lived, is of no great importance. Besides, the goal of bodily attraction is reproduction, the generation of another life. Bringing into existence another life offers us a glimpse of the eternal, because we have for the time being substituted a fresh young life for a decaying, older one. Plato believed therefore that physical love can be construed as a good when it is an expression of the need for contact with what is not the self. It is not a good when physical attraction becomes obsession with the need to own, to possess, to make the other a part of oneself.

After a time, the soul glimpses higher visions. It longs for contact with other minds, with ideas, with art. One can therefore be in love—Platonically—with another person's mind, a painting, a sculpture, a symphony. One can fall in love with the face of another because it represents a perfect arrangement—in short, when it provides aesthetic pleasure, desirable for its own sake, not for the sake of possession. One can find a painting in a museum that strongly attracts the soul and sit before it for a long time, wanting only to remain in its presence, even as one might have, at another time, longed to remain in the exciting physical presence of another person. Why is one said to be a higher good than the other? The answer is that the painting will always be there. The painting is a window through which one sees a little piece of the eternal. With the painting, the soul revisits its home, beyond physical reality, where, if only for a few minutes or hours, one is in the presence of pure beauty that cannot be tarnished like the things of the material world. Platonic love is a ladder that leads past physical pleasure and upward toward the experience of pure beauty, an experience that cannot be expressed in words, but only felt by the soul.

> *the true order of going, or being led . . . to things of love, is to begin from the beauties of earth and mount upwards for the sake of other beauty, using these as steps only, and from one going on to two, and from two to all fair forms, and from fair forms to fair practices, and from fair practices to fair notions, until from fair notions he arrives at the notion of absolute beauty, and at last knows what the essence of beauty is.*[7]

For Plato, the highest form of love is therefore the love of the beautiful: in a mind, in art, in life itself.

Christianity during the Middle Ages preferred Plato to Aristotle, mainly because of his theory of *agape*. Christians believed the Platonist ladder leading from physical desire to a vision of the ideal was a ladder to God. Platonic love thus became God's love for humanity and, conversely, human spiritual, or holy, love divorced from base passions. Whether Christian-based or not, this idea continues to influence vast numbers of people and forms the basis for the popular notion that to love Platonically means to refrain from sexual contact.

Almost none of us can fail to be affected by this idealism, whether overtly labeled Platonic or not. During a long separation, lovers may imagine each other as they once looked, but in a reunion years later, they can face disappointment. Consider the major ideals of Plato's world: the Good, the True, and the Beautiful. Then consider how the world of the flesh conspires against them. To be alive is to change, eventually to be different from before, just as a flower only briefly achieves its potential. The beautiful smiling child in a photograph is for its time the epitome of how a child should look. Part of the pleasure of seeing it is the knowledge that the child has the potential to become something else—larger, smarter, more agile—but different. The separated lovers may compare present reality with old photographs, noting with sadness how the actual person is no longer the ideal person.

The beauties of the body are as nothing to the beauties of the soul, so that wherever one meets with spiritual loveliness, even in the husk of an unlovely body, he will find it beautiful enough to fall in love with and to cherish.

—Plato

Platonism carries with it an ideal worth striving for and yet intrinsically disappointing, even anti-life. (One thinks of the famous aria "The Impossible Dream" from *Man of La Mancha*, the 1967 musical version of *Don Quixote*, in which the virtuous knight declares that he will devote his life to pure and beautiful causes. But we note that even he admits his dream is "impossible.")

Even for the confirmed Platonist, a price must be paid for attempting to live in a world higher than the physical plane. In John Keats's "Ode on a Grecian Urn" (1820), the poet envies the inanimate lovers pictured on the urn as being superior to human lovers because they will not suffer the pains of aging and death: "All human passion far above / The burning forehead and the parching tongue." The pictured lovers will stay the same: "Forever wilt thou love and she be fair." The poem is just one of many, many works to make the Platonist statement that art is better than life because it does not change—one of many works to view the love of art as equivalent to the highest form of love.

A mathematician's love of a perfect equation is an example of Platonic love: a reaching out for the ideal.

The Platonist concept that love in its highest form takes us to the realm of pure beauty, which rules supreme at the top of the ladder, may have sounded inspiring to lovers and the artists who depict them, but they have also been quick to recognize that few can withstand the rigors of the climb. Shakespeare many times commented on the human weakness for sexual pleasure, once calling it "the appetite that grows on what it feeds on." No serenity there!

In his short story "The Birthmark," Nathaniel Hawthorne recognizes the impossibility of reaching pure perfection, of experiencing ideal beauty. In the story, a husband frequently remarks that his wife is beautiful, almost perfect in fact, except for the small birthmark on her cheek. He thinks he knows a way to remove it, but there may be danger. The wife begs him to try. She wants to appear completely beautiful for the man she loves. With the aid of his assistant, the husband performs an experimental operation and manages to take away the ugly blemish. As the birthmark disappears, the wife dies. Hawthorne is saying that we cannot expect perfection in this world. Humankind is born naturally flawed and can never attain an ideal state in which love is pure and untainted and beauty lasts forever. Is the Platonist injured by striving for it?

Family Love

The majority of us, born into a family circle, take for granted having siblings, cousins, and aunts. These are the close kin who sign letters, cards, and e-mails "with love," hug and kiss us at family gatherings, and expect loyalties and favors from us, even as we expect such in return—without asking why. All these actions are performed under the rubric of the word *love*. Loyalty to the family is so much taken for granted that juries tend to disregard a defendant's alibi that depends on the testimony of a family member. Advertisements exhort us to "show how much you care" with elaborate gifts and greeting cards. Supermarkets like to show a happy assemblage of relatives around a festive table, the implication being that, if we would only shop at Food Stuff, somehow all family ties will be restored and all guilt washed away.

Still, we know the truth is rarely as pictured. The French satirist and social reformer François Arouet, better known as Voltaire (1694–1778), once defined the family as a "group of people who cannot stand the sight of each other but are forced to live under the same roof." The American poet Robert Frost (1875–1963) in his narrative poem *The Death of the Hired Man* has one character observe

> *Home is the place where, when you have to go there,*
> *They have to take you in.*[8]

It is in the love of one's family only that heartfelt happiness is known.
—**Thomas Jefferson**

This is not the final word on the subject in the poem, but these lines have become famous and often quoted as if they did indeed express the poet's philosophy. Sometimes they express the thinking of those who quote them!

How important are blood ties? The concept of family love has changed over time. Movies and television programs can barely keep up with the new dynamics. Nowadays schoolchildren easily master a complicated family tree, with visits to and from stepparents, gifts of varying value from one branch or another, and different rules required for dealing with ex-parents and former siblings, as well as the less well-defined zone of "significant others" and their offspring.

Children begin by loving their parents. After a time they judge them. Rarely, if ever, do they forgive them.
—**Oscar Wilde**

Even before the current, fluid state of marriage and family, the humanities have dealt extensively with family love and its discontents, if only because people have enjoyed reading about or watching stories about unhappy, dysfunctional families. One college instructor of playwriting told her class that "if you come from a happy home life, you may never be able to write a play."

Think of the many unhappy children in fiction, eager to escape parents who don't appreciate them or stepparents who abuse them. In popular fiction there is usually a happy ending, in which runaways return, sometimes with a fortune. In more serious work, however, there is seldom a happy ending. Literature features a host of disappointed fathers and mothers and offspring who never manage to find themselves. The bewildered Willy Loman, hero of Arthur Miller's *Death of a Salesman* (1949), wants his son to be more successful than his academically gifted friend, only to be told in a wrenching confrontation scene that he, the son, is "a buck an hour" and is never going to be anything else. The revelation shocks the father into a Don Quixote–like delusion that his son is still "going to be magnificent," impelling the poor salesman to crash his car into a wall so that the son will collect the insurance and become a business triumph.

The humanities are full of epic struggles for family fortunes and hatred between brothers who have had nothing to do with each other for years. Perhaps some people find solace in reading about and seeing portrayals of families a lot less loving than theirs. Particularly during holidays, these solace-seekers have the feeling that everyone else is enjoying a festive meal complete with harmony among the generations. Though greeting cards and illustrations show Grandma setting a turkey on the table to the applause of her loving family, and though that old skinflint Scrooge comes to his senses and supplies the poverty-stricken Cratchits with enough food to sink a ship, others are alone, eating unappetizing leftovers and maybe congratulating themselves, as compensation, that they are disenfranchised.

One not-so wonderful holiday account of family life is found in Amy Tan's *The Bonesetter's Daughter* (2001). The setting is a Chinese restaurant in San Francisco during the Festival of the Full Moon. Because of last-minute invitations, the party is larger than expected, and guests are seated at two tables. The hostess, her mother, her live-in boyfriend, and his two daughters are at one. The boyfriend's ex-wife, her parents, her husband, and their children are at another. Everyone arrives at the same time, so that unity is hard to achieve. One character, noticing the non-Chinese children, asks: "Hey, are we in the white ghetto or what?"

Following Chinese tradition, the hostess offers the first delicacy to her mother, while the non-Chinese children squeal their disapproval of the foreign-looking food with cries of "Take it away!" The mother's boyfriend pays particular attention to his ex-wife, and Grandma shows signs of dementia. A somewhat less than happy family get-together.

Can something be said for societies in which men eat separately from the women, or have separate living quarters? Or societies in which the closest bonds are among children of the same age who are brought up together, without parents? In *The Republic*, Plato advises that in an ideal community, children should be taken from their parents and raised by the state. The idea has interested other utopians (people who map out plans for a perfect society). Parents are not automatically endowed with the best child-rearing skills, so real-life courts and social agencies are often called upon to judge whether a foster family or an institution guided by experts may not be better custodians for a child. Still, removing a child from the biological parent may be desirable only in the early years and could lead to problems later on. Numerous television movies have depicted people obsessed with the need to learn the names and nature of their true parents, or unfit parents who undergo sobering changes, leading them to move heaven and earth to be reunited with their offspring. But what happens to foster parents who may have established a happy home life for children and suddenly discover that their comfortable world is about to come apart?

In The Republic, *Plato advises that, in an ideal community, children should be taken from their parents and raised by the state.*

Perhaps the ancient Hebrews may have given the world its first idea of the family as more than a convenient survival mechanism. In developing the father and children relationship between God and humanity, Judaism also created a model for earthly existence. First came the tribe, a group of interrelated families governed by a patriarch, an older and presumably wiser man with great powers of judgment over all the members. The prominent biblical patriarchs Abraham and Moses are examples. Such an arrangement was logically paralleled by the idea of "God the Father" with the same power over human children. The family circle became sanctified as a means of protecting the larger unit, the tribe. Rules against worshipping false gods or marrying outside the tribe helped to maintain coherence and unity.

Love for God, which included fear and respect, was also demanded for the father of the earthly family. Without obedience there would be no order, and without fear, awe, and respect there could be no obedience. Fear was the means by which the children of a patriarch and humanity as children of God showed their love. The sometimes wrathful imposition of discipline and punishment (as well as unexpected forgiveness) from both fathers was in turn *their* way of showing love.

Two biblical women, Ruth and Naomi, changed a traditional view of the family. Ruth, after the death of her husband, chooses not to return to her original roots but remains instead with Naomi, her husband's mother, thus forming the basis for a new family. "And Ruth said, Intreat me not to leave thee, or to return from following after thee: for whither thou goest, I will go; and where thou lodgest, I will lodge: thy people shall be my people, and thy God my God" (Ruth 1:16).

The biblical concept of family love has created a model of human behavior that is beautiful to contemplate if not easy to achieve.

Scholars who have studied the origins of the Bible tell us that a group of Hebrew elders got together hundreds of years after the historical events mentioned in the earliest portions of the Bible, gathered up all known written accounts of Hebrew history and cultural practices, and embarked on the astonishing project of setting everything down in what they considered proper order. These elders regarded the giving of the Ten Commandments to Moses as pivotal in Hebrew history, and many people since then have believed that those commandments should be binding on all humanity, not merely those of the lineage of Abraham and Moses. One of the commandments—Honor thy father and thy mother—is a restatement and an enlargement of early tribal requirements, but the principle has become universally accepted, whether acted upon or not.

To honor a parent may require specific instructions, and the Chinese sage Confucius (551?–479 B.C.E.) provided exactly that. (A fuller discussion of Confucius is found in Chapter 10.) Almost every detail of living is covered by Confucius, but none in greater detail than the rules for the treatment of one's parents and in-laws. Assuming that most households included several generations, Confucius instructs children to eat whatever food is left over after their elders have finished. They must constantly inquire after the comfort of their parents, whether they are too warm or too cold, and whether they have an itch that needs scratching. There are prescribed visits morning and evening, and always obedience is foremost.

> *When sons and wives are ordered to do anything by their parents, they should immediately respond and reverently proceed to do it. In going forward or backward, or turning around, they should be careful and serious. While going out or coming in, while bowing or walking, they should not presume to belch, or cough, to yawn or stretch themselves, to stand on one foot, or to lean against anything.*[9]

The rules set down by Confucius may sound quaint to viewers brought up in a child-centered home and nurtured with the idea that individual happiness is more important than tradition or loyalty to the family. Today's audiences and readers usually cheer when the obedient (and therefore repressed) young adult leaves home to seek a fortune far from the restrictive rules of the tribe. Nonetheless, respect for the wisdom of the strong patriarch or matriarch remains alive and well in cultures throughout the world—and even here, though it may be limited to the enjoyment of nostalgic glances backward. One of the reasons for the enduring popularity of the 1967 musical *Fiddler on the Roof* seems to be that its subject matter—the strength of the family unit and its ability to survive oppression—appeals to many who might accept the weakness of family bonds but secretly wish it were otherwise.

Two plays by Federico García Lorca (whose poetry is discussed in Chapter 4) illustrate the tragic consequences of strong parental control. In both, mothers claim the right to steer the destinies of their daughters and to have the final say about when and whom they marry. In *Blood Wedding* (1935) a young woman who is promised to a man she does not love runs off with someone else, a solution that cannot end happily in the repressed, traditional Spanish society of Lorca's plays. *The House of Bernarda Alba* (1940) explores the tragic effect of a fiercely dominating matriarch over her daughters in a cheerless household dominated by unbreakable rules of endless mourning, forced chastity, and waiting without joy for an arranged match to materialize.

In a similar vein, a dominating mother in the 1993 Mexican film *Like Water for Chocolate* demands that her daughter marry no one at all in order to continue to cook and otherwise take care of the household. All the daughter can anticipate in life is becoming the caregiver of an aging parent.

Steinbeck's Ma Joad gave the world one of its most memorable portraits of the matriarch who struggles to keep the family together.

John Steinbeck's *The Grapes of Wrath* gave the world one of the most memorable portraits of a matriarch with responsibility for keeping her family together: Ma Joad. In the 1930s, the Joad family lose their farm in Oklahoma and join hundreds of other displaced "Okies" on a grueling migration to California, where they pick fruit from sunup to sundown for a paltry salary. As the men devour the few scraps of food that the Joads can afford, they do not notice that Ma has none of her own. When one of the sons asks if there is any more food, she says in a voice that tries to sound pleasant and hopeful but nonetheless tears at the heart: "No, son, they ain't." The novel has attained the status of a classic, and

Jane Darwell as Ma Joad, Henry Fonda as Tom Joad, and Russell Simpson as Pa in the 1940 John Ford film version of *The Grapes of Wrath*. Ma Joad has become the model of the strong matriarch.

Source: Bettmann/Corbis.

Ma Joad has taken her place among the great archetypes of the family protector. Though Steinbeck has often been criticized for suggesting that a woman's role is solely to look after her family, the truth is that Ma Joad is heroic in the best sense of that word.

All strong parents in American literature are not as self-sacrificing as Ma Joad. One of the most overbearing fathers is the frightening creation of Henry James (1843–1915) in his 1881 novella *Washington Square*, later to become a play and film of the 1940s, both called *The Heiress*. This father makes no attempt to conceal his disappointment in his daughter, reminding her that she is far less attractive in every way than the mother who died giving birth to her. The daughter is told that she lacks grace and charm and the feminine ability to flirt and make small talk. In an age when a proper marriage is the only suitable future for a gentleman's daughter, she is continually reminded of her sad deficiencies.

The father in Henry James's Washington Square *is a memorable portrait of the dominating patriarch who doesn't know how to give love.*

At length a suitor appears, a handsome, charming young man, who woos her and asks her to be his wife. The father decides, however, that the suitor is nothing but a fortune-hunter. Why else would such a handsome person take an interest in his daughter? The father announces his intention of bequeathing his money to a charitable institution if the marriage takes place, but the daughter is confident her suitor will marry her anyway. They plan an elopement, but she is left broken-heartedly waiting for the man who claimed to love her but never comes for her.

Years later, after she has inherited her father's wealth, the man returns. Full of apologies and renewed declarations of love, he again asks her to marry him. Again she agrees to an elopement. But this time she does not open the front door as he stands there pounding on it and calling to her. As his cries fill the empty street, she lights a lamp and goes upstairs to bed. When her aunt asks how she can be so cruel, the heiress replies with a stony face, "I have been taught by masters."

Often the unhappiness caused by dominating parents is treated comically. Countless stories for thousands of years have been built around the desire of an amorous couple to outwit the marriage plans a parent has made for them. Readers and viewers are expected to be (and usually are) on the side of impetuous youths as they outwit their more unbending elders. We delight in seeing a daughter in a Molière comedy find a devious but clever way to marry the man she loves instead of a boorish aristocrat chosen by her father.

Nor should we believe that family domination of children's destiny has been limited to stage and fiction. In her 1984 study of the struggle for women's independence, *The Weaker Vessel*, Antonia Fraser writes about the arranged marriage. "During this period, the emotion we should now term romantic love was treated with a mixture of suspicion, contempt, and outright disgust by virtually all pundits," Fraser tells us, and "that tender passion which has animated much of the great literature of the world . . . received a hearty condemnation. Nor was this a revolutionary state of affairs in seventeenth-century England, the arranged marriage as opposed to the romantic union having been preferred by most societies."[10]

Friendship

Aristotle, unlike his teacher Plato, does not say much about love but is a strong believer in friendship. As we have seen, he includes it among the highest goods of the happy life. For him, friendship is a strong bond between individuals sharing common interests and moral values, and it is thus suspiciously like Plato's ideal of the perfect non-physical relationship, except that Platonist love need not involve interaction with another person at all. Our nature, however, seems to require, whether we like it or not, that we have ties with other people who cause our lives to intertwine with theirs. Some of these ties, as in friendship, are of our own choosing; often, as in the family circle, they are not.

Even if we never ascend to the top of Plato's ladder, close friendship with another person is usually attainable and satisfies the Platonist requirements for a form of love that exists on a higher than physical plane. Experience shows that some of our friendships last far longer than physical obsession. Plato defines friends as "a single soul dwelling in two bodies." Almost as strong a tribute to friendship is this statement from the biblical Book of Revelations: "A faithful friend is a strong defense; and he that hath found one hath found a treasure."

Love is blind; friendship closes its eyes.

—Old proverb

If *kinfolk* is the traditional word for people related by blood, there ought to be a designation for the friendship that has in some ways replaced the bonds of family, a new "next of kin," "superkin," or "kin by choice": people who choose to live together, starting out perhaps for economic reasons as roommates sharing the rent on an apartment. They also share their struggles to begin careers and to make important decisions about romance. Perhaps they find that these special kinfolk understand them in ways their parents do not. The new—usually urban—families depicted in movies and on Broadway and television have found a responsive audience among young people who, overtly or otherwise, may long to substitute a self-selected family for the one into which they were born.

The international stage hit *Hair* (1969), subtitled "The American Tribal Love Rock Musical," ushered in the era of the family with a common bond that is not biological, focusing on a spontaneous family of young men and women, bonded by a mutual hatred of the war in Vietnam. The Broadway musical *Rent*, playing for more than a decade to packed houses, continued the tradition of the new family. The television sitcom *Friends* attracted millions of viewers each week during its ten-year run, and nearly that many in reruns. In fact, it has been called the most successful TV show in history. Audiences ranged in age from the very young to the elderly. Clearly, it struck a responsive note, and that may have had something to do with alarming reports about the gradual eroding of the **nuclear family**. Once considered the foundation of our society, the nuclear family, comprising parents, children, and often one or both grandparents, has given way to the *extended family*, which may include some blood relatives as well as lifelong friends and even recent acquaintances with whom quick bonds are established. *Friends* represented this new family, and perhaps its enormous popularity is evidence that Americans secretly fear the isolation that a swiftly moving, rapidly changing society can bring.

When people join like-minded groups, they tend to become extreme versions of what they were originally. This could mean that consciously choosing a family is another way of affirming individuality. Because one is not living in isolation, there is group support for peculiarities, even though the combined peculiarities of this new family can easily result in bickering and wounded egos. At the same time, there is the tacit realization that the front door is always open.

In times gone by, friendship may not have been as desirable as it now seems to be in our fragmented society. In *Hamlet*, for example, Polonius gives his son Laertes some patriarchal advice before the young man sets out to discover his place in the world: "Neither a borrower nor a lender be; for loan oft loses both itself and friend." This advice is tough-minded, isn't it? The implication is that friendship won't withstand either borrowing or lending. If the loan isn't paid back, chances are neither person will ever speak to the other again.

Friendship is seldom lasting but between equals.
—**Samuel Johnson**

Far more cynical are two recommendations about friendship made two centuries apart. In the novel *Tom Jones* by Henry Fielding (1707–1754), we are told: "when you have made your Fortune by the good Offices of a Friend, you are advised to discard him as soon as you can." In other words, what is a friend if not someone you can use to better your own station in life? One wishes that particular definition were indeed a thing of the past! Just as cynical and self-centered is the presumed wit of this remark from F. Scott Fitzgerald, author of *The Great Gatsby*: "It is in the thirties that we want friends. In the forties we know they won't save us any more than love did."

Close in spirit to the superkin idea of family is the buddy relationship, extolled in two classic novels: Cervantes's *Don Quixote* and Mark Twain's *Huckleberry Finn*. In both cases, we note, the close bond between two men may have something to do with the fact that one outranks the other.

In Cervantes's novel, the buddies are Don Quixote, a crazed old man who believes he is a young chivalrous knight, and his faithful servant, Sancho Panza, who knows exactly what his master is but who deeply loves his idealism, however misguided it may be. If love is sometimes defined as caring more for another than for oneself, Sancho Panza, in dedicating his life to a man who has lost all contact with reality, and nurturing and protecting him from the jeers of the crude world, brings us face to face with the veritable icon of that trait. Whether or not it exists

In the film version of *Driving Miss Daisy*, Danny (Morgan Freeman) lets Miss Daisy (Jessica Tandy) think she is fully independent.

Source: Warner Bros Courtesy Everett Collection.

in the real world between friends, readers may decide for themselves. The servant's love for the master is the more admirable when we consider that the master is too far gone to appreciate it, and it may be that the fragile health of the master makes it easier for the servant to devote his entire being to him.

Love sickness needs a love cure.
—**Chinese proverb**

That relationship has contemporary parallels, as in Alfred Uhry's Pulitzer Prize–winning play *Driving Miss Daisy* (1988). The master in this case is a feisty old woman who belongs to Atlanta's moneyed aristocracy. The servant is her African American chauffeur, who understands and accepts the racial barriers separating them but, like Sancho Panza, has a deep-rooted loyalty toward and genuine love for the woman. He does all he can to protect her from the knowledge that she is close to senility and will soon be utterly incapable of even feeding herself. The popularity of both the play and the movie version may be a testament to audience nostalgia for a vanished past in which such unquestioning devotion could exist. Nor can that relationship be considered racist, because, like Sancho Panza, the chauffeur is superior to Miss Daisy both physically and mentally.

Huckleberry Finn begins with a continuation from an earlier novel of the buddy adventures of Huck and Tom Sawyer, but the author must have realized that Tom was too middle class, too much of a conformist to fully understand the rebellious Huck. That friendship is replaced by the bond that develops between Huck and Jim, a runaway slave. Though once more we have discrepancy in rank and ethnicity, Jim emerges as the stronger of the two, teaching Huck how to survive the hardships of life on the Mississippi River.

The age discrepancy between fourteen-year-old Huck and the much older Jim also became the forerunner of many such relationships celebrated in films and television programs in our era. Italian film directors, in particular, have been fond of pairing an old man and a young boy. The man teaches the youth about the ways of the world, perhaps as another nostalgic glimpse of a past age, when aging persons were less likely to be considered burdens on the young.

Romantic Love

We have seen how the behavior of people said to be in love is strongly influenced by time period and cultural values. Most probably, when you the reader first looked at the title of the chapter, you thought of one kind of love in particular, one that has yet to be discussed: **romantic love**. For many, the words *love* and *romance* are synonymous. Perhaps we like to think that the need for such love is inborn. When friends advise that a current suitor is "not the right one for you," the implication is that the "right person" must surely exist and will come along eventually. How many people have become lost in self-pity because Mr./Ms. Right has never shown up? The "right person" is a mythic archetype indigenous to our culture, but not necessarily universal.

The prototype of romantic love is, undeniably, Shakespeare's *Romeo and Juliet*, performed almost continuously throughout the world. It is the first work that comes to mind when someone is asked to name a great love story. There are few parallels in any of the literature by Shakespeare's contemporaries, and those that come close, such as *The Duchess of Malfi* by John Webster (1580?–1634), are, like Shakespeare's work, considerably ahead of their time. Who knows? Webster may have been influenced by Shakespeare's story of a woman who goes against the wishes of her family, preferring someone of whom the family disapproves, and dies for her love.

Still, as we have pointed out, the famous star-crossed lovers *are* smitten by passionate physical desires in the classical tradition. Near the end of the balcony scene, Juliet tells Romeo she must go inside now, and the anguished young man cries out, "O, wilt thou leave me so unsatisfied?" There is no mistaking what he means. Juliet answers, "What satisfaction canst thou have tonight?" The key word is *tonight.*

The archetype of romance has such a strong influence on us that one must be cautious about calling it a lie or a delusion.

But there is more. Shakespeare is writing at a time when women, at least of the upper classes, were no longer mere commodities. Yes, Juliet is destined for an arranged marriage, and yes, its purpose is her financial security as well as the social advantages of uniting two prominent families. But Romeo, after all, is willing to have Juliet despite the fact that, if they were to marry, both would be cut off without a penny. Hence Juliet is not property in his eyes. The play tells the world there is something more important than financial security or social approval. And that has come to be called romantic—or true—love. The language of the lovers is the language of romance as far as subsequent eras have been concerned. Nobody is saying that romance is an experience entirely separate from sexual passion, but most of us would agree that romance has something more that transcends obsession with sexual union alone. Shakespeare's lovers indeed seem to believe in, to share, that something more, and to give up their lives for it.

Cynics believe the language of romance is all a façade and that lust is always the reality. Yet the archetype has such a strong influence on all our lives—as do many other archetypes—that one must be cautious about calling it a lie or a delusion. Why would romance novels constitute a billion-dollar industry? Why would so many readers be lost without those heroes and heroines who think of nothing but being with each other? Poetry and songs are filled with accounts of the all-consuming emotion defined by the word *romance*, with hearts being won, lost, broken, and crushed. The despairing lover in a classic Cole Porter song cries, "You took my heart and threw it away." The heart, not some other part of the body, is the location of romantic feelings.

Romance continues to be talked or written or sung about in terms that exclude all mention of physical desire. Lovers long for one glance, for the touch of a hand, for an ascent to paradise. Romeo and Juliet elevate their passion through verse. The *West Side Story* lovers in their version of Shakespeare's play do so by thrilling audiences with "Maria" and "Tonight." One real-life young soldier wrote a postcard to his beloved that said "I'd walk around the world barefoot for one hour with you." Even if so many of the pop tunes of today deal with the torments of finding that one's true love is cheating, even if romance is considered a *tragic* state, the fact remains that it is the basis of hopes and dreams for millions, the thing most worth striving for. It must therefore be a real force—and, if it comes from the humanities, what better testament to the power of myth, art, and literature? Where would we be without them?

The language of romance is exactly what we do not find in the writings of Greeks and Romans. Except for Plato they were strictly earthbound, and they saw love as an affliction, often terrible, which drives people into desperate fires of longing. It may be fun for a time, but unless one is willing to suffer, one is better off without it. Plato, with his ladder that leads to the ideal, paved the way for the eventual emergence of the belief that ideal love transcends the flesh.

The notion of the love that transcends lust and lasts through and beyond time may have been glimpsed by Plato, but it grew firm roots in the Middle Ages. We can cite these sources for its growth and spread, and its continued hold on our emotions:

Three sources for the romantic ideal of love:
the cult of the Virgin Mary
the literary genre called the romance
the code of chivalry

1. The celebration of an idealized Virgin Mary by medieval poets and artists, a practice known as *mariolatry*.
2. The *romance*, a sophisticated genre of literature about a (usually) highborn young man and woman for whom physical union is not allowed—one or the other may be married or have obstinate parents—but who nevertheless pledge their hearts for eternity.
3. The code of chivalry, a set of generally elegant actions performed by a knight to honor his lady fair, including possibly laying down his life for her in jousting tournaments.

Mariolatry

The Christian Bible does not say much about Mary, but as the religion spread and the Christian tradition grew during the Middle Ages, the subject of the mother of Jesus became a matter of increasing fascination. Madonna and Child were favorite subjects for medieval and, later, Renaissance painters. Poets waxed eloquent about Mary as the perfect woman, and particularly about her chastity. Though the virgin birth was not always easy to comprehend, no one doubted the purity of Mary. And since Mary was mortal, not divine, her purity and glory encouraged reverence for other women as well, women deemed to be superior to men—literally "above" them if they were on a balcony or in a tower, from which they could wave and provide inspiration to the adoring men below.

Idolatry of Mary, or **mariolatry**, led to innumerable kinds of artistic expression, and it carried over into secular literature as writers borrowed the idea of the virginal heroine, worshipped for her purity as the poets worshipped Mary. Earthly love was thus presented in spiritual terms, even if lust were secretly there as well.

The same period saw a rebirth of interest in Plato's theory of love. It now became readily understood as the pursuit of an ideal—pure, chaste, true, and undefiled by lust—the love that cannot be destroyed, even in the grave. This ideal, we repeat, is still very much with us, despite attacks by an all-pervasive cynicism.

Romance and Chivalry

The **romance** is a literary genre that began with the long fictional narratives popular during the eleventh and twelfth centuries. The word *romance* derives from the French *roman*, which today is translated as "novel." Romances were told rather than written, since there was no printing press, and storytelling had become an art form. Though they usually revolved around a man and a woman, the stories were not always about love but might include perilous journeys to distant Eastern lands at the time of the Crusades. Told from the Christian point of view they presented dangers lying in wait for noble knights in combat with "infidels." Many of the best-loved romances were stories about King Arthur, Camelot, and the knights of the Round Table.

So faithful in love, and so dauntless in war,
There never was a knight like the young Lochinvar.
—**Sir Walter Scott**

The word *chivalry* also had its origin in France, coming from the word *cheval*, meaning "horse." The dashing knight on his horse had many admirable qualities, including a willingness to fight to the death in the name of his lady. All that was required of her was that she allow him to risk his life, perhaps while wearing a scarf she had given him as a token of the honor she bestowed. Thus was born the tradition of placing the lady on a pedestal and of expecting nothing in return, should she be disposed to offer nothing. Chivalry, the knight's code, was the ancestor of the polite gestures that are often performed even today, such as opening doors, pulling out chairs, and in general placing the lady first in any order of events. (The gentlemanly practice of walking nearer to the curb is a latter-day version of chivalry, originally meant to spare the lady from being splattered with mud from carriages racing by.)

In many of the stories, although a lady might be willing to offer herself to a gallant man, they could not form a lasting union because one of them was already married or otherwise unavailable. Typically such marriages were arranged by families more interested in property and financial gain than in the happiness of the offspring. Perhaps the loving couple experienced a few moments of physical gratification in secret, but on the surface was the assumption that love denied was nobler than a loveless marriage. Love outside of marriage was made to seem chaste.

A second assumption was that true love was made in heaven and was therefore elevated above earthly concerns such as bodily pleasure, marriages of convenience, and the wealth they brought. The belief that heaven destines each of us for someone else and that this someone is the right and only mate has persisted through the centuries. Even if no union ever takes place between two right people, the rightness lasts forever.

One of the enduring romantic and unconsummated relationships in the Middle Ages was that of Dante (Chapter 3) and the woman he called Beatrice, whom he presumably first saw when he was nine years old and whom he later immortalized in *The Divine Comedy*.

> *At that moment, I say most truly that the spirit of life, which hath its dwelling in the secretest chamber of the heart, began to tremble so violently that the least pulses of my body shook therewith; and trembling it said these words "Here is a deity stronger than I; who, coming, shall rule over me." . . . I in my boyhood often went in search of her, and found her so noble and praiseworthy that certainly of her might have been said those words of the poet Homer, "She seemed not to be the daughter of a mortal man, but of God."*[11]

Dante's overwhelming attraction toward Beatrice was, he said, the inspiration behind the hundred **cantos** of *The Divine Comedy*. It is the reason he as narrator of the poem is willing to undertake the arduous journey through the Inferno and Purgatory before reaching Paradise. It is understood that they will never be able to enjoy their love in any mortal way.

In Canto V of his poem, Dante visits the circles of hell (the Inferno) in which are the souls of damned, carnal sinners, who must suffer eternal punishment for their unsanctified lust. Because illicit passion swept them off their feet, they can now find no rest. Still, in the tragic tale of Paolo and Francesca, two of the doomed lovers, the poet, while not justifying their sin, nonetheless is compassionate toward them. In fact, the reason that he does not place them in lower circles where punishment is far more severe is that, even though they were misguided, at least they loved. The lowest circle is reserved for Satan, who represents the total absence of love.

Paolo is the brother of a man in an arranged marriage to Francesca, sent to inform the lady of the parents' wishes. One day, however, they are so strongly affected by reading about the passion of an Arthurian knight that they fall into each other's arms, unable to keep from enjoying the strong sexual feelings that overwhelm them. Francesca explains to the poet-narrator:

We were alone and without any dread.
Sometimes our eyes, at the word's secret call,
Met, and our cheeks a changing color wore.
But it was one page only that did all.
When we read how that smile, so thirsted for,
Was kissed by such a lover, he that may
Never from me be separated more
All trembling kissed my mouth.[12]

Yearning and aspiration toward an unreachable beloved is a feature of romantic love. Domesticity is not. Stories about romantic love tend to feature not wedding anniversaries and visits from in-laws and grandchildren, but rather, the death of one or both lovers. Lovers of music are the beneficiaries of their suffering—for example, in the erotic yet also spiritual "Liebestod" (Love-Death) from the opera *Tristan and Isolde*, composed between 1857 and 1859 by Richard Wagner (see Chapter 8) to celebrate his love for a married woman. As in the story of Paolo and Francesca, Isolde, the heroine, has been promised to another, in this case King Mark, and is escorted to the wedding by the king's nephew Tristan. On the ship they drink a love potion that creates feelings too powerful to resist.

Like much romantic art, the opera carries the implicit message that illicit love is short-lived but wonderful enough to make early death worthwhile. Ordinary mortals who live by the rules are shown to live safe but dull lives. True love is therefore often combined with death. In the final scene, Isolde kneels by the body of her lover and sings the "Liebestod," perhaps the most sexually explicit as well as passionately romantic music ever written, its rising melodic line and crescendo, its sonorous chords becoming a musical parallel to the sex act itself (according to many interpretations)—reaching a glorious high note of ecstasy before resolving itself in a serene aftermath, which brings peace and death to Isolde as she rests on the body of her lover.

If, as cynics like to say, romantic love is pure balderdash, we must be proud of a human tradition that can so nobly celebrate and create its reality.

Susan Owen-Leinert sings Wagner's "Liebestod" beside the body of her forbidden but one true love.

Source: Kranich-Foto, Berlin, Germany, Courtesy Susan Owen-Leinert.

Courtly Love

During the twelfth century, Queen Eleanor of Aquitaine, wife of England's King Henry II and mother of Richard the Lionhearted, inaugurated a form of entertainment that eventually spread to other royal courts and became known as **courtly love**. In order to amuse themselves, Eleanor and her circle of aristocratic friends would hold mock trials in which the defendant, a young man who had declared his passionate longing for a reluctant young woman, was given a series of difficult tasks to perform in order to win her approval. The "jury" would hear the case—that is, the young man's account of all he had done to win the lady's favor—and then decide whether such favor should be granted. Most of the time it was not, an outcome that was in no way expected to diminish the plaintiff's devotion.

Courtly love became known more precisely as a set of rules for the proper conduct of courtship, rules based on the recommendations of Eleanor and others as they developed this "harmless" diversion. The idea that a high-bred woman was born to be adored and a man to be her virtual slave was implicit, if not directly stated, in the romances, so that by the time rules were actually set down, there was little objection from the masculine side.

Earlier in this chapter we mentioned Cervantes's *Don Quixote* and the deep friendship between the hero and his servant. In addition, Cervantes created his own version of courtly love. The mad hero, who imagines himself to be a courageous knight, adores a fair lady he names Dulcinea, who is actually a peasant girl named Aldonza. He has no contact with her, but in his delusion he imagines she is pure and unreachable and makes himself her slave. This letter to the imaginary lady fair is the epitome of romantic love carried to absurd extremes. The Don invites her to ask anything of him, even his very life: "I am thine, and if not, do what thou likest, for by ending of my life, I shall both satisfy thy cruelty and my desires." He signs the letter, as befits his self-imposed lowly state, the Knight of the Ill-Favored Face.

A real knight, Ulrich von Lichtenstein, spent 15 years trying to please his lady, who rewarded his devotion with scorn and derision.

The model for Don Quixote's cruel lady may well have been a real person, described in a relatively obscure book of the thirteenth century called *Freudenliest* (The Service of Women) by an actual knight, Ulrich von Lichtenstein. The book contains 30,000 lines of narrative verse, all claiming to constitute the autobiography of a man who sacrificed nearly his entire existence for a princess who for years hardly knew he existed.

When he was twelve, Ulrich, knowing that, if he were to become a knight, he must adopt the role of a courtly lover, became a page in the court of a certain princess. He was so much in love that he would steal a basin of water in which the lady had washed her hands, then he would reverently drink it. Later, he fought in tournaments, developing a reputation as a brave knight willing to defeat all others in the name of his all-consuming obsession.

His only reward for all this effort was a series of insulting rebuffs. Even when he cut off his finger and sent it to her in a velvet-lined box, the princess was unimpressed. After a number of years, the lady finally agreed to allow the poor suffering man to visit her, but only if he came as a leper in the company of other lepers. After spending a long, rainy night outside in a ditch, he was finally allowed to climb a ladder and peer into the window of the lady's chamber, only to find a hundred candles burning and eight maids standing by her bed. After making a few crude remarks about his appearance and stupid devotion, she then pushed him and the ladder back into the moat surrounding the castle. *Freudenliest* concludes with some pretty cynical observations about women—rare for the time but perhaps understandable in this case.

In 1507 the long-standing rules of courtly love were altered in a book called *The Courtier* by Baldassare Castiglione (1478–1529), in which the tempering effect of the Renaissance begins to be felt. The woman, though still powerful, is now less cruel. She is well-educated, charming, witty, and sophisticated, and she requires a suitor to be her match—or nearly so. She still refuses to lose control no matter how much she secretly admires the man, and while he is still expected to sue for a physical encounter, she is not supposed to grant it. The grounds, however, have changed. To surrender to him would coarsen what was thought to be an entirely civilized relationship. She anticipates some of Shakespeare's wittiest and most independent heroines, who adore privately but hurl insults publicly!

Love is merely a madness.
—**William Shakespeare**

Love as a Game

The Roman poet Ovid (43 B.C.E.–18 C.E.), who specialized in writing about the subject, defines love as "a game of seduction." Whether readers of Castiglione agreed and privately enjoyed physical encounters behind bedroom doors we cannot be entirely sure, but during the seventeenth century—again, among the highborn and well-bred—the game of seduction became quite fashionable, often as a way of making the satisfaction of lust more delicious, as Ovid no doubt had in mind, but often as a sparring match between two people who really do love each other romantically. Courtship began as a verbal match between educated and witty partners, and ended in physical or physical-romantic union, only if preceded by stylish playfulness and earnest competition. The game of love has provided us with some of the drama's most memorable dialogue and charming characters. (Whether it will continue to do so depends on the willingness of playwrights and scriptwriters to provide clever talk, and on whether audiences will have the patience to listen.)

And when we meet at any time again,
Be it not seen in either of our brows
That we one jot of former love
retain.
—**Michael Drayton**

In England, especially during the period known as the Restoration (beginning in 1661, when the monarchy was reinstated after twenty years), the sexes reached an equality exceeding even that of the late Middle Ages. Charles II adored women and encouraged them to show their strength. In this period women took two steps forward—before the nineteenth century would take them three steps back.

English theater sparkled with plays about the game of seduction, carried off in high style and delightful banter. Mirabell and Millamant were the most glittering couple to grace the stage of that time in William Congreve's *The Way of the World* (1700). They manage to hide their feelings for each other behind a dazzling display of linguistic skill, yet manage not to hide the truth of those feelings. The play combines the purity of romantic love with the sophistication of courtly love.

Rules of the love game are observed by the couple, who openly scorn sentimentality and sincere vows. They speak in mutually curt tones and throw challenges to each other that would never be understood by people unaware of the game they are playing. Millamant sounds downright cruel when she laughs at her lover's serious face and talks of using his letters to roll up her hair. She is reluctant to entertain a proposal of marriage, despite the fact that she has never wanted to marry anyone else. Yet, according to the fashion of the day, she declares that she really would not want to surrender her cherished solitude. Besides, she has a host of other admirers. (Her name means "a thousand lovers" in French.)

For his part, Mirabell is no saint, and she knows it. He has been the lover of other women in the play, one of whom has accused him of fathering her child (which he probably did). Nor is he foolish enough to suggest to Millamant that they elope without the approval of her aunt and guardian, who would withhold the lady's fortune if marriage were to take place without her consent. Instead, he uses his wits and ingenuity to embarrass the guardian and gain both her approval and her fortune. Neither Millamant nor the audience would have expected Mirabell to be morally perfect. In this sophisticated, essentially hardboiled society one had to be a tough survivor, and true love had to accommodate the fact that it can exist only when love is a game played for high stakes by skillful players.

The play is over three centuries old, and yet audiences today would find it way ahead of its time when it comes to the scene in Act IV in which the lovers draw up a marriage contract, or prenuptial agreement, as it is now called. Millamant demands that, even after the wedding, her husband must respectfully request sexual favors from her, not regard them as automatic rights. She will sleep as late as she wants in he morning, nor will she endure being called pet names such as joy, jewel, sweetheart "and the rest of that nauseous cant" when they are in public. She insists on her privacy and refuses to be "intimate with fools, because they may be your relations." Mirabell, for his part, insists that she limit what she drinks (no strong liquor) and the confidences she shares with her female friends. He commands her not to smear her face with creams and oils at bedtime and reminds her not to squeeze her body into corsets when she becomes pregnant as a result of their "endeavors"—to which Millamant cries "Odious endeavors!" But there is every indication that both are looking forward to them. "These provisos admitted," he concludes, "I may prove a tractable and complying husband." She replies, "These articles subscribed, if I continue to endure you a little longer, I may by degrees dwindle into a wife." This is, in fact, the *Romeo and Juliet* balcony scene in a very different social context, but the underlying devotion between the lovers is still there.

Julianne Moore and Pierce Brosnan as squabbling lovers in the film *Laws of Attraction*, horrified to wake up and discover they have married each other the night before.

Source: New Line/The Kobal Collection.

Allowing for changes in language during the three centuries since *The Way of the World* first appeared, couples determined not to make public parade of their strong feelings for each other no doubt still enjoy the banter of Congreve's famous lovers. They stand as icons of how sophisticated people can hold their own in an unsentimental environment and yet not forego the pleasures of romance. Despite today's high divorce rate and the competition between men and women for success and recognition, there may currently be more Mirabells and Millamants—closet romantic lovers so to speak—than we might suppose.

In fact, love-as-a-game remains a popular theme, especially with audiences who like to show their sophisticated taste by sounding cynical about romantic love but who secretly long for its existence. We enjoy sparring couples like the gender-equal characters portrayed by Spencer Tracy and Katharine Hepburn in films of the 1940s and 1950s (see Chapter 9), who know very well they really love each other. Julianne Moore and Pierce Brosnan are the unlikely lovers, both of them divorce lawyers, in *Laws of Attraction* (2004). Catherine Zeta-Jones and Aaron Eckhart, in *No Reservations* (2007), are two chefs who form an immediate loathing of each other that we all know conceals the customary sexual chemistry. All of these romantic partners enjoy putting each other down and wanting to show disdain for conventional courtship. They quarrel more than they kiss or display outward signs of affection. In *Laws of Attraction*, apparent hostility between the lovers is raised to another level when they wake up in a bedroom and suddenly remember that, after overimbibing the night before, they had "accidentally" gotten married.

Love and Marriage

Notice that marriage has been mentioned sparingly thus far in the chapter. It deserves its own special treatment, because sometimes convenience or prearrangements outweigh love in importance; sometimes romantic love is present at the outset, but diminishes as time goes on; and often, quite often, differences of opinion about gender roles interfere with the course of true love. And yes, true love can remain throughout the course of a lifetime. Clearly, no institution, especially in modern society, is quite so complex.

The Victorian Model

We begin with the period of history and the moral code that grew very strong on both sides of the Atlantic during Queen Victoria's reign (1837–1901). The Victorian era was the heyday of the upper middle class, which decided to forget its humble past and start living "correctly" in what it believed to be the manner of the aristocracies of old. It created the most stringent code of behavior any society had ever known.

As it was first conceived, the Victorian model saw marriage as not only the goal, but the duty of respectable men and women, the prime—really, the only—source of true happiness. Specific **gender roles** were assigned. The husband was to be the breadwinner. The status of men became thus elevated, and women now saw their importance diminished. Even when the wife's inheritance was the original source of a family's income, the husband was still the dominant figure in the household, making the big decisions about where the family would live, what kind of education the children would receive, and of course, when and whom those offspring would marry. If daughters were likely to be married off to promising future

Archetypes in This Chapter

Adonis in Roman mythology, a beautiful youth loved by Venus, the goddess of love; in our own time, the very model of male beauty.

Big Brother a euphemism for an authoritarian leader and the state apparatus in George Orwell's novel *1984*; now symbolizes any form of authority that intrudes into one's life.

Breadwinner originally a reference to a father as the head of a household and its primary source of income; now a reference to anyone earning a paycheck.

Cupid in Roman mythology, the child of the gods Mars and Venus; in our own time, a personification of love as a winged mischief-making cherub who shoots men and women with his arrows, causing them to fall in love.

Don Quixote the hero of Cervantes's novel *Don Quixote*, a man who read too many courtly romances and believed himself to be a chivalrous knight; the iconic figure of a delusional idealist.

Family the fundamental social unit the world over, often incurring a sense of social obligation or guilt if the obligation is not met.

Venus the Roman goddess of love; today, any woman whose beauty causes those who see her to fall in love with her.

Utopia from Thomas More's book of the same name, a carefully planned and maintained ideal society; now an archetype of a perfect place to live or a blissful state of mind.

executives, sons were frequently earmarked for wives who would bring with them generous dowries.

The wife's job was to run a good household, to deal with the servants, to choose the menus (always with an eye to pleasing her husband's tastes), and on appropriate occasions, to show off her husband's success. The still prevalent phrase **conspicuous consumption** was coined in 1901 by economist Thorstein Veblen (1857–1929) to describe the spending habits of the money-conscious society, which included the wife's costly apparel and display of fine jewelry as demonstrations of her husband's success.

Out of this society emerged a **double standard**, by which the woman, but not the man, was expected to remain a virgin until the wedding night. The groom had the right to wed a bride untouched by other men, regardless of his own past (or present) escapades. An adulterous wife was ostracized forever from polite society, but a husband suspected of indulging in extramarital affairs usually incurred only mischievous winks from other men. Novel after novel, play after play during the Victorian Age showed the disasters that befell women who broke the moral code.

One of the best visualizations of the Victorian middle class can be found in *A Sunday Afternoon on the Island of La Grande Jatte* (Color Plate 32), painted by Georges Seurat in what was considered a revolutionary and controversial style known as pointillism. Instead of brushstrokes, the artist creates his images by dabbing at the canvas with the tip of a tightly rolled brush dipped in the desired color. The effect gives the scene an almost unearthly appearance that suggests the lack of substance in this stiff society in which proper manners were everything.

Men marry because they are tired; women because they are curious. Both are disappointed.

—**Oscar Wilde**

Remnants of the double standard remain today in varying degrees of acceptability. They continue to be influential, even admired, especially among those who value traditional institutions, such as carefully specified gender roles that provide clear rules about the obligations of each member of the household. Throughout the world today, in some societies, the patriarchal system remains in place. Marriages are arranged for toddlers, educational opportunities are minimal or non-existent for girls, women are prevented from showing their face in public, and in custody disputes, children are expected to remain with their father.

In the 1930s, when the family unit was in danger of splitting apart because of economic instability, an American play set in the Victorian era was a long-running success. *Life with Father*, adapted in 1938 by Howard Lindsay and Russell Crouse from the memoir by Clarence Day, provided a genial and nostalgic visit to what many considered the Good Old Days. Father Day, stubborn and tyrannical, is the acknowledged ruler of the family domain, believing that his word is law, almost by divine right. Mother Day appears to accept her subordinate role, managing by devious strategies to get her way, but never by bickering or direct confrontation. Sometimes she pretends not to understand what her husband is saying and talks in a disorganized manner that spins Father's head until he backs down. The play became a successful movie in 1947, perhaps because, following World War II, marriage and the family were threatened by shifting gender roles, and nostalgia for a more stable past grew even stronger than it had been a decade earlier. And what about now? Released on DVD, *Life with Father* received this Internet comment from a young viewer: "This movie is too stupid for me to relate to."

New Versions and Continued Misgivings

Despite current cynicism about the way family life used to be shown, the different attitudes toward love that we have reviewed in this chapter, *including* the Victorian Model, continue to influence our hopes and expectations. In discussing a wedding, friends usually want to know if the bride or groom has made a good choice economically, and there are nods of approval (or envy) on hearing that one or the other has "married well."

Books and movies are still described as aimed for male or female audiences, and the handsome, brave hero with smoldering eyes is still the "good catch." Even in a freer age in which the more productive moneymaker may be the wife, the househusband who takes the children to the park and prepares dinner is apt to cause talk. There are still members of the older generation who count backward the number of months between the birth of a first baby and the day wedding vows were exchanged.

At the same time, the twenty-first century has brought greater freedom to choose. Newspaper announcements of recent weddings (or commitment ceremonies) are not confined to members of the same ethnic group, class level, or even the traditional male/female paradigm. Accounts of how the couple met and were attracted to each other may often include shared trips and apartments long before a public exchange of vows.

Feminist thinking sees no reason not to be frank and open in matters of intimate relationships, even if it means denying that love alone makes life complete. The heroine of the late Wendy Wasserstein's Pulitzer Prize–winning play *The Heidi Chronicles* (1988) learns that love need not be the pivotal event in anyone's life. After a disappointing relationship with a gay doctor, Heidi, in a final scene that is anything but poignant, feels totally free to continue her life without a long-term commitment to anyone.

> *Love without marriage can sometimes be very awkward for all concerned; but marriage without love simply removes that institution from the territory of the humanly admissible.*
>
> —**Katherine Anne Porter**

A modern fairy tale, *Don't Bet on the Prince* (1986) by Jack Zipes, begins as a wise and witty (not shy, maidenly, and dim-witted) princess is introduced to a prince from a nearby kingdom. Sitting next to her at a royal banquet, he is swept away by her beauty and charm and falls instantly in love. The families are delighted and look forward to a wedding. When the couple rises to dance, however, he is appalled to discover she is taller than he. The next day, when he shows off on horseback and expects her admiration for jumping hedges and ditches, she gives instead a superior display of equestrianism. After the prince calls off the wedding, she loses the use of her legs and takes to bed. Feeling superior to the princess once more, the prince condescends to visit her but rejects her again when he discovers she converses as skillfully as she had ridden horses. Forlorn, the princess loses her voice, and now that she can neither move nor speak, she becomes an acceptable candidate for marriage. Not to worry! *This* princess decides to reject his offer and accept a different suitor, one who is shorter and less articulate than she but who admires her for all her accomplishments. Her health restored, they live happily ever after but on *her* terms.

Playwright Edward Albee (b. 1928) has been obsessed with themes of marriage, parenthood, and relationships between the sexes. His characters are products of a modern sophisticated society from which the Victorian model is notably absent, though it has not been replaced with other strict codes. Consequently, they are unable to find a secure and stable footing in any kind of relationship, marital or otherwise.

Who's Afraid of Virginia Woolf? (1962) is the story of a modern marriage between two such insecure people: George, the husband, a history professor at a small liberal arts college in New England; Martha, his wife, the alcoholic daughter of the college president, childless, bored with her life, and disappointed that her laid-back husband has never used his intellect to make a name for himself.

At a faculty party they meet a young biology teacher named Nick and his wife Honey. Everyone has been drinking to excess, and Martha, attracted to Nick, invites the young couple to continue the party at their home. As more liquor is consumed, the hostility between George and Martha intensifies. The latter makes an unsuccessful attempt to seduce Nick, who has some remnants of Victorian morality in him. He wards off Martha's persistent advances by asking her to tell them about a mysterious son, supposedly coming home for his twenty-first birthday. George warns her of dire consequences if she talks about the young man. She defies her husband's orders, describing the son in passionate terms. George later informs her they have received a telegram, telling them that their son has been killed, driving his car on a country road where he "swerved to avoid a porcupine" and smashed into a tree.

The mysterious son turns out to have been a fantasy child, the child "we couldn't have," who became central to the game of parenting they have been playing for years, and George has decided to make an end of the game, partly as a punishment for Martha. Albee, adopted when he was eighteen days old, seems, according to his biographer Mel Gussow, to be obsessed with the subject of parents and children. In this play, is the playwright longing for a different society, one in which the home is once more the core unit? Or is he writing the tragedy of alienation within society as it is now, a society of broken homes—as broken as the people who inhabit them?

Love in a Time of Health Hazards

The pairing of love and disease has a long history in the humanities. Some new works may remind us of the romantic operas of the nineteenth century, such as Verdi's *La Traviata*, in which heroines die, usually from tuberculosis (or consumption, as it used to be called). At their deaths they achieve a beautiful spiritual union with their lovers. We have already discussed Jonathan Larson's *Rent*, a modern adaptation of Puccini's *La Bohème*, in which AIDS substitutes for consumption.

AIDS has had a tremendous effect on the entertainment world. Many actors and dancers succumbed quickly to the disease, especially during the 1980s, when medical treatments were less advanced than they are now. Writers gave us plays and films about love that strengthens and deepens under the shadow of inevitable death, about dying men cared for by lovers who might otherwise have never shown the ability to care more for another than they do for themselves.

Larry Kramer's play *The Normal Heart* (1985) contains a powerful and heartbreaking scene. The caregiving lover of a man near death from AIDS returns home with a bag of groceries, hoping to induce his dying partner to eat something, only to find him on the floor, shaking from an unstoppable fever. The caregiver's profound grief suddenly erupts into anger at death and at his lover for leaving him and at the whole complacent society that pretends none of this is happening. In his rage he hurls groceries at the pitiable figure on the floor, screaming invectives through his tears. An equally memorable scene occurs at the end of Craig Lucas's *Longtime Companion* (1990) when a man holds his dying lover in his arms and gives him permission to "let go," even though it means leaving him forever.

Perhaps we can say that the health hazards of the world today have unexpectedly turned many writers away from the cynical attitude toward love that flourished in less troublesome times.

Perhaps we can say that the health hazards of the world today have unexpectedly turned many writers away from the cynical attitudes toward love that flourished in less troublesome times. Perhaps the shadow of death has led to the realization that we cannot afford to abandon a precious ideal. In the musical *Kiss of the Spider Woman* (1992), two prisoners in a South American jail, one gay and one straight, share the same cell, and though death is all around, they transcend their fears through a relationship that at first seemed impossible. The straight prisoner loses his distaste for homosexuality, at least for one night in which he finds that *any* form of love is better than loneliness and abandonment.

Love and Older People

If thousands upon thousands of younger people have been lost to AIDS, thousands of older people have found their lifespans greatly lengthened with the emergence of once unavailable drugs and medical treatments. In addition to experiencing unexpected and continued health, many senior citizens now face a different kind of problem: how to overcome society's and their own stereotyped notions of what is and is not acceptable behavior for people past sixty. Years ago, one never heard, "Sorry, I have to babysit tonight because grandmother has a date."

According to Colombian-born (1928) Nobel Prize winner Gabriel García Márquez, one is never too old to love and be loved. His 1988 novel *Love in the Time of Cholera*—made into a 2007 film of the same title—deals with both disease and aging. In the beginning of the story, Florentino Díaz, a rather unattractive and awkward young man, is overwhelmingly attracted to Fermina Daza. The lady, however, marries a successful doctor, partly because she finds her relentless suitor Florentino peculiar, if not repulsive. Nonetheless, the ardent admirer is loyal to his lady for over fifty years. When at length Fermina's husband dies, Florentino renews his suit, though by now both have reached an age when there should be no question of sexual attraction.

Nonetheless, Fermina agrees to marriage, if only out of weariness from having repelled Florentino's advances for so long. At first she has no intention of sharing her body with him, as they set sail on a long voyage to escape the cholera epidemic that is ravaging the country. One night, however, Fermina submits to his ceaseless demands:

> *Then he looked at her and saw her naked to the waist, just as he had imagined her. Her shoulders were wrinkled; her breasts sagged, her ribs were covered by a flabby skin as pale and cold as a frog's. She covered her chest with the blouse she had just taken off, and she turned out the light. Then he sat up and began to undress in the darkness, throwing everything at her that he took off, while she threw it back, dying of laughter.*[13]

So what is love in this instance? We cannot say the word is inappropriate or has no sexual connotations, for this geriatric couple indulge in passionate sex incessantly after their wedding night. It is their saving grace. Their love is not Platonic: having lost touch for over half a century, they know almost nothing of each other's mind. What they have is, however, assuredly good and seems to be the author's almost mystic answer to the world's problems.

It certainly beats hate, doesn't it?

Imagining a World in Which Only Sex Exists

Warnings about separating love and sex are evident in three works of fiction that attack **utopianism**, the belief that there are ideal ways to plan and run a society. This belief goes all the way back to *The Republic* of Plato, who describes a society in which parents give their newborns into the care of the state, which will raise them to become rational human beings, free of emotional ties, understanding that marriage is for reproduction only.

In Aldous Huxley's novel *Brave New World* (1932), there are no emotional quandaries that cannot be solved by popping a pill called "soma." Sex is easily available for pleasure alone, without guilt or responsibility. Couples get together briefly, enjoy themselves, and move on to other partners. This is not only condoned but demanded by the state. Skilled scientists take care of reproduction through in vitro fertilization. Children are thus conceived and born in the laboratory. The babies have no connection with parents; they immediately become wards of the state, to be carefully conditioned and monitored as productive citizens of the future.

The only taboo is affection for another person. In other words, sex yes, love no. In a world carefully engineered for efficiency, love would only get in the way. Something inside Huxley's main character, however, tells him that there is more to life than this, that he is missing out on something. He manages to escape this utopia and wanders far away, where he finds and joins a group of people living as a nuclear family. For the first time in his life he is happy.

In George Orwell's *1984* (written in 1948), love is again forbidden on grounds of being contrary to the interests of the state, ruled by the unseen Big Brother, who watches everybody constantly. The novel gave rise to the immortal phrase "Big Brother is watching you," now used to describe surveillance technology in public buildings, the monitoring of protest marches, and the proliferation of bugging devices. Two of the citizens break all rules by falling in love and indulging in sexual relations, only to have their most intimate moments and private conversations discovered and exposed. Their punishment is to be sent for brainwashing to a rehabilitation center, called ironically the Ministry of Love. When Orwell wrote the novel, World War II had just ended, and Soviet communism was being declared the next great enemy. The book remains a powerful anti-utopian statement, but more than that: a powerful warning against government intrusion into the right of individual privacy.

In Margaret Atwood's novel *The Handmaid's Tale* (1986), all rights except that of reproduction have been taken from women. They are denied education, careers of their choice, and the ability to choose a mate based on love. The handmaid of the title is a slave who must always wear an identifying garment; her name, Offred means she is owned by a man named Fred. When they have sex, as is required when a woman is in her fertile period, Fred's wife is present to oversee the process. The child will then belong to the husband and wife. Atwood shows that the powers of the state, even in a democracy, can be used as instruments of oppression against those deemed undesirable.

Everything is, everything exists, only because I love.

—Leo Tolstoy

The theme that runs through all of these novels is that love is a natural instinct and cannot be denied or controlled by outside forces. Some may argue that *this* version of love is ultimately based on sexual passion. Or is there more to it than that?

One of the major lessons the humanities teach us is that all of us are free to choose, and that includes the freedom to define love in a way that is most meaningful for us. Will chivalry be an important component? Or a return to the stability of unbreakable family ties? Or a game that is not expected to last? Or an ad in the Personals column?

We may choose to remain single, without feeling the need to travel with or arrive at a social event with a recognizable lifetime partner. We may be comfortable behaving according to the traditional rules requiring us to marry someone from a background acceptable to our family and friends and fitting into accepted gender roles. We may make our own rules, unconcerned about which partner earns more money, which one is considerably older or younger than the other, or even whether a relationship that seems so right at the moment will or must last a lifetime. Or we may decide love is not to be defined, only to be experienced, as the poet Hannah Kahn would have us believe.

SIGNATURE

If I sing because I must
being made of singing dust,

and I cry because of need
being made of watered seed,

and I grow like twisted tree
having neither symmetry

nor the structure to avert
the falling axe, the minor hurt,

yet of one thing I am sure
that this bears my signature

that I knew love when it came
and I called it by its name.[14]

Key Terms

agape Greek term defining actions of the spirit or soul (in an intellectual or aesthetic sense) including love for another's mind; adopted by Christianity as love for God and one's fellow beings; generally understood as the opposite of sexual love.

canto a division of a long poem, such as *The Divine Comedy*, corresponding to a chapter in a book.

conspicuous consumption phrase coined by Thorstein Veblen connoting the desire to make a public display of one's wealth.

courtly love an artificial and codified set of rules governing the mating behavior of the upper classes during the late Middle Ages and the Renaissance; principal among these was the right of the lady to make any demands she wished in order to test the loyalty and devotion of her suitor.

double standard originally a reference to the understanding in the Victorian period that men would have sex outside of marriage but women should not.

eros Greek term referring to the appetites of passion and the flesh; used as the opposite of agape.

gender role the way each sex is defined by society, including expected behaviors and the rights and responsibilities of each sex, especially within marriage.

goliard a medieval troubadour, usually a young man training for the priesthood, who sang lyrics extolling the hedonistic life and encouraging others to enjoy themselves before entering austere holy orders.

mariolatry the idealization of the Virgin Mary as practiced by some late medieval poets and painters; not only did it ennoble the life and characteristics of the mother of Jesus, but it also tended to elevate the status of upper-class women and women in holy orders.

nuclear family a family unit of father, mother, and children; once including grandparents, but less apt to now.

Platonic love originally, an ideal relationship between two compatible minds, one that may have begun as physical passion but moves to a higher plane that involves mutual intellectual and aesthetic interests; it can also define one's love for an idea or work of art or the physical beauty of another divorced from any desire to possess it; in popular usage, it connotes simply a relationship without sex.

romance a genre of fiction originating in the Middle Ages, featuring the exploits of a dashing knight and his pure love for a lady for whom he is willing to die—and often does.

romantic love a relationship that may or may not include sex, which is less important in any case than tender feelings and a desire to be with the other person for the sake of that person, not for the satisfaction of personal desires.

utopianism a belief that the ideal society can be planned and rationally administered.

Topics for Writing and Discussion

1. One of the ways Platonic love has been defined is as a ladder beginning with delight in a physical union and leading upward to the oneness of two minds. Do you believe the concept is still valid? Or is love only a fancy word for lust?

2. Is genuine friendship more, or less, important to you than a satisfying, if temporary, physical relationship? Pretend you are forced to choose.

3. Parents, unhappy because they believe their children show them insufficient gratitude, have been known to say, "After all, look what we have done for you. Don't you think you owe us something back?" Is "owe" a verb that should be used in discussions of family love?

4. American society has been affected by the women's liberation movement, calls for gender equity, increasing numbers of househusbands, and the need for more than one breadwinner in a family. Cite evidence that the Victorian model is still around, or that it appears to have vanished altogether.

5. Tap your creative energies. Write a story in which two of the characters you have met in this chapter meet each other and have a conversation about love. What would Romeo, for example, say to Ulrich von Lichtenstein? How about Mirabell and Juliet on the balcony? Or the princess from *Don't Bet on the Prince* and the daughter from the play *The Heiress*?

6. Still tapping your creative energies, write a dialogue between two people who both use only the word "love" when they refer to their relationship, yet who somehow make it clear to us that each is operating according to a different definition of the word.

7. If, when some people declare love for each other, they really mean they have physical desires and nothing else, would it help matters if one simply said to the other, "I am in lust"? Or do we need to disguise the actual meaning? If we do, explain why.

8. Does romantic love still figure in your expectations of a relationship? Or a marriage? Or both? Or is it only a figment of the imagination?

9. Watch two or three television sitcoms that deal, in one way or another, with relationships that can be classified under the heading "love." Report on the different meanings you find. Talk about the handling of gender roles.

10. Imagine you live next door to an elderly, unmarried couple who indulge in amorous behavior in their backyard, on their front porch, and at neighborhood parties. Suppose that others in the neighborhood, including your parents, want to stop what they consider disgraceful behavior, especially for people in their seventies. Write a speech that you would make either to the elderly couple, explaining why their behavior is inappropriate, or to your parents and other neighbors, explaining why their attitude toward the couple is inappropriate.

14 Death and Life-Affirmation

Overview

A firmly held belief is that the arts worthy of our attention should be consistently life-affirming, reminding us that in the long run, life is good. Why read, view, or listen to material that is depressing? A contrary belief is that the function of the humanities is to reveal the truth of human experience, some of it life-affirming, some of it not, and we harm ourselves by hiding from the truth.

Insisting on never-ending optimism and refusing to acknowledge mortality may bring temporary comfort, but we cannot ignore it forever. The subject of death informs some of the most glorious works of visual art, music, literature, and film. The reason? For many who create the humanities in their multiple disciplines, the omnipresence of death, even at its most tragic, can serve to enhance the appreciation of being alive. Both death and life-affirmation can often be found in the same work.

In this chapter we explore how thinking about mortality has affected artists and philosophers, and how the popular arts have capitalized on both our fear of and fascination with death. How do we benefit from death as a subject? First, experiencing intense creativity is in itself life-affirming for us. Second, we benefit by the reminder that we too may face problems as our lives unfold, and ignoring them is life-denying in itself, for sorrow and, eventually, death are inevitable for everyone. Once recognized and accepted, sorrow and death lose some of their terror.

Inconsistency of belief is one kind of death-in-life. Some beliefs are at cross purposes. For instance, a belief in the happiness to come in an afterlife struggles against the belief that one cannot bear to leave the pleasures of *this* life. Many of us would not mind having both a rich, exciting life filled with fame and wealth and an eternity of bliss.

One reason for despising the thought of life's termination is the importance placed on the self. It seems impossible that there should ever come a time when that self is non-existent. For some people, the next best thing to immortality is the thought of their own funerals. In their fantasy they are actually present, listening to what is being said about them. Facing up to the reality that each of us is only a temporary resident of this world, and that the

A famous artist's visualization of the afterlife.

Source: Gustav Doré, *Paradiso I.* ©Bettmann/Corbis.

world will continue without us, may be difficult at first but more and more acceptable once we get used to the thought.

The idea that life is temporary, however, can be another form of self-preoccupation. Asked whether growing old was unpleasant, one person said: "I don't mind getting old and facing death when I think about the terrible things to come on this earth." This sentiment can be rephrased to read: "The one compensation for my death is that I won't be around to face the awful future. I'll leave that to the people who keep on living." This is not an example of the courage to face life. It is a comment by someone who allows death to cast its shadow each day and who tries to escape from fear by believing that life for the survivors will be worse than death.

It is our hope that this consideration of death in the humanities will encourage you to take stock of where you are at present in the matter of life-denying thoughts and actions. You may discover that death is not always something that happens only once. Unfortunately, many people needlessly die over and over.

Images of Death

We humanize what is going on in the world and in ourselves only by speaking of it, and in the course of speaking of it, we learn to be human.

—**Hannah Arendt**

Death can be thought of in a number of ways. It may be an enemy out to get us; a force that makes us all equal; a glorious finale to the lives of the pious and the brave; a preordained end destined for everyone (but not till our "number is up"); a beautiful woman or handsome man, welcoming arms extended, inviting the dying person to a haven of peace and joy; or a natural event, part of the universal cycle. Or it can be something that happens only to people who deserve it.

Death can be a photo album with pictures of candlelit tombs, skulls, masked killers, and the black-hooded Grim Reaper holding a long scythe. Businesses thrive on such images, believing that, if we didn't enjoy being safely frightened, we wouldn't look at them or attend Halloween parties wearing ghoulish costumes. The thought of possible death provides excitement for people who love to ride roller coasters, standing up, shouting "No hands!" People also love boat rides through dark tunnels with skeletons popping up unexpectedly and bodies moving out of coffins.

Sometimes death is celebrated in a life-affirming fashion to honor the memory of those who have departed. In Hispanic cultures such as those in Mexico and Puerto Rico, the Día de los Muertos, or Day of the Dead, is an annual occurrence. Originally an Aztec custom that took place earlier in the year, it was moved to the beginning of November to coincide with the Catholic All Saints' Day. The holiday is now more often celebrated in rural areas than in the big cities, but wherever it is observed, people tend and decorate the graves of loved ones, after which there is a fiesta, with large quantities of food, including cakes and candies in the shape of skeletons.

In this section we study the many and varied possibilities for thinking about death, taken from art, literature, the popular media, and our own imaginations. The aim is to find the means of affirming life without refusing to consider the inevitable.

Death in the Popular Arts

An unexpected source of life-affirmation may be the way death (including all acts of violence, murder, suicide, and other kinds of self-destruction) is treated in the popular arts. The public that lines up to buy tickets for horror movies, murder mysteries, and perhaps even automobile races may not *know* these events are life-affirming, but in fact, they are in the sense that they turn death into an unreality.

In the nineteenth century, the popular arts included magazines, pulp fiction, stage melodramas, and tented spectacles like the circus and Wild West shows. Monthly journals with mass circulation ran serialized horror tales. Sentimental tear-jerkers featuring the deaths of young children and frail maidens were the staples of melodramas. (Audience members were advised to bring three or four hankies with them.) Pulp fiction, called "penny dreadfuls" by the British press, allowed readers to gorge themselves on lurid tales set in haunted houses, dreary castles, remote inns, all with spider webs, bodies hanging on closet hooks, distant shrieks of terror, and thunderstorms raging outside.

During the 19th century the horror story established the ghoulish images of death that have stayed with us.

A good example is Bram Stoker's *Dracula*, which seized hold of the public imagination in 1897 and has remained popular ever since. We continue to be fascinated by stories about the walking dead. In our own time, the novels of Anne Rice, revolving around the centuries-old vampire Lestat, are surefire bestsellers. Her hero's insatiable thirst for blood has even led him to Miami Beach, where he jumps out of dark alleys and kills innocent old people—a subject one would *think* would be too horrible for readers to enjoy.

The murder mystery, which appeared in the nineteenth century, paralleled the development of the magazine and its insatiable need for suspense stories that could be spread out over several issues and thus guarantee that readers would rush to the newsstand for the next installment. "Who done it?" was the original question posed by the mysteries of Edgar Allan Poe, with his detective Dupin, as well as those of Arthur Conan Doyle, with the immortal Sherlock Holmes. Emphasis was primarily on the detective's logical deductions that invited the reader to "play along" and try to solve the riddle before all was revealed. But Poe and Doyle could also provide horror and enough scary scenes to keep the reader from turning off the lights.

Circuses, rodeos, and similar spectacles continue to lure crowds that evidently love the element of danger faced by performers, not to mention auto races with their death-enticing speeds and the unacknowledged but always present possibility of a fiery crash with a driver trapped inside a burning vehicle. "Confronting" death at a safe distance, whether at a race track or in a movie house, can make us feel that we are strong enough to withstand the real thing. Nonetheless, we tend to glamorize the real thing, endowing it with exotic terrors it usually lacks in order to give us the illusion that we have confronted death fearlessly.

The real thing, however, as described by Dr. Sherwin B. Nuland in his book *How We Die*, is "not a confrontation. It is simply an event in the sequence of nature's ongoing rhythms. Not death but disease is the real enemy, disease the malign force that requires confrontation. Death is the surcease that comes when the exhausting battle has been lost."[1]

In the day-to-day world, directly confronting even the *idea* of death is considered "morbid." The language of insurance salespeople reveals much about how we deal with the sensitive issue. It is filled with euphemisms, such as "In the event that something happens to you . . ." Attorneys can tell you that even though married couples are urged to make out their wills as soon as the first child is born, they seldom do. The very words "death" and "die" are considered poor taste in conversation. Instead, we speak of "passing on" or use other evasions.

Among those who avoid talk of death are people who believe they have plenty of time before they must be "serious" about such matters as wills and burial arrangements. Audiences that gulp their popcorn, entranced by a screen full of blood, love the terror of anticipating what is going to happen to the innocent walker on the lonely street—and they must certainly have a fear of death concealed in their unconscious even as the vampire is concealed in the doorway—but it is a fear that can wait a little while before it is realistically confronted. No one who goes to these movies appears to want the triumph of life over death, at least not in the film. Sometimes improbable happy endings are tacked on, perhaps to make a film seem more acceptable to young viewers. Yet the irony is that minors are the *last* people who want happy endings. After all, the younger you are, the more immortal you feel.

Those who are a little older and therefore apparently less immortal may enjoy the spectacle of violent death, not to mention the many films and television shows about terminal illness, because these disasters are happening to *other* people. As the philosopher La Rochefoucauld cynically remarked, "All of us share a willingness to bear the misfortunes of others"; he includes real-life tragedies.

All of us share a willingness to bear the misfortunes of others.
—**François de La Rochefoucauld**

In recent years, the popular Left Behind novels have heralded the near destruction of the world and the salvation of the good. Balancing these apocryphal books and movies are those describing planet Earth wiped out by natural disasters. Both spring from the same source: the assurance that death can be overcome, either because it is happening to actors who are being paid to pretend to die on the screen, or because a last-minute rescue is possible for those who are pure of heart or at least not completely evil.

Hugely popular also are novels, films, and television programs about the disasters awaiting humanity from global warming and the unpredictable effects of climate change. In some depictions, people huddle together in their seacoast community, waiting to be engulfed by monstrous waves caused by sea levels rising to unthinkable heights.

Why would people seek escape from their fears by immersing themselves in stories in which life seems cheap? The answer is that, in stories and films involving murders and global disasters, deserving people are usually not the ones who die. In one of the early disaster films, *Earthquake* (1974), a street suddenly opens and swallows hundreds of people, except the hero and heroine. In *Titanic* (1997), one of the biggest box-office successes in cinema history, the hero (Leonardo di Caprio) freezes to death in the water, but the lovely heroine (Kate Winslet) survives the tragedy, floating on a piece of wood from the sunken vessel until she is rescued. *Both* lovers could not possibly be lost!

The 2004 film *The Day after Tomorrow*, in which Manhattan is destroyed in a new Ice Age, has become a cult classic for all who find disaster entertaining.

Source: The Everett Collection.

In the 2004 disaster film *The Day after Tomorrow*, global warming has caused catastrophic climate reversals. A new Ice Age sweeps over the eastern United States, burying Manhattan under a hundred feet of snow. The rationale, endorsed by many environmentalists, was to sound a dire warning that disasters could happen unless nations realize that saving humanity is more important than carbon-emitting industrial growth. A significant percentage of viewers undoubtedly took the message to heart, but an equally significant percentage undoubtedly went to the cineplex merely to enjoy another spectacle of suffering and death happening to all except most of the film's stars—and, in any case, to no one in the comfortable safety of stadium seating.

They cut me down and I leap up high:
I am the life that'll never die:
I'll live in you if you'll live in me.
I am the Lord of Dance, said he.
—**Anonymous folk song**

Most horror tales, murder mysteries, and disaster films seem to have one thing in common, regardless of the period in which they were written or produced: deadliness is not random. In the classic murder mysteries, there are apprehended culprits with clear motives. Stories of the supernatural usually end with rational explanations. Climate-change thrillers offer the "comforting" underlying message that reasonable people can still do something to avert the tragedies that engross audiences for two hours before the message is delivered.

The eternal fascination with lurking terror and sudden, violent death and the reassurance that it is not random or personally threatening may not completely strengthen us for the hard chore of facing up to reality. If we are to be strong and skillful in being human, we must still explore meaningful ways to say "Yes!" to life without trying to escape from truth.

Humor

I'm not afraid to die. I just don't want to be around when it happens.
—**Woody Allen**

Would-be funeral directors, studying for state boards that will license them as embalmers, often exhibit a sense of humor about their profession. In one joke, a golfer is asked, "Why isn't your husband playing with you today?"

"He died," she replies.

"Oh, I'm sorry," comes the reply. "When was the funeral?"

Looking up at a procession of cars on the road above them, she says, "That must be it now."

Another joke is about a dying man whose son says, "Pop, what can I do for you? Is there anything you want?"

"Yes," says the man. "I'd like a piece of your mother's apple strudel."

The son leaves the room, goes into the kitchen, then comes back empty-handed, saying, "Ma says it's for after the funeral."

Both anecdotes may actually hold a sane and healthy death attitude, especially for those whose profession is making final arrangements. Though many people take offense at such humor, others find it helpful. Life has to go on. Is it better to confront death in a humorous story than to suppress not only the fear but the very mention of it? Suppressed, the idea of death becomes magnified, and the more terrible is the anticipation of it. Laughing—when appropriate of course—may be better than becoming addicted to the murder tales that actually *deny* the truth of death despite the multiplication of corpses and the darkened streets down which the unsuspecting walk to their doom.

Magnifying and Beautifying Death

We have magnified the place of death in our lives in direct proportion to the emphasis on the self. Most of us want to be recognized, singled out for special achievements. Few of us can think of death in casual terms as a natural event to be accepted whenever it comes. To magnify death—to mark it as a special event that happens only after a person has achieved high status—is to create a mythology for ourselves.

We mask our fears about our own mortality in the importance we place on the death of celebrities. Perhaps many of us, consciously or otherwise, identify

Left, Victorian image of Death as the Grim Reaper; right, a humorous treatment showing Death as budget-minded.

Source: Left: Aubrey Beardsley, *The Pestilence*. Credit: Aubrey Beardsley. Right: Credit: Illustration by Christoph Niemann. First publised in *The New Yorker Magazine*.

They sang alternate measures, not louder than the twittering of the awakened wood-lark before it goes up the dewy air, but dolorous and full of the desolation of death...in a few moments the greensward was smooth as ever–the very dews glittering above the buried Fairy.

—**Christopher North**

with the pomp and majesty surrounding the funerals. Noted personalities, revered authors, often heads of state pay eloquent tribute to the lifetime achievements of the deceased. We are moved, as if this extraordinary homage were being paid to *us*. Empathizing with graveside eulogies often stands as the ultimate summing up of an individual's worth and can dispel—at least for a time—our secret insecurities, our hidden doubts about our own value to the world.

In magnifying the role of death, we also become aware of the pain of death, so we invent strategies for shielding ourselves. The best thing we can say of someone who has just died is that the end was peaceful or that death came during sleep—these representing everyone's fondest hopes.

Greek mythology offers two versions of finality. One is well known as the dark place ruled by Hades, god of the underworld. But the Greeks also had their own kind of Avalon: the Elysian Fields, a bright and sunny land of eternal happiness, reached by heroes who fall in battle. Parisians, wanting to make their major thoroughfare seem like a place of perfect joy, named it the *Champs-Elysées*, the French translation of Elysian Fields; significantly enough, it leads to the tomb of the Unknown Soldier.

In Chapter 3, the passing of the mythic hero is described as unlike that of other mortals. His death is shown to be not one of physical pain, but rather a beautiful passage into a mysterious, nonthreatening realm. Frodo, the tiny hobbit hero of J. R. R. Tolkien's popular trilogy *Lord of the Rings*, meets a peaceful end after a wonderful if brief lifetime of facing up to grave dangers in order to save others. Yet he is never shown to have died at all. He outfits his own little ship and sets sail for the Grey Havens.

> *And the ship went out into the High Sea and passed on into the West, until at last on a night of rain Frodo smelled a sweet fragrance on the air and heard the sound of singing that came over the water. . . . And he beheld white shores and beyond them a far green country under a swift sunrise.*[2]

Magnifying or beautifying death helps to diminish, temporarily, our fear of it. But aren't we better off facing death as the natural termination of our time here and not masking it in mythology?

The Medicalization of Death

The medical profession has made the conquest of death a priority. Medical research has devoted itself to finding cures for cancer and AIDS, prominent among the still unconquered afflictions. And much progress has been made in at least prolonging life or making it as pain free as possible. New drugs and medical technology have raised life expectations, but when they don't work, they add to the sense that death is intolerable. For this reason, members of the medical profession are not only saddened but *outraged* when patients die. Physicians believe they have a duty to save lives at all costs. Sometimes this sense of responsibility continues even when a patient is beyond medical help.

In the midst of the current technological emphasis on the success story of healing the patient whose disease cannot be cured, the human being who is dying is inexorably perceived to be a failure to the health profession.

—Elisabeth Kübler-Ross

Doctor shows on television have enjoyed almost unbroken popularity. In earlier days of television, physicians like Dr. Kildare and Dr. Welby were always ready to put aside their personal lives and sit by the bedside of the sick and dying. Images of death were abundant, but they were usually photographed through special lenses that obscured the stark realities of the medical surroundings.

Medical shows with death themes have become less sentimental over the years, yet shows like E.R. have reassured, not depressed, viewers, possibly because the realistic struggle to save lives is comforting.

One of the most popular medical shows of recent years, *E.R.*, is less romantic in its approach. Its medical staff is far more pressured. Mistakes are made. On one occasion a head nurse inadvertently causes a patient to die after giving him the wrong blood type. Egos are wounded, conflicts between medical personnel erupt over proper procedures—all in an attempt to make the stories truer to real life and to avoid the sentimentality of the show's predecessors. A good many episodes revolve around the torment and guilt experienced by doctors who do not always triumph over death. Nonetheless, the show aims to reassure, not depress, us. The staff of the emergency room is always there, willing to forget personal problems and grief as soon as they hear the ambulance outside. Despite the deaths that occur, *E.R.* is life-affirming, administering to our need for a way to erase the fear of dying.

The fact that *E.R.* lasted more than fourteen years with strong ratings indicates that the need to alleviate the fear of death is ongoing. On the other hand, more sophisticated viewers may be tiring of the formulaic affirmation of life regardless of the quality of the material. The artistic success of a different kind of

Hugh Laurie as Dr. House in a dark hospital show that takes a sobering path to life-affirmation.

Source: The Everett Collection.

hospital show, *House*, which premiered in 2004, indicates that the time had come for an antihero kind of doctor. Gregory House is described by a TV critic as "an almost sociopathic genius who is given to muttering bitter comments such as 'Humanity is overrated.' He's a mess of a man, filled with open disdain as well as Vicodin, which he takes to stop the pain of 'muscle death' in his leg. And yet he is a brilliant diagnostician, a last-ditch doctor who cures people the rest of the medical world has written off."[3]

Gregory House is, in a sense, a medical detective, much like the cynical antiheroes of film noir. He is a hard-nosed realist, obsessively unsentimental. Yet a good many fans of this dark show would rather have a serious illness treated by someone who may have no bedside manners whatever but can be depended on to find a solution, no matter how obscure. This is life-affirmation at a high price, but perhaps worth the money.

If famous actors play cameo roles as dying patients, we know in the back of our minds they will be revived in a different show.

Some critics point out that shows like *E.R.*, a pioneer in deromanticizing hospitals, and even the more intellectually appealing *House*, are always going to be *seemingly* but not *actually* real. If we recognize, as we often do, that a famous actor is doing a cameo bit as a dying patient, we know in the back of our minds that he or she will be revived in a different show. The wise course is to approach the viewing in the knowledge that, true, it isn't real, but still, the subject matter *is* real, and we do well to prepare ourselves for the truth by "practicing" with the fable.

Death in Literature

Death is generally easier to take on the printed page, because there is no realistic scenery or skilled actors playing doctors and patients. Yet some of the most potent insights into the meaning of death have come from novelists and poets. It would take many volumes to do justice to the vast literature. Here are a few representative samples.

A Death in the Family (1938) by poet and novelist James Agee (1900–1955) remains an American classic that should be read by anyone concerned with the effect of death on children. It is especially timely in Western society, where death has been removed from the home. Years ago—including the period of Agee's novel—the viewing (or **wake**) always took place in the living room, with neighbors and friends coming by to pay their respects to the deceased and offer a support network to the grieving family. The sight of death was thus unavoidable for the youngest family members. The book shows how a child approaches death when its reality is not kept hidden.

Rufus, the young protagonist, has never known about death or had it explained to him before his father is suddenly killed in an auto accident. Agee analyzes every minute detail of the little boy's thoughts, feelings, and confusion. At one point the boy even experiences a sense of pride and achievement because he is undergoing something denied to the other kids on the block. One memorable passage is this account of Rufus's first sight of casket and body in the living room of his grandparents' home.

> *Rufus had never known such stillness. . . . Rufus had never seen [his father] so indifferent; and the instant he saw him, he knew that he would never see him otherwise . . . an indifference which would have rejected them . . . in this self-completedness which nothing could touch, there was something else, some other feeling which he gave, which there was no identifying even by feeling, for Rufus had never experienced this feeling before; there was perfected beauty. The head, the hand, dwelt in completion, immutable, indestructible: motionless.*[4]

It could be argued that what a mature writer feels about death is not what an actual little boy would feel, but we can perhaps trust the instincts and compassion of a poet; we can perhaps trust his assurance that children are able to handle early tragedy in their own way and that the exposure will only fortify them for the pain of loss in later years.

Asked about when a child is ready to learn the facts about death, psychologists generally advise that children can deal with loss when they fully understand the concept of time: not how to *tell* time, but time as the unending agent of change. And children may be more sophisticated than we suppose, even though they may not have the words to express their knowledge.

For certain is death for the born
And certain is death for the dead;
Therefore over the inevitable
Thou shouldst not grieve.

In the following poem by Gerard Manley Hopkins (1844–1889) a young girl is staring sorrowfully at autumn's change of leaves. Instead of asking why she is so glum (as many an adult probably would), instead of telling her to come away and "cheer up" (as many adults probably *do* in order to force gaiety on a child rather than taking the time to probe to the heart of the sadness), the poet interprets the emotion she is experiencing and, in so doing, will fortify her for sorrows yet to come.

SPRING AND FALL

To a Young Child

Margaret, are you grieving
Over Goldengrove unleaving?
Leaves, like the things of man, you
With your fresh thoughts care for, can you?
Ah! as the heart grows older
It will come to such sights colder
By and by, nor spare a sigh
Though worlds of wanwood leafmeal lie;
And yet you will weep and know why.
Now no matter, child, the name:
Sorrow's springs are the same.
Nor mouth had, no nor mind, expressed
What heart heard of, ghost guessed:
It is the blight man was born for,
It is Margaret you mourn for.[5]

By contrast, the fact of the omnipresence of death has instilled writers with a deep-rooted cynicism. In Chapter 4 *Gilgamesh*, the earliest known literary epic, was discussed, and it's appropriate to point out here that the tragedy of death is one of its prominent themes. The underlying question is: *Why must people die?* The inevitable end robs life of its joys, as does the acute awareness of time passing. Along with the earliest literary urge was the unbearable fact of mortality.

One of the most famous works of pessimism in the face of death is *The Rubáiyát of Omar Khayyám*, resurrected and translated in the nineteenth century by Edward Fitzgerald. The poem is cast in much the same format as the *Tao Te Ching* of Lao-tzu (Chapter 10): that is, as a set of brief observations about life. Some of it is joyous and life-affirming, as in this famous quatrain:

A book of verses underneath the Bough,
A jug of wine, a Loaf of Bread—and Thou
Beside me singing in the wilderness—
Ah, Wilderness were Paradise enow!

The lines have become a standard way to celebrate life and love, often removed from the context of the entire work. For example, a lively song from a 1940s musical began "A jug of wine, a loaf of bread, and thou, Baby!" followed by a sprightly dance. The entire poem, however, is essentially pessimistic.

Ah, make the most of what we yet may spend
Before we too into the Dust descend;
Dust under Dust, and under Dust, to lie,
Sans Wine, sans Song, sans Singer, and—sans End![6]

For this poet, the oblivion of death is never ending. Still, we need to ask an important question. Is living in the "fast lane" the best way to shield ourselves from the thought of oblivion, avoiding the thought of and the literature of death?

The answer has been memorably given to us in a poem called "Terence, This Is Stupid Stuff" by the English poet A. E. Housman (1859–1936). Speaking to a friend named Terence, who writes cheerful but bad poetry, Housman takes him to task for his blind optimism about life. He denounces the literature of false hope, when it's much better to expose oneself little by little to the fact of sorrow and death, as he explains to Terence in this fable:

There was a king reigned in the East:
There, when kings will sit to feast,
They get their fill before they think
With poisoned meat and poisoned drink.
He gathered all that springs to birth
From the many-venomed earth;
First a little, thence to more,
He sampled all her killing store;
And easy, smiling, seasoned sound,
Sate the king when healths went round.
They put arsenic in his meat
And stared aghast to watch him eat;
They poured strychnine in his cup

And shook to see him drink it up:
They shook, they stared as white's their shirt:
Them it was their poison hurt,
—I tell the tale that I heard told.
Mithridates, he died old.[7]

Housman faces death with humor as well as a profound resignation. Rational acceptance of death as well as other afflictions is also life-affirming.

Death in Music

We associate certain kinds of music with life's final moments and the rituals that follow: hymns played slowly on an organ; a somber march played in drawn-out cadences; a solo voice solemnly assuring the mourners that the deceased is at rest in a better land. The effects of the music vary, depressing some listeners, uplifting the spirits of others.

Out of the earth, I sing for them
A horse nation, I sing for them.
Out of the earth, I sing for them.
The animals, I sing for them.
—Teton Sioux chant

Sometimes music seems to be an exact translation into external sound of the way we feel inwardly; sometimes it seems to impose a mood of its own. The jazz funeral, still conducted in New Orleans, has a dual personality. On the way to the cemetery, mourners follow the casket and walk in time to a slow and sad march, but the return trip absolutely *defies* those in attendance to be consumed with sorrow. The musicians throw off the mantle of grief and break out into joyous jazz. What it says is that the deceased is better off now, is free of life's pain, worries, debts, tangled relations, and the pettiness and hypocrisy of others. The jazz

The return from the cemetery in the New Orleans jazz funeral is an occasion for joyful sound.

Source: Philip Gould/Corbis.

funeral echoes Milton's famous line from *Samson Agonistes*: "Nothing is here for tears."

Great composers have through music explored the tangle of conflicting emotions that all must experience when the end is in sight, when no escape is possible other than to transcend the fear of losing a personal identity and merging with what is timeless.

Richard Strauss (1864–1949), one of those responsible for the transition from romantic to modern opera, is equally famous as the composer who brought the genre of the symphonic poem to new heights. The symphonic or tone poem is an elaborate work that tells a story through sound, belonging to a category known as **program music**, in which the composer has a definite scenario in mind. Repeated melodies represent major characters and events, as in the operas of Wagner. At the age of twenty-six, Strauss contributed *Death and Transfiguration* to the permanent concert repertoire, showing a premature concern for what happens as a person dies. The program notes to an early recording of the work make clear how the composer translates the experience into orchestral instruments, melodies, and rhythms.

> *A muted string figure in a softly pulsing rhythm, heard at the beginning, sets the scene. A sick man lies dying in a dark room, except for the ticking of a clock. The flickering of a candle is represented by an upward flick on the flutes, while the stifled moans of the sufferer are heard on the strings. Presently a wistful phrase on the oboe, known as the motif of childhood, indicates that, with a stirring of consciousness, the innocent happiness of youth is being recalled.*
> (Strauss, "Death and Transfiguration," Artur Rodzinski conducting, Seraphim Records, 1958)

In the next section, the dying man rebels against the coming of death and asserts the will to live. Two melodic lines—one representing the fierce demands of death, the other a desire for life—struggle against each other in a massive and richly textured orchestration, out of which emerge the strands of what will be the beautiful Transfiguration theme, played on cellos, trombones, and horns.

As these fragments of the final theme begin to come together, the protagonist slides peacefully into what we presume to be a coma, in which he returns to his childhood and then his young adulthood, revisiting as well the trials he undergoes as he matures, the pangs of lost love, the anger that wells up when one crisis after another begins to overwhelm him, leading to the worst of all—the onslaught of his final illness. The figure of death finally appears as the strings tremble and fade slowly away and the dramatic stroke of a gong is heard.

The Transfiguration theme now begins, building from near silence to a majestic musical statement of the human spirit freeing itself from the pains of the flesh and the tribulations of the world and ascending into what we have been taught to call the Unknown. But through the great gift that music is able to give us, the Unknown is heard, and visual imagery floods the mind of the listener. If the fear of dying is indeed present in the unconscious of most of us, great works of the humanities, such as those we have been dealing with, can support and comfort.

A Philosopher's Death

Unforgettable images of how some actual people faced death can be as life-affirming as the tone poem of Strauss. Exemplary lives are as much a part of the

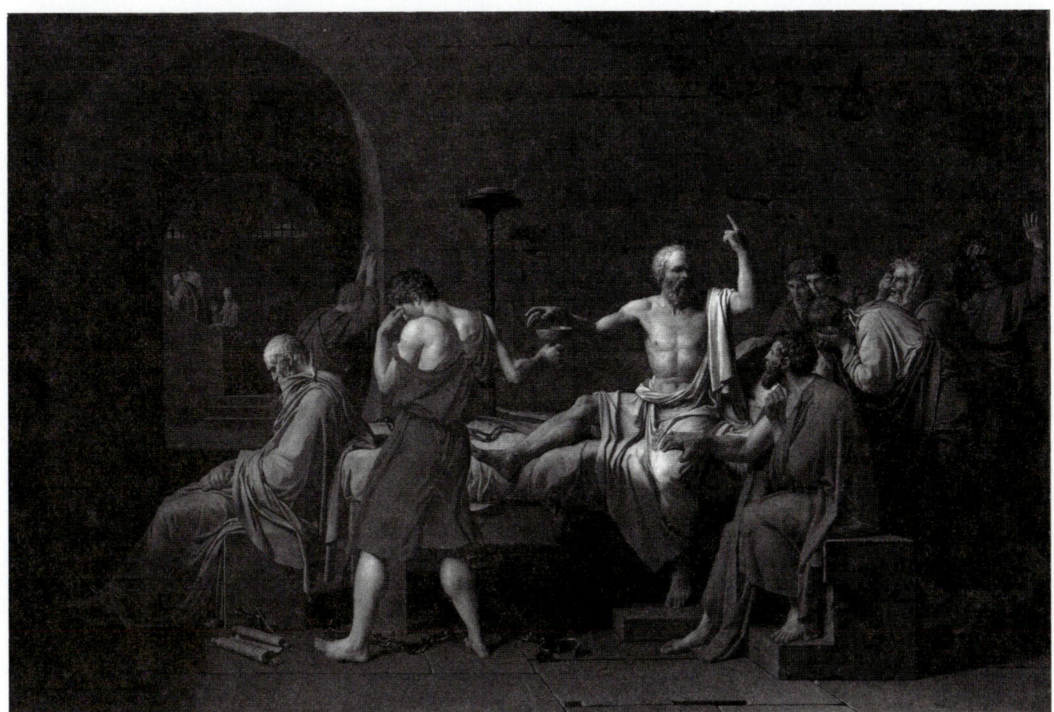

In this famous French painting, Socrates appears to be the only one who is not sorrowful over his impending death. Even the jailer who has administered the poison is in tears.

Source: Jacques Louis David, *Death of Socrates*. Catharine Lorilland Wolfe Collection, Metropolitan Museum of Art, Wolfe Fund, 1931/Image © The Metropolitan Museum of Art/Art Resource, NY.

humanities as works of art. They are in fact *living* works of art. This aspect of the humanities offers shining images of people who endured the continual presence of death without the natural instinct to save themselves at all costs. While such an instinct is not to be frowned upon, it may not be the unwavering law of human existence. What all of these people had in common is the ability to bear the thought of not existing. Preoccupation with the loss of personal identity can underlie the fear of death. An old folk song expresses an attitude shared by many people:

> *Nothing was here before I came;*
> *All that is here now bears my name.*

Earlier, Socrates provided a philosophical way to transcend the fear of death. There is no evidence that this great philosopher was preoccupied with self*ness*. In all the accounts of Socrates that Plato has given us, the mentor seems out of touch with himself in our sense of what *himself* means. His choice of death by poison rather than life in exile without being able to teach indicates that the freedom to think and communicate rational thought was more important to him than simply being alive. In the accounts Plato has written, Socrates, in his final days, is shown to be genuinely interested in seeking wisdom and not at all in making people feel sorry or afraid for him. After he has drunk the hemlock prescribed by law, surrounded by the students who adore and are weeping for him, he shows a singular absence of self-consciousness.

I covered my face and wept, not for him, but at the thought of my own calamity in having to part from such a friend.

—Plato (on the death of Socrates)

When one of those students, Phaedo, observes that the master drank his poison "cheerfully," we have no reason to believe Socrates was struggling to put on a brave act in front of his young friends. And then comes a most telling statement:

> *And hitherto most of us had been able to control our sorrow; but now when we saw him drinking, and saw too that he had finished the draught, we could no longer forbear, and in spite of myself my own tears were flowing fast; so that I covered my face and wept, not for him, but at the thought of my own calamity in having to part from such a friend.*[8]

No pessimist ever discovered the secret of the stars, or sailed to an enchanted land, or opened a new doorway for the Human spirit.
—**Helen Keller**

The passage reminds us that the loss of someone we love can also be tinged with self-interest. Phaedo has not learned from the selfless behavior of his teacher.

One reason loss is hard to separate from self-interest is that only very strong people do not need others to reinforce their identity. You can miss those who die, but you should be able to survive without them. Insecure lovers sometimes test each other with questions like "If I die, would you ever get over it?" A reply like "Surely you would want me to find someone else and be happy" would not be understood, or there would not have been a question to begin with.

Death and an Afterlife

A prevalent idea about death is that it doesn't really exist, that life continues beyond the grave. The arts as well as some religions offer concepts of an afterlife, a place where the dead retain their earthly identities and will one day be reunited with loved ones. Immortality has a different meaning for those who define it as living on in the memory of family and friends or achieving eternal life through the works they leave behind.

An argument against believing life continues beyond the grave is that it prevents us from accomplishing all we might during this one chance given to us. Another is that belief in an afterlife is simply a weak excuse to minimize our failures in this life.

Christianity speaks of heaven as a reward for virtue and hell as a punishment for sin, but the Christian next life has always had an ambiguous nature. Is it an actual place with a geography of its own? Or are the Inferno and Paradise, so vividly described in Dante's *Divine Comedy*, purely *literary* inventions? An afterlife is implied, if not defined, in the Christian Bible. On the cross, Jesus promises one of the thieves that he will be in paradise that same day, but paradise can mean many things, including a state of release from pain rather than a place of eternal life. After his resurrection, according to belief, Jesus appears to his disciples, a story that may perhaps be partly responsible for the idea that physical identity continues beyond death. The idea is reinforced by reports from those who have attended séances and claimed to have actually seen their loved ones. A popular element in films of the 1930s was the after-death appearance of the departed, looking just as the person did in life, except for being transparent.

In the Hindu faith, there is not only *moksha*, the blissful state the soul attains when it is released from the cycle of death and reincarnation, but also a heavenly paradise enjoyed by the souls of those who died with a preponderance of good karma but who must still undergo at least one more stay on earth. They are allowed to remain in this paradise for a certain length of time before revisiting the earth. When they achieve perfection, however, they are not in paradise but become reunited with brahman, the soul of the universe.

Color Plate 34 reproduces an eighteenth-century illustration from India, depicting Krishna, believed to have been the god Vishnu (second in the Hindu trinity—see Chapter 10) in his mortal incarnation. Krishna continues to have many followers, who see him as a mortal incarnation of God. He is the god-hero of the Hindu epic *The Mahabharata*, discussed in Chapter 4. In the illustration, Vishnu is shown in a geographical paradise, dancing to music played by three young women. Buddhism has no such concepts of a physical afterlife.

In Judaism, the afterlife is traditionally the memory of a good person, who lives on in charitable works and the broad impact of a life well-lived. The ancient Hebrews were a realistic, survival-bound people, and in their Bible is the hope of a better life *here*, free of persecution and despair. Canaan, the Promised Land of Abraham and the covenant, is a real place, a highly desirable fertile area over which violent struggles are still being waged. In contrast to the arid desert, it offers green pastures and may possibly have influenced agricultural images of the next world. The depiction of God as a shepherd providing green pastures for his flock reinforces the image.

In remembrance is the secret of redemption.

—Jewish proverb

The Christian vision of the afterlife is often accompanied by feelings of apprehension and fear. The Christian Bible contains, in the Book of Revelations, vivid, even frightening imagery of the world's end, a violent war against the Antichrist, and the terrible suffering that awaits the sinner. Hell, especially as described by Dante, has a tenacious hold on the human imagination. If the perpetuation of the body in heaven is often a vague concept, not so the accounts of the physical torments to be endured in hellfire. The sermons of early New England Puritan ministers are particularly filled with flesh-crawling warnings of the agony to come.

In the final scene of Thornton Wilder's *Our Town* (discussed in Chapter 7), the heroine, Emily, who has just died in childbirth, joins the dead seated at one side of the stage while her funeral is in progress on the other side. Emily is told that very soon she will begin to think less and less of her former life and that eventually she will become indifferent to it: "When you've been here longer you'll see that our life here is to forget all that, and think only of what's ahead, and be ready for what's ahead." Emily does not understand what these words mean, nor do we. How can we? How can anyone? The playwright, who may not have believed in a literal afterlife, is probably unwilling to show Emily passing into an endless void. Instead, he has her return to earth for one last time. While there, she is appalled that the living do not appreciate what they have while they have it. If its vision of what lies after death is a literary device, *Our Town* is nonetheless an affirmation of life, and it teaches that the price to pay for affirmation is first to recognize that life does not last.

Death is only an incident, and not the most important which happens to us in this state of being. I have been happy, and you have taught me how noble a woman's heart can be. If there is anywhere else I shall be on the lookout for you.

—Winston Churchill (to his wife)

The need to believe that life is somehow, if not some*where*, perpetuated beyond death is deeply ingrained in the human tradition. In the humanities of many periods we keep finding the theme of survival through love. If two people are so close that they consider themselves to be one person, then death cannot take away the identity of *that* person. It matters not who dies and who lives on: the survival of one ensures the survival of the other.

John Donne, whose sonnet "Batter My Heart" was discussed in Chapter 4, was death-conscious throughout his life, the more so as love for his wife deepened with each passing year. The thought that so ideal a relationship could end was unbearable to him. In 1612 he had to accompany his patron on a long trip, despite strong protests from his wife, who feared that something tragic was going to happen during his absence. (Her premonition was accurate; while Donne was away, his wife gave birth to a stillborn child.) To reassure her before leaving, Donne wrote one of his major poems, "A Valediction Forbidding Mourning," giving posterity the gift of an amazing metaphor for life beyond death.

Our two souls, therefore, which are one,
Though I must go, endure not yet
A breach, but an expansion.
Like gold to airy thinness beat.
If they be two, they are two so
As stiff twin compasses are two;
Thy soul, the fixed foot, makes no show
To move, but doth if the other do.

Other artists have found that art itself is the gateway to immortality. John Keats, the nineteenth-century Romantic poet, was also death-conscious throughout his life. It was a very short life, marked by ill health and the fervent need to believe that death would not be final. In one of his sonnets "After Dark Vapours," he links death (his own?) to the rebirth of life in the spring—in three startling and immortal words that close the poem.

After dark vapours have oppress'd our plains
For a long dreary season, comes a day
Born of the gentle South, and clears away
From the sick heavens all unseemly stains.
The anxious month, relieved its pains,
Takes as a long-lost right the feel of May;
The eyelids with the passing coolness play,
Like rose leaves with the drip of summer rains.
And calmest thoughts come round us; as, of leaves
Budding,—fruit ripening in stillness,—Autumn suns
Smiling at eve upon the quiet sheaves,—
Sweet Sappho's cheek,—a sleeping infant's breath,—
The gradual sand that through an hour-glass runs,—
A woodland rivulet,—a Poet's death.

Death and Fate

Fatalism—the belief that all events, including the manner, time, and place of one's death, have been predetermined—is found throughout history, religion, and literature. It is a popular way of thinking about and accepting misfortune and death. It was the foundation of Greek mythology in which great and powerful families are doomed by events beyond their control. Without the concept there would have been far less tragic theater in ancient Athens.

Tell him that we shall all bear his memory in the most precious part of our hearts. Tell him he is only before us on the road as he was in everything else, and that we are coming after him.
—**Leigh Hunt (on John Keats)**

These myths saw fate as a mysterious, universal force that preceded the birth of the gods and the creation of the world. Sometimes fate was represented as three women spinning, measuring off, then cutting the thread of life. The snipping of the scissors appears arbitrary and capricious. On the other hand, with the coming of urban society and the establishment of law, people (even the Greeks) were held responsible for their actions, no matter how much they insisted their deeds were preordained. The opposing forces of fate and free will have been a source of confusion for thousands of years. Fatalism in the courts nowadays takes the form of arguments that defendants were driven to commit crime because of a bad family background, a bad neighborhood, or temporary insanity which has robbed them of free will. Fatalism is also involved in religions that stress God's omnipotence. In Chapter 10 we discussed some of the ongoing questions: Does the fact that the deity knows in advance what will happen mean that it *must* happen? Does God therefore will it to happen?

For some, fatalism is the inevitable conclusion that must be drawn from the belief in God's omnipotence. But people of faith adopt different attitudes toward fatalism: one, depression, because a disaster can be just waiting to happen, and nothing can be done about it; two, a willingness to accept the inevitable no matter how unsettling. Besides, if what happened *had* to happen, then it's really nobody's fault, is it? Nothing could have changed the outcome.

Still, it is difficult, if not impossible, to accept dreadful calamities with serenity. In his popular book *When Bad Things Happen to Good People*, Rabbi Harold Kushner has a personal reason for discussing the subject. He lost a young son to incurable disease. In his search for answers, he considers possible errors in the way people think about and attribute motives to God. Perhaps fatalism is a human construct, not in any way connected to God. Kushner suggests that, instead of asking "Why me?" we might say "Why *not* me?" In this, he echoes what was written long ago in the Book of Job: that God gives and God takes away and humanity must accept either action without complaint.

To die is to go into the Collective Unconscious, to lose oneself in order to be transformed into form, pure form.

—Hermann Hesse

A popular brand of fatalism is one that can be accepted or rejected as circumstances dictate. A believer in free will may explain sudden death in terms of fate ("It was his time"). Some people say they don't mind flying despite their fears of a crash, because "if your number is up, there's nothing you can do about it." (The reply may be: "Suppose the pilot's number is up, not yours.") Yet the same fair-weather fatalist might avoid taking unnecessary risks, such as joining a parachute club or riding a roller coaster standing up. An individual might refuse to undergo a delicate operation with a fifty-fifty survival rate on the grounds that the odds are not favorable enough.

Islam has traditionally maintained a strong belief in the will of Allah, allowing for the peaceful acceptance of all that happens. Eastern thought has its own versions of fatalism. Indian religion believes karma determines the circumstances of the next cycle of life, but it also believes the individual is responsible for leading a better life and proving worthy of a brighter future. This outlook surely implies that the will is free to accumulate good or bad karma, but, once the choice is made, there is no escaping the consequences.

To the Buddhist and the Taoist, the *dharma* or the Way is a controlling force that operates through the choices people make. There is no conscious deity arranging the future. The universal order is a dynamic, flowing force that changes as people change. The death of anyone is part of the natural way of the universe and is to be accepted without anger.

Native American cultures show a strong belief in a Great Spirit that rules the natural world and an unquestioning recognition that there is a time to live and a time to die. *Northern Exposure*, a popular television series from 1990 to 1995, took place in rural Alaska, where newcomers to the area discovered the philosophy of the native Inuit people. In one episode a woman in her sixties, who appears to be in good health, informs her doctor that she is going to die. The young doctor, who has moved there recently from New York soon after getting his medical degree, disagrees vehemently, citing the fact that all of her medical tests argue to the contrary. Nonetheless, she gathers her family about her to bid them goodbye. The doctor, desperate to communicate his sound medical opinion, seeks comforting agreement from a townswoman, who shakes her head and says: "No. It is her time." And it *was*. The cause of death was never discovered.

Symbolic Death

However we approach death, we need to remember that we have to die only once. Unfortunately, we often *barely* live because the shadow of symbolic death continually crosses our paths. This is psychological rather than biological, but it is all the more terrible because it *can* be avoided. Here the life-affirming gifts of the humanities would help us if only we would seek them out. In this section we examine prevalent ways of dying psychologically.

Unworth

An inner sense of unworth is the most obvious form of symbolic death. We hang back from taking risks that could have beneficial results. We worry continually about what others are saying, though chances are they have troubles of their own and are not buzzing about *us*. A woman who attended a two-week group therapy workshop hoped to overcome paranoid feelings that people were talking about her behind her back. After days of exhaustive persuasion by the trainer and the other group members, the woman smiled and announced she had made a real breakthrough: "I see now that my neighbors aren't always gossiping about me behind my back. After all, who am *I* that they should do that?"

We often convince ourselves we shall fail before we ever make an attempt to accomplish a given task. Sometimes, because of unresolved guilt from the past, we yield to failure because we secretly believe we deserve it.

The sense of unworth can affect the body's condition and appearance. Often people believe they are not popular because of the way they look. Consequently, they overeat as an escape, become overweight, and bring about the very unpopularity they feared. In rare instances people suffering from an acute case of unworth may harbor a secret wish to escape from living altogether, and sometimes their bodies heed the message. There is a will to live, as we all know. Who has not observed it in action? Who has not witnessed startling recoveries that seemed to defy medical science? But there is also the will to die.

Envy of others is a sign that one has contracted the affliction of self-perceived unworth. To wish for another's looks, financial resources, possessions, or talent is to overlook or devalue one's *own* resources. The British philosopher Bertrand Russell tells the story of a painter who produced fewer works than he might have because of his fear that they would turn out badly. On one occasion Russell asked him how he was feeling. The reply: "I spent a horrible morning comparing myself to Raphael." Envy of others can also mean believing *they* deserve what they have and *we* deserve not to have anything. The self-destructive cycle continues.

Characters in literature and people in real life who suffer symbolic death often withdraw deeply into themselves, become passive spectators of the passing scene, and succumb to the belief that their situation will never change. They are people who abdicate all their power and even lose the emotion of envy. They are jealous of no one, because they attempt nothing.

Symbolic Suicide

Literature and drama have given us many stories of people who beat themselves up inside, or who long to die, even imagining what it will be like. James Thurber's short story *The Secret Life of Walter Mitty* appeared in 1942. Its hero has become a modern archetype, whose life is synonymous with a leading cause of symbolic suicide: *the need to escape from a reality that does not give one a significant identity.* Walter spontaneously, and with no warning, disappears mentally and emotionally into a fantasy world. His shrunken self-image is encouraged by a nagging wife, who tells him how fast to drive, when to see a doctor, and even where to sit while waiting for her in a hotel lobby. On one occasion Walter explains that he has forgotten some errand because "I was thinking." Mrs. Mitty responds: "I'm going to take your temperature when I get you home."

You only live once, and usually not even then.

—**Michael O'Donoghue**

In his perpetual escapes from reality, Walter Mitty lives as an airplane pilot making a perilous landing in a hurricane, a world-famous surgeon, a defendant in a murder trial, a war hero, and in the saddest fantasy of all, as a man about to be executed:

> *He took one last drag on his cigarette and snapped it away. Then, with that faint, fleeting smile playing upon his lips, he faced the firing squad; erect and motionless, proud and disdainful, Walter Mitty the Undefeated, inscrutable to the last.*[9]

Just as there are martyrs who may have died for a cause and may be said to have committed a kind of suicide, not surprisingly there is also *symbolic martyrdom.* When life appears hopeless, one recourse is to become its victim and completely evade responsibility for what has happened. Such "victims" derive a measure of comfort from having others say, "Oh, you poor thing." And they will eagerly seek out ways to keep the pity going: volunteering for tasks nobody else wants to do; making sacrifices of time and money whenever possible, and making sure everyone knows about it; reciting misfortunes in great detail, hoping listeners will make an extravagant show of sympathy. On the whole, however, listeners tire of feeling sorry for someone who demands such a response. For this reason, acting teachers warn students they must never feel sorry for themselves in the roles they play, because audiences will lose interest in them.

Death is not the worst evil, but rather, when we wish to die and cannot.

—**Sophocles**

A subtle form of symbolic suicide is compulsive gambling, at least according to psychologists. Compulsive gamblers secretly want to punish themselves by losing. They suppress guilt over what they perceive as past wrongdoing and, supposedly, do not want to win. Even if they do, even if they gamble because of debt or the desire to improve their lifestyles, chances are that, in losing, they will experience the guilt that will restart the cycle, leading them to gamble more in the unconscious hope of further failure. The 1998 film *Oscar and Lucinda* featured a pair of ostensible lovers who were linked by the need to gamble and who found themselves trapped in a vortex of self-loathing. Had they been real-life people and observed by a psychiatrist, the verdict might have been that, through their gambling, self-loathing is what they were really after.

Victims of social prejudice frequently develop strong feelings of unworth, causing self-inflicted symbolic death. Of course, the very opposite result can occur, whereby at some point the victim refuses to be victimized any longer and rebels, performing an act we may call *symbolic resurrection*. Mark Medoff's play *Children of a Lesser God* (1981) gives us a heroine who undergoes both experiences.

The central character, Sarah, was born without hearing, and though she is extremely bright and has mastered American Sign Language, she resists efforts to make her talk. Sarah harbors deep-seated feelings of inferiority. She knows that others who attend her "special" school and who speak cannot sound like normal people and therefore are undoubtedly derided behind their back. Nonetheless, she falls in love with and eventually marries the new speech teacher, who seems to understand her completely and to treat her as a full equal. His plan, however, is to induce her to talk, believing this would be the final proof that she is *not* a child of a "lesser god" but is capable of functioning as an accepted member of society.

In a harrowing confrontation scene, when the teacher/husband taunts and goads her into speaking—hoping thereby to prove to her that she can do anything—the woman screams out her resentment in a high-pitched wail that doesn't sound normal at all, and she runs off in a convulsive outpouring of tears. The hope that he has engendered in her has died, as she herself symbolically dies when faced once again with the glaring truth about herself. Yet in this fierce assertion of will, Sarah finds that she has not, in fact, died. She functions differently from non-deaf members of society, and she will function as herself. Free of dependence on her husband's hollow support, she has proved that alternatives to symbolic destruction *do* exist.

Symbolic suicide is sometimes the consequence of feelings of unworth because of the aging process. Much of American society seems in the throes of a great campaign against aging. Fitness is a multibillion-dollar industry. Almost any new diet makes the bestseller list. Cosmeticians and plastic surgeons charge exorbitant fees to impart the illusion of youth. Television commercials exhibit product after product guaranteeing the user will look like the young models employed to demonstrate product effectiveness. Older people are shown playing golf, kicking up their heels on a cruise ship, or rehearsing in the clubhouse for a musical comedy. No one ever advertises the quieter pleasures of age. Quiet features such as a well-stocked library are seldom found in ads for retirement homes. Everyone is conditioned to believe that resisting age, not accepting the biological and sociological changes that age inevitably brings, is life-affirming, the sign of a healthy society.

To enjoy looking trim for one's age, to exercise and maintain a sensible diet, to avoid excessive use of life-shortening pastimes like drinking and smoking . . . these *can* be called life-affirming and can be the signs of a creative approach to one's existence. Having attained the age of, say, seventy-five, one is not automatically required to consider oneself *old* or to obey the rule our society has adopted for its "senior citizens": *look young and act young so that the rest of us will not be intimidated by the thought of aging.*

The humanities not only consider the universal fear of aging but have supplied us with memorable images and prototypes. In the final moments of the film *Dangerous Liaisons* (1989), Glenn Close, as an aging aristocrat whose only pleasure in life has come from the game of love, especially with the most sought-after and eligible partners in Paris, finally accepts the fact of her advanced years and works up the courage to confront herself in a mirror. Without speaking one word,

Close removes every bit of her makeup and stares at the reflection of her true physical image: past middle age, wrinkled, and gray-toned. But the image in the mirror brings no acceptance—only misery and contempt for herself.

Alan Parker's darkly comic film *The Road to Wellville* (1994) makes diabolic fun of today's obsession with stay-young health fads and cults. Based on a novel by the celebrated T. Coraghessan Boyle, it disguises its contemporary relevance by pretending to be a period piece about the beginnings of the health craze a century ago. The archvillain is John Henry Kellogg, a physician and nutritionist, who founded the famous (and, as we find out, infamous) Battle Creek Sanatorium, catering to the very rich who are willing to spend fortunes to look and feel young again. Dr. Kellogg—who in real life invented cornflakes—subjects his patients to daily sessions of excruciatingly painful exercises and imposes strict rules, forcing them to abstain from meat, tobacco, alcohol, and even sex. In addition, they must soak for hours in boiling-hot water. One man dies after a wiring malfunction in the water heater electrocutes him.

The Road to Wellville was praised by some critics for its sardonic humor, but it was reviled by others who found it offensive and distinctly unentertaining. Audiences tended to avoid it. One reason may well have been that the public at large was not ready to be told how desperately some search for eternal youth in a society that discourages everyone from getting old.

> *Aging, fatal disease, and dying are not seen as part of the life process but as the ultimate defeat.*
>
> **—Stanislav Grof**

The classic literary treatment of the burning need to stay young is provided by Oscar Wilde in his 1891 novel *The Picture of Dorian Gray*. The protagonist is an incredibly handsome young aristocrat, totally committed to a life of sensuality, leisure, and extravagance. In the opening scene he is observing his portrait, just finished by a major artist of the day:

> *How sad it is! . . . How sad it is! I shall grow old and horrible and dreadful. But this picture will remain always young. It will never be older than this particular day of June. If it were only the other way! If it were I who was to be always young, and the picture that was to grow old! For that—for that—I would give everything! Yes, there is nothing in the whole world I would not give! I would give my soul for that!*[10]

Like Faust, another famous character who barters his soul, Dorian has his wish granted by a mysterious power. He thus remains young while the man in the portrait grows older, but he loses his innocence. He becomes cruel and sadistic, and he develops an addiction to every conceivable pleasure, knowing he cannot do harm to his body. Ultimately, he even commits murder. The possession of eternal youth suggests he might be immortal—and perhaps out of the law's reach. In a grisly finale, however, Dorian is sickened by the knowledge of what he has become and now despises the portrait with its wizened face that shows every evil action he has ever committed. He seizes a knife and plunges it into the heart of the painting. When his servants find him, he is "withered, wrinkled, and loathsome of visage." He has become the very thing he feared most. On the wall, however, the servants see a splendid portrait of their master in all the wonder of his exquisite youth and beauty. Immortality exists in art, but not in life.

The Eastern mind, with its acceptance of the natural cycle of life and death, youth and age, has no literature of symbolic suicide, though the physical act is often performed by people wishing to avoid dishonor. What is taught is to surrender to that cycle and let happen what must. "The way of life is soft, the way of death is hard," say the Taoists, and the death to which they refer is the one we inflict on ourselves. There is in actuality only life, only existence. The individual self just borrows that existence during its brief stay, only to pass it on to someone else. Knowing this, we come to understand that existence is always young. From the *Tao Te Ching* comes this wisdom:

The student learns by daily increment.
The Way is gained by daily loss,
Loss upon loss until
At last comes rest.
By letting go, it all gets done;
The world is won by those who let it go!
But when you try and try,
The world is then beyond the winning.[11]

For the young who have not yet learned the way life works, who are involved in day-to-day struggles to find a secure place for themselves, each day brings new knowledge. And with new knowledge come tension and bewilderment. The older person gains wisdom by realizing that everything passes. Since this is so, what makes that person think he or she will not also pass? The tragic mistake is to hold out for what is impossible.

Symbolic Murder

There are two ways to win a race. One is by being the fastest runner. The other is by tripping your opponent. Too many people deal with their insecurities by killing others symbolically, especially those who appear self-confident and are successful and much admired. The joke, of course, is that the majority of symbolic murder victims are busy committing symbolic suicide.

Symbolic murder can also spring from subterranean hostility that the "killers" do not even see in themselves.

One form of symbolic murder is the verbal knife thrust. There is a famous anecdote in the New York theater about the visit by one actress to another after the latter's opening. The "friend" embraces her and tells her that the performance was just marvelous: "I argued with everyone."

Molière, discussed in Chapter 7 as possibly the greatest of all comic dramatists, was fond of eliciting smiles from the audience with scenes in which one person, professing to be well-meaning, destroys another verbally by pretending to be "merely" reporting what others are saying. In *The Miser* (1668), the tight old codger's cook tells him off indirectly.

Harpagon: I'm glad to hear what the world says of me.
Master Jacques: Sir, since you will have it, I tell you frankly that people everywhere make fun of you; they are never more delighted than when they tell stories without end of your stingy tricks. . . . One tells a story that you ordered a cat of one of your neighbors to be cited in court, for having eaten the remains of a leg of mutton. Another that you were caught one night stealing your horses' oats. . . . You are the laughing stock of all the world, and you're never spoken of, but by the names of miser, skinflint, penny-pincher, and extortioner.[12]

"I'm too old to do that."
"What will they think of me?"
"Nothing ever turns out right."

Molière, who dared not speak out directly and risk angering his aristocratic patrons, often used the device of loose-tongued servants to make fun of their supposed "superiors."

"Darling, I loved your performance. I argued with everyone."

Symbolic murder can also spring from subterranean hostility that the "killers" do not even see in themselves. Often such murder takes place within the family circle. The British author Katherine Mansfield (1888–1923) pioneered the literature of the suppressed self, of people who can never be free to express how they really feel, but whose emotions, including those of hostility and resentment, find other ways to come to the surface.

The title character of her short story "The Man without a Temperament" is constantly at the beck and call of his invalid wife confined to a wheelchair. All day long he wheels her about the garden, responding in monosyllables to her comments. He has become devoid of all personality and interest in life. The wife senses he is keeping everything inside and at one point says to him:

> *"I sometimes wonder—do you mind awfully being out here with me?"*
> *He bends down. He kisses her. He tucks her in, he smoothes the pillow. "Rot!" he whispers.*[13]

Mansfield, who was not a very outgoing person, must have known the pain of unexpressed, and perhaps unexplored, feelings. Should we let those feelings lie dormant? What is the alternative if those feelings are too unpleasant to acknowledge?

Models of Life-Affirmation

If negative attitudes and negative internal imagery act to dampen people's lives, causing them to die many times before the actual and unique moment of their physical death, it should be possible—and indeed it is—to reverse the depression and be driven by positive attitudes and positive imagery. We are not talking here of shallow optimism. The issue is the profound realization that the potential for a productive, exciting life belongs to each of us. *We* control our attitudes, as Zeno the Stoic would be quick to remind us. **Life-affirmation** is recognizing not only that life is worth living but that real death happens only once and, in a sense, does not happen to us at all. In this final section we will look at ways of refusing to allow the shadow of death to eclipse the sunlight of living.

A DEATH MODEL
"I've already taken the qualifying exam for the third time. Now I'm out for good. I'll never amount to anything."
A PHOENIX MODEL
"I'm obviously not suited for that kind of work. Let me see..."

The Phoenix

An ancient symbol of life-affirmation is the phoenix, a mythological bird of rare and exotic plumage and supernatural powers. The Greek historian Herodotus reported that the phoenix actually existed and was known to have visited the Egyptians every 500 years. The Roman belief was that each era bears witness to the birth of one phoenix, that it lives for a very long time, and that at the moment of its death it generates a worm that becomes the phoenix for the next age. Yet another version of the legend is that the phoenix is a bird from India which lives for 500 years and then flies to a secret temple, where it is burned to ashes upon the altar, only to rise from the ashes three days later, young and resplendent.

In folklore, poetry and song, in literature and drama, the phoenix has endured through time as a symbol of rebirth, new growth, regeneration, and redemption. Religions have counterpart symbols: gods who die or descend into the underworld, there to remain for a time and then to rise, reborn and renewed.

The **phoenix model** gives structure to many masterworks, such as Dante's *Divine Comedy*, in which the poet, seeking a vision of God in Paradise, must first travel through the very depths of hell before his wish is granted. The phoenix model has suggested to many people certain ways of thinking about events. Thus "I've been through hell" often prefaces an account of some happier turn of events, or at least invites the listener to effect a happy change for the sufferer through lavish sympathy and compassion. People say "I'm going to pull myself out of this." Even the popular exhortation "Lift yourself up by your own bootstraps" has underlying suggestions of phoenix imagery.

The epic poem *Faust* (published in sections beginning in 1790) by the greatest of all German poets, Johann Wolfgang von Goethe (1749–1832), makes inspiring use of phoenix mythology. In the poem, set in the Christian Middle Ages, Faust is an alchemist—someone who attempts to transform ordinary metal into gold—and gives up his soul in exchange for the ability to discover *all* of the earth's secrets. Goethe turns the old legend into his own version of the phoenix myth, one that echoes nineteenth-century German romanticism and its strong belief in the power of individuals to reinvent themselves.

There are two distinct parts to Goethe's masterpiece, but only Part One is widely read. In it, the protagonist, having wearied of his intellectual efforts to probe the secrets of life, is willing to part with his soul in exchange for a lifetime of unlimited sensory pleasures without having to think. He bargains with Mephistopheles, an agent of the devil, who promises to grant his every wish, but on one condition: *He must never be so satisfied within a given moment that he would want time to stop.* He must live from day to day at a frantic pace, never looking back, never wishing to hold onto anything or anyone.

Mephistopheles agrees to give Faust a life of constant pleasure, but he must never wish to make any moment last.

Source: Private Collection/The Stapleton Collection/ The Bridgeman Art Library.

Faust falls in love with an innocent maiden called Gretchen, then seduces and abandons her. Charles Gounod's opera *Faust* centers on the poignant story of Gretchen, called Marguerite in the opera, and the eventual loss of the hero's soul as punishment for what he has done to her.

Courses in world literature seldom assign Part Two (published after the poet's death). It is less dramatic, as the term is generally understood, and requires many hours of reading as well as studying many complex passages. It eventually rewards the patient reader with the true meaning of the entire work: not the triumph of Nephistopheles, but the triumph of humanity. In its entirety, Goethe's *Faust* offers the perfect phoenix model, a work of ringing life affirmation in the very confrontation of life's harshest realities.

In Part One, Faust readily agrees to the condition laid down by Mephistopheles. He has decided that life has no meaning beyond the enjoyment of each passing moment. There is no truth. There is only continual change. Why should anyone ever want to hold onto a moment? In Part Two, the protagonist is older and has grown tired of a life that offers nothing but a variety of sense experiences without thought. He is beginning to long for some accomplishment, something to show for his having lived. He is also tired of serving only himself, and so he becomes the mayor of a seaside village, situated on land so low that the waves threatens to engulf it and render life there intolerable. His project as mayor is to build a sea wall, but he finds that each time the wall is extended a little further, the sea has already begun to erode what was already built. He sees that he faces an impossible task; the wall will *never* be finished. Yet this realization fills him with a raging passion to challenge the sea. He will continue putting up the wall, then going back to repair the damage. He will keep on, knowing that each day a little more land will be made suitable for agriculture, and though inevitable floods will come, the people will have raised food—perhaps a little more each year.

The thought that the human courage to accept continual change and to meet challenges head on regardless of whether one succeeds or not is greater than success itself—the thought that things are worth doing even if the work of one individual's life is unfinishable—hits Faust with the force of lightning. If he cannot ultimately win, he shall not ultimately lose.

> *He only earns both freedom and existence*
> *Who must reconquer them each day.*
> *And so, ringed about by perils, here*
> *Youth, manhood, age will spend their strenuous year.*
> *Such teeming would I see upon this land,*
> *On acres free among free people stand.*
> *I might entreat the fleeting minute:*
> *Oh linger awhile, so fair thou art!*[14]

Mephistopheles had warned him, however, that "when to the moment thou shalt say 'Oh linger awhile, so fair thou art,'" his doom will be sealed and hell will have triumphed. Faust has asked time to stop so that he can enjoy the beauty of his realization—and has lost the bargain. In a sense, all of us lose the bargain in that we eventually run out of lifetime. Yet it is within our power not to believe we have lost anything, *provided* we know that we reconquer our freedom and existence every day. Faust's original pact is made because he wants it all—wants to experience every sensation life has to offer. His victory is recognizing that "it all" is present completely in every moment and that it is far more than sensory pleasure. It is knowing that one has confronted every challenge and done all that was possible, and thus has not wasted one precious second. Faust knows he has given everything for the good of his people, and what one gives is what one also *has*. To give nothing to life is to have nothing from life.

There Is Only Now

The late Uta Hagen, giving a workshop to several young aspiring actors, asked a young woman to prepare a scene

Archetypes in This Chapter

Fate with origins in Greek mythology, this pervasive archetype suggests that things happen as they do because they were preordained or predetermined; often used today to explain disastrous events.

Ghosts spirits of the dead who for various reasons are still tied to this world. As phantoms they can communicate with or otherwise haunt the living. The term is used symbolically as a reference to guilt for past deeds that inhibits us from living fully in the present.

Grim Reaper a popular image of death as a hooded phantom carrying a scythe with which he cuts down lives as if harvesting grain.

Phoenix a symbol of self-reinvention and renewal based on the fable of the mythical bird that is consumed in flames and then reborn from its own ashes.

Time once thought to be a universal absolute but shown by Einstein and other physicists to be an abstraction that describes the rate of change but has no independent existence; as archetype, a real force that makes the young impatient to grow up and the not-so-young increasingly melancholy over their aging.

in which she would play a fifty-year-old woman. At the appointed time, the student made her entrance and spoke in a cracking voice, sounding much like the witch in *Snow White*. "What in the world are you doing?" Hagen interrupted her. "Trying to physicalize the character's age," was the answer. "Do you feel as though you are fifty?" the student was asked. "No, of course not." Hagen told her to play fifty as she would play sixteen—the student's actual age—because, barring unfortunate accidents of fate, she would feel no different inwardly when she really *was* fifty and therefore there was no reason to indulge in external and false signs of aging *now*.

For me, thinking finally came late that night as I wandered through the shattered house by flashlight. I looked up through where the kitchen ceiling had been and saw a clear sky filled wih more stars than I ever knew were possible. I realized that those stars were only visible now because there was darkness all around; they were no longer lost in the wash of light from Earth.

—**Leonard Pitts, Jr.** (**After Hurricane Andrew**)

Time is physical in the contemporary world of science. It forms part of Einstein's fourth dimension and can be measured. Time for us human beings is a habit, a social construct, something on the hands of a watch that lets us keep appointments. In terms of actual experience, what is it? Can one experience yesterday? In memory, to be sure, but we can also choose *not* to remember. Can one experience tomorrow? Only in imagination, and again we can decide against it. What we cannot control is the presence of the present moment, and regrettably, too often we are so busy with our inner thoughts we lose the sense of that moment. The more we actually experience, the less significant is the myth of time. It has been wisely said: "Time is important only when you're doing it—in prison." Even at that, prisoners can choose not to keep marking their calendars.

Ways of thinking about time are well within our power. In the poem "My Heart Leaps Up," William Wordsworth, to whom we return again and again for his quiet wisdom, has left us with this definitive statement about living in the eternal Now:

My heart leaps up when I behold
A rainbow in the sky:
So was it when my life began;
So is it now I am a man;
So be it when I shall grow old,
Or let me die!
The Child is father of the Man;
And I could wish my days to be
Bound each to each by natural piety.

Did you ever think that life can run a course that is the complete opposite of the popular way of depicting it? Your childhood can be your tomorrow. The future has not yet even begun, and you can choose never to have it. Like Merlin in the musical play *Camelot*, you can live backwards and "youthen" as the years unfold. The great Picasso urged us to remain as children, filled with wide-eyed wonder.

Internal imagery can be adjusted. To break the illusion of time rushing by to an inevitable aging and death, we can replace pyramids with circles. In pyramid imagery, we visualize ourselves rising through the ranks (in school, on the job), reaching a peak or a crest ("Ah! At last I've made it!" Or, negatively, "This is as far as I'm going!") and then feeling we are "over the hill." In circle imagery, on the other hand, life is like a Ferris wheel, rising, cresting, going back down, and then starting up all over again. This is a particularly effective image, because riders of Ferris wheels know that moving around is preferable to being stuck on top for very long.

World tennis star Martina Navratilova retired in 1994 from singles competition but returned in 1995 to win a Wimbledon championship with her mixed doubles partner, and then announced she was thinking of reviving her career—all this at the age of thirty-eight, when most athletes decide, or are told, they've had enough. The effects of time on her game? "I have to think about my shots now," she said. Never did she say she couldn't *make* them. In the 2004 Wimbledon, she played a much younger opponent in a singles match—and won! "I'm not proving anything to anybody," the forty-seven-year-old told an interviewer. "I'm trying to make myself a better tennis player so I can play the best tennis possible."

Jack Benny, one of the great comics of the twentieth century, always gave his age as thirty-nine. Audiences laughed every time he did, reacting to the apparent absurdity of persisting in such a lie. Yet, up to the time of his unexpected death at seventy, Benny exhibited the imagination and energy of the pretended age.

Einstein showed that time is absolute only with respect to bodies moving at uniform speed. If A is traveling in a train side by side with B on an adjacent train and both trains have the same speed, A and B could wave to each other whenever they wished, and for both the length of the trip would be the same. The theory of relativity also demonstrates that, as one travels faster and faster, time slows down. If astronauts could travel at the speed of light, they would never grow old. Though it is unlikely that this particular part of the relativity theory will be tested anytime soon, it does nonetheless remind us that time—absolute time—is a variable even in the universe of science.

In the depths of winter I finally learned there was in me an invincible summer.

—**Albert Camus**

A famous way to explain relativity is to think of identical twins, one of whom takes off in a spaceship that will travel at the speed of light (186,282 miles per second), while the other remains on Earth. The mission lasts twenty years as measured on Earth by the homebound twin. When the space twin returns, he will find his brother looking twenty years older, while he himself looks the same as when the mission began. It is possible to live your life as if moving at the speed of light, because unless you *want* to feel old inside, you need be conscious only of where you are *now* and what you are doing.

The most famous work by the French author Marcel Proust (1871–1922) is titled *Remembrance of Things Past* in its customary English translation, but a closer translation of the French title is *In Search of Lost Time*. Memories are pleasant diversions for a rainy afternoon, but to actually wish we could go back in time (time travel mythology notwithstanding) is not life-affirming. At forty-seven, Navratilova wanted to keep getting better.

In Eastern thought, the mind, or consciousness, is infinite. Awareness is always with us. Even memories of past events are alive within us in the everlasting moment. We carry time with us. There is no such thing as the past, and therefore no reason to lament that it's gone. Those who try to hold onto time are the ones suffering the most, for they come to recognize how quickly it flies by. Those who do not try to seize it are living vividly in the Now.

Eastern philosophers tell us that we become dismayed by the passing of time because we create the illusion of *beginning*, which we date from the instant of our birth, and of *ending*, which is death. Books end, movies end, the party is over—always the same pattern, so that it becomes ingrained in us. The Chinese poet and philosopher Chuang Chou, who lived over 2,000 years ago, had fun with verbal dazzle that is also profound:

> *there is never beginning to have a beginning, there is never beginning to never begin to have a beginning. There is existence, there is non-existence. There is never beginning the existence of non-existence.*[15]

How can the beginning begin? Where was it before? If the beginning cannot begin, then it cannot end either. In this philosophy all of us live between the two poles, but where that is cannot be precisely defined, can it?

Reinventing Ourselves

The world cannot be discovered by a journey of miles, however long, but by a spiritual journey, a journey of only one inch, very arduous and humble and joyful, by which we arrive at the ground at our feet, and learn to be at home.

—**Wendell Berry**

It's easy enough to say that memory imprisons us in time, but not so easy to erase memory. Memory is a distinguishing attribute of our species. It can brighten the darkest of days, offer consolation for loss, and link us to the past so that we don't have the sense of drifting aimlessly through life. But memory can also exert a ferocious hold over us, triggering negativity. Too many of us accumulate self-determined bad karma from the past; we refuse to let go of it and thus see no way of ever changing. What is desirable is that we learn to put memory in proper perspective, to recognize that things we have done or have been done to us in the past may have relevance to the present but *not in the same form*. We do ourselves harm when we act and react *now* as if it were still *then*.

There are those, however, who carry the pain of yesterday into the way today is experienced and finally decide to terminate their existence. Committing even symbolic suicide is in its own way a termination of existence.

Psychologists who treat suicidal patients usually try first to convince them to reaffirm life, to consider what is good in it. Often their counseling fails, and in retrospect, some of them have said that self-inflicted death can be a highly rational act, a meaningful, if somber, way of reinventing oneself that is not to be recommended—only, on occasion, understood.

The Greeks and Romans generally believed self-inflicted death served four purposes: to show bereavement; to preserve honor; to avoid pain; and to benefit the state. Socrates disagreed, warning that human beings did not create themselves and therefore were not at liberty to dispose of their bodies as they willed. Most religions that oppose suicide do so on similar grounds.

Jewish law forbids self-inflicted death, but many Jews did in fact kill themselves to avoid capture by the Romans. Early Christians, also oppressed by Romans, frequently took their own lives, apparently without fear of God's retribution. Christian denominations tend to reject or forbid the act. But a case could be made for regarding the deaths of Thomas à Becket, Joan of Arc, and Bernadette of Lourdes as suicides. Becket, the archbishop of Canterbury who refused to say the king was greater than the pope, was slaughtered on his altar. Joan of Arc, who refused to sign a paper confessing she did not hear heavenly voices urging her into battle, was burned at the stake. Bernadette of Lourdes, the peasant girl who discovered a spring that was said to have cured many hopelessly ill pilgrims, suffered from a terminal disease which she never mentioned until medical help was no longer possible, and she maintained that heaven would not allow her to use the water for herself.

What seems sad, however, is that artists sometimes end their lives prematurely, overlooking the fact that, of all people, they possess the creativity to reinvent themselves. Sometimes the reason is, tragically, the very excess of their own genius. Compulsively driven to create what we now acknowledge as masterpiece after masterpiece, van Gogh was increasingly victimized by lack of recognition and the thought that his work must deserve its obscurity. Earlier in his short life he *was* able to tell himself, defiantly, that he would paint as he liked, no matter what others thought. This was reinvention, but van Gogh ultimately lost the power to do it.

Compulsively driven to create masterpiece after masterpiece, van Gogh was victimized by the thought that his work must deserve its obscurity. He ultimately lost the power to reinvent himself.

Two major poets of the twentieth century, Sylvia Plath and Anne Sexton, took their own lives, thus depriving us of the full flower of their genius. Whereas Hamlet had seen a choice in "to be or not to be," these poets said emphatically "not to be." In both cases the decision appears to have been calculated, inevitable, and not the result of a sudden, uncontrollable impulse. Both women were feminists, believing that women and men are equals. Both were married to intelligent, productive men who may have—or ought to have—understood their creative needs, at least at some points in the marriage. Yet those needs were finally incompatible with the demands that even a flexible marriage can impose.

Sylvia Plath (1932–1963) had two small children and a husband, the poet Ted Hughes, who had his own creative and emotional needs. Many such literary marriages are full of tension, and Plath had a history of emotional breakdowns. Apparently she tried at first to make the marriage work but found that it was stifling her creativity and her personality. As she neared her thirtieth birthday, she began to fear that she could no longer write, and the inner anxiety brought her to a final breaking point, a condition that only worsened when her husband left her.

The poet Robert Lowell once described Plath as being "a little like a racehorse, galloping recklessly with risked outstretched neck, death hurdle after death hurdle topped." While the description makes Plath seem quite out of control, the signs she gave of approaching suicide in her writings tend to be calm and deliberate. There is no reason to believe she did not know exactly what she was doing when she made her final decision.

The following lines, written when Plath was twenty-seven and pregnant, say a great deal about the frustrations she was experiencing:

> *I'm a means, a stage, a cow in calf,*
> *I've eaten a bag of green apples,*
> *Boarded the train there's no getting off.*[16]

It's just speculation, of course, but were there no other options? In using the metaphor of the train, might Sylvia Plath have forgotten that there are stations all along the way, and trains travel through many different landscapes?

Anne Sexton (1928–1974) lived in a sophisticated eastern seaboard world of martinis, smart talk, broken marriages, abortions, and tranquilizers. A wife and mother like Plath, she found she could not balance all of the conflicting strands of her life and decided the rewards were simply not enough to offset the pain. Her decision to end her life was also not a momentary impulse. Sexton struggled for a long time, and she reached middle age. In her poem "Live," she writes:

> *I say Live, Live because of the sun*
> *the dream, the excitable gift.*[17]

I postpone death, by living, by suffering, by error, by risking, by giving, by losing.

—**Anais Nin**

Often quite determined to live, she may have been trying to find a way to reinvent herself. Apparently, the "excitable gift," to which she refers in her poem, was not enough. Yet it is tempting to wonder why a poet who had at least once decided that the sun was reason enough to live could not recapture the feeling again.

Perhaps the best-known literary suicide of the last century was that of Ernest Hemingway. Suffering from ill health and a dramatic loss of creativity, he ended his life with a violent blast from a shotgun. Most of his novels and short stories deal with men who exist without fear on the borders of violence and death. Throughout his work there is admiration for *machismo*, masculine pride and daring. Perhaps when he acknowledged the truth that his life of heavy drinking, prolific sexual activity, and long sessions at the writing desk was no longer working, Hemingway decided to bow out in a heroic way, as if his readers would expect nothing less—a drastic way to reinvent himself, perhaps, but for the writer, it must have made complete sense.

In Marsha Norman's wrenching play *'night, Mother* (1983) a middle-aged woman cleans the house, does the laundry, and announces to her mother that, when she is finished, she is going to kill herself. She is tired of living, tired of her unsuccessful struggle with a weight problem, and depressed after a failed marriage. The mother deals with the decision in a manner usually denounced by psychologists.

> *You're not going to kill yourself, Jessie. You're not even upset! . . . People don't really kill themselves, Jessie. No, Mam, doesn't make sense, unless you're retarded or deranged, and you're as normal as they come, Jessie, for the most part. We're all afraid to die.*[18]

What the mother doesn't understand is that self-inflicted death happens because a person is more afraid to live than to die. One must recognize that the fear of living is not always an indication of mental illness but is a rational position that must be taken seriously and dealt with as rationally as possible. Only in this way might it be reversed. The mother gives every indication of being self-centered, too much so to have read the signs Jessie must have given long before. Had she been sensitive to her daughter's needs, she might then have suggested they sit down and talk through Jessie's problems. Instead, she *adds* to them by continually trying to make her daughter feel guilty for wanting to leave her.

The final line of the play is revealing. Jessie locks herself in the bedroom. There is a silence, then the inevitable gunshot is heard. The mother, overcome by tears, pounds on the locked door. "Forgive me," she says to the daughter who can no longer hear her, "I thought you were mine."

Think back to Chapter 7, to the discussion of Ibsen's *A Doll's House*, the play about a woman who, realizing she has been denied the truth about life, leaves her husband and children, slamming the door behind her—a sound effect that shocked many in the original audiences. That act can now be seen, in retrospect, as the very model of self-reinvention.

Guilt and Forgiveness

Life-affirmation cannot happen until we do something about guilt. First, we must discover that hidden guilt is indeed responsible for anxiety, fear, the sense of unworth. Second, we must determine what is causing the guilt. Is it really deserved? Too many of us suffer from unexplained depression because of actions that often were not as bad as we thought, or were led to believe.

A classic case is that of the only child of parents who are getting divorced. One parent agrees to leave the home, explaining to the child: "Mommy [Daddy] is going away for a while and wants you to be good in the meantime." Eventually the child wants to know when the parent is coming home. After a few more weeks the question is now: "Doesn't Mommy [Daddy] love me anymore?" Finally, the divorce has to be explained, in the gentlest of terms. The child may appear a trifle melancholy now and then, but in general seems to be adjusting rather well—or so the parent believes. The single parent gets on with the task of making a living.

The next thing we know is that the parent finds and spends much time with another companion. Why not? Hasn't the child adjusted nicely? Yet the double loss—the departure of the other parent and now the lack of attention from the remaining parent—reinforces the sense of unworth that small children have to work through anyway. Many children in this quandary grow to adolescence never having faced their anxiety. Secretly they fear that one parent left home because of *them*, and now the other parent doesn't want to be there.

Our parents are an integral part of us, consciously or not, and they are talking inside us all the time. Close behind them might be a teacher, a minister or priest, an older sibling. The existentialist (Chapter 16) advises us we are free to carve our own destinies, but sometimes we cannot find the key to remove the shackles of our early lives.

Good, to forgive;
Best, to forget!
Living, we fret;
Dying, we live.
—Robert Browning

Many people spend hours, weeks, months, even years on the psychiatrist's couch, willing to confront their guilt, only to have it revived, starting up the whole cycle again. Or else they find that original guilt has been joined by a lot of new guilt. After all, *I'm a terrible person, and I know that everything bad that happens is my fault.* The result can be a decidedly neurotic individual (like the character Woody Allen plays so definitively). Many people go through life endlessly apologizing and feeling abandoned because they think nobody wants to be around them. It becomes a self-fulfilling prophecy.

What is known as "survivor guilt" is among the most common sources of depression, whether conscious or not. Testimony from those who escaped death in Nazi concentration camps during World War II indicates that their suffering did not cease just because they were still alive. D. M. Thomas's celebrated 1981 novel *The White Hotel* is a fictionalized account of an actual case in which Sigmund Freud psychoanalyzed a woman afflicted with hysteria, a mental disorder traceable to buried survivor guilt—in her case, for not having gone to the gas chamber while so many others perished. Many survivors have cried, "Why was *I* not the one?"

Too frequent are natural disasters such as earthquakes, mudslides, raging wildfires, tsunamis, and cyclonic winds and seas that can abruptly terminate existence for thousands of men, women, and children. Television reports show anguished survivors walking amid the rubble, dazed and tearfully searching for a wife, a husband, a child. Who knows how many of them may harbor the secret feeling that the punishment for past sins is their being forced to live without their loved ones? It is hard for those of us fortunate enough not to have experienced such unbearable losses to isolate ourselves from the recognition that human existence is fraught with perils and that little can be said to comfort the unlucky. Or it should be. To hope that saying "Life goes on" will take care of the problem is unrealistic and often unkind.

Yet something *can* be done by those whose guilt has been buried for a long time, who suffer needlessly when nothing has long since been able to change the past. A suggestion is to have a Goodbye to Guilt party. Make sure the invitation states clearly what the party is for, and require that attendees show up with a large piece of paper on which, using letters clipped from magazines, they have spelled out the most terrible thing they have ever done or been responsible for. No one else need see what is on the paper. The paper is to be folded up and deposited in a receptacle of some kind. (The hosts of one party made a tiny casket out of cardboard and decorated it with flowers.)

What did it matter if he existed for two or for twenty years? Happiness was the fact that he existed.

—**Albert Camus**

A forgiveness ritual follows that should be developed spontaneously rather than planned in advance. Participants have made up hymns on the spot, have engaged in a ritual dance, conducted a funeral service as they buried the receptacle, and even formed a torchlight procession to a nearby lake, where they set the receptacle ablaze and cheered as they watched it drift away and finally consume itself.

The past and present wilt–I have
fill'd them, emptied them
And I proceed to fill my next fold of
the future.

—**Walt Whitman**

Hebrew tradition has for centuries encouraged a forgiveness ritual.

> *. . . the Jewish practice known as tashlikh (Hebrew for "throw") is derived from a verse from the prophet Micah, "And You [God] shall throw their sins into the depths of the sea" (7:19). Based on the prophet's words, a Jewish custom arose during the Middle Ages. On the first day of Rosh ha-Shana . . . Jews go to a river and symbolically cast their sins into the water. In many communities, people pull out their pockets and shake them, emptying them of the sins they contained.*[19]

If we take no part in such organized functions, we can create a private ritual, which involves sitting quietly in a corner, concentrating very hard on the guilt we don't want to share, gathering up all of it into a tight ball, and then—calmly and deliberately—imagining ourselves hurling the ball straight up into the sky. See? There it goes. The ball of guilt suddenly becomes a bird winging its way over a cloud, becoming lost in an azure infinity, and never being heard from again.

Death itself—biological death, the single stroke that happens only once to each of us—will come as it may. In this chapter we have not been discussing that event only. We have also been talking about *other* kinds of death and how the resources in the humanities can, except in cases of overpowering disasters, help us to affirm the value of life.

Like the ancient phoenix bird, we have the power to reinvent ourselves.

Source: The Granger Collection.

The most distressing aspect of a death-denying culture is the fact that we die (or cause others to die) *symbolically*: that is, psychologically—experiencing the death of self-worth and the loss of the power to reinvent ourselves. We may laugh heartily at the guilt-ridden, anxiety-filled neurotics in movies or on television, but they can also be looked upon as tragic examples of how to waste a life.

We end the chapter, however, on a positive note. The humanities are sources of life-affirming models, such as the myth of the phoenix, models we have the power to use as we reinvent ourselves and continue to be born anew.

Key Terms

fatalism the belief that all events, including the nature, time, and place of one's death, have been predetermined.

life-affirmation the belief that life is essentially good and worth living; the ability to free oneself from unnecessary burdens of guilt and a lack of self-esteem as well as fears of growing older and eventually having to die, and substituting the realization that death happens only once, not every day.

phoenix model a way of living based on the mythical archetype of the phoenix, an immortal bird that goes up in flames and flies up again from its own ashes, reborn; a way of perpetually reinventing ourselves.

program music musical genre including works such as Richard Strauss's *Death and Transfiguration*, an orchestral poem telling a story or following a scenario in the composer's mind.

wake the custom of displaying the deceased person in the home, while the family sits in mourning and visitors come to pay their respects; tends to be replaced now by a "viewing" held in a funeral home.

Topics for Writing and Discussion

1. Identify and explain three of the images of death discussed in this chapter.
2. People not only enjoy watching horror movies, but they will invariably slow down every time they see what looks like a terrible accident. The text points out that these tendencies can be either life-affirming or life-denying. Make the case for both.
3. What is symbolic, as opposed to actual, death? Explain by giving a specific example. Then indicate how one can be resurrected from such a death.
4. Reread Wordsworth's "My Heart Leaps Up" on page 520. Explain the line "The Child is father of the Man." Then indicate in what way it relates to the subject matter of this chapter.
5. Much of the art depicting people's reaction to death shows them grieving. In your own words, define *grief* and indicate whether it is life-affirming or life-denying.
6. The film *The Road to Wellville* was a satire on the lengths (and expense) to which people will go to stay (or think they are staying) young. Isn't the desire to stay young life-affirming? Why make fun of it?
7. From reading the chapter, you should have found hints about staying young. Explain one of them.
8. Write a short paper on this question: Is it life-affirming or life-denying to say that one ought to have as much fun as possible whenever one can because life is so short?
9. Read the account of the Forgiveness Ritual described by Rabbi Telushkin. Then create your own ritual and describe it to the class. Or better still, volunteer to arrange the ritual in which the entire class may participate.
10. The final section of the chapter reminds the reader about the perils in life, from nature and from other humans. One might argue, "Yes, it's all very sad, but what can I do about it?" Is it better not to think about such things but to look instead on the bright side? Explain.

15 Conflicts about Art

Overview

The way of the humanities has not been smooth. Artists and thinkers want their offerings to win acceptance, even praise. They want the assurance that others understand and appreciate what they are doing. Throughout the ages, however, many artists have struggled for recognition, understanding, even survival. The works they created have met with protests of varying kinds, including censorship and outright destruction. Sometimes a work praised in one era is denounced as offensive in another. Sometimes the public art that has defined a city or a nation under one regime is rejected by its successor and can be torn down or defaced.

Artists and philosophers have faced prison, even death, for works regarded as dangerous to a ruling party or to the public it governs. In an earlier chapter we saw how Socrates was condemned to death for allegedly corrupting the youth of Athens, though historians have discovered that his friendship with a man denounced as a traitor may have been partly responsible. At any rate, Socrates and many others who voiced opinions they considered logical have run into fierce opposition from those who had the power to require that *their* views be accepted as the only truth.

In the late 1980s, Iranian-born novelist Salman Rushdie was placed under a sentence of death for what a powerful spiritual leader called blasphemy in Rushdie's novel *The Satanic Verses*. The writer was forced to hide and travel incognito for many years. In 2005, a Danish newspaper cartoonist was denounced, then threatened for what was considered irreverence toward the founder of Islam in some of his work.

Suppression is probably as old as the humanities themselves. It would take many volumes to catalogue works of art and philosophy that have been stifled by people in power. Countless women, slaves, and outcasts have generally been denied education and status in the past and, unfortunately, present societies—human beings who might otherwise have made significant contributions if given the chance.

Outright suppression of the humanities by government is not supposed to happen in the United States, where the First Amendment to the

After the artist's mural for Rockefeller Center was rejected for political reasons, Diego Rivera painted this version in Mexico. Note the portrait of Lenin at the right.

Source: Diego Rivera, *Man, Controller of the Universe* (detail from mural), 1934. Credit: Collection of Mr. and Mrs. Manuel Reyero, New York. Instituto Nacional de Bellas Artes y Literatura, Mexico/© 2005 Banco de Mexico Diego Rivera and Frida Kahlo Museums Trust. Av. Cinco de Mayo No. 2, Col Centro, Del Cuauhtemoc 06059, Mexico, D. F.

Constitution protects the free expression of artists and others. The First Amendment states:

> *Congress shall make no law respecting an establishment of religion, or prohibiting the free exercise thereof; or abridging the freedom of speech, or of the press, or the right of people peaceably to assemble, and to petition the Government for a redress of grievances.*

Even in the United States, however, artists can encounter obstacles to acceptance. The public might disapprove of something in an artist's private life. Or it could be the unfamiliarity of structure or appearance in the artist's work. Or an overly shocking depiction of a revered historical or religious figure. Or the use of language or images considered to exceed the bounds of common decency. The issue of why an audience accepts or rejects is complex. Once a work of art is out there for all to see, hear, or read, it is subject to many interpretations, winning approval from some and disapproval, even hostility, from others.

Mark Twain's *Huckleberry Finn*, a book since hailed by critics and literary historians as one of the greatest of all American novels, met initially with denunciation because of its sympathetic treatment of the friendship between the white Huck and the black runaway slave Jim. The public library of Concord, Massachusetts,—thought the book was coarse and at first banned it, calling it "trash and suitable only for the slums."

Richard Wright's *Native Son* (1940), about an African American youth, Bigger Thomas, who kills a white woman, won raves both as a novel and a Broadway play. However, it ran into trouble with M.G.M., which wanted to film the story but insisted on assigning the African American roles to white actors. The author refused to allow the change and, instead, accepted an offer from an Argentinean company. Despite dictator Juan Perón's angry protests, the film was produced anyway and was a great success in Buenos Aires. Its American release, however, was delayed when the New York State Board of Censors ordered cuts that included the protagonist's impassioned speech to the court, vehemently exposing the prejudices that had put him on trial. Finally, in 1986, an American version was filmed, with Oprah Winfrey as Thomas's mother.

Works have been censored, even banned, because of objectionable language. During the 1940s, a Massachusetts school board refused to allow teachers to assign Dorothy Canfield Fisher's delicate and genteel novel *The Bent Twig*—widely hailed by critics at the time—because of the word *breast*, as in the sentence "Beneath this breast is a heart turned to stone." In 1939, when the film version of Margaret Mitchell's *Gone with the Wind* was released, audiences gasped as the hero, about to leave the heroine for good, tells her he doesn't "give a damn" what happens to her. M.G.M., the studio that released the film, was told by the committee overseeing propriety in the industry to remove the dreaded word "damn," which had never before been spoken on the screen. M.G.M. refused and was fined $50,000.

Even in our supposedly more enlightened era, language is still being censored. The title of Eve Ensler's 1996 play *The Vagina Monologues* caused more than a few raised eyebrows. The author uses the objectionable word repeatedly to illustrate the history of negativity toward women. The play is a series of monologues based on interviews with real women, most of them quite ordinary, but some were abused by husbands or had been raped by strangers during wartime. Ensler's play, lauded by supporters of the feminist movement, has seen over 1,000 productions, especially on college campuses, throughout the world. But acceptance has not been universal. Censors at many schools prevented the play from being performed, supposedly because of its descriptions of violence. One college student reported on the Internet that, in order to buy tickets through her school for a production in the community, she had to ask for "The Monologues." Had the dreaded word been said, the ticket sale, presumably, would have been denied.

Society is not a monolith made up of millions of people in total agreement about what is good or bad in the humanities. Almost always an artist somewhere is being opposed by someone or some group. The aim of this chapter is to examine a few important conflicts that illustrate the difficulties all too often confronting the arts—visual, literary, philosophical, musical, and cinematic. We present this material in the hope that you will be fair and open-minded about what you read, hear, and see. Prejudging something because others seem to dislike it may rob you of the chance to enrich your life. If nothing else, learning to offer the arts a fair hearing can only sharpen your critical skills.

How Some Artists Fared in Their Lifetime

An artist cannot get along without a public, and when the public is absent, what does he do? He invents it, and turning his back on his age, he looks toward the future for what the present denies.

—André Gide

Artists and writers are often stereotypically portrayed as wan creatures starving in an attic, their walls papered with rejection notices. No one deliberately courts obscurity, though a few may have come close. Some artists on the threshold of recognition and financial gains have refused to compromise the integrity of their work, whatever the cost. We must not begin our study, however, believing that greatness is always rejected or, conversely, that rejection is a sign of greatness. Some artists, celebrated in their lifetimes, continue to be admired by later generations. Some, recognized for a time, are rejected when tastes change. Others have been celebrated long after their death. Still others remain unrecognized in life or in death. If only there were a rule. There isn't.

Belated Recognition

The Italian composer Antonio Salieri (1750–1825) was more popular in courts and concert halls than his contemporary, Mozart, whose genius he is said to have envied. There was for a long time a widespread belief, now entirely discredited by music historians, that he poisoned Mozart to stop him from composing. As far as we know, Mozart died from a fever. Still, the rumors appear to have been strong enough to help Salieri's once lofty reputation decline after his death. Hundreds of years later, however, conductors and audiences are rediscovering his work to their delight.

Van Gogh, completely ignored by critics and public, never knew his paintings would one day sell for incredible sums. In 1987, his *Irises* sold at auction for over $50 million. His posthumous success provides a dramatic story of rags to riches that came too late, a story told over and over in novels, films, and plays. The failure, of course, was very real, one of the most complete any artist has ever experienced. Van Gogh encountered rejection even in his personal life, never being able to persuade anyone to marry him. His obscurity and the increasing despair that led him to suicide while still in his thirties have been celebrated quite as much as his genius.

Observer Michael Kimmelman fears that stories of neglected artists greatly exaggerate the truth.

> *The example of Van Gogh, who couldn't sell a picture before he shot himself, has given hope to countless embittered Sunday watercolorists. But contrary to what people believe, the neglected genius of posthumous fame is an extreme rarity in the history of art, basically a Romantic conceit. Things mostly work in the reverse. Call it the Maratta effect. Carlo Maratta was perhaps the most famous painter alive in Europe in the late 17th century. Raise your hand if you have heard of him.*[1]

There are, however, enough exceptions to perpetuate the lore of the neglected artist and his or her post-death recognition. Herman Melville (1819–1891) is a case in point. His masterpiece, *Moby Dick*, sold few copies in the first edition of 1851, most of which was eventually destroyed in a publisher's warehouse fire. (Melville was billed for the loss.) The *New York Times* acknowledged his death with a two-line obituary (which didn't even mention his greatest work), and it wasn't until the 1920s that Melville's genius was duly recognized.

Recognition in Life

> *There are two things for which animals are to be envied: They know nothing of future evils or what people say about them.*
>
> **—Voltaire**

Held to be the greatest literary genius in the English language, William Shakespeare was celebrated during his lifetime and has been ever since (except for a temporary eclipse during the eighteenth century). His plays were immensely popular with Elizabethan audiences, although not always for their literary qualities. Some members of his audiences must have appreciated the intricate poetic images, while others no doubt paid less attention to the subtleties of language than to a rousing swordfight, a suggestive quip by a clown, or the glimpse of a ghost. Shakespeare needed to support himself by his pen, and that meant appealing to both the educated and the uneducated.

In the past, some artists were subsidized, given commissions by popes, monarchs, and aristocrats. Michelangelo (discussed in Chapter 5) was recognized when he was still in his early twenties and was asked to create the Vatican *Pietà*. The Spanish artist Goya (also discussed in Chapter 5) was initially given handsome commissions by many aristocrats as well as the royal family itself.

A frequent pattern, however, is that artists, once accepted and revered by their contemporaries, become supremely confident and demand the right to create as they wish, and this stance can lead to bitter disputes and loss of patronage. Michelangelo defied Pope Julius II, suffering the loss of lucrative commissions. Goya's style became increasingly bitter and satiric, causing the artist to lose favor with the court.

Celebrated artists such as Pablo Picasso (see Chapter 5) have been known not only to win critical and public acceptance but to become wealthy in the bargain. Recognition or otherwise is only part of the story of the artist's relation to society. Picasso, for example, did not live in perpetual harmony with his society, but such was his genius that he altered the public definition of art and forced even nonbelievers to acknowledge his ability. The kind of conflict he experienced may indeed have had a beneficial effect on what he produced. Scorned at first, he set about with renewed determination and a fighting spirit to paint on his own terms. Unlike van

Gogh, whose similar determination resulted only in continuing public indifference, Picasso brought about a change of taste. He *educated* the public while he waited for it to catch up with him.

On the other hand, success has its pitfalls. In the world of entertainment, for example, there have been artists who were recognized early, earned fame and fortune, then lost favor when they were perceived as not living up to their own standards—the American playwright Tennessee Williams (discussed in Chapter 7), for example. Hailed in 1945 as the next great voice in American theater for *The Glass Menagerie*, he followed this up with *A Streetcar Named Desire*, which won the Pulitzer Prize and secured for him an international reputation. Both plays were immediately studied in modern drama courses. Much of his later work, however, was panned by critics for not measuring up to the quality that was expected of him.

Other artists work hard just for the chance to speak with their own voice. Minority artists have struggled not only for the opportunity to be heard but to resist the requirement to do a kind of art that represents protest, as if they were forbidden to paint landscapes or write love poems. The African American artist Henry Tanner, who painted *The Seine* (Color Plate 35), considered himself an Impressionist first and foremost, not an artist with a message. Aaron Douglas (see Chapter 5) came to the fore during the Harlem Renaissance as a distinguished American Cubist in the school of Picasso, not a spokesperson for a cause.

Five reasons for conflict:
Objectionable treatment of religious subjects
Controversial political views
Controversial sexual themes
Artist's personal behavior
Unfamiliar forms

A major obstacle facing contemporary artists has to do with economics. Because spending all day working on a novel or a sculpture rarely entitles the artist to a regular paycheck, there is a need to attract the attention of funding providers, television interviewers, gallery proprietors, literary agents, or theater producers. More than one aspiring novelist has been told: "We never publish first novels." Of course, there have to be exceptions; otherwise literature would soon die out. But rejected writers often abandon their personal, heartfelt mode of expression and try to imitate works with wide public appeal.

Reasons for Conflict

Five major reasons for conflicts about art are: (1) objectionable treatment of religious subjects, (2) controversial political views, (3) controversial sexual themes, (4) the perception that an artist's work or personal behavior is too scandalous to be tolerated by decent people, and (5) unfamiliar or novel forms that challenge accepted artistic expectations and provoke such questions as *You call this art?* and *What is it trying to say?*

Religious Content

At any given time, segments of the population have had to defend their right to dress differently, observe different holidays, and refuse to support public celebrations at odds with their own beliefs. Covering the head with a scarf, chador, or yarmulke, appearing at work with ashes on the forehead, or refusing to engage in sports competitions on a sabbath has generated negative feelings on the part of others who do not understand such practices. In the name of religion, artists have been denounced, censored, or physically harmed. Those who have experienced scorn, even persecution, on religious or political grounds should be able to understand the loneliness of

Willem Dafoe as Jesus in Martin Scorsese's *The Last Temptation of Christ*, a controversial film for portraying Jesus as more human than divine.

Source: The Everett Collection.

the artist who is attacked, sometimes physically, because of perceived heresies in a book, painting, play, or film.

In 1664, the Comédie Française presented a new work by the comic playwright Molière (discussed in Chapter 7). *Tartuffe* is about a self-appointed and fraudulent evangelist, who lies, steals, and makes lascivious overtures to the wife of his naive patron. In its original version, the play shows the main character going unpunished for his crimes (the author's way of indicating that in real life the bad guys often win). The Catholic authorities, however, were not amused, insisting that the play was a slap at the clergy, and for a time were successful in having it banned. The play was saved through the intercession of the king, but only after the playwright agreed to a new ending in which the fraudulent evangelist is exposed and arrested and the victim's property restored.

In 1988 director Martin Scorsese (discussed in Chapter 9) released his film version of the Nikos Kazantzakis novel *The Last Temptation of Christ*. Jesus is presented as a questioning, indecisive mortal, capable of human weaknesses. Only after experiencing what he believes are voices from heaven does he become convinced that he must die on the cross. Then he commands Judas to betray him. His crucifixion is depicted in graphic detail that was unprecedented for its time. In his dying agony, he meets his last temptation, a vision of a normal, happy life. The film shows Jesus released from the cross, marrying Mary Magdalene, and enjoying a fulfilling emotional and sexual relationship with her. He resists this temptation, however, and accepts death on the cross.

Scorsese's The Last Temptation of Christ *shocked many viewers because it showed Jesus as a married man with a family and gave him a sexual fantasy while he was on the cross.*

The film was so at odds with traditional presentations of Jesus as a strong, wise, highly spiritual leader that it was denounced as **blasphemy**, which means in this case *containing material deemed abusive toward a religion or religious sect*. There were demonstrations, marches, and letter-writing campaigns. Entrances to theaters were blocked. In some instances projectors and screens were destroyed, and one movie theater was even burned. There were efforts to boycott *all* films made by the studio that produced the movie. The curious helped increase attendance figures, but even so the film did not fare well at the box office. While some critics gave it mixed reviews, others stamped the film as a truth-telling, genuine work of art.

Equally controversial but in a different way was Mel Gibson's *The Passion of the Christ* (2004), an independent film originally shunned by major studios and ultimately panned by critics, who found that its in-your-face graphic violence and overlong scenes of suffering prevented it from approaching the level of screen art. In this case the public ignored the critics, and the film even had the strong endorsement of some religious groups. Nor is this the only example of conflict between those who judge a work by artistic standards and those who have other reasons for patronizing a work. Religious advocates for the film insisted that the truth was finally being shown and that seeing it was a genuine religious experience. Opponents mainly objected to the negative depiction of Jews and the emphasis on physical torture at the expense of Jesus' message of love and forgiveness.

In some countries there exists a different kind of problem created by religious content. In Iran, for example, religious authorities regulate the film industry. Directors such as the highly acclaimed Jafar Panahi are allowed a reasonably free hand, but police are required on the set to make sure Muslim codes are not violated. Nonetheless, Panahi's award-winning film *The Circle* (2000), which shows the difficulties faced by Muslim women who have been released from prison but are regularly reincarcerated for the slightest offense, drew considerable criticism from religious extremists in the country, who saw the film as an attack on their principles.

Religion in the visual arts is also a sensitive issue. A 1999 portrait of the Virgin Mary by Christopher Ofili (Color Plate 36) caused a furor when it was first shown in London, then was denounced in the United States by public officials, who urged the government to stop funding the museum exhibiting it. In the portrait, Ofili surrounds the Virgin Mary with real elephant dung, which he said was a sign of respect in Africa, where excrement is seen as a symbol of the earth's goodness. Religious groups in this country also objected to "distortions" in the depiction of the Virgin's face and body. Those who supported Ofili argued that an artist's style should not be controlled by either the government or organized religion.

The debate raises the question of whether a painting of a religious subject can be treated solely as art. Can it be admired for its inventiveness and creative technique apart from doctrine associated with it? Visitors to museums enjoy art and artifacts from bygone civilizations and religious practices, but works growing out of a living religion in one culture often give offense in a foreign context. Should there be a universal separation between art and religion?

The American Library Association regularly publishes a list of challenged, banned, and censored books that have been denounced for a variety of reasons, one of which is that certain books contain viewpoints or incidents that run contrary to the teachings of different religions. The non-fiction book *Final Exit* (1991) by Derek Humphrey, for example, has stirred up considerable protests from religious groups because it offers advice on how to commit suicide. Those who argue passionately in favor of individual rights maintain that people should be allowed to read whatever they choose.

Many parents objected to the Harry Potter books for what they considered satanic wizardry at the Hogwarts School and for the young protagonists' disobedience to established rules of authority.

Enormously popular works are not exempt from complaints. The Harry Potter books, which have sold nearly half a billion copies, have aroused the wrath of many parents for two reasons. One is the author's admiring attention to the wizardry taught at Hogwarts School, which they denounce as satanic. The other is the way Harry Potter and his friends frequently disobey the rules of the establishment. When it suits them to go after their evil opponents, they leave school at night and practice their magic arts in forbidden places—as if to say disobedience is all right if it is practiced for good reasons. Children, the detractors argue, should not be the ones to decide whether a reason is good or not. This could lead to disobedience against their own parents or religion.

Sometimes elements in religious rituals have incurred hostility when they are practiced in environments unfamiliar with them. Though Native Americans comprise the oldest known continuing culture on our shores, modern descendants have faced difficulties keeping their rituals intact. In an article originally published in the *Journal of Indian American Education*, Terry E. Huffman reported that only 6 percent of Native American students were graduating from college, despite the fact that many colleges, especially in the northern Plains, award them generous scholarships. Interviewing those who had dropped out or were seriously considering doing so, Huffman discovered that a major reason was campus hostility toward overt religious practices such as tribal dances and drumming ceremonies, along with a pervasive feeling that Native Americans who held onto the traditions of the reservations were regarded as culturally inferior by both the faculty and other students. Some of the "others" included what are called "urban Natives," that is, persons of Native American descent who grew up in the cities, had never set foot on a reservation, and tended to distance themselves from those who still lived on one. A minority of reservation students said they would graduate anyway but added they might move to the cities when they had their degrees and try to assimilate themselves into the dominant culture.

Political Views

Whenever books are burned, men also in the end are burned.
—**Heinrich Heine**

Before the American Revolution, a journalist was tried for printing allegedly libelous remarks against the governor. Because the charges included the word *false*, however, the man was acquitted when the state could not document that the statements made were in fact not true. Years after the Revolution, even under protection of the First Amendment, Benjamin Franklin's grandson, the editor and publisher of the *Philadelphia Aurora*, was arraigned for attempting to expose what he called President John Adams's desire to create a monarchy and to banish immigrants suspected of opposing his policies or joking about the presidency.

Overt attempts at censorship continue throughout many parts of the world today. Customs agents routinely prevent magazines and videotapes or DVDs from being allowed into countries whose governments oppose Western ideas. The list of suppressed and censored books the world over is a constant concern of writers' organizations. Even some supposedly democratic societies lack free access to ideas offensive to a portion of the populace. Governments cite the threat of violence as justification for banning books, lectures, and films.

During much of the twentieth century, the clash between **communism** and capitalism caused considerable turmoil within the humanities. In the 1930s, a furious controversy involved an artist who had been commissioned to produce a mural for the newly built Rockefeller Center in New York City. The artist was Diego Rivera (1886–1957), a Mexican whose political leanings were toward communism; his hero was Vladimir Lenin. The executive who commissioned the mural was Nelson Rockefeller, wealthy grandson of the founder of Standard Oil and very much a believer in capitalism. After Rivera included an image of Lenin in the gigantic mural, which was designed to celebrate the nobility of labor, Rockefeller ordered the figure removed. When Rivera refused, Rockefeller had the entire mural painted over. The angry Rivera insisted that the intentions of an artist are beyond question, and that there is no such thing as inappropriate art.

The writer E. B. White, amused by the conflict, gave this account of it:

> *"It's not good taste in a man like me,"*
> *Said John D.'s grandson Nelson,*
> *"To question an artist's integrity*
> *"Or mention a practical thing like a fee,*

"But I know what I like to a large degree
"Though art I hate to hamper:
"For twenty-one thousand conservative bucks
"You painted a radical. I say shucks,
"I never could rent the offices—
"The capitalistic offices.
"For this, as you know, is a public hall
"And people want doves, or a tree in fall,
"And though your art I dislike to hamper,
"I owe a little to God and Gramper.
"And after all,
"It's my wall."
"We'll see if it is," said Rivera.[2]

Rivera scornfully turned his back on Rockefeller Center and returned to Mexico, where he created a replica of his rejected mural and called it *Man, Controller of the Universe* (1934). (See the chapter opening photo.)

He who joyfully marches in rank and file has already earned my contempt. He has been given a large brain by mistake, since for him the spinal cord would suffice.
—Albert Einstein

Many governments have censored or banned works that questioned their practices. In 1982, the military government of Turkey banned a film called *Yol (The Road of Life)*, written by a jailed supporter of the Kurdish separatist movement. The script had been smuggled out of the prison, and the film had been made in secret. The main characters, all Kurds, stood firm in their defiance of military repression, as well as the outmoded and cruel treatment of women. The film gave the world a Turkey unlike any described in a travel brochure. Fourteen years later, when a civilian government replaced the military one, the film was finally allowed to be seen but still incurred the anger of many Turks, not necessarily sympathetic with the deposed regime, but adamant about its presenting a false impression of their country. One Turkish critic argued that "to view 'Yol' as a representation of Turkey is akin to seeing 'The Grapes of Wrath' or 'Fort Apache the Bronx' as representing life in the United States."[3]

A notorious example of government-run creativity was the 1936 "documentary" *Olympia*, a film by Leni Riefenstahl, Adolf Hitler's favorite filmmaker. The director, acclaimed for her creative use of the camera, lent her powerful artistry to a project intended to show the world that Nazi Germany supported open sports competition, even if Nazi athletes were superior. Riefenstahl's camera is highly selective in its shots. In a sequence showing the high-diving competition, admiring blonde women gaze upward at lean, glistening male bodies poised to cut through the water with surgical precision. As they descend, the divers perform spectacular acrobatic feats. Then, in defiance of gravity, they seem to fly—one, two, three at a time—in silhouettes against a cosmic background, accompanied by stirring music. Though the propaganda intent is clear, Riefenstahl is still admired for her skillful editing techniques. Yet government-run creativity is, to the free world, a form of suppression.

Sexual Content

Do the arts have a duty to encourage what a majority of the population considers moral behavior? If so, then museum curators are justified in using subject matter as a criterion for what is hung on their walls, theatrical and film producers may reject any works with explicit sexual content, and publishers may instruct their

But a work of art is an act of faith, as Michelangelo says, and one goes on writing to the unseen witnesses.
—**D. H. Lawrence**

editorial staff to use moral propriety as one of the major guidelines in determining whether a manuscript is recommended for publication.

Édouard Manet, now recognized as one of the great Impressionist painters in nineteenth-century France, was critically reviled for *Olympia* (Color Plate 37), a painting of a reclining nude woman. Not only was she obviously a courtesan, but her bold gaze seemed to stare shamelessly at the viewer. Exhibited at the Paris Salon of 1865, *Olympia* provoked one critic into writing that Manet had sunk to an incredibly low level "in his plan to replace our traditional values. His ugly portrait of a disgusting whore, brazen and offensive to all decent-minded people, is unacceptable." As we indicated in Chapter 5, Manet had been repeatedly rejected by the authoritative committee that selected works for the annual exhibition, and the furor over *Olympia* appeared to justify the committee's earlier opinions. Now the painting is considered a priceless work of art, but international prestige has come too late for its creator to enjoy its fame.

Violent controversy has erupted over words and scenes we would now consider innocuous. In 1907, during the Dublin opening of John Millington Synge's *The Playboy of the Western World*, some angry audience members threw rocks and bottles at the stage when one of the characters mentioned the word "shift," a reference to a lady's undergarment. The hero has declared to his true love that, if all the girls of Ireland were standing before him in their shifts, he would not give them a glance, not after having met *her*. One critic stated angrily that no respectable Irish girl would stand in her underwear before any man except her husband.

There was nothing explicitly sexual in the content of *The Playboy of the Western World*, but another Irish writer, James Joyce (1882–1941), faced stiff hostility, as did an English contemporary of his, D. H. Lawrence (1885–1930), for pioneer efforts to create fiction that truthfully mirrored sexuality as a dominate factor in every level of society.

Joyce's *Ulysses* (1922), eventually voted by a panel of literary critics as the greatest novel of the twentieth century, was initially banned in Britain (for fourteen years) and the United States (for eleven years). It also was the subject of a court case that did much to bring greater freedom to novelists. In 1933, an American judge named John M. Woolsey was asked by book-sellers to render a verdict as to whether the sexually explicit language of the book was so morally offensive the public should not be allowed to read it. Had Judge Woolsey decided against the novel, there is no telling how long the ban might have lasted. Instead, he stated that in his opinion (after two careful readings!) this "difficult" book was not pornography, but rather, the author had, in the case of the character most objected to, made her express feelings that would have been appropriate for a woman of her station in the time frame of the story (1904). His finding was that the book was written not to arouse sexual thoughts in the reader, but purely to record the truth of human nature.

Track 19

The character in question, who created an almost international furor, was Molly Bloom, wife of Leopold Bloom. As the title suggests, Joyce was writing a modern version of Homer's *Odyssey*, which recounts the ten-year journey undergone by Odysseus—Roman name, Ulysses—following the Trojan War (discussed in Chapter 4). Since that conflict had also lasted ten years, Penelope, wife of the hero, had been waiting at home patiently and faithfully for two decades. Molly is Joyce's modernized Penelope, waiting for her husband—Leopold Bloom as Odysseus/Ulysses—to return from his all-day wanderings in Dublin. But Joyce revolutionized modern fiction by taking us inside the mind of Molly and other characters to show what was really going on. In this he shocked many readers, as well as many more who joined the moral crusade against the novel without having read it.

In an onrushing narrative without punctuation marks, Joyce gives us what has been called **stream of consciousness**, revealing what the character is thinking and feeling from one moment to the next. In a private reverie, for example, Molly is reminiscing:

> *and then he asked me would I say yes to say yes my mountain flower and first I put my arms around him yes and drew him down to me so he could feel my breasts all perfume yes and his heart was going like mad and yes I said yes I will Yes*[4]

These are the closing words of the novel's final sentence, which is forty-five pages long and surely one of the reasons Judge Woolsey commented before stating his verdict that *Ulysses* "is not an easy book to read or to understand." Embedded in the stream-of-consciousness passage are language and images many readers thought highly improper for an author to put into the mind of a woman. Nobody, of course, said Joyce was being untrue to human nature—only that such truths should not be shown.

> *Molly Bloom, despite her triteness, despite the conventional quality of her ideas, despite her vulgarity, is capable of rich emotional response to the superficially lovely things of life.*
>
> **—Vladimir Nabokov**

The verdict, which resulted in a lifting of the federal ban that had been in existence since 1922, is a landmark decision. "If Joyce did not attempt to be honest in developing the technique which he has adopted in 'Ulysses' the result would be psychologically misleading and thus unfaithful to his chosen technique. Such an attitude would be artistically inexcusable."[5]

Some people, offended by Judge Woolsey's opinion, said the real issue was the entire purpose of art, which was supposed "to improve society." Supporters of Woolsey argued that art was intended only to mirror reality. In our own time the conflict continues, especially since all of the arts have become more explicit in the depiction of sexual feelings and sexual acts. Guidelines for television, especially in the daytime, have become increasingly permissive, allowing for graphic displays that make *Ulysses* seem tame by comparison. The appalling number of real-life sexual battery cases and crimes of passion have led many groups to demand federal censorship of works they believe encourage such behavior. Still, a clear correlation between artistic freedom and violent sexual acts has yet to be demonstrated. Many argue that, even if censorship really does improve society, it would not compensate for the *loss* of artistic freedom.

More explicit than James Joyce was D. H. Lawrence in his 1928 novel *Lady Chatterley's Lover*. The lover of the title is a gamekeeper working on an estate where the bored and unhappy Lady Chatterley lives with her crippled and impotent husband. The sexual coupling of the lady and the gamekeeper occurs with no effort to fight temptation or mention of the possibility that "it's wrong." The words Lawrence uses to describe the intimacy—metaphors drawn from the gamekeeper's outdoor life—were, Lawrence said, a tribute to the overwhelming beauty of human sexuality. He renounced society's moral code as "a denial of the purity of love," which was natural, basic to the species, and therefore good.

Once again, there was a court trial to determine whether society was dealing with literature or pornography; once again the verdict was in favor of the author. Before delivering the verdict, the judge in the case pointed out that the novel contained a number of "carnal acts of wanton intercourse" before either the lady or

Archetypes in This Chapter

Witch-hunt a term borrowed from the Salem witch trials of the seventeenth century and applied to the HUAC hearings in the 1950s; now used for aggressive inquiries into alleged violations of patriotism or morality, as in attempts to remove members of the military who are thought to be gay.

Bohemian artist a concept born in the late eighteenth century characterizing artists as struggling or free spirits on the fringes of society but dedicated to their art. Public fascination with bohemian eccentricities and antisocial behavior has often worked to an artist's advantage.

Neglected artist the concept that the most talented artists are usually unacknowledged in their own time and can only be truly appreciated after their deaths. Prominent examples include Vincent van Gogh and Herman Melville. This idea still comforts many a struggling artist.

her companion ever mentioned the word "love." A professor of literature, called as a defense witness, replied: "Sometimes, that's the way it is, my lord." Lawrence, who died in 1930, actually wrote several versions of *Lady Chatterley's Lover*. The final—and most graphic—version of the novel was not allowed to be published in the United States until 1959 or in Britain until the following year.

Despite many signs that the government of China is allowing the population to enjoy greater freedom (DVDs of the explicit *Sex and the City* television series now sell by the millions), government intervention can still occur. With the release of a heavily censored version of Ang Lee's *Lust, Caution* (2007), many Chinese citizens have found a means of peacefully expressing their interest in the freedom to judge the film for themselves by flocking to see the uncensored version in nearby Hong Kong. In another example of Chinese censorship, a hugely popular Internet column was banned because its twenty-five-year-old author spoke openly of her sex life, claiming to have slept with over seventy men and to have had at least one abortion. Her estimated 10 million followers loved to chat with her and each other about their own sex lives and their anger at government restrictions. Censorship, in this case, indicated the government believed too much permissiveness could lead to a desire to rebel against *all* restraints. The central issue here is not whether the columnist, Mu Zimei, is an artist. The point is that, if she *were* another James Joyce or D. H. Lawrence, nobody would ever know it.

The Artist's Behavior

No great artist ever sees things as they really are. If he did, he would cease to be an artist.

—**Oscar Wilde**

Sometimes the public is less offended by the art than by the actions of the artist. Admittedly deviant personal behavior now tends to be less shocking than it was earlier, yet a hefty price can still be paid for straying too far. If the general public considers an artist's behavior inappropriate, the artist's work may be supported only by a small sympathetic audience.

At one time, society could make outcasts of any persons, including famous artists, whose behavior deviated from the norm. For some, however, this did not lessen their popular success. In the late eighteenth century the archetype of the "bohemian" artist was born. Often public fascination with bohemian eccentricities and antisocial behavior worked to an artist's advantage. The poetry of Lord Byron, for example, may have attracted public interest because of the flamboyant, sometimes sexually daring, exploits of the poet himself, including, it is said, an incestuous romance with his half-sister. Artists of the time often became famous for flouting middle-class conventions with their divorces, mistresses, deviant sexual preferences, unpaid debts, hot tempers, and bizarre clothing. The French novelist George Sand was a woman determined to shock society and call attention to the inequality of women. She sometimes dressed like a man and incited gossip for going from lover to lover, including the poet Alfred de Musset and the composer Frédéric Chopin.

All the while, however, middle-class society was emphasizing hard work, thrift, sobriety, and the sacredness of the family. It may have been fascinated by morality-defying artists in secret, but overtly it viewed unconventional behavior as a threat to all the most worthwhile virtues. The classic example of an artist whose personal behavior made him the victim of a morally repressive society is poet and playwright Oscar Wilde (1854–1900). His masterpiece *The Importance of Being Earnest* (see Chapter 7) was widely acclaimed at the time it was written, and despite the scandal once attached to the author's name, it continues to be produced frequently and to entertain audiences.

Nothing about either the content or the form of the play was the cause of the playwright's trouble. Rather, it was Wilde's affair with a young aristocrat, Lord Alfred Douglas, and his angry reaction to the outrage expressed by his lover's father, the Marquess of Queensberry. On the opening night of *The Importance of Being Earnest* in 1895, Queensberry sent a note to Wilde at his private club. The note, accusing Wilde of appearing to be homosexual, contained a spelling error in the address: "To Oscar Wilde posing Somdomite." If Wilde had kept his customary sense of humor, he might have shown the spelling error to a friend with a remark about how even noblemen seemed to have been untouched by education, but instead he sued the marquess for libel. In order to win the lawsuit, Wilde had to prove in court that the charge was a lie. For his part the marquess, having used the word "posing," had only to prove that Wilde's behavior was not what society called masculine.

Queensberry, as it turned out, had an easy time, because Wilde undid himself before the jury, which must have forgotten that the marquess, not Wilde, was the defendant. The playwright, known for his wit, alienated the jury with his apparent self-confidence and cavalier remarks, including the one that destroyed his career and eventually his life. When Wilde was asked by the prosecutor whether he had engaged in a sexual alliance with one of the young men giving testimony at the trial, the playwright denied the relationship on the grounds that the young man was "extremely ugly," adding, "I pitied him for it." He must have thought the answer would elicit a smile. Instead it shocked the jury and the general public.

The jury's verdict in favor of Queensberry led to the arrest of Wilde the next day on the charge of sodomy, a crime in Britain at the time. The evidence against him included a damaging letter written to Lord Alfred and a philosophical defense of "the Love that dare not speak its name." Wilde was convicted after a jury deliberation of only a few hours. He was sent to prison for two years of hard labor. His wife divorced him and changed her name. His children were alienated from him. Lord Alfred denounced him publicly and, after his release, refused to see him. Wilde died soon after, nearly penniless and convinced his name would rust in oblivion.

Ironically, the day after the arrest of Oscar Wilde on immorality charges The New York Times *published a rave review of* The Importance of Being Earnest.

Ironically, on February 15, 1895, the day after the opening of *The Importance of Being Earnest*, the *New York Times* had published a review that included this statement: "Oscar Wilde may be said to have at last, and by a single stroke, put his enemies under foot." The favorable review, which surfaced later, did a lot to build Wilde's literary reputation but nothing to prolong his life. He was a victim of prevailing attitudes toward divergent lifestyles, as well as of his own naive belief that wit could triumph against formidable opposition.

The controversy over Wilde revolves around two important questions. If artists provide pleasure with their work, have we the right to demand model behavior from them? Should artists, because they are artists, have the freedom of behavior often denied the rest of us?

Taste is the enemy of creativeness.
—**Pablo Picasso**

Unfamiliar Form

Thus far this chapter has been concerned with problems created when a given work arouses opposition from society as a whole or a segment of that society because of its subject matter, not the technique employed by the artist. Here we are concerned with style, the handling of the medium, the way the work is done. Opposition may derive from prejudice toward what looks or sounds unfamiliar, what is considered "too" innovative—sometimes in an orchestra's sound, a dancer's movements, a film's failure to tell a story in a linear way. Opposition may result from the artist's apparent failure to work very hard: using pencil or charcoal, for example, instead of oil paint; sculpting with rusty old pipes instead of marble, or assembling found objects and calling the result *art*.

In Chapter 5, we discussed the initial rejection of Marcel Duchamp's porcelain urinal. One negative-voting member of the selection committee insisted that art had to be *made*, not *found*. Though the piece is now permanently installed at the Whitney Museum in New York, viewers and critics still express discomfort, if not ridicule. The apparent assumption behind the continuing controversy is that a work of art must be comfortable and familiar, but never challenging. As you read about artists discussed in this book, note how many of them confused, even shocked, their contemporaries with bold new techniques, moving beyond what the public was willing to accept. We can only imagine how reluctant most people were to accept portraits with unnatural flesh tones or with two eyes on one side of the head, what resistance there must have been (and still is) to a canvas simply painted white, as if the artist had forgotten to paint something on it. Artists continue to insist they have the right to do what they feel they must. As one artist succinctly defined it: "Art is what the artist does."

"I wouldn't give that to my worst enemy." Comment from a viewer looking at a series of horrifying death heads during the 2007 Art Basel exhibition of new art in Miami Beach.

One of the most famous—and always controversial—art fairs in the world is Art Basel, originating in Switzerland but now held annually in Miami Beach. In a cavernous hall as long as several football fields, hundreds of artists display new works for thousands upon thousands of viewers, collectors, gallery owners, and museum curators. In the 2007 fair, a visitor could see a number of canvases painted white, a blueprint for a water treatment plant submitted as art, the sculpture of a woman with foot-long breasts, a mirror that causes viewers to see their reflections upside down, and a series of paintings of horrifying death heads, which evoked the comment: "I wouldn't give that to my worst enemy." One artist displayed an unusual floor and non-symmetrical chairs he had designed, and he was on hand to take orders. An interested patron wondered whether he would use a color scheme and create shapes that would "go with my decor." The artist respectfully declined.

Artists with long-established critical reputations no doubt profit from exhibitions like Art Basel. Yet many whose works elicited raised eyebrows and even some nods of interest would go home with only the satisfaction of having had their work shown.

Each new generation of artists strives for new forms, to speak with its own voice. In literature, experiments with form are many: poems created without rhyme or the expected number of lines; words—sometimes seemingly inappropriate for poetry—placed on the page in no apparent design; ambiguous short stories without a definite conclusion; novels that seem to have no point of view or that take us so deeply into the mind of a character that we soon lose our bearings.

Negative, even insulting, reviews often signal critical rejection of the new, and some reviews later prove embarrassing to their writers. Numerous plays and operas that have gone on to become classics were initially denounced as failures because, for example, the story was told backwards or perhaps disappeared altogether, or the music contained an unpleasing combination of sounds. Films that failed to tell a story in a conventional way have been accused of being confusing, if not downright "crazy," because the director refused to submit to the rules of audience (and critical) expectations.

Pioneer filmmakers often took bold chances, and today many of their films are required study in film schools and academic courses in cinema history. German directors, in particular, influenced by the non-realistic plays of writers such as Bertolt Brecht (see Chapter 7), transferred similar techniques to the screen. Robert Wiene's *The Cabinet of Dr. Caligari* (1920), bewildering to American audiences at first, is now carefully analyzed by young directors eager to seek new possibilities for the cinema. The film concerns the innocent servant of a mad doctor, who turns him into a murderer. The sets, constructed of cardboard, and primitive lighting create vivid imagery of a deranged mind. Still, there is no indication that contemporary audiences were shocked by this early departure from realism.

Even if you are on the right track, you'll get run over if you just sit there.

—**Will Rogers**

An early review spoke of the "remarkable use of delicately distorted perspective—narrow slanting streets that slice across each other at unexpected angles—that are matched by mesmerizingly strange performances."[6] The film came along at a time when the public was eager to see almost anything in the exciting new medium of moving pictures, whether bewildering or not. The strongest objections to the film's bizarre technique developed long after its release. Showings at festivals of early films often generate guffaws from many who see only the cardboard and the weird acting, not the pioneer artistry of the director.

Audience expectations have not become completely sophisticated with time. In 1950, for example, a western called *Yellow Sky* used theatrical scenery such as a single door or window to represent a house, and it failed miserably at the box office, a fact duly noticed by Hollywood studios. Still, in 2004, innovative Danish director Lars von Triers made *Dogville*, a biting indictment of American materialism and greed. Not only was the subject matter offensive to most audiences, but von Triers used skeletal sets, very much like those of *Yellow Sky* half a century earlier, in direct defiance of what he knew American movie-goers liked—namely, total realism. Despite the presence of Nicole Kidman, a major star, in the lead role, the producers decided to give the film only limited release in anticipation of audience rejection. A good many critics warmly praised the work, further widening the chasm between critical and public taste.

Repressive Measures against Art

People working in the arts have struggled against forces that prove difficult to overcome, sometimes amounting to a combination of government or legal suppression and adverse public opinion. The humanities may triumph, but only in the long run. Innumerable artists, not to mention philosophers, have died without knowing their work would eventually be recognized, praised, and studied by future generations.

Suppression of "Degenerate" Art

As mentioned earlier in this chapter, totalitarian states have a history of strictly controlling the arts. For example, certain works by the Russian composer Dimitri Shostakovich (1906–1975), deemed obscure and unmelodic by Josef Stalin, the leader of the Soviet Union, were forbidden to be performed in public. Stalin regarded avant-garde music as depressing and discouraging. The Soviet government believed music should follow traditional forms in order to inspire the listener with positive feelings about their lives and the ruling party.

One of the most infamous conflicts in the history of the humanities, based on both form *and* content, erupted in Germany during the 1930s. Under Chancellor Adolf Hitler and Minister of Propaganda Joseph Goebbels, the Nazi leadership moved to purge the nation of **degenerate art**. They began in 1933 with the burning of books written by "foreigners"—an all-encompassing term for Jews, Bolsheviks, modernists, homosexuals, for anyone at odds with what was called "Aryan purity."

The oldest hath borne most: we that are young
Shall never see so much, nor live so long.

—**William Shakespeare**

Martin Goldsmith, music commentator for National Public Radio, wrote a book called *The Inextinguishable Symphony* (2000), about the life of his father and mother in Nazi Germany. Both were gifted musicians, destined for the Berlin Philharmonic, when the Hitler regime announced that henceforth no Jewish musicians could play with German orchestras, no Jewish actors could perform on the same stage as German actors, and no Jewish work of any kind could be shown or performed for German audiences. In exchange, the Nazi government would permit the establishment of the "Berlin Kulturbund," a performing arts center devoted solely to Jewish music and drama, attended only by Jewish audiences. Musical giants such as conductor Bruno Walter and composer Erich Wolfgang Korngold soon realized that the Kulturbund was simply a propaganda strategy, designed to make the free world believe the Nazis were generous after all, and they emigrated to America. The Nazi leadership gradually eliminated all Jewish culture, deporting some artists and sending others to their deaths in concentration camps.

After the massive burning of books came ridicule of non-German paintings in an exhibit called "Entartete Kunst" (Degenerate Art). Painting was of particular interest to Hitler, who had wanted to become a professional artist but whose superficially "pretty" landscapes had been critically reviewed as no longer fashionable. Rejected by the art world, Hitler turned to politics, benefiting from the despair of the populace in post–World War I Germany.

The Degenerate Art exhibit gathered up paintings from museums and toured the country, attracting enormous crowds. The paintings were displayed with labels informing the public of what was "wrong" with each work. This one was irreverent; that one was grotesque, ugly, and hard to understand. All abstract art was derided and subsequently banned on the grounds that the artists were deranged and hence dangers to society.

Having been an early member of the Nazi party did not save Emil Nolde (1867–1956) from disgrace when he was denounced for such paintings as *The Last Supper* (Color Plate 38), a work that was perceived as irreverent and impure. Despite Nolde's growing reputation and the money that the painting could bring, his town council rejected an offer for it because of an art professor's statement that "the material advantages of such a sale must at all costs be secondary to the higher political points of view."

To replace the degenerate art there was "German art," for which the government built a magnificent museum displaying the Aryan ideal of beautiful blonde women and muscular, heroic men, along with family scenes of mothers smiling down at their infants. Needing money to finance their war effort, the Nazis eventually held an auction in Switzerland, selling some of the degenerate art, including works by van Gogh and Chagall.

As in the Soviet Union under Stalin, atonal and dissonant music was banned in favor of works by composers such as Richard Wagner (see Chapter 6), who represented what the Nazis considered German ideals. Hitler's admiration for Wagner was based on the composer's glorification of Teutonic mythology and on his virulent anti-Semitism. Years after the deaths of both Wagner and Hitler, the music continues to stir up controversy. Israelis who protest against any Wagnerian performances by the Israel Philharmonic or visiting ensembles may recognize the aesthetic value of the music but say it has too many negative associations for survivors of the Holocaust and their descendants. On the other hand, some Israeli factions want to separate the art from the artist. One critic observed, "The man was anti-Semitic, not the music." Jewish conductors have also defended the music. On July 7, 2001, Daniel Barenboim, conductor of the Israel Philharmonic, performed the overture to Wagner's *Tristan und Isolde* as an encore and received a warm ovation.[7]

Music is Life, and like Life, inextinguishable.
—**Carl Nielsen**

Whether called "degenerate art" or not, some artistic endeavors continue to incite anger in audiences and have driven other governments to impose crackdowns. Rock music comes to mind. Though the one-time hugely popular band *Led Zeppelin* can attract over a hundred thousand people for a reunion concert in London in 2007 (a pair of tickets reportedly sold for $170,000!), rock has never found ready acceptance from all music lovers. In free societies, those who say they can't stand the noise simply stay home. In unfree societies, aesthetics and politics get mixed up.

Rock 'n' Roll, the 2007 play by the Czech-born British author Tom Stoppard (see Chapter 7), recounts the history of the suppression of rock music in his native land. During the 1970s, under the Soviet domination of Czechoslovakia, rock music was denounced as Western-style "degeneracy" and viewed as a force trying to undermine socialist ideals. Central to the play is the band called Plastic People of the Universe, composed of strange-looking "long-haired musicians with wild robes and make-up," whose very appearance is viewed by authorities as clearly revolutionary, hence dangerous to the state. The opening of the play, however, has one of these musicians sitting on a wall playing a rock song on a flute. He suggests the innocence of Pan, the Greek nature deity, who was as far from politics as any mythological character could be. Through the play, different styles of rock serve as a kind of musical Greek chorus, pulsing with exuberant energy, loudly proclaiming the underlying theme: art must be exempt from politics; the artist must be free, or civilization will die.

Tom Stoppard's 2007 play Rock'n Roll *loudly proclaims that art must be exempt from politics, the artist must be free, or civilization will die.*

Other restrictive governments, such as that in China, have attempted to quell the popularity of Western rock music, but to no avail. Even those loyal to the philosophy of the ruling party have argued that the joy such music inspires belongs to every human being—at no cost.

Are You Now or Have You Ever Been a Member?

Jewish artists in Nazi Germany were pitted against a repressive government. Oscar Wilde was pitted against an unsympathetic social climate. Before we say this sort of thing could never happen in our free and democratic society, we need to be aware that many of our artists have also suffered suppression, especially those who were cited for suspected leanings toward foreign ideologies.

A powerful institutional indictment of artists occurred during the mid-1950s, when the U.S. House of Representatives convened the House Un-American Activities Committee (**HUAC**), climaxing a decade-long and increasingly intensified wave of anticommunism that swept over the nation after World War II. One of its targets was the entertainment industry. The committee sought to discover who in the entertainment world carried—or had once carried—a Communist Party card or had written or performed in works considered subversive by the committee. The entertainment industry itself was divided. Some supported HUAC's efforts because they considered communism a threat to the nation. Others were appalled by the government's attempts to curb free speech and artistic expression and infringe on other basic rights.

Many of those brought before the hearings declined to answer questions about their affiliations, citing their **Fifth Amendment** rights not to have to testify for fear of self-incrimination. Some, to save themselves from being blacklisted and to protect their livelihood, gave the names of friends and associates who were known to be sympathetic to communist ideology. Those who did so were never forgiven by some segments of the entertainment community. Those who refused to name names were threatened with contempt citations, indictments, even trials leading to conviction and prison. Many artists never worked again or were able to do so only under an assumed name or in a foreign country.

One American artist whose suffered the loss of a great career was Paul Robeson (1898–1976), a gifted singer and actor. The son of a former slave, Robeson had scored highest in a competitive entrance examination for Rutgers University, which he attended as the only African American student. He won prizes for oratory and extemporaneous speaking, earned varsity letters, was elected to Phi Beta Kappa, and delivered the commencement address. He earned a law degree from Columbia University but soon became attracted to the theater, where he believed he would encounter less racial discrimination than he would practicing law. Robeson was cheered as a gospel singer and for leading roles in Shakespeare's *Othello*, Eugene O'Neill's *The Emperor Jones*, and Jerome Kern's *Showboat* (discussed in Chapter 8), in which he routinely stopped the show with his rendition of "Ol' Man River."

Paul Robeson singing "Ol' Man River" in *Showboat*. He was much under fire for his politics.

Source: The Kobal Collection.

Internationally acclaimed but always controversial, Robeson sang for Loyalist soldiers on the battlefield of the Spanish Civil War. Later he traveled to the Soviet Union, which he admired for its devotion to folk music and its apparent freedom from racial bias. Upon his return to the United States, he declared publicly that the Soviet Union had treated him without prejudice. He became even more bitter toward the inequality he saw in America and campaigned vigorously for political candidates who demanded racial equality. He spoke out passionately against lynching and refused to sing before segregated audiences. In his fervor he made the widely criticized recommendation that, as long as segregation remained, African American men should refuse to serve in the U.S. armed forces.

Protests and even a riot now accompanied Robeson's attempts to sing in public. His passport was revoked so that he could no longer sing abroad, before friendlier audiences. His endorsement of a labor union was suspect. Yet he was only one among many victims of the anticommunist fervor.

The question that caused the most trouble was: *Are you now or have you ever been a member of the Communist Party?* Some commentators pointed out that membership in the party was not a violation of the law and that the Soviet Union had been the ally of the United States during World War II. But the political climate was so heated that Robeson and others called to testify before HUAC felt they were in a struggle impossible to win. If they answered "Yes," they were branded as enemies and denied the opportunity to work. If they answered "No" and evidence was found to the contrary, they were accused of perjury. If they invoked the Fifth Amendment, they were unlikely to find employment. Because those summoned by the committee had not been technically charged with a crime, they were not given customary legal protections, nor were they allowed to hire lawyers for their defense or question the questioners. Some fled the country rather than testify. Some committed suicide.

Some are proud of their handful of justice and commit outrages against all things for its sake, till the world is drowned in their injustice.
—**Friedrich Nietzsche**

In 1953 playwright Arthur Miller (see Chapter 7) saw a parallel between the Puritan witch-hunts in Salem during the seventeenth century and the wave of anticommunist sentiments that were evident in contemporary political circles. Instead of making an overt statement of protest, he wrote *The Crucible*, a play about innocent Salem townspeople charged with witchcraft and imprisoned on the hysterical testimony of a few children. To escape hanging, victims had to confess their alliance to Satan and to name others also involved. John Proctor, the protagonist, whose wife is one of the accused, denounces the court and is sentenced to death, but he is given the chance to live if he will reveal the names of people he knows to have practiced witchcraft. Deciding that his good name is more important than his life, he refuses and is sent to the gallows. His pregnant wife is allowed to live, at least until her child is born. In 1956 HUAC summoned Miller to appear and, to save his reputation, name names. Like the protagonist of his play, Miller refused.

HUAC was disbanded soon afterwards, but only after inflicting permanent damage on many reputations. Yet Miller, the artist, put his stamp on the period. Ever since HUAC, similarly aggressive inquiries into alleged violations of patriotism or the moral code have been labeled witch-hunts.

Moral Censorship

The HUAC hearings were a form of censorship. If nothing else, they sounded a warning to writers and directors that pro-communist sentiments would not be tolerated. During the 1920s, Hollywood exerted little censorship on films that featured partial nudity and passionate lovemaking, or that treated outlaws and criminals sympathetically. In response to vigorous protests from organized groups threatening boycotts, the industry became increasingly less permissive. No longer would explicitly sexual content or the glamorizing of wrongdoers be allowed.

Only a still-Puritan society confuses art with self-improvement.
—**Lewis H. Lapham**

The studios knew that, if they did not impose regulations on themselves, the federal government might step in. In 1922, during the silent-film era, they organized the Motion Picture Producers and Directors of America, the job of which was to approve or disapprove of each movie. Because Will Hays was its first chief, the organization was referred to as the "Hays Office." It grew to such power that the mere mention of its name could send shivers through an entire studio.

The Hays Office issued a manifesto called the Motion Picture Production Code, containing three general principles:

1. No picture shall be produced which will lower the moral standard of those who see it. The sympathy of the audience shall never be thrown to the side of crime, wrong-doing, evil, or sin.
2. Correct standards of life, subject only to the requirements of drama and entertainment, shall be presented.
3. Law—divine, natural, or human—shall not be ridiculed, nor shall sympathy be created for its violation.

"Go ahead, make my day."
—Clint Eastwood as Dirty Harry

The Code had great impact on the future of film, but not always in ways it intended. From the beginning, the first principle was not consistently applied. Movie studios would have gone out of business if they had not been able to exploit the unbeatable plot: protagonist plotting clever crime and succeeding—or nearly succeeding. Entertainment was achieved by the threat not the arrival of the law, which, despite the third principle, was seldom portrayed sympathetically. Audiences simply accepted the fact that the cops would be there, but the predictable climax is not what sustained interest. A charming actor playing a clever bank robber or even casual murderer, spending his ill-gotten gains in a country without strict extradition statutes, could usually count on approval from the audience, who reluctantly had to forgive his final capture. If the Hays Office objected to the characterization, the producers could always say, "But justice *does* triumph in the end, doesn't it?"

Gun-toting, sharpshooting western marshals, though technically on the side of right, were rough and ready, not to mention super marksmen. During the early 1940s, war movies gave audiences the chance to identify with grenade throwers and bayonet wielders. There was enjoyment in brutality and carnage as long as the studio could say, "But you wouldn't want us to show a victorious enemy, would you?" The tacit approval of violent methods employed by those just barely on this side of the law and democracy still exists. It could be argued that the early imposition of the Code affected the kind of writing that has become deeply ingrained in our cinema tradition: that is, the continuance of a hypocritical formula in which extreme violence is presented as morally acceptable. Whether this is better than outright defiance of moral restrictions, readers must decide for themselves.

Clint Eastwood as the cop-hero Dirty Harry, whose request to a criminal he wants to kill, "Go ahead, make my day," has become part of our folklore.

Source: The Everett Collection.

The second principle, espousing "correct standards of life," was ambiguous from the outset. There were plenty of loopholes, starting with the vagueness of "correct." Sexual relationships could be strongly implied if not graphically shown. Most popular were the triangle plots, involving a usually unsympathetic wife, a moral but unhappy husband, and a warm, outgoing other woman. Adultery was never mentioned, and either the wife would conveniently die, allowing true love to proceed, or the husband and his lady friend would suffer as a punishment for falling in love. Punishment was mainly a necessary estrangement from each other, as in the 1942 film *Now, Voyager*, in which the sympathetic protagonist is the "other woman," Charlotte Vale, portrayed by Bette Davis. The love of her life, Jerry (Paul Henreid), cannot obtain a divorce from his difficult wife. He and Charlotte will see each other again, but he says, "You understand we can never—." Charlotte's reply: "Let's not ask for the moon. We have the stars." Who knows how many of the millions who viewed and wept over the ending were influenced all their lives by films like this that carefully separated sexual gratification from the "real thing"—that is, true love?

The third principle of the Code banned giving offense to any religious faith. This restriction included a crackdown on mixing religion with flagrant near-pornography. At one time, biblical epics depicted all manner of sadistic acts perpetrated by pagans before their conversion. Scantily clad dancers gyrated sensuously before wide-eyed Roman emperors. But the finale might show a crucified or lion-devoured Christian martyr ascending to heaven in a blaze of light, purporting to be inspirational, thus justifying all the vulgarity that preceded it.

Biblical epics tried to obey the Production Code by having a crucified Christian martyr ascend to heaven in a blaze of light, thus justifying all the vulgarity that preceded it.

Stereotyping as a Form of Suppression

The ultimate measure of a man is not where he stands in moments of comfort but where he stands at times of challenges and controversy.
—Martin Luther King, Jr.

Ours has never been a society in which all persons are equal—except in *theory*. There has always been stratification of one sort or another, and the form it often takes is stereotyping. Stereotyping is discouraged today, but nonetheless it can be subtly there. We hear it in everyday communications in which certain assumptions are buried. We hear it in jokes about different ethnic groups and see it in the depictions of women in books and films. This has led to some bitter debates over the perpetuation of stereotypes in art created in the past or that deals with the past.

Societies as well as individuals seem to progress through four broad stages regarding stereotyping. The four stages as seen in the history of American society can be described as follows.

Stage One. In the first or earliest stage, people probably do not even know that the word **stereotype** means *characterizing a group in terms of very general, unchanging traits and assuming that individual members of the group fit the general description.*

During the first half of the twentieth century, for example, when people in the mainstream of American culture thought about minorities, perhaps they told themselves: "That's the way those people are." They're all lazy, or stupid, or stingy, or they have accents so they obviously have nothing worthwhile to say. They're set in their ways, and they will never make it in society, but of course they are generally happy with their situation.

Magazine advertisements of the time showed a smiling black mammy on a box of pancake mix. She wore a red bandana and wanted nothing more than to make breakfast for her "family." Racial and ethnic minorities were also the targets of jokes in which they behaved in what were thought to be delightfully stupid ways. No one thought of apologizing for telling such a joke, or for including stereotypes in songs and stories. Poking fun at those outside the dominant culture had, after all, a long tradition going for it.

The portrayal of Native Americans in movies and popular magazines of the early twentieth century provides another example of the first stage. American

Indians were invariably portrayed as savages intent on kidnapping the children of God-fearing white settlers after they had scalped their parents. Or else great legions of them, on the "warpath," brandished their tomahawks and screamed from the ecstasy of the kill as they sought to wipe out a wagon train or a courageous band of soldiers. They were usually unsuccessful, except in a film such as *They Died with Their Boots On* (1942), which recounted the annihilation of General Custer and his men at Little Big Horn, filmed as the tragedy of gallant soldiers killed in a just cause.

Four stages in minority stereotyping:
early unquestioning
gentler but still separate
near-assimilation (but not quite)
multicultural (difference with pride)

The work of Frank Mechau (1904–1946), a celebrated artist and muralist of the early twentieth century, illustrates a major dilemma brought about by the growing sensitivity toward the subject of stereotyping. His work was praised by art critics and historians for a careful attention to detail and use of color. But some of Mechau's works—for example, "Covered Wagon Attacked by Indians," "Torture by the Stake," and "The Pony Rider Goes Through"—leave no doubt where viewers' sympathies were meant to be!

No longer representing prevailing attitudes, Mechau's works would ordinarily be consigned to history but for the fact that six of his murals are the subject of a recent heated controversy, central to which is the question *Should the paintings be allowed to remain on the doors of the General Services Administration building in Washington, D.C.?* Those who say yes insist that these works are, after all, a part of our history and are well executed by an extremely talented artist. Opponents, including a number of Native American organizations, want them removed. Many art historians maintain that doing so would be to suppress the reputation and work of an important American artist. As of this writing, the issue has yet to be resolved.

There's the stereotype of the Asian as quiet, courtly, yet not particularly introspective–I've felt compelled to say, "That's not me."

—David Henry Hwang

Minorities from Asia fared little better. Chinese characters usually had sinister smiles, or bowed profusely and rubbed their hands together in phony gestures of humility. They were quick to pull out a knife in a dark alley, dabble in forged works of art, and take advantage of innocent American tourists. One Asian hero in early films was the character Charlie Chan, a wise detective, always played by a Caucasian actor. The detective's dimwitted son was always played by an Asian actor.

The Book says we're all dead level in the eyes of God. Our Forefathers claimed everybody's created equal (of course, by the time you get delivered nine months later, seems like social class, skin color, looks, and health have pretty much knocked the pins out from under Conception's fair shake).

—Allan Gurganus

The list of racial stereotypes from this period could go on and on. Classic films from the past contain a good deal of stereotyping that can be scorned, laughed at, or else ignored by cinema buffs who look for writing, directing, and acting skills and are willing to *overlook* outmoded residues of their times.

Stage Two. During the second stage, people begin to see stereotyping for what it is. For example, those who had laughed at the crude and tasteless stereotypes in films, radio shows, and popular novels of the 1930s and 1940s came to pride themselves on "knowing better." This was the gentler but still separate stage. Minorities could fit in, as long as they knew their place. African Americans were acceptable as entertainers, especially as jazz musicians. Hattie McDaniel took the stereotype of the faithful servant and turned it into one of the unforgettable performances in film history, winning an Academy Award in 1940 for playing a strong, opinionated Mammy in *Gone with the Wind*. Nonetheless, in her acceptance speech, she said she hoped to be a credit to her race. Much was made of her being the first of "her race" to win such an honor. At the same time, Lena Horne, a dazzlingly beautiful and hugely popular African American singer, was denied certain movie roles, cut from scenes in films distributed in the South, and shown on screen singing alone and never in romantic situations.

In 1950 the film *Broken Arrow* provided a genuine break for audiences weary of stereotyping. It centers on a love affair, and eventual marriage, between a white U.S. army scout and an Apache woman. Because of the alliance, the Apaches are willing to sign a peace treaty. Opponents of the treaty and the interracial marriage, however, murder the wife, causing the army scout to condemn his race. The film was a critical but not a box-office success.

Forty years later, Kevin Costner's *Dances with Wolves* dealt with a white army officer who deserts his company and becomes a member of a Sioux tribe. The film bore down heavily on the historical mistreatment of Native Americans. By this time, the public was ready for the message. The film was both a critical and financial success, sweeping the Oscars in 1991.

Stage Three. The third stage is one of near **assimilation**, or blending in, at least in theory. During World War II, for example, both sexes and all racial and ethnic groups worked together and fought side by side out of necessity. The gap began to close. Women were now given important roles in war movies and novels. One film, *So Proudly We Hail*, tells the story of a group of nurses serving with the military during the war. One sacrifices her life to save her company—a role once reserved for heroic males. The screenplay, however, was written by a male, who may have seen in the deed an extension of woman's traditional if mythic role as the self-sacrificing mother.

In stage three, however, awareness of the appalling nature of stereotyping is both genuine and widespread—clear recognition of its unacceptability. During the 1950s and 1960s, there was real ferment in the land. As part of the civil rights movement, African Americans engaged in boycotts and sit-ins and attempted to enroll in previously all white high schools or colleges. Younger people, especially, wanted to break down all racial, gender, and class barriers; older people frequently nodded in agreement but often were less adamant about disturbing the status quo. Parents who expressed an overt belief in school integration might add: "Except that in the case of my child such long bus rides are unfair."

Hollywood made widely applauded movies with the social message that we are all equal. *Gentleman's Agreement* (1947) condemns anti-Semitism by showing what happens to a reporter who pretends to be Jewish. Of course, he isn't really; nonetheless, the anti-Semitism he finds in the professional world and even in his own fiancée made a strong point. *Guess Who's Coming to Dinner* (1966) told the world that interracial marriage is okay. Here the minority hero was an extremely well-educated and handsome scientist with a brilliant and wealthy future ahead of him, and the star, Sidney Poitier, was already a household name with a huge following.

Stage Four. In stage four, discrimination truly begins to vanish, and human beings begin to evaluate each other in terms of individual circumstances and achievements. Whether American society has achieved this stage is debatable. Yet there is little doubt that progress has been made. Stereotyping is socially frowned on, and non-stereotypical roles for minorities, women, and gays have become more prevalent in film and television.

In this stage, minority groups do not wait around for acceptance or to be depicted as equals: they demand the right to live where they please, go to school where they please, enter any profession they please, write their own stories, and produce and star in their own films. Equality, they insist, is *not* a theory, not a principle; it is the only acceptable condition of life.

The Persistence of Stereotypes

Most people recognize that stereotypes still exist. They are slyly there behind seemingly innocent jokes that nonetheless betray unacknowledged sexism or racism. They can still be found in television sitcoms, especially those featuring characters with foreign accents. When comic actor Danny Hoch was invited to make a guest appearance in an episode of the popular sitcom *Seinfeld*, he was directed to sound comically Hispanic as Ramon the Pool Guy. After reading the script, Hoch objected that the character was meant to be "nothing more than a stereotypical, crazy, Spanish-speaking guy." The casting agent assured him that the character could be whatever Hoch wanted him to be. He didn't even have to be called Ramon.

At rehearsal, Hoch played a character of unspecified ethnicity but made the cast and crew laugh anyway, only to be told to say the same words with a Spanish accent, because "it's funnier that way." Hoch thought about the boost his career might receive from appearing on the most popular television show of its time. He thought about other scripts he had turned down because of stereotyping, and about the lack of opportunity for fellow actors, "university-trained, fabulously talented African American, Dominican, Puerto Rican, and Cuban actor friends, and how the only roles they're asked to play are drug addicts, prostitutes, murderers, and idiotic pool cleaners."[8] In the end, Hoch told the assembled group he didn't think it was funnier that way; he didn't think an accent makes someone funny. His role was given to someone else.

In the intervening years, depictions of gays and lesbians have become more and more realistic, and they are shown to have the same problems handling relationships as everyone else.

Many would argue that the public acceptance of homosexuals still lags behind that of minorities and women, though much has been done to close the gap. In the past, male homosexual characters in film and television were identified by stereotyped superficial characteristics, such as a particular way of walking, moving the hands, and speaking with a lisp or in a high-pitched voice. Lesbian characters were almost non-existent. The word *gay* was never used, nor did the stereotyped homosexual male character have close male friends. Still, it was assumed audiences would recognize the traits and ridicule the character. Since the sexual revolution of the 1960s, however, there has been increasing recognition that a gay world exists. A breakthrough work was the 1968 play and subsequent film *The Boys in the Band.* In both versions, a group of gay males gathers together for a surprise birthday party; though surface characteristics could still be played for laughs, the underlying intent is to portray real relationships between men. In the intervening years, depictions of gays and lesbians have become more and more realistic, and they are shown to have the same problems handling relationships as everyone else.

Despite the prevalence of the many pride movements and a continuing trend toward breaking down stereotypes, a society in which all members are totally accepted by each other remains an ideal that is like the "untravelled land" in a poem by Tennyson, a land "whose margin fades forever and forever" and is never reached. The poet spoke of this land with great enthusiasm; it symbolized for him the unbounded opportunities that living gives us, so that we should never be satisfied with where we are and what we have accomplished. In this case, however, we can still hope to reach a land where shining differences are never lost—and never have to be.

Women and the Humanities

As we pointed out in Chapter 1, early histories of the humanities have been mainly male. Women were largely excluded from the arts for many centuries. Even during the nineteenth century, when a number of significant women novelists and poets *did* emerge, training in musical composition, philosophy, and the visual arts was still considered a masculine activity. While no one could have prevented a woman from privately composing music or from privately *thinking*, there would have been little interest in making the products of her creativity available to a wide audience.

Women have had to live down stereotypical images that suggest they are inherently incapable of competing with males. Aristotle advanced the opinion, widely held for centuries, that women could not think logically or concentrate for any length of time and were given to incapacitating illnesses caused by their delicate nerves. In addition, women have had to free themselves from the traditional notion that their role was to go from adoration of the father to adoration of the husband.

But if God had wanted us to think with our wombs, why did he give us a brain?

—Clare Boothe Luce

English novelist Virginia Woolf (1882–1941) grew up well aware of the challenges faced by creative women. The daughter of a famous author, Leslie Stephen, she was determined at a very young age to follow in her father's footsteps and, in her twenties, became a charter member of the Bloomsbury Group—a social circle of radical writers, poets, and artists who consciously created the new style they called *modernism*. In this safe enclave, the rebellious and free-spirited Woolf took up the cause of gifted women denied a place in the history of the humanities and still underappreciated by society at large.

In *A Room of One's Own* (1929) Woolf contrasts facilities offered to males and females at Oxford University. Before achieving fame, for example, she had been denied admission to the Bodleian Library because she was not accompanied by a man. She points out that, historically, most women were not even allowed the privilege of having their own room in the house, a fact which made it virtually impossible for talented women to find the solitude and privacy necessary for the creation of art and literature. She acknowledges the fact that Emily and Charlotte Brontë, George Eliot, and George Sand managed to make themselves heard, but she adds that they might have given us even greater works had they been able to work uninterrupted in a room of their own. All, incidentally, had to adopt masculine names in order to be published.

I decided the one way to seek justice was through the power of words.

—Leslie Marmon Silko

Woolf also imagines what might have happened if Shakespeare had had a brilliant and creative sister who followed her brother to London to carve out a career as a writer and actress. She would have been laughed out of the theaters and, no doubt, forced to take up with any man willing to feed and clothe her—for a price, of course—or else suffered an even worse fate: "any woman born with a great gift in the sixteenth century would certainly have gone crazed, shot herself, or ended her days in some lonely cottage outside the village, half witch, half wizard, feared and mocked at."[9]

Today, most of Western society, fortunately, regards men and women as creative equals, and belated recognition is gradually being given to some of those whose works were ignored or suppressed because of old prejudice. Rediscovered talents such as the British playwright Aphra Behn and the American poet Anne Bradstreet, both of whom worked in the seventeenth century, are a welcome addition to the humanities, but they also cause us to wonder how much creative inspiration was forced to die before a pen ever touched a paper or a brush a canvas.

Early Exceptions to the Rule

In Greek and Roman society, women who were not slaves were homemakers responsible for maintaining the gracious arts of civilized living. These arts did not include fashioning statues out of heavy stone or carving the facades of public buildings. In ancient Athens, the center of a civilization that produced classics of art, literature, and thought, the few women who were remotely educated and curious to develop their minds usually looked forward only to a future as professional, highly paid courtesans, with learned men as their regular clients. Even though some of them achieved reputations for their conversational ability and probably wrote poetry and kept diaries, none could have published her writings.

Early in the sixth century B.C.E., Sappho (see Chapter 4) did manage to become an acknowledged poet and founded the first known school exclusively for women on the island of Lesbos. (The term "lesbian" has been inappropriately derived from this venture.) She was also one of the earliest known women composers, though no examples of her music have survived.

In Europe during the Middle Ages, the closest a woman could normally get to education was learning the duties and prayers of a religious sisterhood or the gracious arts practiced or supervised by the lady of the castle. These included embroidery, tapestry weaving, and playing the lute, but never designing and installing a stained-glass window or painting a triptych on a church altar.

Very recently, however, information has surfaced concerning a woman of African descent who earned the right to be considered an artist of great stature in her time but who has been all but forgotten since then. Teodora Gines, who lived from the late sixteenth to the early seventeenth century, was born into slavery on the island of Cuba and would have remained there had it not been for a chance discovery of her musical talent made by a plantation overseer. Lacking any formal training in music, she nonetheless taught herself how to play a number of instruments and to compose songs. She and her sister, also an untaught but talented musician, were freed and allowed to perform, along with two male Hispanic musicians, at the Cathedral of Santiago de Cuba. Given more and more leeway in what she could do for the church services, Gines began to compose sacred music but with the syncopated rhythm that we now associate with the Latin style. In her native land she is recognized as having been a founder of the modern Cuban beat.

Our knowledge of Asian humanities has been almost exclusively male oriented, but scholars have begun to uncover past treasures of Asian art and literature by women. In medieval Japan, a number of aristocratic women achieved excellence in literature, including the poet Ono No Komachi, the writer Sei Shonagon, and foremost of all, Lady Murasaki Shikibu (see Chapter 4), author of *The Tale of Genji*, considered by many scholars as the world's first novel. While women in Japan, as elsewhere in the world, have faced considerable obstacles to recognition in a male-dominated society, the following nineteenth-century poem, written on a teapot by Buddhist nun Otagaki Rengetsu, suggests that, in some instances, they were able to transform these obstacles into art.

> *Refused at the inn—*
> *but I took the unkindness*
> *as a gracious act,*
> *under the hazy evening moon*
> *I slept beneath blossoms.*[10]

Getting Closer

They thought I was a surrealist, but I wasn't. I painted my own reality.
—**Frida Kahlo**

Almost no women visual artists were featured in traditional art histories before the twentieth century. In a ground-breaking essay entitled "Why There Are No Great Women Artists," art historian Linda Nochlin points out that the paucity of feminine names in art history courses has nothing to do with hormones (as was often believed) and everything to do with social institutions and customs. The primary institution was a male-oriented educational system, and the primary custom, a woman's traditional role as nurturer to the family. During the nineteenth century, women who wanted to study art were not allowed to look on nude models of either sex. Denied the right to learn the fundamentals of anatomy, women were also denied access to art studios and thus to the tutelage of master teachers—something most artists need as they mature.

Edmonia Lewis (1844–1907) overcame the obstacles of being both black and female. Perhaps because of her minority status and a ferocious will not only to survive but to succeed, she was able to avoid traditional feminine "genteel" education and actually took painting and drawing classes at Oberlin College. Running into many difficulties, however, she was forced to halt her academic studies, moving to liberal Boston, where she became determined to achieve fame as a sculptor. Her busts of important men earned her a good livelihood and a limited amount of fame, for a while. For her own subjects she chose Native American themes as well as biblical heroines such as Hagar, cast out of Abraham's tribe after having given birth to an illegitimate son by the venerated patriarch. In truth, Lewis was really a pioneer in dealing artistically with the sufferings of African Americans, though, to be accepted, she had to disguise the subject.

Edmonia Lewis, an African American, dealt with the racism of her time in her art, here through her sculpture of the biblical figure Hagar, ostracized when she bore a child to Abraham.

Source: Smithsonian American Art Museum, Washington, D.C./Art Resource, NY.

The Mexican artist Frida Kahlo (1907–1954) (Color Plate 39), though belonging to the early twentieth century, was nonetheless a child of nineteenth-century attitudes, among which was the belief that her role in life was to be helpmate to her artist husband (Diego Rivera, the muralist discussed earlier in the chapter), not his artistic equal. Kahlo's early exhibitions were advertised as the work of "Mrs. Diego Rivera"; otherwise, gallery owners thought, nobody would want to see paintings by an obscure Mexican woman.

In one marriage of American artists, that of painter Georgia O'Keeffe and photographer Alfred Stieglitz (both discussed in Chapter 5), recognition came late for the wife because the husband insisted that his own art must come first. Their summers were spent at his family retreat, where O'Keeffe had hoped to find time for her paintings, only to be told that she must play the hostess for her husband's visiting relatives. Today O'Keeffe's reputation is as strong as that of her husband. Some would say, stronger.

Mahler recognized just before his death that his wife Alma was also a talented composer, but it was too late for him to do anything about it.

In music, women continue to struggle for recognition. During the last two centuries, women have achieved fame as singers, but rarely as composers. In the late nineteenth and early twentieth centuries there was Alma Schindler Mahler (1879–1964), for whom the history of the humanities has yet to find a significant place. She was forced to subordinate her own considerable talents as a composer to her skills as a nurturing mother figure, which attracted insecure male artists to her. In the latter role—if for nothing else—she exerted so much influence that she deserves a place in any study of the arts.

When she was only seventeen, she fell in love with an artist twenty years her senior and became engaged to him, though he neglected to mention he was already married. Undaunted and driven by her passion for music, she inspired fellow music student Arnold Schoenberg, one of the twentieth-century giants, to compose the music he heard inside rather than what audiences would immediately accept. One of *his* students, Alban Berg, also became a close friend, so close indeed that he dedicated to her a masterwork, his opera *Wozzeck*.

Then she fell in love with and soon married the composer Gustave Mahler, also a giant of modern music. Her expectation was that they would nurture each other's careers, but he had other ideas. He soon demanded she give up composing and live for his music alone, as a wife was expected to do. He was already a recognized genius, who answered to no one but the emperor of his native Austria—and God, to whom he dedicated his last symphony. Mahler, incidentally, was also twenty years older than Alma and assumed the role of father as well as husband. In this role he naturally treated her as was expected of fathers in this time: he was protective and in no way interested in exploring her talents or encouraging her to develop them.

Exerting the same dictatorial attitude with which he directed the destiny of the Vienna Opera, Mahler told his wife that she must nurse the children, create a quiet home with well-prepared meals, and copy all of his manuscripts in her spare time. At one point she wrote to a friend: "I realize that the man who had to spread his peacock train in public wants to relax at home. That after all is woman's fate. But it isn't mine!" Yet her rebelliousness came only in spurts. She was also able to note: "I often feel as though my wings had been clipped. I feel so often how little I have in comparison with his [Mahler's] immeasurable riches."[11]

Feeling a slight twinge of guilt perhaps, Mahler spent an afternoon with Sigmund Freud and told him about Alma's problems. The famous psychoanalyst urged him to look into his wife's work. Quite possibly he would be surprised. After the session, Mahler returned home, began to play some of her songs, and finally cried out to her: "What have I done? These songs are good. You have got to go on working. They must immediately be published."[12]

Mahler unfortunately died before he could follow through on his promised support, but Alma lived to be eighty-four, still without much recognition, except as a woman who had nurtured male artists. Near the end of her life, with no thought of herself, she rejoiced: "God gave me to know the works of genius in our time before they left the hands of their creators."[13]

In the United States a very few woman composers have had their concert music performed, and even fewer women have been or are now conducting major symphony orchestras.

Small wonder that the society in which Alma Schindler struggled for independence gave few role models to inspire her. In 1900, for example, there were few women musicians in the orchestras of the world—and no women conductors. Even now few women are entrusted with wielding the baton before a major orchestra. As of 2002 only two women had ever guest-conducted the Chicago Symphony at the prestigious Ravinia Festival. Kay George Roberts is one of the very few African American women conductors. Zheng Xiaoying is the first female conductor ever appointed in China, and that was just recently. In 2005, Mei-Ann Chen became an associate conductor of the Atlanta Symphony. One musician went on record as saying he would like women conductors to wear uniforms that would disguise their anatomies.

In the United States, a few women composers have had their concert music performed—but only rarely. Libby Larsen, Joan Tower, Augusta Read Thomas, and Judith Lang Zaimont have all won critical praise but have yet to be widely known, even among the most devoted concert-goers. Only one woman, English composer Rachel Portman, has ever won the Academy Award for Best Musical Score (1996, for *Emma*), and that was seventy years after the Oscars began to be presented annually.

Clearly the humanities will be much richer when a gender balance is achieved in all areas; when repression, including stereotyping in all its forms, is a thing of the past; when every viewer, listener, and reader approaches the new and unfamiliar with an open mind; and when we do not allow controversy and contrary opinions to make us pre-judge a given work.

In the first chapter of this book we encouraged you to insist on your own self-expression, your own creativity. If you want to practice the art of being human, don't you want people to give *you* a fair hearing?

Key Terms

assimilation generally, blending in with the mainstream culture by giving up some unique characteristics of one's group.

blasphemy in the arts, any feature—such as character, dialogue, or visual image—considered abusive toward or contemptuous of a religion or religious sect.

communism an economic and political ideology, founded on the writings of Karl Marx, that favors state ownership and control of land, industry, and national resources.

degenerate art a label applied by the Nazi government in the 1930s to art that deviated from acceptable forms.

Fifth Amendment in the Bill of Rights of the U.S. Constitution, a provision for granting accused persons the right not to testify on the grounds that they might incriminate themselves.

HUAC The House Un-American Activities Committee, established in 1947 and headed by Senator Joseph McCarthy, which held public hearings for a number of years in an effort to uncover communists working in the arts, media, and governement.

stereotype the general depiction of a group, often with unflattering emphasis on a few simplistic traits, without regard for significant differences among individuals that make up that group.

stream of consciousness a literary technique associated especially with the work of James Joyce, whereby the author abandons standard rules of grammar, punctuation, and logic in order to present the unorganized inner thoughts of a character.

Topics for Writing and Discussion

1. Write a short report on a book, film, play, comic strip, or television show that you believe may have influenced your early views about gender roles or ethnic characteristics or social class. If you were not subject to early stereotyping, explain how it was avoided.
2. If you had the deciding vote in a Supreme Court review of a case in which parents were suing an Internet service for corrupting their children with pornography, what would it be? That is, where do you stand on issues concerning the First Amendment right of free speech versus the moral responsibility of a public medium of communication?
3. Would you or would you not have voted to deny funding to the museum that exhibited the painting of the Virgin Mary (Color Plate 36) in which elephant dung was used? State your reasons.
4. Should anything ever be banned? If so, what and by whom? If you think nothing should ever be banned, justify unlimited freedom of expression.
5. Herman Melville and Vincent van Gogh were geniuses who never knew their work would belong at the very top echelon of the humanities. Does that matter as long as it is there now?
6. Divide into pairs. One person is the prosecutor in the Oscar Wilde case; the other is the defense counsel. Let the class be the jury.
7. Briefly explain the current rating system for films. Do you find it useful? Dumb? An example of unacceptable moral censorship? A system that needs to be toughened?
8. Why is stereotyping a form of repression?
9. With the permission of a restaurant owner, an artist paints a mural on a wall adjacent to the front door of the restaurant, depicting naked people in a pot-smoking orgy. Passers-by lodge vigorous complaints. The police arrest the muralist and restaurant owner, who contend that the mural is a work of art. The prosecution says that the public has a right to a morally decent neighborhood. Which side are you on, and why?
10. The final chapter of this book is called *Freedom*. Without having read it yet but having read the present chapter and others, predict some of the issues with which the last chapter is concerned.

16 Freedom

Overview

Man is free. This at once a heady luxury and also the source of his discontent.

—Carlton Beck

An artist's whimsical drawing suggesting the forces that control our actions.

Source: Fineart America.

Like love and happiness, freedom is a desirable commodity. The fundamental belief of our society is that everyone is equal at birth, entitled to life, liberty, and the pursuit of happiness. Freedom is vital to the art of being human: the freedom to create and to enjoy what others create; the freedom to think and listen to the thoughts of others, whether in agreement or not; the freedom to examine one's options and then decide on the wisest course of action.

Yet like love and happiness, freedom has not had the same meaning in every historical context. The Greeks, for example, invented the concept of democracy and passed on as their legacy the model of the democratic state, in which citizens are free to think, to question, and to speak out. At the same time, free citizens comprised only about 5 percent of the population. The rest were slaves and women, whom the citizens generally deemed too irrational and irresponsible to be trusted with political decisions. Similarly, the Roman state also denied freedom to the majority of the population and held many thousands in slavery, believing that it had the right to enslave the conquered in the name of civilization, which it was bringing to the barbarian world. But Rome also had its famous Forum, where duly qualified citizens had the right to exchange ideas and debate the laws, even if an emperor such as Caligula ruled with an iron hand.

Christianity struggled for centuries with the complexity of freedom. Like most monotheistic religions, Christianity demanded obedience to the one, all-knowing God. The idea that God was necessarily omnipotent implied, however, that God had to know the result of every human choice before the choice was made. Whether or not the potential thief was inwardly torn between desiring to steal and realizing it was wrong, God could not be imagined as looking down in suspense, wondering what the person was going to do. In the mind of an all-knowing God, the deed was already accomplished. If indeed the choice, known by God in advance, was to go ahead and steal, how then, asked many, could the thief be held accountable for an act he could not avoid committing? To solve the problem, the Christian theologian Augustine, as we pointed out in Chapter 10, said that God gave humanity free will as a gift. To say that the result of choice is known to God does not mean that God *demanded* a certain outcome. Humanity is both free by God's grace and predestined because of God's

In all this he always acts according to necessary laws, from which he has no means of emancipating himself.

—**Baron d'Holbach**

foreknowledge. Detractors argue that Augustine cannot have it both ways. We are either free or we are not free.

The Augustine problem is only one of many recognized by the humanities in relation to that highly valued human state—being able to do what one feels like doing. It seems clear that, before we can insist on freedom, we need to understand just what we are talking about. A close look at the subject raises a very important question: *How free are we?* Can we really do what we please?

Another question: *When we argue that we should be free to do what we really want to do, how do we know what we really want?* Perhaps many forces are pushing us in one direction or another. How much of what we are, what we think, and what we do was determined long before we ever entered this world? A great many scientists, philosophers, sociologists, economists, and psychologists maintain that total freedom is an impossibility, even in a free society.

This chapter focuses on *whether or not the will is truly free.* It also asks *what does it mean to be a truly free individual?* We will look into two major aspects of the debate. **Determinism** is the philosophical belief that complete freedom of the will does not exist, that there are too many factors governing our choices. Its opposite is **indeterminism**, the belief that our actions are not necessarily determined by a prior cause, and therefore we have free will to make choices. Determinist arguments outnumber indeterminist arguments, but readers must resolve the issue for themselves. Besides the philosophical speculation about whether or not we have free will, there is also the political issue of *freedom*. **Libertarianism** holds that one's free will should be unrestricted. Most governments, however, impose some curbs on human freedom.

Determinism: People Are Limited in Their Choices

First, we will consider the many arguments claiming that we are not, or at least not completely, free. Only when we offer a meaningful challenge to these arguments do the words *I am free* acquire true and powerful significance. Growing up and constantly hearing the phrase *free country* is likely to put our rational faculties to sleep, to lull us into the unexamined assumption that, because we are told we live in a free country, we must obviously be free.

We think of freedom as the ability to choose between alternatives, particularly those that strongly oppose each other: obeying the speed limit or driving faster than we should down the highway; spending an entire paycheck for a night on the town or saving a substantial portion; deciding on marriage or staying single. Listing the number of options with which we are faced each day might cause us to think we are indeed free.

Yet stop a moment and reflect on even one of these options. Without an automobile, the first alternatives are reduced to just words. There is a limitation right off. Without the money or adequate credit, we cannot buy the automobile—another limitation. Without a job, we cannot have either money or credit. What kind of job? It has to be a good one if we seek a certain kind of automobile. If we do not have sufficient training, many jobs are out of the question. Of course, money to buy ten cars can be inherited or left by a benefactor, but to qualify, we have to be born in the right circumstances.

Economic considerations encompass only one class of limitations. Suppose one is born without the coordination that makes driving possible: a genetic limitation. In order to go 50 miles per hour in a 40 mile zone, one must be willing to risk being stopped by the police. Even if this were a first offense, one would be forever deprived of the opportunity to commit a first offense again—a legal limitation. As the offenses mount, the limitations on choice become imposing.

Rigid determinists believe the limitations that are integral to our lives are too numerous for there to be any question of making a *free* choice, ever. We are free to vote for whomever we like *from a given list of candidates*. Our social class lays down the parameters of our lifestyle. Responsibilities incurred by marriage and family tell some they must continue reporting to jobs they may not like, or tell others they must put a career on hold in order to care for children. Switching roles results not in greater freedom but in different limitations.

Augustine's concept of predestination Chapter 10) would have qualified him as a determinist were it not for his counter belief in God's *gift* of free will. Had they known the term, the Puritans of the early American colonies would have denied that they were determinists even though they believed in predestination. The reason? They argued that, though people's choices were already known to the all-knowing God, ordinary mortals could know if they were saved or damned by performing good deeds, reading their Bible, and appearing in church—signs they would be welcomed into heaven. And in this way, the good Puritans believed, they were directing their own destinies.

Determinism proper emerged from the eighteenth-century revolution in philosophy, triggered by science—in particular, the impact of the view that every effect must have a cause. Taking this scientific law and applying it to human behavior, some philosophers argued that all choice is limited by a prior condition, limited so severely that it cannot be considered a free choice. Each of us is in fact the product of a chain of cause and effect stretching back to the very dawn of existence.

Despite his own widely publicized life of personal indulgence, the artist Picasso is here drawn to a condition that limits free choice in this portrait of a woman who is enslaved by her designated role either as housewife or employee.

Source: Pablo Picasso, *Woman Ironing* (1904). Credit: © 2003 Estate of Pablo Picasso. Artists Rights Society (ARS), New York/ The Solomon R. Guggenheim Museum, New York, Thannhauser Collection, gift, Justin K. Thannhauser. 1978 Photo David Heald at The Solomon R. Guggenheim Foundation, New York, NY.

Let us examine a few major arguments against the existence or exercise of free will: limitations on freedom of action, past and present; institutional determinism; economic determinism; character consistency; behaviorism; genetics; and sociobiology.

The issue of freedom has haunted philosophers for a long time, and it appears there are more arguments against *freedom than* for *it.*

Past and Present Limitations on Free Action

The most evident obstacles to freedom of choice and action are the restrictions imposed on the individual by groups in power. Enforced slavery is, regrettably, not a thing of the past. In far too many places, for example, young children are either sold to or kidnapped by underground organizations reaping huge profits from offering their services for a price. When driving in certain parts of the United States, one can see prisoners in their orange uniforms hacking away at underbrush under the broiling sun.

The independent film *Chinese Dreams* (2004) deals with uneducated, poverty-stricken young men in China who are lured into signing up for work in the United States with promises of unlimited opportunities but who are smuggled into the country, brought to New York without being told where they are, forced into menial labor for long hours every day in the stifling heat of a restaurant kitchen, and made to live in dirty, crowded, airless dormitories, never seeing sunlight. When the sensitive young protagonist finally escapes one night, he is penniless and bewildered by the roaring traffic and frenetic pace of the big city, a vast neon wasteland in which he will never be free to create his own destiny.

Millions exist in countries that deny freedom to all but a privileged few. Azar Nafisi, now a professor at Johns Hopkins University and author of *Reading* Lolita *in Tehran*, formerly taught in Iran at a university held to be the most liberal in that country. It did admit some women, but they were not treated as the equals of the male students. "I felt helpless as I listened to their endless tales of woe. Female students were being penalized for running up the stairs when they were late for classes, for laughing in the hallways, for talking to members of the opposite sex."[1]

Thwarted in her attempts to enlarge the scope of her students' reading background and their critical thinking skills, Nafisi decides she will never be allowed to teach books that invite a free exchange of ideas and so offers her resignation, which is promptly refused on the grounds that only the university has the right to decide when employment is to be terminated. At length she does manage to leave, but not without a feeling of regret that she has been unable to fulfill her mission as a teacher, one dedicated to opening the minds of her students so that they might think for themselves.

Facing up to the reality that freedom is denied to a large portion of the world's population can be unpleasant. We may be tempted to just shrug our shoulders, as if to say, "But what can I do about it? Let's just be glad *we're* free." Yet understanding that *free* is not a word to be tossed about lightly or to be simply *assumed* is the first, absolutely essential step we must take. Even if we are lucky enough not to be penalized for laughing in the hallway, so goes the determinist argument, too many other forces must at some point be recognized, all the more frightening because they have no human face.

Institutional Determinism

Though he is known as one of the staunchest advocates of freedom from oppression, Jean-Jacques Rousseau (1712–1778), whom many consider the major architect of the French Revolution, is also famous for his analysis of the forces that limit freedom. Since these forces are still at work, he must be considered, in part at least, a determinist. If he could be asked, his answer might well be: "I wish I were not, but the conditions under which we live require me to adopt this belief."

Rousseau's thinking was as radical as that of any activist of the modern era. He was vehemently against any repressive government with the power to limit human choices. The ideal form of government, he reasoned, is something we *should* be free to create. Total freedom, however, was for him impossible, given the uncontrollable forces stacked against everyone. But to take what freedom remained and surrender it to one human being or group of human beings was an affront to all civilized people. He believed the ideal government was answerable to the entire population rather than existing for personal power or prestige.

In fanning the revolutionary flames beginning to sweep through a France increasingly outraged at the decadence of the aristocracy and the injustices suffered by the common people, Rousseau constructed a mythical account of the origin of the human species to back up his claim that freedom was both a natural condition and a natural right. Called *A Discourse on the Origins of Inequality*, the myth draws a romantic picture of a lost age of innocence, when early people lived in peace and harmony, sharing the fruits of the earth through a common realization that nature provided equal bounty for everyone. In this age of innocence, no laws or government existed because, obviously, law and government are not necessary when everyone is happy and there is no crime. In and of itself, the idea of a lost age of innocence was not new. Judaism, Christianity, and Islam all share the belief that our earliest ancestors lived in the Garden of Eden before their fall from God's grace. In Color Plate 40, you will find one of the most famous depictions of the Garden paintings: *The Garden of Eden* by the Flemish artist Jan Brueghel (1568–1625).

I am as free as Nature first made man,
Ere the base laws of servitude began,
When wild in woods the noble savage ran.

—John Dryden

In the Rousseau myth, there came one day *the man with the stick*, the first person to take it into his head to grab more than his natural share of things, the first person to *abuse* nature's gift of freedom by putting it to his own advantage. With his stick he carved out a private piece of territory for himself: "The first man, who, after enclosing a piece of ground, took it into his head to say, 'This is mine,' and found people simple enough to believe him, was the true founder of civil society."

The man with the stick was the founder of society as Rousseau knew it because, by creating the model of the exploiter (the inhuman alternative to natural freedom), he and his followers became an ever present threat to the rights of the others. The exploiters therefore had to be suppressed by the gradual development of law, government, and all other institutions dedicated to the curtailment, or the limitation, of natural rights. But these safeguards of liberty, once in place, become despotic. It is here that Rousseau's position truly becomes revolutionary—literally. Rousseau asserted that revolution, even if violent, is a genuine alternative to exploitation and in many cases may be the only means by which to deal with it.

The man with the stick was the founder of society as Rousseau knew it because, by creating the model of the exploiter, he and his followers became an ever present threat to the rights of others.

Rousseau explains and justifies revolution in the name of natural rights belonging to all, but he fails to account for the *origin* of the man with the stick in his myth. What made this one man decide to become possessive while the others were joyously bobbing for golden apples in an age of sun and fun? Or was he merely the first to manifest himself? Did the potential for exploitation lie deep within *every* member of that "innocent" society? If so, when were institutional safeguards ever *not* needed?

Rousseau justifies revolution in the name of natural rights but fails to account for the origin of the man with the stick.

Rousseau's anti-institutional bias is based on the assumption that in the *state of nature* (a phrase hotly debated then and since), humankind is decent, tame, moral, and benevolent. Only when held in check, only when threatened with punishment for disobedient acts, do people become hateful, aggressive, and violent—except for periods of rebelling in a just cause. But what Rousseau did not know, because he died a decade before the revolution he predicted, was that Napoleon Bonaparte would rise from the ashes of France and, sword in hand, create a new age of exploitation, perhaps even more oppressive than the one it supplanted. History shows us that this cycle of oppression, liberation, and further oppression has been repeated many times over.

How shall we ever put Rousseau's assumption to the test? How shall we ever know whether most people, left on their own without law or government, would remain peaceful and willing to share the fruits of the earth with each other, or whether the *people with sticks* would come along and start once again the cycle of exploitation and revolution? What *does* appear certain is that few revolutions within human memory have been without their exploiters, often the revolutionary leaders themselves.

A tragic example of a revolutionary cause turned lethal occurred on November 18, 1978, when over 900 members of a religious sect called People's Temple were ordered to commit suicide by drinking cyanide-laced Kool-Aid. From all accounts, their leader, Jim Jones, was in the beginning earnest about establishing a communal agricultural society, which, had it come to pass, would have resembled Rousseau's free and benevolent community. But when many became disillusioned and tried to defect, the community turned into a prison. One member was able in secret to contact outside sources, describing Jones's manic, self-absorbed leadership, forced sexual intercourse, and brutal beatings administered to those who disobeyed his rules. Four Americans, including U.S. Representative Leo Ryan and several relatives of Jones's prisoners, visited the camp but were gunned down before they could reboard their plane. Facing exposure and the end of his control over the group, Jones ordered the mass suicide. Among the dead were 270 children. A memorial service was held, and one speaker said: "Remember the people of Jonestown, not for their horrible deaths, but for who they were—people in search of a better world."

If you ask me what I came to do in this world, I, an artist, will answer you, "I am here to live out loud."
—Emile Zola

If a strong-willed person leads a benevolent cause, Rousseau might have said, does it sometimes lead to "forced benevolence," which then must be autocratically monitored? Is the stick inborn in certain people, who become a menace to civilized life and must in turn be controlled? Are the institutions of control inevitable? And can *they* in turn become oppressive, acting as curtailments on everyone's freedom?

Rousseau believed he had solved the problem when he advanced the theory of the *social contract*. By this he meant that the only way to guarantee the protection of human rights was not through unlimited freedom but through each citizen's willingness to hand over some rights to institutions dedicated to the maintenance of order within society. The social contract is a cornerstone of **institutional determinism**, which holds that government controls are needed to protect people from other people.

The problem, unfortunately, did not end there. What happens when institutions insist they must have more and more power in order to do their job? Are they then challenged by those who insist on unlimited freedom? And if unlimited freedom should ever be realized, will a person with a stick suddenly appear? Does the whole cycle begin again?

Economic Determinism

The philosophy of Karl Marx (1818–1883) profoundly influenced the Bolshevik Revolution of 1917 in Russia and the subsequent spread of socialism and communism throughout the world. Despite the failure of the socialist experiment in the Soviet Union and its satellite nations, Marxism continues to be strong in other countries, notably China, North Korea, and Cuba.

Marx believed that money was the key influence in all of our choices. As an economist, he developed a theory explaining that our behavior, our hopes and aspirations, our career choices are all determined by the social class into which we are born. The rich want to hold onto their money and tend to favor legislation designed to keep their holdings intact. The poor desire to better themselves, and in some cases, this desire becomes an obsession, eclipsing everything else in their lives. Lacking money, some who are driven to a life of crime might otherwise have been decent neighbors. If we are middle class, we want to climb to the top, while making sure that those below are not following too closely.

Marx believed that **economic determinism**—which holds that the quest for money and property controls our thinking and dictates our actions—inevitably led to a society divided into two classes: the affluent **bourgeoisie**, or middle class that controls means of production, and the **proletariat**, or workers. Sooner or later the proletariat, made furious by the unfair distribution of wealth, would unite, rise up, and seize the means of production for themselves. Marx envisioned this demand taking place naturally and without violence.

. . . only romantic fools and children of affluence can suppose that being poor is anything but hard.

—**Irving Howe**

His theory was influenced by the thinking of an earlier German philosopher, Georg Wilhelm Friedrich Hegel (1770–1831), who had developed the theory that we reach philosophical certainty through a method he called the **dialectic**, which involves analyzing opposing views and combining them into a *synthesis*. Marx took Hegel's abstractions and applied them to the concrete realities of the class struggle. The opposition of the bourgeoisie, who want to hold onto money and power, and the proletariat, bent on seizing some of it, would lead to a synthesis Marx called the *classless society*.

Communism, a social system based on the idea of the classless society, was the banner of the 1917 revolution in Russia. The Communists disagreed with Marx, however, in the matter of non-violence. They had grown tired of waiting for the *natural* coming of what was described as a workers' paradise. Their leader, Vladimir Lenin (1870–1924), extended Marxism to include the idea that a one-class society might have to be reached through violent revolution. With "The ends justify the means!" as their battle cry, the Communist Party overthrew the czar (eventually executing him and his family) and established a new order whereby all property would be state owned. There would be no private sector, no capitalism with its assumption that clever entrepreneurs had the right to exploit others and get as far ahead as possible.

We don't allow our enemies to have guns. Why should we allow them to have ideas?

—**Joseph Stalin**

Communism entails complete state ownership, usually referred to as *public* ownership. Socialism is nearly the same thing but holds that a limited amount of private business is a necessity. For example, the Soviet Union soon realized that public ownership of all farm lands was not practical. Could farmers be induced to raise crops and livestock for society as a whole rather than for themselves and their families? Since the answer seemed to be no, the agricultural workers were given small farms (about one acre) and told they could answer their own needs first and then sell what was left over. As a result, they were better off than factory workers in the city. The vast majority of the population under communism were given assigned jobs, and everybody was paid what was considered a modest, but decent, wage. The housing program was administered by the state under the strictest of guidelines: so many square feet per person.

The freedom and independence of the worker during the labor process do not exist.

—**Karl Marx**

As time went on, more and more capitalism became necessary. The classless society never really materialized, and because the private sector grew, a few people prospered while the mass of workers looked on with envy. Propaganda was strong, constantly assuring the people that their sacrifices were for the good of all. But as time went by, workers began to wonder when the "paradise" was coming. It began to look as though the separation of the rich and the poor was still there. Without being able to satisfy their self-interest, most workers could not be motivated to produce more goods or provide more efficient service.

A serious consequence of the communist experiment was that the majority of workers were unable to see the products of their labor, unlike the farmers. (Much the same is true of assembly-line workers everywhere.) Salespeople in department stores, without the incentive of commissions, failed to go out of their way to sell goods.

There remains the question: To what extent do economic needs control us and therefore set limits on freedom?

The coming of television was a boon to bored Soviet workers crammed into tiny apartments. They scrimped to buy even the tiniest set, but this enabled them to see how their counterparts in the West were supposedly living. Many of the viewers probably did not realize the sitcoms were not telling the whole truth. The illusion must have been powerful indeed: Workers in a free society, with the help of labor unions, were more than comfortable. Viewers under communism might have seen the American sitcom *Julia*, starring an African American. The series centered on the romantic relationships of Julia, a nurse, presumed to be middle-class, except that she lived in a multiroom apartment that did not seem to reflect a nurse's salary. Modest, but decent, wages eventually did not suffice for a population tired of scrounging around in grocery stores for a few vegetables and the limited supply of meat farmers were able to provide.

When the state exists, there is no freedom. When there is freedom, there will be no state.

—**Vladimir Lenin**

Whether or not the classless society could ever exist, Marxist theory is still invoked by many as a way of explaining, at least partly, what motivates human behavior. The free world has seen the failure of Soviet communism, but we must remember that economic determinism is a major philosophy and *not* the same thing as the failed system instituted by the Soviet Union and its allies. There remains the question: *To what extent do economic needs control us and therefore set limits on freedom?*

In Chapter 11 we discussed Adam Smith's theory that capitalism is the natural driving force behind human life. Smith argues that greed, natural to humanity, is good because it ensures a free market system. If businesses are allowed the freedom to do what they like, they will provide employment, which in turn gives people disposable income, which in turn moves the economy upward. When there is too much money to spend, businesses raise prices, until a point is reached at which buying slows down and prices began to fall.

Marxism and capitalism share a common underlying assumption: economic needs dominate. Others believe both systems are flawed, because there are never enough material resources to satisfy everybody. In a communist society, workers may not be motivated to produce abundantly. In a capitalist society, the affluent can afford to buy whatever they want regardless of price, but inflated costs eventually harm those less fortunate. The case for determinism at this point becomes very strong. Can anybody escape the desire for more money? The more one has, the less one is likely to be satisfied. The less one has, the need for more becomes obsessive. According to economic determinists, all human behavior can be understood in terms of how much money is or is not available.

Traditional humanists object. They find it degrading to suppose that money should be a paramount concern. After all, are not philosophy, literature, and music supposed to be *alternatives* to the accumulation of wealth? Still, finding pleasure in other than material resources is one thing; denying that economic motivation drives enlightened people is quite another.

The art of being human does not entail making a choice between the humanities and money. It *does* require that we observe ourselves in action. If economic motives are not the sole reasons that we do what we do, they *are* sometimes the major ones. Common sense tells us that the poorer we are, the more we look for opportunities to advance.

> *The inherent vice of capitalism is the unequal sharing of blessings; the inherent virtue of socialism is the equal sharing of miseries.*
>
> —**Winston Churchill**

Theoretically, the chronically poor, those who barely survive on the fringes of society, always have the option of giving up thoughts of advancement and deciding instead to enjoy music and art. Yet museums have entrance fees, galleries charge sometimes exorbitant amounts for original paintings, concerts are expensive, and even CDs can strain a modest budget.

Creative artists, once romantically thought to be "above" the vulgarity of seeking money, retain agents, negotiate contracts, charge high fees for television interviews and college lectures, and go on promotional tours to boost the sales of their latest film or publication.

We never know when economics will suddenly assume the dominant role in our life. We are often constrained by economics, such as when our only options are staying in a job we hate or not being able to make our car payments. Still, to be economically determined is not the same as being either a Marxist or a crass materialist. The important thing is at all times to recognize the roots of our behavior (or try to, anyway). We are chronically unfree the more we remain blind to reality when it confronts us. We take a step on the path to freedom when we begin to see the things that limit us—or when we impose the limitations on ourselves.

Character Consistency

> *A foolish consistency is the hobgoblin of little minds.*
>
> —**Ralph Waldo Emerson**

> *Nothing that is not a real crime makes a man appear so contemptible in the eyes of the world as inconsistency.*
>
> —**Joseph Addison**

Enduring characters in memorable works of fiction—Don Quixote, Becky Sharp, Huckleberry Finn, and Scarlett O'Hara, for example—stay in our minds not because they are amorphous, fluid, and unpredictable, but because they have specific character traits that can be summarized and that readily explain what they do. If they were real people, the determinist would say they lack free will, that they are bound by the very traits that make them come alive to us.

We think of each other as we think of literary characters. We characterize our family, friends, and associates as we interpret what they say and do. This person is witty and intelligent; that person is arrogant and pretentious; another is totally amoral. Of course, due reflection tells us that real-life people, unlike many characters in books, are unfairly placed in rigid categories. At the same time, when someone does something unexpected and atypical, we are likely to say, "He isn't himself" or "That is so unlike her." We expect predictability. We expect consistency. A determinist argument often advanced is that, the more people are consistent and predictable, the less they are free. A frequently heard determinist pronouncement is that, because insane people are totally unpredictable, *only the insane are totally free.*

Suppose someone stops a stranger in the street and strikes that person in the face. Imagine a panel of experts on human behavior being told this story and asked to predict what the response of the stricken person would be. Their predictions would surely be based on some cause-and-effect view of human interaction, which they would call *rational behavior*. But what does this mean? Does it not mean that the stricken person is expected to respond in one of certain ways that are accepted and shared by all "rational" persons? Thus, the assaulted person may be projected as (1) striking back out of righteous anger; (2) not striking back, because of pacifist beliefs, but attempting to leave without undergoing further harm; (3) voluntarily deciding against the use of force on his or her own, preferring to call a police officer; (4) turning the other cheek, because of a strong religious upbringing; or perhaps (5) simply staring in disbelief at the assailant, not quite knowing what to do.

Comments like "He isn't himself" or "That is so unlike her" indicate how predictable people are expected to be.

But now suppose the victim does not respond in any of these predicted ways but, instead, suddenly produces a sword and bids the attacker kneel down and be knighted. There is a good chance that not the assailant but the assailed would be hauled away for observation. Such a response would not fall within any *meaningful* category of behavior. The determinist is likely to argue that, of the responses considered, the King Arthur action is the only one rightfully labeled *free*. Under these circumstances, how many of us live in a free world? Or would *want* to if everyone were unpredictable?

The determinist would argue that only the insane are truly free, because their behavior can't be predicted.

Some indeterminists and libertarians not only criticize the character-consistency argument but urge us not to be bound by the character traits instilled in us during the so-called acculturation process. They tell us we can be rational without being continuously predictable. If such were not the case, how could we explain the creative and the imaginative, the divergent thinkers whose oddball notions have in one way or another altered the shape of human experience? Are all of them insane? And, come to think of it, do any of us want to acquire a hard-and-fast reputation for being always and tiresomely the same?

Behaviorism

Founded on the work of B. F. Skinner (1904–1991), **behaviorism** is a school of thought that says we are what we do, and how we behave is determined by a series of rewards and punishments that begins to weave its web as soon as we are born.

Physics does not change the nature of the world it studies, and no science of behavior can change the essential nature of man, even though both sciences yield technology with a vast power to manipulate their subject matters.
—**B. F. Skinner**

If, says Skinner, humanity has a nature, it lies in *the capacity to be conditioned.* Everything we do is the result of a reinforcement of behavior. Those actions that are followed by pleasant consequences tend to be repeated; those followed by unpleasant or painful consequences tend to be avoided. Behaviorism is both a philosophy and a method used by some psychologists to alter patterns of human behavior that need to be changed, according to individual wishes or institutional commands. In both theory and practice, behaviorism believes that what people do is determined by responses to the consequences of their actions. The child who repeatedly drops dishes on the floor is scolded or otherwise punished until the unacceptable behavior is at last avoided.

According to Skinner, freedom is nothing but the effort to escape from the unpleasant consequences of certain actions. We slap at a mosquito that's about to attack to prevent the itching that will follow if we don't. A child who throws a tantrum and is sent to bed without supper may cry so loudly that the parents will change their minds in order that *they* in turn may escape the sound of the crying. Whatever the motive for escape, says behaviorism, the fact remains that the *desir* to escape is a determining force; moreover, if freedom is defined as escape, no such thing as pure and absolute freedom exists because freeing oneself from all unpleasantness is impossible.

People, says Skinner, identify the state of absolute freedom as one in which "aversive control" is absent: that is, if there is no apparent oppression, then people imagine themselves to be free. Skinner calls such people "happy slaves." They are molded by hidden controls and don't know it. Their freedom is an illusion. Victims of oppression are in a sense better off. At least they know where they stand.

Skinner adds that "the literature of freedom has been designed to make men 'conscious' of aversive control, but in its choice of methods it has failed to rescue the happy slave."[2] Activists who fight against oppression are concerned solely with obvious victims, not enlightening those who believe they are free.

Behaviorism is often rejected by those who believe that human beings are distinguished from other animals, and that, while animal behavior can be molded through rewards and punishments, human beings have intellect and free will. Skinner's position is that the desire to hold fast to the ancient and honorable abstraction "freedom" is tied in with the belief that human dignity is lost if it is shown that humanity is not nor ever can be considered free. What happens to the great artists, writers, and philosophers if they are considered only products of conditioning forces? "We are not inclined to give a person credit for achievements which are in fact due to forces over which he has no control," says Skinner."[3]

But, he argues further, *dignity* has no meaning as an absolute abstraction. People do not vibrantly experience an inner something called "dignity" at the thought of being free. Like every other human condition, dignity is a very specific response to a particular kind of stimulus: it is the positive reinforcement given to one who has behaved properly or who has performed some achievement deemed notable. Dignity equals praise. Dignity equals recognition. Robbing people of their dignity is taking away recognition they believe they have rightfully earned. It is their reward, much as we give our pets a treat when they show they have learned the trick we taught them.

Science can point out dangers, but science cannot turn the direction of minds and hearts. That is the province of spiritual powers within and without our very beings–powers that are the mysteries of life itself.

—Chief Oren Lyons
Faithkeeper of the Turtle Clan of the Onondaga Iroquois

Praise and recognition represent very positive reinforcements and, as such, are among the most pervasive of conditioning forces. Moreover, we may push Skinner's idea even further and point out that to win praise and recognition, some people would do just about anything required of them. Many forgive their own lapses of artistic or intellectual integrity when the stakes are high enough. How many writers and composers have said a fond farewell to the novel in the desk drawer or the sonata in the piano bench in exchange for fame and fortune in the world of popular entertainment?

Some believe dignity is personal integrity, and that those who hold fast to their dignity, in this sense of the word, are indeed free. For them, the tortured van Gogh possessed *both* dignity and creative freedom.

Skinner would not agree. The title he gave to one of his most influential works is, in fact, *Beyond Freedom and Dignity*. We need, says Skinner, to take broad terms that mean very little in themselves—like "freedom" and "dignity"—and redefine them in strictly behavioral language. We need to concentrate on creating what Skinner calls a "technology of behavior." Since people are going to be conditioned anyway, the focus should be on the good controls that *can* exist. He maintains that "the problem is to free men, not from control, but from certain kinds of control, and it can be solved only if our analysis takes all consequences into account."[4]

Skinner is also a modern utopian thinker, believing that eventually an ideal society can be designed in which people develop their abilities to the maximum through carefully preplanned reinforcements. In such a society there would be no crime, no aggression, no exploitation. *But would we want such a society?*

Anti-Skinnerians argue that a "technology of behavior" sounds too threatening to all hope of freedom. When "behavioral technicians," as he calls the conditioners, realize how much power they have, what will stop them from using those identical controls that Skinner wants to eliminate? What if van Gogh had lived in a behaviorally engineered community, one in which the residents were rewarded with candy for going to art galleries displaying his work and with free vacations if they bought it? Suppose those who publicly denounced his work were carted off to jail. Suppose further that as an artist, he had the right to file a petition against those who scoffed at him and was rewarded by having the governing body take money from his detractors and give it to him. Would he then have been truly free? If the detractors who lost their money appealed the ruling on the grounds that van Gogh's work was a hodgepodge, totally lacking in artistic value, perhaps the next step would be that the governing body would reexamine the work and inform van Gogh that, if he wished to continue exhibiting, he would henceforth have to paint in an approved style. Once conditioning becomes institutionalized, how long before *it* becomes aversive control?

Genetics

The sequence:
two genomes in each cell (one from each parent)
chromosomes–transmitters of genetic instructions
genes (inside chromosomes)
DNA molecules (inside genes)

Perhaps the major medical science of the future, *genetics* developed from a study of the role played by biological factors in determining how plants, animals, and human beings develop their characteristics. Exhaustive research has found the way to look inside the infinitesimal cells that compose the various forms of life, discovering what they in turn are made of.

There are an estimated 3 trillion cells in a human body. Within each cell are two **genomes** (one from each parent), which are sets of genetic instructions that determine gender, hair and eye coloring, height, and certain tendencies, such as susceptibility to a disease that runs in the family. These instructions are transmitted through **chromosomes**, long stringy bodies in the cell's nucleus, inside which are the **genes**, granular substances containing the **DNA** molecules, long strands of sugar and sulphate that are the actual carriers of the genetic code determining how we will look and how we will sound.

We now know that diabetes, Alzheimer's disease, cystic fibrosis, and certain forms of cancer can be inherited. Arguments have been advanced that one can inherit alcoholism and other dependencies once thought to have been socially acquired. Advances in genetic research can come almost weekly. Now that the strands of DNA (deoxyribonucleic acid) have all been identified and labeled, gene replacement therapy has become a major goal in medical science. The time may not be far off when an inherited birth defect can be stopped in its tracks by locating and replacing the gene responsible.

Opinions are sharply divided about the advisability and the ethics of investing in medical science the power to use such therapy. Many are afraid of where it could lead. Suppose a gene is discovered that governs intelligence. Will science be able to produce a "super" child? Some say that nothing is wrong with making smarter humans. Others say that gene specialists would have too much power.

On the other hand, what happens if society demands that genes must be left alone to do whatever they are biologically suited to do? Preventable birth defects and inherited diseases would continue unchecked. Yet some are disturbed by the idea of interfering with nature or producing a super race. For certain religious sects, such practices substitute the will of science for the will of God.

In the social sciences, the role of genetics becomes intertwined with the long debate about heredity versus environment, also known as the nature versus nurture dispute. Do we owe our personalities and behavioral patterns to our genetic makeup, or to the influence of family, peers, education, and the social structure around us? Replacing a faulty gene is one thing; replacing external influences at will is quite another.

In addition, no one can say for sure how much of what we are is determined by more than the DNA molecule or by the nurturers. Other factors, including—yes!—a person's will can affect even one's genetic destiny. There are documented cases of people with supposedly incurable diseases who have refused to accept a death verdict and whose determination to live has thwarted medical predictions.

Still, despite all the debates, genetic science continues to make powerful strides and seeks to probe ever deeper into once unimagined possibilities for assuring the human species of a brighter and longer future. Gene replacement has already been amazingly successful, particularly in mice and chimpanzees. Using their knowledge of genetic codes, scientists have cloned animals. This means they already have in their hands the process of bringing about prearranged genetic results. Many medical researchers want unrestricted access to stem cells that may, as the technology develops, grow healthier hearts and organs and eliminate diabetes as well as various genetically transmitted diseases. Powerful religious groups lobby against the use of human embryos for the research, but recently a way has been found to extricate stem cells from skin alone. Yet even so, debates over the ethics of interfering with natural processes are likely to continue.

Literature has long been concerned with the danger inherent in out-of-control scientific experiments. One of the earliest literary works to sound a warning was *Frankenstein*, a novel written in 1818 by Mary Wollstonecraft Shelley (1797–1851). The book has become a classic anti-science fable, lending its two central figures—the scientist who creates a live being from sundry body parts and the creature itself—to countless film versions and even comic books, not to mention Broadway musicals.

The subtitle of the novel is *A Modern Prometheus*, from the ancient Greek myth about a man who was half-human and half-god. The human side of his nature caused him to seek liberty and self-determination, to become, in short, as powerful as the gods. In the novel, Victor Frankenstein, the Promethean figure, is a sensitive, gentle person intrigued from childhood by science (then called natural philosophy) and eager to learn everything possible in order to improve the lives of all people, even as his mythological ancestor sought to aid humankind by stealing fire from the gods. As he matures, he finds himself particularly concerned with the way the body functions.

> *Wealth was an inferior object; but what glory would attend the discovery, if I could but banish disease from the human frame, and render man invulnerable to any but a violent death.*

Archetypes in This Chapter

Age of innocence mythical long-ago when people were happier and life was simpler.

Frankenstein originally the name of the experimenting doctor in Mary Shelley's famous novel but now used to designate an experiment gone terribly wrong; also a reference to a protégé who turns out to be the opposite of what the mentor intended.

Freedom can mean liberation from prison, a relationship, or any kind of oppression; also used to mean the major characteristic of democratic societies.

Natural derived from Rousseau's idea of whatever belongs to the perfect state of nature; now loosely employed to describe such things as food that has not been treated with additives and the sexual orientation deemed acceptable by mainstream society.

Prometheus in Greek mythology, the titan who stole fire from the gods and gave it to humankind, and was thereafter punished by being chained to a rock where each day an eagle would devour his liver. The myth of Prometheus has had such great influence on the humanities that it gave rise to the adjective "promethean," which signifies a person who is boldly original in thinking or creativity.

Sisyphus in Greek mythology, a king who was punished for stealing a secret from Zeus by being forever forced to push a huge stone up a hill in Hades only to have it roll down to the bottom every time he neared the top; the adjective derived from this influential myth describes any futile or endlessly laborious action.

Frankenstein *is the archetype of a scientific experiment gone terribly wrong.*

Yet how is he to find the secret of immortality unless he first learns where life comes from? For Mary Shelley, wife of the famous Romantic poet Percy Bysshe Shelley, nature was to be admired, adored, glorified, but not analyzed—and certainly no human being had the right to tamper with its workings. The tragic flaw of Victor Frankenstein is that he wants to be more than a part of nature, existing harmoniously with the rest. Not content with merely understanding how the spark of life enters lifeless matter—from electricity, he is convinced—he must go further. He must assemble parts of cadavers into an eight-foot superman who will represent the perfection of the species and live forever. The outcome of his experiment is not what he expects.

> *I had selected his features as beautiful. Beautiful! Great God! His yellow skin scarcely covered the work of muscles and arteries beneath; his hair was of a lustrous black, and flowing; his teeth of a pearly whiteness, but these luxuriances only formed a more horrid contrast with his watery eyes, and seemed almost of the same colour as the dun white sockets in which they were set, his shriveled complexion, and straight black lips.*

The Creature, as he is called in the novel once he comes to life, is not the scary ogre of movie fame. Instead, he is an innocent, who kills because his ugly appearance causes him to be persecuted. Not understanding his superhuman strength, he defends himself in the only way he can. Nonetheless, he has become an archetype of an experiment gone terribly wrong.

The work seems surprisingly relevant today, and we may not be far from having yet another version, this time about a geneticist who seeks to create a perfect human being only to . . . well, you can fill in the rest. Meanwhile, comic writer Mel Brooks has had fun writing *Young Frankenstein*, first as a 1974 film and then a 2007 Broadway musical, both about Victor's heir, who wants to recreate the experiment and get it right this time. The new monster sings and dances—if this can be called getting it right. Few novelists have given the future public so enduring (and changeable) an icon as Mary Shelley did in creating Frankenstein.

Manipulation of genes in the sports world is already taking place. Some athletes have been using "gene doping." Foreign genes are injected into cells of the muscles; they carry a "growth code," and the muscles become strengthened. Theodore Friedman, director of the human gene therapy program at the University of California at San Diego, told the National Institute of Health that those "intent on subverting the gene therapy will do so. The technology is too easy."

On the other hand, successful gene therapy, performed with the intention of curing once fatal illness or prolonging human life, may silence those who denounce genetic science. If people can live longer, healthier lives, may not they be free to maximize their potential?

Sociobiology

A discipline combining biology and social science, **sociobiology** assumes the absence of free will and studies human behavior in terms of *genetic investment.* Its beliefs are closely related to those of the self-interest philosophies. The basic assumption is that everything we do pertains to our genetic strain. Love between two people is a matter of genes. If a single male wants unlimited sex with different partners, he is showing that he is not ready to make a genetic investment; he has no immediate need to continue his genetic line. A single female may also want unlimited sex, but even with birth-control devices, she has to think about the possibility that she is making more of a genetic investment than her partner. Marriage and family are viewed as a mutual agreement to make the investment. Married people who do not wish to have children are showing that genetic investment is not necessary for their happiness. Everyone is not the same, but everyone can be studied in relation to a "genetic attitude." How we feel about genetic propagation determines everything we do.

Sociobiology redefines love in terms of how much genetic investment people are willing to make.

Traditional definitions of love are thus displaced. People who share the same genetic attitudes are likely to attract each other. Even family ties result from sharing a similar gene pool. Altruism, or self-sacrifice, is also redefined. A mother sacrifices for her children, because they represent the continuing life of her own genes. She would face death to save her own child, but not someone else's—unless she has become so close to another's child that she considers the child part of her family, or unless she imagines the child in danger is her own. Soldiers who die to save their battalion do so because the battalion has become a substitute family.

Sociobiologists contend that not just romantic but *all* decisions—political, religious, educational, financial—relate in one way or another to genetics. If nothing else, genes determine *who* we are, and who we are determines what we stand for, and apparently we cannot decide to walk a different path.

But all of this is only half the story. There are many who advance contrary arguments, many for whom freedom is a reality that can be attained.

Possibilities for Freedom

This chapter has reviewed a great many determinist views, extending far back into the past and continuing strongly into the present. One reason is that determinist arguments are too powerful to be ignored. Another is that, when the summing up is made, we shall find that much of what they say does indeed apply to many, but perhaps not all, people. The state of being a free person may well be a gift not equally shared. Perhaps the art of being human includes the art of being free, where that is possible. Yet like any art, freedom needs to be very delicately and carefully fashioned and preserved.

I have no friends
I make my mind my friend
I have no enemy
I make carelessness my enemy
I have no armor
I make benevolence my armor
—14th century Japanese samurai

Even in free societies, there are many who choose a determinist path. Jeremy Rifkin, in his 2004 book *The European Dream: How Europe's Vision of the Future Is Eclipsing the American Dream*, maintains that Americans in general define freedom in terms of "autonomy and mobility, which requires amassing wealth." We may be free to choose between living for or scorning the pursuit of wealth, but, Rifkin argues, most Americans never feel that they have enough money. By contrast, he finds that "Europeans define freedom in community—in belonging, not belongings." Whether or not this definition is an overgeneralization, we probably need to begin our investigation into possibilities for freedom on a cautionary note, reminding ourselves that we cannot simply *assume* we have a free will or are free.

A Pessimist's Definition of the Will

Many have argued that the phrase "free will" is redundant, that in fact, if one *has* a will at all, it must be free. The existence of will implies freedom. But! Is there in fact such a thing as the will? Or is what some philosophers have called "will" nothing but causation working through our conscious level, making us *think* we are doing what we want, not what we must? B. F. Skinner, for example, argues that the will

Schopenhauer believed that free will was the will to live and could be used for selfish purposes.

cannot be detected, cannot be felt. We cannot say "I have free will" with reference to a specific sensation or emotion. So *where* is will? Not everyone agrees on an answer.

The German philosopher Arthur Schopenhauer (1788–1860) had no doubt that the will existed, but the fact did not fill him with unmixed feelings of joy. First, he tells us how to *see* the will objectified in an action. Stand in front of a mirror. Observe yourself. Think you would like to raise your left arm. Then do it. One instant the desire to raise the arm is locked inside the mind, the consciousness. The next instant, it is visibly present in the action perceived in the mirror.

Whereas many have thought that having discovered the will is enough to dignify the human condition, Schopenhauer went on to ask: *What is the will for?* It is obvious, one might respond. The will makes free choices among available options.

> *Schopenhauer: Indeed, but is that enough to justify optimism about the human condition? (We say we do not understand.)*
> *Schopenhauer: Is a free choice always a good choice? Suppose the choice is to kill someone. Does the fact that it was a free choice in any way soften the horror of the crime? Do we take a measure of comfort in knowing that the decision to murder was determined solely by the will of the murderer? Would it not be far better had the potential killer been conditioned by a religious upbringing that taught benevolence towards one's fellows?*

Schopenhauer believed the will is actually the will *to live*. The will drives us to actions that we think will benefit us, will ensure our survival. Often these are downright evil.

> *Unjust or wicked actions are, in regard to him who performs them, signs of the strength of his affirmation of the will to live, and thus how far he still is from true salvation, which is denial of this will.*[5]

In other words, while not denying our freedom to act, Schopenhauer is also saying that everyone is constrained, is *forced*, to use the power of will to further their own cause, even if that means harm to others. The freedom of not acting also exists, but too often this results from the fear of being caught—or at least, of not profiting from the act—and cannot be construed as a true denial of will.

Yet, if salvation lies in this very denial, Schopenhauer must believe such a thing is possible. While remaining pessimistic about human nature in general, he would not have written his books if he had not entertained the hope that a rare few would understand and would curb their own aggressive drives.

In a dialogue between Man and the World Spirit, Schopenhauer thinks of what he might say to the Spirit: "Should I tell him that the value of life lies precisely in this, that it teaches him not to want it?"[6] The philosopher is not recommending suicide here. He is talking about willfully turning aside from the pleasures and successes life appears to offer, because the free pursuit of them only makes us evil in our intentions: that is, solely self-centered. Yet, he believed, few were capable of abandoning the pursuit of success-regardless-of-cost. A disillusioned idealist, Schopenhauer longed for a world of peace and *good* will, but he saw little chance that it would ever come about.

Feminists disapprove of Schopenhauer's seemingly blatant put-down of women. In truth, much of what he said about women tends to be condescending and insulting. He called them "incurable philistines." He said "the entire sex have proved incapable of a single truly great, genuine and original achievement in art, or indeed of creating anything of lasting value."[7] He also believed, however, that their will to power is much less aggressive and destructive than that of men, and that, while fathers train their children to exercise their wills for evil purposes, mothers impart softer values. For Schopenhauer, in a sense, women are more apt to deny their wills, and by his own definition, are better for the world than men.

Regret and Relief

If everything were predetermined, we would not be able to look back and see that genuine alternatives existed, but we were not aware of them at the time.

The American philosopher William James (1842–1910) reviewed the case for pure determinism as set forth by European philosophers and concluded they were wrong. In fact, James developed the theory he pointedly called *indeterminism*, with a specific meaning that presents the world as a random collection of chance happenings. Determinism, for James, was too coldly logical: cause A leads to effect B. Determinism made people seem like well-run, well-oiled machines. James said, on the contrary, people were indecisive and unpredictable, exactly the opposite of machines.

Take regret, he said. Regret is a universal phenomenon. At any given moment people are able to think back over a hundred choices they wish they had not made. But at the same time, regret cannot be meaningfully experienced unless there exists an opposite—satisfaction—that gives regret its identity. In other words, within the random collection of happenings, people sometimes make what they consider the right move and many times make what they consider the wrong move. If everything were predetermined—that is, if the will were not free—looking backward could not reveal missed chances. We could not see them unless they had existed, though we may have been blind to them at the moment of choice. How often do murderers think back and realize that they did not *have* to carry a pistol when confronting their eventual victim? For James, hindsight is proof that genuine alternatives always exist. The determinist would reply that alternatives not chosen have no real existence. Something always makes us choose one—and only one.

If we were to extend his philosophy of indeterminism, we could say that another revealing exercise is to sit back and think of all of the terrible things we might have done last week but refrained from doing, such as

> Having a confrontation with a friend that could have threatened the relationship.
>
> Lying about something that would have involved a whole series of other lies.
>
> Dropping a course in an impulsive moment, a course required for graduation.
>
> Taking a chance and driving the old car with two bald tires.

We would probably feel relieved we had not done these things. Thus the experience of *relief* is another sign of freedom of will. When we consider the wrong moves that might have been made but were not, we are aware of having chosen wisely. We were free to do so, because we *could* have made the wrong decision. Nothing except our own intelligence determined the choice.

Our lives are probably split down the middle, with good moves on one side and bad moves on the other. That we can say we have made many mistakes is an admission that we know ourselves to be free agents. That we have sometimes chosen wisely may cause us to think, " If the good choice was predetermined, then I freely embrace determinism!"

Psychoanalysis: Freedom through the Conscious Ego

Certain schools of psychology are based on the premise that whatever we think or do is impelled by a previous cause which is not always of our own choosing. **Psychoanalysis**, in examining a patient's dreams, the thought processes evidenced in their conversation, and their free association of ideas, seeks to free people from acting without the knowledge of why they do what they do. It aims to lead people to a rational state of mind in which free choice is possible, to help people integrate their behavior by learning the causes of deviant, antisocial, or uncharacteristic actions. The theory is that, once a cause is discovered, the subterranean forces driving actions can be fully or at least partially controlled. Therapists hold out the hope that, through understanding and proper guidance, people who undergo treatment because they don't like who they are, or what they do, can change and become less "determined" than they were before.

Psychoanalysis and **psychotherapy**, invented by Sigmund Freud (1856–1939) to assist people toward mental health, are based on the assumption that, because of painful events in the past hidden away in our unconscious minds, many of us have bizarre dreams, make odd statements, and perform actions we cannot comprehend. In other words, our lives are determined by unconscious prior causes: sometimes by guilt-ridden emotions we have refused to deal with; often by desires of the *id*, that primitive, animal self human beings possessed long before they developed the rational *ego*.

Psychoanalysis has had a tremendous influence on theater, films, television, and literature. It has replaced the "who done it?" with the "what made him do it?"

In the Freudian view, the ego is the Apollonian conscious mind, and the id is the Dionysian self. In the id are sexual and aggressive drives that society has urged us to suppress. The values imposed on us by family, education, religion, the law, and the opinions of others he called the *superego*, the voice inside that tells us what we may or may not do. Yes, the will is free to disobey this voice, but chances are those who do so will be plagued by guilt. And yes, we are free *not* to think about our guilt, but, for Freud, denying it only makes matters worse.

The aim of the Freudian therapist is to analyze the patient's dreams, characteristic use of language, and free associations, to uncover the hidden self responsible for neurotic—that is, disordered—behavior, and to lead the patient to a happier life dominated by the ego. Presumably the successfully psychoanalyzed patient comes to possess freedom of the will, having been released from the determining phantoms of the past. Will thus resides in the fully conscious ego.

In recent years Freud's theories have been reevaluated. There is growing skepticism about two of his basic assumptions: the first, that all behavior can sooner or later be traced back to significant early experiences, often in childhood; and the second, that the ego, or the conscious self, is capable of rational, sustained thought once the suppressed secrets of the past are brought to light. For many, human behavior is far more complex than Freud suggests, and freedom is not attainable in the therapist's office.

Another objection is that the role of the superego, as defined by Freud, is far less pronounced than it was in his day. Sexual mores, in particular, are far less rigid, violations less apt to instill guilt. Today's therapists often take on the role of friends and counselors, willing to listen when close acquaintances and, especially, family members do not; but they are less apt to search for dreadful skeletons in the closet.

Nevertheless, Freud has received much recognition in the study of the humanities for having created one of the most prominent and influential myths of the twentieth century: *the myth of the liberated self.* Novels, plays, and films, especially in the first half of the twentieth century, display the overwhelming impact of Freud. The

An eighteenth-century painting, uncharacteristic of its time, amazingly anticipates the Freudian view that dreams have a powerful hold on our unconscious.

Source: John Henry Fuseli, *The Nightmare* (1781). Credit: The Detroit Institute of Arts, USA/Founders Society purchase with Mr. and Mrs. Bert L. Smokler and Mr. and Mrs. Lawrence A. Fleischman funds/The Bridgeman Art Library.

most popular plot centers on a man or a woman haunted by nightmarish dreams and held prisoner by past guilt, which the conscious mind refuses to confront. He or she then meets a benevolent, wise (and often attractive) analyst, who forsakes all personal concerns and works solely to free the prisoner from the shackles of tormenting guilt.

The structure of this generic therapy plot is usually that of a detective story. The old question "Who done it?" is replaced by "Why was it done?" or "What is someone afraid to face?" Sometimes (indeed very often) we learn that the victim was responsible for the death of a sibling, as in Alfred Hitchcock's popular 1945 film *Spellbound*. In the film, the victim of suppressed guilt is troubled by nightmarish dreams involving snowstorms. At lunch one day, another therapist, a beautiful woman of course, observes him using a fork to make parallel lines on a white tablecloth. Through therapy, she forces him to confront his buried past, in which he had slid down the wrought-iron railing on his parents' front steps, unaware that his younger brother was perched at the bottom. An inevitable collision caused the boy to be impaled on a spear-like post, a trauma that he has locked deep in his unconscious for many years. As expected, the recognition liberates him from guilt and steers him straight into the waiting arms of the beautiful therapist.

Psychoanalytic films, with their familiar plot structure and predictably happy endings, were extremely popular during and just after World War II. Interestingly enough, the emergence of Freudian-based entertainment coincided not only with the recovery of the American economy from the dismal depression of the 1930s but also with the recognition that the United States had to enter World War II to help free those overrun by fascist forces. The need for the literature and drama of freedom was apparently an insatiable one. Whether on the battlefield or in the therapist's office, characters struggled against overwhelming odds and in most cases emerged victorious.

Freud-based stories are by no means relegated to the war years, however. Pat Conroy's popular 1988 novel *The Prince of Tides*, which became an equally popular 1991 film, hinges on a disturbed man's complex mental journey back to his childhood, under the guidance of a wise female therapist, who helps him to uncover the suppressed memory of violent rape by an escaped convict long ago. Shame, guilt, and fear of social condemnation have prevented him from being a successful husband and father, but when he finally faces the truth that he is not responsible for the traumatic experience, he is able to return to his family, his rational self completely restored.

Writers who remain unconvinced that anybody can readily be freed from a suppressed past show less optimism, and a few have given us memorable modern tragedies. Tennessee Williams's milestone work *A Streetcar Named Desire* (1947) presented audiences with a harrowing study of mental illness culminating in madness. The heroine, Blanche DuBois, tries to give the impression that she is a genteel Southern belle, carrying on the elegant traditions of the Old South, but as the play deepens, she exhibits unmistakable signs of an unstable mental condition that causes her to denounce her sister's uncouth husband while she is at the same time driven by a fierce sexual attraction to him. Recognizing this attraction and thinking of his own sexual gratification, the husband rapes her. The abuse causes Blanche to retreat into a fantasy world from which she will never escape. The author himself was in therapy for a good part of his life, apparently unable to free himself from the demons of his own past.

Dennis Lehane's novel *Mystic River* (2001) is a dark tale about a troubled man who has attempted all his life to absolve himself of the guilt he suffered when, as an innocent child, he was abused sexually. As is so often the case after such childhood traumas, the boy grows up with feelings of worthlessness and an inability to communicate his feelings, even to his wife. His suppressed passion for revenge becomes his tragic flaw when he murders a man he believes to be a child-molester, an act that leads to his own violent death at the hands of his best friend. In 2003, Clint Eastwood directed a powerful screen adaptation of the novel, which won Oscars for Tim Robbins as the troubled protagonist and Sean Penn as the friend. David Denby in the *New Yorker* magazine declared the film "as close as Hollywood has ever come to creating true Greek tragedy."

Freudian psychology has provided subjects for tragedies of nearly classic dimensions, as in Clint Eastwood's powerful screen adaptation of *Mystic River*, starring Sean Penn and Tim Robbins.

Source: Warner Bros./The Kobal Collection/Wallance, Merie W.J.

Of course, thorough-going determinists can always argue that the liberation of the unconscious and the confrontation with reality may provide the illusion of freedom but only for a time. Stamping a patient's chart CURED does not guarantee that the person who walks out of the office for the last time is free from all determining influences. Just as physicists discovered that matter is composed of particles within particles within particles, so too may the self be a circular staircase leading down into an infinity of shadows. Freud understood this and was generally cynical about human existence, but his theories provided hope that many could ascend that staircase into the clear light of day.

Studying the humanities of the past century would be difficult indeed without recognition of Freud's role. Many schools of psychotherapy continue to be rooted in his thought, and millions have been restored to mental health through psychoanalytical methods. That Freud's views may not represent an all-inclusive means to human freedom from the determining past should not eclipse the importance of these views to both the arts and to modern psychology.

Existentialism

After the armistice ended World War I in 1918, European countries exhausted from years of turmoil and a staggering loss of life eagerly sought new ways of thinking and living. Then Roman-style nationalism, the belief that one's country was superior to all others and had a right to subjugate the rest of civilization, reared its head once more. A maniacal dictator named Adolf Hitler decided to take advantage of the chaos that usually follows a large-scale conflict. Thousands were enslaved, tortured, and executed. The freedom to be whatever they wished to be was denied to thousands more.

I know of no more encouraging fact than the unquestionable ability of man to elevate his life by a conscious endeavor.

—Henry David Thoreau

After Hitler and his allies were defeated in 1945, there came a call for new approaches, new values, and a new way of defining freedom that, if difficult to attain, was nonetheless within the reach of anyone prepared to work for it. That definition was provided by the philosophy called *existentialism*, born in the middle of the nineteenth century, but little known until postwar cynicism spread throughout Europe. It took an especially strong hold in France, a nation that once prided itself on being the cultural center of Western civilization but had been brought to its knees by Nazi occupation. After the war, France found itself without a guiding philosophy, and its art reflected hopelessness and despair. But then, existentialism was rediscovered, and with it, a strong light that could be seen at the end of a long, dark tunnel. Existentialism taught that people are free to be anything they want—but that freedom comes with a price.

Religious Existentialism

The first official existentialist was a Dane, Søren Kierkegaard (1813–1855), who was raised in an austere religious environment, rebelled against it for a time, then returned to it as a matter of conscious choice, without the need of mystic revelations. For Kierkegaard, religion became a psychological reality freely accepted rather than a revealed truth with required acceptance. When one reached a point of absolute despair (as indeed he did) and felt ready to turn to God, one could take a **leap of faith**.

In that leap, however, lie undeniable anxieties. The leap must be made over many counterarguments, especially scientific evidence that seriously questions religious beliefs. On one's knees in the darkness of a church, one might feel one's prayers soaring heavenward and have a sense of union with God, but one can never *know* if God is listening—or is even there at all.

So long as the heaven of Thou is spread out over me the winds of causality cower at my heels, and the whirlpool of fate stays its course.
—**Martin Buber**

To dramatize the plight of the believer, Kierkegaard recounts the biblical tale of Abraham and Isaac in his book *Fear and Trembling*. An angel appears to Abraham and tells him God demands the sacrifice of his son Isaac (see Color Plate 41 for Rembrandt's famous depiction of the event). Abraham is appalled, but what can he do? If God wants the sacrifice and he is God's servant, he must obey. His unquestioning willingness to do as God commands is a leap of faith. And in that leap, in that raising of the knife, must not Abraham experience unutterable anguish? Suppose the message was not really from God—what then? The anguish of Abraham represented for Kierkegaard the existential dilemma of all people. An existential dilemma is knowing that one is free to make a choice, but who knows whether it is the right or even best choice?

The philosopher Martin Buber (1878–1965), like Kierkegaard, found his way to religion through non-traditional means. He is most famous for defining two kinds of relationships a person can have. The first is the "I/it"—the objective relationship with objects and events outside, with concrete reality. Here there is no God, but only the existential moment. The second relationship is "I/Thou," representing a bridge to God. For Buber, an "it" must be defined; it has to be justified as concrete reality, otherwise there can be no relationship. A "Thou" is not defined, but addressed. The difference is clear. If you can address someone (whether a person standing in front of you or God, unseen), objective definition is beside the point. The fact that you are addressing anyone means that for you, at least, they exist. When it comes to "I/it," objective proof is possible. The "it" is out there for all to see. The experience of God comes through feeling, through intuition, through an overpowering sense of God's presence, and is not out there for all to see. Hence there can be no challenging it. Buber and Kierkegaard are very close on this point.

According to Buber, if you can address someone (including God) they must exist at least for you. Objects have objective reality, but since you don't address them, they have no actual existence.

Early in his adult life Buber approached religion intellectually. He was a scholar of sacred Hebrew texts, concerned with the interpretation of traditional religious history as being a matter of myth and legend. Yet he sought the fundamental truth behind them. He did not address God personally. God was not a "Thou" until the reading of one particular text—just a few sentences, really—changed his life forever.

> *I opened a little book entitled the Zervaat Ribesh—that is the testament of Rabbi Israel Baal-Shem—and the words flashed toward me; "He takes unto himself the quality of fervor, for he is hallowed and become another man and is worthy to create and is become like the Holy One, blessed be He, when he created his world." It was then that, over-powered in an instant, I experienced the Hasidic soul.*[8]

In Chapter 2 we would have called this a Dionysian religious experience. Buber discovered that truth in religion comes from irresistible feeling, not analytical thought. From that moment on he became a Hasid—a member of a sect that emphasizes joy in God's closeness to humanity and the warm fellowship with other members of God's family.

He was then led to a passionate concern for the sacredness of human relationships, for in human contact he also found God. Every person with whom one connects was for him a "Thou," and every "Thou" contained the spirit of God. In one of his books he tells of greeting a visitor perfunctorily; though he showed the man ordinary courtesy, he was eager to return to a scholarly manuscript he was editing. Upon learning that his visitor later committed suicide, Buber recognized that human beings are more important than any task.

"I/Thou" created a revolution in modern ethics, for here was a philosopher who dispensed with the rules, who challenged the moral absolutes of both the Socratic and major religious traditions, but still found a way to affirm that moral goodness was there in every human heart, provided it was sought. Not everyone would find it, but each of us was free to search for it.

Secular Existentialism

A different kind of existentialism swept over Europe after World War II. It accorded well with the depressed mood of countries that had been devastated by fighting and loss, but at the same time, its belief in freedom as a natural condition helped to stir up some optimism.

Freedom is fragile and must be protected. To sacrifice it, even as a temporary measure, is to betray it.
—Germaine Greer

Secular existentialism does not seek to address a God whose existence we cannot prove. Belief in God entails obeying commandments as well as believing that one is put here for the purpose of deserving God's love and mercy. Secular existentialism believes almost all religions erroneously teach that human beings have an *essence* which defines their humanness, but all we can be sure of is *existence*. Once we recognize that fact, we can begin to work our way out of the sense of abandonment that comes with the understanding that human beings are alone in a bewildering universe that exists for no known reason. Of course, this means that each of us is free in the sense of having no obligation to a higher force or indeed to anything else, but this brand of freedom is at first confusing if not terrifying. Most people, say the secular existentialists, choose religion or some other authority that lays down guidelines for them. Even if they don't obey them, they have at least a perspective. They know what they are *supposed* to be doing.

Central to the secular existential movement is the thought of three French philosophers: Jean-Paul Sartre (1905–1980), Simone de Beauvoir (1908–1986), and Albert Camus (1913–1960). Sartre, the most influential of the three, bases his belief in the human right of self-definition on the absolute certainty that God cannot exist. He is opposed to the acceptance of God as a matter of psychological necessity. Deep down we know that each of us is alone in a world that makes no sense—something that must have seemed all too true to many war-weary survivors in Europe.

Man is condemned to be free.
—Jean-Paul Sartre

Sartre maintains there is no such thing as human nature. People *talk* about human nature, but who has ever seen it? We cannot assume people are fundamentally good *or* bad, when in fact they are *neither* at birth. No one comes into this world to serve any purpose whatever or to fulfill some preexisting definition of what it means to be human. "If man, as the existentialist conceives him, is indefinable, it is because at first he is nothing. Only afterward will he be something, and he himself will have made what he will be. Thus, there is no human nature, since there is no God to conceive it."[9]

Saying that humankind is born without any identifying nature is in direct conflict with earlier philosophies that describe everyone as having an essence. In Christianity, for example, that essence is the soul. For Aristotle, it is rationality. In short, existentialism says you have to work at developing an essence that can be defined as human, an essence that for him includes good will and a strong, clear sense of moral responsibility to one's fellows. For the religious existentialist, one creates an essence that is spiritual and longs for union with God. Thus the ringing declaration of both religious and secular existentialism is *Existence precedes essence.*

According to Sartre, only natural phenomena and manufactured objects have essences from the beginning. A paper cutter was "born" to cut paper. If it doesn't cut paper, you have the right to demand your money back. A storm was "born" to bring wind and rain (or snow) and maybe knock down a few buildings in its path. Even animals have essences, for they too are natural phenomena. A tiger has to growl and be carnivorous. But human beings somehow escaped *having* to be anything.

Ah, but there is a bright side to the picture. We *are* capable of reason, a faculty we develop through experience. Some choose to exploit this capacity more than others do. Some decide they cannot live without an essence, without a purpose, without a way of defining themselves. The bad news is that each person must find the definition all alone. If one borrows an essence from the past, from the traditions and beliefs of one's ancestors, or is influenced by peer pressure or educational or religious institutions, the right to define oneself is forfeited. One's essence has already been predefined.

Once we realize we have no essence, we have to create one freely; or, as Sartre puts it, we are "doomed to freedom." Each of us, having declared our essence, must then take responsibility for it. You cannot decide you are going to be such-and-such, only to deny, when your actions harm someone else, that you ever made that decision. No one is free to be morally unaccountable. True freedom carries a hefty price tag, reason tells us. You cannot argue that reason guarantees the right to behave any way you want to, unless, as Kant (Chapter 11) would say, you can accord that right to everyone else. In that case, you'd have to be careful not to turn your back on anyone. Do we *really* want to live in a society in which no one is responsible for anything?

Many, says Sartre, prefer to believe they serve a purpose and what they do was meant to be. He relates the tale of a young man who could not pass the examinations for various professional careers and decided he was meant to fail because he was truly destined to become a priest. Nonsense! declares Sartre. The young man was always in charge of his own life and should not have turned to the priesthood solely on the hunch that destiny was forcing him into it. Freedom is a painful thing sometimes. If we fail, we try to blame others or circumstances, thus denying the truth of our freedom.

Sartre argues that most people—to avoid difficult choices—prefer to become things and believe they serve a destined purpose, like a paper cutter. Whatever a *thing* does, it must do in order to fulfill its thingness. Things have no moral responsibility. If we cut our finger on the paper cutter, we cannot blame *it* for our clumsiness. People would rather renounce freedom than blame themselves for what happens to them.

The true existentialist—like Abraham—has to make choices, and is always confronted with anguish. An existential ship's officer, faced with the awful decision of having a dangerously overcrowded lifeboat or tossing some of the survivors into the sea, where they will certainly die, might decide to sacrifice certain people to save the others, but he would not be able to argue that he was a victim of circumstances. Of course, he *could* do so, but if he does, he cannot be considered *authentic*. An authentic person is one who defines himself or herself, stands behind the definition, and willingly accepts either praise or blame.

Simone de Beauvoir, a feminist writer and close associate of Sartre, urged women to create bold new essences. Her route to existentialism was the feminist rejection of male rules and the essences males imposed on females.

> *By the time humankind reached the stage of written mythology and law, the patriarchate was definitely established: the males were to write the codes. It was natural for them to give woman a subordinate position, yet one could suppose that they would look upon her with the same benevolence as upon children and cattle—but not at all.*

> *While setting up the machinery of woman's oppression, the legislators were afraid of her.*[10]

If not the most influential of the French existentialists, Albert Camus has surely been the most poetic—and dramatic. In his three major essays, "An Absurd Reasoning," "The Absurd Man," and "The Myth of Sisyphus," he makes the existential case that rationality is found not in the universe but in the human mind. The intellect, attempting to make sense out of reality, realizes it is not to be understood. Why then are we rational? To what end? Reason leads us to the conclusion that living is absurd, meaningless.

Having said this, he begins "An Absurd Reasoning" with his most often quoted statement: "There is but one truly serious philosophical problem, and that is suicide." Where Sartre believed that abandonment in a meaningless universe opened the door to freedom, Camus goes deeper, analyzing that condition of abandonment and insisting that life is not worth living if we cannot assign a value to it. Yet, if life is absurd, what value *can* it have?

Real generosity toward the future lies in giving all to the present.

—Albert Camus

Camus's answer is that it has an absurd value. What we think and do may not make any ultimate sense, but perhaps "ultimate sense" ought never to have been the goal. That there is only this existential moment, this here and now, does not imply that the moment is not worth experiencing. Unlike his colleagues, Camus talks about the colors, the sounds, the continually unfolding wonders of the universe. Absurd, yes, in that they have no meaning beyond themselves, but this fact does not make suicide the inevitable, the *only* recourse.

If we do not, as Hamlet does not, choose suicide, then we must have a purpose. That is, if we *had* chosen suicide, would it not be said that our purpose was to do away with ourselves? People don't kill themselves without reason. Choosing life rather than death is, therefore, purposeful as well. But if the world is absurd and we choose to remain in it, it must follow that we accept the absurdity and move on from there. In that lies our freedom, and with freedom comes an infinite number of possibilities.

To dramatize his point, Camus recounts the Greek myth of Sisyphus, "the wisest and most prudent of mortals," who also questioned the meaning of life. To find the answer, he stole secrets from the gods. They retaliated by condemning him to roll a heavy rock up a steep hill. When, through exhausting labor and physical pain, he reaches the top, the rock rolls back down, and Sisyphus has to start all over again. This is to continue for eternity.

> *I leave Sisyphus at the foot of the mountain! One always finds one's burden again. But Sisyphus teaches the higher fidelity that negates the gods and raises rocks. He too concludes that all is well. This universe henceforth without a master seems to him neither sterile nor futile. Each atom of that stone, each mineral flake of that night-filled mountain, in itself forms a world. The struggle itself toward the heights is enough to fill a man's heart. One must imagine Sisyphus happy.*[11]

There are many American existential writings as well. In *Mother Night* (1972), a novel by Kurt Vonnegut, an American newspaper columnist ostensibly defects to Germany during World War II and gets a job writing anti-Semitic propaganda for a German newspaper. After the conflict is over, he is tried as a war criminal, the charge being that the message of hatred in his inflammatory columns played a part in the Holocaust. The man's defense is that he was actually an American spy sent on an undercover mission by President Roosevelt himself. Of course, since Roosevelt is dead, the journalist cannot prove what he claims. The author's message is that we are what we say we are and thus we need to be very careful about defining ourselves. In the author's eyes, the journalist was guilty because he had created for himself an essence which led, however indirectly, to the deaths of many innocent people. Whether he was secretly anti-Semitic or merely carrying out orders can never be known. He narrates his story from an Israeli prison, his freedom denied. Had he made a responsible use of freedom before?

The view of freedom expressed in much existential philosophy and literature has been widely questioned. Is it the freedom to behave without regard for others? The Norwegian philosopher Dagfinn Føllesdal asks this ominous question: "Can one who creates his own values do anything that is morally wrong?" True, the existentialists insist that one be held accountable for speech and actions, but are people free to lie? To behave toward others in a way that will draw praise and make it easy to manipulate them? And if people use their freedom for their own profit, are they *really* free, or are they victims of their own selfishness?

Freedom within Limitations

Keep in mind always the present you are constructing. It should be the future you want.

—**Alice Walker**

By now it may have occurred to the reader that the philosophies of freedom we have been discussing were all generated by Western thinkers living in comparatively open societies in which freedom of thought and expression are taken for granted. Even Augustine, within the confines of Christianity, was at liberty to express his doubts. Determinists like Marx and Skinner were not threatened with jail for saying that our choices are not freely made.

Sometimes it happens that a philosopher of freedom is in fact living under an oppressive government: Rousseau, for example, in a rigid monarchy; Sartre, during the Nazi rule in France. Both fought against tyranny: Rousseau through his pen, and Sartre through his work in the French Underground, an organized covert attempt to help those being sought or persecuted by the Nazis. Neither philosopher abandoned his belief that freedom was the natural condition of humanity. That belief tends to be echoed throughout the humanities in different ways.

What does freedom mean to those who grow up in societies which have been embroiled in bitter religious and territorial disputes that severely limit choices? Or do those who are born into centuries-old ways of being human resign themselves to some form of slavery? Is freedom a narrowly Western idea? Or may we now extend its possible meanings?

For the Japanese, strongly influenced as they are by Western capitalism and the urgent need to do well financially, there is as well the strong tradition of family honor. Many of us, accustomed to more open pathways, would see this severe limitation as an impediment to the exercise of will. Succeeding in business is often the way for a Japanese son or daughter to win family approval. But in the West, one may well decide that a business career is not the right choice and embark on another. There is the heartbreaking story of a Japanese student attending an Ivy League university who killed herself when she received less than an "A" grade in one subject and thought her family would be disgraced. She left a note saying that because she had not studied hard enough, there was no other course of action open to her.

Japanese society is nothing if not rule-driven, Western influences notwithstanding. We have already studied the principles of Zen Buddhism, a dominant practice in Japan. Zen requires long hours of meditation. To excel in any of the martial arts demands many years of training in body coordination and muscular development. These arts are also products of a civilized society in which ethics and good manners are essential. Opponents must bow to each other as a mark of deep respect. The Japanese love of the beautiful dictates how tea is prepared and served and how flowers are arranged in a vase. All of these requirements might strike some in the West as cumbersome impositions, as jailers imprisoning the will. Yet it is doubtful that the Japanese would agree.

One of the foremost modern spokespersons for Buddhist thought and practice was Chögyam Trungpa (1939–1987), a monk who fled Chinese persecution in his native Tibet and founded a still-thriving American Buddhist community in Boulder, Colorado. Among those who came there to absorb his teachings was the poet Allen Ginsberg, a major voice of the Beat Generation, post–World War II writers, artists, and composers who found themselves disillusioned with the greed they saw on all sides and what they took to be the goal of rebuilding America as a more materialistic version of what it had once been. The Beats proclaimed themselves social dropouts, adrift in a land that called itself the cradle of liberty where people could be whatever they wanted to be yet were really slaves to its shoddy values.

Many, like Ginsberg, saw in Buddhism the one true path to freeing themselves from this enslavement; and the road to true freedom was through the discipline of meditation and the renunciation of materialistic desires. One of Trungpa's major works is in fact titled *The Myth of Freedom* (1976), by which he means that Western definitions of the word often require an absence of external control and the right to disobey the rules whenever it suits—or, better yet, the right to become the boss and impose whatever rules one wants. Trungpa would perhaps have agreed with behaviorists that, for most people, freedom meant getting out from under aversive controls—that is, from all those authorities that wish to shape our lives.

Trungpa maintains such freedom is impossible to achieve. One must first wake up to the reality of pain and suffering. It is absurd to suppose that following the American Dream and striving for wealth and the pleasures it can buy will avoid pain and suffering. If anything, wealth and pleasure only add to the pain because, as Epicurus points out (Chapter 12), there is never enough pleasure to satisfy us. And even if we had all the money we could ever want and spent our life doing whatever we pleased, there would be the excruciating pain of recognizing that death will bring an end to our holiday. According to Trungpa:

> *we must begin by seeing the experience of life as it is. We must see the truth of suffering, the reality of dissatisfaction. We cannot ignore it and attempt to examine only the glorious pleasurable aspects of life. If one searches for a promised land, a Treasure Island, then the search only leads to more pain. We cannot reach such islands, we cannot attain enlightenment in such a manner. So all sects and schools of Buddhism agree that we must begin by facing the reality of our living situations. We cannot begin by dreaming.*[12]

Trungpa defines true freedom as surrendering to reality and, by accepting things as they are, to liberate oneself from pain, which is, after all, the goal of the free person. In his view, one can be free though tightly shackled. Even in a narrow prison cell, freedom is possible, because no one can put chains on our thoughts and feelings. This doctrine of freedom through personal choice despite limitations has inspired hundreds of Trungpa's followers. However, a critic has said it is doubtful that it would bring solace to the many who still live in slavery or under severe autocratic rule.

Perhaps all one can say at this point in time is that there are many paths to freedom and that some of them still have impassable barriers. All the more reason to be grateful if you have the right to choose.

It seems appropriate to close this book with a theory—and it is just that—by means of which we can apply the word *free* to ourselves. According to this theory, derived from a number of sources, freedom is achieved *only* when we place limits on our options.

People who jog know all about the relationship between freedom and limits. They will tell you about a consciousness of freedom in running, pushing against the wind and feeling their arms and legs equal to the demands made by the will—for runners, in contrast to what Skinner has said, *do* feel their will. When there is a sharp incline, runners must draw upon reserve strength. On the downward slope, they know that power needs to be conserved. If they run flat out, they may not have enough left for the final mile. If they are running against others and there is a need to win, they accelerate; if all they want to do is complete the course, they adopt a more leisurely pace.

He who bears in his heart a cathedral to be built is already victorious. He who seeks to become sexton of a finished cathedral is already defeated.

—**Antoine de Saint-Exupéry**

But the vivid experience of will does not happen all of a sudden. In the beginning, jogging is a distinct effort accompanied by pain and soreness. There is the inevitable pulling of muscles, the labored breathing, the tendency to overheat rapidly. In the beginning, joggers often stop running for the slightest excuse. After a time they set a goal: to the end of the road and then back; one mile; two miles; down to the county line. Self-imposed limits are crucial. The goal must be met. Even wind and rain are not likely to keep the determined runner at home. The ultimate feeling of liberation—the sense of floating, the runner's high—occurs when the runner's body is equal to the task set by the will. And the will is experienced when runners feel at ease within the limitations they impose on themselves.

In Chapter 4, we talked about the sonnet form in which the poet's choices are determined by the number of required lines: fourteen. It would be easy for the poet to complain that the length limitation prevents the free expression of an idea, and indeed, many poets have chosen to write in "free" verse for which no restrictions exist. Yet the Romantic poet William Wordsworth does not see the rigid sonnet rules as constraints upon freedom.

Nuns fret not at their convent's narrow room;
And hermits are contented with their cells;
And students with their pensive citadels;
Maids at the wheel, the weaver at his loom
Sit blithe and happy; bees that soar for bloom,
High as the highest Peak of Furness-fells,
Will murmur by the hour in foxglove bells:
In truth the prison unto which we doom
Ourselves, no prison is: and hence for me,
In sundry moods, 'twas pastime to be bound
Within the Sonnet's scanty plot of ground;
Pleased if some Souls (for such there needs must be)
Who have felt the weight of too much liberty,
Should find brief solace there, as I have found.

There is in the poem an implied comparison between *liberty* and *freedom.* Liberty means going anywhere one wants and doing anything one wants. Liberty means that any door can be opened. Yet if we have all possible doors to choose from, would we ever open even one?

Why, one asks, is freedom so vital? If Sartre is right in saying that most people prefer not to be free, why should we *have* to be free? Or if freedom and liberty are not the same thing, what's wrong with seeking liberty for its own sake? What's wrong with going through life unfettered by rules and behaving in any way one desires? Why need we define ourselves at all and then be responsible for what we do?

When you put a tight lid on a pan of boiling water, the energy inside will become intense. So too will the joy of living be intense to the degree that we face a limited number of choices. Liberty is bewildering. Liberty does not know what to choose. Defining oneself as a certain kind of person is the first limitation. Unless we can do that, we become scattered to the winds, at the mercy of every gust. Narrowing the range of possibilities and *then finding the best way to work within that range*—this might, after all, be the answer. And what is the question? It is: *How can I do the most with the one life I have after I take inventory of how much freedom of choice is available to me?*

Of course, determinist arguments are powerful, and one has the right to believe there is no free will and thus one cannot be held responsible for anything. If one adopts that view, one must accept the fact that no one else is responsible either. Determinism is the only logical course for some. Many artists and philosophers do not agree. If a painting is decried by those who fund the exhibit, we don't hear the artist saying, "But I came from a bad environment that forced me to paint that way." Instead, the artist defends the work and decries the funders. Without *this* kind of freedom, there can be no pride in any accomplishment.

Without freedom, no art; art lives only on the restraints it imposes on itself, and dies of all others.
—**Albert Camus**

If determinism is chosen, is the chooser forced to do it? Surprisingly enough, many *do* choose determinism without realizing it. How many people do we know who seem to be happy only when they find someone who will listen to their tragic tales of victimization—by other people, by the law, by the government, by their parents, and on and on? Never by themselves. As Sartre continually reminds us, the only way to be an authentic person is to admit that you are free and to take responsibility for the bad choices you make. We have conceded many times that not everyone is lucky enough to have the right to choose. Those who do and who prefer to see themselves as helpless victims without responsibility would do well to recognize that they were nonetheless free to reject that responsibility.

Authentic people advertise their natures. We always know what to expect from them. Inauthentic people, backed into a corner after being blamed for something, try to plead their innocence by saying something forced them to make a wrongful choice. If free will is a fact of life for many, it cannot be accepted here and rejected there—at their convenience.

In the final analysis, true freedom may reside in the limitations we impose on ourselves freely. To believe that freedom means having unlimited options is to be trapped in infinity. Only by deliberately narrowing our range of options can we experience the exhilarating sense of being truly our own persons. It is freedom to say we can do this or, on the other hand, that. It is not freedom to say we can do this, or that, or perhaps that other thing, or even its opposite, and on and on forever. When we come to this realization, we also see we need not trap ourselves by always choosing the easy way. At a sumptuous buffet we can gorge ourselves or decide to enjoy fully a limited amount of delicious food.

Those who achieve the strength of inner control are not only authentic persons, they are *good people*. They never want to harm others, for doing so would mean being at the mercy of uncontrollable passions, becoming the victims they choose not to be.

A study of the humanities, looking into the minds and hearts of creative and thoughtful human beings, reveals many, many innovations in art and philosophy. Many, many artists and philosophers have changed the course of human consciousness and given us options our ancient ancestors could not have dreamed of: options for experiencing the beautiful, the different, even sometimes the shocking, and of course the thought-provoking. How predetermined were *they*, when the greatest of them did what nobody else had ever done? If they were predetermined, why was there not more than one Beethoven or Shakespeare, people who might have been similarly directed? The humanities would seem to be the study of the free spirit, and from this each of us can know that more can be done with our lives. It is your birthright as a human being to reach up and mentally redo the Sistine Chapel ceiling if you don't happen to like it. Once you have investigated the past, it is your birthright to let go of it, but knowingly and with full awareness of what you want the present to be. It is your birthright to reach into the darkness and from it pull forth a new lantern, however unfamiliar the shape, however irregular the beam of light.

Reaching beyond ourselves is a natural right. Without the risk of failure, there can be no possibility of success. The American novelist and poet Stephen Crane sums it all up:

I saw a man pursuing the horizon;
Round and round they sped.
I was disturbed at this;
I accosted the man.
"It is futile," I said,
"You can never—"
"You lie," he cried
And ran on.[13]

Key Terms

behaviorism both a philosophy and a school of psychology that believes people are what they do and what they do is determined by systems of rewards and punishments.

bourgeoisie the middle classes; in Marxism, those who control capital and the means of production and exploit the proletariat.

chromosomes long stringy bodies in the nucleus of the cell, containing the genes made of DNA.

determinism the philosophical belief that everything has a prior cause and consequently absolute free will cannot exist.

dialectic the philosophical method of Hegel, involving the presentation of one idea, followed by an analysis of its opposite, and then arriving at a truth that combines the two; adopted by Marx to describe the conflict between the proletariat and the bourgeoisie and the eventual establishment of a classless society.

DNA abbreviation for *deoxyribonucleic acid*, which forms long strands of sugar and sulphate within the gene and carries the genetic codes throughout the body.

economic determinism another name for the philosophy of Karl Marx, maintaining that our behavior is controlled by the need for money.

genes granular substances within the chromosome that contain the DNA molecules.

genome the genetic blueprint of a living being, contained within each of its cells.

indeterminism the philosophy expounded by William James, that whatever happens does so randomly, without a clear prior cause, and therefore we have free will to make choices.

institutional determinism name given to Rousseau's belief that the will is governed by restrictive forces of law, education, and religion, all necessary because of the inborn depravity of a few people.

leap of faith phrase used by Kierkegaard to indicate that religion can be freely chosen, but to do so, one must bypass reason and thus can never be sure if the choice was right.

libertarianism a political and philosophical belief in unrestricted free will.

proletariat in Marxism, the working classes who will eventually rise up against the affluent bourgeoisie, leading to the classless society.

psychoanalysis a technique developed by Sigmund Freud that examines a patient's dreams and patterns of free association of ideas in an effort to diagnosis the causes of neurotic behavior and mental illness.

psychotherapy clinical treatments of mental disorders based on the findings of the psychoanalysis, usually involving discussion sessions in which the patient is encouraged to talk openly about his or her dreams and to go from one subject to another without being interrupted or "kept to task."

sociobiology a social science that believes human behavior can be analyzed in terms of genetic investment or the lack of it—that is, the extent to which one is motivated by the need to propagate one's genes, either directly, through a sexual relationship, or indirectly, through the need to survive physically, socially, or economically.

Topics for Writing and Discussion

1. Though the chapter is titled "Freedom," you didn't find anywhere in it a succinct definition of the term. The reason is that the word is used in many different contexts and often quite vaguely. From having read the chapter, give as many versions of "freedom" as you can.
2. Define and describe determinism. Do the same for two philosophies that oppose it.
3. Of the determinist philosophies discussed in the chapter, which ones do you believe have the most bearing on your life? Which the least? In view of your answer, would you call yourself a complete determinist? Partial? Not at all? Explain.
4. Whether or not people agree with B. F. Skinner, most do concur that all of us are subject to a certain amount of aversive control. Describe one or two aversive controls in your own life, present or past.
5. Great strides have been taken in the science of genetics and genetic research, especially in the use of stem cells for the treatment of conditions such as diabetes and Parkinson's disease. Opponents of even limited federal funding maintain that dissecting the cells to learn more about genetic diseases is tantamount to murder. Advocates of funding say the research will result in extraordinary medical breakthroughs. Support your argument for or against federal funding.
6. Rousseau's famous position was that, if it were not for the necessary but oppressive limitations imposed by social institutions, people would be naturally benevolent toward each other. Do you agree that in a state of nature, without any limitations, people would get along? Or is aggression inherent in human nature and must be controlled?
7. On what does William James base his argument to support free will? We can't deny that the conditions he cites actually exist, but do they prove we act freely?
8. The gist of Schopenhauer's free-will theory is that it would probably be better if the will were not free. Why does he believe this?
9. The chapter discusses two schools of existentialism. On what do they agree? Where do they disagree?
10. The chapter discusses a number of religious and philosophical beliefs that say freedom comes only within limitations. Discuss at least two of these limitations. Do they apply to your life at present? If not, would you be willing to try them?

Endnotes

Chapter 2

1. William Wharton, *Dad* (New York: Avon, 1981), 419–420.
2. e.e.cummings, "may my heart always be open to little birds," *Poems 1929–1954* (New York: Harcourt Brace, 1954).
3. Anthony Lane, "Review: A Mighty Heart," *New Yorker*, June 25, 2007, 131.
4. Howard Cohen, *Miami Herald Weekend*, July 3, 2007, 28.
5. Alex Ross, "Review: La Pasión Según San Marcos," *New Yorker*, March 5, 2001, 100–101.
6. William Wordsworth, "The world is too much with us," *The Major Poets, English and American* (New York: Harcourt Brace, 1954), 257.

Chapter 3

1. Anthony Lane, "Review: Eternal Sunshine of the Spotless Mind," *New Yorker*, March 22, 2004, 103.
2. June Singer, *Boundaries of the Soul: The Practice of Jung's Psychology* (New York: Doubleday, 1972), 79.
3. Singer, *Boundaries of the Soul.*
4. Joseph Campbell, *The Myths of God: Oriental Mythology* (New York: Viking Penguin, 1976), 243.
5. Campbell, *The Myths of God*, 342.
6. Campbell, *The Myths of God*, 9–10.
7. Edith Hamilton, *Mythology* (New York: New American Library, 1969), 63.
8. *Paradise Lost*, Book VII, ll. 211–217.
9. Hamilton, *Mythology*, 89.
10. Rose Anna Mueller, "La Llorona, The Weeping Woman," *Community College Humanities Review* 20, no. 1 (1999): 28–33.
11. J.R.R. Tolkien, *The Return of the King* (New York: Ballantine, 1966), 384.
12. Paraphrased from R. H. Blythe, *Zen and Zen Classics* (Tokyo: Hokuseido, 1960–1970).

Chapter 4

1. John Steinbeck, *The Grapes of Wrath* (1940; reprint, New York: Penguin, 1992).
2. *The Iliad of Homer*, trans. Robert Fitzgerald (Garden City, NY: Doubleday Anchor, 1975).
3. Sappho, "Ode to Aphrodite," trans. J. Addington Symonds, in *Our Heritage of World Literature*, ed. Stith Thompson and John Gassner (New York: Dryden Press, 1942), 258.
4. Catullus, trans. Walter Savage Landor, *Our Heritage of World Literature*, 268.
5. "Llagas de Amor," trans. John K. Wilde and Francisco Aragon, in *Federico Garcia Lorca: Selected Verse*, ed. Christopher Maurer (New York: Farrar, Straus and Giroux, 1989–1994).
6. Jaron Lanier, "Jaron's World: The Meaning of Metaphor," *Discovery*, February 2007.
7. *Collected Sonnets of Edna St. Vincent Millay*, ed. Ruth Bornschlegel and Norma Millay (New York: Harper and Row, 1987).
8. *Red Dragonfly on My Shoulder*, trans. Stkvua Cassedy amd Kunihiro Sustake (New York: HarperCollins, 1992).
9. *Red Dragonfly on My Shoulder.*
10. Attributed to Isabel Crawford (1865–1961), a Baptist missionary to the Plains Indians.
11. Emily Dickinson, *Complete Poems*, ed. Thomas H. Johnson (Boston: Little Brown, 1966).
12. Georgia Douglas Johnson, "Black Woman," in *The Portable Harlem Renaissance*, ed. Daniel Levering Lewis (New York: Penguin, 1995).
13. *The Collected Poems of Archibald MacLeish, 1917–1982* (Boston: Houghton Mifflin, 1995).
14. Billy Collins, *Sailing Alone around the Room* (New York: Random House, 2001).
15. *The Bread Loaf Anthology of Contemporary American Poetry* (Hanover, NH: University Press of New England, 1985).

16. F. Scott Fitzgerald, *The Great Gatsby* (New York: Scribner Paperback, 1995), 160–161.
17. Khaled Hosseini, *The Kite Runner* (New York: Riverhead, 2003), 324.
18. Nadine Gordimer, "A Beneficiary," *New Yorker*, May 21, 2007, 66–73.

Chapter 5

1. Walt Whitman, "There Was a Child Went Forth," *Leaves of Grass* (New York: Barnes and Noble, 1993), 305.
2. William Fleming, *Art and Ideas* (New York: Henry Holt, 1959), 307–308.
3. Bruce Cole and Adelheid Gealt, *Art of the Western World* (New York: Summit, 1985), 271.
4. Jan Garden Castro, *The Art and Life of Georgia O'Keeffe* (New York: Crown, 1985), 25.
5. Amy Helene Kirshke, *Aaron Douglas: Art, Race, and the Harlem Renaissance* (Jackson: University Press of Mississippi, 1995), 10, 77.
6. John Perrault, "Forging Ahead: A Sculpture Conference Diary," *Village Voice*, September 21, 1982, 84.
7. Jonathan Lipman, *Frank Lloyd Wright and the Johnson Wax Building* (New York: Rizzoli, 1986), xii.

Chapter 6

1. Abraham Veinus, Syracuse University, line notes for Ludwig van Beethoven, Symphony No. 3 in E Flat Major, *Eroica*, Philharmonic Promenade Orchestra of London, Adrian Boult cond., Vanguard.
2. Joan Baez, "Joe Hill," http://www.ilyric.net/Lyrics/J/Joan-Baez/Joe-Hill.html/.
3. Alan Bullock and R. B. Woodings, eds., *20th Century Culture* (New York: Harper and Row, 1983), 212.
4. Charlie Gillett, *The Penguin Book of Rock and Roll Writing*, ed. Clinton Haydin (London: Penguin, 1992), 14.
5. Gillett, 11.
6. Gillett 212.
7. J. Decibel.
8. Decibel.

Chapter 7

1. *Henry V*, IV, Prologue, 1–9, 22–28.
2. *Twelfth Night*, II, iv, 14–19.
3. *Othello*, V, ii, 91–97.
4. *Hamlet*, III, iii, 80–82.
5. *Hamlet*, II, ii, 1–9 (abridged).
6. Molière, *Tartuffe*, trans. Richard Wilbur (New York: Roundhouse, 1997).
7. John Simon, "Holy Sanctimony," *New York Magazine*, January 13, 2003.
8. Henrik Ibsen, *A Doll's House*, trans. Rolfe Fjelde, in *Literature of the Western World*, ed. Brian Wilke and James Hurt (New York: Macmillan, 1988), 1303.
9. "Edward Albee Returns to the Zoo," *New York Times*, May 16, 2004, sec. 2, 22.
10. *Aristotle*, trans. Philip Wheelright (New York: Odyssey, 1951), 296.
11. *Hamlet*, V, ii, 230–236.
12. *Macbeth*, V, v, 17–28.
13. Sophocles, *Antigone*, trans. Dudley Fitz and Robert Fitzgerald (New York: Harcourt, 1946).
14. *Othello*, V, ii, 92–97.
15. *King Lear*, V, ii, 306–308.
16. Tom Stoppard, *The Real Thing* (New York: Faber and Faber, 1983), 53.
17. *Henry IV, Part II*, V, 51–54.
18. Harold Bloom, *Shakespeare: The Invention of the Human* (New York: Riverhead, 1998), 271–272.
19. Bloom, *Shakespeare*, 272.
20. Eugene O'Neill, *Long Day's Journey into Night* (New Haven, CT: Yale University Press, 1955), 165–166.
21. Oscar Wilde, *The Importance of Being Earnest*, in *Twenty-Three Plays*, ed. Otto Reinert and Peter Arnott (Boston: Little, Brown, 1978), 526.
22. John Lahr, *Notes on a Cowardly Lion* (Berkeley: University of California Press, 1962), 264–265.

Chapter 8

1. John D. Drummond, *Opera in Perspective* (Minneapolis: University of Minnesota Press, 1980), 15.
2. Drummond, *Opera in Perspective*, 278.
3. Edward A. Berlin, *King of Ragtime* (New York: Oxford University Press, 1994).
4. William G. Hyland, *Richard Rodgers* (New York: Yale University Press, 1998), 127.
5. Hyland, *Richard Rodgers*, 131–132.

Chapter 9

1. Gerald Mast, *A Short History of the Movies* (New York: Macmillan, 1986), 68.
2. Ephraim Katz, *The Film Encyclopedia*, 3rd ed. (New York: Harper Perennial, 1998), 121.
3. David Denby, *New Yorker*, July 23, 2007.
4. Harriet Quick, "Review: Lost in Translation," *British Vogue*, January 2004, 101.
5. Edward Jay Epstein, "The Second Coming of Jim Garrison," *Atlantic Monthly*, March 1993, 89.
6. Edward Rothstein, "Connections: To Homer Iraq Would Be More of Same," *New York Times*, June 5, 2004, A17.

Chapter 10

1. Walt Whitman, *Leaves of Grass* (New York: Heritage), 25.
2. John A. Hutchinson, *Paths of Faith*, 2nd ed. (New York: McGraw-Hill, 1975), 79.
3. Justice Thomas Berger, "Mackenzie Valley Pipeline Inquiry," Briefs and Transcripts, October 1976, available online at gateway.uvic.ca/micro/.

4. *Buddhist Scriptures*, trans. Edward Conze (London: Penguin, 1959), 51. Some say that Siddhartha was born into the Shakyas, a warrior tribe living near the foothills of the Himalayas. They refer to him as the Buddha Shakyamuni as well as the Shakya sage.
5. A. A. Milne, *The Complete Poems and Tales of Winnie the Pooh* (New York: Quality Paperback Book Club, 1997), 81.
6. Milne, *The Complete Poems and Tales of Winnie the Pooh*, 82.
7. Plato, *The Republic and Other Works*, trans. Benjamin Jowett (New York: Doubleday Anchor, 1989), 470. "Apology" as used here means "defense."
8. Plato, *The Republic*.
9. *Aristotle*, ed. and trans. Philip Wheelright (New York: Odyssey, 1951), 4–5.
10. Joseph Telushkin, *Jewish Literacy* (New York: William Morrow, 1991), 102.
11. *The Confessions of Saint Augustine* (New York: Airmont, 1969), Book VI, 213.
12. Edwin Arlington Robinson, "The Man against the Sky," in *American Poetry and Prose*, ed. Norman Foerster (Boston: Houghton Mifflin, 1947), 1275–1276, ll. 305–314.
13. Charles S. Peirce, "How to Make Our Ideas Clear," *Popular Science Monthly*, 1878.
14. Charles S. Peirce, "The Fixation of Belief," in *The Search for Meaning*, ed. Robert F. Davidson (New York: Holt Rinehart Winston, 1967), 259.
15. Peirce, "How to Make Our Ideas Clear."

Chapter 11

1. Plato, *The Republic*, trans. Benjamin Jowett (New York: Doubleday, 1973), 44.
2. Plato, *The Republic*, 44.
3. Plato, *The Republic*, 46.
4. Thomas Hobbes, *Leviathan*, in *Basic Problems of Philosophy*, ed. Daniel Bronstein, Yervant Kriokorian, and Philip Weiner (Englewood Cliffs, NJ: Prentice Hall, 1964), 155.
5. Thomas Hobbes, *Leviathan*, 159.
6. Ayn Rand, *Atlas Shrugged* (New York: Dutton, 1957), 661.
7. John Donne, *The College Survey of English Literature*, ed. Alexander M. Witherspoon et al. (New York: Harcourt Brace and World, 1947), 340–341.
8. Steven Pinker, "The Moral Instinct," *New York Times Magazine*, January 27, 2008, 36–37.
9. John Rawls, quoted in Donald Palmer, *Does the Center Hold?* (Mountain View, CA: Mayfield, 1996), 262.
10. "Arguments: Should Opera Be Subsidized?" *Dissent*, Summer 1999, 96.
11. "Arguments," 98.
12. In Palmer, *Does the Center Hold?* 342.
13. Hans J. Morgenthau, "The Sanctity of Moral Law," *New Republic*, December 2, 1959.
14. Huston Smith, *The World's Religions* (San Francisco: Harper, 1991), 290–291.
15. John A. Hutchinson, *Paths of Faith*, 2nd ed. (New York: McGraw-Hill, 1973), 121–122.
16. Isabel Allende, *Of Love and Shadows*, trans. Margaret Sayers Pedern (New York: Knopf, 1987), 115.
17. Allende, *Of Love and Shadows*.
18. Studs Terkel, *Working* (New York: Pantheon, 1974), 48.
19. Terkel, *Working*.
20. From an article by Colin Nickerson, which appeared originally in the *Boston Globe* and was reprinted in the *Miami Herald*, September 17, 2000.
21. Nicholas D. Kristof, "In Japan Nice Guys (and Girls) Finish Together," *New York Times*, April 12, 1998.
22. Sui Sin Far, "The Americanizing of Pau Tsu," in *Asian American Literature*, ed. Shawn Wong (New York: HarperCollins Literary Mosaic Series, 1996), 68–69.
23. Cullen Murphy, "Was Jesus a Feminist?" *Harvard Magazine*, September/October 1998.
24. Matt Ridley, "A Boy or a Girl," *Smithsonian*, June 1993.

Chapter 12

1. Kurt Vonnegut, "Joe Heller," *New Yorker*, May 10, 2005.
2. Epicurus, *The Extant Remains*, trans. Cyril Bailey (London: Oxford University Press, 1926), 64.
3. Epicurus, *The Extant Remains*, 65.
4. *The Complete Short Stories of Ernest Hemingway* (New York: Scribners, 1982), 289–290.
5. Viktor Frankl, *Man's Search for Meaning: An Introduction to Logotherapy*, preface by Gordon W. Allport (New York: Washington Square, 1998), 90.
6. Anne Frank, *The Diary of a Young Girl*, ed. Otto J. Frank and Miriam Pressler, trans. Susan Massotty (New York: Doubleday, 1991), 281.
7. Frank, *The Diary of a Young Girl*, 54.
8. Frank, *The Diary of a Young Girl*, 190.
9. Dalai Lama, *The Path to Tranquility* (New York: Viking Arcana, 1999), 163.
10. Dalai Lama, *The Path to Tranquility*, 303.
11. Dalai Lama, *The Path to Tranquility*, 395.

Chapter 13

1. Petronius Gaius, "Doing, a Filthy Pleasure Is, and Short," trans. Ben Jonson, in *99 Poems in Translation*, eds. Harold Pinter et al. (London: Faber and Faber, 1994).
2. Francine Prose, *Gluttony* (New York: Oxford University Press, 2003), 8.
3. William Shakespeare, *Venus and Adonis*, in *The Annotated Shakespeare*, ed. A. L.Rowse (New York: Clarkson N. Potter, 1978), II, ll. 7–12, 1141–1144.
4. Geoffrey Chaucer, "The Wife of Bath's Tale," in *The Canterbury Tales*, trans. from the Middle English by the authors.
5. *The Rubáiyát of Omar Khayyám*, trans. Edward Fitzgerald, in *The College Survey of English Literature*, revised ed. (New York: Harcourt, Brace and World, 1951), ll. 393–396.

6. *The Rubáiyát of Omar Khayyám*, ll. 217–220.
7. Plato, *The Republic and Other Works*, trans. Benjamin Jowett (New York: Doubleday, 1989).
8. "The Death of the Hired Man," *The Poetry of Robert Frost*, ed. Edward Connery Lathan (New York: Holt, Rinehart and Winston, 1969).
9. Confucius, "Classic of Rites," in *Anthology of World Scriptures*, ed. Robert E. Van Voort (Belmont, CA: Wadsworth, 1999), 151–152.
10. Antonia Fraser, *The Weaker Vessel* (New York: Knopf, 1984), 26.
11. Dante, *La Vita Nuova*, trans. D. G. Rossetti (New York: Viking, 1947), 547–548.
12. Dante, *The Divine Comedy*, trans. Lawrence Binyan (New York: Viking, 1947), 30.
13. Gabriel García Márquez, *Love in the Time of Cholera* (New York: Knopf, 1988), 339.
14. Hannah Kahn, "Signature," in *Eve's Daughter* (Coconut Grove, FL: Hurricane House, 1962), 17. Reprinted by permission of the poet.

Chapter 14

1. Sherman B. Nuland, *How We Die* (New York: Knopf, 1994), 10.
2. J.R.R. Tolkien, *The Return of the King* (New York: Ballantine, 1966), 849.
3. Review of *House* by Matthew Gilbert, *Boston Globe*, November 16, 2004.
4. James Agee, *A Death in the Family* (New York: McDowell, Obalensky, 1957), 307–308.
5. Gerard Manley Hopkins, "Spring and Fall," *The Experience of Literature*, ed. Lionel Trilling (New York: Holt, Rinehart and Winston, 1967), 1213.
6. *The Rubáiyát of Omar Khayyám*, trans. Edward Fitzgerald, in *The College Survey of English Literature*, ed. Alexander M. Witherspoon et al. (New York: Harcourt, Brace and World, 1957), 1028.
7. A. E. Housman, *The Collected Poems of A. E. Housman* (New York: Henry Holt, 1965), 88.
8. Plato, *The Republic and Other Works*, trans. Benjamin Jowett (New York: Doubleday, 1989), 551.
9. James Thurber, *My World and Welcome to It* (New York: Harcourt, Brace, 1942), 61–62.
10. Oscar Wilde, *The Picture of Dorian Gray* (New York: Dell, 1977), 33.
11. *Tao Te Ching*, trans. R. B. Blakney (New York: New American Lbrary, 1955), 101.
12. Molière, *Four Plays*, trans. Carl Milo Pergolizzi (Boston: International Pocket Library, 1999), 234.
13. Katherine Mansfield, "The Man without a Temperament," *Ten Modern Masters*, ed. Robert Gorham Davis (New York: Harcourt, Brace, 1953), 61–62.
14. Johann Wolfgang von Goethe, *Faust*, trans. Walter Arndt (New York: Norton, 1976), 294.
15. *The Essential Tao*, trans. Thomas Cleary (San Francisco: Harper, 1991), 75.
16. Sylvia Plath, "Metaphors," in *Collected Poems*, ed. Ted Hughes (New York: HarperCollins, 1981).
17. Anne Sexton, "Live," in *Live or Die* (Boston: Houghton Mifflin, 1966), 87.
18. Marsha Norman, *'night, Mother* (New York: Hill and Wang, 1983), 17–18.
19. Joseph Telushkin, *Jewish Literacy* (New York: Morrow, 1991), 566.

Chapter 15

1. Michael Kimmelman, "Life Is Short, Art Long," *New York Times Magazine*, January 4, 1998, 20.
2. E. B. White, "I Paint What I See," in *Poems and Sketches of E. B. White* (New York: Harper and Row, 1933).
3. Stephen Kanzer, "Turkey, Relenting, Shows the Work of a Kurd Patriot," *New York Times*, April 14, 1999, 26.
4. James Joyce, *Ulysses* (New York: Random House, 1992), 768.
5. From John M. Woolsey's decision lifting the ban, reprinted in Joyce, *Ulysses*, xi.
6. Ronald Berger et al., *Cinema Year by Year, 1894–2000* (New York: Dorking Kindersley, 2000), 146.
7. Joel Greenberg, "Playing a Bit of Wagner," *New York Times*, July 9, 2001, 22.
8. Danny Hoch, "The One Where Jerry Disses the Pool Guy," *Harper's Magazine*, March 1998, 26.
9. Virginia Woolf, *A Room of One's Own* (San Diego, CA: Harcourt, Harvest, 1989), 49.
10. Otagaki Rengetsu, "A Trip during the Cherry Blossom Season," from *Lotus Moon: The Poetry of Buddhist Nun Otagaki Rengetsu*, trans. John Stevens (Berkeley, CA: Shambhala, 1994).
11. Walter Sorell, *Three Women: Lives of Sex and Genius* (Indianapolis, IN: Bobbs-Merrill, 1975), 15, 16–17.
12. Sorell, *Three Women*, 27.
13. Sorell, *Three Women*, 69.

Chapter 16

1. Azar Nafisi, *Reading* Lolita *in Tehran* (New York: Random House, 2004), 9.
2. B. F. Skinner, *Beyond Freedom and Dignity* (New York: Bantam, 1972), 37.
3. Skinner, *Beyond Freedom and Dignity*, 41.
4. Skinner, *Beyond Freedom and Dignity*, 39.
5. Arthur Schopenhauer, *Esssays and Aphorisms*, ed. and trans. R. J. Hollingdale (London: Penguin, 1970), 65.
6. Schopenhauer, *Esssays and Aphorisms*, 65.
7. Schopenhauer, *Esssays and Aphorisms*, 86.
8. Martin Buber, *Tales of the Hasidim* (New York: Schoken, 1992), viii.

9. Jean-Paul Sartre, *Existentialism and Human Emotions*, trans. Bernard Frechtman (New York: Philosophical Library, 1947), 15.
10. Simone de Beauvoir, *The Second Sex*, ed. and trans. H. M. Parchley (New York: Knopf, 1969), 79.
11. Albert Camus, *The Myth of Sisyphus and Other Essays*, trans. Justin O'Brien (New York: Vintage, 1995), 123.
12. Chögyam Trungpa, *The Myth of Freedom* (Berkeley, CA: Shambhala, 1976), 1–2.
13. Stephen Crane, "I Saw a Man," *Readings in Stephen Crane*, ed. Bonnie Szumski (San Diego, CA: Green Haven, 1998), 194.

Credits

"may my heart always be open to little". Copyright 1938, © 1966, 1991 by the Trustees for the E. E. Cummings Trust, from *Complete Poems: 1904-1962* by E. E. Cummings, edited by George J. Firmage. Used by permission of Liveright Publishing Corporation.

From "Resurrection: The Passion According to Osvaldo Golijov" a review of *"La Pasión Según San Marcos"* by Alex Ross in *The New Yorker*, March 5, 2001. Used by permission of the author.

Excerpt from Homer *The Iliad* translated by Robert Fitzgerald. Translation copyright © 1974 by Robert Fitzgerald. Renewed translation copyright © 2002 by Ughetta Fitzgerald, Barnaby F. Fitzgerald, and Benedict R. C. Fitzgerald. Reprinted by permission of Farrar, Straus & Giroux, LLC.

"Wounds of Love" from *Federico Garcia Lorca: Selected Verse* edited by Christopher Maurer, translated by Francisco Aragon, Catherine Brown, Cola Franzen, Will Kirkland, William Bryant Logan, Christopher Maurer, Jerome Rothenberg, Greg Simon, Alan S. Trueblood, John K. Walsh, and Steven F. White. Translation copyright © 1994 by Francisco Aragon, Catherine Brown, Cola Franzen, Will Kirkland, William Bryant Logan, Christopher Maurer, Jerome Rothenberg, Greg Simon, Alan S. Trueblood, John K. Walsh, and Steven F. White. Reprinted by permission of Farrar, Straus & Giroux, LLC.

"Llagas de armor" (in Spanish) by Federico Garcia Lorca. Used by permission of William Peter Kosmos, Esq. as attorney for the Lorca heirs.

"Haiku" by Matsuo Basho, translated by Sylvia Cassedy and Kunihiro Suetake, from *Red Dragonfly on My Shoulder*, New York, HarperCollins Publishers, 1992. Translation reprinted by permission of Ellen Cassedy.

"Haiku" by Kobayashi Issa, translated by Sylvia Cassedy and Kunihiro Suetake, from *Red Dragonfly on My Shoulder*, New York, HarperCollins Publishers, 1992. Translation reprinted by permission of Ellen Cassedy.

Reprinted by permission of the publishers and the Trustees of Amherst College from *The Poems of Emily Dickinson*, Ralph W. Franklin, ed., F372, Cambridge, Mass.: The Belknap Press of Harvard University Press, Copyright © 1998 by the President and Fellows of Harvard College. Copyright © 1951, 1955, 1979, 1983 by the President and Fellow of Harvard College.

"Ars Poetica" from *Collected Poems 1917-1982* by Archibald MacLeish. Copyright © 1985 by The Estate of Archibald MacLeish. Reprinted by permission of Houghton Mifflin Harcourt Publishing Company. All rights reserved.

Billy Collins, "My Number" from *The Apple that Astonished Paris*. Copyright © 1988, 1996 by Billy Collins. Used by permission of the University of Arkansas Press, www.uapress.com.

"Ev'ry Time We Say Goodbye" words and music by Cole Porter. © 1944 Chappell & Co., Inc. Copyright Renewed and Assigned by John F. Wharton, Trustee of the Cole Porter Musical and Literary Property Trusts Publication and Allied Rights Assigned to Chappell & Co., Inc. All Rights Reserved. Used by permission of Alfred Publishing Co., Inc.

"Joe Hill" music by Earl Robinson, words by Alfred Hayes. Copyright © 1938 (Renewed) by Music Sales Corporation (ASCAP) and MCA Music Publishing. International Copyright Secured. All Right Secured. Reprinted by permission. **(only half of credit line, rest to come)**

Excerpt from *Tartuffe* by Molière, English translation copyright © 1963, 1962, 1961 and renewed 1991, 1990 and 1989 by Richard Wilbur, reprinted by permission of Houghton Mifflin Harcourt Publishing Company. CAUTION: Professionals and amateurs are hereby warned that this translation, being fully protected under the copyright laws of the United States of America, the British Empire, including the Dominion of Canada, and all other countries which are signatories to the Universal Copyright Convention and the International Copyright Union, are subject to royalty. All rights, including professional, amateur, motion picture, recitation, lecturing, public reading, radio broadcasting, and television, are strictly reserved. Particular emphasis is laid on the question of readings, permission for which must be addressed to Peter Franklin, William Morris Agency, 1325 Avenue of the Americas, New York, NY 10019; inquiries on translation rights should be addressed to Harcourt, Inc., Permissions Department, Orlando, FL 32887. The stock and amateur acting rights of *Tartuffe* are controlled exclusively by the Dramatists Play Service, Inc., 440 Park Avenue South, New York, NY. No amateur performance of the play may be given without obtaining in advance the written permission of the Dramatists Play Service, Inc., and paying the requisite fee.

"A Doll House", from *Four Major Plays, Volume 1* by Henrik Ibsen, translated by Rolf Fjelde, copyright © 1965, 1992 by Rolf Fjelde. Used by permission of Dutton Signet, a division of Penguin Group (USA) Inc.

From *Long Day's Journey Into Night* by Eugene O'Neill, 1955. Reprinted by permission of Yale University Press.

"Joe Heller" by Kurt Vonnegut, *The New Yorker,* May 14, 2007. Reprinted by permission of Donald C. Farber, Esq.

Excerpt from "You, Andrew Marvell" from *Collected Poems 1917-1982* by Archibald MacLeish. Copyright © 1985 by The Estate of Archibald MacLeish. Reprinted by permission of Houghton Mifflin Harcourt Publishing Company. All rights reserved.

Excerpt from "The Death of the Hired Man" from *The Complete Poetry of Robert Frost* edited by Edward Connery Lathem. Copyright 1958 by Robert Frost, © 1967 by Lesley Frost Ballantine, copyright 1930, 1939, © 1969 by Henry Holt and Company. Reprinted by permission of Henry Holt and Company, LLC.

"La Vita Nuova", translated by D. G. Rossetti, copyright 1947, renewed © 1975 by The Viking Press, Inc., from *The Portable Dante* by Dante, edited by Paola Milano, translated by Laurence Binyon. Used by permission of Viking Penguin, a division of Penguin Group (USA) Inc.

"Terrence, this is stupid stuff" from "A Shropshire Lad" authorized edition from *The Collected Poems of A.E. Housman.* Copyright 1924, © 1965 by Henry Holt and Company. Reprinted by permission of Henry Holt and Company, LLC.

From *The Miser* by Molière from *Four Plays,* translated by Carl Milo Pergolizzi, 1999. Used by permission of Branden Publishing Company.

From *Faust: A Tragedy* by Johann Wolfgang von Goethe, Cyrus Hamlin, editor, translated by Walter Arndt. Copyright © 1976 by W. W. Norton & Company, Inc. Used by permission of W. W. Norton & Company, Inc.

"A Jug of Wine" (from "The Day Before Spring"). Lyrics by Alan Jay Lerner, Music by Frederick Loewe. © 1945 (Renewed) Chappell & Co., Inc. All Rights Reserved. Used by permission of Alfred Publishing Co., Inc.

From "Metaphors" from *Crossing the Water* by Sylvia Plath. Copyright © 1960 by Ted Hughes. Reprinted by permission of HarperCollins Publishers and Faber and Faber Ltd for The Sylvia Plath Estate.

Excerpt from *Night, Mother: A Play* by Marsha Norman. Copyright © 1983 by Marsha Norman. Reprinted by permission of Hill & Wang, a division of Farrar, Straus and Giroux, LLC.

"I Paint What I See" from *The Fox of Peapack and Other Poems* by E. B. White. Copyright 1932 by E. B. White. Reprinted by permission of HarperCollins Publishers.

Excerpt from "Live", from *Live or Die* by Anne Sexton. Copyright © 1966 by Anne Sexton, renewed 1994 by Linda G. Sexton. Reprinted by permission of Houghton Mifflin Harcourt Publishing Company. All rights reserved.

Index